The Making of the Black Working Class in Britain

Ron Ramdin

VERSO
London • New York

This updated edition first published by Verso 2017
First published by Gower Publishing Co. Ltd 1987
© Ron Ramdin 1987, 2017

1 3 5 7 9 10 8 6 4 2

Verso
UK: 6 Meard Street, London W1F 0EG
US: 20 Jay Street, Suite 1010, Brooklyn, NY 11201
versobooks.com

Verso is the imprint of New Left Books

ISBN-13: 978-1-78663-065-0
ISBN-13: 978-1-78663-067-4 (US EBK)
ISBN-13: 978-1-78663-066-7 (UK EBK)

British Library Cataloguing in Publication Data
A catalogue record for this book is available from the British Library

Library of Congress Cataloging-in-Publication Data
A catalog record for this book is available from the Library of Congress

Typeset by Acorn Bookwork, Salisbury, Wilts.
Printed and bound by CPI Group (UK) Ltd, Croydon, CR0 4YY

THE M  CLASS

For Irma and Ronnie

Contents

That England, that was wont to conquer others,
Hath made a shameful conquest of itself.

William Shakespeare

Labour with a black skin cannot emancipate itself where labour with a black skin is branded.

Karl Marx

The problem of the twentieth century is the problem of the colour line.

W. E. B. DuBois

... none of us can shrink from the challenge of racialism ... this Bill [The Race Relations Bill 1968] ... is to protect society as a whole against actions which will lead to social disruption and to prevent the emergence of a class of second-class citizens.

James Callaghan

The reorganisation now of society on classless lines by the proletariat will release immense energies in an uninhibited environment. It is a miserable, cringing mentality, confined to the 'higher standard of living of our people', striving to hold on to what it has and to keep people where they are, which does not understand that the only way out is to give people new visions of themselves, so that they will find new ways to express them and to create new ties, new bonds and a new understanding between those who are now so divided.

C. L. R. James

Preface

This book is an attempt to put in historical perspective the Black presence in Britain as it relates to the development of British capitalism and its control and exploitation of black labour. The making of the black working class in twentieth-century Britain has been a long process, reflecting essential changes in Britain's labour needs over time, both at home and abroad.

As overseas trade expanded, the discipline and control of labour (both black and white) became imperative to Britain's economic well-being. To ensure the continued exploitation of colonial labour, an ideology based on racial differences, which bred an inferior/superior nexus both in interpersonal relations and in international trade, was constructed to keep Blacks in subjection.

Thus, plantocracy racism supported by British capitalists, politicians, historians and influential people of letters, engendered dogmatic belief in white supremacy and institutionalised racism in Britain and her colonial 'possessions'. Consequently, the cultural transmission of racist ideas was handed down over generations. Historically, as Blacks in the colonies laboured under the inhuman and deplorable working conditions endemic in slavery, indentureship and trade union-regulated working conditions, in response, they resorted either 'spontaneously' or in an 'organised' way to various forms of resistance, creating in the process, their own ideologies of Indian nationalism, Pan Africanism and Black Power, and autonomous organisation. This tradition of struggle has, in

turn, informed and strengthened the black working-class movements both in the colonies and Britain in recent years.

In order to avoid any confusion that might arise in the reader's
mind, it is perhaps necessary to define the 'black working class' in
the context of this book. In general, 'black' refers to non-white
persons, particularly those from former colonial and Commonwealth countries. Within this usage, there are sub-divisions denot-
ing the various constituent groups: these are Africans, Asians, West
Indians, Afro-Americans, Afro-Caribbeans, Asian-Caribbeans and
Black British. 'Working class' refers essentially to those unskilled
and semi-skilled Blacks who came to Britain throughout the
period, but particularly during the heavy post-war immigration in
search of jobs.

The task of writing this book has been made less onerous by the
encouragement of many people, particularly Tim O'Keeffe and
Louise Floyd; Ziggi Alexander, Jane Anthony, Crispin Cross,
Ghazala Faizi, Moira Ferguson, Peter Fraser, Peter Fryer, David
Hill, Peter Hogg, David Paisey, Lina Patel, Brian Rooney, Allen
Synge and Rosina Visram. I would also like to thank many of my
colleagues and members of staff in the British Library (at the
Reference Division, Bloomsbury, the Newspaper Library, Colin-
dale and the India Office Library); the staffs at the Public Records
Office Library (Chancery Lane and Kew); the Library of Economics and Political Science; the Institute of Commonwealth Studies
Library; the Labour Party Library, and A. Sivanandan, Director of
the Institute of Race Relations for permission to use the Institute's
unique collection of material. My grateful thanks to Jen Scallan for
her assistance.

Finally, I am grateful to my parents, brothers and sisters for their
invaluable support.

Ron Ramdin
Bloomsbury, London
14 April 1986

Introduction to the Second Edition

On 16 April 2016, a special event was held at Congress House in Central London to celebrate the thirtieth anniversary of the completed manuscript of *The Making of the Black Working Class in Britain*. The occasion was filmed and a clip titled 'An Audience with Ron Ramdin' was put online. Prior to the event, I was approached by Verso Books about republishing the book. For both the book and myself to be so honoured made me pause for reflection.

On its first publication in 1987, a book reviewer in *New Society* described it as a 'pioneering and valuable work of scholarship and interpretation'. I was struck by 'valuable work of scholarship and interpretation'. Why? Because hitherto I'd not read such a positive reference to any book on the history of Black people in Britain, especially one featuring Black workers. Even more encouraging educationally, the book was widely read and used by researchers, students, and writers. As one author put it, he had 'cannibalised' the book for his own work. As time passed, in-depth academic book reviews appeared in the *British Journal of Sociology*, the *American Journal of Sociology* and *History Today* among others; and the *Times* newspaper included it in its 'Pick of Paperbacks'. Given that hitherto British historians had largely ignored the long-standing existence of Black and Asian people in Britain, from the outset, I'd intended that *The Making* should take a long view of this hidden presence, certainly long enough to show continuity. In the context of an expansive history, this 'presence' and contribution, I felt, would make more sense than it would in any short, largely general account and, at the same time, correct a widespread misunderstanding that Black people began coming to Britain only in the 1950s. Thus, given that there had been Black people in Britain since Roman times, I structured the book in three parts to cover the period from 1555 to 1986; a perspective which I thought was preferential if one was to better understand not only the pre-twentieth-century Black presence, but also the interwar period and the turbulent forty years prior to 1986. Overall, such a long view of Black people in Britain would, I felt, not only incorporate their multifaceted contribution both in war and peacetime, but also place *The Making* as an integral study relating to a deeply ingrained attitude and therefore to all aspects of British society.

After I'd published *From Chattel Slave to Wage Earner*, a work on labour history in the Caribbean, I was surprised that there was no book on Black workers in Britain. Thereafter, I became increasingly fascinated by the pre- and early-twentieth-century contribution of Black and Asian people to the British economy. As I stated in the preface to *The Making*,

> To ensure the continued exploitation of colonial labour, an ideology based on racial differences, which bred an inferior/superior nexus, both in interpersonal relations and in international trade, was constructed to keep Blacks in subjection ... Historically, as Blacks in the colonies laboured under the inhuman and deplorable working conditions endemic in slavery, indentureship and trade union–regulated working conditions, in response, they resorted either 'spontaneously' or in an 'organised' way to various forms of resistance, creating in the process, their own ideologies of Indian Nationalism, Pan Africanism and Black Power, and autonomous organisation. This tradition of struggle has, in turn, informed and strengthened Black working-class movements both in the colonies and Britain in recent years.

As these ideas and struggles evolved, I continued to question aspects of social orthodoxy – namely race, tribe, caste, colour, class, gender, culture, religion and so on – categorisations reflecting aspects of divisive social behaviour that were more often than not to be found in various academic journals and books. Indeed in relation to one of these forms of totalisation – class – I was surprised to find that after years of research contrary to my understanding, one famous textbook, *The Making of the English Working Class*, had entirely overlooked the presence and contribution of Black leaders who were prominent in English working-class struggles.

For the purposes of *The Making of the Black Working Class in Britain*, my definitions of 'Black' and 'working class' were clear. Thirty years on, those descriptions are still relevant and often used today by trade unionists, socialists, politicians and social commentators. In recent years, however, the influx of migrants (including those seeking asylum and refugees) from all over the world has added to an even more diverse working population; an extraordinary commingling of people speaking a large number of languages, especially in London and the larger British cities.

Soon after I'd completed the manuscript there was no doubt in my mind that *The Making* (for so long a hidden story) was an essential and timely text which not only broadens and gives depth to our understanding of the past, but also foregrounds an evolving multicultural Britain. It was also very rare that a book of this kind should become a bestseller and quickly go out of print at a time when academics were still largely disinterested in the growing populations of Black and ethnic minorities as integral to British history. But while *The Making* has been informative for students and general readers, for a new generation of those born and bred in Britain, as well as new immigrants from outside the Commonwealth, a great deal was (and is) taken for granted! Some fundamental 'rights' (for example, the Race Relations Act, affecting people at the workplace and in communities) enjoyed by today's citizens were not achieved overnight. In fact, such 'rights' became law as a direct result of insistent, bitter campaigns against racism and sexism waged by Black and Asian workers in the 1960s, 1970s and 1980s. But while there has been change, racism and sexism have persisted.

This year marks the fortieth anniversary of the Grunwick strike. The 'Grunwick 40' exhibition currently on display in the Brent Museum and Archives at the Willesden Library retells the celebrated story of the 'Strikers in Saris'. Thus, by the 1980s, the heightened consciousness of Black workers had generated the need to form autonomous organisations which pointed the way ahead. For me as a writer, *The Making* was a watershed, the beginning of a new phase in my intellectual development. My quest was for a deeper truth about people and society for, in spite of their relevance, I felt there was too much of a cosy woolliness about the prevailing ideas such as race, class, colour, gender, culture and religion. Something vital was missing. Thus I committed myself to an intense exploration of these ideas while I continued to write about histories, cultures and identities. The result was that twelve years after *The Making*, I published *Reimaging Britain*, which helped to clarify in my mind the idea of difference, of celebrating 'the creative potential of human difference'. So far so good, I thought, but not good enough.

And so fifteen years after the publication of Reimaging Britain, I took a further step and confronted head on the totalising effect of social categorisations such as race, class, tribe, colour, gender, culture and religion which stymies individuals ('Striker in Saris', for example) instead of freeing them. Thus since *The Making of the Black Working Class in Britain*, given the making and remaking process, my ideas continued to evolve crucially from autonomous organisation to respect for difference.

Today, the fundamental question that confronts us is this: where are Black and ethnic minority workers located in the employment structure? As if to confirm the persistent, stark daily lived reality of many working people, a few reports on pay and disadvantage have recently appeared. 'Analysis of pay data by the Trades Union Congress (TUC) suggests that the difference in average pay rates amounts to a gap of 23 percent,' stated a BBC Education and Social Affairs report titled 'Black Workers "earning less than white colleagues" ', adding that Black graduates earn less than their white counterparts, the average pay gap between Black and white workers with A-levels being 14 percent; and at GCSE level, the gap is 11 percent. So many issues raised and dealt with in *The Making*, including the inequities in relation to race, education and pay, still confront us. A generation on, how should we address the problem?

Frances O'Grady, the TUC General Secretary identified the problem: 'Race still plays a huge role in determining pay.' She added the 'harsh reality is that at any level of education, Black and Asian workers are getting paid LESS than their white counterparts. The Government cannot afford to ignore these figures and must now take genuine action to tackle pay discrimination.' And what role could or should the government play? One way forward was urgently needed 'interventions'. When dealing with the deprived and disadvantaged, the last Labour Government was convinced throughout its long reign that the key to social mobility was 'education, education, education'. Alas, whatever the beneficial effects of the Labour Government's policies, though masked by self-righteous rhetoric (and, at times, exaggerated political correctness), deep-seated problems remain. While disproportionality in the number of disadvantaged Blacks and Asians attending universities was flagged up repeatedly as a major hurdle, beyond this, there were other consequential inequal-ities to confront. Various researchers, including those at the BBC and the race equality think tank the Runnymede Trust have found that 'pay gaps are not due to the type of university attended, they even extend to Black workers with degrees'. In fact, the TUC's anal-ysis, based on the Labour Force Survey figures from 2014 and 2015, shows the pay gaps were widest among the more qualified. And so education is not working for the benefit of the aspirant as it should. This is shocking. Such evidence of 'pay gaps' is confirmed by recent findings of the University of Essex and the Institute of Economic and Social Research. The implications of these workplace inequal-ities on the rest of society are significant. Furthermore, the British Referendum on 23 June 2016, which resulted in the British people's decision to leave the European Union, will, no doubt, have unknown consequences for migrant workers, especially Blacks and Asians.

Given repeated demands for change, indeed the need for 'interventions', the Prime Minister, concerned with developing a race-equality educational strategy said, 'Transparency would force top universities like Oxford to work harder to broaden their intake.' Fine words from the leading politician, but in spite of his 'intervention' a few weeks later, on 14 September 2016, an *Evening Standard* headline read: 'POLICE DO TARGET BLACK PEOPLE.' In the article Scotland Yard's new diversity chief, Victor Olisa, a Black man, admitted 'stop and search' on the streets targeted Black people. Thirty years earlier in *The Making*, I had written at length about 'sus charges', Black youth and confrontations between Black people and the police. Now, with great interest, I read that the police were still 'routinely discriminating against Black people in stop and search operations in London as part of a misguided performance culture'. Furthermore, the diversity chief attested that 'it was accepted practice to stop young black men to try to boost arrest rates for drugs such as cannabis'. To avoid the 'negative stereotyping of black people', he felt stop and search should not only be based on intelligence, but most importantly officers should be able 'to explain as an individual why you stopped Joe Bloggs'. This official statement points to the very essence of the evolving ideas contained in *The Making* that culminated in the recent publication of my original essay *On Respect for Difference*. Given that 'difference is the DNA of social relations', crucially I concluded the essay in relation to migrations and the globalized world thus: 'Like Britain, few countries can claim to have an "indigenous" population. But wherever human beings congregate in so-called civilized communities and societies, the insistent calls for "freedom" and "human rights" would indeed remain elusive, meaningless slogans, unless people *genuinely* relate to each other with *respect for difference.*'

Against this background, in scope and depth, educationally the value of *The Making of the Black Working Class in Britain* is as timely now (if not more so) as it was when it first appeared: an instructive, informative text for readers regardless of age, race, class, colour, gender, culture or religion about a crucial period in our past. It is at once of major historical and contemporary significance; an educational resource that crucially adds to our understanding of neglected aspects of British history. The oft-quoted historian Peter Fryer, in his 'Suggestion for Further Reading' on Black history stated, 'Some gaps in this cursory reading are due to gaps in the literature ... One at least of these gaps will be filled by Ron Ramdin's forthcoming history of the black working class in Britain.' In fact *The Making* is about a great deal more. Significantly this new edition is the first book to incorporate a 'forgotten' and little known aspect of 'British' history which hitherto chroniclers of the Black presence have either not known about or had overlooked: for many people, Dadabhai Naoroji, elected in 1892 is known as the first Black MP. But new research refutes this. The first Black Member of Parliament was James Townsend, whose election to the House of Commons predates Naoroji by some 125 years. He was also the first Black Lord Mayor of London. (For more on the fascinating story of James Townsend, see Appendix VI.) And so *The Making of the Black Working Class in Britain*, described thirty years ago by *The Times* as a 'pioneering' book continues to enlighten us. Its republication is a rare event which gives due recognition of its place in British history, culture and society.

RON RAMDIN
The British Library,
21 May 2017

PART ONE

The 'Blackamoores'' Presence (1555–1900)

1 Profits, Slavery and the Black Poor

The long standing presence of black people in Britain dates back to Roman times. By the seventeenth century many were employed as servants, pageant performers, court jesters and musicians. Later, this black presence would become significant as trade and economic expansion forged a fundamental connection between the demands of British capitalism and black labour. Indeed, it was argued that Negro slavery and the slave trade were responsible for providing the capital which financed the Industrial Revolution in England and of 'mature' industrial capitalism which, in turn, destroyed the slave system.[1] Since this thesis was propounded, it has been hotly disputed and debated by historians. The purpose here is not to pursue this argument, directly. Nevertheless, a significant consequence of the commerce and trade in slaves, cotton and sugar was that black people began to appear in England in increasing numbers. And throughout the period of slavery, and thereafter, black labour has remained a crucial factor in the development of the British economy.

The rise of African slavery

The arrival of Christopher Columbus in the New World had far-reaching consequences. England joined Spain and Portugal in

their rivalry over actual and potential colonial possessions as a result
of Cabot's voyage to North America in 1497. By 1580 the English
government sought to implement the principle of effective occupation in determining sovereignty. In the struggle for possession in
the West Indies, the 'Iberian Axis' was challenged by England,
France and Holland. In this struggle for a 'place in the sun', as Eric
Williams put it, 'The negro, too, was to have his place, though he
did not ask for it: it was the broiling sun of the sugar, tobacco and
cotton plantations of the New World.'[2]

In the ensuing years, the English claim to colonial possessions
grew. The major economic determinant of prosperity in a new
colony, according to Adam Smith, the English economist, was
'plenty of good land'. Not surprisingly, by 1776, British colonial
possessions were already divided into two types, the self-sufficient
and diversified economy of small farmers and the colony with
facilities for the large-scale production of staples for an export
market. The northern colonies of the American mainland were in
the first category, while the mainland tobacco colonies and the
sugar islands of the Caribbean fell in the second. Given that both
land and capital were useless unless labour could be controlled and
disciplined, labour became of primary concern to the British colonial planter.

To achieve the maximum gains, the kind of labour required on
the plantations had to be constant and able to work in co-operation.
These demands resulted in a dispersal of the rugged individualist
small farmers. The alternative for the Caribbean colonies was
slavery. This system was an economic institution of the first
importance, a key factor in large-scale plantation production. As
one historian saw it:

> In modern times it provided the sugar for the tea and coffee cups of
> the Western world. It produced the cotton to serve as a base for
> modern capitalism. It made the American South and the Caribbean
> islands. Seen in historical perspective, it forms a part of that general
> picture of the harsh treatment of the underprivileged classes, the
> unsympathetic poor laws and severe feudal laws, and the indifference
> with which the rising capitalist class was 'beginning to reckon
> prosperity in terms of sacrificing human life to the deity of increased
> production'.[3]

While slaves and land-hunger moved in tandem, the role of the
African in slavery became crucial. Although slavery in the Caribbean has been narrowly identified with the African, it is clear that a
racial twist had been invented and superimposed on what was
fundamentally an economic institution. For slavery was not the
result of racism but rather, racism was the consequence of slavery.[4]
Before the African, unfree labour in the New World was brown,
white, black and yellow. In fact, the first instance of slave trading
and slave labour developed in the New World involved not the

'Negro' but the Indian. Indian slavery, never sufficiently extensive in the British Dominions, did not interfere with African slavery. The planters demanded sheer physical strength for the future production of the New World staples, sugar and cotton. This, they felt, the Indians lacked. Indeed, the Spaniards had already sought in 1518 that 'permission be given to bring Negroes, a race robust for labour, instead of natives so weak that they can only be employed in tasks requiring little endurance, such as taking care of maize fields or farms'.[5] The epithets 'cotton nigger' and 'sugar mules' became common usage. While the supply of Indians was limited, that of the African was plentiful. Thus, with time, the system of slavery forged an inseparable link between West Africa and the West Indies.

It is important to point out, however, that the immediate successor of the Indian was the poor white, not the African. These white servants comprised indentured servants, 'redemptioners' and convicts. Between 1654 and 1685 a regular traffic developed in these indentured servants; ten thousand sailed from Bristol to the West Indies and Virginia.[6] In 1683, one-sixth of Virginia's population were white servants. As the trade in white servants prospered, commercial speculation encouraged abuses. Kidnapping in London and Bristol became part of a regular business. Convicts provided another source of steady labour. While Benjamin Franklin opposed this 'dumping upon the New World of the outcasts of the Old' the West Indies was prepared to accept 'even the spawn of Newgate and Bridewell'. In effect, these colonies became the dumping ground for the 'riff-raff' of British society.[7]

Moreover, the political and civil disturbances in England between 1640 and 1740 helped to supply white servants. Transportation, mostly to the sugar islands, was the penalty imposed on political and religious non-conformists, such as Cromwell's Irish prisoners who were sent to the West Indies. Transportation was actively associated with the West Indies to the extent that to 'Barbadoes' a person became a verb in the English vernacular.

As trading links grew stronger, the transportation of servants and convicts produced a powerful vested interest in England. Indeed, when the Colonial Board was set up in 1661 one of its more important duties was to control the trade in indentured servants. By the end of the seventeenth century, the aim of economic policy in England was the development of industry, the promotion of employment and the encouragement of exports. But, the question of emigration from the home country to the colonies produced a serious debate. In the context of the argument that 'whatever tends to the depopulation of a Kingdom tends to the impoverishment of it', a British population drain was costly and had to be stemmed. A policy of drawing on cheap labour from elsewhere to people the colonial plantations was under serious consideration. By then, the Royal Family had already given patronage to the Royal African

Company and the African slave trade. Thus, Africa aided British capitalism in launching its process of industrialisation.

By 1680 there was already evidence[8] (in Barbados) that the African was more suited to the demands of production than the European. It seemed clear then that white servitude had no place in a system of chattel slavery. The servant's loss of liberty was for a short period of time, while the African was a slave for life. Furthermore, the servants' status was passed on to their offspring, but African children assumed the status of their mother. The servants also had rights. In the final analysis, the fact that the Negro slave was cheaper proved to be decisive. The cost of securing a white man's services for ten years could buy an African for life![9] The Governor of Barbados stated that 'three blacks work better and cheaper than one white man'.[10]

The experience of one trade served as a rough guide for another. Not surprisingly, therefore, Bristol, the hub of the white servants trade, played the role as one of the centres of the slave trade.

The reason for the origin of negro slavery then, was economic, not racial; it was the cheapness of labour rather than the colour of the labour which was decisive. Features such as hair and colour were the subsequent rationalisations to justify the simple economic fact that to fill the vacuum of colonial labour requirements, African labour was resorted to because it was cheapest and best. Moreover, it is important to understand that where the whites disappeared, the cause was not the climate, but the replacement of the small farm by the large plantation and its consequent demand for a large, cheap and steady labour supply. African slavery's origin can be expressed in terms of three plantation products: sugar, tobacco and cotton. A change in the economic structure produced a corresponding change in the labour supply. In the Caribbean slave society King Sugar reigned supreme. This was a society in which there were only two necessary classes – the wealthy (absentee) planters and the oppressed slaves, the exploiters and the exploited.

Profits

In comparison with the wealthy planters of the sugar islands, the planters in the tobacco colonies came a poor second. The West Indian sugar planter was among the biggest capitalists in the mercantilist era. Indeed, the West Indian (with wealth beyond dispute) was dramatised in a play at the Theatre Royal, Drury Lane, London in 1771.[11] He became a familiar figure in the English social scene in the eighteenth century. But why was he lording it in England when he should have been attending to his fortune-making sugar plantations in the West Indies? The answer must be sought in absentee landlordism;[12] the 'curse of the Caribbean'.

Absenteeism affected the prosperity of the islands. One of the more serious consequences was the mismanagement of the plantations by overseers. There was also the growing imbalance between the whites and the black slave populations. The slave population increased making the prospect of rebellions real. Nevertheless, risk-taking was incidental to the fundamental fact that slavery meant wealth.

Among the absentee landlords of the sugar plantations, the most prominent were the Beckfords, an old Gloucestershire family. Sir Thomas Beckford was among the first absentee proprietors, getting £2000 per annum net (of all charges) from his Jamaican holdings.[13] Another member of the family, Peter Beckford, became the most distinguished of the new colonists, holding military and civil positions in Jamaica. When he died in 1710, he left 'the largest property real and personal of any subject in Europe'.[14] In 1737 William, his grandson, with the inheritance of the family wealth became 'the most powerful West Indian planter in England'.

Another family with West Indian interests were the Hibberts. They operated as planters and merchants, supplying cotton and linen checks for the plantations and the African market. The income received from his West Indian property was enough to enable Robert Hibbert to live comfortably in Bedfordshire. The abolition of slavery brought its compensation to the Hibberts. They received £31,120 for their 1618 slaves.[15]

The Long family were also connected with Jamaica. When Charles Long died he left property in Suffolk, a house in Bloomsbury and 14,000 acres of property in Jamaica. His income 'by far the largest enjoyed by any Jamaican proprietor of that period'[16] entitled him to live in splendour.

Planters and merchants both reaped vast profits from the West Indian trade. The merchants were particularly fortunate. Professor Namier argued that there were 'comparatively few big merchants in Great Britain in 1761 who, in one connection or another, did not trade with the West Indies, and a considerable number of gentry families had interests in the Sugar Islands, just as vast numbers of Englishmen now hold shares in Asiatic rubber or tea plantations or oil fields'.[17] Relations between the two groups however, were not without problems. Planters and merchants belonged to separate organisations. And in spite of their common bond (credit), their interests were, at times, opposed. The basic area of conflict was the planters' determination to maintain monopoly prices. In 1793 conflict between them increased considerably as the planters' struggled for a grant of direct trade to Europe. Ultimately, as the capitalist class, their common interests outweighed their intergroup antagonisms. About 1780, planters and merchants combined in an effort to defend their monopoly against the gathering forces of free trade.

In the eighteenth century planters and merchants, working with colonial agents, became the powerful West India interest. Together, they exploited West Indian resources to the hilt, making large fortunes. To maintain the level of profitability in the age of rotten boroughs, the wealth of those with West Indian interests very often proved decisive during Parliamentary debates. Votes and rotten boroughs were bought. Once in Parliament their competition (and who could successfully compete against them!) increased the price of seats. Elections were no longer foregone conclusions for the English landed aristocracy. In fact, they were indignant and baffled by the West Indians at elections. This was not surprising especially when one recalls that in the 1830 elections a West Indian planter was elected in Bristol having spent £18,000. [18] Money, however, could not buy every Parliamentary seat. Nevertheless, a large fortune more often than not was the barometer which measured political power and influence. The Beckford dynasty, for example, was well-represented in Parliament in accordance with their wealth. [19] In addition to the Beckfords, Richard Pennant represented Liverpool, one of the Barbados Codringtons was an MP in 1737, Edward Colston held the Bristol seat from 1710 to 1713, George Hibbert represented Seaford from 1806 to 1812 and John Gladstone represented Woodstock and, later, Lancaster.

Because of the impulse given to trade and agriculture in England, Henry Goulburn in 1833 was still pleading with Parliament to look at the towns that had sprung up as a consequence of the connection with the colonies. [20] It was difficult to ignore the West Indians; their presence mattered. Ten out of fifteen members of an influential Committee of the Society of Planters and Merchants held seats in Parliament. [21] In effect, the slave traders and slave-owners were entrenched both in the Commons and in the House of Lords. From these powerful positions they were able to repel attacks on their plantations and their social structure. In the balancing act of give and take, peerages were conferred in return for political support. There was a hard ring of truth in the statement that there were few, if any, noble houses in England without a West Indian.

The slave-owners not only dominated Parliament, but they had an all-pervasive effect as aldermen, mayors and councillors. William Beckford was not only an Alderman for the City of London, but also twice Lord Mayor. [22]

Nevertheless, the West Indian interest was the 'enfant terrible of English politics until American Independence struck the first great blow at mercantilism and monopoly'. [23] In 1764 there were fifty or sixty West Indian voters who held the balance of power. [24] The West Indian sugar interest was enjoying the heyday of its power. But although sugar (and monopoly) would be replaced by cotton (and laissez-faire) in the eighteenth century, sugar remained supreme throughout this period. The vast profits made by the slave traders, slave-owners, planters and merchants were openly displayed in England. Indeed, such West Indian wealth courted the displeasure of King George III who, on a visit with Pitt, having encountered a wealthy Jamaican is reported to have said, 'Sugar, sugar, eh? all *that* sugar! How are the duties, eh, Pitt, how are the duties?'[25] Duties or no duties, given absentee landlordism, the fact remains that West Indian profits were spent in England. In short, it was all to the benefit of the home country.

As the slave trade developed and sugar became King (later succeeded by cotton in the United States) many Blacks were brought to the mother country by their masters; a living reminder of the slavery–profits nexus. On the question of this fundamental relationship two distinguished black historians have reached significant conclusions: C. L. R. James suggested in his history[26] of the Haitian Slave Revolution and the rise of Toussaint L'Ouverture that Britain abolished the slave trade and slavery for economic reasons. Six years later, Eric Williams in *Capitalism and Slavery*[27] also showed how economic rather than humanitarian reasons led to the abolition of the slave trade and slavery in Britain. While few would dispute these conclusions, logically, one might well ask: how did the black slaves in Britain live and how did they become 'free'?

Pets and domestic servants

Before John Hawkins sold his first group of Africans into slavery in 1563, towards the end of 1555, John Lok had already returned from his second voyage bringing to England with him 'certaine black slaves, whereof some were tall and strong men, and could wel agree with our meates and drinkes'.[28] Naturally, the 'colde and moyst' air offended the Africans. This was the inauspicious beginning of the importation by the Merchant Adventurers of Blacks from West Africa into England. Over the next two and a half centuries the trade between West Africa, the Caribbean, the Americas and England grew enormously. Consequently, the number of Blacks in Britain increased.

The commercial probings of the Merchant Adventurers opened up a new world, the world of the black peoples. Thus from the 1550s, the Blacks became a haunting and focal point of political debate among the ruling class in England. By the late sixteenth century, the Englishman no longer resorted to reading exotic and fantastic tales about the African. Indeed, the African had become human, a real presence on the streets of English seaports, in London and more particularly, as 'pets' and domestic servants in wealthy English households.[29] Among some members of the English working class, the Black had become an object of envy who, it was argued, did not have to worry about the next meal.[30] By the end of the century, as cheap black labour was sought, there had been a considerable increase in the number of Blacks in England.[31] Initially, these Africans were brought to assist English traders who ventured to Africa. A rare sight, the English were curious about the black persons they saw. Indeed, in social circles they were highly valued. Increasingly, black slave domestics became part of noble households. This early contact with West Africans was to have far-reaching consequences. Queen Elizabeth I gave her blessings to African slave-trading, bestowing a knighthood on the slave-trader, John Hawkins, who used one of the Queen's ships, the *Jesus* on his second slave-trading voyage.[32] As the trade in human cargo between Africa and the New World developed, more Africans arrived in England as the property of whites, 'human ballast' for sale or to be used at will.

During the first two centuries of black settlement in England, the most common form of work for black workers was found within the servant class.[33] As their numbers grew, their employers became less exclusive. By the late sixteenth century, for example, black servants were employed not only close to the Court, but by those of humbler status.[34] Many years later Samuel Johnson's black servant, Francis Barber, was fortunate enough to receive an annual income of £100 after his master's death. This, however, was an exceptional case of good fortune.

Among the Africans, most of whom lived in London (a reflection of the mercantile importance of the city), a few became 'relatively prosperous residents'. In fact, a group of Blacks were able to build their own house in London in 1597.[35] Although they did not conform to 'building regulations', they nevertheless showed an independence quite at variance with the received attitude of contemporary Englishmen.

By the end of the sixteenth century, the black presence had become noticeable to no lesser person than the Queen. The growth of a black minority in London was, to say the least, assuming the proportions of a real problem. The social problem which faced England, as poverty, famine and hunger spread over the country, had adverse effects on the Blacks who were singled out for special treatment. Queen Elizabeth alerted the mayors of the major cities 'that there are of late divers blackamoores brought into this realm, of which kind of people there are allready here too manie considerynge howe God hath blessed this land with great increase of people of our owne nation as anie countrie in the world'.[36] Accordingly, she ordered 'that those kinde of people should be sente forth of the land'. In her deportation order, she identified the Africans imported by Sir Thomas Baskerville.[37] She had objected to black settlement in July 1596 and repatriation was already becoming a preoccupation by the beginning of the seventeenth century. An order was issued to hand over all black servants to the Lubeck merchant, Van Senden, emphasising that Her Majesty's subjects should 'be served by their owne countrymen (rather) than those kind of people'.[38] The Blacks had become a 'problem' to the extent that in January 1601, the Queen issued a proclamation to deport 'such Negroes and blackamoores which . . . are carried into this realm . . . who are fostered and powered here, to the great

annoyance of her own liege people'.[39] Already Blacks were being
set apart from the rest of the British people. As the slave trade
entered into high-gear, in addition to direct importation from
Africa, more and more Blacks entered Britain via slavery in the
West Indies and in North America where, particularly after the War
of Independence, the black slaves who had fought on the British
side were promised their freedom.

Liberty

The presence of black slaves in Britain introduced a new social
'problem'. The ownership of human beings as property was a
challenge to the common law. This was reflected in a number of
slave cases in which contradictory decisions were taken, indicat-
ing confusion and uncertainty in the law. In 1729, however, in an
attempt to clarify any misunderstanding about slaves becoming
free on entry to England or Ireland, or as a result of being baptised, the Solicitor-General and the Attorney General were of the
opinion that a slave coming from the West Indies to Great Britain
or Ireland, with or without a master was not free, and that the master's property or right in the slave was not thereby determined or
varied; and that baptism did not bestow freedom on him or made
any alteration in his temporal condition. They added, 'We are
also of opinion that his master may legally compel him to return
again to the plantations.'[40]

Known as the Yorke–Talbot opinion, this view prevailed,
upholding slavery in England until 1772, when the case of the
runaway slave Somerset was heard in the Court of King's Bench
before Lord Chief Justice Mansfield. The case is regarded as a
'watershed' in English legal history. In the case Lord Mansfield
effectively decided that a slave could not forcibly be taken abroad
by his master against his wishes. The case also had historical
significance in showing the positions of contemporary schools of
thought on the slave question.

The verdict on the Somerset case was indeed of great significance
to the anti-slavery movement. In spite of this decision, however,
the practice of taking slaves forcibly from England continued after
1772. The law remained defective, offering no protection to the
'free' black person in England from unlawful enslavement. Slavery
in the colonies then was a rude reminder to the Blacks of their
confused status in Britain. As F. O. Shyllon argued, it was not until
1834 that it can truly be said that black slaves in Britain were
emancipated, as were their fellow Blacks in the West Indies.[41]

Free black voices

Among the 'free' Blacks there were a few who spoke out on the
intolerable conditions of slavery and the plight of the black poor in
Britain. Having come 'Up from Slavery' in the upsurge of

abolitionist sentiment in the 1780s outstanding contributions came from three Africans, Ignatius Sancho, Ottobah Cugoano and Olaudah Equiano, amongst others. They were all men of letters. Cugoano and Equiano both wrote essentially for publication, while Sancho was published posthumously. Indeed, Sancho became the best known African in London. He was the author of a book on the theory of music and appeared on the stage. These talented Blacks appealed to the liberal instincts of a few distinguished Englishmen. In fact, at this time, the pro-abolition campaign to arouse British public opinion against slavery through petitions (given missionary zeal, the growth of non-conformism and humanitarian agitational pressure) had begun to receive widespread support from radicals and the British working class.

Such men as Garrick and Sterne were among Cugoano's friends, and his portrait was painted by Gainsborough.[42] He was best known, however, for the representations made on behalf of his unfortunate fellow Blacks. In his campaign, he solicited the help of Laurence Sterne by drawing attention to the acute distress of the black poor in London. They needed food, clothing and shelter, and many were desperate and dying he argued. In 1797, in his *Thoughts and Sentiments* Cugoano denounced the evil of slavery and pleaded for human dignity; for kindness and mercy, not transportation to Sierra Leone.[43] Moreover, he cited the appalling lack of consideration of the British government by elaborating the real difficulties of the ill-advised plan of settlement in West Africa for London's black poor.[44]

More political than either Sancho or Cugoano was Equiano. His autobiography, published in 1789, made him famous.[45] He gives a detailed and moving account of how he and his sister were kidnapped in Africa and taken aboard a slave ship. After years in slavery, he was employed as a sailor and gained much experience on vessels plying the Caribbean waters and beyond. He travelled as far as the North Pole.

In 1774 he set out with Captain John Hughes from the Thames, on a ship called *Anglicania* bound for Smyrna, in Turkey. On the journey he acted as steward and John Annis, a 'clever black man' was the cook. Equiano told how Annis, after two months on board ship was hounded by a Mr. William Kirkpatrick, a 'gentleman' of St. Kitts, from whom he had parted by consent. Kirkpatrick nevertheless sought to have Annis back in bondage. After several unsuccessful attempts to 'trepan him' (and when all attempts at kidnapping proved abortive) Kirkpatrick with six men and two boats boarded Equiano's ship, tied Annis and forcibly took him away as the crew and the chief mate looked on. This lack of response on the part of the ship's company to retrieve Annis, troubled Equiano. 'I believe', he wrote, 'that this was a combined piece of business.'[46] And any vague ideas he might have had about the goodness of the Captain were now clearly revealed. He added, 'but, at any rate, it certainly reflected great disgrace on the mate and captain also, who, although they had desired the oppressed man to stay on board, yet he did not in the least assist or recover him, or pay me a farthing of his wages, which was about five pounds'.[47]

Given his own suffering and experience of slavery, and having borne witness to the suffering of others, no wonder Equiano was moved to give voice to the voiceless.

Enemies and friends

Enemies

While the black writers pleaded the cause of the slave and the black poor, between 1750 and 1838 the anti-abolitionists' arguments centred on the personality traits and physical features of the African slave. Over generations, the prejudice of white racists against the African had imbued the popular consciousness with certain 'characteristic' traits peculiar to the African. A desperate anti-Black campaign was mounted on behalf of the planters' interest to counteract the struggle for black freedom.

In their accounts of slave life and 'scientific observations' of the African in West Africa and the West Indies, bourgeois writers furthered the planters' propaganda. The literary talents of these propagandists were supported by West Indian properties and metropolitan interests that were interlocked. Indeed, the absentee planters offered their explanations (or prejudices) based on past experiences on the plantations.

Edward Long was one such planter. Born in 1734, he lived in Jamaica for twelve years. His *History of Jamaica*, published in 1774, became 'a classic description of the machinery of colonial government on the eve of the American Revolution'. Long certainly had strong views about the African. While he must be credited with being outspoken, his feelings about Africans were instructive and must not go unnoticed. In fact, as a respected author, he made 'scholarly' references to support his arguments, and was widely read by a captive audience. In a burst of unscientific nonsense, revealing a preoccupation with black sexuality, he wrote: 'I do not think that an orang-outang husband would be any dishonour to an Hottentot female for what are these Hottentots?' In describing the Hottentot Black as 'one of the meanest nations on the face of the earth',[48] Long, the successful exploiter of black slaves, betrayed much about himself and his society of British planters. Having attempted a debasement of the black man's physique to a sub-human level, he went on to insult his intellectual faculties, his diet and eating habits, (and most interestingly) expressed his alarm over their alleged sexual capacity. 'Their hearing is remarkably quick', he observed, adding 'their faculties of smell and taste are truly bestial, nor less so their commerce with the other sex; in these acts they are libidinous and shameless as monkies, or baboons. The equally hot temperament of their women has given probability to the charge of their admitting these animals frequently to their embrace.'[49] So much for Long's sexual fantasies! A pleasure rooted in racism; the oppressor justifying oppression and exploitation through his own weakness?

Another pro-slavery book, a *History of the British Colonies in the West Indies*, was written by Bryan Edwards in 1793. In recognising the simple fact that the degrading nature of slavery had the effect of conditioning the behaviour of the slaves, he made pronouncements on the morality of sex. Edwards denied that, in reality, the Negro had any 'visions of romance' or capacity for a caring relationship with the opposite sex.[50]

Fifty-six years later, *The Nigger Question*, written by Thomas Carlyle, was published. He was particularly abusive and dismissive of Blacks. As far as he was concerned, from his comfortable bourgeois perch, Africans were 'all very happy and doing very well'. West Indian Whites, on the other hand, were unhappy. One might well ask how he arrived at this incredible conclusion. The clue to the answer, it would seem, is in the fact that this relative concern over the slave/white relationship in the West Indies afforded him the opportunity of a larger bone to pick nearer home. He contrasted the impoverished Whites with the Blacks thus:

> But, thank Heaven, our interesting Black population – equalling almost in number of heads one of the Ridings of Yorkshire, and in worth (in quantity of intellect, faculty, docility, energy, and available human valor and value) perhaps one of the streets of Seven Dials – are all doing remarkably well. 'Sweet blighted lillies' – as the American epitaph on the Nigger child has it – Sweet blighted lillies, they are holding up their heads again! How pleasant, in the universal bankruptcy abroad, and dim dreary stagnancy at home, as if for England too there remained nothing but to suppress Chartist riots, banish united Irishmen, vote the supplies, and wait with arms crossed till black Anarchy and Social Death devoured us also; as it has done the others; how pleasant to have always this fact to fall back upon: our beautiful Black darlings are at last happy; with little labour except to the teeth, which surely, in those excellent horse-jaws of theirs, will not fail![51]

He saw oppressed Blacks and Whites as being forced by hunger to labour for their living and feared that an emancipated West Indies would be turned into a 'Black Ireland'. Further, he likened such a reality to be stronger than a nightmare dream.[52] He refused to explore the question of African rights. And with a facile consideration, he excused himself from further discussion by saying what 'a complex' thing it was.

In 1859, Anthony Trollope joined the chorus of racist writers with the publication *The West Indies and the Spanish Main*. He, too, showed a preoccupation with 'the black skin and thick lip' of the 'Negro', drawing a distinction between that strange race of creole 'Negroes' born out of Africa and those born within. He derided the black slave for having 'no language of their own' and for speaking 'broken English' as uneducated foreigners always speak a foreign language. The lack of educational opportunities was the farthest thing from his mind. In fact, his view of the African was that he was capable of the hardest physical work which could be endured 'probably with less bodily pain than men of any other race'. Nonetheless, he was 'idle, unambitious as to worldly position, sensual, and content with little'.[53] This was his *raison d'être* for not educating the black man who was forced to eke out the barest existence, yet was seen as being 'content with little'! Trollope bowed to the deity of profits, emphasising his concern for competition and the labour market. One might well ask, what indeed did the rich planters and merchants (whom Trollope and others have so staunchly defended) give in return for the vast profits they reaped at the expense of the cheap, mercilessly exploited labour of generations of enslaved Blacks?

Friends

The slave trade and Negro slavery had been a matter of conscience for many English philanthropists who sought to educate public opinion about the black slave. The pro-planters and merchants lobby had to face a countervailing force described as 'The Humanitarian Impulse'. Granville Sharp, one of the guiding lights among the philanthropists gave shape and direction to the humanitarian movement. He was in close contact with the slaves in London and became controversial in dealing with their problems. In 1765, he rescued an ill-used slave Jonathan Strong, who in 1769 was recaptured and jailed. Sharp's determination in rescuing him again was followed by Strong's 'owner' David Lisle taking legal action against Sharp whose lawyers advised him that because of the Yorke–Talbot opinion of 1729, Lisle had a strong legal case. Not to be outdone, Sharp undertook research to prove that slavery in England was unlawful. In 1769 the result of his research, *A Representation of the Injustice . . .* was published. His fight against English slavery was rewarded with the famous judgement on the Somerset case in 1772. Throughout the case, Sharp played a crucial role, directing popular attention to the illegality of slavery in England. This case was used as a platform for political organisation and propaganda in the campaign for abolition and emancipation.

John Wesley also rallied crucial support for the philanthropist cause. In *Thoughts Upon Slavery*, published in 1774, he attacked British involvement in slave trading. This publication had a huge circulation in the 1780s. It was influential in turning the growing body of Methodists against the slave trade. Moreover, it led to extensive missionary work in the West Indies. His description of the Negro helped to restore a 'human image' which played an important part in the campaign of the abolitionist cause.

Another influential campaigner against the evils of slavery was James Ramsay. His decision to do so was the result of a visit to a disease-ridden slave ship and the appalling treatment meted out to the slaves. He took Holy Orders and became a missionary in the West Indies. His involvement with the slaves brought inevitable displeasure to the planters. This experience served him well. On his return to England, Ramsay wrote his *Essay on the Treatment and Conversion of African Slaves*. He worked together with William Wilberforce, Thomas Clarkson and the abolitionist Quakers.

Thomas Clarkson, regarded as the greatest of all the abolitionists, undertook the demanding and dangerous task of gathering evidence (from the slave traders themselves) against the slave trade. As a student at Cambridge, his prize-winning *Essay on the Slavery and Commerce of the Human Species* was first published in 1785. This aroused a wave of public indignation against the slave-traders. Further, it evoked sympathy for the slave that was 'never to be surpassed'. And after Henri Christophe (the King of Haiti) died, his wife and daughter stayed with the Clarksons. Clarkson's friend, the poet William Wordsworth (who also went to Cambridge), aware of Clarkson's essay on slavery, recognised both Toussaint L'Ouverture and Clarkson in the following sonnets:

> Toussaint, the most unhappy man of men!
> Whether the Whistling Rustic tends his plough
> Within thy hearing, or thy head be now
> Pillowed in some deep dungeon's earless den;
> O miserable Chieftain! Where and when
> Wilt thou find patience! Yet die not; do thou
> Wear rather in thy bonds a cheerful brow:
> Though fallen thyself, never to rise again,
> Live and take comfort. Thou hast left behind
> Powers that will work for thee; air, earth, and skies;
> There's not a breathing of the common wind
> That will forget thee: thou has great allies;
> Thy friends are exultations, agonies,
> And love, and man's unconquerable mind. [54]

On the final passing of the Bill for the abolition of the slave trade in March 1807, he wrote:

> Clarkson! it was an obstinate hill to climb:
> How toilsome – nay, how dire – it was, by thee
> Is known; by none, perhaps, so feelingly:
> But thou, who starting in thy fervent prime,
> Didst first lead forth that enterprise sublime,
> Hast heard the constant voice its charge repeat,
> Which, out of thy young heart's oracular seat,
> First roused thee – O true yorke-fellow of Time,

> Duty's intrepid liegeman, see, the palm
> Is won, and by all Nations shall be worn!
> The blood-stained Writing is forever torn;
> And thou henceforth will have a good man's calm,
> A great man's happiness; thy zeal shall find
> Repose at length, firm friend of human kind![55]

In *Letters on Slavery*, published in 1789, William Dickson challenged the widespread belief in the inferiority of black men. He too had first hand experience of the debilitating effects of life on the plantations in Barbados. He pointed out that planters failed to see that the qualities they complained of in the slave stemmed directly from the life to which the slaves were subjected.

Finally, we turn to the activities of William Wilberforce. His struggle in the cause of emancipation was spread over half a century. Like Granville Sharp, Wilberforce was involved at every level in the campaign for the abolition of slavery, from the late 1780s to the time of his death before Emancipation. Against the impression created by the planters and their influential apologists, 'that the indolence of the Negro race was utterly incurable, and that without the driving whip they never would willingly engage in agricultural labour', Wilberforce argued that it has been 'shown to be utterly without foundation'. Among others, he cited a 'striking instance' in Trinidad where the many hundreds of American 'Negroes' at the close of 'the late unhappy war with the United States, were, by the humane policy of Sir Ralph Woodford, received into Trinidad, to no small alarm to the planters'.[56] Wilberforce's overall contribution to end the system of slavery has become well-known. What is less well known, however, is his highly questionable position as a 'humanitarian'.

Following Carlyle's 'Discourse', John Stuart Mill entered the debate on the 'Negro' question in 1850. Despite the collapse of the sugar producing colonies, his overall argument in support of black freedom is interesting. He wrote:

> Were the whites born ever so superior in intelligence to the blacks, and competent by nature to instruct and advise them, it would not be the less monstrous to assert that they had therefore a right either to subdue them by force, or circumvent them by superior skill; to throw upon them the toils and hardships of life, reserving for themselves, under the misapplied name of work, its agreeable excitements. . . . That this country should turn back to the matter of Negro slavery, I have not the smallest apprehension. There is, however, another place where that tyranny still flourishes, but now for the first time finds itself seriously in danger. At this crisis of American slavery, when the decisive conflict between right and iniquity seems about to commence, your contributor steps in, and flings this missile, loaded with the weight of his reputation, into the abolitionist camp. The words of English writers of celebrity are

words of power on the other side of the ocean; and the owners of human flesh, who probably thought they had not an honest man on their side between the Atlantic and the Vistula, will welcome such an auxiliary. Circulated as his dissertation will probably be by those whose interests profit by it, from one end of the American Union to the other, I hardly know of an act by which one person could have done so much mischief as this may possibly do; and I hold that by thus acting, he has made himself an instrument of what an able writer in the *Inquirer* justly calls 'a true work of the devil'.[57]

In the long debate between the 'enemies' and 'friends' (whose arguments weighed in the balance the future of the slaves) the bedrock of the slave system remained its economic viability. Taking the issue from there, the struggle was strengthened by winning public opinion. For as Walvin argued: 'What ultimately doomed slavery was the anti-slavery movement and the irresistible pressure it exercised via the public, over Parliament and Governments'.[58] Indeed, it was clear that this economic issue with all its political implications would only be resolved by Parliament.

The struggle of the black poor

The black people living in England during these years were engaged in a daily struggle for survival. Apart from being 'alien', their blackness emphasised their conspicuousness. The grim reality of poverty pushed many to desperation. They fought on two main fronts; some became political activists and some pugilists.

The fight for survival was the essential experience of the black poor. Street life bred the art of self-defence but most of the black poor were the victims of adverse circumstances. Blacks were abused indiscriminately.

Those born or brought to Britain were treated, to say the least, indecently. In short, many in the 'circus' were displayed like animals.

Poverty was, in general, synonymous with being black. The black poor were among the 'poorest of the poor' in London. Not surprisingly, therefore, a large proportion of London's black poor were beggars in the mid-1780s and during the nineteenth century. It seemed wherever there were beggars, black people were among them. According to the Society for the Suppression of Mendicity, there were approximately 400 black beggars between 1820 and 1826, a ratio of one in every 40 beggars.[59]

Barely eking out an existence (and in many cases close to death) the gradual decline in black beggary reflected a decline in the black population as a whole due to a high death rate in London and the fact that there was little fresh immigration.[60]

Given that remunerative employment was hard to come by, many blacks had to live by their wits. Necessity being the mother of invention, some mendicant Blacks were able to elude the Society's strictures. One important reason for keeping out of reach of the Society was the severe treatment Blacks received. Inevitably, some Blacks were caught and punished as were a Jamaican and a Barbadian in 1819 and 1820 respectively.[61]

Deportation of Blacks loomed large as the final answer. Financing such a remedy was clearly no problem. (This was attempted earlier in the 1780s when the black poor were deported to Sierra Leone.) But deportation to the West Indies meant slavery. Blacks were caught in a dilemma. On the one hand, hunger and poverty forced them to beg and steal, while on the other, they were faced with the possibility of deportation and slavery. By all accounts then, the position of the black poor in English society was a desperate one. Cornered like animals, they had to fight for the barest existence.

As they fought in the boxing ring, or on the streets, or against prosecutions, at various times, they faced the real possibility of being imprisoned, flogged or deported.

Given the difficulties, not many Blacks were prepared to remain beggars. Many, however, seemed to have begged at one time or another. A few who 'turned professional' did well enough to become heroes. Tribute was paid to these outstanding beggars by their peers. The black one-legged fiddler, Billy Waters, was elected 'King of the Beggars'.[62] Another well-known 'successful' black beggar[63] was Charles McGee. Born in Jamaica in 1744 he begged at Ludgate Hill.

In the fight for survival, another section of the black community – the Lascars – were faced also with extreme hardship. The Lascars in London were Indian seamen. These men, who found England cold and inhospitable, managed to join the professional beggars.

From 1814, about 1500 Lascars living in barracks received support from the East India Company.[64] In fact, the Company paid 1s. 6d. a day for their board and lodging.[65] In spite of this gesture, an estimated 130 Lascars died in Britain each year from 1790 to 1810. This death rate doubled in 1813. In the winter of 1813–14, the Company admitted that at least two Lascars died each week and, on one exceptionally cold day, five died.[66] Naturally, these men complained at the treatment they were receiving. The Company responded predictably. The grumblers were to be deported on the first ship.[67] In spite of the fact that the Lascars' grievances were many, once again repatriation was used as the ultimate threat. But such threats were no solutions to the problems of the black poor. A Parliamentary Committee found that men slept on bare planks on the floor and that the barracks were often overcrowded.

Moreover, the Company openly admitted that the men in their care were the victims of acts of violence by the administrators.[68] The missionaries and magistrates showed little sympathy or understanding for the Indian seamen or their religious beliefs. But of course, tolerance was never enough. Racism lurked everywhere. A dark complexion was clearly objectionable. And when members and friends of the African and Asiatic Society met for dinner at a Tavern in 1816 (even with the humanitarian and friend of the Blacks Wilberforce acting as Chairman) tokenism and discrimination was seen very clearly.[69] Alas, such gross prejudice did not prevent intermarriage. Of the estimated 10,000 black people living in Britain at the beginning of the nineteenth century, many black males had taken white wives.

According to Peter Fryer, while black immigration to Britain dwindled, intermarriage was widespread. Consequently, these two factors contributed to a decrease (how large would be pure guess-work) of the black community during the last two-thirds of the nineteenth century. Nonetheless, there was a continuous black presence. In Liverpool (the slave port and centre of the cotton trade) research has shown that there never was a time, throughout the century, when the city did not have black citizens and that these citizens were always united by common problems and interests.[70]

Despite a decrease in the number of the black poor in Britain during the nineteenth century, their essential poverty remained unaffected. So much so, that action of another kind became necessary; action based on common causes shared to some extent by the wider British working class.

2 Black Radicals and Black Women in Service

Common problems and common interests indeed. Through aiding the common causes, by the turn of the nineteenth century the anti-slavery campaign, in church and chapel and especially among the British working class (although there is evidence during the early 1830s of radical working class hostility) won steadily growing support. In fact, the mass anti-slavery movement emerged at the end of the 1780s, reaching peaks in the campaigns for abolition of the Slave Trade (1788, 1792 and 1814), for Emancipation (1823, 1830 and 1833) and for the end of 'Negro' Apprenticeship in 1838.[1]

Paradoxically, in spite of this shift in British public opinion, the black people in Britain were, in various ways, forced to submit to the prejudices inherent in English society, as their fellow Blacks endured the agonies of slavery on the colonial plantations. Significantly, the black struggle had merged into a larger movement, with the black slave being used as an argument against white slavery in Britain. Not surprisingly then, black working class leaders were acceptable and became an integral part of the vanguard of the radical working class movement between 1800 and 1850. During this period, four exceptional Blacks emerged to channel their particular grievances and arguments into the mainstream of British working class agitation. Two of them, William Davidson and Robert Wedderburn, were revolutionary socialists. They were 'members of the far left of all the radical organisations of the time', and followers of Thomas Spence (Secretary of the London Corresponding Society (LCS) and editor of radical papers), who was imprisoned for his radicalism.

It is more than likely that, apart from the fact that the Spenceans were the 'farthest left of the radicals', these black radicals were also attracted to their group which was the 'most solidly working class in composition'. Most of its members were 'mechanics and manufacturers', factory workers and shoemakers and a few soldiers and sailors. The small numbers of its membership did not detract from the quality of their group which was the only radical organisation to maintain an unbroken continuity throughout the Napoleonic wars. [2]

The Spenceans, the only socialist organisation in the country, had the reputation of being 'the most serious, and influential group of conspirators during the post-war radical agitation'. [3] Spencean activists were involved in the Spa Fields riots in December 1816 and some of them had contacts in Manchester, Stockport and Bolton. In terms of formal organisation, the Spenceans were divided into sections, structurally similar to that of the old LCS. This influence on the Spenceans was not surprising since the last Secretary of the LCS was Thomas Evans* (a colourer of prints and later, patent brace-maker)[4] who became leader of the Spenceans after Spence's death in 1814. [5] Inevitably, the splits and disharmony led to various Spencean groups operating along independent lines during 1817–1820. Robert Wedderburn led one of these groups while William Davidson led another. The other outstanding black radical devoted to the British and colonial working class struggle was the deported London Chartist, William Cuffay. Lesser known (and understandably) is Matthew Bogle who was involved in the Scottish Insurrection of 1820.

---

* According to Iain McCalman, George Canon (alias Rev. Erasmus Perkins) Evans, Wedderburn and Davidson, among other working class radicals, were involved in the pornographic press (see *Past and Present*, August 1984).

Robert Wedderburn

The English working class had, by the early nineteenth century, become sufficiently aware that their freedom was crucially dependent on their own forms of agitational organisation. Like the slaves on the colonial plantations, they could not wait for 'a dispensation from above'. Those who followed the radical tradition risked everything; ultimately, their lives. Prison sentences were served on those who challenged the ruling class on political, religious or trade union matters, for example. Although there were 26 prosecutions for seditious and blasphemous libel in 1817, radicals of all shades of opinion were united in one aim: to bait authority until certain freedoms were won. Among the black radicals was Robert Wedderburn. A tailor by trade and leader of a London-based Spencean Group, he had printed *The Forlorn Hope*. Seen as a threat to the ruling class, he was imprisoned.

This black man had come a long way to join the working class struggle in Britain. Wedderburn's mother was a slave in Jamaica. His father was James Wedderburn, a Scot who owned large sugar plantations in Jamaica.[6] What we know is that Robert was born in Jamaica in 1762[7] and brought up by his grandmother. As a child he bore witness to both his mother and grandmother being flogged. This had a profound effect upon Robert.[8]

A witness to many atrocities, Wedderburn, a lad of 17, arrived in England in 1778. His first employment was at sea, before becoming a jobbing tailor. He was aware during his life, particularly in England, of the great divide between rich and poor, and the importance of social status in English society. He had begun to see much of his earlier life in historical perspective. Prejudice and social injustice in his workaday experiences had sharpened his perception and honed his intelligence to a militant edge. He felt his earlier work experience could have been better.[9] Indeed, he was a social man. Having heard a Wesleyan preacher at Seven Dials, he sought to relate fringe groups like Armenians, unorthodox Christians, Calvinists and Unitarians with the rest of the Christian flock. Togetherness, brotherhood and unity was superficial. He wanted to get to the heart of the Christian religion. He became a Unitarian preacher which acted as a cover for his radical activities. Thus, he became 'Reverend' Robert Wedderburn. His work as a Unitarian preacher proved fruitful. His findings in a pamphlet Truth, self-supported; or a refutation of certain doctrinal errors, generally adopted in the Christian church, led him on to unorthodox directions. A few months before Thomas Spence died, Wedderburn came into contact with him. Wedderburn was then about 51 or 52 years old. In fact, Wedderburn became a member of the Society of Spencean Philanthropists.

Wedderburn's activities in the Spencean group became prominent in March 1817 with Parliamentary legislation aimed at suppressing the Spenceans. Following the Act, Thomas Evans, the Spencean leader, and his young son were imprisoned for high treason, for publishing anti-landowners views. Wedderburn was now in the front line. In an effort to arouse English workers from their lethargy, he launched in 1817 *The Forlorn Hope*, a periodical through which he hoped 'to establish something of a free Press'. He used the first issue to appeal for help on behalf of Evans and his son. This was a clever move designed not only to draw out those who were supporters of Evans, but also an attempt to establish the principle of a free press.

Among the radicals leadership was a quarrelsome issue. On his release from jail, Evans clashed with Wedderburn. Young people approved of Wedderburn's teachings, applauding 'anything that he ridiculed in the Scriptures most violent'.[10] He was sensitive about his African ancestry and was pleased with the decision of a debate concerning the right of a slave to kill his master. This outcome in favour of slaves freeing themselves from their Christian masters was widely welcomed. Wedderburn's undoubted influence led to his prosecution for 'sedition and blasphemy'.

Soon after Wedderburn's incarceration, the Peterloo massacre took place. The factory owners, merchants and shopkeepers in Manchester, amassed their strength against a defenceless working class. The violence and enormity of events of Peterloo and its implications were the subject of political debates and discussions on 'class war' throughout the country.[11]

In Wedderburn's view the revolution was imminent. The ministers and Prince Regent, he said, were 'bloody tyrants'. There were no two ways about it. His commitment to the revolution was clear. He was 60, and three years earlier he had engaged in physical training in readiness for a confrontation with and the eventual overthrow of 'those bloody murdering thieves'.[12] He had an abiding faith in 'the poor' emerging victorious.

Given his Jamaican background, Wedderburn was able to put in perspective the English working class struggle in the context of the Empire. As Fryer correctly states, he was the first black activist to disseminate revolutionary writings from Britain in the West Indies. While urging slaves to acquire lands, Wedderburn felt the plight of White European poor and Black slaves integral to the revolutionary struggle.

By the 1820s, Spenceanism had given precedence to the

National Union of Working Classes, and other organisations in the early 1830s. Indeed, the ideas of Spence, were highly influential on the Socialist theories of Robert Owen. Moreover, old Spenceans played an 'important and continuous' role in London Chartism.[13] How did Wedderburn figure in these movements?

Little is known about the rest of his life, and the date and circumstances of his death, but one thing shines through in his life: the son of a slave, he was unwilling to accept slavery in any form, either among the English working class or the slaves on the plantations. The class struggle was his main concern; race and colour, it seemed, were secondary. His commitment to the class war was uncompromising. Though incarcerated twice for his beliefs, criticised by fellow working class leaders and spied on by informers, this black radical's revolutionary fervour on behalf of the poor and oppressed remained uncompromised. This kind of commitment resulted in the role of the Spenceans being an important and continuous one. Indeed, Spenceanism survived as a revolutionary idea in radical politics long after it ceased to function as an organised party.

William Davidson

Born in 1786, William Davidson came to England from Jamaica.[14] Like Wedderburn, Davidson was the offspring of a black woman and a white man. His father was 'Mr Attorney General Davidson', a man of considerable legal knowledge and talent, who had several children. William, his second son, was sent to England at an early age to be educated at a level suited to the rank of his father and to further his own career prospects. In spite of his mother's opposition to her son being sent to England, his father's mind was made up: he should proceed to study law.

After study and a stint at sea, Davidson became a cabinet-maker. He had read and supported the ideas of Thomas Paine[15] and had joined the Marylebone Union Reading Society, formed as a direct result of the Peterloo massacre. Like Wedderburn in his Hopkins Street chapel, Davidson called meetings which were held in his house. Davidson's associates and activities (and his colour) singled him out for special surveillance. He was introduced to George Edwards by the radical John Harrison. Edwards, (a 'modeller of statuettes' by trade) posed as a radical to deflect attention from his double role of police spy and *agent provocateur*.[16]

In the deliberations over an uprising or attempts to dislodge the government, Edwards was not short of plans for dealing with guilty government officials. He suggested that the House of Commons should be blown up. This, among other plans, was rejected by the radical leader Arthur Thistlewood on the ground that the innocent should not 'suffer with the guilty'. As it happened, an opportunity approximating something they were waiting for presented itself. It was announced that the Cabinet as a whole would be dining at Lord Harrowby's house in Grosvenor Square. Davidson had worked for a time for Lord Harrowby who described him as 'a damned seditious fellow'.[17]

The group's plan was to kill all the ministers as they dined together. This, they hoped would initiate an insurrection and lead to the formation of a provisional government. Edwards' double-dealing had begun to affect Thistlewood and his supporters who agreed to 'every detail' of a plan he suggested.

Thistlewood's group delegated to Davidson the responsibility of raising money and buying weapons at a time when working men in various parts of the country were arming to defend themselves against further attacks on radical demonstrations. Moreover, the group relied on Davidson to guard their home-made grenades, muskets, pistols, etc. which were kept in the Cato Street loft, near Edgeware Road. Uncannily, the loft was pounced on by police as the group made its final deliberations before setting out for Grosvenor Square. In the shouting and scuffling that ensued, Thistlewood stabbed a policeman to death and fled. His escape was however, only temporary. He was arrested the next day at his hiding place which was known to the spy Edwards.

As it was, the long-awaited insurrection in London did not eventuate. Elsewhere in Barnsley, Huddersfield and Sheffield insurrections failed. In Glasgow and Paisley however, about 60,000 weavers went on 'spy-fomented' strike.[18] And in the Battle of Bonnymuir during the Scottish Insurrection the radicals were defeated.[19] The spy Alexander Richmond played a key role in the downfall of the Scottish Radical Movement. Thereafter, the Movement collapsed.

In the aftermath Thistlewood, Davidson and their three companions were put on trial for high treason. Davidson pleaded not guilty and when he suggested his colour might lead to his conviction, one of the Judges said: 'God forbid that the complexion of the accused should enter, for a single moment, into the consideration of the jury.'[20] In his defence, he told the Court that although his house had been ransacked, no incriminating evidence had been found. This was supported by a Bow Street constable who reported that Davidson's 'Hovel' was carefully searched.[21]

The five men accused in the Cato Street conspiracy were all sentenced to be hanged early on the morning of 1 May 1820.

The dream of revolution harboured by these desperate men had failed miserably. Indeed, the legend on the banner (a black flag with skull and cross-bones) which Davidson guarded from capture by the police was a fitting epitaph, 'Let us die like men and not be sold like slaves.'[22]

William Cuffay

Like Wedderburn and Davidson, William Cuffay (called Cuffey, Cuffy and Coffey) stood out among his contemporaries in the English working class movement and was penalised for his activities and political beliefs.

His grandfather, like so many Africans, was a slave on the plantations in St Kitts. His father, apparently a free man, brought the family to Britain when Cuffay was a child. William grew up with his mother and sister.

There is uncertainty as to when Cuffay first became active in the working class movement. He 'disapproved of the Trades Union Movement in 1834, and was nearly the last of his Society in joining the lodge'. [23] It must not be presumed however, that this reference to the Owenite Grand National Consolidated Trade Union and Cuffay's hostility to it, extended to trade unionism as such. In fact, Cuffay went on strike with his fellow members. As a result of this involvement, he lost a shop where he had worked for many years, thereafter finding it very difficult to get a job. With the difficulties of unemployment, the die was cast; the direction already charted.

Cuffay joined the Chartist Movement in 1839 and became prominent in the London leadership. In October 1839 he helped to form the Metropolitan Tailors' Charter Association, which recruited 80 members on the first night. [24] He supported the People's Charter, drawn up by the cabinet-maker, William Lovett, and Francis Place, demanding universal male suffrage, annual parliaments, vote by secret ballot, payment of MPs, abolition of property qualifications for MPs, and equal electoral districts.

Cuffay emerged as one of the dozen or so most prominent leaders of the Chartist movement in London. The Chartists in London were essentially artisans. In fact, Chartism in London was, 'a sustained movement which produced its own leaders, stuck to its traditional radicalism yet worked out its own class attitudes'. [25]

Within this movement Cuffay's popularity grew. In 1841 he was elected delegate for Westminster to the Metropolitan Delegate Council. [26] A few months later, in 1842 when George Julian Harney and other national leaders were arrested, the Council appointed Cuffay, together with Morgan, Dron and Knight to form an 'interim executive.' [27]

Cuffay, the tiny tailor, during his Chartist years was always among the most militant of his contemporaries. In the mid-1840s he advocated the interruption of the middle class Complete Suffrage Meetings and Anti-Corn Law demonstrations. As expected, the press singled him out for his militancy and his intransigence. There was no doubt about Cuffay's influence among London Chartists. Indeed, The Times had referred to London Chartists as 'the black man and his party'. [28] This bad press led to Cuffay's wife losing her job as a charwoman. [29] The ruling class had to have their scapegoat, but their sneering attacks could not deflect the onward march of this black radical leader, who went from strength to strength in his representation of an important section of the English working class. His stature was such that by 1844 he was a member of the Masters' and Servants' Bill Demonstration Committee.[30] In this capacity he was opposed to the power vested in magistrates to imprison a neglectful worker for two months on his employer's oath. To the poor working man this was indeed adding salt to the wound. One of those who fought against the Bill was the radical MP Thomas Slingsby Duncombe, who saw it as 'one of the most insidious, oppressive, arbitrary, iniquitous and tyrannical attempts to oppress the working classes.[31] Support of this kind (few and far between) was vital in the working class struggle and needed to be recognised. Cuffay, the Tailors' delegate, was among those who met to arrange a soirée for Duncombe in support of his fight against the Bill.

On other issues such as the Chartist Land Plan, Cuffay was always a vigorous supporter, representing London at the Manchester Conference in 1845. In essence the Plan was to 'take the unemployed out of the slums and allocate to each family two acres of good arable land'. His life as a Chartist leader was hectic. In 1846 he served as one of three London delegates to the Birmingham Land Conference, and was an auditor to the National Land Company. He held this position until his arrest. He was also one of the ten directors of the National Anti-Militia Association and a member of the Democratic Committee for Poland's Regeneration. In 1847, Cuffay was on the Central Registration and Election Committee, and in 1848 he sat on the management Committee for a Metropolitan Democratic Hall.[32]

The year 1848 was significant for Cuffay. He was a London Chartist delegate to the National Convention which opened at the Literary Institution in Fitzroy Square, on the morning of Tuesday 4 April 1848. Whatever of value Cuffay might have learned from past experience, he intended to adopt. From the outset he took a hard line. His militancy left no room for flexibility. He was suspicious of opportunists. He questioned G. W. M. Reynolds' standing as a Chartist, and totally opposed granting credentials to Charles McCarthy of the Irish Democratic Federation. Eventually, the McCarthy dispute was settled.

During the Convention, Cuffay's militancy was in the ascendant. The Convention's main concern was to call a mass meeting on Kennington Common and a procession that would take the Chartist petition of almost two million signatures to the House of Commons. Cuffay seconded Reynolds' amendment 'That in the event of the rejection of the Petition the Convention should declare its sitting permanent and should declare the Charter the law of the land',[33] and expressed opposition to a body declaring itself permanent that represented only a fraction of the people. However, he directed the Convention's attention to presenting the petition, and that a National Assembly be called instead. In due course the idea of a National Assembly was accepted.

Cuffay's militant stand at the Convention could not accommodate moderation. When the Committee for managing the procession was set up, Cuffay was appointed Chairman.

Significantly, Cuffay, the militant Chartist organiser was no hot-head. His sense of responsibility came through. In the 'crisis', he expected Chartists to act with cool determination. Cuffay was ahead of the Executive which had 'shrunk from their responsibility'. Their lack of spirit did not inspire confidence in those who would follow them.

The procession was declared illegal by the Commissioner of Police, and the Queen journeyed to the Isle of Wight in search of safety. In defence of their class interests, lawyers, shop-keepers and government clerks, volunteered as special constables. Seven thousand soldiers were detailed along the Embankment and 'heavy gun batteries' were deployed. Thousands of police were drafted in to guard the sealed-off bridges.[34] This impressive, intimidating show of force had the desired effect.

The Commissioner of Police who interviewed O'Connor, the Irish confederates' leader, said he had never seen a more frightened man. After this interview, O'Connor decided, at that advanced stage, to end the procession. When this decision reached the large crowd assembled at Kennington Common it was met with anger.

At the forefront of those who protested was Cuffay who was opposed to O'Connor and the platform's abandonment of the procession to Parliament. He recognised the stupidity of congregating south of the river, with the bridges under complete control of the police and the military, and he spoke in the strongest language against O'Connor.[35] He regarded the whole Convention as a set of 'cowardly humbugs' with whom he did not ever wish to be associated. He then left the vehicle he was in and joined the crowd. He told the crowd that O'Connor must have known all this before and that he ought to have informed them of it so they could have taken the petition at once to the House of Commons, without crossing the bridges. As it was, they were completely trapped.[36]

This defeat was a severe blow which Cuffay would not forgive or forget. When he was elected as one of the Commissioners to promote the campaign for the Charter following its rejection by Parliament, he saw an uprising as the only way forward. Insurrection being preached by a black man in England was indeed anathema. But, the question arises, was Cuffay the instigator? According to one historian, although Cuffay was secretary of the 'Ulterior Committee' on 16 August, he had only occupied that post since the 13th of that month. Indeed, the 'true leaders' and originators of the revolutionary attempt were Payne, Mullins, John Rose, Brewster and James Bassett.[37] To the ruling class, Cuffay was clearly a dangerous man. Police spies kept a close watch on his activities, as they did with the other black radicals Wedderburn and Davidson. Here again, spies found their way into the inner circles of working class organisations. A police spy was actually a member of the seven-strong 'secret' Committee that was planning an uprising. A group of 'luminaries' were arrested at the Orange Tree Tavern, Bloomsbury, on 15 August 1848 for allegedly plotting to set fire to 'certain buildings as a signal for the rising.' Seven Dials was to be one of the four stations from which the outbreak on 16 August was to be attempted.[38] Cuffay was arrested the next day. He refused to go underground 'lest it should be said that he abandoned his associates in the hour of peril'.[39]

Evidence for Cuffay's conviction for waging war against the Queen was given by the police spies: Thomas Powell and George Davis. Cuffay had remained intransigent throughout his trial and made a powerful speech before sentence was pronounced.

Found guilty, Cuffay and his fellow Chartists were sentenced to transportation 'for the term of their natural lives'. *The Times* in its attempted balanced judgement commented, 'A severe sentence, but a most just one.'[40] The radical press, however, found in this black man steadfastness and courage.

Cuffay's transportation on the ship *Adelaide*, lasted 103 days. After he landed in Tasmania in November 1849, he was allowed to work as a tailor for wages.[41] Mindful of his earlier experiences of unemployment before he became a political activist, he practised his trade until the last year of his life. Cuffay's working class activities brought him into prominence and in the full public view. He was a larger than life character, who enjoyed great popularity. So much so that social commentators found him interesting, even to the point of distorting his character and contribution to the Chartist movement.

While the black radicals Wedderburn, Davidson and Cuffay, among others, (i.e. Matthew Bogle, Benjamin Prophitt and David Duffey) waged war against the English ruling class, the struggle of black women, in the nineteenth century, to achieve self-respect from the degradation of slavery and in displaying unusual loyalty and devotion in the service of the British was exemplified in the lives of Mary Prince and Mary Seacole.

Mary Prince: slave and 'servant'

Mary Prince was born a slave in Bermuda on a farm owned by Charles Myners. Her mother was a household slave, as was her father, a sawyer, whose name was Prince.

In this household Mary's violent owner flogged her repeatedly for what he considered to be her misdeeds. Her mistress beat her too, not only instructing Mary in her household tasks, but also impressing upon her the difference between 'the smart of the rope, the cart-whip and the cow-skin'.

Later in her life Mary was sold into the service of Mr and Mrs Wood, where among other tasks she had to nurse their child. Years of work, washing clothes and standing in the water of the salt ponds took their toll and Mary developed rheumatism. By the time she arrived in England with Mr Wood, who had brought his son to attend a British school, her rheumatism had worsened and her body was 'dreadfully swelled'.

Unfortunately for Mary, her increasing disability was met with increasing anger and impatience from the Woods. She was ordered to leave and finally did so, seeking refuge with the Moravian missionaries in Hatton Garden. Given her destitution and her determination to obtain her freedom, Mary went first to the Anti-Slavery office in Aldermanbury towards the end of November 1828 and her case was referred to George Stephen to be investigated.

In spite of the Anti-Slavery Society's efforts, Mr Wood stubbornly refused to let her go or to return to her husband in the West Indies. This was chattel slavery with a vengeance. After working for a while as a charwoman, Mary finally went into the service of Mr and Mrs Thomas Pringle, where she remained, at least until the time when she related her full story in *The History of Mary Prince: A West Indian Slave Related by Herself*.

According to Pringle, the idea of writing her story was Mary Prince's own suggestion. Throughout her story, a unique view is presented of every facet of the life of a black woman in the service of her oppressors, first as a slave and then, more charitably, as a 'servant'. Indeed, black women were so used to being taken for granted that they were disgraced and, in Mary's words, 'thought no more of than beasts'. Mary's service in England was both tangible evidence and a reminder of that human debasement. Although her master had returned to the West Indies, he refused to set Mary free. Legally, she was still in his service; his property for the rest of her life.

Nothing more is known of the life of Mary Prince. The unanswered questions remain. Did she get her freedom and return to her husband in Antigua? Or did she spend the rest of her life in England? Whatever the answers, Mary Prince, slave and 'servant' was the historical precedent of her sister in service, Mary Seacole.

Mary Seacole: 'nurse and doctress'

Known as 'mother' to many white soldiers and civilians in many countries, Mary Seacole was born in Jamaica by the turn of the nineteenth century. Her father was a soldier of Scottish background and her mother, a black woman, kept a boarding house in Kingston. In her role as 'doctress' her mother achieved high repute among the officers stationed in Kingston.[42]

At an early age, Mary showed both an independence of mind and a desire for medical knowledge and practice. After nursing dogs and cats when she was about 12, she began assisting her mother who attended to the invalid officers and other sick persons who came to the boarding house. As she grew older, she developed a great desire to travel.

One of her impressions on her first visit to England was the vivid recollection of London street-boys poking fun at her complexion. After a year in England, the enterprising Mary returned to Kingston. Soon she was back again in England for another two years with a large stock of West Indian preserves and pickles for sale. Journeys to New Providence, Haiti and Cuba followed before she was again at her mother's side learning creole medical art. [43]

About this time, she married a Mr Seacole with whom she had established a store. This enterprising experience would serve her in good stead later in life. She patiently nursed her husband who was dogged by ill-health. His death, a severe loss to Mary, was followed by the bitter blow of her mother's demise. After this, Mary resolved to take life as it came. When her house was burned down in the great fire of 1843 which swept through Kingston, she set about the practical task of rebuilding.

Like her mother, she had gained a reputation as a skilful nurse and doctress. The loneliness which might have ensued was pre-empted by the continuous presence of invalid officers and their wives. Much knowledge was gained from naval and military surgeons who occasionally worked in her house.

When cholera swept Jamaica in 1850, Mary Seacole gave invaluable service. Later travels took her to the Isthmus of Panama, Navy Bay, Gatun and up the river Chagres to Gorgona and Cruces. She confessed to having 'a little prejudice' against some Americans. Given that her complexion was a few shades of deeper brown which showed she was related to the black slaves (a relationship she was proud of) she asked, 'Is it surprising that I should be somewhat impatient of the airs of superiority which many Americans have endeavoured to assume over me?' [44]

The outbreak of cholera at Cruces led to Mary Seacole attending successfully to the sick, thus earning herself the title the 'yellow doctress'. She tirelessly braved the primitive conditions under which she worked. Unfortunately, she was not immune and cholera attacked her overworked body. Her high spirits and medical knowledge helped towards a quick recovery. While at Cruces, she also had the invaluable experience of running a 'hotel' where she served dinners, but had no lodgers. This experience would also serve her well later.

After Cruces, she went to Gorgona before returning to Kingston where she stayed for eight months in 1853. According to Mrs Seacole, that year the ravages of yellow fever nearly exterminated the English in Jamaica. Yet again, she was on hand to administer and comfort the sick and dying. She turned down proposals of marriage from many men of high and low rank, because her lasting love seemed to be a yearning to travel and to nurse. About that time, war was declared against Russia and in Jamaica news was expected of a 'descent upon the Crimea'. This news seemed to have affected her little at the time. She returned to Navy Bay, where she opened a store and got caught up in the 'gold fever'.

Each new trip abroad reinforced Mary's confidence in her nursing ability. In the face of sickness and death, she showed initiative and great courage. Indeed, she met many challenges and was now preparing for the ultimate challenge: a longing to join the British Army at Sebastopol. After hearing the news of war at Sebastopol she wrote: 'Now, no sooner had I heard of war somewhere, than I longed to witness it; and when I was told that many of the regiments I had known so well in Jamaica had left England for the scene of action, the desire to join them became stronger than ever.'[45]

Preoccupied with Sebastopol and the Crimea, she arrived in London in the autumn of 1854, soon after the battle of Alma. In London, she devoted herself to a visionary 'new scheme'. With no friends and limited funds, she speculated on a 3000-mile journey that would take her to Balaclava. The fundamental question remained: how would this unknown 'creole' woman persuade the British authorities that she would be useful to the British army in Sebastopol? Although achieving this seemed highly improbable, she persisted.

There had been reports of mismanagement, overcrowding in the hospitals, want and suffering in the Crimea. After the Russians had inflicted heavy casualties, the hospitals needed disciplined staff to attend to the hundreds of wounded and dying. This need reinforced Mary Seacole's resolve to offer her services in the Crimea.

Indeed, she did go to the Crimea, but only after repeated rebuffs and disappointments which reflected her total commitment to the cause. A lesser person might not have made it. Her determination to serve her British 'sons' eventually took her to the battlefront, and into history as a 'Crimean heroine'.

Mary Seacole, the black nurse, felt she was well fitted for the tasks that awaited her. Indeed, she was 'the right woman in the right place'. Although she was well qualified, through her past experience, to deal with the diseases most prevalent in the Crimea (cholera, diarrhoea and dysentery) British officials at the War Office referred her to the Quartermaster General's department, who in turn, referred her to the Medical Department. The British bureaucrats were not convinced. Colour had again become a factor. She complained that the authorities would not listen to a motherly 'yellow' woman, before changing her plans.

Her next scheme was to offer herself for recruitment as a nurse, following Florence Nightingale's departure for the Crimea. She was convinced that she was 'one of the very women they most wanted', possessing the requisite experience and fondness of the work. Enrolment, she reasoned, would be no problem. Here again, during this period of waiting, her colour was clearly resented. This plan of going through the normal nursing channels also had to be abandoned when she was told that the full complement of nurses had been secured. Following an interview with one of Miss Nightingale's companions, Mrs Seacole got the same negative reply. Disappointed, she wrote: 'I read in her face the fact, that had there been a vacancy, I should not have been chosen to fill it.'[46]

In desperation, she applied to the managers of the Crimea Fund for information as to whether they would help her to get to the camp, where she hoped something would turn up. Unfortunately, this attempt also failed. She felt a sense of cruel disappointment in view of the unselfish motives in going to the Crimea and the value of her service to the sick soldiers. Indeed, she found it most difficult to convince the authorities of these qualities. In that hopeless predicament she began to have doubts and suspicions as to the possibility that American prejudices against colour might have had some root in England. She asked, 'Did these ladies shrink from accepting my aid because my blood flowed beneath a somewhat duskier skin than theirs?'

Clearly, there was no way of making the trip through British official agencies. Her only hope was to get to the Crimea at her own expense, on her own initiative. She took comfort in the fact that some of those she had cared for (and doctors she had worked with) in Jamaica, were there. They would vouch for her skill and experience, she reasoned. Rejected as a nurse by British officialdom (at a time when the nursing profession was an occupation for the well-to-do classes) she entertained the idea of opening a hotel for invalids in the Crimea to be run in her own way. She acted upon her decision by printing cards which read:

BRITISH HOTEL
Mrs Mary Seacole
(*late of Kingston, Jamaica*)
Respectfully announces to her former kind friends, and to the
Officers of the Army and Navy generally

That she has taken her passage in the steamer *Hollander*, to start from London on the 25th of January, intending on her arrival at Balaclava to establish a mess-table and comfortable quarters for the sick and convalescent officers.[47]

While still preparing to leave England Mrs Seacole met again a Mr Day who was travelling to Balaclava to attend to some shipping business. Together, they decided to open a store as well as a hotel near the camp. She emphasised, however, that 'These new arrangements were not allowed to interfere in any way with the main object of my journey.' In fact, in anticipation, most of her limited funds were invested in medicines which she believed would be useful. How thoughtful. Still with the British soldier in mind, she used the remaining money to buy 'those home comforts' which would be difficult to get outside England.

Finally, she left England on the *Hollander*, passing through Malta, Gibraltar and Constantinople, before visiting the Scutari hospital. On a tour of the wards, she was greeted with shouts of 'Mother Seacole! Mother Seacole!' by an Irish sergeant she had known in Kingston. She sat at his bedside and tried to cheer him up and, at the risk of offending hospital officials, she gave a helping hand. The suffering at the hospital was unlike anything she had ever seen. 'But if it is so here', she wrote, 'what must it not be at the scene of war . . . I must be useful three or four days nearer to their pressing wants than this.'[48] Thus, she was ready for the greatest challenge of her life.

On this journey she carried a letter of introduction from a doctor ('Dr F—') to Miss Nightingale. To one of Miss Nightingale's assistants, Mrs Seacole was more of an object of 'curiosity and surprise' than a deeply committed volunteer for service. Assuming that Mrs Seacole sought employment at Scutari, this assistant kindly told her that Miss Nightingale already had the entire management of the hospital staff and that there was no vacancy. When Mrs Seacole interrupted her by saying that she was bound for the battlefront in a few days, the assistant was left even more surprised.

About half an hour later, Mary Seacole met Florence Nightingale. This is how she described the English nurse who would achieve world renown:

> A slight figure, in nurses' dress, with a pale, gentle, and withal firm face, resting lightly in the palm of one white hand, while the other supports the elbow – a position which gives to her countenance a keen inquiring expression which is rather marked. Standing thus in repose and yet keenly observant – the greatest sign of impatience at any time a slight, perhaps unwitting motion of the firmly planted right foot – was Florence Nightingale.[49]

After reading Mrs Seacole's letter of introduction, Miss Nightingale in a gentle, practical and businesslike way asked, 'What do you want, Mrs Seacole – anything that we can do for you? If it lies in my power, I shall be very happy.'[50]

Although overcrowding in the Scutari hospital presented a problem, Mrs Seacole was able to find a bed for the night in the hospital washerwoman's quarters, before resuming her journey on the *Hollander* to Balaclava. The six weeks she spent at Balaclava were 'rough'. Nevertheless, with permission from the authorities, she set up a store and gave English language lessons to a Turkish Pasha. Mrs Seacole's British Hotel, never fully completed (indeed a year later, it still needed shutters) gained a great reputation.

The written records of many testify to Mary Seacole's work in the Crimea. Given the comments of those well-placed to make a judgement, it is clear that she had achieved the goal of serving as camp doctress, nurse and 'mother'. Her natural concern, which seemed boundless, facilitated flexibility in activity demanded by the war. Not surprisingly, her many patients turned to her firstly, because these men had serious objection to going into hospital (except in urgent cases) and secondly, because they were able to get the 'sick-comforts' and nourishing food available at Mrs Seacole's store. An additional reason why many came to Mrs Seacole's British Hotel for medical treatment was, in her own words, because she was 'very familiar with the diseases which they suffered most from and successful in their treatment'.

After Sebastopol was taken, she wrote, 'the great work was accomplished'. Indeed, her great struggle to get there was also accomplished in the teeth of 'official indifference, hauteur and prejudice'. It was for her, a great triumph, a moment to savour.

Mrs Seacole returned to England and worked for a while in Aldershot. The acclaim she received subsequently was a well-deserved bonus. Financially, however, she was in a precarious position, for some time. In fact, she was ready to 'journey to any place' in search of employment. Although poor, she was proud of the service she had given for others.

In England, she reflected on the results of her Crimean campaign: she was in poor health, bankrupt and unemployed. What, in fact, Mary Seacole had gained was friendship, particularly from those she had met before and after Sebastopol. In London, she enjoyed being recognised. She derived great pleasure and satisfaction, having achieved her goal of getting to the Crimea and back, through her stubbornness to serve the cause of Britain, in keeping with the legacy of her Jamaican past.

Nevertheless, the 'Crimean heroine' was poor and unemployed. In recompense for her 'charities and incessant labours' among the Army, as she put it, a number of 'noblemen and gentlemen' who knew her in the Crimea had set up a Committee to aid her. Yet in spite of the courage and the indomitable spirit displayed by this extraordinary woman in the service of Britain, sadly, one can't help recalling the problems which confronted British charities some seventy-five years earlier, in assisting the black poor in London.

Some, however, remembered and stood by her. For Mrs Seacole's benefit, a friend, Lord Rokeby, to whom her book was dedicated, among other well-to-do friends, organised a four-day musical festival at the Surrey Gardens, with one thousand performers, nine military bands and an orchestra. At this event, Mary Seacole took 'pride of place', seated in the front of the gallery flanked by Lord Rokeby and Lord George Paget. Unfortunately, this massive effort raised only £228 for Mrs Seacole.[51] Although she never realised a fortune, her fame was unquestioned. Cheers greeted her wherever she went and publication of her autobiography, *The Wonderful Adventures of Mary Seacole in Many Lands*, helped to maintain her popularity.

After 1857, she spent most of the rest of her life in England and continued to enjoy the friendship of members of the English aristocracy. Indeed, Queen Victoria's kinsman, Count Gleichen, the sculptor, did a small bust of her; and Lord Rokeby and his daughter were all remembered in her will. When the firm of Day and Seacole was wound up, Mary Seacole needed all the financial help she could get. While little is known of how she recouped her fortunes, she left over £2600 when she died on 14 May 1881.

After her death, she seemed to have been 'totally forgotten' in England. By chance, her grave was recently discovered in a 'complete state of disrepair, stones cracked and crumbling, headstone with mildew and dirt'. Efforts were undertaken to restore the headstone by the Lignum Vitae Club (an association of Jamaican women in London) and the British Commonwealth Nurses War Memorial Fund.

If the 'yellow doctress' was forgotten in England, she was remembered in Jamaica, where the Nurses Association of Jamaica Headquarters was re-named 'Mary Seacole House'. For the Association, Mrs Seacole has remained a source of great inspiration. Recently, a reconsecration ceremony was held at her graveside in London. In accordance with her wish, she was buried 'in the Catholic portion of the cemetery at Kensal Green, London'. The restored headstone read: 'Here lies Mary Seacole (1805–1881) of Kingston, Jamaica, a notable nurse who cared for the sick and wounded in the West Indies, Panama and on the battlefields of the Crimea, 1854–1856.'[52]

Mary Seacole was an outstanding nineteenth-century example of a black woman from the Caribbean who, through service in the imperial cause, found her way from the colonial periphery to the metropolitan centre. While her struggle reflected the oppression of women generally in the nineteenth century, she was the precursor of an exodus of Florence Nightingale-oriented black nurses who came to serve Britain in the twentieth century, only to realise the harsh reality of race and colour prejudice.

3 Post-Emancipation Developments: Indentureship and the Rise of Pan Africanism

The Indian diaspora: 'a new system of slavery'

The abolition of the slave trade did not end slavery on the plantations. In the British sugar colonies, sugar and servitude remained tied together, dictating the economic, political and social structure.

In the aftermath of full Emancipation of the slaves in 1838, the labour vacuum on the plantations was filled by East Indian indentured labour. In Mauritius, one of the most oppressive territories during the period of Apprenticeship (which came on 1 February 1835, later than in the Caribbean) it was estimated that as many as one-seventh of the slaves were from South India.[1] Not surprisingly therefore, Mauritius planters turned to India for their plantation labour force. In 1840 Mauritius received 18,000 Indian labourers.[2]

The West Indian sugar islands, with no immediate supply of labour, went through a period of decay. Pressure from the planters was mounted to get the British government to induce East Indians to labour for deplorably low wages. Thus, 'Negro' slavery in the Caribbean and the Mascarenes was replaced by a 'new system of slavery' – East Indian indentured labour.

The actual functioning of the institution of slavery and of indentured labour and other forms of bondage which followed can only be understood by reference to the plantation products, and by some account of how this form of production evolved. Given the opening up of the New World and the acquisition of tropical colonies by the warring European powers, and the high priority given to the cultivation of tropical products in the metropolis, a new unit of production, the plantation, emerged.

During the eighteenth century, until the end of the Napoleonic wars, British West Indian sugar enjoyed a preference against the tariff on foreign sugar and sugar from elsewhere in the British Empire. With the capture and occupation of Trinidad and Demerara (British Guiana) new competitors within the British monopoly were accepted. By 1830, there had been a change in the relative importance of the sugar producing colonies. For example, that year, Jamaica exported only 68,962 tons (having exported a record 99,600 tons in 1805), Trinidad's total was 10,244 tons, British Guiana produced 59,790 tons and Mauritius 32,750 tons. Further, the new undeveloped colonies surged ahead. In 1840, Mauritius exported 36,559 tons with British Guiana 35,619 tons, Jamaica slipped further down with 26,453 tons and Trinidad 12,258 tons.[3]

During the 1840s, the free trade campaign led to a lowering of tariffs protecting British and British colonial produce in line with the duties on foreign imports.[4] Given the hard times which hit the British West Indian plantations between 1840 and 1950, the English capitalists were faced with the challenge of producing a larger volume of sugar at cheaper prices. To do this, given the state of technology, cheap labour was the only way possible. Thus, Mauritius, in close proximity to the Indian labour market was able to increase its exports. In 1855 the area under sugar production was 81,000 acres, rising to 122,000 acres ten years later. While production in British Guiana and Jamaica had levelled out, Trinidad's output increased steadily. Mauritius, however, was the principal British sugar producer, dramatically increasing its exports from 55,163 tons in 1850 to 134,048 tons in 1860. Five years later, a record crop of 165,000 tons was achieved.[5]

Given the changes in the sugar industry in the various islands, in terms of the mode of production, little had changed in Mauritius since the days of slavery.[6] As the ruling power in the Empire, Britain owned and controlled production in the tropical territories. And although free trade was substituted for mercantilist monopoly between the 1840s and 1860s, colonial dependency on Britain was much the same. While some colonies experienced a degree of prosperity such as Burma (and to a lesser extent Ceylon and Malaya) British economic policies and practices had adverse effects upon other colonies. Thus, India succeeded Africa in providing the insatiable capitalist demand for cheap and disposable labour on the plantations and mines to maintain the British/colonial relationship.

Because most of India's population, an estimated 80 per cent, were engaged in agriculture and because of the instability of the rural economy, due to the loss of land of peasant farmers falling into debt, or through illness, many found themselves landless labourers. Predictably, there was a desperate drift that took on added significance in times of famine, flood or invasion. Consequently, a large pool of floating, casual labour was to be found in India's large cities.

Towards the end of the eighteenth century there were Indian labourers in the ports of south-east Asia. In fact, the East India Company's attempt to establish a trading station in lower Burma on Negrais Island in 1753–9 was dependent on Indian labour. When the settlement was withdrawn, the families of the 'Coolies' sent to Negrais complained that the 'Head Cooly' was paid 'what money those who died there left behind them'.[7]

Labouring far from home was an acceptable part of the reality of life for thousands of poor Indian families, perhaps because such employment, usually short-term, allowed a return to their homes. However, different and disturbing patterns began to emerge with the export of Indians further afield. Forced banishment killed hopes of a return home. In addition to the domestic slavery prevalent in India during the eighteenth century, there was a trade in slaves to supply the sugar plantations of the Mascarenes. South Indian slaves from Kerala were taken by the Dutch to Mauritius. By the latter part of the eighteenth century (in spite of the proclamation in 1789 by the Governor-General, Lord Cornwallis, prohibiting the export of people as slaves to different parts of India and beyond) slaves were regularly sold to French planters in Mauritius and Reunion. Kidnapping men, women and children was part of that trade. There were some 6000 Indian slaves in 1800 on the Mauritian estates, with thousands of enslaved Indians in Reunion where slavery was not abolished until 1848.[8] Moreover, convicts were transported to Mauritius in 1815 at the request of Governor Farquhar.

In spite of the Hindu objection to crossing the 'Black Water', emigration was already regarded as a natural progression in the early nineteenth century. Among those lured to servile labour abroad (to Mauritius and British Guiana) were the Dhangars or Hill Coolies, who were regarded as good workmen and preferred by the planters. During the 1840s and 1850s they formed a substantial number of those taken abroad under the indentureship system. From the 1850s, however, their proportion dwindled. It was estimated that from two-fifths to one-half of the emigrants were Dhangars.[9]

Travelling to Mauritius was in itself, a formidable proposition. But that long hazardous journey to the West Indies was another matter. During the 1850s, the mortality rates on voyages to the West Indies reached an appalling level. Apart from the incidental humanitarian concern, at this time, in the reckoning of the capitalist log-book, the loss of a quarter or a third of the cargo of coolies was 'a major commercial loss' on the voyage. And interestingly, the 'better workmen', the Hill Coolies, were at the greatest risk. The death rate among them was considerably higher than among the plains people. Significantly during the long sea voyages, suicide was a common form of death.

Apart from the sugar colonies, from the 1860s, the tea industry began to make labour demands. With the drying up of the supply of Hill Coolies, demands were made on the 'flotsam of humanity' in Calcutta, Madras and Bombay. Most of these simple country people were herded towards the Emigration Agent's depot where their muscles and hands were examined for the rigours of manual labour. Despite these checks (were they mere formality?) the most 'outlandish' emigrants were taken aboard to fill the ships, which was clearly the object of the exercise.

Calcutta was the main port of embarkation during the first 30–40 years of organised emigration until about 1870. Labourers were drawn particularly from Banaras Province and Bihar where, as the people at the bottom end of society, they were economically and socially inferior. These low-caste people were at the mercy of the superior castes. In effect, many were, as in Bihar, in a state of semi-slavery known as *Kamiuti*, by which the poor people sold their services, and sometimes those of their children in years to come, in order to meet their pressing needs. These people were most vulnerable to the recruiters of indentured labour.[10]

Among the early emigrants, many were from what was then known as the Western Districts of British India: those between Banaras and Allahabad. A major push factor, the 'awful famine' of the early 1840s in Upper India resulted in a mass exodus, first to Bihar, where they were 'persuaded to embark'. To this point, people came from as far as Delhi. Also, during the 1840s, emigration built up at Madras and in Bombay.

Overall, the main movement of indentured emigration occurred in the years before 1880. By 1871, Mauritius had a population composed of 216,258 Indians and 99,784 Creoles, mainly of African descent. Thereafter, as fewer went to Mauritius, the flow was deflected to fill a steady demand in the Caribbean, with growing numbers going to Natal during the remaining years of the nineteenth century.[11] Emigration from Madras expanded during the 1870s to satisfy the growing demands of Ceylon, Burma, Mauritius, the Straits Settlements, Natal and the Caribbean.

By 1900, British Guiana had a larger Indian population than Malaya. The Malayan rubber boom, however, siphoned-off a considerable number of the labourers from Madras to the rubber estates. Moreover, Fiji became a significant importer of Indian labour. While Madras also supplied the heavy demand in Natal, emigration from Calcutta continued.

Towards the end of the nineteenth century, the Indian diaspora had stretched far and wide as the planters' demand for labour was satisfied. In the West Indies, St Lucia, St Kitts, Grenada, St Vincent, Martinique, Guadeloupe, Jamaica, Trinidad and Tobago and British Guiana all called on Indian labour. Further, Fiji, the Straits Settlements, Burma, Malaya, Mauritius, Ceylon and Re-union had large infusions of labourers. And in South Africa, they went to Natal and Durban. In East Africa, they went to Kenya and were called upon to build the Uganda Railway.

According to one estimate 525,482 Indians emigrated under indenture to French and British sugar colonies between 1842 and 1870. Of these, 351,401 went to Mauritius, 76,691 to British Guiana and 42,519 to Trinidad, with 15,169 to Jamaica. Natal received 6,448 and Reunion imported 15,005; both these importations were between 1860 and 1870. The other French colonies took 16,341 Indians in the same decade. One calculation made in 1869 showed that immigration from India during 1843–67 amounted to 1,446,407 of whom 89,897 returned to India. An estimated 250,000 had settled in Ceylon (now Sri Lanka), while the 350,000 unaccounted for were presumed dead. Overall then, between one to two million Indian labourers went overseas to the tropical plantations during 1830–70.[12]

Although the Anti-Slavery Society had expressed its concern in 1872, there was general complacency in Britain, but eventually protest against the system, undertaken during a very long period of questioning, was to overcome even the massive inertia of the Government of India. Many aspects of the system aroused concern, but always much too slowly. The deadly diseases (cholera, typhoid and dysentery, among others) plagued the indentured labourers. The passage over the menacing oceans on sailing ships was a difficult ordeal for passengers and crew. Those who arrived alive at the end of their journeys, were both shattered and strengthened.

Having suffered a tortuous passage to the plantations, for various reasons, only between one-third and one-quarter of the emigrants to the distant colonies ever returned. Basically, the right of a return passage to Indians was only reluctantly conceded by the colonial authorities. In Mauritius, for example, this was granted only to the 'indigent, the sick and the misfits'. Underlying this return was the fact that those who did so were 'either the defeated, or the winners, either poor or rich'.

Apart from the rich and poor groupings among the returnees, there was another category of Indians from the diaspora who came back on holiday. The children of indentured Indians, having traced their ancestral village, were shocked to find that their parents were only vaguely remembered or in some cases forgotten in caste-ridden India. The effect on these second-generation Indians during their genealogical visit to the Motherland was to lead to a preferable, hasty retreat back to the familiar colonies! Although some Indians returned to India with a spirit of independence, they were the exceptions. While generations of human beings had laboured and died, the old slave plantation system had remained largely unchanged since the eighteenth century. Into the twentieth century, work on the sugar estates was still a gruelling experience as it was intended to be (closely monitored by the watchful eyes of the Protectors and Magistrates of the estates who identified with the interests of the planters); the Indian indentured labourers were monitored and exploited to the hilt. Under this extremely oppressive regime, they laboured throughout their terms of indenture for a pittance.

That some survived this ordeal was due largely to their resilience, or closer to the truth was the fact that they had no alternative. They relied on a community spirit: organising a social life in relation to the 'lost India'. Thus, their festivals and feasts were crucial safety valves which aided their survival. But these were occasional moments of cultural release. Their grinding poverty and the constant demands on their labour, were ever present. As sickness and premature death took their toll, many resorted to drunkenness to temper the boredom and emptiness of their lives. In effect, they were lost and a long, long way from home. The feeling of betrayal among them was strong. According to descendants of indentured labourers in Trinidad, 'They had spent their first year in Trinidad "crying" as they remembered their homes and realised how badly they had been "tricked".'[13] This story had echoes elsewhere, such as in the Straits Settlements.

On the estates, the 'task' was the assignment with which newcomers had to come to terms. Not only was it an 'un-Indian' way of working, it was grossly unfair in that newcomers who failed to complete their assignments forfeited any payment for the day's work. Thus, the labourer was liable to the daily imposition of maximum hours of work. Moreover, the strong were played off against the weak. For example, a task might require a 15-hour working day for the weaker or less experienced coolies, while a stronger, more capable worker could do it in about half the time.

Like the slaves before them, the coolies ('a compulsory labour force') had to be kept by their employers. Thus, the indentured labourer in earning his keep became the 'all-purpose work animal' as the primitive system of manual labour took precedence over the more extended use of implements worked by steam machinery or by animal (mules and oxen) power. Given the wear and tear of the system, generally, the coolies were either at work, in hospital or, more often than not, in gaol. Few were free of either the threat, or the actual fact, of some form of punishment. This attitude towards them as convicts was a mark of their bondage under the plantation indentured labour system.

To maintain obedience to the demands of the plantations, flogging was a common form of discipline. Planters were all powerful; some taking the law into their hands. As one of them put it, 'Every man is a magistrate on his own estate, you know, and therefore as long as the man is working for you, you have a right to do what you like with him – that is, anything short of killing him.'[14] Indeed only just 'short of killing him' was a clear statement of the treatment meted out to the Indian coolies. According to the Mauritius Royal Commission, during the period 1867–72, 50 Indians had died of rupture of the spleen as a result of severe beatings. There was no record of punishment of those responsible.

Given all the atrocities committed by planters and their managers, there were few official comments either in India, in Britain or in the colonies. Indeed, it was the Sanderson Committee which drew attention to the alarming number of convictions of indentured labourers in the sugar colonies. Was this passive disobedience in the face of planters' oppression and exploitation? Or was it a wilful act on the part of the employer to instil obedience through fear into an already 'docile' and 'submissive' labour force? Given the abuses of the system, the Sanderson Committee underlined the various labour codes applying to both indentured and 'free' Indians.

The stereotype image of the vagrant Indian labourer was reinforced in colonial reports. As it was, the system which brought them to the colonies as workers now condemned them as vagrants. In 1878, there were 20,000 vagrants in Mauritius, and predictably, a 'Vagrancy Committee' was set up. Most interestingly, however, if a time-expired indentured labourer refused employment (as a 'free' man) he was classed as a vagrant. And if he was still without registered employment after three months, he was regarded as an 'incorrigible vagrant'. Hemmed in from all sides, a considerable number of Indians who should have been hospitalised or receiving medical care were woefully neglected, and left to die and end their indentureship prematurely.

Taken together, disease, bad housing, lack of medical attention and care, and malnutrition contributed to suicide. In 1871, Sir Arthur Gordon, the Governor of Mauritius, commenting on the 'extraordinary frequency of suicides among Indian immigrants' in the colony, attributed this partly to the shortage of women. He added however 'I myself believe that a very large proportion of the suicides are due to nostalgia or an intense desire to return to India which they have no means of gratifying.'[15] As a result of the agitation of Indian Nationalist, Dadabhai Naoroji, officials began to take notice of the suicide statistics. In fact, the indentured labourers' lives were monotonous and unattractive; indeed, many had quarrelled over the lack of women in their communities.

As in slavery, under indentureship, marriage or 'companionage' was an unstable relationship. Although a wife was a status symbol (of security and prosperity), the low-status poor man was liable to have his wife taken away by a man of superior status. This dearth of women aroused much concern and comment. In fact, disputes over women constituted the main cause of murders and suicides.

In addition to the hostility which surrounded them, Indian labourers also had to contend with the rising antagonism of the Creole Blacks, on and off the plantations.

The ex-slaves were conscious of the Indians as labour which was replacing them on the plantations. Indeed, Indians were used by planters as strike-breakers in Jamaica and other West Indian islands. Soon, both Indians and Creoles developed stereotyped views referring to each other as 'nigger' and 'coolie'. In colonies where the Indians were a small minority they were 'Creolised'. And where they complemented Creole Blacks economically, as in Trinidad, they achieved a partnership. A major point of contention between the two groups, however, was Indian immigration. In fact, as early as 1857, Blacks in Jamaica encouraged by Baptist missionaries, petitioned against Indian immigration. In 1866, there were strikes by native labourers for higher wages. It was argued that without the reserve supply of Indian labour, employers would have been compelled to raise wages by 25 per cent.[16]

In spite of the antagonism between Creole Blacks and the Indians, some integration and intermarriage had taken place, particularly in the smaller islands. In general, however, the Blacks did not allow them into their community. This was especially marked in the French colonies.[17] To Blacks in the West Indies, the Indians were 'Coolie Slaves'.[18] It seemed the Indians were almost always stigmatised as the dregs of their country: 'low-born, even criminal'.[19]

Through all this, they showed an almost limitless patience and capacity to suffer. Although it seemed the Indians were pacified by small concessions, this approach was balanced by the severe punishment meted out to 'ringleaders' by the Immigration Department. Moreover, reflecting their total subservience, 'It was an absolute principle of the system that no Indian labourer should ever acquire a recognised position as a leader or even as a negotiator. Their only recognised role was that of petitioners: and humble petitioners too.'[20]

But such revolts as there were, were 'sad and sordid' as in 1869 in British Guiana. In 1903 there was, in the always highly charged atmosphere of British Guiana, a wave of strikes, and in Surinam there was industrial unrest where an attempt by Dutch troops to arrest the Indians resulted in 13 dead and 40 wounded.

It has been argued that the rise of protest in the Caribbean reflected the fact that the Indians were becoming conscious of their rights. On the other hand, the absence of mass protest in Mauritius, Ceylon, Malaya and Natal (prior to Gandhi's efforts) is evidence of successful organisation in these territories. Together, these protests demonstrated the potential solidarity of the Indians. The one factor which gave the 'coolies' an advantage over the slaves was that one day their 'slavery' would be ended. It was this expectation, not escape or revolt, which generated hope by the close of the nineteenth century.

Thus, in response to the global demands of British capitalism, an Indian diaspora had come into being and settled (albeit uneasily) next to the African diaspora. Capital's advantage in creating and widening schisms and divisions between these two major colonial labour groups, would become a major manipulative weapon during the twentieth century. Already, however, the questions of race and colour, on which colonial exploitation was based, were uppermost in the minds of both African and Indian nationalists. The black intelligentsia from both the African and Indian diaspora would continue to challenge the questions of race and colour, and demand the fundamental right of self-government.

Pan Africanism: origins and early development

Given the deep roots of the Pan African tradition, a pre-history which could be dated back to Cugoano and Equiano in the eighteenth century, it was only in the nineteenth century that the Pan African idea put forward by Delany and Edward Blyden, achieved some clarity and form in Britain when the African Association came into being on 24 September 1897 with Henry Sylvester Williams as honorary secretary.[21] This was merged into the new Pan African Association following the first Pan African Conference called in London in 1900. Williams was the moving light behind the Pan African Association and the brain behind the Pan African Conference. Preceding him were Celestine Edwards and J. A. Thorne. Apart from Blyden's pioneering work, the efforts of both men had an important bearing on these formations in support of the 'Black Race'.

Celestine Edwards

Celestine Edwards was born in Dominica in 1857. Having there developed 'burning convictions', namely the truth of fundamentalist Christianity, the cause of temperance and a strong belief in human rights and brotherhood,[22] Edwards came to live in Britain. The date of his arrival cannot be ascertained. It is clear, however, that he lived with his cousin William in Edinburgh where he became active in the temperance movement. He then moved to Sunderland before settling in the East End of London about 1880.[23]

He was proud of his blackness and showed a dedication to the theme of Black self-betterment throughout his life. In fact, he

distinguished himself by being the first Black man to become
an editor in Britain, preceding such Pan Africanists as Sylvester
Williams, Duse Mohamed Ali and John Eldred Taylor. He edited
the magazines *Lux* and *Fraternity*, which reflected his political
commitment to a Pan African press.

Edwards had heralded a long list of remarkable Blacks in Britain
who contributed to the Pan African movement, but who are less
well-known than their twentieth century successors, namely C. L. R.
James, George Padmore, Ras Makonnen, Kwame Nkrumah,
Jomo Kenyatta and Wallace Johnson, among others. One such Pan
Africanist of note, during the nineteenth century, was J. A. Thorne.

J. A. Thorne: the 'preliminary stage' 1894–7

In the 'preliminary stage' of Pan Africanism, J. Albert Thorne played
a central role in Britain. As a 'descendant of Africa and Barbados'
he had hoped eventually to establish a colony of one hundred
West Indian families on the banks of the Zambezi. His African
Colonial Enterprise provides an important focus in the development of Pan African nationalism. Indeed, Thorne is (and must be)
regarded as a precursor of Marcus Garvey. His repatriation scheme
and general philosophy in relation to Africa 'would have been
most likely to have fertilised the embryo of Marcus Garvey's racial
nationalism'.[24]

Thorne was born in Barbados on 2 May 1860, the last of 13 children born to George and Jane Thorne. Albert was one of the five
children who survived smallpox and cholera. His father rose from
labourer to become a highly respected small landowner and also
a devoted member of the Anglican Church. Thus, hard work and
a religious upbringing had a powerful influence on young Albert,
who did exceptionally well at school and served as a pupil-teacher
from November 1873 to December 1876. Having made considerable
progress he became disenchanted with his career as a teacher. If he
had the choice, he would have preferred being a printer. It was clear,
however, that he had a great respect for scholarship.

In 1879, when he was 19, he arrived in British Guiana and
after enrolling for a course at the Colonial Hospital, he received a
diploma as a principal dispenser and dresser. He also did missionary work for the Moravians in Demerara. Soon after his brother,
who ran a respectable druggist establishment in Georgetown, had
left for Scotland, Albert returned to Barbados. In 1884 he arrived
in England.

After making 'a host of friends', some of whom were in high positions, Thorne was impressed by the force of commitment of 'these
good people' to the moral advancement of their own race. Thus, he
set out to work for 'the temporal and spiritual advancement of our
race'.[25]

He registered as a medical student at the University of Aberdeen
in Scotland on 31 October 1887 and graduated with the degree of

Bachelor of Medicine and Master of Surgery on 28 October 1893.
Later, he recalled that it was about two or three years before his
graduation that the plan of African colonisation was conceived.
According to Robert Hill, it was highly likely that Thorne was
influenced to some degree by Edward Wilmot Blyden's work,
Christianity, Islam and the Negro Race, a fundamental theme of which
was 'African colonisation'.

About this time, Thorne met Dr James Johnston (the Scottish
missionary) who had arrived in England between February and
April 1891, with a party of six Jamaican missionary assistants on
their way to South Central Africa. In spite of Thorne's argument
that his plan was 'a purely original experiment', Robert Hill stated
that Thorne could probably have been influenced by the pioneering
work of Dr Johnston between 1891 and 1892.

The years between 1891 and 1893 were crucial to British colonial
consolidation in Central Africa. In the scramble for African territory, Thorne felt West Indians should stake their claim. The Rev
Fergus Ferguson of Glasgow wrote that Thorne might become 'the
Moses of our day to lead his people back to the land of promise'.
Unfortunately, Thorne's promising plan was beset by problems.
For instance, the African Sub-Committee made it clear that 'he
would be shut out from intervening in the sphere of missionary
operations on the Zambesi'. His idea of an African fatherland and of
'a great movement of enterprise' was what ultimately Marcus
Garvey was to realise, but it should be clear that 'the seed was
planted and watered quite some time before it came to fruition in
the Universal Negro Improvement Association'.[26]

Thorne's scheme to take West Indian settlers to his African Zion
received a decisive setback from which it did not recover. Following an editorial in the Jamaica *Daily Gleaner* on 13 March 1897
entitled 'The Fall of Dr Thorne', the members of Thorne's Preliminary Committee 'resolved to withdraw entirely from the scheme'.
This action by the Committee dealt a severe blow to the chances of
success of Thorne's scheme. Further, an attempt was made to
discredit Thorne's personal character. In the muckraking which
ensued his alleged marriage was seen as a means to financial gain,
and *Truth*, published in London, stated 'Not only is it extremely
doubtful whether any nigger will be better off in the land of his
ancestors than in the West Indies but the fitness of the Ethiopian
Moses to lead this exodus is open to considerable question.'[27]
Following the acrimony, the only support Thorne received came
from the *Illustrated Missionary News*.

Given these problems, Thorne's plan to select ten 'pioneer
settlers' and gather whatever support he could obtain in the West
Indies in order to take them to the Zambezi in British Central
Africa was never realised. Nonetheless, for Thorne this experience
was one of self-discovery and racial awakening. Before leaving
England, he wrote to Bishop Henry McNeal Turner in America,

whose *Voice of Missions* he had read. Moreover, Thorne's 'Africa for Africans' letter to the *African Times* was reprinted in full in November 1896 in the *Voice of Missions*. Given the problems of the Pan African Triangle (or quadrangle), his letter to Bishop Turner stated:

> The first great lesson we have to learn, I think, is unity. It does not matter whether we are born in Africa, in the United States of America, in the West Indian Islands or in any other part of the world. It is enough that we are all members of the African race, whose past history has been the same, whose future is also identical, and whose present, though it may differ in a few individual instances, nevertheless is, in the main, beset by the same racial disabilities. [28]

This constituted the essence of the ideology of Pan Africanism as the racial vanguard of the African diaspora. Three years after writing to Turner, the first Pan African Conference was called in London with Turner being one of the leading participants. Had Thorne stayed in England, it is more than likely he would have attended the Pan African Conference, and thus, his work would have become better known. What is clear, however, is that his work and idea of a 'Zion on the Zambezi' was the preliminary phase which had laid some of the essential groundwork in the years 1894–97 in England and Scotland for the emergence and later development of Pan Africanism.

The influence of Henry Sylvester Williams

Having laid the groundwork and departed, Thorne's idea of an African homeland remained to be acted upon. The black radicals in Britain during the nineteenth century had seen, as products of the colonial plantations, the relevance and importance of the British and colonial working classes. Indeed, exploitation was relative. The small group of black people in Britain, because they were easily identified and alien, suffered from discrimination as no other group before them. The degradation of Blacks and the pseudo-scientific arguments constructed to cast the black man as sub-human, inevitably resulted in certain black responses. Pride in blackness was lacking, and among black men of achievement, it was vital that a sense of dignity, and pride in race, in the face of degradation should be emphasised and organised.

Among those in the African diaspora, there had to be a 'son of Africa' committed to redeeming the good name and humanity of the African and his people as a whole. In response to James Anthony Froude's negrophobe travel book *The English in the West Indies* (1888), J. J. Thomas, a Trinidadian schoolmaster wrote *Froudacity, West Indian Fables by James Anthony Froude Explained*. This well stated argument, however, was not enough. While many had thought of the idea, few or none had acted on behalf of the

African peoples until Henry Sylvester Williams, a Trinidadian, became aware of this need while he was in London.

Williams was born in Arouca, Trinidad, in 1869 where the villagers were mainly of African descent. At that time, slavery had been abolished for some 30 years. In fact, there were people alive when he was growing up who had experienced the 'middle passage' and others who had been born in slavery in Trinidad. Moreover, there were those who had come to Trinidad as 'recaptives'. Many of these Africans were taken from slave ships by the Royal Navy's anti-slave squadron and transported to Sierra Leone for settlement. In Williams's young mind, Africa and his Africanness were real. The African form of worship, African drums and dances formed part of Trinidadian village life. All this, however, was being increasingly undermined.

British colonial rule had the effect of making Trinidad (and other West Indian colonies) less African, less French and more English. For some, like Williams, Africa was indelibly written in his youth and early manhood. Issues affecting Africa and Africans did not go unnoticed in Trinidad. The Rev Henry Doughlin told a meeting in San Fernando on 1 August 1888 that it was the duty of every African man in Trinidad to help in Africa's conversion. The fact that Williams knew there were African princes in the land of his ancestors raised many questions. He was particularly concerned with the fact that he had heard only the praises and rituals of white royalty. This troubled him even more because he lived under the British Crown and had received a British education. At the time, agitation for self-government was growing. There were riots and clashes in the early 1880s when James Anthony Froude (the Oxford University Professor of Modern History) derided Trinidadians and their aspirations to self-rule in his book *The English in the West Indies*. Among other things, this sneering observer considered a constitution with a Black minister and a Black legislature as unthinkable. What the ill-informed Froude did not know at the time was that Trinidad was regarded as the land of chronic agitation for reform.[29] His view of self-government and Trinidadians (as a people) was a reflection of what English politicians and officials (who controlled the political destiny of the island) firmly believed. Williams came to realise this later when he tried to press upon the Colonial Office the case for reform of the Trinidad legislature. Following the 'great reform meeting' black consciousness was heightened during 1888 and 1889.

J. J. Thomas's book *Froudacity* was a clear exposition, which left no doubt of pride in his blackness and concern for his race, wherever its members lived. Williams, then only 20 years old, was one of many black readers of *Froudacity*. During this period, Thomas's thoughts had an influence on Williams, then a young schoolteacher. Thomas was preoccupied with Africa, the birthplace of his parents and 'the cradle of our race'. He felt, as would others after him, that black people in the Western hemisphere would be better off in Africa. Thus, the back to Africa and Pan African thoughts of Thomas had a major influence on Williams who in turn developed and set the idea in motion, through practical organisation.

After some teaching experience in Trinidad, at the age of 22, Williams went to the United States. As a newcomer, he took a keen interest in the situation of Afro-Americans who were discriminated against, denied equal rights, terrorised and lynched. He was also concerned with the increasing disenfranchisement of Blacks in the South. In 1891, there were only three Blacks in Congress. But the independence of Blacks was evident in religion and in the formation of a black press. This impressed him. The *New York Age*, for example, focused attention on black church activities, black politics and significantly A. M. E. Bishop Henry McNeal Turner campaigned for black emigration to Africa. It was a time when 'Africa fever' was spreading among Blacks in the South. Among many there was a strong desire to emigrate to Liberia.

It is more than likely then, that given the wide publicity surrounding it, Williams was aware of Bishop Turner's back to Africa plan which was criticised by the *New York Age*, although it was admitted that the idea had 'stirred up unusual interest'. Turner advocated the emigration of '100,000 to 150,000 of the coloured race'. [30]

Such factors as racial barriers and the lack of congenial work ended Williams's study in the United States. He had earned enough money to begin his studies when he moved to Canada, where he entered Dalhousie University in 1893. There he was registered as a general student in the faculty of law during the 1893–4 session. Unfortunately, very little is known of his activities as a student at Dalhousie.

In 1896, however, he arrived in England and enrolled at King's College, London where (as at Dalhousie) there has been no trace of his enrolment from the college records. By all accounts Williams had to live frugally. It was not long before he immersed himself in events concerning Africa. His interest was encouraged by the protests of the humanitarian and liberal interests with which he was to identify. As it was, 1896 was especially notable in African affairs. [31]

While atrocities were being committed in Africa, the English publicist, William J. Stead, editor of the *Review of Reviews*, pleaded for 'lenient judgement' for his fellow Englishmen who were 'at the front bearing the heat and burden of the day'. Ironically, Stead also believed in the 'civilising mission' of his race. [32]

Although Williams was active in public affairs, he pursued his ambition of reading for the Bar, enrolling at Gray's Inn on 10 December 1897. It was at Gray's Inn that he delivered his first address as Honorary Secretary of the African Association which he had formed. Having forged this link of black brotherhood, it seemed he felt free to enter the bond of inter-racial marriage. He considered no race to be superior to the 'Negro' race. In 1898, at the age of 29, he married a white woman, Agnes Powell, in spite of her father's disapproval.

In order to fill the need for a 'body of Africans in England representing native opinion on national matters affecting the destiny of the African race', he founded the African Association on 24 September 1897. The purposes of the Association were:

> to encourage a feeling of unity and to facilitate friendly intercourse among Africans in general; to promote and protect the interests of all subjects claiming African descent, wholly or in part, in British colonies and other places, especially in Africa, by circulating accurate information on all subjects affecting their rights and privileges as subjects of the British Empire, by direct appeals to the imperial and local Governments. [33]

Moreover, the Association's scope was restricted to British subjects and it proposed to protect their rights by appealing to both the British and colonial governments to redress their wrongs.

Predictably, good wishes for the future of the Association were counteracted by other comments. The detractors – 'certain English persons' – did not expect the Association to last more than three months, essentially because they could not see black people uniting for such a purpose. However, Williams was confident, insisting that the Association would act on its own, draft its own rules, and not be led by Europeans. Although the Association was beset by difficulties, it managed to survive for four years.

Williams acted in keeping with the Association's pledge to protect the interests of his African brethren by contacting well disposed MPs to ask questions about colonial conditions, particularly in South Africa. He wrote to Chamberlain about the welfare of Africans in Rhodesia and to newspapers such as *The Leader* on behalf of the Association. He criticised the British government for condoning the introduction of slavery in South Africa under the leadership of Cecil Rhodes. British policy was clearly questionable and he appealed to the nation on behalf of the African Association, to lobby their representatives to bring about fairness and justice to Blacks. He carefully trod the racial path. He did not advocate a complete westernisation of Africa; he was prepared to adopt only what was of value in the European culture while retaining the best of his own. This balancing of the modern with the traditional would become a recurring theme in the development of Pan Africanism.

In seeking a reversal of British policies in the colonies, as imperial power expanded, Williams's task seemed hopeless. Nevertheless, he was optimistic; indeed, he had bigger plans.

The African Association's activities spurred the call which was issued as early as 1898 for a Pan African Conference in 1900. Williams had, in fact, conceived of the idea of a world conference of black people in 1897, well before the formation of the African Association which gave it credibility. But he was aware that his plans could only materialise if he could get people to come to London. He thought that the Conference could only get off the ground if he could induce 'representatives of the race' to make the trip. Some other important event in Europe might be helpful. The great Exposition which the French were planning to open in Paris in April 1900 was an occasion which might attract Blacks. Williams reasoned that those Blacks who were going to Paris might be induced to combine their trip with a visit to London for the Conference. This they did.

As preparations for the Conference got under way on 19 March 1898, the African Association issued a circular announcing the intention 'to hold a conference in the month of May (1900) ... in order to take steps to influence public opinion on existing proceedings and conditions affecting the welfare of the Natives of the various parts of the British Empire, viz. South Africa, West Africa and the British West Indies'.[34] Attention was focused on conditions in those lands under British rule for which the British government was responsible and for which it was answerable to Parliament.

The original Conference date, set for May 1900 because of the Paris Exposition, was changed on the advice of a number of 'leading men' of the race from Africa, the United States and the West Indies who, while visiting London for various reasons, attended a preparatory meeting of the Pan African Conference Committee on 12 June 1899. July was more suitable to them and the Committee agreed that the dates should be 23, 24 and 25 July, noting carefully the opening of the World's Christian Endeavour Convention on 16 July. Some of the 'leading men' who advised the Committee constitute 'a galaxy of remarkable men': Bishop James T. Holly, Bishop James Johnson, Bishop Henry McNeal Turner, the Rev Dr Majola Agbebi, the Rev C. W. Farquhar, Judge David Augustus Straker, Professor W. S. Scarborough, Henry Richard Cargill, J. Tengo Jabavu, J. Otonba Payne and Professor Booker T. Washington.[35]

In naming the Conference, it would seem that Williams and his associates were aware of the Pan-Slav movement, the oldest of the 'pan' movements which held a demonstration in Prague in 1898. Of course, there was also the pan-German movement which sought to stimulate the patriotism of race, to emphasise the solidarity of all German speaking peoples and to prepare for their political union.

Africans from the diaspora had increasingly begun to question the validity of European oppression. J. M. Bourne was perhaps the only English member of the African Association, and it is possible that sharp criticism of British imperial policy was not always well received by him. However, as the date of the Conference drew near, the task of organising it was entrusted to the Pan African Committee.

The lack of support from the Anti-Slavery Society did not discourage Williams and his supporters. Funds were coming in and the arrangements were going as planned. The Conference was well-timed for those who were also attending the Universal Paris Exposition and the World Christian Endeavour Convention in London. These two events increased the credibility of actually holding the Pan African Conference. For example, W. E. DuBois who prepared part of the American Negro exhibit at the Paris Exposition travelled to London. Similar coincidental factors were to recur at the historic 1945 Pan African Congress. Thus, the stage was set.

At a meeting held before the opening of the Conference Williams said that the Conference would be 'the first occasion upon which black men would assemble in England to speak for themselves and endeavour to influence public opinion in their favour'. He specified the position of Blacks in South Africa, warning that their interests must not be overlooked in any settlement reached after the South African war.[36]

When the Pan African Conference finally met in 1900, imperialism had reached its zenith. By then Britain had added the following territories to its Empire: Nigeria, Asante, British East Africa (Kenya), Uganda, Nyasaland, Rhodesia and Bechuanaland in Africa; the Sudan, Somaliland and Zanzibar in the Islamic world; and North Borneo, Sarawak, Pahang, Kowloon, Wei-hai-wai and Burma in the Far East. Further, Britain also held extra-territorial rights in thirty-five Chinese cities. Of these territories, none was self-governed. War was everywhere.[37]

Bishop Walters opened the first Pan African Conference on 23 July 1900. His opening address dealt thoughtfully with 'The Trials and Tribulations of the Coloured Race in America', thus setting the tone of the Conference. 'For the first time in history', he said, 'Blacks had gathered from all parts of the globe to discuss how to improve the condition of the race; to assert the rights of blacks and to organise them so that they might take an equal place among nations.' He argued that in the United States it had been their misfortune to live among a people whose laws, traditions and prejudices had always been against Blacks. It had taken the Black two hundred years to gain personal emancipation and one hundred years to attain standing as a soldier. It would hardly be expected, therefore, that he would get his complete social and political rights in 35 years. The black people in the United States had been able nevertheless to eliminate 45 per cent of their illiteracy and they now owned $735 million in real estate and personal property. And they were now engaged in a long and severe struggle for full social and political rights.[38]

In opening the proceedings of the third and final day, Walters spoke in recognition of the services Whites in England and the United States rendered to the cause of black people. He closed the discussion by saying that the object of the Conference was to secure moral, political and civil rights for Blacks. The force of numbers, he argued, was on their side. The Conference was just the beginning of the work, and it meant that Blacks everywhere would organise for their betterment.

The first Committee report (read and adopted) recommended the formation of a permanent Pan African Association with headquarters in London and branches overseas. The intention was that the Association would convene a general meeting every second year in a large city in Europe or America or in an independent black state. It was decided that the next meeting would be held in the United States in 1902, and in Haiti in 1904 'to add to the solemnity of the centenary celebration of Haitian freedom'.[39] Agreement was also reached to the effect that the African Association would merge into the new Pan African Association and that other organisations, in existence, whose aims were similar to those of the Pan African Association would be affiliated on formal application to the Executive.

The aims and objects of the Pan African Association were:

1. To secure to Africans throughout the world true civil and political rights;
2. To ameliorate the condition of our brothers on the continent of Africa, America and other parts of the world;
3. To promote efforts to secure effective legislation and encourage our people in educational, industrial and commercial enterprise;
4. To foster the production of writing and statistics relating to our people everywhere; and
5. To raise funds for forwarding these purposes.[40]

A matter of importance was the fact that the Conference unanimously adopted an 'Address to the Nations of the World'. The Address appealed to the great powers of the civilised world, expressed faith in 'the wide spirit of humanity and the deep sense of justice' and called for an end to colour and race prejudice. The delegates of the Conference also sent a separate memorial to Queen Victoria calling for an end to the discrimination against Blacks in South Africa. Moreover, the Address called on Britain to give 'as soon as practicable the rights of responsible government to the black colonies of Africa and the West Indies'. The questions of race and colour weighed heavily on the mind of Joseph Chamberlain who regarded Blacks in the West Indies as 'totally unfit for representative institutions'.

The Address also called for protection of the American Negro from oppression and to grant him 'the right of franchise' and 'security of person and property'. It also called for the Congo Free

State of King Leopold to 'become a great central Negro State of the World'.

Finally the Address called on the imperialist nations to respect the integrity and independence of the free 'Negro' States of Abyssinia, Liberia and Haiti. In addition the Conference sent a memorial on the ill-treatment of Africans and coloureds in South Africa, directly to Queen Victoria. It stated that the Pan African Conference comprising men and women of African blood and descent, respect-fully invited her 'august and sympathetic attention to the fact that the situation of the native races in South Africa is causing us and our friends alarm'. In fact, the delegates expressed many concerns. [41]

After the Conference, organisation of the new Pan African Association was Williams's main task. Among his immediate duties were arranging for the submission of the memorial to Queen Victoria, despatching the 'Address to the Nations', the memorials to Emperor Menelik and the Presidents of Liberia and Haiti, and the resolutions passed and letters of thanks for the assistance given. Williams found time to attend the Anti-Slavery Congress in Paris. In addition to completing the Conference report, he was engaged in completing his studies for the Bar final examination. Between his finals and the Paris visit, the Association was able to establish a permanent headquarters with a bureau 'to disseminate facts and statistics relating to the circumstances and conditions of members of the African race wherever found'. [42]

Financially the Conference was unsuccessful, although Williams solicited and received contributions from many sympathetic per-sons. In spite of the problem of the lack of funds, Williams was especially concerned about the 'acute ill-treatment of the natives of South Africa' and in line with the Pan African Conference decision, he sent a memorial to Queen Victoria. The fact that there was no reply to this memorial disturbed the Executive Committee. Conse-quently, Williams was instructed to write to the Queen early in 1901 enquiring whether she had received the memorial. On 17 January, he received a letter from Chamberlain's Secretary, saying that Chamberlain had received 'the Queen's commands to inform you that the memorial of the Pan African Association regarding the situation of the native races in South Africa has been laid before her Majesty and that she was graciously pleased to command him to return an answer to it on behalf of her government'. Chamberlain asked Williams to assure the members of the Pan African Confer-ence that 'in settling the lines on which the administration of conquered territories is to be conducted, Her Majesty's govern-ment will not overlook the interests of the native races'. The letter also stated that a copy of the memorial was sent to the High Commissioner in South Africa.

Satisfied with this reply that 'the interests of the native races' will not be overlooked, Williams sent the text of the letter to *The Times* which published it the following day under the heading 'The South

African Native Question' with an introductory paragraph referring to the Pan African Conference and to the General Secretary as 'The Rev Henry Sylvester Williams'. Unfortunately, while the memorial mentioned conditions among the natives of South Africa, Chamberlain's reply referred only to the settlement in the 'conquered territories' such as the Transvaal and Orange River.[43] The fact that this was not a direct reply to the memorial was not surprising since Chamberlain's views on Blacks generally were well known. Acknowledgement of the letter was clearly not enough. Soon after Williams received the reply, the Queen died. During her reign the British Empire expanded by robbery, violence, deceit and forced labour, taking the wealth from the less advanced lands. Yet Williams, the Anglophile, felt that black people should revere the memory of the Queen 'because her first act on ascending the throne was the absolute emancipation of their people and her very last act was in connection with them'.[44] Relying on favourable British public opinion, Williams was later to see that such an opinion was formed precisely by the promises and deceit of such men as Chamberlain.

Williams continued his work for the Association by travelling to Jamaica, Trinidad and the United States in an effort to spread the word. Branches were formed and, at meetings, subscriptions were collected to fund *Pan African*, the monthly magazine that Williams hoped to publish in London. While he was in Trinidad, a month after leaving the Association's headquarters in London, 'certain colleagues' had dissolved the Pan African Association 'on the pretext of lack of funds' and announced it to the press.[45] Although this 'illegality' affected Williams deeply, he made no public announcement in Trinidad.

Soon after Williams returned to London on 4 September a meeting was convened with members of the Association on 13 September, and they announced that the Pan African Association would continue and that the members elected to the Executive Committee would replace those who were 'considered to have resigned'.[46] It was also announced that Williams would continue as General Secretary until 1902 when the next Conference was due in the United States.

Although Williams notified overseas members, the Association never appeared to have functioned. And while little was known of the fate of the Anglo-Africa Association there is no evidence that it functioned either in Jamaica or in Trinidad. The Pan African Association branches, however, continued in operation until mid-1902.

In an effort to keep the Association alive, Williams sought publicity which he hoped would help to enlighten the Whites and expose racial inequities. There was no black press through which grievances could be expressed. Since Blacks had no representation in Parliament, a black-owned newspaper was essential. Conscious of these failings, Williams published the first issue of *The Pan African* in October 1901. This monthly journal dealt with matters 'concerning the interests of the African descendants in the British Empire'. Although this approach was similar to the position of the 'Anglo-Africans', it was argued that 'this stance was probably adopted merely for convenience and was not an abandonment of the Pan African idea'.[47] Be that as it may, Williams was the editor.

Whatever lessons he may have learnt about an independent black press in the United States was of no avail in England. The history of the *Pan African* was short and obscure. Ambitiously, the *Pan African* sought a wide public among Africans, Afro-Caribbeans and Afro-Americans. So much so that in February 1902, a printer in Trinidad, Edgar McCarthy, was appointed local agent. But, by mid-April of that year, Williams's brother was the only person who had to hand 'the back numbers' of the six issues that were printed. No more was heard of the magazine.

While working on the *Pan African* Williams prepared for his call to the Bar. In the meantime he continued to give public lectures on the status of the African in the British Empire. On the question of the Boer War, Williams, who felt that the treatment meted out to Blacks by the Boers was one of the principal causes of the war, expected the situation to be resolved following a British victory. Was he yet again being naive about British imperialism?

Williams later became involved in municipal politics as a member of the Marylebone Borough Council. His mind was set on a political career. To further his ambition he became a member of the prestigious Liberal Club. While his scope in Borough Council politics was limited he held out the brave hope of parliamentary representation for Blacks. With a tiny black electorate in London, Williams needed a white majority to be elected. He was fortunate in that his links with the trade union members among his colleagues appeared to have been closer than his fellow Progressive candidates, and he had the backing of the General Secretary of the Workers' Union. Eventually, he won a seat, 'becoming probably the first Negro man to be elected to public office in Britain'. For the Progressives in Marylebone, however, and especially the Ward 3 area, the election was a disaster. The Conservatives were jubilant. The *Pall Mall Gazette* commented on the 'sharp reverses' of Keir Hardie's party whose policy was based on 'an arrogant and ambitious communism'. The Progressives were described as 'socialistic'.[48]

As a municipal councillor, Williams settled down to work serving on two standing committees, legal and parliamentary and housing. Service as a councillor, however, did not deflect his interest and devotion to African affairs. After a spell of 'protecting Liberian interests' Williams left Africa. Moreover, he had to abandon an unfinished project for a black students' club in Oxford – a kind of Pan African students' club – and discontinued his role as black spokesman in England. For some unexplained reason, he chose to return to his native Trinidad, a small white-dominated colony on the periphery of the British Empire. As it was, Trinidad and Africa were the focal points of interest during his organisational work and representations. To further the ambitious cause of Pan Africanism from this setting was most unlikely. According to his biographer, Williams 'perhaps prematurely, popularised the vocabulary of black grievance, coined a useful phrase, challenged conventional notions regarding Africa and called for a new sort of British Empire. Today's Commonwealth would have seemed to him a logical outgrowth of his ideas. He was certain that black people were the equals of any set of humans, and he could point to a large number including himself, who already had demonstrated the proposition. He sought justice and fair competition. He was, finally, a decent and generous man.'[49] Indeed, it can be asserted that he influenced W. E. B. DuBois.

His biographer concludes, 'One who writes about Pan African-ism must write about Williams, but none of the literature has.'[50] Like Thorne and others (until recently) his work in calling the crucial Pan African Conference remained largely unknown. These early beginnings initiated in Britain, particularly by Thorne and Williams in the nineteenth century, led to the development and 'dilemma' of Pan Africanism in the twentieth century.

PART TWO:

The 'Black Man's' Burden (1900–1962)

4 Britain, Empire and Labour

After the Second World War, one observer wrote that British imperialism, in extreme decay, was not yet finished but strove to adopt many new forms and techniques to meet new conditions, not in order to commit suicide or liquidate itself, but to continue to promote the age-old aims of extracting the super-profits of colonial exploitation.[1]

While the British colonial system is older than British capitalism, the post-war Empire, essentially a modern growth, dates back to the late eighteenth century. Indeed, it was through the 'old colonial system' that the primary capital accumulated, making possible the Industrial Revolution. As Marx put it, 'The colonial system ripened, like a hothouse, trade and navigation … The treasures captured outside Europe by undisguised looting, enslavement and murder, floated back to the mother country and were there turned into capital.'[2] In turn, the old colonial monopoly was overtaken by world-industrial monopoly. Thus through manipulation of the means of production and the improvements in communications, the bourgeoisie of the 'uncivilised' nations (India, Africa and the East and West Indies) were drawn into 'civilisation'. The exploitation and oppression endemic in this binding relationship was expressed in Marx and Engels' *Communist Manifesto*.

Through these developments then, Britain's nineteenth century world industrial monopoly effected a new phase in the colonial system. This was also a dual system: on the one hand, there were the Dominions (Canada and Australia) where British settlers either exterminated or displaced the original inhabitants to become the colonial wing of the British; on the other, there were the conquered and the enslaved colonial countries which served as sources of cheap raw materials extracted through the plantation system and by peasant labour under semi-starvation conditions. These colonies also served as markets for British exports. Flooding the local markets with British goods led, in large measure, to the ruin of the native handicraft industries.

Britain's economic power seemed enviable until the Great Depression of the 1870s when, for the first time, the supremacy of British exports was weakened by powerful new industrial rivals – first the United States, then Germany. This competition resulted in an extension of the export of capital and the scramble for new colonial possessions. Thus, the way was prepared for the twentieth century era of imperialism.

In 1880 British steel output stood at 1.3 million tons, that of the USA at 1.2 million and Germany's at 700,000. By 1900 American steel output had reached 10.2 million tons, German 6.4 million and the British 4.9 million. By 1913 American steel output reached 31.3 million tons, German 18.9 million and British 7.7 million. However, Britain still maintained the first position in the export of manufactured goods although with a lessening proportion. But, in the export of capital and colonial expansion, Britain was far ahead.

Between 1884 and 1900 Britain acquired 3,700,000 square miles of new colonial territories. By 1914 the British Empire covered 12.7 million square miles, with a population of 431 millions, of which the White Dominions totalled 60 million. A further one and a half million square miles were acquired through the imperialist war of 1914–18. Thus, by the eve of the Second World War the British Empire's protectorates and dependencies, covered approximately one-quarter of the earth's surface and one-quarter of the world's population.[3] In effect, the era of industrial capital gave way to the era of finance capital. Britain still remained the great colonial exploiter.

This exploitation was vital to Britain. In the face of a rising challenge from the British working class, Lenin quoted Cecil Rhodes as saying in 1895:

> I was in the East End of London yesterday and I attended a meeting of the 'unemployed'. I listened to the wild speeches which were just a cry for 'bread', 'bread', 'bread', and on my way home I pondered over the scene and I became more than ever convinced of the importance of imperialism . . . My cherished idea is a solution for the social problem. In order to save the 40,000,000 inhabitants of the

UK from a bloody civil war, we, colonial statesmen, must acquire
new lands to settle the surplus population, to provide new markets
for the goods produced by them in the factories and mines. The
Empire, as I have always said, is a bread and butter question. If you
want to avoid civil war, you must become an imperialist.[4]

East Indian labour: the abolition of indentureship

The change in the Indian indentured labourers' circumstances came
only with the change in sugar production. The shift towards fewer
estates and larger, central sugar mills resulted in a movement from
an estate-based population into a rural small-holder or peasant
population. This modification of the plantation system gave some
freedom from its pervasive grip. The system came under increasing
scrutiny and pressure. There was a 'long, long period' during
which it was questioned and challenged. Mohandas K. Gandhi was
right in identifying Lord Curzon as the first Viceroy of India to see
that the indentured Indians were mere helots of the Empire and the
first to question the system. Gandhi's own attempts in South Africa
helped to highlight some of the problems of the Indians as an
important political issue. Thus, both Gandhi and Curzon called the
system into question.

The movement to abolish Indian indentureship was gathering
momentum. In South Africa, the Indians were on the march; in
Mauritius, they were moved to periodic protest; but in the Caribbean the only political movement was that of the Creole Blacks. In
Trinidad, the Working Men's Association was opposed to further
Indian immigration as a threat to wages and living standards. And
in British Guiana, the Peoples' Association, a black organisation,
protested against taxation levied to promote immigration.[5] It was
against this background of colonial resistance to indentured labour
that the Sanderson Committee began its work.

Gandhi's struggle against oppressive laws in South Africa had
become a mass campaign of Satyagraha, in which the majority of
participants were indentured and ex-indentured Indians. At last,
through exceptional leadership, given the historical moment, the
coolies were being mobilised. By 1913, the atmosphere was highly
charged by the news that Gandhi had launched his most massive
Satyagraha campaign. His main appeal was to the indentured
coolies employed in the Dundee and Newcastle districts of Natal.
The labourers abandoned their work and marched with Gandhi to
the Transvaal border. Over 200 were arrested, including Gandhi
who was sentenced to nine months' imprisonment.[6]

This news reached Whitehall and Delhi quickly. Lord Hardinge
responded in an extraordinary speech stating that the Indians in
South Africa 'have violated, as they intended to violate, those laws,

with full knowledge of the penalties involved. . . . In all this they have the sympathies of India – deep and burning – and not only of India but of those who like myself . . . have feelings of sympathy for the people of this country.'[7] Having made this pronouncement which, understandably was 'open to criticism' (because it came 'straight from the heart'), the British Cabinet considered his recall from India, but did not want to precipitate an Indian backlash. Against this background of events, the McNeill and Chimman Lal Report on the *Condition of Indian Immigrants in Four British Colonies: Trinidad, British Guiana, Jamaica and Fiji* and in the Dutch colony of Surinam was considered.

While Gandhi (who was preparing to return to India) recognised the importance of the Viceroy's intervention, with Indian independence in mind, he attached greater importance to Satyagraha. Subsequently, the McNeill and Chimman Lal report was circulated and the First World War intervened. By 1915, Indian feeling about emigration was only partly aroused. In January, Gandhi had returned to India. There, several organisations were founded especially to fight coolie emigration. Among them were the Indian Coolie Protection Society and the Anti-Indentured Emigration League of Bengal. Later, other organisations joined in the protest such as the Home Rule League, the Bengal Province Congress, the UP Congress, the League for the Abolition of Indentured Emigration, the Anti-Indenture League of Madras and the Punjab Provincial Moslem League.[8]

Moreover, during January and February 1917, Gandhi continued to speak out against indenture. He was suspicious that the Government of India might keep the system going for another five years and pressed for a definite early date for complete abolition.

Finally, in 1917, Indian indenture had officially ended. But, Indians were still bound by indenture in the sugar colonies: a continuing servitude that was unacceptable to the Indian public. In December, 1919, all outstanding indentures were terminated in British Guiana. Still outstanding, however, was the fact that the indenture system as a working reality had to be cleared away, once and for all. In theory, at least, the labourers were free. Ironically, many Indians having pined for their homeland, eventually returned to India to find that industrial conditions there, after the famine of 1920, had been unfavourable. The returned emigrants experienced great difficulty in obtaining suitable employment. Many of them were colonial-born and found themselves utter strangers in the country. The India-born found that their long residence in the colonies had rendered them unfit for the old social conditions. These repatriates, after spending all their savings drifted back to Calcutta in the hope of finding ships to take them back to their homes in the sugar colonies.[9]

Thus, the indentured coolies, many of them long forgotten, returned home to realise a state of hopelessness. Strangely, the familiar bounds of the plantations offered the only hope. And so the Indian diaspora, achieved a settled, permanent foothold, existing side by side with Africans in Africa and in the African diaspora.

Thereafter, Indians continued to emigrate. Their concern was not with the colonies where the Indians remained the working poor. Instead, they looked towards East and South Africa where the Indians were trying to establish themselves as urban middle class communities. Their attention was directed especially to East Africa, to Kenya and Uganda.

The first major threat to reduce the status of overseas Indians emerged in Kenya where the white settlers plotted to force the hand of the British government. The Indians were now mostly traders. Despite protest and non-co-operation, the East African Indians were forced to accept an uneasy middle position between the Europeans, at the top, and the Africans at the bottom; clearly an unsettled and unsettling buffer position.

In South Africa during the 1920s, the Indian community came under attack as legislation eroded their rights; those who left the country could not return, and dependants were denied entry. They were profoundly affected by the Class Areas Bill, introduced in 1925, which confined Indians to separate residential and commercial areas. The Indian government and politicians protested loudly. Yet, they could do little to confront South African racism effectively. Motilal Nehru told the Indian Congress in 1928 that the best way to help Indians overseas was to act 'to gain our freedom here'. Clearly then, colonial exploitation had to continue, though it would be tempered by grudging concessions to colonial labour.

Twentieth century politicians, certainly by the end of the Second World War, were unanimous that the Empire was the essential economic base on which the British working class would be saved from starvation. In 1929, Winston Churchill, then Chancellor of the Exchequer, was able to say that the social services in Britain was dependent on the income from imperialist exploitation.[10] Lord Cranbourne, the Dominions Secretary, reminded the British people that their employment and standard of living depended mainly on the existence of the Empire. And in 1946, the Labour trade union leader, Ernest Bevin told the House of Commons that he was not prepared to sacrifice the British Empire for if it fell it would mean a considerable fall in the standard of living of 'our constituents'.[11]

It emerges very clearly from these statements that the exploitation and degradation of the colonial working class was an indispensable requirement in maintaining the standard of living of the British working class. Implicit in this argument is the fact that the British economy is really a 'parasitic economy' dependent on colonial revenues for its maintenance. The concentration on foreign investment, as opposed to industrial renewal, and neglect of home investment would have serious repercussions. For so long as the

British ruling class could amass huge profits (at the expense of minimum and starvation level standards of living in the colonies) attention was deflected from the growing neglect of industrial and agricultural investment in Britain. Indeed, there was every reason for optimism that the British working class would continue to benefit from colonial exploitation. Before the First World War nearly one-fifth of British imports were no longer paid for by exports of goods. And on the eve of the Second World War nearly two-fifths of British imports were no longer paid for by exports of goods. The import surplus (or invisible balance of trade) rose from £30 million in 1855–59 to £134 million in 1913 to £302 million in 1938, and £438 million in 1947. Initially, this import surplus was covered by income from overseas investment such as financial commissions and shipping. Later, however, the tide had turned to the extent that even the overseas income could not cover the unpaid imports. Consequently, in the late 1930s, a net deficit on the balance of payments reached £380 million and £630 million in 1947.[12]

If imperialism means violent aggression, then the imperialist basis of the British economy was clearly founded on an unstable dependence on colonial exploitation. Repressive force exerted over the colonial working classes was, sooner or later, bound to lead to violent reaction. The disturbances or 'riots', as they were called, in India, Africa, Trinidad, Jamaica and elsewhere in the West Indies, during the decades before the Second World War, were symptomatic of the weakness of British imperialism. Increasingly, as cracks appeared in the system, costly military manoeuvres were required to maintain law and order in the colonies. Consequently, there was neglect and decay of British home industries. Thus, the first industrial nation, once 'the workshop of the world', lagged behind the United States of America and Germany, with an accumulation of obsolete machinery and equipment. The coal industry, for example, was 'worse than stagnant' before 1900, and textiles machinery was notoriously obsolete in the majority of factories. This lag was both absolute and relative.[13]

Between the wars this deterioration accelerated. Coal production fell from 287 million tons in 1913 to 230 million in 1938. Between 1920 and 1935 fourteen million spindles were destroyed; one-third of the British shipyards were closed down and British shipping capacity was reduced from three to two million tons annually. Moreover, in agriculture between 1918 and 1938, over two million acres of arable land went out of cultivation.[14]

But in spite of the decay of the basic industries, secondary and luxury services expanded. As the proportion of the working population engaged in production in the basic industries fell from 23 per cent in 1851 to 13.6 per cent in 1929, the numbers employed in commercial and financial operations, distribution, office employment and a variety of 'services' rose continually. Thus, from these secondary industries a 'new middle class' emerged. By 1937 the 'foreign investment' which made this prosperity possible was described by the *Economist* as 'the nation's greatest single industry'. [15]

The consequence of this 'new middle class' was to act as a buffer between the decline and depression of the productive working class in industry. This transformation in the productive base of the British economy had restructured and divided the British working class. In the labour hierarchy, based on imperialism, British working class solidarity was difficult to achieve, with the upper section opposing the lower. Lenin's observation of this in the early twentieth century was revealing:

> In Great Britain the tendency of imperialism to divide the toilers . . .
> to encourage opportunism amongst them and to give rise to a
> temporary organic decay in the working class movement, revealed
> itself much earlier than the end of the nineteenth and the beginning
> of the twentieth centuries. For two big distinctive features of imperi-
> alism applied to Britain from midway through the nineteenth cen-
> tury: vast colonial possessions and a monopolist position in the
> world markets. Marx and Engels systematically followed, over
> some decades this relation between working class opportunism and
> the imperialistic peculiarities of English capitalism. [16]

The British labour movement and imperialism

Thus, Labour imperialism brought workers of both factions of the working class under closer control of capitalist policies. In forming this alliance, those in the labour movement who fought for the advance of socialism (with few exceptions) became converts who hammered out their own brand of imperialist labour policy. Both the MacDonald Labour governments between the wars, and the third Labour government's policies demonstrated this.

The early socialists, Keir Hardie and Tom Mann, fought against capitalist policies and an alliance with capitalists. Both men had travelled abroad and seen the effects of imperialism on the colonial working class. They, like Lenin and Stalin, had observed (under capitalism) the shift from old Labour reformism to Labour imperialism. In effect, this meant an 'open' alliance of Reformism with imperialism. Churchill's declaration that the social services was dependent on overseas investment income received full recognition as Labour reformism accepted the permanency of the 'income' as the basis for its social services, which they preferred to label the Welfare State.

To get a better understanding of Labour imperialism, let us take a brief look at official Labour policy in the Empire. In effect, the Labour leaders in government had become connected with the ruling class. Indeed, there was little to choose between the arguments of Labour imperialism and the Conservatives on the colonial question. Whatever charity or welfare the Labour government would dole out to the working class was clearly calculated. Although the Labour Party had formed a government, they had not seized power. In effect, they had become the protectors of the *status quo*, of British imperialist interests. Indeed, they did well to project a pro-working class image.

Before looking at the main themes uttered by Labour government ministers and official Labour Party spokesmen on the Empire, let us consider the general approach of the main sections of the Labour movement to imperial issues between 1899 and 1924.

During this period there were both objective changes taking place in the Labour movement and new and old influences which accompanied them. This was a time of rapid change within the Labour movement, from being industry-centred to being Parliament-centred. Whereas in 1899 the annual convention of the movement was the Trades Union Congress, it was emphatically the Labour Party Conference in 1924.

As a Parliamentary force, Labour was hard-pressed to play the role of a national party. This meant involvement in debates on the major issues of economic policy, imperial policy and labour conditions. Thus began the process of change from a party of protest to a party ready to participate in government. Moreover, this twenty-five year period saw the beginning of its involvement in the sphere of imperial policy.

Given this change in status, the Labour movement in Parliament meant that mere working class slogans could no longer be accepted as a substitute for policy in Parliament. The Labour movement had to adjust itself to Parliamentary demands both for knowledge of the problems and the ability to present an alternative policy. Overwhelmingly, the Labour movement took the Parliamentary road to socialism. Thus constrained by the grip of ruling class politics, by 1924 they were still casting about for an agreed method through which policy could be devised.

These objective changes in Labour's role and status in British society were accompanied by old and new influences. Firstly, when the 'Little England radicalism' was put to the test before 1914 in the Boer War over South African Union, Labour was on the side of the radicals (within the movement) in the tone of their arguments, in lobbying and voting. The differences were in emphasis.[17]

After 1914, the interaction between radicalism and the Labour movement became more complicated. The clear shift of the Union of Democratic Control, resulting from the new alignments brought about by the war, was a rapid move to the left. By 1924, the UDC was absorbed by the Labour Party. Radicalism and advanced liberalism after 1914 was no longer just an influence on the Labour movement, but an integral part of it. This reinforced the position of

those like MacDonald who advocated a reformed Empire and
Labour's interest in imperial problems. The new internationalism
of 1918 afforded Labour a chance to argue that the world had
changed, and that imperialism was a greater danger to world peace.
In spite of the diversity of views within the Labour movement in
general, it could be said that there was a minimum set of assumptions which all Labour men could have applied to the Empire.
Firstly, the Labour movement believed that the Empire should be
reformed and not abandoned. This immediately put Labour into
the category of a bourgeois reformist party; secondly, most Labour
men, after 1914–18 believed that a reformed British Empire should
not only have 'Home Rule All Round', but also economic justice.
The concept of trusteeship for native races in the economic sphere
was in line with the Labour movement's demand for social justice
at home. This had been advocated by Hardie and MacDonald
before the war. Indeed, Labour and the New Social Order urged
colonial development in the interests of the natives; and thirdly,
with the exception of South Africa, the Labour movement adopted
a position of 'absent-minded friendship' for the white settlers of the
Empire. Australia, Canada and New Zealand were immigration
outlets for the British working class who wished to 'escape' from
economic depression and social oppression.

On the question of the Labour movement's attitude and policy
towards the Empire during this twenty-five year period, given that
'Labour' describes the organisations and functions of a group of
people and not a doctrine, Labour parties can be doctrinally collec-
tivist like the British Labour Party after 1918, or individualist, like
the South African Labour Party. When, therefore, we look for
something 'distinctively labour' in Labour's imperial policy, we can
expect it to be doctrinally neutral. [18]

According to one observer, 'this indeed is what we find'.
Significantly (and paradoxically), British Labour has consistently
backed, at least verbally, labour movements and parties in the
Empire, whether they practised racial discrimination, as in South
Africa, or civil disobedience against Britain, as in India. This
certainly is a distinctively 'labour' policy. During this period there
was very little criticism of the Empire from the ranks of British
Labour. As a corollary, British Labour opposed all attempts by
governments or businessmen in the Empire to practise anti-trade
union labour and strike-breaking. However, this doctrinal neutral-
ism adapted itself poorly to Labour's status as a national party. Not
surprisingly therefore, the distinctively 'socialist' element in
Labour's imperial policy has been more lasting and has produced a
more coherent set of attitudes.

After 1918, the socialism professed by the British Labour movement was social reformism: in other words, the policy of greater
social and economic equality through redistributive measures
aimed at the wealthy, individuals or capitalist organisations. While

the nature and timing of these measures was a matter for debate within the movement, the objectives were agreed.

On the basis of this definition, it was only after 1918 that Labour's policy for the Empire became distinctively non-socialist. Before this, Hardie's views on India were readily accepted. But few Liberals would have agreed to dispossess the white Kenyan settlers after 1918. Similarly they would have opposed Labour's policy of a rapid approach to manhood suffrage in India. Such policies, aiming at rapid and fundamental social change and attacking the possessors of wealth, were the policies of egalitarian socialism. But even so, post-1918 socialist policies were not so very different from radical policies. Indeed, the men who were advocating socialism in the Empire were ex-radicals disgusted with the Liberal Party. The Labour Party owed far more to British radicalism than to continental socialism. The Fabians, socialists with a strong tinge of British radicalism, reinforced the ex-Liberals in the conviction that the Empire should not be immediately abandoned, but reformed. Such a reformation, they argued, would strengthen rather than weaken Britain. In this traditionally British way the Labour Party reconciled equality with patriotism. It was an uneasy reconciliation, open to attack from the right and left, but it is only by understanding this objective that we can begin to understand the hesitation and mistakes of Labour's policy after 1924.

One of the themes emphasised after the Second World War on the old Labour imperialist line was that the Empire was essential to the economic interests of British workers. Repeatedly, contradictions appeared in the speeches of Labour ministers, combining the philanthropic aims of Empire with the aims of economic exploitation. In this, the true relationship of the British and colonial working classes are revealed. Justifying this Labour imperialism, one of the champions of the British Labour movement, Ernest Bevin said in Parliament on 21 February 1946: 'I am not prepared to sacrifice the British Empire [because] I know that if the British Empire fell . . . it would mean that the standard of life of our constituents would fall considerably.'[19] Thus, the exploitation of the British working class and the colonial working class was relative. Indeed, the government's Four Year Economic Plan for 1949–53, submitted to the Marshall Plan organisation in December 1948, was aimed at achieving economic recovery and balancing Britain's trading deficit. In fact, they contemplated a large increase in the contribution of the colonies to European recovery.[20] That same year Mr Bevin, as Foreign Secretary, told the National Union of Manufacturers on 14 October 1948: 'We have ceased to be an Imperialist race; we dominate nobody.' Yet he went on to state:

I believed and still believe that
If we can organise Western Europe with its direct connection with
the Middle East,

If we can use the great resources of our Colonial Empire in Africa,
If we can work out our co-operation with our great Dominion of
South Africa,
If we can arrange matters correctly with Pakistan and India,
If we can maintain a correct position in South-East Asia, and
If we can make our proper contribution to the revivification of
China, then with a little planning we somehow occupy the position
of a general balancing factor as between East and West, and may
provide the correct equipoise and the correct equilibrium for the
maintenance of peace and prosperity in the world.[21]

This fallacious emphasis on peace (and prosperity, for whom?)
was contrary to the dynamic of imperialism which, in effect, means
war! Thus, as the post-war Labour government moved to implement policies at home, to appease working class tensions and
demands through a British Welfare State, abroad, they adopted
rapacious plans to solve Britain's economic problems by assuming
a 'seven-fold' increase in net invisible earnings between 1948/9 and
1952/3. Of course, this goal was to be achieved through intensified
exploitation of the working classes in the colonies. It must also be
remembered that Britain had also exploited black labour during
both wars, at home and abroad. Indeed, the year before Bevin
delivered his 'peace and prosperity' speech, there were racial 'riots'
in Liverpool, and a 'colour bar' had emerged as a 'problem' in
Britain whether or not Bevin knew it.

Moreover, in 1948 the *SS Empire Windrush* had arrived in Britain
with some four hundred West Indian immigrants, including former
volunteer workers who had worked in British munitions factories
during the war. This group of immigrants added to the earlier black
settlements of Liverpool, Cardiff, Hull and in various parts of
London; a legacy of British Labour imperialism. It is against this
background that we must look at the experience of black workers
prior to, and after the First World War, particularly in Cardiff and
Liverpool.

Cardiff: black seamen and soldiers

In the centuries of British trade with Asia, Africa, America and the
West Indies, many black men were employed on British ships.
Bristol and Liverpool were two British ports where black seamen
settled. By the turn of the century, the port of Cardiff had begun to
join the ranks of British ports with a growing black community. In
this maritime community, the Blacks in Cardiff inhabited the dockland area, known as Bute Town. This population was highly concentrated in the neighbouring South Ward. On the whole, black people in
Cardiff lived within the boundary of Bute Street and the Glamor-
gan Canal, and between Greek Church Street and Hodges Row.

Cardiff became a port of mercantile significance at the end of the

First World War clearing a net registered tonnage of vessels from over one million in 1857 to 12.6 million before 1914. The shipping depression between the wars did not stop imports and exports which continued, albeit on a downward scale. Imports included iron ore, fruit, vegetables, pitwood and grain; and exports were coal, coke, patent fuel and flour. [22]

In addition to the trading activity the port was attractive to black seamen, because of the mildness of the climate. It is more than likely, however, that the deciding factor was the employment conditions in the shipping industry. Cardiff offered employment to both white and black seamen. (Although tramp employment served a longer voyage than a liner, it had the disadvantage – if it be so considered – of no job permanence.) Liner routes, on the other hand, were necessarily less casual in their demands.

Employment in the dock area for the black seaman was all-important, since other forms of employment were denied him. Historically, the first decade of the twentieth century is important for the black community. In 1911, Havelock Wilson led a national strike of seamen in order to form a national union. This strike was of major significance. The seamen demanded the right to industrial recognition and complained of low wages and deplorable working conditions. In his attack, Wilson and his colleagues in the union used the employment of foreign seamen on British ships as a major grievance. They argued that employers in shipping had adopted a policy of discrediting white seamen abroad, who were replaced by black seamen at lower wages. [23] Moreover, when the laid-off white British seamen returned home and signed-on, they had to accept the lower going rate for the job.

The unions had good reason for complaint. For one thing, labour in the shipping industry was dependent on a workforce of various nationalities which was incapable of organisation. Captain Edward Tupper explained the difficulties: 'The men of the Tyne, say, had in many respects a different sense of values from the men of the Mersey, or Southampton water. Even now a ship owner would avoid putting a mixed crew of Liverpool and Southampton on a big ship; a friction would set up. Just as a ship would not man with both Madras and Calcutta lascars.' [24]

Indeed, the union's objective was to organise all seamen serving on British ships. In this it was successful. Employment on British ships between 1890 and 1903 of foreign seamen had been increased from 27,000 to 40,000 while the number of British seamen had decreased by 10,000. By 1912, the situation had changed with an increase of about 30,000 British seamen and a reduction of 9000 foreign seamen. The decline in the casual employment of foreigners on British ships was even more drastic, falling from 40,000 in 1902 to 8000 in 1935. [25]

During the First World War, the unions ensured that an alien employed on a British ship must be paid at the going British rates.

This ruling continued under the National Maritime Board. It applied however only to seamen engaged at home ports or on European articles. There were exceptions to this rule. Black seamen, for example, sailing on the West African liner trade from Liverpool could be engaged at lower rates than white seamen. The NMB acted as the Trades Council of the industry since its function was to negotiate with the employers.[26] It did not deal with ships which sign on their crews at a non-British port. Consequently, in Asiatic and Lascar articles there was a wide gap for wage manipulation. Later, this was to have extremely adverse effects on the black community in Cardiff.

Moreover, merchant seamen employment at the beginning of the century, according to Tupper, was a system of 'slavery and starvation'. Wages, he argued, 'were from £2.15s. to £3.15s. a month; £1.7s.6d. to £1.10s. a week . . .; it was generally inadequate, often enough disgusting.'[27] The system constituted low wages, debt, occasional drunkenness, fraud, graft and unemployment. In short, the full catastrophe of depression. Times were particularly hard for the black seaman who sought continued employment in a depressed industry in which there was little public interest during the inter-war period. The world economic slump had brought misery to Tiger Bay and elsewhere. Blacks in Cardiff, the victims of social and economic circumstances in which they lived and worked, were caught in a vicious circle of racial prejudice and discrimination in employment.

During the 1890s black people had settled in small numbers in Loudon Square. During 1914–18, the black community increased through waves of immigration. The demands of war brought to Britain those who in normal circumstances would have been repatriated by the government to 'their own country'. The abnormality of war-time conditions then legitimised their entry and stay. During the war 200 men from black troops in Mesopotamia were transferred by the government to work in the merchant navy. A smaller number of black seamen arrived in England after 1914 as internees from Germany.[28] British ships employing black seamen operating on the West African and other routes were 'requisitioned by the government for transport service and their crews left behind'. Blacks went also to Manchester and other cities to work in the munition and chemical factories, and in the ports of Liverpool and London, a similar situation obtained. As a consequence, large numbers of Blacks were domiciled in Britain.

With the closure of the war industries and other forms of employment, many black workers went to Cardiff where they were employed as seamen. The laying-up of ships in Cardiff contributed to the increased number of West Africans and West Indians. Taken together, this influx of more Blacks had changed the character of the district to the extent that Loudon Square and the street surrounding it came to be known as the 'coloured quarter' of the city. Confined to this space, living accommodation for Blacks was poor and overcrowded. By the end of the First World War, single dwelling houses became apartment houses with two or three persons living in the space hitherto occupied by one. During the war, and up to 1919, there was 'good money' to be earned as seamen. Through hard work and thrift, some black men prospered. Demobilisation resulted in large numbers of Navy seamen returning to their pre-war trade in the depressed shipping industry.

Given job scarcity, ship-owners and ship-masters took the provocative line of adopting the principle of 'our own people first'. In fact, in September 1919, the Trades Union Congress passed a resolution condemning Asiatic labour; preference to be given first to British white, then British black labour.[29] This divisive action caused hostility between Blacks and Whites. The British strategy of 'divide and rule' so successfully practised overseas was now being implemented to separate 'colonised' Blacks from the rest of the British population. Consequently, 1200 unemployed Blacks faced severe economic hardship. They received unemployment pay of 29s. per week which contrasted sharply to earnings of £15 per month during the war.[30] The prosperity which a few of the black seamen enjoyed provoked great resentment among white seamen who, on returning home to Cardiff, earned less for seamen's work than the better-off black man. This discrepancy, plus the fact that the soldiers were themselves unable to find employment, contributed to rising tension between white and black seamen in the area. Given these factors and undercurrents, serious racial riots broke out in Cardiff in June 1919, with wide repercussions. There were disturbances in almost every port area of Britain where Blacks had settled or resided.

The 1919 racial riots and after

Prior to the Cardiff riots there were disturbances in Liverpool and Newport in February and March. Earlier in 1911, there were race riots in Cardiff involving the Chinese community.[31] The Cardiff riots of 1919 had a profound effect on the black community for whom these were bitter experiences.

The trouble started on 10 June 1919 with a scuffle involving some white and black men. In the commotion a gun was fired. Soon a crowd of about 2000 people had gathered. A second shot was fired and several fights broke out (at the town end of Canal Parade) along Bute Street and its side streets. More gunshots followed. The mob was angry; they were out to get black men. They attacked shops in Bute Street, completely demolishing one – where black men lived.[32]

In the same street two other houses were badly damaged while fire broke out in a black-owned boarding house. After an hour of violence and destruction, the fire brigade intervened. In the aftermath, one person was killed, while 14 others were injured. There was more savagery to come.

With time to plan, a better-organised attack was mounted on the evening of 11 June. This assault, described as the 'Sidney Street Affair', started early in the evening when a large crowd assembled near the Hayes Bridge. They proceeded to attack a house in Millicent Street where eight black men lived. Gunshots were fired at these men from nearby warehouses. Leading the charge were two uniformed soldiers. Confronted by 'armed' black men, they retreated and regrouped before advancing with a table for protection. In response to this attack, the besieged black men used razor blades and a revolver to defend themselves. While this battle raged in the house, a large crowd which had gathered outside, ghoulishly, 'looked on admiringly'. Clearly, the racists had many supporters.

When the police and fire-brigade eventually intervened, they took the Blacks into protective custody. The tension and excitement generated by these incidents showed no signs of abatement. For some days, outbreaks of rioting continued. The mob were confronted with a large police presence and 'soldiers in full fighting order'. In spite of this show by the forces of law and order, the angry crowds pursued unlucky Blacks. Finally, the mob dispersed. Several black men who lived in Cardiff at this time said that for several days during the riots, they were forced to remain in their houses behind boarded windows and barred doors.[33]

While these racist attacks on the black community might have been organised by a relatively small number of persons, there was no doubt that it caused the maximum physical and psychological damage to the black community. Black men were hunted and beaten by the mobs and yet one sociologist has suggested that 'Not one out of twenty members of the crowd could explain why the trouble arose.' This is particularly incredible when the chief comments heard were 'why should these coloured men be able to get work when it is refused to us?' Furthermore, sexual relations between black men and white women were also cited.[34] In general, the mood was kill and/or lynch black people. The bogey-man was always black; the scapegoat who was 'rooted out' and rushed upon by the mob.

In counting the cost (the claims for damage, mainly to property, after the riots) the City of Cardiff Corporation paid out about £4000. But in terms of damage done to race relations in the area, the effects of the riots were incalculable.

In effect, the black community was placed in a precarious position. Their sense of oppression was compounded by the fact that some 1500 Blacks were unemployed. With little or no income, in this maritime setting, they were caught, as it were, between destitution and the deep blue sea. In desperation, some applied to the government to be repatriated. Needless to say, such moves by Blacks were most welcome by the large majority of Whites who viewed the sensitive question of racial mixture with 'an awakened conscience'.

While the idea of getting rid of Blacks was uppermost in the minds of the townspeople, there were serious difficulties in the way of effecting repatriation. For one thing, family ties among black people were particularly strong and could not be easily disengaged in the event of separation. Then there were the strong protests of the keepers of boarding houses to whom payments for rents already in arrears were not forthcoming. The black lodgers and tenants were in great debt. Since their employment ended they had been indebted to their landlords who had virtually kept them since the Armistice. The real prospect of ejection by the boarding house keepers was not a welcome prospect for the Blacks or the local authorities. The situation was allowed to persist to this hopeless stage before a partial settlement was revealed. On the one hand, the boarding house keepers were assisted by an official grant, while those Blacks who had not established an English domicile were repatriated. Thus, the black community, echoing a past experience, remained persecuted and depressed.

To a large extent, the misfortunes of the British shipping industry were reflected in the black communities in British ports. Cardiff was no exception during the period between 1921 and 1938. Foreign competition adversely affected British shipping, resulting in falling profits and high unemployment. This economic depression brought human misery and social tension between black and white seamen who competed for a steadily diminishing number of jobs. But to compound the problem of unemployment, the shipping industry was only one area affected by a general slump in world trade. As it was, unemployment among seamen coincided with that of other occupations (particularly manual ones) which made industrial migration among seamen virtually impossible. For example, one possible outlet, the South Wales coalfields, in which a number of black men had previously worked, was also suffering from an unusual state of inactivity.

Unemployment in the steam coal valleys was paralleled by depression in Cardiff. [35] In the struggle for employment in these circumstances, the white majority possessed a clear advantage over the alien black minority. The black seaman's position in the port of Cardiff was worsened by the fact that 'The only course open to British shipowners remaining in the market was to keep down labour costs as low as possible, and coloured firemen and stokers, provided they could be signed on abroad, were considerably cheaper than white seamen.' [36]

Whether resident or domiciled in Britain, the black seaman was caught in a dilemma. On the one hand, he was not wanted by the shipowners and employers, while on the other, he was discriminated against by the white unions who viewed him conveniently 'not as a section of the same labouring class striving for a livelihood on exactly the same basis as any other union member, but as the representative of an altogether different and competitive category, which directly or indirectly was responsible for keeping white seamen out of work, and forcing down their standards of living'.[37]

This was the union's attitude for many years during which relations between white and black seamen became more embittered. The racial bias of the trade unions would become more starkly evident in later years with the growth of Britain's black working class.

There were political repercussions in the dispute. The struggle by the unions and their spokesmen was taken both inside and outside the House of Commons. The battle which began in February 1919 and continued throughout the depression altered little from the original points. The basic argument took the form of a complaint from Neil Maclean MP to the effect that the British crew of the liner *Malancha* had been paid-off in favour of an Asiatic one. For example, in the old crew the British chief cook was paid £20 per month, the Asiatic one was taken on at £5 per month. This case, typical of many others, illustrated one of the gaps left by the National Maritime Board machinery.

The Labour or opposition representatives' role politically was to direct the government's attention to three points. Firstly, the number of alien workers employed in the industry; secondly, the displacement of British seamen by black crews; and thirdly, to suggest various legislative measures of correction, through the employment of additional British seamen or by a rise in black seamen's wages. The government's response on these matters were firstly, that the amount of alien labour of the British Empire (though non-European) was very small indeed; secondly it was not policy to discriminate between British subjects; and thirdly that as an industrial matter, it was best left for employers and unions to decide.

On the question of 'British subjects', Dr Burgin, a parliamentary secretary, felt that a large percentage of black men were British subjects, and that it would be a long time before any attempt was made to examine British nationality and put it into grades and classifications. He added, 'It is no good talking about the brotherhood of man and suggest that there is some difference between a white British subject and a coloured British subject.'[38] To this, Mr Greenwood interjected, 'a difference in wages'.

In their attempts to discredit black labour, the pro-white labour lobby put forward additional reasons for the elimination of black labour such as moral undesirability of its presence in Britain and its cost to the taxpayer. Given the dearth of statistics, government officials, in an effort to provide exact figures of the number of black seamen, laboured vainly. According to one source in 1919, there were about 5000 black seamen in Cardiff. It had already become clear that black labour had to be controlled, contained and disciplined, if not removed entirely to suit the changed requirements of British capital.

Legislation and its application

It is within the context of the many complaints and popular debates that legislation such as the Alien's Order of 1920 and the Special Restriction (Coloured Alien Seamen) Order of 1925 should be seen. The SRCASO was, in effect, the enforcement of the earlier Alien Restriction Act of 1914, designed to keep aliens resident in Britain, under supervision. The object of the Aliens Order of 1920 was to restrict alien immigration, except in cases where they could support themselves and their families.

The main thrust of the Order lay in the power invested in the police to arrest aliens without warrant, and to close certain clubs and restaurants. Moreover, the Act was to place on the Alien an obligation to register with the police and obtain a registration certificate which the police could demand to be shown. Separate articles provided also that every alien should be in possession of a passport furnished with a photograph and duly issued not more than five years before the date of arrival or some other document establishing his identity and nationality.

The Order of 1925 was essentially concerned with checking the flow of alien seamen into Britain. In certain cases its effects were more far-reaching. In short, black seamen were categorised with other aliens, thus forcing their registration in accordance with provisions in the Order of 1920. The crucial feature of the Order of 1925 was its application to all black seamen in Cardiff obliging them, irrespective of nationality and domicile, to register with the police. In effect, this meant that alien seamen who wanted to be domiciled in Britain had to both prove their nationality and carry around a registration card. Further, the real intention behind the Order lay in the fact that in Cardiff the onus was on all non-white individuals to do the same. This meant that an alien who had been in Cardiff before 1925, and in possession of a registration certificate from the police, was in fact better-off than the black British subject who could not prove his identity by documentary proof. Indeed a number of the men involved came from districts or tribes in colonial countries where few, if any, could write, and where there was no system of registration. Inability to prove one's identity led to a passport being almost invariably refused by a prejudiced examiner. (And who could be certain it was not policy that colour prejudice should lurk among officials in the immigration and passport offices?) In such cases, the black person was categorised an alien and could only be granted a certificate if he could prove residence in Britain before the Order was issued. Given his status as an alien then, he was liable to deportation at any time. Ironically, in this position he was able to make a small gain over the passport-holder in terms of employment. And what precious little employment!

The position of passport-holding British subjects left much to be desired. For if such a passport expired during a voyage, it could be withdrawn, and the person not allowed to land in Britain. His employer would then have to bear the expense of transporting him back to his own country or any other that would accept him or her. As it was, a large number of alien black seamen in Cardiff had evidence of nationality such as British passports, birth certificates, army and naval discharges from the First World War. Yet they were harrassed by the police who zealously tried to make them register. If a man refused to produce a passport on demand, he was threatened with arrest and imprisonment. One cannot discount the pervasive effects of personal prejudices in these circumstances.

If there was confusion among some officials, it was clear that much of what was said and interpreted to Blacks was designed to mislead. The West Indian section of the community was told quite simply that the Act did not affect them at all but was aimed at the Arabs. Under this falsehood, the trusting West Indians willingly registered. Others were led to believe that registration was no more than a mere formality which automatically affected every seaman. With little to argue against (given these assurances) Blacks were victimised. So convinced were they that their status as British subjects would not be affected by the procedure that the few who had, until then, managed to escape detection, voluntarily registered as aliens, to be sure they were on the side of the law. In extreme cases, not surprisingly, the police pushed black seamen to compulsory registration. And very often under threats to with-hold payment of wages, black men were compelled to accept Aliens Cards at the end of a voyage. According to a report of an inquiry carried out by the League of Coloured Peoples, in the majority of cases, the shipowners adopted the policy of acting in concert with the police, using refusal to pay a black seaman until he produced an Alien's Certificate of Repatriation.[39]

In the witch hunt, black men in Cardiff had no means of asserting their British nationality. Ignoring the malpractices contributing to the injustices perpetrated on the black community, the Home Secretary played it safe. He supported various kinds of police actions by taking a legal line. In instances where passports were out of date (or otherwise invalid) the holder was advised to register, if he had no satisfactory proof of his identity or nationality. The Home Secretary felt the marking of registration certificates with the word 'seaman' would be enough to distinguish holders from those persons possessing certificates issued under the ordinary provisions of the Aliens Order.

Thus, the alienated Blacks became a moral problem. More pressure was exerted against the black community in Cardiff. One of the main sources of this pressure came from the trade unions, who were supposedly defenders of the poor and oppressed working man and the wider economic and social context within which they operated. Indeed the unions were the mainspring of the legislative measures designed to contain and harass the black community.

The League of Coloured Peoples maintained that the decision to employ white labour exclusively in the shipping industry of Great Britain was not arrived at suddenly or with undue haste. It was the outcome of a mature consideration of the trend of certain events intimately connected with the shipping industry. Clearly, the plan of having these men registered as aliens was devised and put into operation by legislative measures enacted through the influence of the trade unions and other labour organisations. [40]

Given a crippled shipping industry and consequent rising unemployment which by 1931–3 was one out of every three registered seamen in Britain, there was little sympathy for the isolated black community. So far as local conditions at Newport, Cardiff, Penarth, Barry and Swansea were concerned, in 1930, 41.4 per cent of the insured seamen were unemployed, and in December 1937 (two years after the Shipping Assistance Act) there were still 32.3 per cent unemployed. [41]

Economic decline found its scapegoat in the depression of the 1930s, and the replacement of white seamen by Lascars over tropical routes, helped little.

Anger over practices favouring Blacks awakened righteous indignation on 'moral' problems arising from the presence of black men in the ports. The muckraking that ensued invoked many distortions and prejudices. The Home Secretary's attention was drawn to the alleged dependence of black children on the Public Assistance Committee, not only in Cardiff but also in Swansea and Liverpool. Almost as if Blacks who constituted the 'Aliens' group were synonymous with sedition, he was asked to close loopholes in regard to aliens (communists and anarchist leaders from Spain) from entering Britain. [42] Indeed the wider implications of the 'problem' was a source of great concern for the local councils. The 'fairly general consensus of opinion' was that the increasing size of the problem was the result of 'certain laxities in the regulations governing supervision and control of the licensed houses and cafes in the dock area'. The Report of the Special Watch Committee records the following resolution: 'That in view of the grave social evils resulting from the presence in the ports of this country of large communities of coloured seamen, HM Government be urged to promote legislation to deal with the matter . . .' [43]

Similarly, a few months later at a joint conference of the British social Hygiene Council and the British Council for the Welfare of the Merchant Marine, it was decided to draw the attention of the government to the fact that in view of the increase in the number of half-caste children in the seaport towns, and of the future difficulty of finding employment for sons and daughters of black seamen who visit these shores, the government should immediately take steps to enquire into the problem in order to mitigate the evil. Furthermore, the Chief Constable of Cardiff urged the government to support the recommendations of a report of the Watch Committee which he was convinced would 'have the effect of abolishing the undesirable cafes which form the cloak for the conduct which gives rise to the greater problem of the half-caste children. Nothing short of legislative action will deal with this part of the problem, and it is a responsibility which the Legislature will sooner or later have to face.'[44]

In the storm of protest, however, it became evident that the dependence of black children on public assistance was not only the result of the poverty of the households to which they belonged, but also to a general prejudice against employing them 'in virtually any sphere but seafaring'.[45] Things had changed little since the first black seamen settled in Cardiff. Their children were regarded as social outcasts. As the Cardiff Juvenile Employment Committee emphasised: 'It is a very sad commentary on the Christian spirit shown, and indicates that the colour Bar is still very strong in this country.'[46]

The setting-up of special sub-committees had no real effect on the gloomy prospects. Although there was an increase in existing social activities, finding work for the children of both sexes, more particularly the half-caste girls, remained a difficult problem. A more extensive inquiry into 'the colour problem in the ports' of Britain produced evidence to support the above finding on employment. In Liverpool also the prospects of employment for black juveniles were poor. Having written to 119 firms in that city, an inquirer received no reply from 63, and negative replies from 45.[47] In addition, similar letters were sent to employers of domestic servants, with the result that very few women were willing to make the experiment of engaging coloured girls. In contrast to this situation, the Juvenile Employment Officer stated that about 50 per cent of the white boys applying from this area were eventually placed and openings for white girls from the district where most of the black people lived were 'distinctly good'.

But what were the possibilities of shore labour for adult black men? Nineteen 'appropriate' firms were circularised. Out of the 17 which replied, 13 did not employ any black men and had never done so; two had done so during the war, but had replaced them with white labour when this was available. Only two employed 'Negroes' and these had only eleven black employees between them.[48] Predictably, the report was met with a good deal of hostility from the black community.

A further source of pressure on the black community was the effect of the Shipping Act. Through the British Shipping (Assistance) Act of 1935, the government provided a compromise by which shipowners and seamen were to be subsidised at the taxpayer's expense. The purpose of the Act was to enable the tramp owner to meet foreign competition, and by limitation of shipping to raise freight rates. The shipowners were to scrap 'surplus tonnage' and in return the government would grant them a number of subsidies, amounting in all to £2 million. Trouble began when two ships of the Tatham Shipping Line (which had previously employed all black crews of Malays on deck and West Indians and Africans below) changed their policy. They refused to employ men who could not identify themselves, in spite of the fact that a Board of Trade official was willing to grant passes to anyone brought to him by the captain who had a continuous discharge book. The trade unions' position in the circumstances was most interesting. The local union officials felt that shipowners had a right to sign on whom they wished. Previously the 'donkeyman', a West Indian, had always picked the crew. This time, he did the same and took them to Barry to sign on. The Shipping Federation Officer (representing the owners) asked each man for his birth certificate or passport and if unable to show these the men were not signed on. The ship was delayed for a day in order to get in touch with the superintendent of the company, whose reply was that these were owners' orders and must be carried out. In the meantime, a sister ship at Cardiff which had signed on two Malay sailors brought them ashore two days later and paid them off with a month's wages. They were told they could not sail without passports. The matter was solved that afternoon, however, when the Company signed-on a black crew without passports, and the ship sailed. [49]

These industrial developments on the docks led to more political debate. In the House of Commons, Mr Greenwood rejoiced to hear that alien seamen would not be given places on British ships. Another Labour MP, Mr West, mounted a strong attack on Chinese, Lascars and black seamen, as a whole. In the mounting tension at the port, union officials intervened. By opposing the employment of black seamen, a serious disturbance at the docks was averted. The ship involved was the *SS Ethel Radcliffe* which through the intervention of the League of Coloured Peoples, the Chairman of the Tramp Shipping Administrative Committee and the Shipping Company, eventually sailed with black seamen on board. In the daily press, under the headline 'Cardiff Colour Bar Causes Riot', the incident was seen as having 'averted serious rioting' between black and white seamen. [50]

The black seamen were alarmed and with good reason. The events which followed had drastic effects. Many hundreds of families lost their only means of livelihood. One gets an idea of the enormity of the problem from the fact that by 11 June 1936, from a total of 690 unemployed firemen on the Cardiff Docks Register, 599 were black men. In the face of common difficulties, to a large extent, religious and other differences were superseded by a feeling of solidarity among the various groups. A community was formed representing Africans, West Indians, Arabs, Somalis and Malays. This organisation, called the Coloured Seamen's Union, delegated one of its representatives, H. O. O'Connell to seek assistance for their cause in London. The assistance received was that of an inquiry into the vexed question of naturalisation. O'Connell also received the help of the League of Coloured Peoples and members of the House of Commons. Commenting on the government's rearmament proposals in 1935, Mr Maxton pointed out that in the case of the black seamen, their rights and liberties as subjects of the British Empire had been usurped rather than defended.

The inquiry studied 35 extreme cases in an attempt to prove misapplication of the Special Restriction Order. Of the 12 cases brought to the attention of the Secretary, seven men had their national status restored. At the time, the Order forced some 1500 men to carry the Aliens Card with them. In the subsequent readjustment between 1935 and 1937 approximately 1600 names were removed from the 'Live Register' (a term used to indicate the active register which contained the names of black seamen either at sea or ashore, at the time it was taken). Of these, the majority had their national status restored to them.[51]

The role of the white unions

The trade union rhetoric of the 'brotherhood of man' had little bearing on the situation. Indeed, the role of the white unions was invidious as the black seamen were attacked from all quarters. The Aliens' Order and its consequences had the support of the trade unions. Yet, in the serious conflict of interests which arose the National Union of Seamen argued that far from wishing to dispose of the British-born black men (or at any rate the West Indians and Africans) they were actually fighting their battles. In support of this argument, they cited their recommendation drawn up in conjunction with the Transport and General Workers' Union (prepared for the Trades Union Parliamentary Committee) on the question of shipping subsidies and the conditions of seamen against domiciled British crews. This joint trade union memorandum stated:

> No government assistance of any kind should be given to those shipowners who are now making a practice of employing alien crews for their vessels, to the exclusion of domiciled British crews. It should therefore be a condition of any subsidy or other form of assistance that the crews of the vessels concerned should be entirely manned by domiciled British seamen.

If indeed, the word 'British' conveyed to the ordinary working man in Britain only white citizens of the British Empire, then it was possible to blame this interpretation for the misunderstanding. But, if this was a genuine misunderstanding the union's own report helped to foster it. The *Seaman*, the official journal of the National Union of Seamen, admitted that union officials and other white members of labour organisations had made too much of the employment of aliens.[52]

Racial prejudice was the determining factor at the Cardiff Docks. For regardless of the views of the problem taken at union headquarters, a few of the local officials exploited to the full the opportunity to encourage black repatriation. They aroused public animosity by citing the argument of the black community's expense to the public rates. In this connection, the *Western Mail* and *South Wales Echo* reported that George Reed, secretary of the local branch of the NUS, said thousands of imported black men had unrestricted entry into Cardiff. He had no doubt that if these men were going to be displaced they should be repatriated.

The black community: struggle for survival

Clearly, the depressed community, precariously placed on the Cardiff Docks, was being pushed further to the edge. As the Second Industrial Report pointed out, the community had undergone severe hardship. In fact, the history of Blacks in Cardiff hitherto, was essentially one of hardship. The League of Coloured Peoples estimated that about 80 per cent of the men had been on unemployment benefit during most of the year from April 1934 to April 1935. More strikingly, their home life had reached the level of bare subsistence.

While social development and cultural advancement were almost nil, even church attendance was denied one family, whose black father and brown children were not welcome. Moreover, secondary education and industrial employment were practically closed to them, essentially because the sentiment of the city was to reject and restrict the 'half-castes'. In fact, a Cardiff public official was accused of calling for legislation to 'put a stop to the breeding of such children'.

In effect the 1935–6 trouble aggravated an already chronic condition within the black community. How did black people manage to live? Seen in perspective, a large number of men were continuously unemployed. Inevitably, their unemployment benefit, quickly spent, forced them to rely on the Relieving Officer for support. In 1930, relief of 5s per person per week was granted to about 250 Arabs and 300 Somali seamen and firemen, whose destitution during the shipping depression had brought their boarding house keepers to the end of their resources. The payments were made direct to the boarding house masters, to cover the bare cost of food. The proprietors were willing to continue to provide lodgings. In fact, they approached the Public Assistance Committee and undertook to remove the Arab seamen from chargeability, if the Committee would take no further action to deport them. The Committee agreed and the relief was discontinued.

The impoverished position of the black community during this period was to some extent reflected in these out-relief payments.

On the pretext that Blacks were accustomed to a lower standard of living than their white workmates in the trade, the grants were adjusted accordingly. Indeed, the same practice was adopted when the Unemployment Assistance Board was set up. This meant that instead of the basic allowance of 15s. per week for a man living alone, a payment of 12s. per week was made to those judged to be living 'communally', for example, those sharing a 'communal pot'.[53] Differentiation had its special difficulties, and not surprisingly, became a source of dissatisfaction among members of the black community. They particularly resented the implication that because a black man necessarily had to live more cheaply his needs were less great. It was pointed out that the benefit was barely sufficient.

Moreover, it was argued that in practice, a differential scale was adopted not only between white and black, but also between the various black nationalities themselves. This was designed to set Blacks against each other and, of course, it was possible that differently scaled payments were made according to the circumstances of the case, but there was no evidence which indicated that the principle of adjustment was extended in the way suggested. Thus, it was regarded as an illustration of the working of the 'racial myth'. Nevertheless, the policy of adjustment was approved by the Minister of Health. Justifying their relief programme, the Cardiff authorities claimed that 'their treatment was more generous than that of most other ports'. In fact, a large number of seaports refused to grant outdoor relief at all, and offered only institutional relief. Ravaged by poverty, many fought for their self-respect and dignity. In South Shields, for example, it was claimed that after a few days in the Institution, the seamen took their discharge and did not seek further assistance there.

In the wake of the 'riots' and the shipping depression then, the black community had become a 'problem', paradoxically arousing 'censure' and the 'curiosity of social investigations'. The weight of opinion was against Blacks. Social investigators and the media were uninhibited in displaying their prejudices. Black/white sexual relations and half-caste children were haunting themes. Immorality, they agreed, was endemic in the black community. Richardson's report, for example, quoted in the *Western Mail* and the *South Wales News*, alerted the people of Cardiff:

> Morality and cleanliness are as much matters of geography as they are dependent on circumstances. The coloured men who have come to dwell in our cities are being made to adopt a standard of civilisation they cannot be expected to understand. They are not imbued with moral codes similar to our own, and they have not assimilated our conventions of life. They come into intimate contact with white women, principally those who unfortunately are of loose moral character with the result that a half-caste population is brought into the world.[54]

Furthermore, he emphasised hybridisation and disease which helped matters little in a city which had openly showed its hatred for its alien guests. And according to the *Western Mail*, 'The problem of the coloured population in our seaport towns . . . demands immediate government action.' For not only the social amenities of the white man's country, but the best interest of black people themselves were at issue. In spite of the fact that 'many of them are citizens of the British Empire; many did fine work in the war', there was no room for 'sentimentality' in the matter. For although 'Repatriation may involve hardships, and it is our obligation to make it easy for them to return to their homelands, where we will continue to carry the 'White man's burden'? The newspaper concluded emphatically, 'We can no longer tolerate that burden on our doorstep.'[55]

This attack and government apathy (although a few white residents wrote letters describing the report as misleading) led to a 'mild revulsion' in popular attitudes towards black people. The black community was not quick to react violently, but remained spirited. Visitors to the community found that black people were 'patient and peaceful in the face of their difficulties'. A *Daily Express* journalist on a tour of British cities commented on the lack of opportunity and the degree of colour prejudice in Cardiff.[56] In spite of the obvious problems confronting them, there was little public sympathy for black people in the distressed area.

Yet, given the experience of unemployment in their country of origin, and in spite of the onslaught against them, many black people in Cardiff still had an unshakeable belief in their rights as British nationals. Repatriation for the majority was impracticable. Indeed, some of the older men had 'grown into the place', having settled in Cardiff for 30 and in some cases for 40 years. Their 'determination to persist was generally evident, and the sentiment of local association seems to be amongst the strongest psychological characteristics which the younger generation have acquired'.[57]

In sum this was the background of the black experience in Cardiff until the Second World War. In historical perspective, the experience had been shared (to a greater or lesser degree) by other black communities in Britain. Significantly, in economic terms, in some ways, it had similarities with white workers of the same occupational class. The colour bar has been a general feature of the larger ports. And more often than not, Blacks had been pushed and confined in the slums of the towns, as a direct result of the policies and practices of the British government, and the racism of the employers and the trade unions. In Liverpool, as in London, there were race riots at the end of the First World War. Discrimination against black seamen had become widespread. What characterised Cardiff from other ports was that concentration of black families in one small area of the town resulted in 'the creation of a special focus of prejudice, broken up only by rather sporadic attempts at amelioration'.

If peace had brought unemployment, poverty, prejudice, violence and desperation to the black community, the prospects of the Second World War offered the hope that at least things could not get much worse. Hitler could not be as menacing as the race-hate that Blacks were faced with in Cardiff.

Liverpool: 'negro' workers and race relations

The old slave port of Liverpool has had a continuous black presence; stretching from the period of slavery into the twentieth century. Between the World Wars, there was a small black population in Liverpool. This black presence had conditioned the attitude of white people in the city who responded accordingly to the new arrivals. Liverpool had grown enormously as a result of migration from other ports in England, from Wales, Ireland and from overseas. In spite of a diverse racial mix, the city had acquired a distinctive Merseyside character and mode of speech. During the period 1941–51, however, there had been clearly marked in-group/out-group divisions. Nationality and religion divided people in Liverpool. The Irish and Welsh, for example, displayed a high degree of national consciousness. In fact, there had been outbreaks of antagonisms between such groups as Protestants and Catholics, and outbreaks of feelings of anti-semitism.

Given this complexity of inter-group relations in Liverpool, the arrival of increasing numbers of black immigrants to join the indigenous black settlement after 1918 added a new dimension. While the number of black people was not large, they were nonetheless, highly visible, even though one estimate before the Second World War put the Chinese and 'Negro' populations at just over one in a thousand of the total population.[58] In time, 'African' immigrants came to be regarded with suspicion and hostility, particularly after being discharged from the armed forces and the Merchant Navy in 1919. Antagonism between Blacks and Whites grew. And, as in Cardiff about this time, serious disturbances broke out. In the aftermath, public opinion was in favour of the repatriation of Blacks to the colonies. In fact, many (in the face of impoverishment and racial discrimination) were persuaded to return to their homelands. Others, however, adamant in spite of hardship, demanded their rights as British subjects to live in Britain. In spite of the Blacks' minority status in Liverpool, they were nevertheless seen as a threat by the white population, particularly in terms of competition for employment. This threat led to stereotyped opinions of black people. Not surprisingly, then, attempts were made to prevent the further flow of 'Negro' immigrants into Liverpool and to discourage the employment of black labour on British ships.[59] Fortunately for racist decision-makers, it seemed essential economic factors were significant in preventing this policy from being implemented.

Nonetheless, 'Negroes' faced prejudice daily. With these massive disadvantages, the 'Negro's difficulties were compounded by the high unemployment in Liverpool between the wars. Unemployment made the absorption process of the newcomers a very difficult one given the economic insecurity on Merseyside.

Historically, Merseyside is characterised by its dependence upon overseas trade. The predominant industries contributing to its prosperity have been those connected with shipping, shipbuilding and transport. In the wake of the First World War, the area suffered from the severe effects of the depressions of the 1920s and 1930s. The casual labour system on the docks aggravated local unemployment which figured among the largest in the country. The social tensions generated led to unrest.[60] The understandable widespread feelings of insecurity aroused by the unemployment on Merseyside during the 1930s were related to the severe competition for a limited number of jobs. Nevertheless, by the 1930s the black worker had advanced marginally in that West Indians had become employed in English factories doing skilled work on a par with English workers in a working relationship that would have been unthinkable in the pre-war period. Nonetheless, black workers were usually the last hired and the first fired.

The onset of the war, however, brought a change in their position. The existing unemployment was quickly eliminated in Merseyside, and in other areas of the country. The 'enemy' brought work for black seamen who were urgently required to man the Atlantic convoys, as workers for the Merchant Navy. Although they received the same rates of pay, black workers were still restricted to certain ranks in the merchant service.

Industry was also affected as workers of all grades, regardless of colour, were in demand. The war demand for munitions led not only to the building of many factories (concentrating on war production) but also to a great demand for skilled workers. It was this emergency development which influenced the Ministry of Labour to direct skilled labour into the Merseyside area. Some of these workers were refugees from Europe, others were the West Indian volunteers. Once again, in wartime, the British authorities had devised a plan through which they could exploit their labour needs.

The wartime immigration scheme for West Indian workers

Against the backdrop of war, West Indians came to Britain under a scheme organised jointly by the Ministry of Labour and the Colonial Office, with the object of increasing war production. And to legitimise it, the scheme was regarded as making a small contribution towards relieving the unemployment in the colonies.[61]

In the West Indies, men and women ravaged by poverty were eager to offer their services almost at any price, to help the mother country, regardless of the fact that black soldiers had bitter experiences of racial prejudice in the British forces during the First World War. Although there were few openings in the armed forces, at the time, it was felt that the colonies could be called upon to help in filling the urgent need for skilled workers in the factories. The presence of black workers in Merseyside, over a long period of time, led to a policy of employing most West Indians in this area.

In Liverpool, these volunteer workers were selected by the authorities in the West Indies and provided with a passage to England and the guarantee of free passage home again at the end of the war. From this statement, it seemed quite clear that if these black workers were lucky enough to be alive after the war, they would be favoured with the 'guarantee of a free passage home'.

They arrived in England in 11 separate contingents: five from Jamaica, the rest from British Honduras, the Bahamas, Barbados, British Guiana, the Leeward Islands and the Windward Islands. The first three contingents from Jamaica were technicians who had training and experience on the island. The men from the other contingent, despite their 'experience' in the West Indies, were relatively unskilled on arrival, and were sent to one of the Government Training Centres where they received basic training in certain aspects of engineering before being placed in the factories as semi-skilled workers. It was not long before all the men were either skilled or semi-skilled. At the outset of the scheme, it was recognised that special welfare provision had to be made for these workers.[62]

The Ministry of Labour did in fact make special arrangements and the men were put under the charge of a Welfare Officer and his assistant. The man appointed to take charge of the scheme as a whole had previously been involved in an inquiry in 1940 into alleged discrimination against black British subjects in this department. Faced with racial prejudice, the Ministry of Labour had set the pace in pointing the way to the employers by refusing to allow prejudice to influence the appointment of the best qualified men for the job, regardless of their colour. Officially, there was a strong desire to make the scheme work. Naturally, black workers turned to the Welfare Officer for advice and assistance whenever any difficulty occurred particularly on matters of colour prejudice and discrimination. Overseeing the Scheme were officials from the International Labour Office and the Colonial Office who paid periodic 'visits of inspection'.

Among the West Indian technicians and trainees, diversity was the most outstanding characteristic. Their backgrounds reflected varying educational qualifications and skill. However, determination among them was not lacking. They were employed primarily under six headings: engineering (skilled), engineering (semi-skilled), electrical trades (skilled), electrical trades (semi-skilled), building, and civil engineering. Those who could not be so trained, were classified as clerical and miscellaneous grades.

Discrimination in the employment of 'Negroes'

The arrival of these West Indian workers must be seen in the context of discrimination against black people in British industry which was widespread before the Second World War. In spite of the fact that the state of full employment reached by 1940 had created an enormous demand for labour, there was strong resistance to the employment of Blacks among employers. Despite this resistance among several firms, demand for labour at that time far outweighed the supply. Consequently, in spite of prejudiced employers, black workers were able to find employment, primarily in the public sector. Indeed, in time, the mass of black workers were condemned to these low status jobs, essentially because black labour was regarded as cheap, disposable, and as such could not be unduly resisted.

Given the intransigence of employers, some form of labour direction was necessary. In Britain, during the war, the Ministry of Labour in directing black labour, provided one measure (the Essential Works and Control of Engagements Orders) to be used if necessary against employers who discriminated against Blacks. Essentially, these Orders were introduced to deal with the urgent manpower shortage in general and, according to one observer, 'were not drafted with Negroes or any other minority group in mind'. This may have been true, but difficult to believe particularly in view of the fact that these Orders did assist Ministry of Labour Officials in dealing with discriminating employers.

Armed with these powers for the duration of the war, West Indians were kept fully employed. In fact, unemployment and discrimination were not serious problems between 1941 and 1945.

Pay and conditions

In the employment of black workers in industry, the questions of rates of pay and working conditions were vital. Payment at less than the standard rates would have raised serious objections from the trade unions. The West Indian technicians and trainees, sensitive to the demands of the trade unions, joined the following unions: the AEU, UBISS, ETU, NUSMWB, ASW, NUPGDE, TGWU, and NUGMW.[63] As it was, no attempt was made to undercut wages. Indeed, it was the cornerstone of the official Scheme that the black workers should receive no less than the standard rates paid to English workers. In fact, this was agreed by the men before they left the colonies. Subsequently, the disputes concerning wage rates were attributed to 'misunderstanding' on the part of the West Indians rather than any deviation from the principle of a fair day's pay for a fair day's work.

Given the 'misunderstandings', wage rates remained a source of dispute from the outset, and throughout the operation of the Scheme. But, what were these misunderstandings? And why the concern about wages? According to one commentator, the reasons were firstly that the West Indians, like the trade unions, did not wish to be used to undercut standard rates, and secondly, rates of pay were vital in determining satisfaction with working conditions. This was essentially the case when consideration was given to the question of a relative rather than absolute rates of pay. This was crucial because wages were closely linked with status in industry. This relationship, underscored by the desire to maintain and improve status which governed much of the behaviour of individuals and groups in industry, was also a cause of much dissatisfaction and anxiety.[64]

The outcome of 'hurried negotiations' established a special expatriation allowance of £1 per week per man which would be paid later directly into an account for them in the colony. This gesture was not enough. Bad feeling was aroused by the fact that the equivalent sum paid to an English worker required to work 'away from home' was £1.4s.6d. It would seem that the airing of these matters had a beneficial effect. In the months that followed, skilled West Indians were able to earn 'very large wage packets', particularly at the height of the war when they worked many hours of overtime. Some technicians earned as much as £13 or £14 per week; others earned even more at the peak of the munitions drive. But these abnormal earnings were considerably reduced as the war neared its end. The disparity in earnings was a source of complaint. A more realistic standard of living without overtime was difficult to accept. One of the effects of the loss of overtime earnings was that the men who had saved large sums and made regular remittances to their families at home were unable to do so.

Furthermore, wage differentials presented a severe problem among a number of trainees because of the large differentials in the earnings of different groups. The highest earnings in certain factories amounted to £10 per week or more for trainees, while for those denied the opportunities of bonuses and overtime, earnings amounted to no more than £5–6 per week.[65] The arbitrary allocation of the men meant that these differences did not represent any distribution in merit or skill. Thus, the differentials justifiably aroused deep discontent.

One of the more serious effects of these arbitrary wage differentials was the way it affected morale in the hostels. These differences aggravated the other grievances West Indians had about life in the hostels and also in the way they were treated outside. One form of protest was refusal to pay the outstanding debts at the hostels. Under the circumstances, the practice spread and became chronic.

In a foreign land, the West Indian workers (with families abroad) felt alienated; they felt no sense of security or community – only an all-pervasive sense of discrimination. However, one researcher has argued that 'The sense of discrimination under which some of the men laboured with regard to wage rates was completely unfounded, [and that] in no case was a West Indian paid less than the agreed trade union rate for the job.' But, he conceded that it was 'more difficult to assess the complaints with regard to aspects of working conditions'. Allegations from black workers included the tendency to be selected for the more unpleasant jobs, the lack of promotion through seniority and merit, and the tendency to place men in a new shop to get it operative, but when the opportunity arose in their jobs to be upgraded to that of charge-hands or foremen, these men would be moved to another new shop and the responsible posts would be filled by other men. Taken together, these complaints indicated that the West Indians (whatever the merits of the Scheme) did not always identify with the practices in the factories where they worked, and, as Richmond admits 'did sometimes labour under a sense of discrimination and deprivation'.

Before the end of the Scheme in 1946 many changes in employment (the result of trial and error) were introduced. There was greater flexibility between contingents and among different firms. By the end of the Scheme some of the employers had employed one or more West Indians. While in some cases these changes suited individuals, more often than not they were in accord with the demands of the labour situation. But in spite of the changes, there was stability. The hard facts were that towards the end of 1944, some 55 out of 77 technicians originally drafted to two Royal Ordnance Factories were still working there. And in March 1951, the remaining ROF (the others having been closed) had 12 of the original West Indian contingent. Clearly, there was no lack of commitment. The West Indians who arrived in 1941, when the factory was only just beginning to expand, had some of the longest service records in the factory.[66]

Post-war problems: redundancies and loss of earnings

The end of the war had a profound effect on the position of West Indian workers in Britain. They faced an uncertain future. In addition to the loss of overtime earnings and bonus payments, redundancies were threatened as white ex-servicemen returned to their homes. The prospects were very poor indeed. By November 1944 'an atmosphere of unsettlement was beginning to show itself amongst technicians and trainees, which was attributed to the termination of the war and repatriation'.[67] The increased war-time earnings meant that adjustment to basic wages created difficulties, particularly among those with family responsibilities, high rents and travelling expenses. Most of the men knew only war-time Britain and continued to have high expectations. The Welfare Officer's repeated warnings failed to persuade the men to see the post-war situation realistically. Consequently, as their debts mounted, they blamed the authorities.

As expected early in 1945, redundancies grew and jobs for the semi-skilled West Indian became a serious problem. In July, there was further evidence of tension. And later in the year, the WO reported that the relaxation of the provisions of the Essential Works and Control Engagements Orders made it difficult to get employers to accept West Indians, when vacancies were notified. Relaxation of the Orders was controversial. In fact, the trade unions had pressed strongly for this measure. They had accepted 'direction of labour' with the proviso that it be removed as soon as the war had ended.[68] Moreover, as the election approached, while the government felt it necessary to rescind these Orders, they subsequently reaffirmed them during the economic crisis of 1947.

It was clear that the employment of black workers was made more difficult during this period. In a number of instances, a colour bar in employment was practised early in 1946. In the aftermath of war many employers were determined to keep black workers out.

Elsewhere, in the United States, for example, black workers were also beginning to lose ground, which they had gained during the war, and discrimination was beginning to appear on a larger scale again. By 1946 then, there was still no machinery through which a black worker could obtain redress as a victim of discrimination.

Unemployment

From 1946, unemployment remained a central issue in Liverpool and the Northwest. Unemployment in Merseyside at the end of the war remained 'considerably above the average' for the country as a whole. The policy of setting up new industries in the area did not move at a pace fast enough to compensate for the decline in employment. This decline was stemmed when rearmament started again. Employment at the end of 1951 had reached the 'highest in the post war period'. A special count in January 1950 and February 1951 showed that there was some 'improvement in the employment prospects' of black colonials in Liverpool.[69] Although there was some improvement in the unemployment among semi-skilled and skilled West Indians, there was an increase in unemployment among the unskilled. Among West Indians and West Africans, unemployment was about 17 per cent in January 1950. The figure in 1951 was approximately 12 per cent. By comparison, the figures for the total working population of Merseyside were 5 per cent declining to between 3 and 4 per cent in 1951. This was above the national average of approximately 1.5 per cent.[70]

Discrimination

Overall, there was undeniable evidence that discrimination in employment against 'Negroes' occurred, although, at the time, it was not possible to quantify its extent and degree. Among the reasons given by employers for their refusal to employ Blacks were essentially a past unfortunate experience and fear of strikes by their present (white) workers as a result. The latter reason was a powerful determinant, for while there had been no instances officially recorded of an industrial dispute involving the employment of Blacks, there were instances of threatened strikes on these grounds. Needless to say, the prejudiced employer found this useful. Unfortunately, it was argued that the irresponsible behaviour of a minority of Blacks tended to reinforce prejudices.

In the face of these difficulties in employment, it was not surprising then to find a considerable number of West Indian technicians, trainees and unskilled workers leaving Liverpool for other towns, particularly in the Midlands and Southeast where work was plentiful. Accommodation, however, acted as a real deterrent to black workers on the move. Once one or two of them had established themselves in a new town, they searched for accommodation for their colleagues.

Unemployment in Manchester after the war was not as serious as on Merseyside. In March 1949, there were 150 'Coloured Colonials' registered as unemployed at the Oldham Street Exchange. Of this number, only 26 were West Indian, and of these only seven appeared to have come to Britain under the original Scheme. The others were discharged ex-servicemen or men who paid their way and arrived in Britain during 1948. In Manchester also there was discrimination. The Employment Exchange confirmed the unwillingness of employers to accept black workers because of the difficult behaviour of a few of them.

The closure of the colonial hostels at the end of the war resulted in the original residents moving to Liverpool, Manchester and other areas. In Bolton, a new group of West Indians emerged as private lodgers. Apparently well-adjusted, they were employed in the cotton industry as motor mechanics, motor drivers and labourers. In spite of the fact that there had been no disturbances since the end of the war (and given the Chief Constable's endorsement of the men's good behaviour) employers were still reluctant to employ black workers on any large scale. This attitude was supported by the local trade union officials.

After 1946, the poor employment prospects of Blacks in the Northwestern areas led to a substantial migration to the Midland region. In Birmingham, a small black community amounting to 'a few hundreds' had grown. Here, in the post-war situation, the local authority took an interest in the welfare of the Blacks and set up an Afro-Caribbean Centre which provided educational and recreational facilities.

In the pottery districts, some Blacks were being accepted and a few found their way into the mining industry. It seemed, in these areas of full employment and labour scarcity, there were few employment problems. Accommodation, however, remained a serious problem and acted as a strong deterrent to migration, particularly to those with families.

West Indian workers, employers and managements

The relations between West Indian technicians and trainees and the managements of the various firms employing them varied widely from factory to factory. The personal qualities of the workers and the attitudes and policies of managements were crucial determinants in these relationships.

For both the government and private employers, black labour was worrisome, now that their colonial war contribution had been made. On the one hand, black workers had certain standards. Many of them were very sensitive (by and large they were made to feel so) about work which was 'unpleasant or below their dignity'. They interpreted being given such work as an example of prejudice and discrimination against them. They also disliked 'outdoor work'. Their main grievance was that they were singled out for special treatment; a more equitable distribution of certain jobs would have alleviated the problem. Later, this discrimination in certain kinds of jobs, against black workers, would become a continuing theme in British industry.

On the other hand, those in management were prone to hold grudges. While there were many issues directly related to West Indian workers, there were also common issues affecting both black and white workers. For example, West Indians who interpreted disciplinary action or dismissals as based on colour prejudice also, in some cases, identified themselves closely with English workers against management if they felt strongly about some other injustice. Overall, the essential effect of discrimination practised by management against individual West Indians tended to engender strong in-group solidarity among black workers.[71]

Some incidents stirred deep feelings. On one occasion, white workers threatened to strike if the black workers were not suspended or punished in some way for their 'walk out'. Understandably, security of employment has always been a major preoccupation among West Indian workers in Britain. By 1951, in the last remaining government factory in Liverpool, nine out of twelve West Indians were established civil servants who enjoyed the benefits of that status. As one worker put it: 'Establishment gives a man a feeling of security and you get certain benefits and gratuities. You know that you will be the last to be sacked. On the other hand, it is a bit of a tie, because you cannot leave without sacrificing those benefits you have accumulated and you have to be prepared to go anywhere or do any job the Ministry likes to send you on.'[72]

In some factories black workers were compared favourably with the members of other minority groups employed. One labour manager said, 'I would rather employ a coloured West Indian any day to an Irishman: they are much cleaner and more reliable altogether.' In justifying their prejudices, it seemed, employers resorted to exploiting any differences (real or imagined) between groups of workers.

Relations between black and white workers and with the trade unions

The relations between the West Indians and white workers were dependent on conditions which varied from place to place, and upon the local situation at the time and the personnel concerned, both for West Indians and other workers. However, three main stages had been identified in the relations between employers and employed. Firstly, there was the stage of initial surprise and shock to find a group of Blacks doing skilled work; secondly, there was the period when the West Indian group tended to be treated as a scapegoat for the things that went wrong in the factory and thirdly, a stage in which the West Indians gained acceptance as part of the natural order of things (and whilst not always completely integrated into the life of the factory) they were, at any rate, tolerated and respected as individuals on merit. A fourth change took place when the war ended; with increasing redundancies, the West Indian worker tended to be rejected.

During the initial stage of surprise at black workmanship, the black stereotype as a person of primitive habits, little knowledge and completely uncivilised, was the norm. One West Indian was asked where he kept his tail! At the workplace, there was astonishment when West Indians began work on the machines. One black worker recalled his first day: 'I remember the first day I started at the factory. I was put on a machine I was quite familiar with because we had used it a lot at home. I began work straight away, but before long I had a crowd of spectators around me all of them wide-eyed!'[73] The novelty did not last long. Soon there was animosity and a series of grievances. Among the West Indians there were excellent workers who received praise from management and in some cases, earned more than white workers. According to one worker this recognition inevitably aroused bad feelings.[74]

West Indians had to be particularly careful in their relations with their white co-workers. The atmosphere was, more often than not, charged with tension. There was considerable ambivalence in the attitudes of some whites towards the West Indians. While there was genuine recognition of skill, workmanship and other abilities, yet there was reluctance to give full credit. Indeed, the English worker could not accept the black worker as an equal; he was bound, gagged and tied by the notion of the black man as being inferior. A case in point was provided by a Jamaican technician who became a shop steward, and later, deputy convenor for the trade union in one factory. In this role he was called upon to represent white employees. When the Jamaican had succeeded in reversing a decision by management which involved a white employee, the employee concerned remarked: 'Well that damn nigger certainly spoke up well for me!'[75] Forthrightness and honesty in West Indians was met with puzzlement and surprise.

Moreover, relations with the trade unions were revealing. Trade unionism, so integral a part of the industrial structure in Britain, was in its infancy in the West Indies about this time. Indeed, the West India Royal Commission of 1939, Major Orde Browne's and the Forster Commission Reports,[76] all emphasised trade union organisation in view of the deplorable labour conditions in the West Indies. Walter Citrine, General Secretary of the TUC (and a member of the Moyne Royal Commission) in spite of the difficulties, was the most insistent advocate of the formation of Trade Union Councils in the West Indies.[77]

Given this background then, the majority of West Indians coming to Britain did not immediately see the significance of trade union membership and its value to them. The trade unions themselves were not altogether welcoming. Their attitude was, take it as it is, or leave it. In fact, one union was especially slow to recognise that West Indians were competent and qualified for full membership. Further, a West Indian was removed from his employment in the shipyard because the shop steward had orders from the union involved, the United Society of Boiler Makers and Iron and Steel Shipbuilders (UBISSS). Subsequently, a number of West Indians gained full membership only after providing credentials from their employers in Jamaica. Unfortunately, the situation affected some to such an extent that their experience of the union was difficult to eradicate.

The other two unions directly concerned, the Amalgamated Engineering Union and the Electrical Trades Union, were much more welcoming. The Ministry of Labour officials received the co-operation of the District Secretaries of these unions. Moreover, the West Indians themselves spoke highly of the way in which the unions tackled any sign of colour prejudice among their members. 'In the union I am a Brother', said one man, 'and there is no distinction of colour, class or creed.'

In time, a number of West Indians became actively involved in the Amalgamated Engineering Union, holding several offices for varying periods of time. Significantly, this meant acting on behalf of all factory workers, both black and white. Unfortunately, these black trade union activists were few; the majority of West Indians were apathetic and tended to get in arrears with subscriptions. According to the Ministry of Labour records for 1944, there were nine unions representing the West Indian technicians.[78]

The end of the Scheme and after

At the end of the war, a number of administrative problems arose as the Scheme was wound up and many of the workers were repatriated to the West Indies. One of the immediate effects as the Scheme was brought to an end in 1946 was that the West Indian technicians and trainees ceased to be a special group. In effect, they merged into the wider West Indian and black community in Britain, with all its attendant disabilities.

As early as 1944, a scheme of post-war training was envisaged. High expectations were not fulfilled. Indeed, the original proposals were modified and the final version of the Scheme provided for 'Further Education and Vocational Training'. In this context, further education meant education beyond secondary school (for example at a University or other establishment of higher education), undertaken on a part or full-time basis. On the other hand, vocational training was intended to give training essentially in technical work for those who were unable to undertake proper training. The precondition for receiving either an education or vocational training grant was 'effective full-time service in work of national importance during the war'. On these grounds, the West Indian volunteers would qualify. Such training was also related to the benefit accruing to the worker on return to his colonial home. In fact, 'the colonial office wished to be satisfied that there would be employment available in the Colony.' But what if they could not be satisfied? Apart from these crucial background questions, a further stipulation made was that the West Indians 'must not be in debt to the hostel'.[79] As it was, this proved a troublesome issue.

To get the training plan off the ground, the West Indians received letters explaining the details, and applications were invited. At the outset, it was clear that most of the technicians would not qualify for grants, since they were already trained. Many accepted repatriation. Others postponed repatriation by applying for training. The final tally showed that only about 12 men who were under the Scheme received grants provided for by the Further Education and Vocational Training Scheme.

The percentage refusing repatriation was high for technicians, some 43 per cent. On the other hand, the number of trainees from British Honduras who accepted repatriation was also above average.[80] Those men who had arrived earlier were more anxious to return home than those who arrived later. On their return home to the colonies, these early expatriates found they had, in effect, jumped out of the frying pan into the fire. They found conditions in the West Indies very poor indeed, and urged their friends to remain in Britain. Judging from the experience of the early expatriates, repatriation had proved to be a bitter disappointment.

Yet, by the end of 1946 many technicians and trainees had accepted repatriation. Those who refused repatriation were struck-off the Scheme and were no longer qualified for an expatriation grant. Further, they were no longer under the special jurisdiction of the Welfare Officer. By October 1946, 94 men in the Merseyside area were still 'on the scheme', 32 of them were unemployed. Morale among the men had deteriorated thereafter.[81] In discharging them, the government had freed itself from all responsibility. Thus, the least fit to survive were left to eke out an existence in an economic system founded on the survival of the fittest.

Conditions in the West Indies

Sir Frank Stockdale who said at the beginning of the Scheme that it would make 'a small contribution towards relieving unemployment in the colonies', seemed to have conveniently forgotten the implications of repatriation. Unemployment in Liverpool and elsewhere in Britain had alerted West Indians to the same problem in the West Indies.

All the official reports upon the social and economic conditions in the West Indies supported the men's anxiety over employment prospects on their return there. In 1943 and 1944, Sir Frank Stockdale reported that unemployment problems had become more difficult to resolve year by year, particularly among town dwellers. The position in Jamaica had been quite acute for several years, and in Barbados there was a measure of underemployment at certain times of the year, while St Lucia usually had unemployment problems to face from time to time, especially in Castries and elsewhere. In Belize, British Honduras, there were unemployment problems.[82] Further, Sir John MacPherson confirmed the seriousness of the post-war situation in his report for 1945 and 1946: 'Towards the end of 1945 unemployment in Jamaica and Barbados threatened to become acute mainly because of large-scale repatriation of British West Indian workers from employment in the United States of America and to a lesser degree the return of demobilised servicemen.'[83]

The percentage of unemployment for Jamaica in 1943 was 25.6 per cent and was probably 'higher still' in the post-war years. According to the 1946 Census for the other colonies unemployment ranged from 2.5 per cent in British Guiana to nearly 10 per cent in St Lucia. In addition, all the colonies had a considerable measure of under-employment and seasonal unemployment.

Although it was not until the beginning of 1946 that the full details of the training scheme and the arrangements for repatriation were announced a few technicians and trainees were repatriated during 1945 on health grounds or for unsatisfactory behaviour. Interestingly, those technicians and trainees who readily accepted repatriation did not hesitate to warn their colleagues still in Britain of the poverty at home. They advised that they should prolong their stay in England.

Taken together, the facts regarding unemployment in the West Indies, and the sentiments expressed in individual letters, showed that a resettlement of the men returning home posed a serious problem. In Britain the authorities provided special advice and assistance in adjusting to civilian life and sought appropriate employment for the demobilised men. To implement this, the Ministry of Labour set up a Special Resettlement Advice Bureau. Fortunately, their work was helped by full employment conditions which existed in most parts of the country after the war. In fact, there was a general demand for labour. This contrasted sharply to the depressed conditions in the West Indies. For one thing, there were few of the official arrangements that could be compared with the Resettlement Advice Bureau service in Britain. Moreover, high unemployment compounded the difficulties in the way of returning colonial ex-servicemen and volunteer workers.

The West Indians return to England

The war had offered opportunities for workers from the West Indies to escape from unemployment, low wages and poverty to the relative security of the war effort in England. Repatriation was the sad realisation of the return to impoverishment. Adjustment in the colonies was a forlorn hope. Consequently, it was not long before West Indians, particularly Jamaicans, began to find their way back to Britain. By March 1947, the Welfare Officer stated: 'In the consequence of the conditions prevailing in the West Indies, several men previously repatriated by this department have returned to this country; and a few have already been in touch with this office with a view to being placed in employment.'

The arrival of the West Indians in peacetime Britain, not only exposed them to the difficulty of being placed in employment, but also of obtaining reinstatement in their trade unions. Inevitably, disillusionment in the colonies led to a growing number of West Indians seeking employment in Britain during the post-war years. This number constituted those members of the Scheme who refused the offer of repatriation, and stayed in Britain. Among them were a few demobilised ex-servicemen, repatriated workers, ex-servicemen who decided to return to Britain once more, and finally there was an influx of men and women who came after the war for the first time, essentially in search of work.

The majority of West Indians coming to Britain at this time, paid for a passage on a ship. This flow of immigrants reached a high-point in July 1948 when approximately 400 West Indians disembarked from the SS Empire Windrush. Two hundred and two persons from this group found jobs immediately. The majority of them were skilled or semi-skilled workers. The remaining 198 dispersed throughout the country, and to a few towns, Liverpool and Manchester in particular. In October 1948, 180 West Indians arrived in Liverpool on the SS Orbita including students and wives joining their husbands. Another 39 Jamaicans (including 15 women) arrived at the port in December 1948 on the SS Reine Del Pacifico. And in June 1949 the SS Georgic brought 253 West Indians, including 45 women. Thirty-four of the men in this party were unskilled, but the remainder were skilled or semi-skilled tradesmen in search of work.[84] The flow continued as several hundred West Indians arrived during 1950 and 1951. Given these waves of immigrants, post-war immigration from the West Indies was estimated to have reached as high as 1750 per annum. [85]

The inter-war and post-war years saw an increase in the black population in Britain. Constituting a small but important minority, as a group, the Blacks were largely disorganised. Often they sought representation for their grievances from black organisations, few of which had any real credibility. The middle class black intelligentsia, more concerned with the ideology of Pan Africanism, did not ignore the problems of racial discrimination against black workers. One organisation which did make an attempt at black working class representation during this crucial period was the League of Coloured Peoples.

5 The League of Coloured Peoples and Black Radical Groups

During the 1920s there were several black organisations in Britain. The most notable were the African Progress Union (which later had close connections with the League of Coloured Peoples) led by John Alcindor of Trinidad, the West African Students' Union dominated by Ladipo Solanke, the Union for Students of African Descent, and the Gold Coast Students' Association.[1]

After the race riots in Cardiff in 1919, colour prejudice was to rear its ugly head time and again in that port as in Liverpool. Discrimination against black seamen (as we have seen) was no secret; indeed it had almost become a way of life! By 1925 feelings against black workers were so strong that with the support of the National Union of Seamen, Blacks were denied employment. Given the battering they received, black workers mainly in the dockland areas of the major ports were, instead of being disorganised and demoralised, drawn together as a community. Beleaguered, they lacked wider support. Racial feeling had stirred many, and not least, Dr Harold Moody, a Jamaican doctor who founded and became the first and only President of the League of Coloured Peoples.[2]

Given that there were comparatively few black students in Britain at the time, Moody felt there was a great need for an organisation which would bring together not only students (as the West African Students' Union had done) but different people as well from as wide a range as possible.[3] According to Ras Makonnen (a radical Pan Africanist) the LCP group was an extension of the English charitable tradition, inter-racial, involved in 'mild protest' and harassing the 'goody-goody' elements in Britain.[4]

This was the first major black organisation which aimed to bring the black races together. The League's original objects were:

> To promote and protect the Social, Educational, Economic and Political interests of its members;
>
> To interest members in the Welfare of Coloured Peoples in all parts of the world;
>
> To improve relations between the races;
>
> To co-operate and affiliate with organisations sympathetic to coloured people.[5]

By the time of its Tenth Annual General Meeting, 'To render such financial assistance to coloured people in distress as lies within its capacity'[6] was added to the list. The officers were Ansah H. Koi – Vice-President (West Africa); Stephen Thomas – Secretary (West Africa); Miss Una Marson – Assistant Secretary (Jamaica); David Tucker – Publicity Secretary and Editor (Bermuda); K. L. Gordon – Treasurer (Jamaica), and Miss Stella Thomas (West Africa).[7] During the first two years, apart from Ms Marson and Ms Thomas, Christine Moody was also an officer of the League. Other women involved were Mrs Sylvia Lowe, Ms Dorothy Clarke, Mrs Amy Barbour James and Ms Viola Thompson. By 1934–35, J. A. Barbour James (formerly of the African Progress Union) and K. A. Chunchie from Ceylon, were Vice-Presidents. C. L. R. James, Louis Mbanefo, Arthur Lewis, Learie Constantine and Peter Blackman,[8] among others, were also associated with the LCP.

This nucleus of well-educated black people was confronted with the difficulties in bringing together disparate groups of black people in Britain. In an effort to do this, the League issued a quarterly magazine, *The Keys*, which was sold at 2/6 per copy. The LCP's essentially middle-class leadership assumed that this literature would inform and mobilise the black population in the dockland areas. Through this organ, the League consistently appealed for funds. Financial troubles, more than anything, at least initially, hampered it from being a more vigorous organisation. The LCP's officers nevertheless gave willingly of their free time since initially there was no prospect of employing paid officers. Their commitment and expertise guided their readers, pointing to cases of colour-prejudice and discrimination wherever they existed. The League focused its attention on Cardiff's (as well as that of Liverpool, London, Newcastle, Hull and Glasgow) black population, highlighting some of the glaring inequities of the black communities.

What was beyond question was the fact that the colour bar in Britain was all-pervasive, reaching every level of British society. Those who suffered from it individually had no recourse but to seek solidarity on common issues. Organisations within the black population in Britain were few. Apart from the Coloured Colonial Seamen's Union, formed in Cardiff in 1935, the LCP was the only organisation able to bring any degree of co-ordination to the black worker's experience in Britain and elsewhere. Indeed, the CCSU sought the help and advice of the League, the Executive Committee of which unhesitatingly voted the necessary money to enable an investigation to be made on the spot. In fact, it was this initiative by the CCSU which alerted Moody personally (and the League) of the deep-seated problems of the black working class in Britain. The League acted quickly. On 13 April 1935, George W. Brown and P. Cecil Lewis, members of the League, arrived in Cardiff and the same day began their investigation, returning to London with a full report on 19 April.

The report revealed a scandalous situation. The authorities were accused of wilful misapplication of the Aliens Order of 1920 and the Special Restriction (Coloured Alien Seamen) Order of 1925. Apparently all coloured men were classified as aliens, in spite of indisputable evidence of their British nationality.[9] The League had to face the police and the shipowners who were supported by the trade unions. Once the facts were established, the League quickly got to work. Spearheading the attack was Moody. He contacted the Unemployment Branch of the Board of Trade and the Unemployment Assistance Board, and visited Cardiff where he made strong representations to the authorities on the matter. In the fight against this injustice, Captain Arthur Evans, MP for Cardiff, forwarded details of 12 cases to the Home Secretary who cancelled their alien registrations.

Moody was thorough in his efforts to redress these gross grievances. He met W. R. Spence, officials of the National Seamen's Union, and Sir Vernon Thomson, chief of the shipping subsidy. Further, a memorandum was presented to the British Shipping Federation and G. H. Hall MP. These efforts brought the matter to the attention of the highest authorities and the British public. Consequently, large numbers of black seamen had their British nationality rightly restored to them.[10] The leading light in this matter (as indeed in so many other issues involving the League) was Moody. To understand the true nature of the League of Coloured Peoples, why it came into existence and how it developed, it is necessary to understand the life of Harold Moody.

Harold Moody: black moderate (founder and leader of the LCP)

Harold Moody arrived at Paddington Station as a 22-year-old student in September 1904.[11] From the moment he said goodbye to his family in Kingston, it seemed he became progressively aware of his colour. He did not, however, allow this to deter him. Although his natural merry humour helped him, it was not long before he had his first brush with colour prejudice in London.

On arrival at the Young Men's Christian Association in London, he was given several addresses where he might obtain lodging. Significantly, everyone turned him away. He spent hours wearily wandering the streets of London (as so many immigrants before him had done) before he found himself in the top garret of a house in St Paul's Road, Canonbury. As a prospective student in the mother country, he naturally expected more from her, but she had given him anything but a warm welcome.

Moody was born in Kingston, Jamaica on 8 October 1882. His mother was denied the privilege of scholastic education but she learned quickly. During his school days, Mrs Moody insisted that young Harold should make friends 'with those fairer than himself and harbour no feelings of race distinction'. Mrs Moody was very religious and it was no surprise that her son became a diligent student of the Bible, and a devout Christian. She tried to get the best education for her son. Fortunately, she succeeded and he was set to become a medical student in London, a rare achievement for a black man at that time. Before he left Jamaica, one of his friends asked what was his greatest ambition. Harold replied. 'To do something for the Race.'[12]

In London Moody realised how little he knew of Jamaica. London gave him the right perspective. He found that he was more familiar with the names and places in Britain than those of Jamaica. This disturbed him deeply, and was a factor in determining many aspects of his later advocacy and agitation. It was clear to him that he had been brought up in a British and not a West Indian tradition, as such. Indeed, he was almost completely ignorant of the culture and history of his own race. He had been educated away from his native heritage and towards the country which he had learned to call home. In other words, the white bias was predominant. This revelation had serious repercussions on his attitude and personality. He was black, but refused 'to admit that he was an African or that he was in any way related to Africa'.[13] For him and his race, this was tragic. He was disturbed by the fact that he was English in education and upbringing, but in temperament he was not. The nagging question was: Where did he really belong?

Moody the activist was a popular speaker at students meetings and was honoured with election to the Presidency of the College Christian Union. When he left King's College, he moved to King's

College Hospital, then situated in Lincoln's Inn Fields where he did his clinical training. There, he again confronted colour prejudice among his fellow students. He resolved to stand his ground (rather than bow to the pressure) particularly in view of the many black students who were given tickets of leave from the hospital so that they could pursue their studies elsewhere. His perseverence paid off. His academic successes during training were glittering; he won the Warneford Prize and Medal and the Barry Prize in 1906, the Leathes Prize in 1907, the Tanner Prize in Obstetrics, and the Todd Medal and Prize in Clinical Medicine in 1910. During this year, he was a qualified MRCS and LRCP but could not, for financial reasons, obtain an actual Diploma until the following year. He completed his academic qualifications in 1912 by securing the degrees of MB and BS of the University of London. In 1919 he was awarded the 'coveted' degree of MD. Moreover, he was elected as a member of the Fellowship of the Royal Society of Medicine, and in 1925 contributed a paper on 'The Case for Diagnosis' for the Society's journal. [14]

As a fully qualified doctor he made a trip back to Jamaica in 1912. On his return to London, he began his practice at Peckham, London. Later he married a white nurse, Olive Tranter, whom he had worked with at the Royal Eye Hospital. This marriage of black and white caused such deep anxiety in the families on both sides that some twenty-five years later Moody reflected:

> I have always held that marriage is an individual, private and personal matter concerning only the two contracting parties with which no one has the right to interfere as long as the parties are of age and independent. This does not seem to be the general point of view of the English people and at almost every meeting I am asked the question 'What about intermarriage?' as if a girl could not do anything worse than to marry a man of colour. Disparity of union be it racial, social, economic or educational, is to be deplored, but I see no reason why two persons, more or less equal in their educational and social opportunities, who believe that they love each other sufficiently to overcome any differences of temperament and to contract marriage, should be prevented from entering upon such a contract. [15]

After nine years in England, Moody had an established practice, a home of his own and a wife and four children. Indeed, his family responsibilities were many. Christian service, however, had always been 'the breath of life' to him. He devoted much time and energy to the work of Clifton Congregational Church on Asylum Road. It was here that he first made contact with the people of Peckham. Through his practice and ministerial duties he aroused a deep affection among the local people.

In July 1919, Moody set out with his wife and four children for a holiday in Jamaica. Because of a coalminers' strike in Britain, the ship called at an American port to fill her bunkers. While this was being done, passengers were allowed to visit the beach with their children. When Moody attempted to do so, he was told that it was reserved for white people only. This colour bar stirred deep feelings within him. He wrote in his diary,

> I pray that God will help me to do something to alter this awful state of things. It is a huge problem with many intricacies but I pray God to give me grace, strength, ability and tact to do something to show the world that character and not colour is the thing of ultimate importance. *I will not and shall not apologise for my birth.* [16]

In Jamaica, he took the opportunity of travelling beyond the geographical boundary of his youth in Kingston. The experience brought a clearer vision in his mind of his responsibility to his own kith and kin. He felt he was on the threshold of a great undertaking. He returned to London with a clear commitment to fight in the name of his Christian faith and his beloved race. Earlier, in the 1920s, his fellow Jamaican, Marcus Garvey, though in a quite different way, also taught the black man to see beauty in himself.

The formation of the League

In putting his campaign into effect, Moody was mindful of the need to use every means at his disposal. His missionary work was important in tackling the issue of race. No one could discredit his work for the Colonial Missionary Society. In 1912, he was elected as President of the Young People's Branch of the Society and that same year was also appointed a member of the Board of Directors. This afforded him access to the inner councils of British Congregationalism in the Dominions and Colonies of the Empire. He was the first Black person to enter the inner sanctum.

Moody felt this campaign should express itself through the CMS. He began to put all his experiences of the problems of Blacks in perspective, drawing together his own experiences at college and hospital, the appeals made to him during the First World War by black men serving in the British armed forces and his growing knowledge of the practice of the colour bar at many levels of human society. On top of it all, he placed his concern for his people in Jamaica.

Soon he was depressed to find that his burning passion to eradicate injustice was rebuffed and met with calmness and complacency in those to whom he had appealed. He could not come to grips with the fact that big organisations moved slowly and that often the watchword in the hierarchy was careful consideration and caution. This realisation forced him to concede that the time was not right for the action which he desired. He felt he could not rely on others; he would carry the message himself. In fact, there was no shortage of opportunity for him to do so. Invitations to preach and speak came increasingly from all parts of the country. He was well received wherever he went to speak. His natural eloquence held the close attention of audiences. And so willy-nilly, his one-man crusade pressed on and grew in popularity.

In 1921 he was highly honoured. As if to compensate for its failure to give full, unqualified commitment to Moody's racial equality crusade, the Society elected him as Chairman of the Board of Directors. Thus, he became the first black man to occupy that position. He did not see this as tokenism. Through this act, the CMS was seen to free itself from racial prejudice, to show its opposition to the colour bar, and display its Christian belief that there is 'neither bond nor free, black nor white and all men are brothers'. [16] Moody used his new office to proclaim the Society's commitment. His reputation as a champion of the rights of black people, and a fearless fighter against all race prejudice became firmly established. Word of his campaign reached the distant colonies of the Empire. Many were impressed and hopeful that he would gain for them full British citizenship which they regarded as their minimum right.

In the fight for such rights, his home became the hub of activity and fellowship and often the place of call for many who came to Britain to gain further education, training and wider experience in their vocations and professions. Moreover, black workers turned to Moody in an ever increasing stream for help in the many difficulties they encountered due to their colour. Moody offered his counsel to all, particularly on jobs and housing. His telephone rang frequently.

Prejudiced employers posed enormous problems and while Blacks suffered gross indignities, Moody remained receptive, sympathetic and helpful. He believed that reason rather than threats and bullying should be the approach in dealing with prejudiced employers.

In fighting his cause, Moody was always Christianlike. He was supported by 'white Britishers' who were disturbed by the existence of racial prejudice and were willing to join him in his fight against the colour bar and every manifestation of unjust discrimination. The majority of those who joined him were fellow Christians. He also sought the assistance and prestige of high officers of the church where he was 'accepted as an equal amongst them and was conscious of no barrier in their company'. [17] Indeed, he had come a long way and made a full adjustment (unlike his unlettered black brothers) in British society. He used the respect he had gained to enlist, during the addresses at large assemblies, sympathetic forces for his campaign. He used his Chairmanship of the Board of Directors of the Colonial Missionary Society to full effect. Meanwhile his personal reputation and prestige continued to grow.

In 1931, he was elected as the President of the London Christian Endeavour Federation. While he realised he could not put any narrow or sectarian construction on his leadership, he was able to preach freedom from any attitude of racial distinction and belief in the brotherhood of man in a 'vivid and practical way'. He rose to the challenge of proclaiming his message of racial equality. But he did this tactfully, always in the context of the Christian gospel, for he was an exponent of the whole of 'Christian truth' and an advocate of the 'Christian way of life'. He saw his special mission not as a restriction, but as liberty. With this deep belief, he committed himself with great enthusiasm to his work. News of the honour of leadership, conferred on Moody, spread throughout the 'Negro World' and beyond. With time his influence grew. The number of those who expressed support for his racial ideals multiplied amongst Blacks and Whites. However, while audiences caught his inspiring message and enthusiasm at meetings, at the end, they found there was nothing specific that they could relate to. They were left only with 'the right attitude of mind'. He called men and women to fight for the cause of racial justice, but could not mobilise their ready response. The drawback here was that the Christian church had more urgent business to perform and could not concentrate on race. While the Missionary Society was concerned with this question (which had a real bearing on its work) it could not accept it as the reason for its existence. This was precisely the attitude of all the other sympathetic organisations and societies. The result was that Moody found himself heading considerable forces which lacked the direction and fighting power of an organised and disciplined group. Without the full and sincere co-operation of his compatriots, he realised that his objectives could not be achieved. At this stage in his campaign Moody's ambivalence was evident.

Of the racial groups being formed at the time, he wrote, 'They meet in the white man's premises, accept and enjoy his hospitality and at the same time breathe out wrath against him.' He was dissatisfied and distressed after addressing one of these groups. 'How damaging is the result', he said, 'and how futile for a group of coloured people, a mere handful, to meet in this way. They cannot hope to achieve anything of value this way and they are damaging their own souls.'[18] On their own, these disparate bodies could achieve little. Moody was acutely aware of the need for co-ordination.

He met with officials of several sections to explore the possibility of uniting to form a big organisation which would bring together both black and white peoples. This unity was his great hope. One of the people Moody met at this time was Dr Charles Wesley, an Afro-American Professor of History at Howard University who was visiting England. After Dr Wesley had spoken to the Central Young Men's Christian Association, Moody put forward to the meeting (an unusually large congregation of his own people) the idea of one united organisation in the interests of the welfare of all black people. Although nothing positive resulted (apart from Wesley's keen interest in the scheme) Moody's proposals received a general welcome. He was encouraged. Later, a mass meeting was arranged at which Dr Wesley spoke on the question of a united organisation of black peoples, with Moody presiding. A 'full and keen' discussion followed and a committee was set up to examine the possibilities of establishing the kind of organisation advocated by Moody. This committee met at 164 Queens Road, and again on Friday 13 March 1931 at the Central YMCA, Tottenham Court Road, London, where it was decided to form the League of Coloured Peoples. This positive move was a step forward of great significance. Personally Moody had won an important victory in the campaign he had been conducting virtually single-handedly, with occasional confrontations on specific issues, for a number of years. With rank and file support, he could hope for the solid support and co-operation which he desperately needed to effect a successful campaign. Through the LCP he was now able to channel the interest, sympathy and zeal aroused in members of the congregations and audiences which he addressed.

In effect, the LCP was the focal point, providing the necessary thrust in his campaign. Thus fortified he could make representations to government authorities, hospital managements, medical faculties, commercial concerns, factory proprietors, hotel and boarding house keepers, among others, not only in his own name, status and reputation, but also in the name of the black community in Britain and throughout the Empire. Thus, he became the recognised leader of his people in Britain, being elected the first President of the League of Coloured Peoples. With devotion and sacrifice he served the League's cause, holding the post of President continuously until his death in 1947. In many senses, 'the League was his life and it would not be untrue to say that he was the life of the League'.[19]

The LCP: development and issues

The first two years of the League's existence involved strenuous efforts but meagre results. Many of its activities centred on the needs of students in London; for example, in arranging social functions, meetings and conferences on their behalf. Achievement of the League's objects seemed remote then. It was hampered by a lack of publicity without which it was difficult to maintain the interest of its members and attract the attention of others. The League's only means of exposure was through occasional short reports in the press of its main activities and publication of some letters to newspaper editors. This was a major obstacle to growth. A regular periodical of its own was indispensable. But finance was the problem since its members were largely students with limited resources; those few working class members of its essentially middle-class membership were even less well-off. Moreover, large donations could not be expected, though many appeals were made. Finally, in spite of the financial risks involved in undertaking such a project, the League had to be positive. Eventually, a decision was taken.

And so in July 1933, the first number of *The Keys* appeared as the official organ of the League of Coloured Peoples. This quarterly publication received its name from the inspiration of the African Dr Aggrey who asserted that the fullest musical harmony could be expressed only by the use of black and white keys on the piano. Indeed, the League explained in the first issue that the name was symbolic of what it was striving for, namely, the opening of the doors now closed to coloured peoples and the harmonious co-operation of the races.

Earlier that year, the League held its first weekend conference at High Leigh, Hoddesdon. This was attended by representatives from Bermuda, Great Britain, Kamboli, Ceylon, Barbados, the Gold Coast, East Africa, India, Jamaica, Australia, St Lucia, Sierra Leone, Trinidad and the USA.[20] The issues discussed at the Conference covered a wide range, such as 'The American Negro', 'The West African', 'The West Indian', 'The Indian Student', 'The East African' and 'Co-operatives in Africa'. Moody glowed with satisfaction over the fellowship displayed and the serious application of alert minds to the problems of his own race by his own people.[21]

After the Conference, the League's future seemed assured. While the publication and launching of *The Keys* and the Conference at High Leigh were high spots, most of the League's work, though monotonous, comprised the day-to-day work of assisting individuals in their difficulties and with their problems. Occasionally, people from the colonies found themselves in difficulties in Britain through no fault of their own, and by means of cablegram, letters, interviews (and in other ways) the League was able to help them. Moody's personal influence played a large part.

The League's work could not be restricted because of the wide range of issues brought before it. For the many less fortunate members of the black working class in London, the League cared. The social value of the League was, at least, increasingly being recognised. Many important contacts were made. Indeed, it was at one of these parties of the LCP that Kenyatta first met Gandhi, who was visiting England.[22]

Three years after the League's formation, Moody's responsibilities had grown heavier. He attended numerous meetings and made numerous representations on behalf of black workers. But there was a limit to his work rate. In *The Keys* of October 1934 he informed readers that after a very stormy three and a half years,

I have been compelled to inform my Executive that owing to the great demand made upon my time and my finances I feel constrained to ask them to accept my resignation from the Presidency as from March next.

He was nevertheless confident of the League's future adding:

I now appeal to the African and West Indian to cease bickering among themselves about things which do not matter, to put aside all petty jealousies and childish petulances and seek to co-operate one with the other for the good of the race. The Englishman may have certain views about us which I have not been slow to state on many platforms up and down the country, but I am more than convinced that a great many of these views are fostered by ourselves. By far too many of us are lacking in pride of race and are quite content to be thought English. How can the Englishman respect us if we do not respect ourselves? Also by far too few of us are prepared to put in any solid work for racial development . . .

There can be no self-enrichment without self-sacrifice. If you really are anxious to serve your race, come in and get your training in the League and if you will give unselfishly of your best then I can assure you that you will get such self-improvement as will almost surprise yourself. [23]

On the face of it, if the League seemed to have been running smoothly, this statement by Moody was a revelation. There were many violent disagreements among members of the Executive Committee. Even during the period 1945–53, the LCP's 'inner circle' represented a wide divergence of political views. For example, according to one of the League's last secretaries, two of the founder members on the Executive were Dr Belfield Clarke of Barbados (his name was not listed in the 1933–34 Executive printed in *The Keys*) and Sergeant Roberts of Trinidad who were both right-wingers. George Padmore and Ras Makonnen were Marxists, Sam Morris, General Secretary, a committed anti-colonialist ('always have been, always will be'), Desmond Buckle, an active Communist, and Robert Adams, 'a combination of the lot'. No wonder then, that Executive meetings were 'rough and hectic'. [24] This mixture was formidable opposition indeed for Moody, who coped by adopting a reasonably flexible approach if he felt it would help to achieve his objectives.

Commenting on the efforts of white liberals to improve 'race relations', one observer felt that they worked from a middle-class perspective. Thus to them, 'racial equality' implied equality essentially for 'cultured Europeanised' Blacks such as Paul Robeson and Moody. Indeed, many black members of the LCP who mixed in white circles were 'too elitist' to identify with the problems of the black working class. Thus, for the more radical Blacks, such as Padmore and Makonnen, multi-racial organisations such as the LCP only deflected Blacks from a more radical line. [25]

Moody, then, was hitting out at some of the radical young students in the Executive who had revolutionary ideas but lacked the experience which brought as he saw it, wisdom. Cocooned within their schools and colleges, Moody felt they needed to be exposed to the realities of ordinary life. In this conflict between Moody and his detractors on the Executive, the radical faction were convinced that a more militant approach could become operational were it not for the intransigence of vested interests, power and authority. Moody had no confidence in revolutionary methods which he regarded as more destructive than creative. But, was not destruction also a creative force?

It was clear that Moody loved Britain and the British, although he often expressed anger over British policy. He firmly believed that only by mutual understanding and trust could they see their responsibilities to the 'coloured peoples'. Given these opposed views of the contending parties in the Executive, they were bound to quarrel.

There was also disagreement over the phrase in the League's title: 'Coloured Peoples'. What exactly did it mean? To Moody it meant members of the 'Negro race', particularly those in Africa and the West Indies who were under British rule, though there were cordial relations with the National Association for the Advancement of Coloured Peoples in America. Some members of the Executive, on the other hand, held that the title should include Chinese and other Orientals. Moreover, they claimed that the League should accept Indians in Africa and British Guiana where 43 per cent of the population were Indians. In spite of these arguments, Moody won the day, carrying the Committee with him. But the disenchanted faction remained unconvinced. In effect, as Moody saw it, they hampered the unity, purpose and action on which the League's future depended.

Divisions and differences of opinion, though necessary, were blamed on external factors. For Moody the divisive issue was the fact that many of his young Committee members had been conditioned by the environment and the philosophy of pragmatism and materialism. They were attracted to the experiments of Russian Communism and its Marxian economic doctrines. This was anathema to Moody who believed that the 'foundation of all things was the Christian religion and the true realities were spiritual and not material'.[26] It was abundantly clear then, given Moody's leadership, that the aims of the League could and would be attained only through the Christian way.

Nevertheless, the sharp criticisms of Moody's opponents hurt him deeply. While he cared about 'the absence of unity' he was not willing to compromise. Although this dichotomy discouraged and depressed him, 'he maintained his outward geniality and carried his sorrows in the secret of his own heart'.

Admirable as his bearing was, he made no peace with his critics. At the expense of disunity, he was content to wallow in self-righteousness, though aware of the damage he could do. The months between October 1934 and January 1935 were painful for Moody. Eventually, he made his decision 'to part company with the child of his dreams'. While the split in the Executive remained, the final separation did not actually take place. In April 1935 *The Keys* proclaimed that it was happy to announce that 'Dr Harold Moody has reconsidered his decision to relinquish the Presidency this year and was unanimously re-elected at the Annual General Meeting.' The journal reminded readers that Moody had been President of the League throughout most of its critical years and had gained an insight into its problems which would prove invaluable in the task ahead: 'A man of courage and ability', it added, 'he will be able to impart the touch of leadership which is the strength of every organisation.'[27]

Given this confidence in him, Moody responded:

> The overwhelming expression of opinion opposing my decision to resign and other happenings have compelled me to alter my decision and to accept the unqualified mandate of the League of Coloured Peoples and to continue in office a while longer . . . The objective of the League is, as it has been since its inception, to unite the various elements of our race and kind for the teaching of Jesus Christ and I willingly lend a part of my life and work to the League in this fight to serve in accordance with his standards of goodwill and morality. Present happenings in neurotic Europe point to the re-disturbance of peace on earth by another war. What is to be the attitude of negroes throughout the world to this new conflict?[28]

These last words were indeed vital as Blacks faced an uncertain future.

The League's work continued under Moody's 'wise and vigorous' leadership. Christian people were generous subscribers to the League's funds. Members of the League were welcome at all kinds of church functions and many black (middle class?) people were received in Christian homes 'as guests without suspicion or prejudice'.

The wider interests of Africans, however, were always in the mind of Moody and the League. Moody led a deputation to see J. H. Thomas, the Colonial Secretary in London, following the Governor's suspension of the Tshekedi from his position as Paramount Chief of the Bamangwato Tribe in Bechuanaland. Moody also sent a strongly worded letter to Thomas concerning the proposal to incorporate Bechuanaland, Basutoland and Swaziland in the Union of South Africa, and pointed out the unsatisfactory nature of the policy of the Union government in matters of native affairs. In Britain, at Moody's instigation, questions were asked in the House of Commons and all decisions and actions were monitored.

Sixteen years after the Cardiff race riots in 1919, there were an estimated 3000 black seamen, most of whom were in distress.[29] In

1935, British merchant shipping in this Welsh port, among others, was depressed.

Among the working class issues on which the League intervened following the Cardiff racial 'riots' and the subsequent depression in the shipping industry were the call for repatriation of the black community and the unemployment and distress of black seamen as it related to pressure and deliberate trickery by the police, employers and trade unions to get all black seamen to submit to compulsory registration as 'Seamen' aliens. Furthermore, the LCP published a report of its findings after investigation of the inadequate Unemployment Assistance and depressed conditions of the black community, particularly in areas of serious and urgent need such as the social, cultural and educational underdevelopment.

So devastating was the destitution and oppression of the Blacks that the representations of the League were questioned. Clearly, *The Keys* was then, and remained throughout its existence, the organ of a well-intentioned but distant black elite. The black seamen, aware of this, and having themselves formed the Coloured Colonial Seamen's Union, would have preferred to participate fully in the representations made by Moody on their behalf. It is therefore not surprising that black workers in Cardiff resisted being led from above by 'superior' outsiders.[30] More particularly, they may have resented *The Keys*' appeal to readers to help by employing black girls as *domestics*.

Opposition from black workers to this form of employment is understandable when one considers that the very people who were baying for repatriation of the Blacks from Cardiff (some of them liberal social investigators) were the very people who regarded this occupation as the upper limit of black womanhood, decency and capability. Why not more education, social facilities and better opportunities?

Interestingly, and regrettably, although the League recruited many members, it tried unsuccessfully to establish a permanent branch in Cardiff. This was partly due to the fact that seamen were continuously toing and froing, and also because there was deep suspicion among black workers of the LCP's middle-class leadership. The local black leaders 'were not prepared . . . to have a middle class London organisation control the Cardiff race relations situation'.

For the black population comprising Africans, West Indians, Malays, Somalis, Indians and others, discrimination meant they were precluded from employment on subsidised ships.[31] In effect, by the stroke of a pen, hundreds of these men were denied their only means of livelihood. Their common grievances led to organisation in the form of the Coloured Colonial Seamen's Union.

Naturally, this union turned to the LCP for help on such matters as the Alien Order (1920) and the Special Restriction (Colonial Alien Seamen) Order (1925). The League, at least, was determined to establish the facts. Moody thoroughly involved himself on behalf of the black seamen in an effort to rectify the gross injustices of these Orders. Moreover, when the officers of SS *Eskdalegate* refused to sign on five Jamaicans, though they had been regularly employed on that ship, Moody immediately contacted Messrs Turnbull, Scott and Company, the London owners of the ship, and Sir Vernon Thomson of the Tramp Shipping Subsidy Committee. While the shipowners simply confirmed the facts, Thomson assured Moody that if the men were Jamaicans they would be allowed to sail. The men were re-engaged and sailed. This was one of many cases on which Moody had been successful on behalf of members of his race in the manual trades and 'could no longer be accused of interest only in the student and professional classes'.[32] It is surprising that he took so long to come to their aid. In fact, the conditions of black seamen in Cardiff and Liverpool docks were eyesores which could not have failed notice. Nevertheless, the League's investigation brought to light startling facts about the social and economic condition of the black community in Cardiff and elsewhere in Britain. Put simply, these people were left to languish. Practically no provision was made for the social and cultural life of black people and many of them were on or below 'a very low poverty line'.[33]

Moody's spiritual beliefs were now assuming a more material form. Mindful of his own children, he was disturbed and anxious about the welfare of the children of mixed marriages. On the prospects for jobs for 'coloured' children between 14 and 18 years of age, he felt it was a well-known fact that no black boy or girl could procure a job in any office no matter how qualified. No engineering works was willing to employ them, and apart from shipping, they had no outlet. He asked, 'Is there no Christian man big enough to tackle this task and blaze a trail for the kingdom of God? Surely there is?' Unfortunately, Moody's attention was on the individual rather than the system which produced and showed every sign of prolonging this tragedy.

In the interests of these adolescents, he wrote to the authorities in Swansea, Hull, South Shields, Glasgow, Liverpool, London and Cardiff, and held discussions with the officers of the Juvenile Employment Bureaux. Moreover, the British Social Hygiene Council made an investigation into the wider aspects of the problem. A tireless worker, with missionary zeal, Moody visited Cardiff several times to assess the situation. Increasingly, the black populations of the British seaports became the centre of his concern. (We shall return later to Moody's relations with local black groups during the 'Cardiff Crisis'.)

But, in spite of the gravity of these problems, Moody was not parochial in his concerns. His Pan Africanist approach took precedence. At the time, African affairs were of central international interest because of the Italian attack on Abyssinia. A mass meeting of the LCP, held on 4 September 1935, unanimously adopted a resolution which reflected not merely an expression of opinion on the invasion, but a statement of policy on the future of Africa. In it the League expressed its utmost co-operation with the Emperor of Ethiopia and the Ethiopian people 'in the deep shadow of war', which hung over their beloved country and felt that this attitude of a European country towards an African people was a reflection of a deep-seated conviction in the minds of most European peoples that African peoples were ordained to be serfs. The League hoped that this idea would be dispelled once and for all, and that Europe would begin to recognise Africa and the African peoples as equal partners with her in the great task of human development, and that the European would no longer exploit the African but would concede his demands of directing his own affairs. Moreover, he urged the European countries which wielded authority in Africa that 'the time is now ripe for them to consider a plan for the future of Africa which should be nothing less than the ultimate and complete freedom of Africa from any domination whatsoever'.[34]

While the League was struggling against the colour bar and race, world events reflected these issues. Hitler was implementing a policy of racial superiority against the Jews in Germany. And in the United States, the case of the Scottsboro boys was another aspect of racial discrimination. With the start of the blitz, many members of the International African Service Bureau refused to be recruited in the war effort. According to Ras Makonnen, the radical Pan Africanist, 'There is only one war we will fight. It is the war against Britain. So don't tell us about Hitler. We are not interested. We are only concerned about the man who is on our shoulders now.'[35]

Authoritative measures taken by the colonial governments in St Vincent and the Gold Coast introduced powers of censorship. Whatever the merits of these imperial directives elsewhere in the Empire, matters had already gone beyond recall. A series of disturbances in Trinidad and Tobago, St Kitts, British Guiana and St Lucia resulted in many civilians being killed, wounded and arrested by the repressive imperial and colonial forces.

To say the least, labour conditions in these colonies were deplorable.[36] The low price of sugar led to the collapse of the sugar monoculture; an industry on which so much was dependent. Several hundred thousand labourers and their families faced starvation. After a long gestation period in ferment, they rebelled. Then there was the special case of South Africa where the Union had introduced a new native franchise policy which in effect denied Africans the right of a direct vote. They were to be represented by four white men in the Senate, 'an effective chamber'. Moreover, a new body, a 'Native Advisory Council' was to be established with, predictably, no executive or legislative powers.

There were also serious risings among workers in the copper mines of Northern Rhodesia against a poll-tax equal to a month's wages. In the confrontation, government forces were reinforced by support from Southern Rhodesia. Tear gas was used to control the workers.[37]

Given black rebellion in the colonies, Moody used his undoubted influence in Britain by sending letters and cables and making speeches and giving interviews on these international matters. As a colonial himself he was particularly concerned.

When the representatives of the Dominions, colonies and other territories came to Britain in 1937 for the Coronation of King George VI and Queen Elizabeth, Moody, the opportunist, played an active part in cementing the bonds of fellowship between the peoples (white and black) of the British Commonwealth.

Among the English upper classes, Moody was well-received. But this did not actively help him to reach the objectives he sought. In the midst of many pleasantries, he was patient. But all this was marred by events in Jamaica and other parts of the West Indies, where the deplorable living conditions of the working class provoked unprecedented riots. High unemployment and low or non-existent poor relief were indefensible.

Furthermore, the education system was in need of reforms, and bad housing was prevalent. Following major strikes in Trinidad and Barbados, Moody contacted a 'sympathetic' Secretary of State, Malcolm MacDonald and led a deputation of representatives of the League, the Union of Democratic Control, the National Council of Civil Liberties, and the Colonial Information Bureau. He seemed to be the spokesman for the black population in Britain. The position of black people in Britain was reflected by that of their fellow Blacks in the colonies. Moody seized every opportunity to develop this relationship. In doing so he had willing accomplices. *The Times* published three of his letters and at a meeting held (in June) at the Memorial Hall, Farringdon Street, a resolution was sent to the press and colonial office, which expressed horror at the bloodshed in Jamaica, where since 3 May 1938, no fewer than 11 persons had been killed and a large number wounded in the disturbances which arose from the effort of the Jamaican workers to improve their intolerable conditions. It called on the British government, on the basis of an economic survey and a full enquiry into the political and economic structure of the islands, to take immediate active steps to improve the economic condition of the population; in particular, to ensure and protect a market for West Indian products at reasonable prices and by redistributing the land so as to establish a large and prosperous peasantry. Moreover, the resolution called upon the British government to give universal free education up to university standard and to establish a University of the West Indies; to ensure that these measures were not thwarted by local vested interests; to grant the people of Jamaica and of all the British West Indian islands the same constitutional rights and the same civil liberties as those enjoyed by the people of Britain, including universal adult suffrage and the removal of the property qualification for members of the Legislature; to form a Federation of the West Indies with complete self-government, with the hope that on the Commission to be appointed by His Majesty's Government there would be at least two representatives of West Indian labour.[38]

When the Royal Commission was appointed under the chairmanship of Lord Moyne, it contained two representatives of the British labour movement, Walter Citrine and Morgan Jones MP, but no representative for West Indian labour. The Commission's terms of reference were to investigate social and economic conditions in the British West Indies 'and matters connected therewith and to make recommendations'. It was found, however, that political questions were not included nor was the constitutional issue. Moody pointed this out to Malcolm Macdonald who said that the words 'and matters connected therewith', were deliberately included so that consideration of the constitutional or any other aspect should not be excluded.

The League took every opportunity provided by the appointment of this important Commission to further its cause. It drew up and gave wide publicity to a document which set out a minimum programme of change and development in the West Indies. This attributed the discontent there to the widespread poverty of the people, the failure of the government to take appropriate steps to improve conditions and the absence of machinery through which the people could press their claim and express their grievances – in other words, the lack of constitutional liberty. Further, it stated, 'For one people to dominate another is unchristian and cannot but have evil results. The time has now come to put an end to this domination, to remove the distinction between a commonwealth of free, prosperous, self-governing peoples and an empire of poverty-stricken vassals.'[39]

The League was using strong language and becoming more insistent in its demands. In support of these demands Moody received the sympathy and backing of the Congregational Union of England and Wales, the National Free Church Council and the Fellowship of Reconciliation, among other bodies. Moody himself travelled to all parts of Britain to address meetings.

While Moody and the League awaited 'radical' recommendations arising from the Commission's investigation into all aspects of West Indian life, events in Europe took a gloomy turn. As Hitler and Mussolini dominated the political scene, Moody and the LCP monitored the anti-semitic policy in Germany. Racial persecution disturbed Moody for he well understood that persecution of the Jew and persecution of the African were inseparable matters. Both were wrong for the same reason, namely that they violated and denied the basic natural rights of the human personality.

World-wide colour conflict and racial prejudice kept Moody and the LCP busy. In the process of making representations, they received wide publicity. Due to the cancellation of the League's Annual Christmas Sale in 1939, its finances were depleted. The League was forced to cut back on its expenditure. Consequently, its work was put on a voluntary basis and the offices were now the home of Moody. In the circumstances, *The Keys* was suspended and *News Notes*, a monthly duplicated 'Newsletter' first appeared in October 1939. In that issue Moody wrote:

> In common with other organisations, the League has been badly hit as a result of the sudden and unfortunate onset of War. It is our fervent hope that it will be of short duration, and that from it will emerge freedom for all people, not only in Europe but also in Africa and Asia. True peace cannot reign over the world until the liberty and freedom of the individual is fully recognised and respected and men and nations acknowledge God as their supreme and only Dictator. In the meanwhile the LCP propose to carry on. [40]

Given Marx's view that religion was the opium of the masses, Moody was interestingly prepared to trade in one kind of bondage for another! It is therefore not surprising that the Executive Committee was split between the Moody faction and the radicals who wanted a more materialistic approach in tackling the problems confronting Blacks.

The League's work continued nevertheless, and it was soon evident that the need for such work had not diminished, but increased as the 'colour bar' was being practised at the highest levels. The League chided the British government for stipulating in its advertisements for all responsible and executive posts in the colonies that applicants must be of European parentage. As the Second World War loomed large, this question was of central importance in granting commissions in the British Armed Forces. It was felt that a full memorandum on the subject of the 'colour bar' in the forces and in the civil administration should be prepared and copies circulated to all MPs.

In spite of such devotion, changes in the colonies came slowly and grudgingly. When the Colonial Office stated on 19 October 1939 that 'British subjects from the colonies and British protected persons in this country, including those who are not of European descent, are now eligible for emergency commissions in His Majesty's Forces' Moody, although thankful, was not satisfied. He said, 'We do not want it only for the duration of the war we want it for all time. If the principle is accepted now surely it must be accepted for all time.'[41] But clearly, this was only the first step on a long journey.

The new policy was tested and Moody's son, Arundel, was one of the first to be accepted as an Officer–Cadet in the British Army. Later, he became a major in the Royal West Kent Regiment, and Lieutenant in the Royal Artillery. He concluded his war service as a major in the Caribbean Regiment, commanding it on the return to Jamaica for demobilisation.

During the war (a time of great hardship) Moody felt the League's grievances should be muted. Nonetheless, branches of the League were set up in Jamaica, Sierra Leone and British Guiana. Moody was now seeking the help of everyone. He sought to balance independence with co-operation. Thus white people were admitted as members of the League, but could not serve in any of its offices on the Executive Committee. At the Annual Meeting that year he pointed out that the League's publications were quoted extensively in the overseas press, and that no other 'coloured' organisation in Britain had such wide acceptance. He claimed that the British goverment recognised it as the main body representing the needs of the coloured peoples.

Moody was right about the League's prestige. At the request of the Secretary of State for the colonies it was given the important responsibility of preparing a memorandum setting out its views of the Recommendations of the West India Royal Commission. While the League commented on 'certain aspects of social welfare' and was in 'substantial agreement' on education, public health, housing, industrial legislation and transport, its emphasis was mainly on economic and political questions.[42]

When publication of the Report was withheld on the grounds that the conditions in the West Indies revealed in the Report were such as to have been useful to Germany and her propagandists in her anti-British publicity, the League protested against this secrecy, alleging that it hindered West Indian progress. Although at the time it was difficult to judge the influence of the League's comments and suggestions on the final recommendations, subsequent events have proved their wisdom.

The use and abuse of black people in Britain and abroad was the focal point of the League's concern. During the war, Moody questioned the use of the word 'nigger'. He wrote to the BBC in 1940, after one of their announcers when interpreting some records made use of the offensive term 'nigger'. 'There is no need for me to remind you that this is one of the unfortunate relics of the days of slavery, vexatious to the present day Africans and West Indians and an evidence of incivility on the part of its user. I hope you will take some steps to repair the damage done.'[43]

The fault was acknowledged. Moody received an apology and was assured that everything was being done to prevent a repetition. This incident was particularly relevant since an increasing number of West Indians and Africans were arriving in Britain to render their services in all spheres of the war effort. Yet, a colour bar existed, rearing its ugly head in an incident involving Learie Constantine, the well-known West Indian cricketer who was also a welfare officer in the Ministry of Labour. Constantine, his wife and daughter and three friends had booked accommodation at a hotel for four nights. When they arrived they were told bluntly that because of their colour and the fact that Americans were staying there, they could remain only one night. Needless to say, this infuriated Moody who described the incident as a 'gross insult'. Moody's calmness and moderation were beginning to run out. He wrote, 'Surely the time has now arrived when we should ask our Government to bring in suitable legislation in order to prevent such unfortunate occurrences. We have been against legislative action in the past and have relied on education, but this process seems tragically slow in its progress towards the goal if indeed it will ever arrive there.'[44]

For this comment, Moody was compensated with British press front page publicity, even in the midst of the war. Indeed, the war was being fought on two fronts. With black and white troops fighting on the same side against Nazi Germany, influential British officials were sensitive to Moody's comments, particularly on the colour bar and racial prejudice, both in Britain and abroad. His prominence among British Liberals was undisputed. One of the many honours he received was his election as Chairman of the Board of Directors of the London Missionary Society in 1943, after being elected a year earlier as Deputy Chairman. He was the first black man to hold this position. As head of the British Missionary Society he was concerned with matters relating to Africa, India, China, Madagascar, New Guinea and the islands of the South Pacific Ocean, apart from the West Indies. In these lands, Moody's Presidency brought great hope. The world's press noted the great satisfaction it gave to Africans and their descendants everywhere.

Following his induction, Moody suggested that the religious bodies of Britain and America should immediately meet to consider in detail a speedy plan for the complete emancipation of Africa, which should include the educational, social, economic and political liberation of the continent and the rapid emergence of Africa as an equal partner in the family of nations. He appreciated that such a plan would demand nothing less than full co-operation from all the governments concerned. He urged that immediate steps should be taken to form a competent and responsible council of Africans which should act in concert with a similar body of Europeans and Americans to define the future of the African peoples. In this grandiose plan, Moody aimed to achieve the unity of all Africans and the fullest development of their country's resources, materially, intellectually, morally and spiritually. Since the end of the war in 1945, events and needs of Britain and Europe had made Africa, in many new ways, the centre of their interest.

Political power had become increasingly a central part of his vision. He was invited to serve as a member of the Colonial Office Committee, 'To examine the question of training at home and overseas, for nurses who are to serve in Colonial territories and to make recommendations for increased public health activities and for the fostering and development of community welfare'. [45]

He sat on many other bodies, making his presence felt. In February 1947, he became (at the request of the Colonial Secretary) a member of the Colonial Social Welfare Advisory Committee to consider problems affecting urban and rural communities in the colonies, the training of social welfare workers and related questions. (Sadly he did not live to attend a meeting.) He was also Vice-Chairman of the Child Protection Committee of the Save the Children Fund, bringing to bear his abilities and influence on the cause of unfortunate children in Africa, the West Indies and Britain. He was now in a position to influence policies on colonial matters. But was this to deflect his attention away from a deeper commitment to the black community in Britain?

Moody's grasp of world events was quick. Indeed, it had to be for this was a major part of his strategy as leader of the League. Important decisions were being made at a high level. Following the promulgation of the Atlantic Charter, by statesmen at the United Nations, which was intended to outline the form and character of the post-war world, Moody arranged a conference in London in July 1944 to draft a 'Charter for Coloured Peoples'. The Charter called upon the governments of the UN to adopt the following:

1. The same economic, educational, legal and political rights should be enjoyed by all persons, male and female, whatever their colour. All discrimination in employment, in places of public entertainment and refreshment, or in other public places shall be illegal and shall be punished.
2. Governments administering dependent territories shall proclaim this acceptance of and give effect to the following:
   (a) that comprehensive plans be made and put into effect in accordance with a definite time schedule for the economic, educational, social and political development of the dependent regions and their peoples and adequate funds provided;
   (b) that all such development shall be in the interests of the regions concerned;
   (c) that the educational plans shall in the shortest possible time enable the peoples of such territories to play their full part in all spheres and at all levels of activities in their own countries;
   (d) that the indigenous peoples of all independent territories shall have immediately a majority on all law-making bodies, and shall be granted full self-government at the earliest possible opportunity;
   (e) that imperial powers shall be required to account for their administration of dependent territories to an international body with powers of investigation, and to make regular reports on the steps taken towards self-government. [46]

This 'revolutionary' document was sent to every government of the United Nations and to almost every responsible leader and national organisation in church and state in many countries. It was widely publicised in the British press and especially in Africa and the West Indies where it was enthusiastically received.

While the Charter achieved no immediate results, it kept attention focused on the needs and rights of the coloured peoples. In subsequent years, however, many steps were taken in the direction which the Charter pointed. A committee of the League was appointed to investigate the influence of school textbooks and teaching on the formation of the attitude of British people to race questions. On his last visit to Jamaica Moody had left a manuscript with the intention that it should be printed and circulated so that the work he had begun would continue. Unfortunately, this pamphlet never appeared. On his return voyage, Moody wrote a full report of his experiences and his observations of the problems in the West Indies for the Colonial Secretary and the Conference of British Missionary Societies. Sadly, he could not present or expand on them. In fact, Moody was ill when he arrived in Liverpool. His condition rapidly deteriorated and he died on 24 April 1947.[47]

Although he had little time for extensive writing, he wrote many letters to *The Times* and other leading British newspapers, occasional articles for various periodicals and many of his sermons were published. He edited, for extended periods, the League's journal, contributing a lengthy Presidential letter regularly. He was also the author of four booklets, *Youth and Race, Christianity and Race Relations, Freedom for All Men,* and *The Colour Bar.*[48]

Moody was a man of thought and deed. He directed the League on the stand taken on various issues. As the leader of the LCP, he was not accountable to a rank and file, since the League could not be said to have had such an organisation. In effect, he was the League's motivator and activist. Through sheer force of personality (his undoubted gifts of oratory and intellect) and religious conviction, he became 'acceptable' and from this pulpit, he announced his plans for 'coloured peoples' and the issues affecting them, on a grand scale, starting at Cardiff. To this extent he succeeded. Organisationally, however, his greatest test as a leader of the black community was with black leaders and groups in Cardiff and elsewhere.

The Cardiff crisis: local organisations and the LCP

In 1935, following the black seaman's forced registration, during a period of 'extreme depression' in the shipping industry, the union was at it again forcing a bill through Parliament which provided quotas on the number of black seamen who could sail on British ships. In effect, virtually all black seamen became unemployed. So serious were the effects of the Cardiff Crisis of 1935 that it became 'one of the most important events in the history of race relations in the British Isles'.[49]

In this depression the black community had to rely on its resourcefulness. The 'Crisis' itself attracted strong views from various interested bodies. While the 'Liberal-humanitarians' and white labour leaders called for a check on black immigration and voluntary repatriation of black seamen, the Communists insisted on the right of black seamen to stay in Britain and took the opportunity to argue that race prejudice would not disappear from Britain until the colonies were freed. One of the staunchest proponents of this Communist challenge was the Indian activist and Communist for Battersea, Saklatvala.[50] In the circumstances, the question of colour could not be avoided. For the Communists. imperialism was the cause of the 'colour bar'. In post-war Britain, the Communist-Socialist utopia, in its most extreme form, was represented by members of the Comintern, an organisation devoted to bringing about world revolution. Through its front organisation, the Seamen's Minority Movement, it championed the cause of the black seamen. Another front organisation in Cardiff at the time was the Colonial Defence Association, formed in 1927. Moreover, the League Against Imperialism also occasionally fought the black seamen's cause.[51]

Given their strong arguments, the Communists aroused much sympathy and a small following. The spectre of black labour in the port of Cardiff had its 'red' implications. For although difficult to prove, as one observer put it, 'it is likely that concern over the growth of the Communist movement among coloured people was one factor in stimulating humanitarian circles to begin action on the colour question in the early 1930s'.[52]

While the above-mentioned humanitarian and communist associations interested in race relations were white-controlled, between 1931 and 1937, the LCP became an accepted part of the structure of British race relations. The League advocated a Pan African brand of humanitarianism in carrying out its functions as a social club, housing bureau, pressure group, investigative agency and employment agency. Moreover, it served as a 'middle-class validator' and attempted (without success) to play the role of co-ordinator of all race relations agencies.

Harold Moody, ever vigilant to exploit a situation to the advantage of the LCP, became an adept manipulator. As we saw, he not only stressed international co-operation but also called for the unity of the black race. He used Pan African sentiments to engender solidarity in order to achieve LCP objectives. He felt that black people 'will never be free until they unite among themselves'.[53] Moody, the 'Race Man', constantly pleaded for the unity of people of African descent everywhere. He saw race pride and race loyalty as crucial to achieving racial solidarity. Although Whites were

allowed to become League members, Moody considered the
League to be an essentially black organisation with 'white allies'.
He asked, if black people who sought the uplift of the race could
not reach agreement among themselves, and with 'those English
folks who are working on our behalf, how then can we ever hope
to obtain our objectives?'[54] And in accordance with his objectives,
he was able to maintain an Executive Board which always constituted representatives from the United States, the West Indies and
occasionally, an Asian.[55]

With the publication of *The Keys* in January 1933, the Pan
African orientation of the LCP reflected Negro news and personalities; injustices as well as achievements were reported.[56]
Through *The Keys*, the LCP spoke for the race everywhere.
Moody's attempt to get unity was frustrated by other Pan African
organisations because of cultural differences, not only national,
tribal and ethnic, but also in economic and social class. For one
thing, Moody's LCP was essentially a middle-class organisation.
Moreover, Africans were suspicious of West Indians, among
whom there were inter-island rivalries. And within the African
group there were further groupings, such as the West African
Students' Union, and the Gold Coast Students. To compound the
difficulties of effecting unity, the British-born Blacks were essentially working-class and of lower standing in terms of the social
status of the students and professional classes.

Recognising these difficulties, the left-wing black intellectual
elite tried to bring Blacks together in the various Labour and
Marxist groups.[57] The 'dictatorial' Moody was saddened by the
dissension in the small black community.[58] The criticisms levelled
against Moody's leadership moved him to respond in various ways
to ameliorate and threaten to resign or dissolve the League. All
these tactical moves helped. Both the League and Moody survived;
indeed, he remained President until 1947.

Ladipo Solanke, leader of the West African Students' Union, also
wanted to unite Blacks everywhere. Clearly, at least for the first
seven years of the League's existence, WASU (given its radical
student membership) was one of the League's most serious rivals.
In fact, there was much hostility from nationalist organisations in
West Africa to the League and its branches. WASU's credibility
was reflected in the fact that, for a time, a fairly successful branch
was set up in Sierra Leone.

Moody and Solanke, unwilling to give ground, fought for the
'moral and financial' support of Blacks in Britain and the colonies.
Their differences had become so entrenched that in May 1934, two
representatives from the LCP and four from WASU met but failed
to reach any agreement.[59] A major bone of contention between the
two organisations was Aggrey House, a student hostel, set up by
the Colonial Office and the missionary society. WASU proposed

that the League should join its boycott of the hostel, stating that failure to agree on this point meant other matters would not be discussed.

In true accommodative fashion, the LCP was prepared 'to go more than half way to meet our sister organisation', but it could not accept the terms of the report.[60] While many students opposed Aggrey House as a paternalistic gesture designed to monitor and control their movements, Moody defended it. His dream, however, was the establishment of a Cultural Centre run by the LCP.[61]

The dispute over Aggrey House was a turning point in the League's relationship with other groups, particularly WASU. Moody's religious fervour and success in influencing those in high places, served to alienate Blacks who distrusted missionaries and officials. In the face of the real divide which separated him from so many Blacks, Moody, the 'Accommodative Leader' could do little to effect unity, precisely because he was 'a firm believer in the aristocratic virtues and in the essential fairness of Britishers with breeding'. Moreover, he had great faith in Christianity. In the mid-1930s, he tended occasionally to mix 'absolute pacifism' with 'racial messianism'.

For his 'racialism', he received criticism not only from white Christians, but also from the Communists. *The Negro Worker*, an international monthly magazine, attacked the League. The magazine appealed to working class Blacks in Britain and was sold in left-wing bookshops. In 1931, the Communist-affiliated, Negro Welfare Association was formed, establishing its headquarters in London. This 'specialised' organisation never acquired a 'mass base'. Indeed, it remained a small group of intellectuals and militant workers before it petered out on the eve of the Second World War. The continuous propaganda churned out by the NWA and its affiliation with the international Communist Movement, brought pressure to bear on the accommodative 'race leaders'. The NWA played an active part in organising many large 'Scottsboro' demonstrations in England.[62]

Aware of the differences and dissension among the black community leaders, one of the Association's goals was that all organisations should co-operate. Moreover, it attacked the *Joint Council to Promote Understanding between White and Coloured People in Britain* because it failed to view race relations in Britain within the imperialist context. The LCP was also taken to task for not agitating for an end to British rule. On the Aggrey House issue, the NWA joined WASU in denouncing the 'Jim Crow' hostel. On the question of race prejudice in democratic England, *The Negro Worker* mounted a strong attack on Quakers and other pacifists for their lack of organisation (among rank and file workers), traditionalism and lack of militancy. Furthermore, Moody who was always under a strong Quaker influence, although a Congregationalist, was referred to as 'Uncle Tom Moody'. Stung by this jibe, he replied that communism was not the answer. 'We don't want to fight, we are pacifists – but we know what we want.'[63]

Between 1929 and 1935 'opposing the colour bar' emerged as the major preoccupation of the various black associations and interested individuals.'[64]

The Cardiff Crisis of 1935 and its consequences

The Cardiff Crisis of 1935 was of major importance. In the face of racial discrimination on the part of the NUS and employers who refused to sign-on black seamen, an *ad hoc* committee was formed. Consequently, the Communist leader of the Colonial Defence Association was sent to London to seek the support of the LCP for their cause.[65]

Already the LCP (under pressure from Communists and Marxists within its own ranks) had been, for two years, discussing the question of aid for the Cardiff seamen and the overall condition of the 5000 black people there. The time had come for the League to act, and it did so with vigour. Apart from its investigative and lobby efforts, as an integral part of their activities, Moody tried to organise a branch in Cardiff, although he and his middle-class organisation were far removed (geographically, economically and socially) from the local Blacks in Cardiff. Nevertheless, he felt his leadership was necessary. Before the 'crisis' he stated that plans were being prepared by the League to help 'our coloured' working population, in Cardiff and throughout the British Isles and would go a long way toward helping to solve the problem of the race.[66]

Unfortunately for Moody and the LCP, the local leaders were not prepared to have a middle-class London organisation in control of 'race relations' in Cardiff. More emphasis will be placed on this crucial relationship between the rank and file workers and the LCP leadership later.

During and following the Cardiff Crisis of 1935 competition and co-operation involved individuals representing four main types of organisations: firstly, those with a Christian–humanitarian orientation, composed mainly of white leaders; secondly, those with a Christian–humanitarian orientation controlled by black leaders; thirdly, Communist-influenced groups; and fourthly, Pan African groups.

Underlying these relationships however, even when they were co-operating, there was 'diffuse tension and latent antagonism'.[67]

Pan Africanism and the Marxists

Pan African sentiments were ever present within the various working class groups in Cardiff, at this time. Such sentiments appeared in their most 'extreme' form in the United States in the 1920s, with Marcus Garvey's 'Back to Africa' movement, the UNIA.[68] Following the UNIA's collapse, Garvey was jailed in 1925 and deported back to Jamaica. Interestingly, Garvey was anti-socialist. In fact, he emphasised the development of black capitalist enterprises. After entering politics in Jamaica, he came to England in 1934. In the hope of re-establishing the movement, he published a magazine called *The Black Man*. In spite of Garvey's efforts his London UNIA had little appeal for black seamen or students. When he died in 1940, there was no branch in existence.

Although Garvey's brand of Pan Africanism declined during the 1930s, Pan African sentiments had become an integral part of black organisations in Britain. One of the most important was a Marxist group led by George Padmore, then a young West Indian intellectual, who edited the Communist journal *The Negro Worker*. Padmore became disillusioned with the subordination of colonial revolutionary movements to the demands of the Soviet Union. Refusal to toe this line led to his expulsion from the Communist Party in 1935. That same year, when he arrived in London, he joined forces with C. L. R. James, Ras Makonnen and Jomo Kenyatta, among others. Later, they founded the IASB and the Pan African Federation. And in 1938, they began to publish *International African Opinion*.

Both these organisations differed from the Liberal–humanitarians and the Communists. Their goal was the united action of all the organisations in the 'Pan African aggregate'. This meant Pan African solidarity to reinforce the nationalist movements in Africa and the West Indies. These radical Pan Africanists attacked the LCP 'on principle'. Moody, in true paternalist fashion, considered them to be 'young and misguided'. As it was, they were anything but misguided. He said, however, they served a useful purpose in raising black consciousness, and thus black protest.

Not surprisingly, the attackers had themselves to face strong criticism from the Communists who regarded them as 'renegades and Trotskyists'.[69] In spite of attack and counter-attacks, this small group of radical Pan Africanists was in tune with the impatient colonial masses. In effect, they gave voice to Blacks in the Metropole and elsewhere in the Empire.

The impact of the Second World War

Between the Cardiff Crisis of 1935 and the outbreak of the war, there was closer co-operation between the League, a 'wide segment' of the British Labour Movement, and the Communist Party on such issues as Spain, protest against the Italian invasion of Ethiopia, and racial discrimination in Britain. Significantly, also during this period, the LCP's Cardiff Branch was 'killed off' by the opposition, on the one hand, of the Liberal–humanitarian forces and the Communists there, and on the other, by the 'apathy' of the people in the area. Given this position of stalemate there seemed little that anyone (certainly from outside, short of government intervention) could do to improve the black seamen's status. The prospects for their children seemed graver.

The depression of the 1930s had the effect of aggravating an already serious problem of colonial poverty, disease and unemployment. Not surprisingly, the cumulative effect of these tragedies accelerated the sense of desperation among colonial peoples. By 1938, the acute problems of colonial workers led to serious riots in the West Indies, Africa and India. Indeed, many of the indigenous labour leaders were also nationalists. Their agitation for self-government (so that the dispossessed masses could at least have control of their problems) reflected the essential sentiments of Pan African groups in Britain. Thus, the colonial 'disturbances' became a rallying point from which the radical Pan Africanists could hammer home their primary demand of black nationalism.

The League, through Moody, seized this opportunity. Through its representations a Royal Commission was appointed, and Moody played a part in helping to set the Commission's terms of reference.[70] This was an important step towards achieving other Pan African objectives.

Gradually, the League grew in stature and influence. During the war, it emerged as the most important organisation in British race relations. During the early stages of the war, however, there were important differences between the LCP and the radical Pan Africanists and the Communists. The advice given to Blacks by Pan Africanists and Communists was not to support the war effort because they did not have full democracy. More precisely, when the Soviets were attacked, the Communists called upon Blacks and colonials everywhere to fight against Fascism. On the other hand, while the Pan African group gave 'half-hearted' support to the war effort, the LCP's support was 'whole-hearted'.

In 1943, the LCP had reached the peak of its influence and popularity. The League had also moved to new offices in central London. With its hard-won credibility, Moody the vigilant opportunist, was poised to exploit the war for the benefit of the League. He used a dual strategy, firstly employing the soft-soap technique of appealing to the Liberal–humanitarian 'sacred sanctions'; and secondly, by projecting Communism as the dreaded alternative if reforms were not introduced. Moody used the circumstances of the war, for example, the fight against Hitler and Fascism, to highlight his fight against the colour bar. The good behaviour of the black American troops reinforced his arguments.

The war then, brought Pan African activity to a peak. The League had worked closely with a number of black leaders and organisations in spite of their ideological differences.

As the war drew to a close, the LCP concentrated on the problem of the illegitimate children of black American soldiers. When Moody died in 1947, there was a struggle for control between the 'Christian–humanitarian' group and a 'more aggressive' group.

After its successful Congress, the radical Pan Africanists had a major influence over the controlling group for about three years, before the League disintegrated. When it was revived again in 1951, it functioned as a 'very feeble organisation'.

The Pan African Federation also declined. But, it had sowed well the seeds of black nationalism in the colonies. During 1947 and 1948, there were only about 12 organised associations among people of African descent in the London area. One of these groups, a pressure group representing the interests of the black working class (with a membership of less than 100 members) was the ambitious Coloured Workers Association of Great Britain and Ireland. Among the other organisations were students' groups (WASU and the East African Students' Association) and a 'rather weak' Caribbean Club, The West African National Secretariat; and of course, the oldest and most influential was the LCP.

On reflection, then, between 1935 and the close of the war, all the major ideological and utopian organisations were concerned with race relations in Britain. Indeed, during the period significant changes tóok place at the demographic level. The presence of over 200,000 black American soldiers, and several thousand Africans and West Indians who had come to Britain, meant that more black people than ever before were brought into contact with the British public. [71] This was a rude awakening; a preamble of things to come, as Black and White in a 'world crisis' fought for democracy.

Cardiff's black leaders (1947–48)

During 1947 and 1948, there were three major black leaders in the Cardiff community. They were 'Larry' (also known as 'left-wing leader'), a Guianese over 60 years old. He was Chairman of the Colonial Defence Association. Jack (also known as Pan African leader), head of the Coloured International Athletic Club, was also over 60 years old and from Guiana. The third leader, 'Old Man Jacob' (alias 'Elder Statesman') was president of the United Committee of Coloured and Colonial Peoples Organisations, which was active in 1945 and 1946. A fourth leader, who had suffered a loss of influence was 'Nelson' (the 'Accommodative leader') from Sierra Leone. He was president of the Sons of Africa. [72] Almost 'hounded out' of the community (he lived outside Bute Town), he regained some of his lost influence (though nowhere near enough) by running the Bute Town Social Welfare Club in the centre of the black community. None of the other leaders spoke to him. Each of these men's characters gave an insight as to their role, not as leaders, but as personalities.

Larry came to Cardiff in 1914. He did a 'shore job' during the war, but was basically a seaman who was proud of his affiliation to the Communist Party. He seemed obsessed with the 'corruption' of capitalists, the police, public officials, trade union bureaucrats, missionaries, social workers and a few local Arab businessmen. The butt of many of his jokes was the 'corruptness' of Islamic religious leaders. A fierce protector of the black working class, he was (as were most West Indians) suspicious of Arabs and their collusion with the Colonial Office. For his rivals, the Pan Africanists and Trotskyites, his hatred was 'uncompromising'. He was particularly critical of Padmore, James and Makonnen. He tagged Padmore a 'Trotskyite', Makonnen, 'a plain racketeer' and James as one of that 'set of renegade Communists'.

Larry founded the Colonial Defence Association in 1927, and during the Crisis between 1927 and 1939, he had become the most popular, aggressive and vocal leader in the community. Later, in 1947 and 1948, the CDA declined. Unfortunately, Larry never gave a full account of the number of dues-paying members in the CDA. Asked what he considered to be the most important events during the CDA's existence, Larry noted: the fight to restore the nationality of seamen in 1935 and 1936, deputations received by the Lord Mayor protesting against differential relief allotments in August 1937, and publicity by the BBC in a broadcast publicising the problems of the people of the Bay in March 1939.[73] According to Larry, the CDA had never had any salaried officials and its membership fees were one shilling to join and four pence a week dues. He was proud of the several successful compensation claims that the Association made on behalf of its members. At the height of the Crisis, during the 1930s, Larry claimed that the CDA had a thousand cases on file. He took the view (and given the trend he seems to be correct) that people respond only when there is an issue that touches them such as the fight for benefits.

Larry's past leadership had brought him respect and admiration from his followers, even among those who resented his 'dogmatic air' and 'tendency to lay down the line on all issues'. His commitment on behalf of the community was reflected in the number of times he had been arrested. This suffering for the cause elevated him to the status of 'Hero'. His prestige was such that although the CDA was inactive in 1947 and 1948, Larry had around him about five or six men who remained loyal to the Party line.

The other black leader from Guiana, Jack, 'The Pan African Leader', regarded himself essentially as a race-leader in the Marxist–socialist tradition. Interestingly, he also held office in the CDA and the United Committee of Coloured and Colonial People's Organisations. Formerly a Communist, but still a Marxist, as one of the officials of the Coloured International Athletic Club (CIAC), he had achieved leadership status.

Occupationally, Jack was involved in two lines of business: as a salesman of newspapers and running an illegal 'bookie business'. Interestingly, while his illegal business devalued his leadership among some Blacks and all of the white middle-class leaders, it clearly did not weaken his standing among the rank and file in Bute Town. As far as the police was concerned, Jack was cast again in a dual role: that of 'agitator' and 'law breaker'. Over the years he had been arrested on several occasions on both counts. Not surprisingly, therefore, he harboured a hatred and suspicion of the police. Few Blacks, certainly among the older men in 'The Bay', would disagree with Jack's hostility towards the police.

Jack's commitment as a Pan Africanist was clear. His intellectual hero was George Padmore. And interestingly (given Larry's antipathy towards Padmore) Larry labelled Jack a 'Trotskyist'.

Then, there was, in the early 1940s, the Sons of Africa, an association of the Mutual Aid type, which had more than 400 dues-paying members. By 1947 the organisation had disintegrated. Nelson, the founder and president was blamed. According to Nelson the club's decline began in 1945. The demise of the Sons of Africa led Nelson to found the Bute Town Social and Welfare Club which was still functioning in 1948. The social and sports activity orientation proved attractive as the Pan African leader, Jack, found after the war when he based his CIAC on members interested in athletics. Nelson placed the emphasis on black youth, particularly the British-born. Music and dancing constituted an integral part of the club's activities.

Unlike Larry and Jack, Nelson was a conservative, accommodative leader. While Larry and Jack consistently opposed the colour bar in Britain, Nelson felt, 'There is no colour bar here. There is colour prejudice in individuals, but there isn't any colour bar.' He added that although the other black leaders tended to blame the middle and upper classes for prejudice, 'It's only the ordinary people we see in the every day life that don't want us.'[74] Moreover, Larry and Jack favoured government action to fight the colour bar. Nelson disagreed. He felt that the main trouble in The Bay was irresponsible leaders – the 'fools' as he called them.

The last of the notable community leaders during the period was Old Man Jacob, known as the Elder Statesman. Unlike the other black community leaders mentioned Old Man Jacob was a college graduate. In 1945, he had been the head of the United Committee of Coloured Peoples Organisations in Tiger Bay. But hope gave way to disillusionment. He said: 'This is a white man's country, and he may be ever so polite about it, but he lets you know it. No one wanted black engineers in the Valley. There was no colour bar in social intercourse – only some curiosity about the "blackie" – but to handle important affairs that was different.'[75] To educated Blacks, this expression of race and colour prejudice would in time become a recurring and major theme at the workplace.

From the vantage point of holding a number of official posts in every African and West Indian organisation in the community, he summed up the rise and fall of organisations in the Bay thus, 'It's mighty hard to get a host behind you in a place like this.' In 1945, he was the only leader to unite the community. He was chosen Chairman of the United Committee of Coloured and Colonial

Peoples Organisations. Unfortunately, the UCCCPO declined. Commenting on this, the Elder Statesman echoed a well-known fact among the black leaders, 'when the pressure is off, we fall apart.'

In effect, the situation during 'normal' times in Tiger Bay was that most people were not members of any associations or in cliques. And leaders had frequent interaction with each other. On the other hand, during 'crises' in Tiger Bay, people came together 'around their leaders' and were more closely integrated with each other.[76]

The LCP's Cardiff branch

The Cardiff Crisis of 1935 had brought together a number of interested groups, both black and white. Indeed, the local black seamen formed an *ad hoc* organisation, and the LCP activity supported the seamen. The intention was that the League should exploit the crisis by organising a branch in Cardiff; a deliberate ploy to use the Cardiff Crisis to begin a national fund-raising campaign to help the League out of its financial difficulties. Caught in the middle, the black seamen were flanked on the other hand by another organisation representing the local white Christian–humanitarian group. Whatever the League's motivation, it was clear that none of the local leaders, black or white, cared for LCP control of race relations in Cardiff. Thus, the local groups combined to get rid of the London-based League. Both Larry and Jack took a strong line against the League's opportunism. Moreover, they were keen in competition with the London Square Mission for Coloureds. This was an on-going struggle and when the League intervened Larry gave Moody his support. This gesture of black solidarity was attacked by the Mission which tried to weaken the newly-organised LCP branch's influence. In turn, Larry's supporters attempted to get the LCP branch leaders against the Mission and the meddling, troublesome parson.

Moody was in an awkward position. In spite of his need to protect the new branch, as a prominent church leader, he could not pick a fight with the denomination that had financed the Nancy Sharpe Report on the black community. Surrounded by hostile forces, the new LCP branch leadership turned to the left-wing black leaders for advice.

Public officials were becoming increasingly active. Captain Evans, MP for Cardiff South wrote to the LCP Branch Secretary informing him that Sir John Harris of the Christian–humanitarian Anti-Slavery and Aborigines Protection Society and the Africans in Europe Welfare Fund was due to speak on behalf of the seamen at the local Methodist Church. In the full knowledge that the black organisations were in need of funds, Evans stated that Sir John's intervention meant that money would be doled out to assist in any ameliorative work connected with the welfare of Blacks in England. Why England when the Cardiff crisis had become a crying need? It seemed there was something in the 'Crisis' for everyone, including several 'very important Englishmen from London' who would 'share the platform'.

Eventually, the meeting did take place and the President reported to Moody that both Jack and the Secretary of the Cardiff LCP branch were annoyed over the meeting. The President felt it was a generally good meeting in spite of the fact that references made to the LCP were ignored. Non-committal throughout, he ended feebly, 'The only fault with the meeting seems to be the ignoring of the LCP. Well, I don't think I have more to say except that instead of expressing the opinion of various members I have invited them to do so to you themselves, so expect to hear some more.'[77] Thus, the President had done his bit following a meeting which presented perhaps the greatest threat to the survival of the local LCP Branch.

The two black leaders, Larry and Jack, participated in the meeting. Generally, they were concerned with asking embarrassing questions and they had no intention of defending the LCP. More precisely, they were interested in exposing the link between the church and the shipping interests.

Meanwhile, a Cardiff case that was being fought in London by the Communist-affiliated League Against Imperialism moved Moody to get in touch again with the local LCP branch a week later. Following the inquiry as to why the local League branch had not fought the case, he appealed for information. 'I have heard nothing from you recently,' he wrote. On 10 April 1936, the branch's silence was broken when the Secretary wrote to Moody: 'I am more than sorry that it (the LCP branch) should have gone phut because coloured folks in this town is (sic) in need of organisation and qualified representation badly. But you know better than I do that you cannot help a man more than he is willing . . .'[78]

The inability of the League to espouse causes that the local black communities (not only in Cardiff, but also in London and Liverpool) considered to be important was a major factor in the League's failure to mobilise mass support. Here the class aspect of the organisation is clearly reflected. Moreover, the League's financial problems prevented the pursuit of individual cases which, if won, could well have engendered greater interest. Taken together, these factors, and the combined effect of competition from the Mission and such leaders as Larry and Jack, put paid to any hopes of survival for the Cardiff LCP branch. Moreover, in time, Moody's 'moderate' approach would be tested as other more radical black groups came into being.

The League and other black groups

Although during its earlier phase, ideological and philosophical differences separated the LCP from the Negro Workers' Association, WASU and the IASB, on the issue of the working class disturbances in the West Indies, both Moody and Arthur Lewis showed a willingness to find common cause with other black groups in Britain. Indeed, a number of issues during the 1930s and 1940s led to agitation either jointly or in parallel action.

The International African Service Bureau was organised in the mid-1930s by George Padmore, C. L. R. James, Ras Makonnen, Jomo Kenyatta and I. T. A. Wallace. The relationship between the LCP and the IASB was regarded as one of convenience. [79] Although the LCP was recognised as a powerful organisation among Liberals, it had little effect on the IASB since the Bureau had already taken an independent course. The India League ran parallel with the LCP in terms of its influential expatriate Indian nucleus which worked closely with Labour Party intellectuals.

The IASB emphasised service to the people of African descent on educational, economic, co-operative and political matters. Indeed, the movement towards the founding of the Bureau was the direct result of the Ethiopian crisis. As the movement grew, a rota of Hyde Park Speakers was organised and experts were called in to give an address at one of the many meetings held by the Left. The IASB also published a journal, *International African Opinion*.

Both Padmore and James wrote for the journal, while Makonnen concentrated on raising money for it. Makonnen was particularly resourceful selling the paper at Halls where leftist and peace meetings were held. If his presence and activity at these meetings meant embarrassment for the organisers, to him it meant pounds sterling.

Given the 'convenience' of the relationship, the radical IASB, led an attack on the LCP obstructionists, who used the balm of aid, and garden parties to seduce young men. WASU was also more outspoken than the LCP, providing a social outlet in the form of WASU House, 'a homely place' where one could always get a groundnut chop, and where dances were held on Saturday nights. By comparison, the LCP (now financially better off) was much more of an administrative centre with two offices on St Andrews Street, near Buckingham Palace; a long way from the black communities!

An important issue between the LCP and WASU was the projected Aggrey House which reflected the more suspicious attitudes of WASU to the Colonial Office. About this time, Marcus Garvey was trying to make a come-back on the English scene, having been expelled from the United States of America. WASU, particularly concerned about the need for a hostel, fortunately received the assistance they needed. Indeed it was Marcus Garvey 'who made the really generous gift to WASU. He gave that house of theirs in Camden Town, and of course this put a number of the more conservative members in a difficult position; they were not sure whether this rabble-rouser Garvey was an even more dangerous person to associate with than the Colonial Office.'[80] Ladipo Solanke and other more political members of the WASU Committee recognised this debt to Garvey.[81]

Another black group which related to the LCP was the working class Colonial Seamen's Union. The Union's leader, Chris Jones worked closely with the militant IASB to persuade black seamen to join the union. There was at the time a real fear among white trade unionists that the Blacks would act as scabs. This was understandable since the victimised Blacks received no support from the white unions.

The black seaman's position was particularly precarious in that the Union was 'not really a union in the strict sense'. According to Makonnen, the IASB did not want a separate black union. Thus, the CSU functioned more on the lines of a welfare and propaganda grouping in order to bring the colonial seamen together so that they would be persuaded to join the white unions. The intention was to show the weaknesses of remaining un-unionised. The argument was that by not joining the union bosses would always pay lower wages 'and this will separate you from your comrades'.

As leader of the 'Union' Chris Jones was the mouthpiece, representing any grievances. Apart from connections in the LCP and the IASB, Jones also had contacts in the Labour Party. Clearly, his grass-roots leadership was crucial in engendering a sense of confidence among black seamen. On the question of delayed payment of black seamen's wages from Greek shippers, Jones played the important role of go-between. So impressed was Makonnen by his leadership that he wrote: 'he was looked on as a leader in the same way as some of the outstanding Irish dock leaders in New York.'

Political agitation and economic discontent in the West Indies provided common ground for inter-group co-operation. In particular, the widespread disturbances in Trinidad and Tobago (beginning earlier with the 1919 strikes and later with the oilfield 'riots' in 1937, and a series of strikes in Jamaica in 1938) led to united condemnation.

In addition to the LCP's statements, the IASB and the NWA also sent highly critical memoranda to the Colonial Office.[82] They condemned the conclusions of the Forster Report. Moreover, both the League and the IASB responded quickly to the strikes in Jamaica and the violence which involved the police and the military.

A further shift in the League's position brought it closer to militancy, as reflected in the radical content of a resolution passed at a meeting held at Memorial Hall in London.[83] Moody was particularly active at this time lobbying the Colonial Office and joining a deputation to see Sir Henry Moore. In response to the combined pressure of the LCP, IASB and the NWA, the government appointed the Lord Moyne Royal West India Commission. This pressure was reinforced by the influential political, religious and humanitarian contacts of Moody and members of the IASB.

Once the Commission was set up, the League concentrated on its membership and noted that there was no announcement of any representative of labour on the Commission. One further observation was the 'very serious and significant omission from the terms of reference . . . of any provision for enquiry into the political aspect of the life of these territories'.[84] Moreover, the League's militancy was seen in the firm statement that only when economic improvement is accompanied by political freedom 'will the West Indies be freed from the stultification of all progress by those who at present controlling the political machinery prevent even the most elementary change in the lot of the West Indian people'.[85]

Further, the League in conjunction with the IASB and the NWA submitted a joint memorandum to the Moyne Commission. The people on whose behalf these representations were made declared their appreciation, when Alexander Bustamante (the Labour leader) telegraphed that 'tens of thousands organised Jamaican workers are standing firm behind you'.[86]

This shift towards militancy in the League continued. When the war started, the League, IASB and WASU came together on the colour bar issue, especially within the British Armed Forces. They were particularly concerned that black citizens of the British Empire were not given commissions as officers.

Significantly, the League had indicated that it could coexist with other groups, in spite of differences in philosophies and ideologies. So much so that when Marcus Garvey died, the LCP *Newsletter* paid tribute to him, stating 'His work has not been in vain.'[87]

During the war, the League ceased to concern itself with social activities. From the publicity it had received, increased support for the League came from the West Indian technicians and trainees who came to Britain, and from 'substantial numbers' of Blacks generally who enlisted in the armed forces. Additionally, there was a massive presence of black American troops.

The League's next major concern was discrimination within the Colonial Service. Arthur Lewis noted that 'the League of Coloured Peoples will not rest until this iniquitous system is ended.'[88] Agitation continued. In 1943, the League had reached its 'high water' mark of influence and effectiveness. As St Clair Drake put it, the League 'was the most important institutional increment in the action-structure oriented toward race relations on the eve of the Second World War', influencing public policy on a wide range of issues involving the West Indies and Africa.[89]

Moreover, by 1943 Moody's personal influence had grown. He was Chairman of the Board of Directors of the London Missionary Society. The League had grown much stronger and had John Carter as its full-time Secretary; and in 1944, instead of Moody's home, new offices were established at 21 Old Queen Street near St James's Park Underground Station. Most gratifying to Moody was the setting up of two Commissions namely, the Asquith, concerning the development of higher education in the colonies, and the Elliot, to consider the development of Universities in West Africa which included three West Africans in its membership of twelve.

In July 1944 the League convened a conference to draw up a 'charter for the League of Coloured Peoples'. Among its participants were Arthur Creech-Jones. A year later, the radical Pan Africanists (Padmore, James, Makonnen and Kenyatta among others) called the historic Fifth Pan African Congress in Manchester. The wide publicity given to the 'Charter'[90] and the arrival of substantial numbers of Africans and West Indians in London, as a direct consequence of the war, moved Moody to find a way of establishing a Colonial Cultural Centre. In spite of his best efforts to raise £50,000, this ambition was never realised.

When Moody died 'a struggle for control broke out between the Christian humanitarian group and a more aggressive group. The Pan African radicals exerted great influence on the group for three years and then the League disintegrated, to be revived in 1951 as a very feeble organisation.'[91] In retrospect this was inevitable for the radical Pan African Federation (incorporating the leaders of the IASB) had grasped the nettle of the post-war colonial situation.

With Moody's death in 1947, a 'unique' organisation and personality were lost. In one fundamental respect, Moody and Garvey (both Jamaicans) shared a firm belief in the upliftment of the black race. Although Garvey was a charismatic leader, Moody was not. As Sam Morris, General Secretary of the LCP from 1945 to 1953 (with a short break), put it, 'If Marcus Garvey could be called a visionary, which he was, the name could no less be applied to Dr Moody.' Indeed, both men possessed magnetic qualities. Following Moody's death, many League members continued to pay their subscription, 'not because they were all that interested in the League, but because they liked and respected Dr Moody'. In time, this was proven: the membership fell, enthusiasm flagged, and eventually the organisation petered out about 1954–55.[92]

Pan Africanists in the twentieth century

Following Celestine Edwards, J. A. Thorne and H. Silvester Williams were the Pan Africanists Samuel Coleridge-Taylor, Duse Mohammed Ali and J. R. Archer. Samuel Coleridge-Taylor was the son of a medical student from Sierra Leone and a white woman. He was taken care of and raised by a white family in Croydon, when his father returned to Africa.

His exceptional gifts as a musician and composer made him famous. By 1900, he was brought into contact with not only cultured but also politically conscious Blacks. Indeed, he participated in the Pan African Conference in 1900, and was also a member of the Pan African Association. J. R. Archer was also a member of this body.

On his concert tours of the USA in 1904, 1906 and 1910, Coleridge-Taylor became more acquainted with the persecution and oppression of Blacks. He valued highly the achievements of Blacks. Moreover, he was politically committed to black self-determination and freedom. He sided with DuBois's more militant Niagara Movement[93] as opposed to Booker T. Washington's willingness to accept the American racial bias.

Duse Mohammed Ali, like Sylvester Williams, also met (and at least initially) was impressed by the Indian Member of Parliament, Dadabhai Naoroji. Apart from his work on Pan Africanism, he also knew Garvey and worked for the Universal Negro Improvement Association.

Ali was born in Alexandra in 1866 and lived in England between 1883 and 1921. Between 1882 and 1909, he worked as an actor and journalist, and travelled widely to the USA, the Caribbean, South America, West Africa and, of course, to his native Egypt.[94]

While working as a journalist, he became aware of the Indian nationalist Naoroji. In fact, he was glad to meet the first 'coloured' man to be elected to the British House of Commons. As it was, when Naoroji first contested a Parliamentary seat in Holborn in 1886, colour consciousness was evident.

During a period of growing curiosity and questioning of the position of Blacks in Britain and elsewhere, Ali, on his doctor's advice, sought to regain good health in a warmer climate. He travelled to South America, visiting Port-of-Spain, Trinidad, where he met members of the 'coloured' middle class, among whom was a group of lawyers. Given that Sylvester Williams was in Trinidad at the time, one might well speculate on a meeting between the man who organised the first Pan African Conference and the African who would later make an important contribution to the development of Pan Africanism.

When the multi-talented Ali returned to Britain, he showed a determination to settle down. He set up in business as a literary agent off Shaftesbury Avenue, London. Gradually, his work as a Pan Africanist took precedence over his theatrical interests. His journalism brought him to the attention of men of influence such as A. R. Orage, editor of the prestigious *New Age*. By then, Ali's writings had already appeared alongside famous men, and those who were to become so, namely G. B. Shaw, H. G. Wells, G. K. Chesterton, Hilaire Belloc and Ezra Pound.

His interest in launching the *African Times and Orient Review* led him to appeal not only to successful black businessmen, but also to G. B. Shaw, a 'patron of the New Age'. Increasingly, Ali's articles were concerned with the questions of race and colour. He attacked

Edwardian racism. Moreover, he sharply criticised British political, religious and social life.[95]

An important event in Ali's life was the Universal Races Congress held in London (1911) which symbolised and instilled in him a firm belief that something could and must be done for the black masses. It is this vision that spurred him on to launch his greatest achievements, the *African Times and Orient Review* and the *African and Orient Review* published between 1912 and 1920. These reviews, printed in the heart of the Empire, and circulated internationally, had a major influence on the black intelligentsia in Africa, North America and the Caribbean. In spite of financial troubles, the quality of these publications was 'persistently extremely high'. Their columns supported colonial nationalism and attacked imperialism and racism. Underpinning these themes was the significant call for Afro-Asian solidarity, and more precisely, black economic solidarity or 'economic Pan Africanism'.[96]

Moreover, these magazines drew attention to Ali's Fleet Street office where many Blacks met in London. It was here in 1912–16 that the young Marcus Garvey had met Duse Mohammed Ali and became conversant with black politics.[97] The major achievement of Ali was that in the face of difficulties he had over many years, consistently, through his *African Times and Orient Review* and *African and Orient Review*, brought black men and ideas together with far-reaching consequences in developing Pan Africanism and an international black consciousness.

J. R. Archer was Ali's contemporary, although there is no record of any contact between the two men. Archer had attended the 1900 Pan African Conference and, having served as a Labour councillor, was elected as a London borough mayor in 1913. Archer's career reached its apogee when he became first President of the London-based Pan African Group, the African Progress Union, in December 1918.

Archer attended both the 1919 and 1921 Pan African Congresses. At the second Congress, he introduced the radical Indian, Shapurji Saklatvala, who later became the Communist MP for North Battersea. Clearly, Archer who chaired a session of the Congress was involved at a high level in the formal Pan African movement. Following his resignation as Chairman and President of the APU, Archer was succeeded by Dr Alcindor.[98] Significantly, thereafter, Ali became one of the members of the new Committee. It is no wonder that Archer and Ali did not get on together, for with Archer's departure, the APU's policy had changed and Ali's economic Pan Africanism took precedence over the Archer–DuBois emphasis on political Pan Africanism,[99] at least, in the British context.

By the early 1920s, however, Pan Africanism seemed to have declined and so too did the APU. Up to this point, with few exceptions (if any) it seemed that the Pan Africanists were prepared to work within the imperial framework. Inevitably, as depression set in and the Abyssinian War stirred black militancy, the later 1920s, 1930s and 1940s were to witness a radical change in thinking among Pan Africanists in Britain. This shift in thinking from the late nineteenth to the early twentieth century was decisive, particularly after the Second World War.

In Britain, while the League of Coloured Peoples had made representations on behalf of black seamen in Cardiff and Liverpool, through the persistent efforts of DuBois, the first Pan African Congress was held in Paris in 1919.[100] Indeed, DuBois was instrumental in planning the first four Congresses, and had a profound influence (through his writings) on the black movements in Africa, the USA and the West Indies.

Before the fourth PAC was held in 1927, Garvey's Black Zionism had collapsed. Ideologically, DuBois and Garvey were diametrically opposed. Pan Africanism, DuBois style, differed from Garveyism in that 'it was never conceived as a Back to Africa Movement, but rather as a dynamic political philosophy and guide to action for Africans in Africa who were laying the foundations of national liberation organisations'.[101] Another source of conflict between the two men was the concept each had of political philosophies and economic systems. DuBois was against Garvey's Back to Africa movement. Indeed, he opposed transportation of American Blacks back to Africa, but was strongly in favour of complete self-government for Africans in Africa organised on the basis of socialism. Thus, national self-determination, individual liberty and democratic socialism were the essential elements of the Pan Africanism of DuBois, while his influence was exercised largely through his writings and in the classroom, as a teacher of economics and social history. On the other hand, Garvey, the agitator and organiser had generated mass appeal as an orator. In spite of these differences, both Garvey's and DuBois's Pan Africanism had become well-known in Africa and among Blacks in the diaspora. However, while Garvey's Back to Africa movement had a meteoric rise and decline, DuBois was at the centre of the planning of the first four Congresses. Garvey had appealed to the black man's emotions, DuBois to his intellect. Indeed, at this time, many British intellectuals sympathised with Pan Africanism. When the Third PAC met in London in 1923, Lord Olivier, Professor Harold Laski and H. G. Wells, were among the British Socialists to address the Congress.[102] Moreover, J. Ramsay MacDonald, Chairman of the Labour Party sent his greetings to the Congress. 'Anything I can do to advance the cause of your people on your recommendations', he wrote to DuBois. 'I shall always do gladly.'[103] Unfortunately, the Africans' great expectations of MacDonald and of impending improvements, were not fulfilled.

It was clear, however, that these gestures of goodwill symbolised recognition of the black man's cause.

What was restated at the fourth PAC was the right of Africans in the diaspora to be governed under the elective principle, thus giving them a voice in government. Indeed, this had been one of the basic demands of the PAC. Significantly, at this Congress representatives of women's organisations constituted the majority of the American delegates. Thereafter, as economic depression engulfed the United States of America, with devastating effects throughout the West Indies, Africa and Asia, Mussolini's invasion of Ethiopia engendered greater interest among Africans in international affairs. Following Mussolini's act of aggression against Abyssinia, the International African Friends of Abyssinia (IAFA) came into being with the central purpose of arousing sympathy and support for the victims of fascism.

Predictably, the Ethiopian war rankled deeply among Africans. Cynicism towards the great powers was aroused among black peoples everywhere. Africans felt they could not rely on Europeans for protection; they had to protect themselves from further aggression.

The failure of the League of Nations to respond to the Ethiopian Emperor's appeal for help put the onus on Pan Africanists to renew their efforts at Pan African organisation. Consequently, the International African Friends of Abyssinia Society joined forces in 1937 with others such as T. R. Makonnen to form the International African Service Bureau. The chief officers of the Bureau were George Padmore, Chairman; Wallace Johnson, General Secretary (also a major West African trade unionist); Chris Jones, Organising Secretary; C. L. R. James, Editorial Director; and Jomo Kenyatta, Assistant Secretary. Makonnen who was Honorary Treasurer helped to launch the *International African Opinion* and was also responsible (through his business dealings as a restauranteur) for raising most of the funds in making possible the Fifth Pan African Congress. Moreover, Makonnen established the journal *Pan Africa* which constituted the 'principal medium' in furtherance of the ideology of Pan Africanism throughout the black world.

The years before the outbreak of the Second World War were most stimulating and constructive in the history of Pan Africanism. In fact, there was a growing tide of anti-fascist feeling. This posed an ideological challenge to the Pan African Congress of 1945. It had to meet the communist opportunists, on the one hand, and the racist doctrines and fascists, on the other. Moreover, it had to defend the principles of Pan Africanism, encapsulated in the fundamental right of black men to be free and independent of those who supported acceptance of the *status quo* in the interest of power politics.

Coincident with this period, was the emergence of African

personalities in colonial nationalist movements. These intellectuals studied and evaluated the prevailing doctrines (liberalism, socialism, communism, anarchism, imperialism, fascism) as they related to the cause of Pan Africanism. Through this process, upon the foundation laid by DuBois and his predecessors, these leaders forged a programme of dynamic nationalism, constituting 'African traditional forms of organisation with Western political party methods'. [104]

By the time of the Fifth Pan African Congress held in Manchester in 1945, although DuBois (the 'father' of Pan Africanism) was in the Chair, it was the radicals (Padmore, James, Makonnen, Nkrumah, Kenyatta, and Wallace Johnson, among others) of the Pan African Federation who took charge of the Congress. By then, it had become clear that a new path to black nationalism was the adoption of an anti-imperialist line. We turn now to the men and ideas that came together, after the First World War, to assist the development of a black radical ideology.

6 The Development of a Black Radical Ideology

The black intelligentsia in Britain during the 1920s and 1930s

Socialist movements and socialist thought in Britain during the late eighteenth and throughout the nineteenth centuries have helped to consolidate the English working class and prepare them for electoral politics in the twentieth century. Increasingly, the British working class had, during the 1920s and 1930s developed strong trade union links.

Marxism, having found expression in the 1917 Revolution in Russia through Marxist–Leninism, found more ready acceptance among the English middle-class and upper class liberals and socialists than among the English working class. Class cleavages (and a native distrust of foreign ideas and workers), deeply ingrained in English social values, prevented widespread working class acceptance of the British Communist movement.

By about 1930, however, British Marxism and British socialism became strong influences in Labour Party and Independent Labour Party politics. In spite of these seemingly liberal influences, entry of black Africans, West Indians and Asians into Britain was difficult.

Indeed, more so than the access afforded by France to black French subjects. Thus, many of the black 'ideologues, theorists and activists' who arrived in Britain did so indirectly. For example, George Padmore, Azikiwe, Nkrumah and P. K. I. Seme of South Africa came to Britain from the United States of America, and Ras Makonnen came via Denmark. [1]

If 'reds' were feared, Blacks who ventured outside the colonial elementary school-based education system for higher education and training in the Metropole were particularly marked. As it was, most of those who found their way to Britain during this period were from the colonial middle classes. This included many of the Pan Africanists such as Thorne, Sylvester Williams, Duse Ali, Moody, Padmore, Makonnen and James who were among those committed to black politics in Britain.

By 1931, this black intelligentsia had achieved much. Duse Ali had established his influential *African Times and Orient Review* (with which Garvey was connected before setting-up his UNIA) and Makonnen had set up the Pan African Publishing Company. Moreover, between 1900 and 1931, five social and political organisations were formed: the Afro-West Indian Literary Society, the Ethiopian Progressive Association, the Union of Students of African Descent, WASU and the League of Coloured Peoples. Taken together, this initiative prepared them for the events of the 1930s. [2]

Of this group, Padmore was involved with the Third International, until 1933; James was 'the most active' black Trotskyist; R. Palme Dutt was the leading theorist in the Communist Party of Great Britain (CPGB). This black nucleus had left-wing support from William Gallagher (Communist MP), Fenner Brockway, Reginald Reynolds and Reginald Sorensen of the ILP.

Although these Blacks were committed to the broad Left, the Third International's disbanding of the International Trade Union of Negro Workers in 1933 and the Soviet Union's trade in war materials with Italy during the Italian-Ethiopian War brought about serious questioning of their alignment with European Communists. Thus, the black ideologues accepted Pan Africanism while retaining a Marxist approach in their critique of capitalism and imperialism.

For most of these two decades, the black intelligentsia (who viewed the problem in global terms) intervened on behalf of black workers in Britain and in the colonies. For example, the doctors, barristers and one restaurant and club-owner, among them, provided essential social welfare and professional services for the black and white working classes in the 'industrial ghettoes'. The intellectuals were aware that these services were being rendered at 'the centre of gravity'. Within the Empire, as this black middle-class elite saw it, there were 'two Englands – the England of the colonies and that of the Metropolis'. [3]

It was clear that among this black intelligentsia only a few had come for 'larger political purposes', such as Makonnen and Pad-more. Earlier, H. Sylvester Williams and later, C. L. R. James both acquired their politics while in Britain. These men formed the nucleus 'of that generation of black intellectuals' who had focused attention on Britain. Their goals were decolonisation and black liberation.

Makonnen, with Padmore, was one of the central organisers of the Fifth Pan African Congress held in Manchester in 1945, which brought together DuBois, Padmore and Nkrumah, the last time they met as 'ideologues without power'. Having set up a publishing house which he registered as the Pan African Publishing Company Limited, Makonnen first published a pamphlet by Jomo Kenyatta and later one by Eric Williams, *The Negro in the Caribbean*. He also started a bookshop called the 'Economist' which catered for Man-chester University students. While this was not a 'race bookshop' Makonnen sent many Oxford University Press publications to African countries. Books about Blacks were given a 'big push'. For instance, Kenneth Little's *Negroes in Britain*, George Padmore's *How Britain Rules Africa* and Eric Williams's *Capitalism and Slavery*.[4]

Makonnen who came to Britain in 1935 was aware of the debt that colonial radicals owed to the radical traditions of the English working class, namely free speech and a free press. Whether or not he understood that these traditions were established by artisans and working classes during the late eighteenth and early nineteenth centuries, he was clear about the benefits accruing to black radicals such as himself.

James's English public-school upbringing in Trinidad led to his two obsessions of cricket and English literature which, as he later discovered, were expressions of the same social order. As a developing Marxist, the conjunction (and relationship) of culture, class power and economic dominance, as he put it, 'hit me as it would have hit few of the students of society and culture in the international organisation to which I belonged'.[5] Put simply, James understood the relationship between politics and organised games.[6]

Whatever were James's preconceptions of English society, his arrival in the early 1930s brought him face to face with reality. For one thing, the English working classes 'had become detached from identifications with the ruling class. English workers were mili-tantly unpersuaded that their future and that of the ruling classes were identical'. Indeed, they would no longer fight imperialist wars. According to Cedric Robinson:

And despite the repeated betrayals of the leaderships of the Labour Party and the trade union movement, the material crises of world capital and the political incompetence of the ruling classes provided a basis for a certain integrity in the working class movement. The Labour Party in disgrace in 1931, once again received massive support (8 ½ million votes) from the labouring classes in 1935. The organised Left, however, was not to be a beneficiary. The CPGB, never a mass party in any sense, was further weakened by the Comintern, directly and indirectly.[7]

Given a left wing in disarray, according to James, the radical black intelligentsia was forced to liberate itself by its own means. Padmore and Makonnen disagreed with this view. This difference of opinion provoked new ideas and new writings. Padmore wrote *How Russia Transformed Her Colonial Empire*, Eric Williams, *The Negro in the Caribbean*, Kenyatta, *Kenya – Land of Conflict*, and James, *The Black Jacobins*. The first three were Pan Africanist proposals for national independence, while James's book, 'a declaration of war for liberation', also dismissed 'the need for trusteeship of either the left or the right'.

Before the 1945 Pan African Congress, Padmore had made an ideological shift from Communism and the 'Negro' to Pan Africanism.[8] Garvey's Back to Africa movement in the 1920s received enough support in the United States to be able to resist Communist infiltration. In their frustration, the Communists conceived the idea of a 'Black Republic'. Padmore saw this 'fantastic scheme' as a cohesive force which could bring together disparate elements within Garvey's movement.[9]

By 1930, Padmore was at the forefront of international Communist activity. His role was the supervision of the black diaspora. More precisely, he was not only responsible for the recruitment of young colonials to Moscow, but also gained election to the Moscow Soviet, participated in party work in Africa and had been on the reviewing stand with Stalin. Given this commitment, he was opposed to Garveyism, Pan Africanism, national reformism and trade union reformism.[10] In effect, this meant opposition to DuBois and Garvey, among others.

Padmore was now faced with the major dilemma in the political thought of the colonial intelligentsia. As one commentator observed, 'Padmore had thus begun to rethink the classical theories of Marxism on the problem of working class solidarity. He had already begun to rebuke Profintern supporters and sections of the 'white' working class for their failure to recognise the specificity of the negro problem.' Garveyism, he felt, was the major battle facing Negro workers in America and in the African and West Indian colonies. Moreover, DuBois and his followers were dismissed as 'office-seekers' and demagogues'. In sum, Padmore saw the African as suffering from a major disability in terms of class and race.[11]

Given that the failure of the black intelligentsia was, in part, the failure of Marxism to accommodate the problem of minorities, it is clear that in Marx's writings, 'a separate theory on minorities would have constituted a serious breach with the basic postulate of the primacy of economic factors on the consciousness of man and its concomitant of the 'class' struggle as the motivating factor in history'.[12]

Since Marx stated, 'White labour can never be free while black labour is enslaved', Marxists have been unable successfully to integrate 'race' with 'class'. Eventually, the competing issues of 'nationalism' and 'class' led to Padmore's break with the Soviet Union in June 1934, and the beginning of his career as a Pan Africanist. He chose this course rather than accept the call 'to endorse the new diplomatic policy of the Soviet Government, but to put a break upon the anti-imperialist work of its affiliate sections and thereby sacrifice the young national liberation movements in Asia and Africa'.[13]

The years immediately preceding the outbreak of the Second World War coincided with what was known on the Left as the 'anti-Fascist Popular Front Period'. According to Padmore,

> This period was one of the most stimulating and constructive in the history of Pan Africanism. It was then that Pan Africanism had to meet the ideological challenge from the Communist opportunists on the one hand and the racist doctrines of the Fascists, on the other, and to defend the programme of Pan Africanism – namely, the fundamental right of black men to be free and independent and not be humbugged by those who preached acceptance of the *status quo* in the interest of power politics.

By the end of the 1930s, after two decades of thought and activity in Britain, the black intelligentsia was poised to take their slowly crystallising ideas of education, organisation and involvement of the masses back to the colonies. But, in order to do this they had to raise the level of black consciousness. This they attempted to do during the 1930s and 1940s. In fact, these decades constituted an important transitional period when the mood of the small black community moved from a large measure of grudging acceptance to rising consciousness and radicalism. An integral part of this process of a heightened awareness was the role of London's black press. Among the more important publications were *WASU, the Negro Worker, The Keys, The Black Man, The African Sentinel* and *International African Opinion*, the LCP's *Newsletter, The New Times & Ethiopian News* (edited by the Pankhursts) and *Pan Africa*.[14]

This body of writing, broadly circulated during this 20-year period, helped to create new attitudes and approaches in the post-war world. Black radicalism was in the ascendant. Moreover, heightened awareness of national identity clarified the fact that political freedom was not enough; economic self-sufficiency was also of primary concern. Furthermore, from this composite of approaches (reflecting a multiplicity of views) was crystallised the urgent need to 'educate, organise and involve the masses' towards achieving the ultimate goal of self-government and national independence. Freedom from colonial domination was the major theme. Two of the chief advocates of achieving this goal were Shapurji Saklatvala (the Indian nationalist and Communist) and the black radical George Padmore. First we turn to Indian nationalism and the Home Rule League advocates, particularly Joseph Baptista.

Indian nationalism

Joseph Baptista: 'father' of the home rule movement in India

Since Raja Rammohun Roy's representations in the nineteenth century there has been a list of outstanding Indians who helped to engender a growing nationalism among the Indian people. Among them were Phirozeshah Mehta, Dadabhai Naoroji, Gokhale, Tilak, Lala Lajpatrai, Surendranath Mbanerji and Shrinivas Shastri Jayakar, who preceded the later champions (Gandhi and Nehru) of Indian nationalism.

Among the outstanding men who worked towards self-government is the comparatively less well-known Joseph Baptista now recognised by some as the 'Father' of the Home Rule Movement in India. Baptista was the link both between different levels of leadership and between India and England.

The educated Indian elite which had remained aloof during the 1857 mutiny had ambiguous feelings about British rule in India. By 1870, however, the year of 'famines and agrarian unrest, trouble between landlords and tenants, between workers and money-lenders',[15] the nationalists criticised the government's failure to reduce wasteful expenditure and for not acting to restore the equilibrium of the rural population of India. By contrast, this was a time of literary and intellectual activity which helped to engender higher aspirations in the succeeding generation.

In the 1870s, Baptista belonged to a group of people known as the 'angry young men'. Among this group of middle-class agitators were the 'Moderates' and the 'Extremists'. Their differences were fundamental in aim and methods.[16] The 'Moderates' claimed social equality and participation in the British government in India, placing their reliance on English history and English political ideas. They emphasised the need for political apprenticeship under British rule. On the other hand, the 'Extremists' demanded social equality and political emancipation as a fundamental right. They rejected England's mission in India, and the constitutional agitation of the Moderates, and stressed apprenticeship as being an acceptance of the end of political servitude. Indeed, they called for self-reliance and self-apprenticeship through *Swadeshi*, boycott and passive resistance.[17]

In 1914, the Indian National Congress passed a resolution calling for 'measures as may be necessary for the recognition of India as a component part of the Federated Empire in the full and free enjoyment of the rights belonging to that status'. Further, speakers and writers helped to spread the message of the liberation movements in the West, for example, the Home Rule Movement of Ireland and the movement of Italian unification and freedom. In

June of that same year, Tilak was released (after being incarcerated by the British authorities) and with Baptista's help made efforts to start a mass Home Rule agitation. Tilak's three-point programme was (i) the Congress compromise; (ii) the reorganisation of the Nationalist Party; and (iii) the setting afoot of a strong agitation for Home Rule.[18] Baptista proved to be an able co-ordinator. Under his presidentship, nationalists attended a conference in Poona which demanded Home Rule. Consequently, the Home Rule League Headquarters was established at Poona.

Both Tilak (at that time 60 years old) and Baptista started the Home Rule League on 23 April 1916, six months before Mrs Annie Besant started hers. Mrs Besant was a tireless worker in support of Indian nationalism. At the Indian National Congress session in 1915, she had tried to get the support of the Congress to form her own Home Rule League. In this, she met resistance from Bannerjea who argued that formation of a Home Rule League would 'overlap and weaken the Congress'. A year later, militancy for Home Rule had increased. At the Lucknow Congress the Extremists, Tilak, Gandhiji, Mrs Besant and Bipin Chandra Pal won control of the Congress from the Moderates. Tilak voiced the Congress demand 'for India to be a self-governing Dominion in which Indians would have control over the Central Legislative Council and complete Indian control over all matters in the provincial governments'.[19]

Significantly, while Baptista and Besant were engaged in setting up their Home Rule Leagues, Gandhi hoped to establish a new socio-economic order in India based on truth and love; a saint-like approach envisaging 'the establishment of the Kingdom of God on earth'. In fact, as far as the Home Rulers were concerned, the atmosphere, generated in the country by the non-violent movement launched by Gandhi was most unfavourable to them.[20]

Against this background then, Joseph Baptista, (later known as 'Kaka' uncle) became one of the foremost advocates of the Indian Home Rule Movement. He was born on 17 March 1864 in Bombay's East Indian community. He was educated at Bombay and Cambridge Universities, and had taken part in politics in England since 1895. After being called to the bar at Gray's Inn and enrolling as an advocate of the High Court at Bombay in 1899, he became Professor at the Government Law School in Bombay.

On his return to India in 1899, he quickly realised the political stagnation in Bombay and gravitated towards Sir Phirozeshah Mehta and Tilak. He was particularly drawn to Tilak. According to his biographer, Baptista may be claimed to have been the first Home Rule advocate in India. In 1900, he suggested to Tilak that a Home Rule League should be formed. Tilak felt the idea was too premature. Both men met again in 1906 at the Congress in Calcutta. In 1908, Tilak was imprisoned for six years, and in 1909, the Morley-Minto Reforms were introduced. After the outbreak of war in 1914, a series of events stimulated the dormant and latent nationalism of India. Immediately Tilak was released from prison in 1915, he called a Provincial conference at Poona. Baptista was invited to preside and took this opportunity to suggest again the establishment of a Home Rule League. This time Tilak agreed, but added, 'Yes, but would it be right to raise the issue of Home Rule now while the war is raging?' Finally, in 1916, the Home Rule League was inaugurated at the Belgaum Conference, and became the first such body to be established. Baptista was elected President of the League which he led for several years. Indeed, he was the first to see the possibilities of British Labour Party connections in helping to further the cause of Indian nationalist aspirations. Thus, in 1917, he arrived in England, 'as the vanguard of· the Indian delegation'. His appeals to the Labour Party were successful to the extent that the party pledged itself to support the principle of self-determination.[21] Baptista's confidence in the Labour Party was based on his belief that the party was democratic in principle and in practice.

Moreover, he was encouraged when Annie Besant followed his lead by forming her own Home Rule League. The agitations of both organisations helped to disseminate the idea of Home Rule which spread like wildfire. In 1916 the Home Rulers were able to capture the Indian Congress at Lucknow. Although Baptista recognised the national status and leadership of Gokhale, his political hero and guru was B. G. Tilak. It is fitting that both Baptista and Tilak should come to Britain to work as ambassadors of the Indian Home Rule Movement.

In spite of the growing awareness of nationalist feeling in India, Baptista never lost sight of the importance of support from British Labour. Thus, at the Annual Conference of the Home Rule League in 1917, a resolution was passed urging the necessity and urgency of sending a strong deputation of representatives and influential men to England. Tilak's choice was Baptista.[22] About the same time, Annie Besant announced the need for support for her own Movement in England. Consequently, Ramswamy Aiyar came to Britain.

Baptista, the first man to go to England for the noble cause of Home Rule agitation, had the task of making propaganda for Home Rule in India among the British people. Both Aiyar and Baptista had to explain the Congress-Home Rule Scheme to the English. Among the London Home Rule League's prominent members who held meetings and interviewed newspaper editors were George Lansbury, Lady Emily and Graham Pole. One of Lansbury's meetings was with Montagu, Secretary of State for India. He suggested Annie Besant's release from internment. Moreover, the London branch of the League also arranged meetings for Baptista who spoke for Besant's release.

Soon after arriving in London in September 1917, Baptista made close contacts with the Labour Party and British working class leaders. He not only addressed meetings, but also wrote articles for the *Herald*. He wrote regularly to Tilak, informing him in October 1917 that he had accompanied Lansbury to six important centres and had spoken on Home Rule and that he was attending the Annual Conference of the Labour Party as the Indian Home Rule League's representative.

Baptista continued to make good progress. There was a great demand from labour leaders for him to speak. He was aware of 'a splendid feeling in favour of the union of India and the British people', and that there was an inquisitiveness among the English about India's political problems. Thus, he again underlined the need for 'half a dozen influential Indian volunteers for propagating the Home Rule movement in England'.[23]

With these despatches, Tilak had grown even more enthusiastic. Simultaneously, he placed much importance in educating English voters and on the creation of favourable public opinion for the Indian Home Rule Movement. For this, the time was right in that the English were already discussing India's needs and rights. Having declared his position as a foreign agitator, it would have been incredible if Baptista's movements were not monitored by the forces of law and order. He reported to Tilak that the police attended all his lectures and passed on their reports to the government.

Outside London, his lecture tour took him to Glasgow, Dundee, parts of Lancashire and Hull, where Labour Party leaders passed a resolution in favour of Indian Home Rule. Although he was confident that 'when the Labour Party is on our side . . . we shall get complete Home Rule', even then he felt that this agitation for Home Rule must continue in England.

Finally, in accordance with Baptista's wishes, it was decided to send a large deputation to England including Tilak, Khaparde, Karandikar, Bipin Chandra Pal and Kelkar. Much was expected of this deputation. When they arrived in Madras (on their way to England) Annie Besant received them, accompanied by prominent Congressmen and Home Rulers. Tilak addressed the 20,000 people who showed their support. He told them that the deputation was not going to England to appeal to the generosity of the British people, but rather to tell the British to save the Empire by trusting India instead of Japan, and granting her Home Rule. When, however, the deputation reached Colombo, Tilak was informed that their passports were cancelled. This evoked protests from all parts of India. Tilak, in particular, was black-listed. He was not invited to the War Conference called by the Viceroy at Delhi. The victimisation of the Home Rule Movement leaders, Tilak and Besant, who were excluded from the Conference, resulted in numerous public meetings throughout India in protest. In response, on 22 April 1918, Tilak, Besant and their followers signed a manifesto which was sent to the British government, stating that 'if India is to make great sacrifices for the Empire, it must be as a partner in the Empire and not a Dependency'.[24]

Baptista felt it was fortunate that he was in England, 'otherwise there would have been nobody to take India's side'. Later on, however, Tilak was permitted to visit England in connection with the Valentine Chirol case, on the condition that he would not engage in political agitation in England. He arrived in London on 19 October 1918. While in England, Tilak was elected President of the Indian National Congress. He could not accept this, but when the delegations of the Home Rule League and the Indian National Congress went to England, Tilak became a member of both.

With Tilak in England, Baptista felt great confidence that their Home Rule mission could be achieved. Tilak met the British Prime Minister, Lloyd George, and got the ban on his political work removed. Moreover, before the elections, he ensured that the British electorate was adequately supplied with important pamphlets on Indian politics. During the election campaign, the Labour Party repeatedly pledged its support for Indian Home Rule. They suffered a landslide defeat, to Baptista and Tilak's disappointment.

Later, when the Montagu–Chelmsford Reform Scheme was announced, Tilak was disappointed. It was not even a close approximation to *Swaraj*. He regarded the proposals as 'only one more hesitant step in the long process toward self-determination'.

What irritated Baptista was the progress by stages approach adopted by the British government. He reminded British readers that their parliament did not apply it in the case of the abolition of slavery.

Tilak sent Baptista and Karandikar (who had accompanied him) back to India. Tilak took Baptista's advice that closer friendly contacts with the Labour Party should be developed. For the rest of his stay in England, his concentration on political work, 'one mad rush', was spent largely attending social functions and holding political discussions with Indian and British friends. He returned to India in 1919.

Thus, after doing more substantial work in England (during a period of 20 months) than any of his predecessors, Baptista, the President of the Home Rule League was back in India. His work with the Labour Party was 'so successful' that the Party was 'now irrevocably committed' to the cause of winning Home Rule for India. His achievement was one of the greatest landmarks in the history of India, and one cannot be too grateful to him for that. The Indians were unanimous in their praise for his work in England.

After Tilak's death, Mahatma Gandhi joined the All India Home Rule League and became President. Thus his splendid isolation ended. He explained that the causes which he wanted to promote through the Home Rule League were *Swadeshi*, Hindu–Muslim unity with special reference to the *Khilafat* and linguistic redistribution of the Provinces. He was particularly careful that he should not be misunderstood. Since he belonged to no party, he promised that he would not treat the All India Home Rule League as a party organisation. Indeed, he was also aware of the League's constitution but never argued that he would try to mould the League's policy to make the Congress retain its national character. He was most concerned about winning the confidence of League members. But, changes were inevitable. Gandhi felt that the Home Rule League had to match the changed political situation in India. Consequently, a sub-committee, appointed in early September 1920, to revise the League's constitution, recommended certain changes which were made on 3 October 1920. The Home Rule League was re-named *Swarajya Sabha*. Among those who opposed this move was M. A. Jinnah. With time, as the *Swarajya Sabha* (Home Rule League) lost its identity, it merged into the Indian National Congress. As the movement for Home Rule became a spent force, the prestige of Baptista also declined. [25]

Tilak's death, then, was an irreparable loss to Baptista. The new leadership of Gandhi, opposed to some aspects of the political ideal of Baptista, led to the rise of Gandhi and the eclipse of Baptista in Indian politics. This was the turning point in Baptista's political career. In the 1924 elections he was elected for North Bombay, to the Bombay Legislative Council, and in 1926 was elected (uncontested) to the Bombay Legislative Assembly. [26] He remained an advocate of Dominion status and the British connection. He dissociated himself from unconstitutional methods which were employed in the cause of political progress.

Moreover, Baptista had devoted much time in the service of the Indian trade unions. He was not only President of several unions, but also one of the founders of the All India Trade Union Congress in 1921. Furthermore, in 1924 he was the Labour delegate to the Geneva Labour Conference, under the League of Nations constitution. After 1926, his failing health forced his retirement from active politics. Whatever influence he had in both politics and civic affairs was, in the face of rising militancy and unconstitutional methods in achieving the goal of *Swaraj*, greatly at risk. Nonetheless, as a Home Ruler – indeed, the 'father' of the movement – he had made a major contribution in helping to stir the Indian masses. He died on 18 September 1930, leaving the struggle to others.

One of the most devoted and militant Indian nationalists to visit England was Shapurji Saklatvala. He was also a tireless worker in the cause of workers everywhere, immersing himself in both trade union and political struggles, particularly in Britain and India. On both counts, Saklatvala was more radical than either Baptista or Gandhi. Indeed, his work in Britain both as a Communist Member of Parliament and at grass-roots level far exceeded that of Joseph Baptista or any other Asian, at least before him.

Shapurji Saklatvala: from capitalism to communism

Saklatvala played a glorious role as one of the pioneers of the international working class movement. If, as Lenin said, 'Capital is an international force. Its defeat requires an international brotherhood',[27] then Saklatvala symbolised such an international brotherhood of workers. R. Palme Dutt recognised him as a heroic figure who fought on many fronts: for international communism, for Indian national liberation and for the causes of the British working class movement.[28] Indeed, he became the first Indian to be accepted and loved by British workers.

His development from capitalism to Communism reflects a spiritual odyssey. From a wealthy family background, he was able to make a passionate commitment towards finding a means to end the poverty and misery of the masses in India. As he told Palme Dutt, there were four stages in this spiritual odyssey. First he sought in religion the key that would unlock the door to a new awakening and advance of the nation. He realised, however, that instead of providing a solution, religion led only to passivity and a sanctifying of the existing unacceptable order of society. Second, he turned to science as a means of helping the Indian people. After years of scientific studies (and having been an active welfare worker in the plague hospitals and slums of Bombay) he found that science alone offered no solution unless it was applied in practice to the economy. Third, he felt that in order to end Indian poverty, industrial development was necessary. This led to the establishment of the Tata iron and steel industry in India. Soon, however, his open advocacy of Indian national liberation ran afoul of the authorities. Consequently, the Tata firm sent him to Britain as their departmental manager. Finally, to climax his spiritual pilgrimage, he entered the world of the National Liberal Club, but quickly found among its members a narrow outlook and snobbish hypocrisy. After confrontation with Morley, then Secretary of State for India, he gravitated towards British working class politics.

Saklatvala was born on 28 March 1874 in Bombay. Since the 1830s the Saklatvala family was a well-known *parsee* family in Bombay. He was intensely sensitive to human suffering. Thus, in spite of being born with 'a silver spoon in his mouth' he moved inevitably towards the working masses and a radical ideology. After leaving college, he was devoted to industry and was instrumental in setting up the Tata Iron and Steel works under the guidance of his maternal uncle, J. N. Tata. During this time, there was rising national consciousness in India. The Indian National Congress, already established in 1855, sought British goodwill in order to redress Indian grievances. Saklatvala's interest in politics which brought him in conflict with the British authorities, embarrassed the Tatas. To forestall growing militant nationalism in Bengal and elsewhere in India, British force became more repressive. After this transitional period in Indian politics, Saklatvala began his political life in England.

He interestingly moved from being a Liberal (believing in British goodwill) to an 'arch-enemy' of British imperialism. Indeed, he bravely held on to this uncompromising commitment and attacked imperialism 'in the heart of its stronghold'.[29] After a brief spell of work in the Tata's Manchester office, he came to London where his especially concerned family made him a life-member of the National Liberal Club. This concern was essentially that Saklatvala would become 'respectable' by meeting 'friends' of Indian freedom. Among those whom he met was Lord Morley of the Morley-Minto Reforms of 1909 (which arrived 'to rally the moderates' in the face of militant nationalism) that contributed towards the division of Indian nationalism along communal lines through the introduction of separate Hindu and Muslim electorates.

Saklatvala saw this division and its implications clearly and did not deviate from his argument, which was further strengthened by his familiarity with Liberal bankruptcy and hypocrisy concerning the true interests of the Indians. An argument with 'Honest Jack' Morley, resulted in Saklatvala's resignation and his departure from the liberal 'mausoleum'. In 1910 he entered British working class politics through the Independent Labour Party.[30]

Involvement in the ILP proved an unsatisfactory experience. Saklatvala was disappointed by the Party's gradual shift from being Marxist to anti-Marxist. He was in fact in search of a group of true internationalists. Narrow nationalism was redundant; he sought support for the national liberation movement in India. Thus, the ILP was found wanting in that (though championing the cause of British workers) it did not attack the cause of capitalist exploitation and failed to link the British working class with the international working-class movement. To Saklatvala, India's oppression was clearly linked to British capitalists and their exploitation through British imperialism. This belief received a fillip in 1917 when the Russian Revolution stirred his imagination and pointed to the possibilities. According to one biographer, he saw this as the precursor to 'a new civilisation – a new social order' which would, in the end, bring liberation to the exploited millions living under the heels of capitalism and imperialism. Alerted to the dangers of the Russian Revolution and its effect on working class and colonial national liberation movements, predictably the British imperialists used every means to discredit it. But in the wave of anti-Soviet propaganda, Saklatvala and others tried to present the other side of the story before the British public. He consolidated his position in 1918 by joining the People's Russian Information Bureau, which spread the message of the Russian Revolution.

At the war's end, the Russian Revolution had the beneficial effect of engendering hope in British and colonial liberation movements. Indeed, colonial working-class movements became more assertive, leading to widespread disturbances in 1919. These colonial developments were not lost on Lenin who formed the Third International in 1919. Saklatvala's response was that the ILP should be affiliated to the Third International to work towards the unity of the workers of the world. This proposal was not accepted by the ILP. Frustrated, Saklatvala moved irrevocably towards the ideals of the Communist Party, which he joined in 1921. To his lasting credit, he remained a Party member to his death.[31]

Three years after the Russian Revolution, the Communist Party of Great Britain was founded at a time of growing militant activities in the trade union movement. The central political struggle during this new era of militant working class struggle in Britain was support for the new Russian Republic. Thus, the Hands Off Russia Committee established in Britain in the spring of 1919 inaugurated a campaign against British intervention. Moreover, in April 1919, the Trades Union Congress and the Labour Party at a joint conference called for the withdrawal of British troops from Russia. Further, the British government's ultimatum to the Soviet Union resulted in radical elements in the British working class threatening a general strike.[32]

Both the Amritsar Massacre and suppression of the Egyptian national liberation movement drew protest from the young Communist Party and from the Labour Left. In the CP Saklatvala found what he was looking for: an organisation which took a strong stand on international solidarity on national liberation and for ending exploitation.

According to one observer, it is no exaggeration to claim that Saklatvala was a product of the British working–class movement. Indeed, his devotion to this movement was undoubted. Historically, this international aspect of working–class unity was a continuing theme of the British working class movement. In the struggle for the reform of Parliament, the London Workingmen's Association was formed 'to secure political rights for the workers after the failure to win working–class representation in 1832'. In fact, it was this organisation which in 1838 produced the People's Charter,[33] which in turn became the rallying point for a revolutionary movement which, at the outset, recognised the working–class struggle as an international one.

Soon after Saklatvala came to England, he took an interest in the trade union movement. After joining the CP he became a keen and active trade union member. This involvement was noted by the *Daily Worker*: 'Night after night, year after year, in all parts of Britain he carried out his task of working class agitation, education and organisation. No comrade ever did more of his work so uncomplainingly as comrade Saklatvala . . . No call was ever made upon [him] to which he did not respond.'[34] In spite of bad health, a 'dicky' heart, he displayed unusual vitality. This unselfish commitment was observed by both organisers and workers. He cared about reaching the workers, travelling widely on speaking tours and sleeping rough 'even on the floor of the corridor in a crowded train – certainly never in a first class sleeper'. [35] Soon this dedication brought him deserved recognition from British workers. This was evident when Saklatvala was able to draw a crowd of 1500 people, while one of the Blackshirt 'stars' spoke to a 'small audience'. In fact, as soon as Saklatvala began speaking, the small crowd deserted the Fascist and turned to listen to the Communist.

Saklatvala's involvement in the trade union movement had deepened over the years, forming the essential base of his politics. Indeed, he was not only an active member of the General Workers' Union, he also joined the Clerks' Union and the Co-operative Union. Moreover, he was elected as a delegate by the Trades Union Congress of India to represent them at various trade union congresses in England. His popularity among rank and file workers had grown enormously.

In the General Election of October 1922 he contested the seat of Battersea North. His candidature aroused much debate and discussion. Eventually, however, he received the support of the Battersea Trades and Labour Council, and the endorsement of the Labour Party NEC. It was agreed that Saklatvala should run as a Labour candidate. Indeed, he pledged himself publicly to support the Labour Party's Constitution and policy. In his election address, he wrote:

In spite of desperate and ludicrous efforts on the part of Liberals and Tories alike to split the Working Class Movement into hostile fragments, THE LABOUR PARTY IS TODAY THE ONLY PARTY IN GREAT BRITAIN THAT STANDS SOLIDLY TOGETHER. The scare-cry of 'Communist' which is sure to be raised by eleventh-hour leaflets will fortunately not frighten the electors of North Battersea . . . [36]

This statement is understandable, given the fact that those were the years when the CP was trying to obtain affiliation to the Labour Party. [37] In fact, at this time, Saklatvala's statements and general attitude towards the Labour Party were fundamentally in line with Communist Party policy. During this campaign he found in Mrs Charlotte Despard a most active supporter. Saklatvala won the seat by a clear majority of 2000 votes but lost it in the November 1923 Election by a narrow margin. In the interval between the 1923 election and that of 1924, which brought the first minority Labour Government to an end, the Labour Conference of October 1924 banned Communists from standing as Labour candidates, and excluded individual Communists from Labour Party membership. Saklatvala, who had attended this conference as the St Pancras Labour Party delegate was, in effect, forced to contest the Battersea North seat as a Communist candidate in 1924. With the overwhelming support of the Battersea North LP, he narrowly defeated his Liberal opponent to win the seat in the Zinoviev Letter election.

During both terms as an MP, Saklatvala worked closely with the left-wing Scottish ILP members. With his broad outlook, he emphasised the connection between the workers' struggle in different parts of the Empire. Naturally, he was concerned with the problems of colonial workers and peasants, particularly those in India. There were two organisations in Britain which provided connections between the British Labour movement and India. There was, of course, Annie Besant's Home Rule League. Towards the close of the First World War, the League had aroused support for its aims among ILP branches and trades councils in Yorkshire, South Wales and in some of the larger industrial towns.

Although Saklatvala was a member of the Home Rule League, he sought to fill another need by forming the Workers' Welfare League in 1916. Its original aim, to work with Indian seamen in London, was broadened to include matters affecting the working conditions of all groups of Indian workers. Moreover, when the All-India Trades Union Congress (AITUC) was established in 1921, the Workers' Welfare League became its agent in Britain. Apart from Saklatvala, among the WWL's leading members during its early years, were Arthur Pugh (until about 1924) J. Potter-Wilson and George Lansbury. Predictably, given Saklatvala's political perspective, by the mid-1920s the WWL was identified with the Communists and the Left generally. After the political rupture of the 1926 General Strike, the League's shift to the left was viewed with considerable hostility by both the Labour Party leadership and the TUC General Council. If Saklatvala's activities in Britain were monitored, thereafter, he was closely watched.

Apart from being a black Communist MP in Britain, his political career had always been controversial. However, he remained undeterred in his passion to end oppression. During this turbulent period, he played a full part in the many industrial and political disputes. As an outsider, he was the perfect scapegoat. In October 1921, his home was searched; in 1925, although appointed a member of the British delegation to the Inter-parliamentary Union Congress in Washington, the American Secretary of State revoked his visa;[38] and on the first day of the General Strike (4 May 1926) he was arrested and charged with sedition for a speech he made on May Day urging the Army not to fire on the people.[39] Forty years later, a *Sunday Times* writer described Saklatvala as one of the instigators of the General Strike. In the face of this onslaught, he remained unbowed. He refused to be bound over and was sentenced to two months' imprisonment, which was served in Wormwood Scrubs. Moreover, during the period of his arrest and trial, his home (and those of other well-known Communists) was again raided.[40] These experiences seemed to have strengthened Saklatvala's resolve. After his release he continued to be active by addressing meetings on behalf of the locked-out miners. His imprisonment in Britain served only to heighten the struggle of workers elsewhere in the Empire.

Since he settled in England, he had been back to India three times: in 1912–13 (a family visit), in 1913–14 by himself; and finally (after some difficulty in getting permission to enter the country) he arrived in Bombay on 14 January 1927. On his third visit, he received a hero's welcome from most sections of the Indian nationalists. Like Gandhi, he supported organised labour in South Africa and directed attention to the need for trade union and peasant organisations. Moreover, he attended the AITUC Conference as a fraternal delegate, was officially welcomed by several large municipal corporations, and addressed huge audiences. Whilst the official authorities tried to divide the people, he appealed for communal unity in the essential struggle for an independent India. In this, he urged the left to work within the Congress Party. His experience and involvement with British working-class politics made his appeal to the Indian people more passionate and memorable. He was fully aware of Gandhi's presence and influence. Before he left India, he published an Open Letter to Gandhi whose policies he severely criticised. In the correspondence between them, Gandhi's reply was published on 17 March 1927 in the Bombay *Daily Mail*. More letters passed between them, all of which were published in 1970. During this last visit, Saklatvala spent three months in India.

When he returned to Britain, India became a no-go area – it was excluded from the list of countries for which his passport was valid. He became so dangerous that he was refused entry to Egypt on his way to India. As he found out, his real enemies, ironically, were Labour members such as Wedgwood Benn, Secretary of State for India and Arthur Henderson, Foreign Secretary, who upheld the ban on his entry into India when the Labour Party was returned to office in 1929. He was also refused admission into Belgium in 1929, while on his way to attend a League Against Imperialism meeting. The League had an important bearing on Saklatvala's politics. Earlier in February 1926, the League was founded after meetings in Berlin and Brussels. Thereafter the organisation became the League Against Imperialism, with George Lansbury as Chairman. After his resignation, two months later, James Maxton replaced him. Willi Munzenberg became one of the two international secretaries, and Jawaharlal Nehru, Saklatvala and Diego Riviera of Mexico were members of the Executive Committee. Reginald Bridgeman, the former British Foreign Office diplomat, was secretary of the British section. Clearly, the LAI was not popular with the world's press or the Indian government which banned all its literature. More witch-hunting was to come. In January 1929, Saklatvala, Maxton, Bridgeman, A. J. Cook and Alex Gossip, on their way to attend a meeting of the League in Cologne, arrived in Ostend where Cook and Gossip were allowed to continue their journey, while the other three were arrested and sent back to Britain. Saklatvala, with no illusions, was right about the international conspiracy of capital.

Unfortunately at this time, the political divisions on the left had hit a new low. Before the Communist International had taken a hard line against reformism Saklatvala had already been critical of the Labour Party. He argued that since the Party had turned itself into a liberal reformist group, the CP, given that it was the only anti-capitalist party, should seek trade union affiliations.[41] Moreover, at the Sixth World Congress of the Communist International in the summer of 1928, Saklatvala, with R. Palme Dutt and Harry Pollitt, demanded a radical change in policy. This was achieved at the eleventh Congress held between November and December 1929 at Leeds. Earlier, in the General Election of 1929, Saklatvala lost his seat to the Labour candidate, who polled twice as many votes. The following year, Saklatvala stood again in a by-election in Shuttleston, Glasgow, but lost. In 1931, he again contested a Battersea seat, but failed miserably, polling only half the number of votes he had received in 1929. It was a sound victory for the Conservative candidate, and a reflection that the political tide had turned their way.

During the remaining years of his life, Saklatvala kept up a gruelling schedule, speaking at meetings across the country. Among others he was particularly concerned with unemployment, the central issue at the time. Together with Reg Bishop, his friend and secretary, he visited the Soviet Union for the third time. He was impressed by the changes he had seen among the non-Russian peoples in central Asia. A year later, he was again active in electioneering. This time, he campaigned for Harry Pollitt in the Rhondda, and Willie Gallacher in West Fife. Indeed, he continued to address meetings until two weeks before his death from a heart attack on 16 June 1936.

The radicalisation of Pan Africanism

George Padmore: from communism to Pan Africanism

Perhaps the most vital advocate of radical Pan Africanism was the globe-trotting, black revolutionary George Padmore, who after the first triumph of Pan Africanism, Ghanaian Independence, has remained relatively forgotten. His wide travels, however, led eventually to the crucial years of feverish activity and historic organisation in Britain between 1935 and 1957.

George Padmore was the adopted name of Malcolm Ivan Meredith Nurse, who was born in the Arouca district of Tacarigua in Trinidad, in 1902.

One of Malcolm's closest friends at school in Port of Spain was C. L. R. James. His undistinguished school career in Trinidad led to his employment shortly after graduation with the Trinidad Publishing Company as a reporter of shipping news for the *Weekly*

Guardian. His working relationship with the editor, Edward Partridge, an Englishman with an authoritarian approach to his staff, set the tone for Malcolm Nurse's passionate involvement in anti-imperialist journalism and politics.

His desire to achieve higher education, such as that gained by a few locals for example the barrister Henry Sylvester Williams (who called the first Pan African Conference) led to travel abroad. In September 1924, given the immigration quota system, Nurse went to Fisk University, Tennessee, with the intention of studying medicine.

When he arrived at Fisk, he changed his mind about studying medicine. Instead, he decided to study law for which he prepared by reading political science. Journalism held a special attraction. He not only joined the *Fisk Herald*, the student newspaper, but played a leading part as an exceptionally able speaker who was sought after to speak on colonial questions. Already in 1926 his grasp of international issues was becoming pronounced. He was one of the 75 state-wide delegates attending a conference on 'religion and the world' organised by the Student Volunteer Movement. He shared the platform with Dr Mordecai Johnson, President of Howard University. The following year, he attended another conference. By then he had become well-known and regarded by a conference organiser as 'one of the outstanding students in Nashville today'.

From here he established contact with the Nigerian Benjamin Azikiwe who was at Howard University. The idea was to form an African student organisation to encourage racial consciousness and a spirit of nationalism aimed at protecting the sovereignty of Liberia. The 1920s was a particularly troubled decade at Fisk: student activities were restricted and the Ku Klux Klan looked for scapegoats among agitators, communists and 'new negroes'. In fact, there was also a student strike. Whatever effects these factors might have had, Malcolm Nurse did not take his degree. However, with a 'first rate record' he arrived in New York where he entered one of the City's universities. In 1926, his wife had joined him in New York from Trinidad and in 1927, he asked Azikiwe for help to establish an African student organisation 'to foster racial consciousness and a spirit of nationalism aiming at the protection of the sovereignty of Liberia'. In time, he would become preoccupied with Liberia and the rest of Africa.

His absence at classes and examinations at the Law School of New York University led to his being 'dropped'. He had, however, enrolled at the Law School of Howard University 'presumably because the Communist Party, which he joined shortly after reaching the Greenwich Village campus, wanted him to do so'.

This involvement with the Communist Party would have far-reaching consequences. At the time a large number of students from the British colonies were concentrated at Howard University. Of the 200 foreign students, 150 were from British territories.

Nurse, under party discipline from mid-1927, had by 1928 adopted the name George Padmore (a compound of his school friend's surname and his father-in-law's christian name, George) while engaged in party business. He wrote: 'You see, all revolutionaries are compelled to adopt false names to hide their identity from the Government.'[42]

This double life was quite successful in concealing Nurse's real identity. One of his instructors at Howard University who knew him well, Dr Ralph Bunche, was not aware of his Communist connection. During this Nurse/Padmore phase, Padmore as secretary of the International Anti-Imperialistic Youth League criticised Sir Esme Howard (who was on a visit to the campus) as a representative of 'history's most bloated Empire' and for his alleged part in Marcus Garvey's deportation from the United States. At the time, there was a campus Garvey Club. Padmore's behaviour was outrageous. The institution's President Johnson, who apologised for this embarrassing incident, explained that it was the act of an outsider (one of the 'new negroes!') since an examination of the record showed that no George Padmore was registered at Howard. Thus, the well-known young man at Fisk became hugely popular at Howard. His penchant for opposition was remarkable. Bunche recalled a speech Nurse made in the campus in which he denounced just about everybody and everything connected with the University in fluent ringing rhetoric. Indeed, he won the admiration of both the faculty and student body achieving the honour of being 'our favourite speaker'. Thus, in a short space of time, he had achieved unusual prominence both as a student and a youth leader. While American racism troubled him, he was encouraged by the 'new Negro' reaction, the kind of spirit which he hoped to see more of in Trinidad. Towards the end of the 1920s in America, he was poor, but enthusiastic and 'keen on winning his way in the world'.[43]

During that part of the decade while he was in America, he travelled extensively on party business. His journalistic work, by 1928, was important enough to appear in New York's *Daily Worker* and collaboration with Richard B. Moore led to editorial work of the Party's Harlem paper *Negro Champion*. Of note during this period was Padmore's concern for black workers, as seen in his involvement in the Harlem Workers' Centre and the workers' school connected with the Party. The education of workers would continue to preoccupy him between his other activities throughout his life.

Moreover, in his work he relied on the new left-wing trade unions. He observed the real problems of inter-racial working class unity and felt that the distance between black and white workers in the southern states was equal to that between Jews and Russian peasants under the Czarist dispensation. Until that point, he had paid little attention to Africa. Within the CP it was assumed that

Afro-Americans would provide the leadership because there were few capable Africans. A generation later, the reverse was assumed: a strong Africa was necessary for the freedom of Afro-Americans. About this time, Nurse, the selfless worker, had fully adopted the name George Padmore.

In March 1928, delegates at the Fourth Congress of the Profintern (or Red International of Labour Unions, RILU, the first genuine participation by Africans), called for more activity in Africa and instructed the Executive Bureau to bring together representatives of the Negro workers to work out 'immediate practical measures for carrying into effect the policy laid down in regard to the question of organising Negro workers in the United States and in Africa'.[44] There was nothing new in this, only a reiteration of a resolution passed at RILU's Second Congress in 1923.[45] At this stage, however, action was taken initially by Willi Munzenberg, a German Comintern member which resulted in a conference held in Brussels 10–15 February 1927 to co-ordinate anti-colonial measures and to reconcile the differences between the antipathetic Amsterdam (or Second) and Red (or Moscow) international labour union bodies.[46] This successful conference was attended by 34 delegates from five continents.

As a direct result, the League Against Imperialism and for National Independence was formed, with Fenner Brockway as General Secretary.[47] Although Brockway resigned, the League remained an important Communist International (Comintern) body until the line changed in 1935.

By the time of the Sixth Congress of the Comintern (15 July–15 September 1928) with Stalin in control of both the Party and the state, the fundamental 'Negro Question' was raised. Padmore thought that Stalin's spokesman, Kuusinen's (who had never seen more than a dozen black people before the Congress) proposal of a 'black republic' was a 'fantastic scheme' intended to secure sections of the Garvey organisation; a peculiar form of 'Negro Zionism which . . . toys with the aristocratic attributes of a non-existent "Negro Kingdom"'. Hitherto, Padmore's speeches reflected a belief in the Party's aid to the black man in America, not to set him apart from it. From here on, he became increasingly preoccupied with Africa. Liberia, in particular, was to him a beacon in the dark continent.

According to Hooker, Padmore did not participate in the Sixth Congress. He was, however, in attendance with James W. Ford at the Second Congress of the League Against Imperialism held in Frankfurt 20–31 July. Padmore was elected a member of the organisational committee, and assigned to get together the names of all West Indian labour organisations. He also wrote articles for the revolutionary press in America and Europe.[48]

The Frankfurt Congress was significant, marking Padmore's entry into international communist activity and brought to an end his activities in America. Indeed, his final contribution to the Party's efforts in the Negro labour struggle was as a delegate to the Trade Union Unity League (TUUL) convention in Cleveland, where he spoke out against white chauvinism and black Uncle Tomism.

Padmore had become an important Party member and had reached the threshold of a great career when he went to Moscow to report on the Cleveland convention. He impressed Party officials and became an important official of Profintern. During 1930, he lectured on colonialism at Kutvu, the University of the Toilers of the East. Although there is doubt as to whether he collaborated with Stalin, it is clear that he did move in important circles, first as an American specialist, and then as head of RILU's Negro Bureau. He also wrote articles on Negro and African affairs to the English language Moscow *Daily News*.

Moreover, Padmore sat on the Commission which investigated the ultra-left deviationist charges levelled against Li Li-san and Mao Tse-tung. Li-Li-sanism was the doctrine which called for the Chinese revolution to be led by the urban proletariat because the rural masses were inert. Interestingly, Padmore agreed with the Commission that the accused was 'fundamentally a young romantic adventurer'.[49] Clearly Padmore had become 'a top person, one who pulled strings and did not move among lesser fry'.

Padmore was instrumental in planning the First International Conference of Negro Workers in Hamburg, 7–9 July 1930. The meeting was originally recommended to be held in London, 'the centre of imperial power', but was refused permission by the Labour government of Ramsay MacDonald. While this stand by the government was understandable in view of the Labour Party's reformism and their paternalistic views of colonial trade unions, it was hypocritical that MacDonald should issue a Circular Despatch urging colonial governments to set up Labour Departments.[50] Of course, such departments were designed to forestall labour unrest which nonetheless exploded thereafter, particularly during the 1930s and 1940s.

In spite of the restrictions in granting colonials passports, 17 delegates managed to attend, including a white representative of black workers in South Africa and workers from Trinidad, Jamaica, Nigeria, Sierra Leone, Gold Coast, the Gambia and the Cameroons. This strong African representation was in contrast to the non-representation of the French, Portuguese and Belgian territories in Africa and the British East African territories.

Given Padmore's broad sweep view of the international struggle, he stressed the connection with revolutionary movements of coloured peoples in Asia, and interestingly, warned against 'Garveyism, Pan Africanism, national reformism and trade union reformism'. The conference ended with the appointment of a new international commission.

Padmore's central role in these revolutionary developments had not gone unnoticed. Fenner Brockway, who was impressed with Padmore when they met later, identified the value of this work as 'encouraging the demand for political independence and stimulating among the native conscripts the idea that when a suitable opportunity came they should fight for their own national freedom'.[51]

Moreover, this conference had an effect on RILU which passed a 'special Resolution on work among Negroes in the United States and the colonies', when the Congress met in March 1931. Earlier, RILU had set up a new arm, the International Trade Union Committee of Negro Workers which began the monthly publication of the *Negro Worker* (the first two issues titled the *International Negro Workers' Review*). It was printed in secrecy in the waterfront district of Hamburg and distributed primarily by black sailors. Following dissolution of the German CP, the missionary society took charge of the house and copies of *Negro Worker* were, fittingly, bound into religious tracts to escape police notice.

In 1931 the Liberian-American and Liberian-League of Nations dispute led to the editor and secretary of the ITUC-NW denouncing imperialism; he saw the Firestone concession as a new phase of imperialist rivalry. Padmore took the opportunity to point out that the Americo–Liberians showed the weakness of Garvey's view that a black bourgeoisie should be trained. He wrote: 'I have always considered it my special duty to expose and denounce the misrule of the black governing classes in Haiti, Liberia and Abyssinia, while at the same time defending these semi-colonial countries against imperialist aggression.'[52]

As a principal spokesman, it was becoming difficult for Padmore to avoid racial references. He maintained, however, in relation to the ITUC-NW that the purpose of the Committee was to build up Negro unions along class rather than race lines. He wrote prolifically and effectively during his first year on the Committee. His output included six of the Committee's twenty-five pamphlets,* and many essays and articles. In his writings, Padmore ridiculed Garvey, criticised the 'petit bourgeois Negro intellectual' DuBois for his anti-communism and attacked Blaise Diagne for supporting French imperialism.

In 1932 Padmore arrived in London and came into contact with C. A. Smith, Chairman of the Independent Labour Party and the Common Wealth Party and editor of *Controversy*.

A year later, while in Germany, with Hitler in power and the German Communist Party on the defensive, Padmore was jailed and deported. On arrival in England he was met by Special Branch officers who were wary of his presence in Britain.

---

* *What Is the International Trade Union Committee of Negro Workers?*; *Life and Struggles of Negro Toilers*; *Negro Workers and the Imperialist War*; *Forced Labour in Africa*; *American Imperialism Enslaves Liberia*; and *Labour Imperialism*.

By mid-1934, Padmore's expulsion notice was served by the Comintern Control Commission. And by the mid-1930s, anti-colonial activity within the Comintern was reduced as the Russians tried to gain greater acceptance in the West. Earlier, in August 1933, Comintern disbanded the ITUC-NW which was welcome news among Western imperialist powers. This act had a major influence on Padmore who immediately resigned the positions he held. Thereafter there have been many versions of his defection. But, perhaps he should be allowed to speak for himself as one who had been holding

> a responsible position in the higher councils of the communist international, which was called upon not only to endorse the new diplomatic policy of the Soviet Government, but to put a break upon the anti-imperialist work of its affiliate sections and thereby sacrifice the young national liberation movements in Asia and Africa. This I considered to be a betrayal of the fundamental interests of my people, with which I could not identify myself. I therefore had no choice but to sever my connection with the Communist International. I formulated my position quite clearly in a political statement which I submitted to the Comintern Executive, and which was subsequently published by the Negro Press, so that my case would be put before my own people. With that the matter was closed as far as I was concerned, and I have never permitted my political objectivity in regard to the Soviet Union to be influenced by my experiences with the Comintern. These are the circumstances in which I resigned from the Communist International, and it is only necessary to add that, in keeping with communist practice, a formal statement of my expulsion followed. But this did not disturb me in the least, for no one whose disassociation from the communist ranks might give rise to any political embarrassment is allowed to make his exit without vilification. Sometimes you are a 'Trotskyist', other times a 'left-wing deviationist', or a 'right-wing deviationist', depending upon the particular period; but I got away with it lightly, as my sin was merely 'petit bourgeois nationalist deviation'.[53]

Thus, Padmore, the 'Top Negro', had descended from the dizzy heights of the CP but he continued to argue for 'Negro Unity' on race rather than on class lines, and attempted an association with DuBois, whom he had earlier attacked.[54] Since his expulsion from the Party, he remained silent under attack and refused (except occasionally) to defend himself. Indeed, he maintained his belief that only the Russians through Communism had succeeded in decolonising and in eliminating racial prejudice.[55]

Black brotherhood in London

In London Padmore became involved with the West African Students' Union. He wrote to DuBois (perhaps the first time he did so) asking for help 'to create a basis for unity among Negroes in Africa,

America, the West Indies and other lands'.[56] Padmore was optimistic about Negro seriousness and cynical about the motives of
middle-class Negro Americans, sentiments which were reinforced
when Dr Willis Huggins came to London from New York, later in
1935, to raise funds for Ethiopia. Huggins was put in touch with
WASU, which, in turn, directed him to C. L. R. James's International
African Friends of Ethiopia, which procured the necessary credentials from the Ethiopian Minister in London. Huggins was not heard
of again.

DuBois was already keen about the idea of a militant youth
movement for the world liberation of 'coloured peoples'. In fact, he
had outlined similar ideas at a conference in New York sometime in
1933 which was resisted by the older NAACP leaders; a resistance
which led to DuBois breaking away from that organisation and to a
closer involvement with the wider perspective of the 'new-style'
Pan Africanists such as Padmore. Thus, by 1934, co-operation
between Padmore and DuBois seemed likely.[57]

Moreover, the LCP had called a conference (on 14–15 July) at the
Albert Hall to consider 'The Negro in the World Today'. The 43
'reformers' headed by Moody, aroused contempt from the militants. Occasionally, however, Padmore and Moody had co-operated, for example in 1938 when the Bledisloe Commission considered the possibility of 'closer association' of the Rhodesias. In
general, however, (and this clearly separated both men) Moody
preferred to be associated with more respectable groups.

Further interest in the 'Negro Question' was engendered by the
worsening of race relations between Italy and Ethiopia which
resulted in Italian aggression in 1935. That year Padmore came to
reside in Britain permanently. He contacted James (who led the
IAFE, a defence committee in support of Ethiopia) whom he had
not seen for three years. About this time, Padmore lived first at the
Vauxhall Bridge Road, then moved to Guildford Street near Russell
Square. He met Ras Makonnen and Eric Williams (then a student
and later Prime Minister of Trinidad and Tobago) who 'followed
Padmore and James closely but never joined their organisations,
preferring instead to prepare for an Oxford first'.[58] T. B. Subasinghe (later to become the Ambassador of Ceylon in Russia),
who was also close to Padmore during 1935–45, recalled that
Padmore 'went through very difficult times in that period. He
conducted political study classes for some colonial students, including myself. Those participating in the study classes made small
contributions to pay him for his lectures. But these were very small
sums of money'.[59] Padmore then met Fenner Brockway, F. A.
Ridley of the ILP, and Reginald Reynolds and his wife Ethel
Mannin.[60]

Padmore, the ex-Comintern member, was not free of the surveillance of British Intelligence agents. A secret circular sent out to the
colonies, advised that 'George Padmore former secretary of the

International Trade Union Committee of Negro Workers has now formed, in conjunction with Tiemeko Garan Kouyate, a prominent French Negro Communist, his own organisation for revolutionary work in Africa, entitled the "Pan African Brotherhood" and already had issued a manifesto on the Ethiopian crisis.' This statement was inaccurate. There was no such organisation in existence, Kouyate was no longer a communist and Padmore was no longer in close contact with him after leaving Paris for London. Nevertheless the Nyasaland government, which had been alerted through the editor of the *Nyasaland Times*, banned the Association's publications. Thus, Padmore's notoriety had extended to the colonies. This did not worry or deter this black revolutionary who had become, if anything, increasingly concerned with the crisis in Ethiopia. His commitment to Africa intensified. This was evident in the fact that after the ITUC-NW, though close to the ILP, he never joined a non-African organisation. Although close to his friend James, he did not become a Trotskyite and the contempt with which he held the British CP was 'boundless'.[61] This detachment from white organisations marked Padmore's clear preoccupation with essentially African affairs.

Nevertheless, the concerns of Africa necessitated maximum publicity which he found through contact with white-controlled organisations and journals in Britain. Through F. A. Ridley he developed a close relationship with the ILP and frequently wrote for its journal the *New Leader* which was edited by Brockway. He never joined the ILP, and repeated efforts by the ILP to secure his candidature for Parliamentary election were unsuccessful.[62]

His enthusiasm and commitment had not wavered since his early years in the United States; Padmore argued that when Europeans expressed horror at General Franco's use of Moorish troops they were not only being inconsistent since substantial numbers of Blacks had been welcomed by the Allies during the World War, but also implicitly racist. Why should they be chilled at the thought of black troops? And did they not see that the black soldiers themselves were a function of imperialism, an aspect of exploited humanity?[63]

The publication of his book *How Britain Rules Africa* in 1936 received generally favourable reviews. He was much respected by other colonials in Britain. That year Padmore met K. D. Kumria, founder of Swaraj (Freedom) House in Percy Street, at an Indian Congress rally. Despite his hostility towards the Congress during his Profintern phase of activity (he always felt they were moving in the wrong direction), he had 'a high regard for people like Jawaharlal Nehru and Subash Chandrabose. But as a Marxist, he also pointed out the limitations of these leaders and of the Indian Nationalist Movement which was under the dominant influence of the Indian bourgeoisie'.[64] Padmore had also developed a warm friendship with Krishna Menon. These ties in later years, especially after 1947, led to Swaraj House becoming a venue for protest meetings of African groups.

In 1937, Padmore's third book, *Africa and World Peace*, was published and the pamphlet *The West Indies Today* was produced in association with Arthur Lewis, then a young student at the London School of Economics. That year, Padmore met Dorothy Pizer (an English woman), his 'wife' with whom he lived before they moved to Cranleigh Street, London NW1 and then to Ghana in 1957. Padmore's residence became the 'headquarters' of anti-colonial agitation for many Africans during the 1940s and the early 1950s. Significantly also in 1937, Padmore had founded the International African Service Bureau (an essentially West Indian organisation); a reconstitution of what was left of James's IAFE defence committee. There was a tendency among Padmore's close friends to minimise the importance and potential of the IASB whose motto was 'Educate, co-operate, emancipate. Neutral in nothing affecting the African people.' Was the IASB too ambitious? One observer wrote that the organisation, formed in March 1937, 'has possibilities for doing constructive work if it limits its field of endeavour, which at present seems too wide for effective work'.[65] In October James went to New York on a speaking engagement and remained in the United States during the war.

Of the seven-member Executive of the IASB, only I. T. A. Wallace-Johnson and Jomo Kenyatta were African. These men felt this 'ginger group' could stimulate publicity to highlight colonial grievances. Fortunately, they had allies such as Brockway who from 1938 placed IASB notices and Padmore's essays in the *New Leader*. In this respect, C. A. Smith helped with *Controversy*. The Bureau was well favoured by members of the British Left, for example Reginald Sorensen, D. N. Pritt, KC, Sylvia Pankhurst, Arthur Creech-Jones and Victor Gollancz. So close was this association that after leaving their 94 Gray's Inn Road premises, the IASB was allowed to use the offices of the ILP before the outbreak of the war. Indeed, Padmore acted as the 'colonial section' of the party.[66]

He was not the only marked man among colonial activists. In a report entitled, 'Wallace-Johnson and the International African Service Bureau', British Intelligence thought Wallace-Johnson to be the Bureau's creator. His connection with Padmore's 'Pan African Brotherhood' further implicated him. After Wallace-Johnson returned home, allegedly over a 'money dispute' among executive members, the Bureau was dominated by Padmore until 1944 when it merged with the Pan African Federation.

If the threat of war in Europe afforded some leverage to colonial agitators, the IASB was ready to exercise it. In September 1938, the Bureau published the manifesto 'Europe's Difficulty is Africa's Opportunity' and stressed that this should not be regarded as a racist view, but a realistic one; opposition was aimed at exploitation, rather than the colour of the exploiter's skin.[67]

Padmore's services in left-wing circles was in great demand. Raymond Postgate, who was editing the journal *Fact* at the time, asked Padmore to write on 'Negro' African Revolt. Padmore, fully occupied with IASB's activities, declined. Postgate managed, however, to get James's essay on 'Negro Slave Revolts'. Padmore was also involved in the joint petition (IASB, LCP, NWA) presented to the Royal Commission to investigate conditions in the West Indies under the chairmanship of Lord Moyne.

When Padmore visited Germany in November, he reported on a mammoth rally at Berlin University, observing a growing colonialist sentiment and how such developments in Germany, tolerantly viewed by many, nevertheless raised real fears among colonials. According to Hooker, scholarly opinion pointed to the conclusion that the Chamberlain government seriously considered attempting to satisfy Hitler with some African territory. Even if this was exaggerated, he argued, the fundamental point was what in fact did Africans think. The IASB editorial secretary, William Harrison (a black American student at the LSE), wrote that the growing race prejudice in Britain was disillusioning subject peoples who, increasingly, were inclined to discount British aims. Further, the former editor of WASU, Ohenenana Cobina Kessie of Ashanti, whose pamphlet *Colonies: What Africa Thinks* went through two editions in two weeks, found white labour invariably racist, saw a European war as being of no concern to Africans and strongly criticised the reported hint that Nigeria might be transferred to the Germans to satisfy their African aspirations. During the year, Padmore emphasised labour matters in South Africa, calling on Africans to show greater race awareness. Ever vigilant, he condemned the likelihood of the three High Commission Protectorates Territories being transferred to South African control. And to forestall such an eventuality the IASB organised a protest meeting in Trafalgar Square.[68]

By the turn of 1939, the IASB helped to call a conference at Friends House, Euston, where continental and British Socialists gathered to discuss the popular front and warn colonial peoples of the dangers.

As the war approached, Padmore's movements continued to be closely monitored. By April, the Special Branch discovered more internal troubles in the IASB. In the absence of Wallace-Johnson, the Bureau's new secretary was Babalola Wilkey, who because of financial difficulties left the IASB to form the Negro Cultural Association which was affiliated to the National Council for Civil Liberties. During the war, the enterprising Wilkey had opened a Colonial Peoples Club in Frith Street, Soho. Whatever truth there might have been in these internal troubles, the IASB had moved from Grays Inn Road to 12A Westbourne Grove, then to the ILP office at St Bride's. Given these hard times, as the police correctly assumed, Padmore virtually ran the ILP Negro affairs.[69]

In June 1939, Padmore expounded his views on military service, a touchy subject, as the war machine was being set in motion. In 'Why I oppose conscription'[70] he argued against support for imperialist war and against co-operating with capitalism because 'the enemy is at home'. Other concerned black leaders and organisations met at a conference of coloured peoples from 7 to 9 July at the Memorial Hall, Farringdon Street. Padmore had to face the Communists who attempted to control the proceedings. Speaking as representative of both the IASB and (Wallace-Johnson's) Sierra Leone Youth League, he objected and during a 'rough session' he impressed one observer as he maintained a dignified bearing 'under fire'. Many who had met Padmore over the years attested to this restraint under attack which was particularly indicative of his attitude to relations with the Communist Party.

In the last days before the war a 'Warning to the Coloured Peoples' was issued, a final statement that Nazis, fascists and democrats were all imperialist bandits whose conflict had no heroes or villains as far as oppressed colonial people were concerned.

By the end of 1939, the 'phoney war' had broken out and Padmore wrote in his article 'The British Empire is the Worst Racket yet Invented by Man' that 'if imperialism means a certain racial superiority, suppression of political and economic freedom of other peoples, exploitation of resources of other countries for the benefit of the imperialist countries, then I say those are not characteristic of this country'. Padmore reiterated his request that British workers should cease their tacit support of the Empire. He was, as he had always been, unsparing in his attack on imperialism. He and the ILP were agreed:

> We were against Hitler and all he stood for when he was being supported by the City of London and when British merchants were flooding Germany with the war goods and munitions he wanted. We were always against him and any form of Totalitarianism and the best and only way to beat him and the Nazis was 'to make Britain Socialist now'.

Particularly galling was the involvement of black colonials in the white imperialist wars.

While Padmore opposed the war, he paradoxically demanded that the colour bar be removed from the services. He refused to make any contribution to the war effort, unlike his friend Jomo Kenyatta who worked as a 'directed labour' farm-hand in Sussex. In October 1943 Padmore told Ernest Bevin, Minister of Labour, of his refusal to undertake directed employment. Although he was offered a post in the Ministry of Information, he declined. He said he would rather go to prison than 'help in any way the war effort of British Imperialism or any other Imperialism'.[71] Interestingly, Bevin ignored Padmore's stubborn refusal, perhaps because the authorities were determined not to make a martyr of him.

During the early months of the war, Padmore spoke frequently against the capitalist and imperialist war. Moreover, he was alerted to the use of the word 'nigger' by a BBC broadcaster. Both the IASB and the LCP complained and the Corporation apologised. This issue led to Padmore's brief co-operation with the LCP. He spoke at their annual general meeting.[72]

Events in Africa and the West Indies continued to preoccupy him. He drew a distinction between national independence and freedom in the West Indies and Africa: 'We demand full self-determination not as an end in itself – for we are not narrow nationalists – but as the historic pre-requisite for the free and voluntary co-operation between all nations and peoples and races.'[73]

In his repeated protests Padmore received the support of West African students who refused to accept that the Allied war aims did not affect them. Thus WASU organised its second conference on West Africa in the summer of 1942 on democracy and its application to that area. The resolutions demanded self-government now and freedom within five years. Given that the majority of colonial students in Britain were from the upper and middle classes (the sons and daughters of the native bourgeoisie, professional men, government officials, chiefs and other petty rulers), Padmore regarded that generation of students as a prelude to freedom. However, this evidence of anti-colonial agitation encouraged Padmore's hope that after the defeat of fascism, a socialist Africa might co-operate with a federated, socialist Britain and Europe.[74]

In 1943, Padmore wrote a number of essays for the *New Leader*: he saw indirect rule as a fraud, the creation of a Colonial Development and Welfare Fund as a hoax. Most of the Moyne Commission recommendations had been shelved 'for the duration' while the big corporations continued to exploit the colonial economies and reap huge war-time profits. He predicted a post-war world that would be ready-made for capitalists.

The achievement of Russia in effecting mass education for her people has had a powerful impact on WASU writers. Thus, the relationship between Russia and colonialism was fundamental to an understanding of Padmore. He was optimistic about the Russian revolutionary achievement which had upset the social, economic and political arrangement between social classes. One of his admirers, Subasinghe, who knew him well wrote:

> He often pointed out that a multi-national state like the Soviet Union could and would maintain its solidarity and hold out against a powerful enemy because of the gains of the people and the manner in which the national question had been solved. This view and his supreme confidence were justified as subsequent events showed.[75]

He was aware of the Russian industrial achievement and was impressed by the co-operation between the various races and peoples. He argued strongly that the Soviet Union had done more to 'liquidate illiteracy and raise the cultural level of the former subject races of Central Asia within twenty-five years than the British Government has accomplished in India or Africa in two centuries'. In effect, the disappearance of the capitalist–imperialist Russian regime meant the disappearance of the oppressor-oppressed relationship between the imperialist metropolis and colonial periphery. [76]

In the light of today's problems of multi-racialism, Padmore's views on socialism and imperialism are worth noting at length: he argued that socialism unites but

> Imperialism divides. Under Imperialism, the native races of Asia and Africa are being kept as illiterate as possible, for history shows that as soon as an educated minority emerges among such subject people it becomes the voice of the national aspirations of the backward inarticulate masses. The idea of national and cultural independence and political unity among multi-racial and national groups is possible only along the lines of a socialised planned economy. And that is why we are witnessing today a tremendous heroic stand of a multi-national state (which because of its many, many different peoples cannot be called 'Russian') which is the marvel of the whole world. [77]

As an anti-Stalinist, Padmore defended the Soviet Union. He insisted that only socialists had the right to condemn Stalin. 'We must while repudiating Stalin's Finnish adventure, dissociate ourselves from all entanglements within the imperialist warmongers and their anti-Soviet campaign.' [78] Nevertheless, Padmore regarded Stalin as a 'harsh tyrant', and harboured the fond memory of having spent three years in the Soviet Union and never encountered 'the slightest manifestation of racial chauvinism or colour bar'. More pointedly one is reminded that he sat on the Moscow Soviet, whereas he could not have aspired to the Port of Spain City Council! In spite of Stalin, he argued, he generally followed Lenin's view of the right of self-determination for national minorities. [79]

Towards the Manchester Pan African Congress

The prospect of a real 'British Socialist Common Wealth Federation – white and coloured' seemed dim to Padmore in October 1944. A survey of the British Socialist scene showed that the ILP lacked a revolutionary basis; the Ernest Bevin and Aneurin Bevan conflict was a quarrel to be expected between socialists and trade union capitalists who controlled the Labour Party, a reflection of Engels' well-founded warning of the progressive bourgeoisification of the British working class. [80] And whatever hope there might have been of building a socialist Britain was strangled by the open 'love affair' between the Colonial Office and the trade unions. [81]

If this was the case in Britain as the hostilities were coming to an

end, what was the future of post-war Africa? American interest in
Africa had become evident. The University of Pennsylvania produced the Office of Strategic Services handbooks to stimulate
interest in the continent. And, of course, business magazines such
as the appropriately named *Fortune* hoped for a good return.
Moreover, the Council on African Affairs organised a conference in
April 1944 in which Kwame Nkrumah played an important part.
The Council was the outcome of a meeting in London before the
war between Paul Robeson and Max Yergan (a lecturer and one of
the sponsors of Padmore's IASB). Their International Committee
on African Affairs was established in New York with a board of
directors including Ralph Bunche, Channing Tobias, Mordecai
Johnson, Rene Maran, Leonard Barnes and, later Alphaeus Hun-
ton, who DuBois described as the 'son of the greatest Negro
secretary the American YMCA ever had'. [82]

During the war, the number of Africans in America, still small,
was nonetheless influential. The African Students Association of
North America was in touch with WASU. Africa House, bought in
Harlem in 1942, served as headquarters for visitors such as
Nkrumah who, in 1943 met C. L. R. James there. Nkrumah was a
graduate student and Fante language informant at the University of
Pennsylvania. James (in the United States under the name Johnson)
gave Nkrumah a letter of introduction to Padmore. [83] Subsequently
James was deported.

When the Council of African Affairs met in New York on 14
April 1944 two proposals seemed particularly promising: firstly the
establishment of an African press centre (put forward by K. A. B.
Jones-Quartey of *The African Interpreter*) and secondly, an international African development authority. Interestingly, at the time,
even the communists believed that the Africans were unable to rule
themselves. One of them, Benjamin Davis felt that most of Africa
was 'not ready for self-government, but nothing will teach these
people faster than a war for world-wide democracy for which they
provide the battleground'. [84]

In post-war Britain, African and colonial matters became a
central theme among Pan African groups, as Moody convened a
conference on the colonial question. At this conference (the first
sponsored by the LCP for some ten years) a background paper was
drafted by the National Council for Civil Liberties Overseas Sub-
Committee. It cited the colour bar, unjust taxation, restriction of
speech and movement, and Wallace-Johnson's case. The conference
called for an end to discrimination in Britain and that immediate
steps be taken to ensure colonial freedom. A 'Charter for Coloured
Peoples' was sent to the Prime Minister who high-handedly felt
that their concern was misplaced. At this point, it seemed that
Moody moved closer to Padmore's position that the Soviet Union
had solved the race relations problem. [85]

Of major significance to the development of radical Pan Africanism was the formation of the Pan African Federation (the last and most ambitious of the pan bodies he was connected with) late in 1944 by Padmore and others such as Peter Milliard and Makonnen (both from British Guiana) who were based in Manchester.

In effect, the IASB had merged into the Pan African Federation, which became the British section of the Pan African Congress Movement. This merger took place in 1944, when representatives of black and colonial organisations in Britain assembled in Manchester to form a Pan African united front movement. The objects of the PAF were broadly based on the principles proclaimed at all the earlier Pan African Congresses:

1. To promote the well-being and unity of African peoples and peoples of African descent throughout the world;
2. To demand self-determination and independence of African peoples, and other subject races from the domination of powers claiming sovereignty and trusteeship over them;
3. To secure equality of civil rights for African peoples and the total abolition of all forms of racial discrimination; and
4. To strive to cooperate between African peoples and others who share our aspirations. [86]

According to Padmore, by pooling resources and liberating themselves from the weakening influence of doctrinaire Marxism which British communists operating through certain Negro fellow travellers were trying to impose upon the African national liberation movements in order to exercise Stalinist control over them, the Pan African Federation was able to take an independent ideological position on the colonial question. The Federation concerned itself with such theoretical problems as the methods and forms of organisation to be adopted by colonial peoples; the tactics and strategy of the national freedom struggle and the applicability of Gandhian non-violent, non-co-operative techniques to the African situation; these were all openly discussed and debated in their journal, *International African Opinion*.

The PAF's publications branch, the Pan African Institute, published a series of booklets. At that time, a young academic at Howard University, Eric Williams, produced a manuscript *The Negro in the Caribbean* which was thought to have 'no market' and Padmore was asked to help its publication in England. Padmore's colleague Dennis Dobson (an English teacher involved in publishing) felt that the work would be more readily intelligible in America. Eventually Padmore (conscious of the stops and starts in publication of his own books) brought out the manuscript himself by persuading the PAF to give the necessary £200.

Early in 1945, after ILO discussions in Philadelphia, a meeting was convened in London to establish a world trades union organisation. The Pan Africanists had not lost sight of their goal – black freedom and independence. Not surprisingly therefore when the conference opened on 5 February in County Hall, London, it quickly became clear that 'peripheral' issues such as colonialism would take precedence. Wallace-Johnson was among the seven colonial trade unionists who attended. He explained that he had made the trip to London because the British recognised that the 'years of their oppression are numbered'. During the proceedings there were real differences: the colonial delegates naturally wanted to discuss the peace settlement and the future of colonial workers, while the British representatives tried to avoid such issues.

When the conference ended on Saturday 17 February, Wallace-Johnson and Ken Hill, the delegate from Jamaica, were asked to stay on to assist in the drafting of a colonial programme for the British TUC. The meeting held on 26 February at Transport House was of major significance, marking the beginning of a new involvement of British labour with colonial workers. After this, the trade unionists were invited by the IASB and members of the PAF to Manchester. There, it was suggested by Padmore that since there had not been a Pan African Conference since 1927, the time was right for another one to be held that September, perhaps in Paris. Although Padmore had talked about such a meeting in the mid-1930s and DuBois had hoped for one since his 1927 Congress, according to Hooker, 'this was the first proposal for the Fifth Congress'.[87]

The idea had caught Padmore's imagination and, as usual, he acted positively. Two weeks after meeting the colonial trade unionists, a 'provisional committee' was set up and a manifesto was drafted (a copy of which was sent to DuBois) and invitations sent to various organisations scattered around the world. At this point, there was a marked emphasis in Padmore's concentration on African affairs. He spent most of his time with African and Afro-Caribbean students. He already knew Kenyatta and became a friend of Nkrumah who had arrived in London from the United States with James's letter of introduction during the war. According to Subasinghe:

> He was becoming more and more cynical about the role of the working class and the so-called anti-imperialists of imperialist countries. He began to advocate the theory that the liberation of the colonial peoples was their own responsibility and that they had to rely on their own resources for their emancipation. Following from this he became more and more interested in the Pan African movement although he was critical of some of the early Pan-Africans. He held Professor DuBois of the United States in great respect and veneration.[88]

Next, an All-Colonial Peoples' Conference organised by the PAF and the Federation of Indian Associations in Britain, WASU, the Ceylon Students' Association and the Burma Association was held on 10 June 1945 in London. By now colonial demands had become unanimous: an end to imperialism, the application of the Atlantic Charter to the colonies, the release of political prisoners, and a universal end to the colour bar, among others. Some delegates felt an All-Negro Conference was necessary and that it should be held jointly with the NAACP in September. Padmore, having expressed this view earlier was optimistic that the outcome of such a meeting could lead, in the near future, to a Pan African conference in Africa.[89] Hitherto, Paris and Africa were mentioned as possible venues; London or elsewhere in Britain was not yet in the reckoning.

As it was, attention was turned to the struggle in Africa where Nigerian civil servants and technical workers were on strike against the cost of living and the marked lack of promotion for Africans. The PAF did not hesitate to support the strikers; an act of solidarity for which Chief A. Soyemi Coker of the Nigerian Trades Union Congress was grateful. Moreover, at a WASU meeting held in Conway Hall in July, Padmore, as the main speaker, spoke forcefully against the suppression of Azikiwe's newspapers. Later that year, WASU again invited him to address their study group.[90]

There was a marked consolidation of Pan African brotherhood and activity. Padmore's growing involvement in African affairs meant a lessening of Asian concerns. The 'Toilers of the East' did not have the immediate importance that the problems of his ancestral home Africa had. According to Hooker, Indian Independence had several consequences for those concerned with African freedom. With much plausibility, it was argued that while Indians could devote attention to the cause of independence elsewhere in the colonial world, often they were more concerned with their own problems than with those in Africa. Indeed, Padmore's Indian friend, Kumria found a steadily widening gap between Indians and Africans in London after Indian Independence in 1947. And despite his long friendship with Brockway's group, Padmore was almost totally immersed in Gold Coast affairs.

Of the Pan African developments in 1945, the September issue of the LCP newsletter reported on a meeting held at the Pan African Institute at 66 Oxford Road, Manchester, on Sunday 12 August, to discuss preliminaries of a congress to be held in England during the month of October. This meeting of representatives of the various 'coloured' organisations in Britain was chaired by Dr Milliard. Padmore, Makonnen, Kenyatta and Peter Abrahams (a South African) were among those on the 'provisional committee' which worked zealously in contacting 'Negro' organisations around the world, drafting an agenda, making the necessary arrangements for delegate accommodation and accreditation and in getting publicity.

A significant addition to this group of organisers was Francis K. Nkrumah who, on his arrival in London in May, with James's letter of recommendation, met Padmore. They liked each other and quickly developed a warm, brotherly friendship and working

relationship. Soon, Nkrumah became Padmore's 'co-political Secretary'.[91] Thus, a 14-year working relationship had begun.
Although many of Padmore's friends were not as impressed,
Padmore almost instantly recognised the single-mindedness of
purpose in Nkrumah's commitment to Africa. Until then, Azikiwe
was Padmore's man in Africa. Now his attention was shifted to
Nkrumah whose commitment and activity in London-based organisations offered real prospects of African freedom. As it was,
Padmore was only three years older but with a greater fund of
experience to draw from. According to Professor John Phillips,
Padmore's influence was clearly a source of help to Nkrumah, but it
was not his but Nkrumah's genius that inspired and waged the fight
for the political, economic and spiritual freedom of Africa.[92] Thus,
George Padmore the elder had met and soon began work with the
younger revolutionary towards freeing Africa from the stranglehold of imperialism.

According to Immaneul Geiss, DuBois had earlier been in touch
with Moody about the prospect of such a Congress, but of course,
to be held at a much later date.[93] It is therefore not surprising that
an LCP member, Sampson Morris, made the announcement of the
Congress by writing in the *Defender* that the conference would take
place in London. This seemed to have been the first public statement that the Congress was to be held in Britain. DuBois was also
trying to organise another Pan African Congress, but was unhappy
about the difficulties, namely the transportation problems of bringing together delegates and his reluctance to allow the planning of
another African meeting to overseas 'Negroes'. In fact, WASU also
had doubts about convening another Pan African conference outside Africa. It came as no surprise then that when DuBois heard of
the British plans of Padmore and his associates, he wished them
well. Indeed, it would seem that he saw these developments in
September 1945 as the forerunner of the Pan African Congress he
had in mind for a later date. Thus, he announced on 29 September
he was coming to London as the NAACP representative. He was
pleased and expected, given his age, 'nothing too spectacular'. He
remarked that 'There is no reason to think that the present Congress is going to be more "Pan African" than the others'. Indeed, he
considered the Congress 'a preliminary one'. The composition of
delegates at this conference represented a change in emphasis from
previous Pan African Congresses. Previously attendance had been
overwhelmingly educated and middle- and upper-class Africans,
whereas now, invitations included a number of African trade
unionists who had already spoken eloquently on colonial matters.
This coming together of the two groups would test the true
character of the Congress. Padmore, in charge of planning may
well have perceived this likelihood in making the arrangements so
that the base of representation could be broadened; a necessary

prerequisite in mobilising the colonial masses in the struggle for national independence.

Finally, the Pan African conference opened on Monday 15 October in Chorlton Town Hall, Manchester, attended by an estimated 100 delegates. Peter Abrahams disputed this figure claiming twice as many. The flags of Haiti, Liberia and Ethiopia were placed in the hall where Mrs Amy Jacques Garvey (widow of Marcus Garvey) chaired the first session on the colour problem in Britain. By now, the problems were a familiar cry: unemployment ashore and at sea, the support of illegitimate children fathered by black Americans and discriminatory treatment by the police. The Nigerian WASU delegate was forthright in encapsulating the problems of black people in Britain: 'If the British people think they have the right to live in Africa', he said, 'then we have the right to stay here. We have the right to get together and see that something is done for us here.'[94] Another speaker representing the Coloured People's Association in Edinburgh pointed out that the African 'student class' in Britain had separated itself from the general body of black people in Britain and that this made the struggle 'more difficult'.[95]

The Tuesday session was chaired by DuBois whom Padmore introduced. Nkrumah was the rapporteur. DuBois had been to all five Congresses but was never treated to the kind of speech he was about to hear from Joe Annan, a trade unionist from the Gold Coast who said:

> I am here as a workman, a man who wields tools, a man who knows no colour. I want you to feel that nothing we can do here is of any avail unless we are in a position to implement the resolutions that we are going to make. . . . So I suggest that before this Congress breaks up on Sunday we set up administrative machinery to cope with the difficulties which lie ahead of us. My workers have given me this mandate: to inform you that they are prepared to spend their last penny in order to maintain an office in London. That is a practical issue.[96]

This kind of speech struck responses in Nkrumah which he said, 'Shot into limbo the gradualist aspirations of our African middle classes and intellectuals and expressed the solid down-to-earth will of our workers, trade unionists, farmers and peasants who were decisively represented at Manchester, for independence.'

On the third day, the Congress rescinded the appointment of chairperson for each session and Padmore declared DuBois permanent Chairman 'as a token of esteem and respect'. The Congress passed resolutions on West Africa, the Congo and North Africa, East Africa, the Union South Africa, the three British Protectorates, the West Indies (urging West Indian Federation), another on the problems of black seamen in England, one on race relations in the United Kingdom and one on South Africa. Delegates were urged to implement all Congress resolutions. Nkrumah felt that the Congress was important because 'for the first time, the delegates who attended it were practical men of action and not, as was the case at the four previous conferences, merely idealists contenting themselves with writing theses but quite unable or unwilling to take any active part in dealing with the African problem. Like Garveyism, the first four conferences were not born of indigenous African consciousness.' Thus, it was this Fifth Pan African Congress that provided the outlet for African nationalism and brought about the awakening of an African political consciousness, which became a mass movement of Africa for the Africans.

Significantly Nkrumah emphasised that the seizure of political power was the first step, the necessary prerequisite to 'complete social economic and political emancipation'; and that the strike and boycott were the weapons. However, unless colonial intellectuals realised their own responsibilities, the masses would not realise their strength. He added: 'Today there is only one road to effective action – the organisation of the masses. And in that organisation the educated Colonials must join. Colonial and subject Peoples of the World – Unite!'[97]

At the final session of this historic Congress, DuBois was elected International President and Liberia was to be host for a Sixth Congress. Having achieved a notable Pan African success, Padmore had not forgotten the toilers of the East. He proposed that greetings be sent to the 'masses in India' and a statement to the peoples of Indonesia and Vietnam. DuBois returned to the United States convinced that he had participated in an important event; there was a new colonial abroad, he wrote in the *Defender*.[98] For Padmore, who had via Communism been central in convening this successful Fifth Pan African Congress, the end of the Congress marked the beginning of a new dawn in Africa. This post-war turning point deserved a fanfare but significantly, with the exception of the *New Leader* and the black American press, the white British press ignored the Congress.

After the Congress, the PAF remained in Manchester but the 'Committee' was located in Padmore's London residence. Wallace-Johnson suggested the formation of a West African Secretariat which Nkrumah welcomed. Thus, the West African National Secretariat was established with Nkrumah as Secretary. Based in Gray's Inn Road, WANS published a journal *New African* which was short-lived. At the end of August 1946, a joint conference was called by WASU and WANS. The delegates (including West Africa) reaffirmed the goals of the Fifth Congress and felt that a West African federation was an indispensable first step towards a Pan Africa. It was agreed to call another meeting which never took place. According to Padmore, their aim was a United Socialist States of Africa.[99] The conference was not held because Nkrumah was called home to work with the United Gold Coast Convention. [100]

During the summer of 1946 Padmore was asked by the Free Indian Press to report on the Paris peace conference. While in Paris he distributed copies of his new book *How Russia Transformed Her Colonial Empire*. From a journalistic viewpoint he was fortunate in meeting Ho Chi Minh who gave him a two-hour interview. According to Padmore's nephew, Dr Luke, Padmore had met Ho during his Comintern days. Hooker has argued that although this may be true, Padmore's references to Ho 'rather contradict the notion'. However, the connection was close enough: thereafter, he became 'the unofficial guardian of Viet-Minh interests in London'. [101] On the question of the peace conference, Padmore had misgivings, in spite of the fact that it was more democratic than the 1919 conference. Overall he saw little hope of serious consideration of African affairs and was concerned with the encroaching threat of American global strategy.

Significantly, the British Centre Against Imperialism came into being in February 1946 – a post-war counterpart to the League Against Imperialism. Padmore spoke at their first meeting on 'Africa and the West Indies', referring to the Fifth Pan African Congress as the first step in the long struggle. A month earlier, he had launched his newsletter *The Colonial Parliamentary Bulletin: A Monthly Record of the Colonies in Westminister* (produced in his Cranleigh Street flat by the African Press Agency for the IASB) which lasted two years. During this period Padmore was optimistic that the second Labour government would combat racial discrimination and tended to blame American troops for racial conflict in Britain. His unusual optimism was reflected in the fact that he felt government action would come about directly and largely from the agitations of the PAF. [102]

After the war, the shift in Padmore's thinking towards West African affairs had become more marked. Ever concerned with relating the struggle in Britain to Africa he was again involved in the joint sponsorship of an anti-colonial meeting between the LCP and the PAF in December 1946. Padmore's wide interests had brought him in contact with many well-known Blacks. Earlier, in 1944, through membership of the Coloured Writer's Association, Padmore met Richard Wright the American novelist, thus beginning a long friendship and collaboration.

The next year, in May, Padmore, concerned with the growing unrest in East Africa attacked Arthur Creech-Jones, the Colonial Secretary. This helped their relationship little. After Padmore's new alliance with Leslie Hale in the House of Commons, Brockway returned to the House and 'became the very natural and very distinguished leader of the group interested in colonial affairs on the labour back benches'. [103] That same month, Harold Moody was buried. Thus ended the uneasy alliance between the black 'Moderates' and the black 'Radicals'. Padmore attended the funeral as the PAF representative. In effect, this was the end of the LCP which had worked dedicatedly for reforms. Predictably, after Moody's death, Padmore had little to do with the LCP, although Dorothy Pizer remained on the editorial committee.

Soon after, when a delegation from the National Council of Nigeria and Cameroons, led by Azikiwe, arrived in London to protest against the Richards Constitution in Nigeria, Padmore, acting as Press Secretary, put Azikiwe's group into direct contact with Nkrumah's WANS, WASU and PAF. Nkrumah was active in all three. The minimal involvement of the NCNC at the Manchester Congress had, through Azikiwe's endorsement of the Congress's aims, a closer involvement. The coming together of Nkrumah, Azikiwe (Padmore's great African hopes) and other representatives in London, consolidated West African aspirations and interests. It must be remembered that in all this Padmore's role was essential.

The major break came for African aspirations when Nkrumah was offered the UGCC Secretaryship. With Padmore's strong approval, Nkrumah accepted. According to Brockway, 'Padmore exerted a considerable influence in getting Nkrumah to go back to Ghana, despite the reactionary leadership of the Gold Coast nationalist movement.' In February 1948 riots had broken out in Accra, marking the beginning of Nkrumah's positive action campaign. Evidently, Britain's continued control over the Gold Coast was at risk. Padmore condemned the police who were responsible for the violence, and at a rally in Trafalgar Square he challenged Rees Williams, the Colonial Under-Secretary, who argued that the rioters were not nationalists but communists. Padmore argued that the Labour government showed more concern for the United Company of Africa than the real needs of colonial peoples. Padmore's radical stance received the support of the reformist LCP, when he argued that the 'spectre of Pan Africanism is haunting the "dark continent"'. The confrontation in Accra following Nkrumah's return to the Gold Coast had set in train a process of enlargement of Nkrumah's past. Already he was being referred to as 'Professor of Philosophy at Pennsylvania University'.

In the summer, Padmore had reported on the Paris Congress of Peoples (an international socialist conference) attended by Brockway, McNair of the ILP, and Bob Edwards of the Chemical Workers Union. Significantly, several delegates attended 'the last international socialist gathering to which Africans were attracted in significant numbers'.[104]

Between 1948 and early 1957, Padmore continued to speak and write. After speaking at the ILP Summer Schools at Bangor on the topic 'Is Imperialism Dead?' in 1950, he was invited to visit the Gold Coast at a time when Nkrumah felt confident that the Convention Peoples' Party would win the elections in February

1951. Indeed, he wanted Padmore to write the history of the post-war events. During this visit, Padmore also went to Nigeria. He was optimistic that Azikiwe 'could emerge as a truly national figure in the Nkrumah sense only if tribalism were eliminated'. [105] Padmore was invited back to Accra (in August 1951) to witness Nkrumah's installation as Leader of Government Business at the re-opening of the Legislative Council.

On his return to London in early October, he began work on a new book, *The Gold Coast Revolution*, which was printed in spring 1953. In the book, Padmore depicted Nkrumah 'as the embodiment of the hopes which international socialists had for renascent Africa and claimed that the Gold Coast colony had gone down a road all Africa would follow'. [106] Another book to consider with Nkrumah's call for a Pan African Congress early in 1955 was Padmore's last and best known work, *Pan Africanism or Communism?*

He regarded Richard Wright's book *Black Power* as 'a very good book indeed'. In 1956 Padmore seemed preoccupied with the Gold Coast elections. Even at that stage, he feared that the tricky British imperialists were likely to pull a 'fast one' given the opportunity. [107] Indeed he was ever aware of the dangers, and was one of the first to identify the 'new danger' of neo-colonialism.

Padmore's hectic work-rate had continued. During the summer of 1956, his health had deteriorated to the extent that he had to cancel his summer school lecture. He was admitted to hospital and confined to bed with a severe chill on the bladder.

His friend Dr Clarke recommended a warm climate. In the meantime, his work *Pan-Africanism or Communism?* was published with a strong preface by Richard Wright. And significantly, the radicalisation of Pan Africanism had brought about its first triumph in Ghana, the 'Black Star' of Africa.

In March 1957 Padmore, Dr Clarke and Professor Arthur Lewis were among the prominent West Indians invited to attend the Ghanaian Independence ceremonies in Accra. Other guests included his former teacher, Ralph Bunche. Hugh Smythe wrote in the *Crisis* that Padmore 'is the silent hero of Ghana and a figure venerated and respected throughout black Africa'. By August, although he had started yet another project for the *Pan African News Agency*, he announced that he was moving to Accra. One of his concerns at that time was the prospects of West Indian Federation and the role of Eric Williams. [108] He responded to the lies in the British press about Nkrumah by stating that Nkrumah was 'the George Washington, the Father of his country'. Now that Ghana had achieved Independence, Padmore monitored its progress and retained a close interest in Nigeria. He was now fully committed to consolidation in Ghana and liberation in Africa as a whole.

By the autumn of 1957, he was appointed as Nkrumah's adviser on African affairs. Before he left London, Dr David Pitt, who was active in Labour Party politics, whose surgery was used as a meeting place for nationalist groups, organised a small party in November, at which Padmore was surprised with the presentation of a briefcase. [109] Among the guests was C. L. R. James, the only representative from the pre-war crowd. Most of those present never saw him again. In effect, Padmore's days in London were over. He had travelled through America, Europe, Asia: now, he was heading 'home' to Africa.

In Ghana, he was disturbed to discover substantial opposition to his presence. If Padmore was treated this way, one wonders how Garvey and his followers might have been received in Africa. In July 1959, as Nkrumah's personal adviser, Padmore attended a meeting of the heads of state of Liberia, Guinea and Ghana in the village of Saniquelle in Liberia. In this 'miserable location' he contracted dysentery which seriously undermined his delicate health. By then, he had already felt a sense of discouragement at the obstacles in the path of Pan African unity. Overall, he was sick, disappointed, uncomfortable in public life and 'unhappy in his private circumstances'. Moreover, his deteriorating health could no longer be ignored. In September, he took leave and arrived in London for medical examination. Dr Clarke diagnosed a severe liver deterioration and Padmore was admitted to University College Hospital on Sunday 20 September. Three days later, though he fought for life, he died. In his foreword to *Pan Africanism or Communism?* Wright wrote that Padmore was the greatest living authority on the African nationalist movements, who not only understood their leaders' aims, structures and ideologies, but whose life embodied those movements, aims and ideologies. [110]

After a funeral service at Golders Green Crematorium on Monday 28 September, Padmore's ashes, at Nkrumah's request, were flown to Ghana where they were interred at Christianborg Castle on 4 October. Moved by this loss, Nkrumah said:

> When I first met George Padmore in London some fifteen years ago, we both realised from the beginning that we thought along the same lines and talked the same language. There existed between us that rare affinity for which one searches for so long but seldom finds in another human being. We became friends at the moment of our meeting and our friendship developed into the indescribable relationship that existed between two brothers. [111]

In death the Ghanaians began to institutionalise Padmore; but the man himself was quickly forgotten. In fact his entire pre-1957 career was put aside by friends and enemies alike who preferred to concentrate on the seemingly glamorous last years in Ghanaian employment. Padmore, the 'black revolutionary', 'father of African emancipation', was much more. According to Hooker, he was 'the expositor of the black man's dignity, the nagging conscience of a white man's world'. Indeed, for most of his life he moved in the white man's world, traversing the physical and intellectual Pan African quadrangle and beyond in a searching journey from the periphery to the centre; from Communism to Pan Africanism. In effect, he had joined the ranks of the Pan Africanists Blyden and Sylvester-Williams, whom he held in such high esteem.

The place of Pan Africanism in history

Pan Africanism, seen by one observer as a twentieth-century historical phenomenon with nineteenth-century roots and precursors, in most cases, involved small and weak groups which came together to form ephemeral organisations. Their ideas and plans printed in transient journals, to some extent, explain the scarcity of research material and the dearth of historical scholarship on Pan Africanism until recently. Of course, Pan Africanism is also a product of history, particularly in relation to decolonisation in Africa which brought its first successes.

It has been argued that a tendency to emotionalism, lack of precision, general lists of demands or declamatory statements, a lack of attention to clarification of the movement's basic theoretical principles, resulted in a lack of committing anyone to a specific course of action. Together, these factors contributed to the fundamental weaknesses of Pan Africanism. Moreover, instead of becoming the ideology of consistent modernisation, Pan Africanism, according to Geiss, was either romanticised or merged into the 'lost paradise' of Africa, [112] or attempts were made to integrate both modern and traditional elements.

Geiss, however, in making a valid criticism of this contradiction, neglected the fundamental fact that without an understanding of traditional Africa and the black man's history, it is remarkable that a historical movement such as Pan Africanism could begin at all, never mind cope with the problems of modernisation. Therefore, it is no good attacking DuBois's enthusiasm for Liberia in 1923–24 (a brief period given his long life) and Nkrumah's pagan ritual at Aggrey's grave in November 1942, as 'manifestations of this inner contradiction'. Indeed, the presence of this dynamic was a reflection of the historical shifts and flexibility in the development of Pan Africanism. Cut and dried principles, given this hazardous course, simply could not be applied. Unfortunately, Geiss chose to ignore the consistent principles within which most Pan African organisations operated. With few exceptions, the goal of all of them was hardly in doubt; there was a fundamental continuity.

In spite of its organisational 'weaknesses', Pan Africanism has had a major impact in bringing about the decolonisation of Africa. Pan Africanism and African nationalism benefited from two basic factors: firstly, the lack among colonial powers of a colonial policy of modernisation in their colonies; and secondly, the fear of revolt in the colonies if African nationalists became disillusioned and turned to Communism. [113] Geiss argued that the suddenness with which post-war developments led to the long-awaited triumph of Pan Africanism, Independence, also brought its post-Independence problems. But, either a short or long period of adjustment would have mattered little in the face of the looming problems of neo-colonialism, which troubled Padmore.

Pan African leaders have also been criticised for 'pushing ahead so impatiently'! After a long history of slavery and oppression, how else could they proceed? Clearly, the Pan African nationalists after 1945, felt it was better to govern themselves badly than go on being governed by foreign imperialists. In concluding his study of the Pan African movement Geiss wrote:

> All 'Pan' movements in the underdeveloped societies face the same basic problem, the clash between the traditional world and modern influences. In trying to solve this conflict, universal to our age, the modernized elites of each country have acted in very different ways, according to their specific historical circumstances. . . . It offers an approach to the history of Africa and of the Afro-Americans. It throws light upon new aspects of European racism and colonialism, against which Pan Africanism rose in revolt. [114]

But, the essential Pan Africanist Marxist historian and thinker, C. L. R. James (85 at the time of writing), in his conclusion to *A History of Pan African Revolt*, commenting on the fact that Dr Nyerere had broken to pieces the old system of education and substituted a genuinely socialist and humanist procedure for youth in Tanzania, wrote: 'It can fertilise and reawaken the mortuary that is socialist theory and practice in the advanced countries. "Marxism is a Humanism" is the exact reverse of the truth. The African builders of a humanist society show that today all humanism finds itself in close harmony with the original conceptions and aims of Marxism.'[115]

The black radical intelligentsia had, by the late 1950s, left Britain. They returned to the colonies to educate, organise and involve the masses. As they expected, the post-war colonial world had not changed materially. The problems were of massive proportions: poverty, malnutrition, high unemployment, low wages, deplorable standards of living and working conditions enforced by local and foreign capitalists. In Britain, however, the reverse was true.

In the post-war prosperity, Padmore was one of the first to recognise the effects of neo-colonialism. British capital demanded cheap black labour, as the British working class achieved upward occupational mobility and social status. The vacated, low-paid, low-status, dead-end jobs, at the base of the occupational pyramid were filled by black migrant newcomers – the black working class. This substitution would, in time, weaken working class unity and increase the racist tendencies of white workers who formed part of the substantial middle class in post-war Britain.

7 Post-war Immigration: Racism, Riot and Legislation

The newcomers who arrived in Britain between 1947 and 1962 dispersed to several parts of the country. Although the majority stayed in London, many went to Liverpool, Manchester, Cardiff, Birmingham, Bristol, Nottingham, Bradford, Leeds, Leicester, Wolverhampton and other towns and cities. In short, at least initially, they joined family and friends who had preceded them. This chapter will concentrate essentially on the problems West Indians faced in Nottingham and Notting Hill in London, where white racism greeted them, increased and exploded into racial riots. In terms of both geography and time, the focus of British racism had shifted from Cardiff and Liverpool to Nottingham and Notting Hill. And interestingly, given a larger and growing black presence, the same repeated calls for black repatriation now had a similar and unprecedented urgency. Let us now examine the developments in these specific areas and, most importantly, how the outcome profoundly affected all black people in Britain and indeed, elsewhere.

The main causes of the migration of West Indians in the post-war period were the pressure of population and the high level of unemployment and under-employment. Furthermore, low wages and the lack of opportunity had caused West Indians to look beyond the Caribbean for economic development. Moreover, doors to other countries were closed.[1] The 1952 McCarran–Walter Act, for instance, reduced considerably the number of West Indians going to the United States.

As British subjects, West Indians naturally turned to the more accessible British prospects. They were brought up in the British tradition, held British values and they had a legal right of free entry into the United Kingdom. Britain's post-war economic development held real promise. Job opportunities in Britain were clearly greater than in the West Indies. News of West Indians (some 8000 of them) who had served in the Royal Air Force and in the munitions factories during the Second World War, became well-known in the Caribbean. Optimism was engendered by the fact that some West Indians had reached commissioned rank and in spite of evidence of discrimination, the majority of those who served were able to admit 'the absence of discrimination in the armed services'. Through their war-time experiences, West Indians were introduced to an advanced industrialised economy. The precedent they set made it easier for their fellow West Indians (and indeed some who had returned home) to come to Britain after the war.

By 1950, West Indian immigration to Britain had already begun in a small and unorganised way. There were no regular steamship services between the Caribbean and Britain. In response to a growing demand, these services soon expanded. Going to Britain became a new line of enterprise for local businessmen and travel agents, which in turn had a snowball effect. Moreover, while West Indian governments did not encourage emigration, most of them permitted it. Indeed, in one case, the government was actively involved. In view of it having 'the most densely populated territory' of the West Indies Federation, with 'high unemployment' and a long history of emigration, the Barbados government actually gave assistance to migrants and helped to arrange jobs and accommodation in Britain. The number receiving such aid, however, was small. In general, West Indian migrants made their own arrangements to get to Britain. Warnings of housing and employment difficulties did not deter prospective migrants. Those who eventually made the trip were determined to succeed.

On arrival in Britain, the authorities did not ignore the immigrant, at least initially. Whatever help they received became increasingly politically motivated. The British Caribbean Welfare Service established in 1956 was one such body designed to help migrants. Two years later, the BCWS, granted a 'more definite social status', was renamed the Migrant Services Division of the Commission in the United Kingdom for the West Indies, British Guiana and British Honduras. This body (supplied with information from West Indian governments) increasingly supervised the arrival of migrants to Britain.

In the 1950s, more West Indians came to Britain than did

Africans, Indians and Pakistanis. According to an official estimate, there were about 210,000 black people, a small minority, less than half of 1 per cent of the total British population.[2] Though similar to the black population of London in the late eighteenth century (in that it was relatively small) the circumstances in 1958, in many ways, presented a 'new situation' of a black population that was growing, that came to Britain 'voluntarily' and was 'free'.

Moreover (with this increased West Indian immigration) during the 1950s black people became far more visible. In recent times no other minority group aroused emotions and controversies of the same intensity and on the same scale as the Blacks. For example, when the Poles migrated to Britain during and after the Second World War (indeed this was a conscious British policy to avoid black settlement) there was far less interest, although the number of Poles settled in Britain in 1960 was roughly equivalent to that of the West Indians. The difference between the two was that West Indians in Britain were (and are) more visible, by virtue of colour, than the Poles. Whatever truth there is in the argument that the difficulties of all newcomers to Britain are alike, it must be remembered that it is also true that the difficulties of black people confront them in an accentuated form. It is futile to argue that they are simply immigrants. As black migrants they were made to feel alien in almost every way. The dilemma of colour prejudice stalked black people wherever they went in Britain. White newcomers, by contrast, had alternatives: they could, for example, fade into the rest of the population and in time lose the more obvious marks of foreignness such as accent. Dark-skinned migrants, however, could not get rid of their colour, even if they wanted to. Given this fact, black migrants set about making a living in Britain. Firstly, they had to find accommodation and, crucially, the employment for which they came.

In London, through sheer necessity, West Indians tended to concentrate in six main areas, two of which continue to be of particular importance. Significantly, each contained well over one-fifth of all West Indians in the London group. The first was the West area stretching from Paddington, through North Kensington and Notting Hill to Shepherd's Bush and Hammersmith. The second, was the South West area with migrants' settlements in Brixton, Stockwell and South Lambeth. Since 1955, there have been slight shifts in the importance of these two areas, with more West Indians moving to the South West area. From 1956 to the end of 1958 more migrants went to Brixton than to Notting Hill, thus belying the popular assumption that Notting Hill was the main reception area for black migrants.[3]

In spite of the concentrations there were very few dense geographical clusters of West Indians in London. Indeed, such 'clusters' existed only in a few districts, particularly in and around Brixton and North Kensington. It was estimated that less than one in five of all the migrants in London lived in these clusters, while over 40 per cent lived in streets where by 1960, there was no indication of multiple West Indian tenancy. According to one observer, these dense concentrations were not 'ghettoes'. Thus, it was argued that the images of Notting Hill and Brixton as 'Harlems' in London was far removed from reality, for only a small proportion of Blacks lived in these places and in most of these districts it was not black people but Whites who were predominant.[4]

Be that as it may, these districts were not considered for re-development and would, in time, become 'decaying' areas. With a substantial and growing black presence in London, the problems of the inner city (already decaying and depressed) had its effect on the newcomers in such areas as housing, education and the crucial area of employment. Indeed, these were the core problems of settlement and adjustment of a steadily accumulating black working class in Britain.

Housing

On arrival in Britain, employment and housing were clearly the two crucial problems facing black migrants in London. These were indeed problems of a personal kind. Whether major or minor, their difficulties were rooted in race and colour prejudice which was (and still is) essentially the black experience in finding jobs and houses. Between 1954 and 1958, housing was at least as serious a problem as employment. Indeed they were directly related. In fact housing appeared to be the more intractable of the two. The Migrant Services was rarely able to assist the migrants (to their satisfaction) in finding accommodation. Consequently, mutual help within the migrant community was the only real alternative.

West Indian newcomers to London initially tended to spend one night at least with a friend or relative. Few migrants arrived without an address. Temporary accommodation was found occasionally in Salvation Army hostels and by welfare officers (from the Colonial Office, the London County Council and the Red Cross) who met them. Similar arrangements were made for nurses and for those Barbadians who came to Britain under their government's scheme. The West Indian Welfare Officer, employed by the London Transport Executive was charged with finding accommodation for workers recruited by the Executive. Few migrants, however, had been helped in this way. Indeed, the vast majority found accommodation through personal contacts and sheer determination.

Fortunately, the newcomers were not only able to draw on the help of recent migrants, but also from those who had earlier established themselves in London. In effect, their houses became 'hostels' for newcomers. Unofficial 'reception centres' of this kind were established; one in North Kensington, several in Camberwell and Brixton, one in Islington and one in Hampstead. Outside London, two became well-known to Welfare Officers as 'Sloobucks' (Slough, Berkshire) and 'Baldockerts' (Baldock, Hertfordshire).[5]

The scattered locations of these 'reception centres' (most within a radius of six miles from Charing Cross) avoided the creation of a 'coloured quarter'. Migrants had, however, frequently tried to get more permanent accommodation as close to their first bases as possible. The inertia of the islanders was evident in this. 'We're all in the same boat now, boy', West Indians often repeated.

Another factor in the location of these 'first bases' was due to chance, as in the case of West Indian settlement in Brixton. For example, when the first large group of West Indian migrants arrived in 1948 on the *Empire Windrush*, 242 were temporarily accommodated in Clapham Common Underground Station which had been used as an air-raid shelter. Blacks who sought a living in Britain presented officials with a problem.

The Colonial Office was now seriously concerned about the *Windrush* men. Mr Creech Jones wrote to Councillor Jack Simpson, Mayor of Lambeth, whose borough was close to Clapham Common, and asked if some welcome could be arranged. Councillor Simpson with an allowance of £600 for the whole year said he could entertain only forty Jamaicans. So, on the afternoon of Wednesday, 3 June, in a room over the Astoria Cinema, Brixton, a representative group of Jamaicans were invited to tea by the Mayor. Local officers and two MPs were also there. In expansive mood, Colonel Marcus Lipton, Labour Member for Brixton, told the men that they should regard Brixton as their second home. The Mayor offered his good wishes and commented: 'When I heard of your coming here I was moved. A journey like yours does not take place without good reason.' Afterwards, the migrants were treated to a free cinema show. On their return to the air-raid shelter that evening the forty men described the reception to their friends. According to Joyce Eggington, 'They spoke with enthusiasm, joyous that a few people had taken the trouble to make them feel welcome. The limited sum of money spent was not important: tea and cakes had been as effective as champagne. In the unknown and perplexing vastness of England, the Jamaicans now felt they could be sure of one place. Brixton was friendly. In Brixton they would make their homes.'[6]

After this welcome most of the men were employed locally which was an added incentive to stay in the district. This was only the beginning of migrant settlement.

The areas of West Indian settlement in London (North, West and South) had several common features. These areas, by virtue of their history and location, offered accommodation (albeit shabby) to the mass of migrants who constituted a low income group. In the main, West Indians could not find accommodation in the working class districts of the East End and the southern riverside boroughs where, because of the stability of the population and tenancies, there was no room for sub-division. The ranks of the white working class were effectively closed. Moreover, the newcomers at that time were not eligible for the new municipal flats and houses built by the LCC and the Metropolitan boroughs. The middle class and upper class districts of Hampstead, Chelsea, Westminster and South Kensington, among others, were closed to most of the West Indian migrants, except a small minority who were more prosperous.

Indeed many old streets and squares became fashionable and expensive, particularly because, in general, the residential capacity of Central London had been (and is still being) depleted. Office blocks, stores and hotels competed with each other for space in central London. Meanwhile, the scarcity of residential accommodation and space was not effectively counteracted by official planning policy. In fact, the London planners' objective was not to encourage population but to discourage it; patterns of development had been designed accordingly.

For the West Indian newcomers, such a policy was hardly accommodating. In these circumstances, they could only be housed in restricted areas. They had no choice. Of necessity then, they had to stay as close to the central London labour market as possible. Coralled into bad housing, these migrants lived in neglected patches of London, which had been in the process of 'decline and social downgrading'.

The rooms they inhabited were in a state of decay. Nineteenth century basements, in an advanced stage of deterioriation, clumsy and ugly, became the homes of the migrants. Some accommodation near the Portobello Road and Paddington Station were 'so forbidding that they were a mistaken speculation from the start; they were never, or only briefly occupied by the fairly prosperous families for whom they had been intended'.[7]

In spite of these conditions, among the more enterprising West Indians necessity brought invention. Many applied themselves industriously and soon the drab surroundings assumed a colourful appearance. But for all their native inventiveness (apart from those which were beyond repair), some lodgings could only be temporary and as such, presented an even more depressing prospect.

In the continued expansion of London's commercial centre, it was not unusual to see both decay and rejuvenation existing side by side. Such contrasts were pronounced in North Kensington where the front of the buildings indicated that migrants might be living there. Moreover, the condition of the streets and their surroundings revealed 'an important aspect of the so-called "colour problem"'.

Since Charles Booth's *New Survey of London Life and Labour* in the 1920s, there had been a rapid deterioration in this area with gaps along streets of terraced housing. According to one observer, the 'missing house seemed to have fallen down'. These were the so-called 'streets of transition' where a large number of West Indians found rooms. Not surprisingly bombed out sites formed part of the surroundings. At the periphery of one of these zones of transition are Notting Dale and Kensal New Town, which were in transition in the late nineteenth century. Since then they came to be called 'the rotten parts of the Royal Borough'.[8]

These districts became notorious for their poverty, overcrowding and crime. In 1924 Kensal New Town presented a dismal picture as one of the worst districts in London. Social workers regarded bad housing in Southam Street (with its nine-roomed houses in which 2500 people were living in 1923, an average of two persons in every room in the street) as surpassing the Special Area of Notting Dale. Some rooms were described as 'slum basements, where rheumatism and consumption and drink scribble their names on the dirty wallpaper'. Not surprisingly, this part of North Kensington figured weekly in the police news.[9]

By 1951 Kensal New Town had the highest rate of overcrowding in London, some five times greater than the average for the London area as a whole. In Golbourne Ward (which includes Kensal New Town) 12.7 per cent of the population were living at a density of more than two persons per room at the 1951 Census date. The comparable percentage of overcrowding for the whole area of North Kensington (consisting of four wards) was then 6.8 per cent; that for the borough of Kensington (North and South) 4.6 per cent; while that for the county of London was 2.5 per cent.[10]

Growing immigration made the 'zones of transition' denser. Consequently, housing conditions deteriorated and rents increased. West Indians lived in poor accommodation and paid high rents. Given their low incomes there was no alternative. This led to overcrowding. Several migrants sharing one small room was not uncommon. In the limited living space, they slept, cooked and ate, staying indoors (except when the weather was warm) for most of their free time. Generally, furniture was bare and simple and washing facilities were shared with others. Under these cramped conditions, West Indians used to the open air, found their accommodation in London suffocating and hard to accept. In their rooms they felt 'home-sick'.

For such accommodation as they had, these migrants paid a standard rent ranging between £2 to £2.10s. and £3 per week. The West Indian writer, Sam Selvon, living in London at the time, coined the phrase, 'a two and ten room'.[11] Within this rent-band however, there were a number of variations upwards, never or rarely downwards. Landlords exploited migrants mercilessly. Black tenants were threatened with violence to prevent them from seeking a reduction in their rent from a rent tribunal. These so-called 'shark' landlords plagued migrants exploiting their real and worst fears of homelessness. In spite of overcrowding (however unattractive their rooms) many West Indians kept clean houses and took pride in making their living quarters as comfortable as possible.

In perspective, it was clear that West Indians were pushed into a decaying environment which became their permanent homes. In effect, prejudice and discrimination limited their opportunities for better accommodation. The migrants' complaints were, in time, echoed by many observers. Thus, the vicious circle became well-known: 'While high rents overcrowding and sharing are in part caused, and certainly accentuated by colour prejudice, such conditions, in turn, create prejudice. There is thus further deterioration, and more of the same.' This was a classic case with West Indians competing for scarce space and amenities with white tenants who were themselves, for a long time, badly housed. Consequently, physical and social claustrophobia was attributed to the black newcomers. Dissatisfied Whites were hypersensitive. Accordingly, migrants were classified and an image of the black person was built up as an 'intruder' to be blamed for the frustrated hopes of improvements. But, as The Times reported: 'It is often said that working class white people resent an influx of coloured neighbours because they "lower" the district with their crowded houses, ignorant behaviour, and rowdy habits. This is emphatically not a satisfactory explanation of the interracial resentment in North Kensington at the present.'[12]

Nevertheless, a scapegoat was found and the witch-hunt proceeded. A few weeks later in July 1959, the Chief Housing Officer for Kensington said: 'Immigration into densely crowded areas made people on the [housing] waiting list suspicious and sensitive to the colour problem.'[13] The image was stronger where housing conditions were worse, for example in the old slums on the periphery of the 'zones of transition' or in adjacent streets that were in the early stages of transition. Moreover, noise was synonymous with crowded rooms. Taken together then, irritations were infectious and hardship was cumulative. Consequently, the disputes were many between black and white tenants and landlords. Strained relations became an integral part of the migrant zones. Increasingly, Blacks turned to each other.

But how does a black landlord become one? The money for a house was often raised by a co-operative. Several migrants pooled their savings, thus raising the deposit. Once acquired, the rooms in the house were let to 'relations and friends', to new arrivals and to 'refugees' from other lodgings. Accumulated rent receipts went towards buying another house. In this way, a chain of ownership was formed. Naturally, black migrants tended to prefer black landlords to white, even though in some cases, the rents (a 'colour tax') charged were higher. White people on the other hand, (especially in North Kensington) blamed their increased rents on the West Indian influx. White landlords ready to exploit the newcomers, bought property in the zones of transition for the specific purpose of 'rack-renting' black tenants who had few alternatives. Indeed, cases were known of such landlords who brought in West Indian tenants and encouraged them 'to behave in an anti-social way in order to get rid of sitting tenants so that higher rents can be charged'.[14]

Housing migrants then involved a maze of exploitative relationships. Within this, discrimination became increasingly pronounced. West Indians were apprehensive when they saw advertisements for vacant rooms such as 'coloured welcome' or 'coloured only'. And rightly so, for such exclusive welcome was not in their experience. They suspected that they could only be welcomed because of the inflated rents they would have to pay. As it was, these 'welcome' advertisements were rare. 'Anti-coloured' advertisements, more frequent, made the migrants even more conscious of their colour and oppressive discrimination.

Discriminatory advertisements seemed to confront them everywhere. A detailed count of the housing advertisements in the *Kensington Post* showed that in the 13 issues analysed (from 7 November 1958 to 30 January 1959) there were a total of 3876 advertisements of vacant furnished rooms and flats. Of these, 1431 were inserted by estate agents, most of which were neutral; they said nothing about race, colour or nationality. Ten were 'pro-coloured' and eight were 'anti-coloured'. Most of the 2445 advertisements inserted by private householders or landlords were also neutral – 2061 were in that group. However, some 322 had an 'anti-coloured' tag; and 62 had a 'pro-coloured' one. The main kinds of 'anti-coloured' statements were no-coloured, 106; Europeans only, 142; white people only, 25; and English only, 49. The evidence indicated a fairly wide range of discrimination, expressed crudely and, at times, apologetically.

Numerous as they were, the statistics on anti-coloured advertisements did not indicate the amount of prejudice which West Indian migrants encountered. There were, in fact, more examples of the kinds of overt discrimination displayed in respectable local newspapers, and also on the notice boards at shop windows. It was clear that these published restrictions were only a small fraction of the total which the migrants met in their search for lodgings. Most of the neutral advertisements without reference to colour, nationality or social class, were misleading in that most of the estate agents and landlords involved refused to accommodate Blacks. In the black experience, this was an established fact of everyday life. Discrimination in these advertisements was subtle. Landlords also resorted to the introduction of a colour scheme to keep black men away from calling at the door, or indeed, from inhabiting one of their shabby rooms.

In the desperate struggle to find accommodation, there were few operators who could help the black migrants. One manager of a small agency near Piccadilly Circus which did find accommodation for Blacks, but ceased to operate, said that he had as many as 200 West Indians a week asking for accommodation, but he had only been able to help about seven a week. Such was the magnitude of the problem. Increasingly Blacks were forced to rely on members of their own exploited groups. A *Times* correspondent wrote: 'Even the most educated coloured people in London normally find flats or houses in London through friends. It is not unknown for property companies to put a stipulation against coloured tenants, or against foreigners, in leases.'[15] Xenophobia in housing was rampant. What is more, those who found unskilled and semi-skilled, low-paid jobs were faced with a truly major area of racial disadvantage. Indeed, black migrant labour was important in the designs of British capital.

Employment

Unlike the situation in housing in which an overt colour bar was advertised, the recruitment of black migrant workers was more disguised. Nevertheless, racial discrimination and racial prejudice in employment were entrenched; the personnel officer was inclined to act in a most personal way. However, once a job was found, it brought about a 'new chain of frictions'.

The English workman had an entirely different attitude to Blacks as workmates as opposed to them as neighbours or prospective neighbours. For while a white man was prepared to work with a black person, he was still reluctant to accept their living nearby. For 'he is far more likely to be aware of their dark skin at home than in the factory'. As workers, some white men were not reluctant to praise the migrants. 'Well, definitely, there's some good working men amongst them . . . and I've got some good working men now.'[16] But, for others, the vast majority, the black man was shiftless and lazy, living off national assistance and off the immoral earnings of prostitutes. West Indians were conscious of this ambivalence among their white co-workers. While recognition of 'good working' might have reduced the chance of discord at the workplace, it certainly did not eliminate it where there were black workers. For the immigrant, getting a job was vital; after all he came to Britain essentially for economic reasons. Getting on with white workers was of secondary importance. Employment, and the attendant indignities in securing and enduring it, was therefore the hard reality for the mass of black workers who were joining the British workforce during this period.

In the field of employment, a large number of Barbadian migrants had received help either directly or indirectly from the official agency set up in London for the Barbadian government and for a few British industries. In the rare cases where migrants secured jobs in advance, the Barbadian government was prepared to lend the passage money. Under this government scheme, Barbadians were recruited by several British firms such as the British Transport Commission, the London Transport Executive and the British Hotels and Restaurants Association. Domestic work in hospitals was catered for by the Regional Hospital Boards. The direct recruitment from Barbados in 1955 came at a time when there was a severe shortage of labour in the transport and catering industries.[17]

The prospect of large numbers of black workers working in British industry and its implications for race relations, did not go unnoticed. To avoid the black problem, the British Transport Commission proposed the employment of Italians on the railways, but this was turned down by the National Union of Railwaymen.[18] Subsequently, the Transport Executive focused its recruiting efforts on Ireland and the Caribbean.

In spite of the economic urgency of the labour problem, much careful thinking had gone into the matter. The Executive had to consider its status as a nationalised industry as it related to the fact that as a mass employer of black workers it might be regarded as reflecting government policy. They need not have bothered, the British government had already reckoned up its labour requirements. Nevertheless, the Executive had previously employed Blacks but not many were in the operating grades. When the decision was taken to employ them in these grades a recruiting team was sent to Barbados in 1956. Thereafter, an elaborate organisation was set up on the island. Thus, via slavery and indentureship the black migrant, deliberately manipulated by British industrial policy, came from the bondage of the declining sugar monoculture to labour in the metropolis, the centre of a declining Empire which now needed workers, not settlers.

The newcomers had travelled to London totally unaware of the realities awaiting them. By the end of 1958, London Transport had employed about 4000 black workers.[19] Some 3000 were recruited in London, while almost 1000 came directly from Barbados. After receiving two extra days of training, the West Indians (like other newcomers from other parts of the Commonwealth) started work in the lowest grades, hoping for promotion. By 1960 some had become bus drivers, train guards and booking office clerks and, in a few cases, station foremen. Those in junior supervisory posts were in charge of white and black workers, but they were only a token few. West Indian workers were good for London Transport in that their turnover of staff was 'exceptionally low'. Thus, black labour was there to be exploited to the hilt and this was done regardless of the consequences.

The employment of migrants by London Transport was exceptional. In other places they were received with hesitation or treated with antipathy. The employers' views of black workers had not changed fundamentally, although they continued to vary marginally. While some gave good references to West Indian workers, others hesitated, describing them as slow and sloppy workers. The overlap of fact and fiction cannot be discounted, for although black workers were not classified as a separate group of workers, colour was significant. Some firms kept an 'unofficial' tag.

The diversity of the migrants' backgrounds and aspirations, and the diversity of the attitudes and conditions which they met in the London labour market, reflected a wide range of experiences. The few success stories were dampened by the more realistic hardship and failures of the majority.

Another aspect of the newcomers' experience was occupational downgrading. In the light of the prejudices directed against them, at least the outlines of the employment situation of Blacks were clear. The newcomers found a variety of low-paid jobs in London. A considerable number were in nursing, some (male and female) were employed as doctors, teachers, journalists or as black-coated workers. Others worked as skilled manual workers or in the field of entertainment. There were also a number of barbers, tailors, cleaners, laundrymen, shopkeepers and cafe-owners whose establishments were largely patronised by West Indians.

Significantly, only a few West Indians, however, were in such middle class and skilled positions. Most were employed in London as semi-skilled or unskilled labourers. In London the migrant was confronted with the real possibility of doing work which was of lower occupational prestige *vis-à-vis* his former position in the West Indies. Not all newcomers, however, regretted their downgrading, for there were benefits. For some this downgrading was involuntary, while it was voluntary for others. Financial compensation was the reward for such a change. For example, a man could earn more if he was employed as a semi-skilled manual worker than he could earn as a clerk.[20]

Having said this, there were many West Indians who had to accept inferior positions to the 'white collar' and skilled occupations which they had held before. In effect, this was a step downwards to the very lowest rank of the unskilled labourers. Bitter disappointment was the result during a period of adjustment which was long and very painful.

Another explanation for the downgrading experience of so many West Indians and other black workers, at the time, was the fact that they had to take menial jobs because of colour prejudice and discrimination. While some observers agreed that this allegation was difficult to prove, they could not deny that there were 'colour bars' and often 'colour quotas'. Clearly, colour prejudice was a major factor which, given the intricate web of circumstances, more or less played its part.

Newcomers and the trade unions

Paradoxically, the growing grievances of black workers at the workplace, posed a challenge to the Trade Union Movement, and its belief in equality and brotherhood. Indeed, the official trade union policy was opposed to discrimination. This was unequivocally emphasised in a General Council statement submitted at the Trades Union Congress (held soon after the disturbances in Nottingham and Notting Hill) in September 1958, which read:

> The Trade Union Movement has been forthright in its condemnation of every manifestation of racial prejudice and discrimination in any part of the world. Here in Britain, immigrants from many countries have been freely accepted into membership of trade unions and in general have been integrated into industrial life. Satisfactory housing and social integration have been more difficult to achieve. Decent people will appreciate that this is a matter which calls for understanding and that many immigrants arrive in Britain with a limited knowledge of its social and economic environment and pattern of life which is so different from their own, and which they require to accustom themselves. Here is the field in which joint efforts in local communities can do so much to further tolerance and an appreciation of the difficult problems which are involved.[21]

Many individual unions and branches submitted similar resolutions denouncing discrimination. Within the trade union movement, however, there was a disparity of views reflected in the approach of policy-makers and the attitudes at other levels. Sometimes the gap was very wide indeed. In fact, as the trade union 'high command' passed resolutions deploring colour prejudice, some local branches operated colour quotas. Furthermore, there was no united approach on the colour question among the local branches of any one trade union. The ambiguity within the labour movement was reflected in this resolution:

> The coloured people coming to England are British subjects only seeking a means of existence which is denied them in their place of birth. We implore all trade unionists to do all in their power to help them obtain employment and join their respective trade unions, thus enabling them to work and live as decent human beings.
>
> It is time a stop was put to all foreign labour entering this country: they constitute a danger to the workers of this country. In the event of a slump occurring, the market would be flooded with cheap foreign labour and a serious deterrent to trade union bargaining power.[22]

Here then we see trade unionists asking black workers to join the trade unions but also calling for a ban on black immigration to Britain. Did they not know of the labour shortage in the British economy (which was the issue) rather than the hypothetical, 'In the event of a slump occurring the market would be flooded with cheap foreign labour'? This was a thin disguise for their own colour prejudice. In fact, black workers proved no serious deterrent to trade union bargaining power. It had been argued that the attitudes of white workers and trade union branches to the 'colour problem' was most pronounced in the Midlands and in the North where memories of the depression were still vivid and where xenophobia was strong. They feared that black workers would cut overtime earnings and weaken agreements, that employers would use them as a pool of cheap, sweated labour and in the event of strikes, use them as 'blacklegs'. This had been, and would become a recurrent sequence in the white workers' argument against Blacks. This time-worn traditional British prejudice towards the foreigner was real; it was rooted in the fear of economic competition and the racist legacy of imperialism and colonialism.

In London, the geographical contrast in attitudes towards the recruitment of Blacks was highlighted in the public transport services. While in London there were few initial difficulties when Blacks joined London Transport, in several provincial cities, there were unofficial strikes or threats of strikes when Indians, Pakistanis and West Indians were recruited for the buses. To influence attitudes towards black workers, members of the Birmingham Transport Authority told a BBC interviewer:

> We did face the difficulty that a number of staff thought that we should get so many coloured and that they would cause trouble between the black and white . . . I am pleased to say that we've got positive proof in our everyday working that those fears were very largely unfounded. . . . And although on the Birmingham City Transport at the moment we've got probably more [coloured] people than any other undertaking of a similar kind in the country anywhere, we can say with some degree of pride that they are now working with the white crews, working with the white public, and I think we can almost say that very often they're not even noticed; no one is conscious that it's a coloured driver or a coloured conductor. [23]

In spite of these assurances, seemingly 'tolerant' people, among them trade unionists, supported discrimination.

During the 1950s relations between Blacks and Whites were distinctly uneasy. There were many cases of disharmony at the workplace. Outside London, two in particular took place in the Midland towns of West Bromwich and Wolverhampton in 1955 involving Asian workers. The first dispute occurred in February 1955 when workers at the West Bromwich Corporation Transport system started a series of token Saturday strikes in protest against the employment of an Indian trainee conductor. The strikers said the strikes would continue until agreement was reached with management on the question of 'coloured labour'. Paradoxically, the official union policy was opposed to discrimination on the grounds of colour, while the management intended to recruit any suitable person regardless of colour.

The strike had aroused much local interest. The Bishops of Birmingham and Lichfield intervened asking the strikers to reconsider their action. They argued that enforcing a colour bar was not reconcilable with Christianity.[24]

The General Secretary of the strikers' union (TGWU), Arthur Deakin, argued that the strike was not a question of colour prejudice but rather that the men were conditioned by a fear of unemployment.[25] Be that as it may, the fact remains that the Indian trainees were not white but black and 'foreign'. Would they have reacted the same way, had the trainees been white?

In the dispute at Wolverhampton which occurred a few months later, transport workers in the Corporation decided to ban all overtime from 1 September in protest against the increase of black recruits. In defence of its action, the Union branch secretary said: 'We are not operating a colour bar. The men have made friends with the coloured men on the job, but we don't intend to have the platform staff made up to its full strength by coloured people only.'[26]

There were 68 black workers employed among a total of over 900. This was clearly well above the colour quota. The branch secretary said the union was prepared to accept 52 blacks but the Transport Committee of the Corporation denied giving such a promise.

When the overtime ban ended on 18 September, the men wanted a 5 per cent quota of 'coloured labour' and demanded that there be no recruitment of Blacks while negotiations were in progress. The Transport Committee refused these requests. They argued that if, in fact, the men were not asking for a colour bar, then their opposition was simply an attempt to keep the department short-staffed, thus maintaining overtime earnings. In the end, the men dropped their demand for a 5 per cent quota and a panel was set up to 'consider all recruits'.[27] In this dispute, as in the first, the official union policy was opposed to colour discrimination. This was difficult to accept, when they were in fact practising it.

Relations between black and white workers

Given this background, relations between white and black work-mates, put simply, were strained. One observer concluded that race relations in British industry were full of ambiguities and contradic-tions. While some white workers opposed the employment of black workers, others protested against the dismissal of black workers. These conflicting attitudes contributed substantially to the insecurity of the black migrant's position.

As black immigration to Britain proceeded, white workers began to distinguish between different kinds of immigrants, shifting from the general to the specific. Serious difficulties remained for some migrants. The problems for West Indians, for example, were not so acute as for migrants from India, Pakistan and Africa. One writer stated that the difference between the previous and the new en-vironment was not so radical for the West Indians as it was for many of the others. By and large the men from the Caribbean territories were already more conditioned for life and work in England than those from Asia and Africa. And, most importantly, they had no major language problem. It was argued that the direct cause of industrial disputes about black people had been more often the employment of Indians and Pakistanis than that of West Indians. This was seen as a reflection of the special problems which the Asian migrants had because of their language difficulties. While West Indians did not speak 'local' English, and their distinct accents and phrases occasionally caused misunderstanding or mutual irritation, there was no greater barrier to communication. Minor differences in speech and habits however were often even more annoying to both sides than major ones particularly when mutual strangeness was taken for granted.[28]

A source of irritation and resentment on the part of English workers was the fact that West Indians, on the whole, in spite of their familiarity with the English language, were not familiar with trade union organisation. The main reason for the West Indian's attitude was the fact that the trade unions in the West Indies were new and 'seditious' organisations. The newcomer to Britain was therefore hesitant to apply for union membership. In fact, he was sometimes unable to do so because he lacked the qualifications necessary to be accepted by a craft union which he wanted to join because of his previous skilled occupation. On the other hand, many West Indians participated in trade union activities in London and the provinces. Some of these activists became shop stewards and a few were elected as secretaries of union branches which questioned the views of white workers about black participation in trade unions.

Moreover, in the relations between black workers and white at the workplace, external factors played a part. The West Indian's prowess at sport – cricket, for example – made him well-known and respected by his workmates with an interest in cricket. In much the same way, the folklore of the black man's sexual prowess enters into reactions at the workplace. The tangle of sexual images about the black man, and of sexual competition with him, was invariably transferred to the workplace, thus affecting adversely the working relationship.

The Senior and Manley Report of 1955 stated that white workers were much more reluctant to accept black workers in establishments where both men and women were employed than in those which only men were working. The Report also said that white workers were more likely to object to 'coloured' workers in job situations 'where they might be thrown into contact with white women' than in others.[29]

As late as 1959 the employment of black shop assistants was rare. In fact when one was employed, it was of such outstanding importance that it featured on the front page of the *West Indian*

Gazette.[30] Colour was a crucial factor in employment. Both employers and unions often demanded a 'colour quota'. In view of this their actions were far less noticeable. Thus, the colour quota remained a significant issue among employers.

Given the 'colour quota' and 'colour bar', the galling fact was that the conduct and performance of black workers were heavily criticised quite often by firms which had no experience (or very little) of employing Blacks. In the preliminary unpublished survey 'On Integration of the Coloured Population of Willesden' some 20 managers of large firms, each employing over 200 workers, were questioned. It was found that among the employers questioned all reported that they had no serious difficulties in employing black workers from the point of view of racial relationships. However, management policy on questions of racial intolerance appeared to differ considerably as between one organisation and another. One firm, for instance, had in the past dismissed both black and white workers who had been involved in 'some kind of conflict', and seemed to think that this had not only effectively prevented any further trouble but had, in their view, helped to improve relationships in the factory. Other firms were less confident in their outlook and seemed more susceptible to the complaints of white workers if merited, while others used black labour wholly or mainly on unskilled work, since they believed that this seemed to placate, or to avoid trouble with their white workers.[31]

The black worker was always reminded that it was the colour of his skin which exposed him to the prejudices of white workers and employers. This increased the stresses and strains of life which they bore. The contradictions among employers were many. It would seem in given circumstances that they suited themselves. Some said the migrants were not very robust, while others felt they were 'tough'; that some lacked initiative while others were 'ambitious and self-reliant'; that black people were 'slow and lazy' and that they 'work hard and quickly'; that they were 'lethargic' and 'energetic', that they 'cannot adapt themselves' and that they were 'remarkably adaptable'.

Without denying the diverse experiences that a few employers had of black workers, their generalisations revealed more about their own attitudes to colour than about the characteristics of the migrants from the West Indies, Africa and Asia.

Overall, the adjustment of the migrants in the local communities in which they concentrated, and the process of integration at the workplace presented the black worker with innumerable difficulties, most of which arose from the reactions of white officials, workers, trade unions and employers. Moreover, since a considerable number of West Indians who migrated did not belong to the lowest ranks in their society, many of them had never thought of themselves as members of the working class before they arrived in Britain. As it was, men who were employers in Port of Spain had become factory-hands in London; women who had their own servants had become kitchen maids.

Very quickly then, the migrants became disillusioned with the pre-immigration rosy images and notions of the British. Their dreams of economic betterment were shattered in the face of the British stereotyping of black people. Of necessity, and partly because of an innate West Indian characteristic of 'flexibility', the newcomers adapted to the 'new images' of the British, offering resistance all along the way. Although stereotypes on both sides made for an uneasy *rapprochement*, mutual strangeness was only gradually modified by personal experience. Where stereotyping was maintained, suspicions became more rigid, thus increasing the difficulties of communication between black and white people.

During the decade of the 1950s, colour prejudice, whether ambiguous, concealed or open, led to discrimination primarily in housing and jobs and tended to be self-perpetuating. This had disastrous effects on the lives of the newcomers to Britain. Yet, no serious consideration was given to the growing tension that had already accumulated.

The riots of 1958

Nottingham

In 1958 an estimated 2000 to 3000 black people were living in Nottingham. A considerable number were concentrated in a 'decaying' district. It was here in The Chase (a public house) on Saturday 23 August 1958 that a fight took place between two men, one black, the other white, before closing time. The fighting spread quickly. Several men were stabbed. The attacks led to counter-attacks. Dozens of men and women were injured. Reinforcements were called in to aid the two or three policemen in pacifying a 1500 hostile crowd which had gathered. The fire brigade was also called in for fear that the 'ugly riotous crowd' would have started fires. And, as was the case in Cardiff in 1919, several black men with cuts and bruises were taken away by police 'for their own safety'. Some 90 minutes later, order was restored and by midnight the crowds were dispersed. The events of this night were not a case of 'spontaneous combustion'. Tension in the area had been running high for a long time as black people were molested, humiliated and beaten up by 'Teddy Boys'. There were many cases of violence committed by Whites against Blacks, two weeks before the Saturday night brawls. The police had been aware of this, for they regarded the Saturday night fights as a reprisal for earlier attacks on Blacks. The Assistant Chief Constable of Nottingham confirmed that there had been assaults. He said that two white men were on remand charged with robbery with violence against a coloured man and that the attacks made by 'Teddy Boys' in the previous 15 days were responsible for the Saturday night outbursts. He regarded the black community, apart from a few isolated cases, as being 'very well behaved'. [32]

The disturbances were given wide press coverage. *The Times* reported that the race clash in Nottingham was alarming. [33] Other national newspapers, less optimistic and less restrained, told the Teddy Boys' story in a distorted form.

It seems clear then that before the fighting broke out, relations between Blacks and Whites in The Chase were tense. And after the fighting more trouble was expected the following Saturday. A large crowd of Teddy Boys and local white people, sightseers and reporters, had assembled where the trouble had taken place the previous Saturday. There were no black people in the crowd; they were advised to remain indoors, while police patrols moved the crowd along. In a mood of expectancy, the 'milling mob' had grown to about 4000 during the course of the evening. No black person was in sight until, presumably unaware of the crowd, a car with three West Indians passing through the area was stopped. The crowd went wild. Cries of 'let's lynch them', 'Let's get at them', went up as the crowd, many of them Teddy Boys, poured from public houses and tried to smash their way into the car. Beating on the windows, they tried to overturn it. Finally the police forced a path through them and told the black men in the car to 'go like hell'. They did. [34]

After the West Indians had escaped, with the crowd in 'lynching mood', tension remained high; it seemed inevitable there had to be some release. According to one report, the trouble started when a cameraman lit a magnesium flare to 'film a scuffle between a small party of youths'. At that moment, the dispersing crowd rushed back, anticipating a fire. In the commotion, there was 'great agitation' and shouting. The call was to 'find some niggers'. With no black people in the streets, Whites fought against Whites and the police. Over 50 people were arrested and 24 teenagers and men were charged under the Public Order Act. The next day the Chief Constable said: 'This was not a racial riot. The coloured people behaved in an exemplary way by keeping out of the way. Indeed they were an example to some of the rougher elements. The people primarily concerned were irresponsible teddy boys and persons who had had a lot to drink.' [35]

But, was the violence attributable simply to drink? Among those sentenced to three months' imprisonment each, were the 'nigger-chasing' men aged between 24 and 45 years. Two Saturdays after the initial trouble, a crowd had again assembled. In the ensuing 'nigger-baiting' incidents, the homes of some black people were besieged. In defence, tenants threw milk bottles from the upper floors while the mob below attacked the houses with a hail of bricks and bottles. In a dark street, the mob chased black men assaulting five of them. The violence was stopped when the police vans arrived.

Once again, colour prejudice had reared its head. Nottingham was marked by it and, for various reasons, many would not forget it. But even the seriousness of the violence had a ghoulish side. A bus company trying to capitalise on the misfortune of black people, advertised coach tours to see the 'terror spots' of Nottingham. The Sheriff of Nottingham was horrified by this latest development. He said: 'It comes at a time when we are striving to eliminate racial conflict. I understand that chalked notices have been displayed outside bus garage booking offices in Leicester . . . giving full details of the trips. More disturbing, however, was the rumour that the same thing is being done in other cities and towns.'

The police were asked to request that the trips be withdrawn.[36]

The London riots

More serious than the 'riots' in Nottingham was the simultaneous violence in London. Unlike the Nottingham troubles, the riots in London continued uninterruptedly for several days and were also spread over a wider area. The trouble started in Shepherds Bush and adjacent Notting Dale and spread to several areas in Notting Hill, Kensal New Town, Paddington and Maida Vale. The London riots also differed from the Nottingham experience in that it did not occur in the centre of a district with a dense black population. Indeed, the main explosions occurred outside the black settlements, and the worst offenders were from white housing estates and districts.

While, as in Nottingham, the large-scale London disturbances were preceded by a number of 'sporadic assaults' on black people, in London there was no retaliation by black men which started the crowd outbursts, nor was there a definite chain of incidents during the turbulent days. There was no set pattern. As 'nigger hunting' spread, a growing number of people, 'active forces and passive spectators', became involved in several districts. Overall, an atmosphere of 'menace and fear' pervaded the area. Between July and early August 1958, apart from fights between individuals, there were many attacks by gangs of white youths on black people.

Shortly after the disturbances in Nottingham, on 23 August, the heightened tension had brought about aggression in several places in West London. Black people had had the ugly experience of 'one weekend of sport' – attempts by drivers of taxi cabs to run them down after nightfall. Fear of this among black people was real. White attitudes were, at the time, reflected in such fascist slogans as 'Keep Britain White' and 'People of Kensington Act Now'. Furthermore, fascist agitators stirred up the racists in and around Notting Hill, where the White Defence League and the Union Movement held meetings and distributed leaflets. In these circumstances, the racists were poised for violent attacks on black people.

On Saturday evening (23 August) the homes of several black people were attacked and in the small hours of Sunday morning, nine white youths from Shepherds Bush cruised along their and the adjacent districts in a car, intent on 'nigger hunting'. Their armoury consisted of iron bars, starting handles, table legs, pieces of wood and a knife. Their strategy was to attack black persons walking alone, or at most two. After their attacks, five black men (three of them seriously injured) were admitted to hospital. One of them, with a chest wound, was taken into the Magistrate's Court on a stretcher to give evidence, but was not allowed to do so. The magistrate said, 'I have never before seen a man in that state brought into a court. I don't think he is fit to give evidence.'[37]

The case became notorious for its 'nigger-hunting' youths. Later, they were tried at the Old Bailey and sentenced to four years' imprisonment each.

Although the *Manchester Guardian* noted, 'Other Cities Not Perturbed About Nottingham It Could Happen Here Feeling',[38] a few days later, violence did break out, this time on a much larger scale. As previously, the trouble occurred on Bramley Road and the vicinity of Notting Dale, where few black people lived. In the attack on several houses, one was set on fire. An aggressive crowd of some 200 milled about the streets. As fighting broke out, a variety of weapons including iron bars were used.[39] The next day in Bramley Road between 400 and 700 people had gathered. Feelings ran high. The furious fighting was punctuated with the shouts 'We will kill the blacks . . .' and 'We will get the blacks'. This 'lynch mob' exchanged blows with black people and the police. In the affray several people were admitted to hospital with injuries and two police cars were damaged. The disturbances had spread to several other places. Under the railway arches near Latimer Road Underground Station a gang of 100 youths with sticks, iron bars and knives, had gathered.[40] There were fights also on the Harrow Road and in Kensal Rise. The rioting continued day and night. Most black people stayed at home. They fought back as the attack on their homes intensified. By Monday and Tuesday, 1 and 2 September the riot had reached its peak; it had become continuous and widespread.

Thereafter, it ran its course for several days, with 'sporadic outbursts' until mid-September in Notting Hill, Notting Dale and Paddington. By September then, the public was reading sensational headlines in the press. At the height of the riots the dramatic impact of individual experiences were reported.[41] There were also reports of incidents throughout the affected areas. According to *The Times* 'a crowd of youths went through Oxford Gardens . . . smashing windows in houses where coloured people live. "They didn't miss a house", said one white resident . . . A police official said earlier: "There are thousands of people milling around the Notting Hill area . . . a black couple took to their heels pursued by the crowd crying 'Let's get the blacks' ".'[42]

The British public was now fully informed of the drama of

Notting Hill. Some initiative had to be taken. George Rogers, MP for North Kensington, appealed for common sense, decency and tolerance in race relations and asked the people to 'remain calm, to stay indoors in your homes tonight, and to obey the police'. Rogers carried this message on his tour of the area. There was also a 'nigger-hunting' tour undertaken by five white men in a car who drove around shouting, 'Stir them up'.[43] And later that day, the Union Movement maintained its presence outside the Latimer Road Underground Station. The Movement was active in the district. In fact, on 4 September, one of their members was arrested for insulting behaviour in Ladbroke Grove, while distributing pamphlets.

Although some black people were militant during this period, most of them obeyed the police and stayed indoors. But, this could not last, for some had to face the public at their peril. Black bus conductors who lived in the troubled area were given police escort at the end of their journeys. Moreover, black people were subjected to vicious taunts from the racists who hawked *Action* (the Union Movement paper) and youths chanting 'Down with the niggers', 'Deport all niggers'. Others adopted the motto: 'Keep Britain White'.[44]

On 2 September, when Scotland Yard announced that the Metropolitan police 'will continue to carry out their duty to preserve the Queen's peace without fear, favour or discrimination', at least 55 people were arrested. In spite of the hope that a change in the hot weather would 'damp the trouble', when rain did fall on 3 September, 'after four of the most turbulent days that London had seen for a long time', its effect was to disperse the crowds. It did not 'damp the trouble' which became 'more localised'.[45] The next day, hot and tense again, saw the continuation (though on a restricted scale) of petrol bombs being flung into the homes of black people in Notting Hill and Paddington. The anti-nigger shouts and bottle-throwing had by then become commonplace.

News of the riots travelled fast. On 5 September, two West Indian political leaders, Norman Manley, Chief Minister of Jamaica, and Dr Carl LaCorbiniere, the Deputy Prime Minister in the Federal Government of the West Indies, arrived in London. Dr Hugh Cummins, the Prime Minister of Barbados, followed them. They had talks with the British government, addressed meetings of their fellow countrymen in London and visited the troubled areas in London and Nottingham.[46] As fear decreased, black people ventured on the streets again. Unfortunately, occasional attacks on black people and their properties in the affected districts and elsewhere in Greater London continued.

On 15 September, when the riots died down, Justice Salmon gave judgement on the nine 'nigger-hunting' youths; this 'severe' sentence was controversial.

Fenner Brockway, having asked the Home Secretary to recommend the exercise of the Royal Prerogative to reduce the sentences said: 'These youths were as much the victims of the hysteria which swept over Notting Hill as the West Indians.'[47] The whole concept of punishment came under review with strong comments from all quarters. The fascist papers referred to Justice Salmon as that 'Jewish Judge' who, according to one report, received a threatening letter.

The youths appealed unsuccessfully. Their local MP raised the question in the House of Commons in February 1960. He asked that 'further consideration . . . be given to a reduction in these sentences if it is not possible to quash them altogether'. Although he received support from both sides of the House, the government spokesman replied that he was 'unable to indicate a prospect that the Home Secretary will find it possible to recommend any revision of the sentences which the Court considered right and which were upheld on appeal'.[48]

It was hoped the sentence would have a deterrent-effect, which it did for a time. However, in the uneasy truce that ensued, Justice Salmon's words to the charged youths were appropriate:

> It was you men who started the whole of this violence in Notting Hill. You are a minute and insignificant section of the population who have brought shame upon the district in which you lived, and have filled the whole nation with horror, indignation and disgust. I am determined that you and anyone anywhere who may be tempted to follow your example shall clearly understand that crimes such as this will not be tolerated in this country, but will inevitably meet in these courts with the stern punishment which they so justly deserve.[49]

In the aftermath of the disorders, the process of identifying the causes began, and blame was allocated accordingly. While there was general agreement that a small group of Teddy Boys were responsible for the troubles in Nottingham and Notting Hill, some sections of the press were blamed for 'sensational treatment' of the news which had a snowball effect. There was also the influence of fascist agitators, particularly in Notting Hill. And according to an American columnist in the *New York Herald Tribune*, the disturbances in Nottingham and London were the result of a Communist conspiracy of the same kind that had accentuated racial conflict in Little Rock and fomented riots in the southern United States. In response, the *Manchester Guardian* reported that this theory had not occurred even to the most 'Right minded commentators in Fleet Street'.[50]

But while all these explanations had relevance, at the heart of the matter was 'the colour problem'. The number of black migrants, it was argued, determined the 'quantity of friction', since there would be no friction if there were no Blacks in Britain. As the debate gathered momentum, and comparison was made with the American experience, it became clear that there was no one simple or single explanation as to the causes of the disorders. It was clear, however, that, 'The trouble makers of Notting Hill acted out tendencies which were latent in all social strata. They were shouting what others were whispering.' That was the lesson of the 1958 race riots which revealed not two but several nations which were separated from each other. Furthermore, both the riots and the comments on them clearly revealed the British ambivalence on the question of colour. The riots also proved that in such a situation the aggressive fringe groups were not insignificant.[51]

If government practices and policies had brought about inner city decay and the advent of black immigration, was there a political solution? What were the reactions of responsible officials to the 'race riots'?

Reactions: prelude to control

The 'colour problem' in Britain had become world-wide news. The first effect, following the riots in August–September 1958, was a flood of reports and comments. This reaction revealed the thinking of official institutions. The press unanimously censured the 'hooligans of Notting Hill' and *The Times* pontificated on 'A Family of Nations'. Race relations was hot news not only in the media but at local and national conferences. Political parties and trade unions felt bound to state their views on black and white people.

But there were voices elsewhere. The British Council of Churches and many ministers denounced the 'dastardly attacks'. Moreover, a host of new organisations were formed and specially prepared pamphlets and memoranda were issued by the Labour Party, the Fabian Society, the Bow Group, the Conservative Commonwealth Council and Oswald Mosley's Union Movement. The Labour Party stated: 'The Labour Party utterly abhors every manifestation of racial prejudice, and particularly condemns those instances which have recently occurred in this country.[52] The Bow Group feared comparison with the foreign reputation of the United States as a result of Little Rock, while the Conservative Commonwealth Council warned, 'We cannot retain the integrity or the cohesion of the Commonwealth unless we can solve and eradicate colour prejudice here in Britain.'[53]

Apart from some extreme groups, the opinion leaders were agreed that 'racial discrimination is unBritish'. These were the terms of reference within which further discussion would follow, at least for a while. Aggressive racial prejudice was a fact in Britain. This startled some, arousing 'shame and anger'.

During the late 1950s the question of colour was already an internationally sensitive issue, featuring in the daily news from Africa, Asia, the West Indies and America. Indeed it was of particular political importance to the changing British Commonwealth. Comparisons between Little Rock and Notting Hill caused great concern not only in Britain, but in the United States of America. The American newspapers in the North and South, gave prominence to the race riots in Britain. In fact, in the deep South, it was thought that Notting Hill had become an 'outpost of Alabama'.

In Britain, white commentators generally sought a balanced appraisal of the 'riots'. George Rogers, Labour MP for North Kensington (which includes Notting Hill and Notting Dale) said, '. . . it was wrong to say this trouble had been started by hooligans. It was the reaction of people sorely tried by some sections of the coloured population.'[54]

In the continuing debate, there emerged a polarisation of opinion. On the one hand, there were those who saw racial tension as a British responsibility which required new measures to counteract it, for example, more training for low income groups, improved education for citizenship and legislation against racial discrimination, among others. On the other hand, there were those who argued that being essentially a 'colour problem', it was aggravated by the growth of a black immigrant minority which was undesirable. Thus, they demanded the control of black immigration to Britain and that Commonwealth migrants convicted for criminal offences should be deported.

Among policy makers, the control of Commonwealth immigration was nothing new. It had been debated in the House of Commons before the riots on 3 April 1958. In essence, the discussion was centred on 'coloured Immigrants'. Speaking for the government Miss Hornsby Smith said:

> We cannot ignore the rising potential of this immigration. In view of the size of the populations of the countries from which these people are coming, we have to take stock of the position as it now presents itself, and to realise that it could in the future possibly constitute a very grave burden on this country if the trend were to increase, or if the numbers arriving in this country were to become out of proportion to those that the country can reasonably absorb.

She cited rates of employment, sickness and crime among black people in Britain, and argued that 'Although the coloured immigrants are not, on the whole being assimilated into the country', generally, they did not create any 'special' employment, health and police problems. However, there had been discussions with the governments of India and Pakistan to discourage 'unsuitable immigrants' and the British government was reluctant 'to receive all citizens' who had the status of British subject.[55] Given these arguments, India and Pakistan imposed stricter control on immigration to Britain.

After the Nottingham disturbances, two local MPs asked for

control. Their demand drew sharp criticism from the *Manchester Guardian* which deplored the fact that they 'should have spoken as though the entire onus rested on the coloured community and talked of restricting immigration to this country as if this might be the prime remedy'.[56] The views of these two MPs, however, received considerable support which was reinforced by the Notting Hill riots. Other MPs joined in the chorus for an immigration 'quota'. Together they exerted enough pressure to get a response from the government.[57]

Since the demand for restrictions referred not to the immigrants who were white but to those who were black, immigration control was a polite term for a colour bar. All sorts of measures were being considered to lessen their numbers in Britain and to keep black people out of Britain. Enough had been said and done towards the expression of strong views by those who felt the time was right. The Conservative Party Conference in October 1958 resolved to revise the immigration laws 'irrespective of race, colour or creed', and the feeling was that immigrants convicted of serious criminal offences should be deported.[58]

Debating immigration control early in December 1958, the government spokesman concluded: 'Both the Government and, I am glad to record, the opposition Front Bench do not see the necessity for any general control of immigration. The Government are considering very carefully the possibility of legislation to deport criminals but, as I have pointed out, that gives rise to great complexities.'[59]

At this stage, it seemed the government's position was to leave 'control' and to concentrate on the deportation of 'undesirable' black people.

The Conservatives were not the only politicians preoccupied with immigration control. In fact, the question cut across party lines. There was mixed reaction in each of the parties. The Labour Party, however, took a stand: 'We are firmly convinced that any form of British legislation limiting Commonwealth immigration to this country would be disastrous to our status in the Commonwealth and to the confidence of the Commonwealth peoples.'[60]

The Liberal Party denounced racial discrimination and rejected any restriction of immigration. Even the liberal wing of the Conservatives, the Conservative Commonwealth Council, said it would be wrong to 'deny Commonwealth citizens their traditional right to come to Britain [for] if we were to legislate against colour we would in the end bring about the disintegration of the Commonwealth'.[61] But the forces of disintegration had already been set in motion, moving irrevocably forward. The idea of restrictive legislation was shelved for the time being. Instead, it was decided to explore the possibility of informal agreements with Commonwealth countries, since their co-operation was necessary in reducing the numbers. Ultimately, however, the British government reserved its rights. As Lord Elton put it, 'We should not seek to exclude, but rather should wish to be able to exercise some power of selection and regulation. And in that way we should not be exposing ourselves to the invidious and everdreaded charge of colour prejudice. . . .'[62]

The possibility of introducing legislation during the late 1940s and early 1950s to make discrimination a punishable offence was debated. Before 1960, no government was prepared to do so. Three main arguments were put forward against it. Firstly, it was unnecessary. It was argued that some of the sanctions implicit in existing common and criminal law were adequate. For example, in November 1949 the Attorney General of the Labour government, Sir Hartley Shawcross, felt it was unnecessary to legislate against restrictive covenants in leases which exclude coloured tenants. He thought such covenants 'may well be void under the existing law as being contrary to the rules of public policy upheld by English Courts'.[63] Secondly, discrimination was not a fit subject for legislation because it was difficult to draft an Act, defining the offences, and to enforce it, without interfering with certain common law privileges of individual freedom. And thirdly, and most importantly, discrimination could only be eradicated through the influence of 'enlightened public opinion', not through the law.

After the 'riots', these arguments were weakened. And as the group of black immigrants increased, there were frequent complaints of 'colour bars'. By the autumn of 1958 then, with a growing body of 'enlightened public opinion' it was thought that legislation would complement public education and that censure of discrimination should be written into the law. In September 1958, Labour politicians made a commitment:

> The Labour Party urges Her Majesty's Government now to introduce legislation making illegal the public practice of discrimination. In any case, it pledges the next Labour Government to take an early opportunity of introducing such legislation. . . . It will use the full weight of Government influence against all such discrimination.[64]

The Conservative Party and the government disagreed. They warned that discrimination might be increased rather than diminished by a formal prohibition against it.

Regardless of the differences it seemed there was much to be learned from the United States. References were made to state legislation against discriminatory restrictive practices in the northern states. It was assumed (as though the problems in both countries were the same) that such American law was ineffective and that its experience was not relevant to similar issues in Britain.

Before the riots in April 1958, Fenner Brockway had headed a group of Labour MPs in sponsoring a Private Members Bill 'to make illegal discrimination to the detriment of any person on the grounds of colour, race and religion in the United Kingdom'.

Brockway's Bill (his third attempt, uncannily anticipating trouble) to introduce legislation defined 'discrimination' thus: '. . . a person exercises discrimination where he refuses, witholds from or denies to any other person facilities or advantages on the ground of colour, race or religion of that person'.[65] If enacted the Bill was so designed as to have an educational rather than a punitive purpose. The Bill did not get a second reading in the House of Commons. Determined, the same group of MPs introduced it once more, but again without success. By the summer of 1959 'anti-colour bar' legislation was still regarded as unnecessary. Indeed, the government had not ratified the ILO Convention 'to pursue a national policy designed to eliminate any discrimination on the basis of race, colour, sex, religion, political opinion, national extraction or social origin in respect to employment or occupation' and to introduce appropriate legislation 'where necessary'.[66]

Racial tension

Political debate on the pros and cons of legislation did nothing to diminish tension in some parts of North Kensington. If anything, the politicians who called for control were also legitimising the fascist groups' race-hate campaign to keep Britain white. In this 'climate of conflict' warnings were given of potential violence. In the build-up, there were a series of minor rows and incidents. Predictably, 'Keep Britain White' was scrawled on walls and lamp posts, and offensive and provocative leaflets posted through letter boxes. In addition, there was agitation at street corners, where Mosley meetings whipped up race-hatred. While there was major confrontation there were deeper rumblings in an environment of physical decay and social discontent.

The tension exploded on the night of 17 May 1959. Kelso Cochrane, a 32-year-old West Indian carpenter was murdered near a street corner in Kensal New Town, when about five or six white youths attacked him.[67] While the police thought robbery was the motive for Cochrane's murder, black people firmly believed that he was killed because he was black. It was clear, however, that the murder increased 'race tension'. Much of what was submerged now came to the surface. Notting Hill and its environs was again in the spotlight. Notting Hill was headlined and dramatised in the press, and the White Defence League referred to Cochrane as 'this manufactured martyr'.[68]

In the face of rising animosity, the vulnerable black minority felt a profound need to organise and fight. An emergency meeting of representatives of West Indian and African organisations in Britain was held in London. Their open letter to the Prime Minister stated, 'Coloured citizens of the United Kingdom and possibly throughout the Commonwealth have lost confidence in the ability of the law-enforcing agencies to protect them.'[69] Furthermore, they asked

Mr Harold Macmillan to condemn the murder of Cochrane publicly, and appealed to the trade unions and churches to denounce the
killing. In fact, although Macmillan did not make a public statement he convened a special meeting of ministers. Subsequently,
after Cabinet deliberations, a new co-ordinating machinery on the
'colour problem' was set up in Whitehall.

Soon after, representatives from the black community with a
number of delegates of English Associations formed a joint Committee for the 'immediate protection of our persons and property'.
They also set up an 'Inter-Racial Friendship Co-ordinating
Council'.[70]

Cochrane's death was symbolic of the need for black unity. The
new council sponsored a memorial meeting for Cochrane, which
was attended by about 40 organisations from the three major
political parties. At Cochrane's funeral, about 800 people marched
behind the coffin from the church in Ladbroke Grove to Kensal
Green cemetery. Among the members of the congregation were
the Prime Minister of the West Indies Federation, the High Commissioner for Ghana and the Mayor of Kensington. The lesson was
read by the Bishop of Kensington. Many ordinary people watched
the procession.

In the wake of the murder, attention was centred on the causes
and symptoms of tension, such as the housing shortage, crowding
and blight, casual employment, the shortage of police, manifestations of social disorder and violence generally, and particularly
the promoters of aggressive prejudice. Government policy had a lot
to answer for. Several aspects were stressed. Firstly, as was the case
in the 1940s in Liverpool and in 1958 in Nottingham, it was said on
the whole black people did not trust the police; a view that was
mentioned by the Labour Secretary of the American Association
for the Advancement of Coloured People.[71] This private view was
now 'openly' stated by representatives of the black communities.
Some of the allegations made were that they knew of instances of
police brutality against Blacks, that the police tended to be harsher
with Blacks than with Whites. These public statements came at a
time when there was concern about certain aspects of police procedure. In fact, at the time, two detective officers in Birmingham,
charged with assaulting a Jamaican in the CID room at the local
police station, were found guilty, fined and asked to resign. Secondly, there were complaints that there were far too few policemen
in the back streets of North Kensington. The Inter-Racial Friendship Co-ordinating Council suggested the appointment of
'coloured and white special constables'.[72] And the Socialist Labour
League talked of setting up 'Workers Defence Squads' for Notting
Hill. Thirdly, and most importantly, special attention was given to
organisations which stirred up colour prejudice and race hatred.
Among these were the Mosley Union Movement, the National
Labour Party, the White Defence League, the League of Empire

Loyalists and the Ku-Klux-Klan who used every opportunity to put their theory into practice.

Post-riots organisations

The role of the racist groups

The agitation by the Mosley Union Movement and kindred bodies helped to keep race hatred alive. Indeed their share of responsibility for the troubles could not be dismissed. The TUC commenting on the disturbances stated: 'Evidence is accumulating that elements which propagated racial hatred in Britain and Europe in pre-war days are once more fanning the flames of violence.'[73] In the weeks that followed the disturbances, although many local authorities refused to give the Union Movement permission to hold their meetings in the schools or town halls, in February 1959 this ban began to be relaxed and after the summer of 1959 Mosley held several meetings in town halls, particularly in Kensington Town Hall.

After the autumn riots in 1958, Mosley concentrated in the North Kensington area. The Union Movement's first issue of the monthly broadsheet, the *North Kensington Leader*, appeared in October 1958. It called for 'Action with Mosley', insisting that 'Now is the Time to Act'. The Movement opened an office and bookshop to serve its activities in North Kensington. On his return from South Africa, Mosley was adopted at a 'greatly packed historic' meeting early in April 1959 as the Movement's candidate for North Kensington. In a no-nonsense speech, Mosley predictably said, 'he would send all coloured immigrants back to their homelands'.[74] He described the Union Movement as 'quite a go-home-party'.

Also in existence, before and after the disturbances, was the National Labour Party. The NLP published a journal, *Combat*, the first issue of which appeared in the autumn of 1958 when tension was high. The Party exploited the situation by holding three open air meetings in 10 days at Notting Hill Gate.[75] Another organisation, The White Defence League, circulated racist literature. Its newsheet *Black and White News* was sold in North Kensington during the outbreak of violence. Its headlines were provocative: 'Blacks Seek White Women', 'Blacks Milk the Assistance Board', 'America Pouring Negro Troops into Britain'.[76]

The White Defence League, closely associated with the National Labour Party, made every effort to distribute and display their racist propaganda. These groups were publicly expressing the private fears of white residents. The propaganda they had been circulating and the racial hatred they preached was, to say the least, dangerous. And before Cochrane was murdered, some organisations expressed anxiety over the 'Keep Britain White' groups. Among them were the British–Caribbean Association and the

Conservative Commonwealth Council. But relying on the police to stamp out fascist activity was no solution. In fact, the black community was apprehensive of both the police and fascist elements.

Two kinds of organisation

Between 1958 and 1959, among the fascists there was a 'division of labour'. On the one hand, there was the Union Movement which aspired to join, or work with, the existing body politic (although they condemned party politics for making Britain 'the dustbin of the world'). On the other hand, there was the National Labour Party, the White Defence League and the Ku-Klux-Klan among others who regarded themselves as 'outsiders'. They took an inflexible, extreme and uninhibited stand. They welcomed the label 'fascist'. They agreed with Colin Jordan, National Organiser of the White Defence League, who said, 'If a Fascist is a person who wants to Keep Britain White, then I am a Fascist and proud of it.'[77]

In contrast with this kind of unbridled racist language, the Union Movement used 'emotive innuendo and insinuation' before the General Election in 1959. The Movement's policy called for 'the establishment of a Europe–Africa economic, cultural and military force to stand between the state capitalism of Russia and the almighty dollar-worshipping United States of America'.[78] It also sentimentalised the so-called bullying of white women, calling for the housing of Britons first and alerted its readers of *Action* to a 'Big Coloured Threat To Britain's Health'. The Movement also put forward a three point policy:

1. send the coloured immigrants home, with their passage paid by the people who brought them here;
2. send them home to good jobs in their own countries, which can be secured by giving them the guaranteed market in Britain for which they have always asked. Give them this market, not for the 10 years they originally suggested, but on a permanent basis;
3. give Britain at the same time the same rights as the British Dominions which have long exercised the right to choose which immigrants shall be allowed through their ports. The right of entry for students coming here for a definite period, after which time they would go back to their own countries.

Under this policy the minority of crooks among them would be expelled because of their habits. The majority of decent people among them would be sent home to good jobs among their own families.[79]

The National Labour Party (and the White Defence League) was, however, more openly offensive than the Union Movement. The NLP's *Combat* quoted from Hitler's *Mein Kampf* and asked 'Was Hitler really our enemy?' The Party's paper described as 'The Voice of British Nationalism' was enough to confuse those who had lost dear ones as Britain fought off Nazi aggression. The Party's leader, John Bean, was also the Party's Director of Policy and editor of *Combat*. Its President was Andrew Fountaine, a Norfolk land-owner.

The Party's 'principles' were:

> A new union of the Dominions of British blood in place of the Coloured Commonwealth. An alliance with our racial kinsmen of Western Europe. This, in essence, is the alternative that the National Labour Party offers to both Communism and Liberal Democracy, fighting its last rearguard action.

Moreover, the Party was anti-semitic and haunted by Blacks, arguing that black immigration must be stopped for it not only aggravated the housing problem and constituted a serious threat to workers' living standards in view of increasing unemployment but, most important, it would turn our nation into 'a race of mongrels'. [80]

For the Party's President, race mixing meant the end of 'our race and our culture'. On this premise, he argued, 'If it is Fascist to try to stop that, then Fascism is a bloody good thing.' In effect, they could not align themselves with any group whose racial views were not 'sufficiently extreme'. [81]

After Cochrane's death, the White Citizen's League (which had the full approval and support of the NLP) implied that the West Indian was killed in order to turn public opinion against white resistance organisations in Notting Hill. The League joined the NLP in a protest meeting in Trafalgar Square, where the cry was: 'Stop the Coloured Invasion! . . . The nation is being Mongrelised . . .'

The other of the 'Keep Britain White' groups, the Ku-Klux-Klan (denounced by the President of the NLP as a 'Communist organisation') did not meet in Trafalgar Square – they operated less openly. They were the dangerous introverts among the racist groups. 'Secrecy is our defence', they said, 'against those who desire to mongrelise our proud heritage.' Again we see eighteenth century racist arguments of white superiority being repeated. Underlying the slogans in 1958 were insistent threats. Five days before the violence erupted in Nottingham in 1958, they sent a letter to the editor of the *West Indian Gazette* which read:

> My Dear Mr B. Ape,
> Kindly post two copies of your paper to the above address every month until ordered to cease.
> Possibly you are wondering why we have so-far failed to pay attention to your audacity in setting up this filthy hack-trash of a paper? Pray good Sir, We, The Aryan Knights miss nothing, close attention has been paid to every issue of this rag, and I do sincerely assure you, the information gleaned has proven of great value to the Klan.

May we take this opportunity to wish your . . . . . . paper every
success whilst you are able to continue printing it.

Aryan regards,

A. Whiteman[82]

The General Election

As the General Election of October 1959 approached, Mosley kept
up the anti-black propaganda. The other contestants from among
the major parties for the North Kensington constituency were
George Rogers (Labour), Bob Bulbrook (Conservatives) and
Michael Hyndelman for the Liberals. A fifth candidate, Dhanaraj
Nandawar, an Indian restaurant owner stood as an Independent
candidate to oppose Mosley so that the people of North Kensington
would have the chance to vote for racial integration. He withdrew
his nomination just before the election 'in the interest of unity and
the fight against racialism'. [83]

The election contest became well known as the 'ugly' election,
with Mosley making an unpleasant address. While Blacks and
'nigger lovers' and 'Jews' were attacked in North Kensington, the
White Defence League and the NLP were active elsewhere as the
election drew near. They agitated to 'Keep Hampstead White'
because a black local doctor, Dr David Pitt, was the Labour Party
candidate. While Pitt was speaking at a meeting in Hampstead
Town Hall he was heckled by a small group shouting 'Keep Britain
White'. Two MPs connected with the British Caribbean Association protested in a letter to *The Times*.[84] Colin Jordan, the
National Organiser of the WDL, replied that 'better race relations is
a euphemism for racial treason'. During his campaign Pitt was
subjected to much racial abuse. He received insulting telephone
calls and his election posters were defaced.

When the votes were counted, the Labour candidate, George
Rogers was re-elected in North Kensington. David Pitt, however,
lost in Hampstead. Several thousand people had cast their votes for
the fascist organisations, the Union Movement and the NLP.
Mosley, however, felt this was not enough. His petition to the
High Court as 'the first legal step towards obtaining a judicial
inquiry' into the conduct and validity of the North Kensington
election was dismissed.

Liberal groups

While the extremist organisations with strident voices preached
racial hatred, there was some activity devoted to integration of the
black minority through the 'Keep Britain Tolerant' groups. Following the events of 1958, social, educational and welfare activities
continued to grow.

Social activities

Naturally, some West Indians (in general a friendly people) became friends with their neighbours. Many black people also joined churches, political parties, trade unions, student organisations, sports, jazz and social clubs. Throughout London there were branches of the International Friendship League. There was also the Overseas Social Centre, the All Nations Social Club and the Linguists Club. The programmes of these clubs, reflecting their cosmopolitan and inter-racial nature, included dances, socials, lectures and tuition.

Given the discord aroused by the pre-and post-riot events and murder, harmony was the keynote. Thus social organisations were formed, particularly after the disturbances of 1958, to assist in the process of integration of black people. In the existing frosty atmosphere, some came into being enthusiastically, flickered and died quickly. For example, Harmony Club (the mixed youth club) which started well lasted only six weeks. Among those who set up organisations were the Quakers, the Methodists and the young socialists. The more persistent of these organisations were those based on inter-racial social activities. Most of these were found in South London. In Brixton, the Racial Brotherhood (one of the best known) was formed by a member of the Society of Friends. Further, the meetings and socials in Lambeth Town Hall, initiated years before by the Mayor to bring Blacks and Whites together continued.

There were also clubs intended primarily for black people. It was assumed that 'the newcomers are often too shy to join clubs because organised social activities are not a feature of West Indian society, and that they need therefore a period of initiation by themselves'.[85] In this context, the churches became involved, holding services and organising meetings for West Indians. Local associations were also involved. For example, the Paddington Overseas Students and Workers Committee which was associated with the London Council of Social Service opened an afternoon club for West Indian mothers. Apart from this direct, self-help approach, there were other organisations. Some acted in an advisory and welfare capacity and some were largely concerned with educating the public, while others concentrated on holding social functions.

Education and welfare

The education and welfare organisations operated at various levels. At the local level, the Colonial Advisory Panel of the St Pancras Borough Council was resurrected after the 'riots'. In Willesden, early in 1959, the Mayor formed an International Frendship Committee 'to undertake the work of helping the newcomers'. One of its practical functions was that assistance was given by members of this Committee who investigated disputes between black landlords and white tenants. In Kensington, a West Indian social worker was appointed in the autumn of 1958 and the Mayor set up a 'Racial Integration Co-ordinating Committee' which was representative of local organisations and churches, and white and coloured 'public persons'. The Committee was meant to promote harmony locally.

The work being done was important, but limited. Co-ordination of their various activities was vital to effectiveness. Unfortunately, these organisations were little known and stability was lacking, except in a few cases. One such case was the Universities and Left Review Club which organised the 'Notting Hill Project'. They were interested in local youth (black and white) 'inter-racial in theory but hardly in practice'; in assisting tenants with their rent and housing problems; and with the establishment of a Residents' Association.[86]

Another attempt at co-ordination was a federal body, the 'Committee for Inter-Racial Unity in West London' which was launched by a Conference held in July 1959.

In attendance were 100 delegates from local branches of the Labour Party, the Co-operative Movement, trade unions, trade councils and black organisations. The Conference resolved to 'carry out activities against racialism in all its forms and in support of greater inter-racial unity in West London', to 'Co-ordinate a drive of watchful pressure and propaganda to improve welfare services and housing policies in areas of changing population, and to ensure that local authorities use to the full, the powers that they already possess.' A 'Unity' leaflet was published, followed by another conference a few months later. Indeed there was a multiplicity of conferences, committees, associations, all providing advice (all well-meaning) to promote inter-racial harmony. As it was, there were 'far more organisations and resolutions in North Kensington than concrete efforts'. This had begun to cause some embarrass-ment. Their effectiveness was questioned. In theory there was no problem, but how practical were they? Thus one local newspaper asked 'Will Too Many Do-Gooders Pave the Path to Notting HELL?'[87]

In this Kensington borough, local organisations proved inad-equate. Much was dependent on other organisations in the wider society of London. There were many enthusiastic organisers whose attentions had been focused on the events in Kensington. Among these groups was the Advisory Committee on the Welfare of West Indians in London. It was established in 1956 by the London Council of Social Service to help and to co-ordinate the work of the various bodies dealing with West Indian immigrants in London. Also in existence was the Metropolitan Coloured Peoples Housing Association, formed in 1957, to alleviate the housing difficulties of black immigrants and their families in London. The purpose of the Association was to buy and convert houses into flats to be let to black people at 'reasonable rents'. By doing so, the Association hoped 'to assist in the real integration of newcomers from overseas into the whole of London'. By 1960, very little progress was made in this direction. Only one house, with five flats, had been opened in Hackney – a long way from Notting Hill but equally depressed.[88]

Much more successful was the Race Relations Committee of the Society of Friends whose function was essentially educational. It advised Quakers to participate in inter-racial clubs. In turn, a Quaker group gave practical assistance (scrubbing and painting houses) in the 'miserable' Kensal New Town district.

There were many other groups which showed general concern for race relations in Britain. Among these were the Institute of Race Relations. Unlike other organisations which pronounced, and indeed campaigned for, the active disapproval of intolerance, 'the Institute is precluded by the Memorandum of articles of its incorporation from expressing an opinion on any aspect of the relations between races'. There was also the Council of Christians and Jews, the National Council for Civil Liberties, the Haldane Society, the Movement for Colonial Freedom, the Campaign Against Racial Discrimination in Sport, and the Stars Campaign for Inter-Racial Friendship. At the national level, the British Caribbean Association was formed during the riots of 1958 in order firstly, 'To develop and increase friendship and understanding between the people of the West Indies (including British Guiana and British Honduras) and the people of the United Kingdom', and secondly, 'To stimulate and encourage all forms of mutual aid between the West Indies and Great Britain.'

West Indian and Asian organisations

If there was a lack of the sense of 'community' among Blacks after the riots and Cochrane's murder, there was every reason for them to form their own organisations. Yet, it was doubtful whether the migrants would, or could develop their own organisations on a large scale. It was argued that only a minority of West Indians who were living in Britain took an active part in organisations though all were more familiar with the concept of formal association than the newcomers were. And also that the duality of West Indian attitudes (should they take part in separate or in joint 'integrated' organisations?) presented a problem. But this 'duality' was not peculiar to West Indians in view of the ambiguity and diversity of English attitudes. Not yet used to being 'organisation men' it was not necessary for West Indians to be organised to express their sociability. Indeed they brought with them a talent for spontaneous, informal social contact. Thus, the pattern of West Indian social organisations was not clearly defined. In fact, they were 'unstable'.

Informal contacts were made through meetings held in rooms, in basements, street corners, markets, cafes and barber shops. The barber shops, in particular, served as community centres where

West Indian newspapers were read and discussed, where all the latest news was heard, where one could get information about new arrivals, about possible vacancies for jobs and accommodation, about threats of unemployment, and the announcements of meetings and dances. Apart from the barber shops, migrants (particularly newcomers) met in their own licensed clubs and in shopping centres such as Brixton Market, Camden Town and Portobello Road.

Formal associations

The formal social links among West Indians were less widespread than the informal ones. There were four main types of organisations: student groups, church groups, 'harmony' clubs (which stressed integration); and associations primarily concerned with the rights of black people in Britain and their liberation in other parts of the Commonwealth.

West Indian students joined various organisations – those in their own colleges and universities, those concerned with all overseas students in London, and the West Indian Students' Union. Generally, it seemed, there was a clear separation between the students and working-class migrants. The majority of students belonged to a different social group. Their stay was not only more limited, but generally more comfortable and hopeful. In short (and in effect) black students posed no threat whatsoever to British society.

Religious groups reflected the social and cultural diversity among newcomers. In London, there were about eight gospel halls with West Indian congregations whose services were essentially evangelical. These services contrasted sharply to the more austere atmosphere of the established church in Britain.

The Harmony Clubs and the Associations which emerged in response to the disturbances of 1958 gained new support after Kelso Cochrane's murder in 1959. Official West Indian policy favoured the Harmony Clubs rather than separate associations. When Norman Manley visited Britain in September 1958 he felt there was a need for a full-scale programme of integration; a 'Grassroots Plan'. He wanted a better community spirit, integration and inter-racial harmony, to be effected through a network of British and West Indian committees working together in every community in Britain.[89]

In the new trend which followed, inter-racial clubs were established by West Indians themselves. The Blacks had come through their phase of fear and were extending friendship to Whites. Thus, the Harmonist Movement was founded by MacDonald Stanley (a black West Indian) to bring about 'inter-racial harmony amongst all peoples of the world'. The first Harmonist Club was opened in November 1958 in a church hall in Stamford Hill where social evenings were held on Saturday nights. The Movement also issued a newsheet, *The Harmonist*.

The Clapham Club, another inter-racial club, was founded after Cochrane's murder by a Jamaican post-office worker who had served in the RAF. The Club aimed 'to promote good will between peoples of all races: to foster and encourage a spirit of mutual understanding and respect . . . by study of their backgrounds – social, cultural, historical'. With a total membership of 70 there was said to be an equal number of white and black members.[90] As a model, this was success indeed.

Most of the organisers of inter-racial clubs were also active in the associations, primarily for Blacks committed to promoting their specific interests. This dual participation was inevitable for those concerned with race relations in London. Very quickly, these organisers found that it was necessary to operate at both levels.

Although small, the various black organisations were 'alert, active and well-connected' to exercise some influence. Among the organisations strengthened after August 1958 were the Association for the Advancement of Coloured People, the Coloured People's Progressive Association, the United Kingdom Coloured Citizens Association and a branch of the People's National Movement (the Party then – and still – in government in Trinidad and Tobago). Although membership was open to Whites (indeed white people were among their officers) these organisations were founded and run essentially by black people, mainly West Indians.

The AACP was, however, in some respects in a category apart. It was presided over by Mrs Amy Dashwood Garvey, the widow of Marcus Garvey. She ran a hostel and club in North Kensington. This was a case in point where one leader worked at several levels. There were also several groups primarily established by and for Africans.

The CPPA, on the other hand, had a list of about 500 members. Its motto was 'United We Stand – Divided We Fall'. Its objects were 'To protect the rights and privileges of its members as citizens; to strive for their social, economic and political advancement; to work for inter-racial understanding'.[91]

This Association's officers were also connected with other organisations furthering the interests of black people. In order to lead, the black leader had to co-ordinate a number of activities in order to get a perspective and direction.

A great deal depended on leadership. Many West Indian leaders were involved in essentially black or 'integrated' organisations of various kinds. This group of black leaders, particularly West Indian leaders in London, was drawn from the ranks of workers, clergymen, intellectuals, professional politicians and welfare workers, among others. Most of them were in the 30–40 age group and had already lived in Britain for some time. As the network of inter-relationships between organisations grew, West Indian leaders assumed increasing importance which, unfortunately, did not reflect the strength of the individual organisations which they represented.

In order to bring together newcomers and to cement this multiplicity of small, unstable black organisations, it was necessary to have a two-way flow of communication between the leaders and the mass of migrants. The importance of a journal reflecting essentially the black experience (to identify the major problems and views) was grasped by Claudia Jones, the editor of the *West Indies Gazette*. In its first issue, which appeared in March 1958, the monthly *Gazette* stated that West Indians in Britain 'form a community with its own special wants and problems which our own paper alone would allow us to meet'. In the summer of 1957, a group of West Indians, concerned with problems of unemployment, housing and colour prejudice spoke to some 2000 West Indians in their homes, at dances and at socials. They found that the migrants 'wanted an organisation to represent their interests' and 'welcomed efforts to unite and further British–West Indian unity'. As a result and for this purpose, the *West Indian Gazette* came into being. By 1960 the *Gazette* had established itself with a total circulation of 15,000 copies. (Another monthly, *Link*, first published in November 1958 was less successful and was discontinued after a few issues. Encouraged, a year later, in November 1959, one of the people who had been concerned with the production of *Link* brought out a new monthly, the *Anglo-Caribbean News*.)[92]

The *Gazette* carried news about race relations in Britain, focusing on questions such as prejudice and discrimination, reports of the existing, relevant organisations and on the personal successes and hardships of black people.

In spite of the fact that England 'is no bed of roses', migration continued at an increased rate because of population and economic pressures in the Caribbean territories. Moreover, the *Gazette* informed the black community in Britain of developments in the West Indies, the United States and Africa and on general political issues in Britain. Its advertisements included the announcements of meetings, of steamship lines to the Caribbean, of West Indian shops, clubs and restaurants in London. Indeed, it was the *West Indian Gazette* which organised the first 'Caribbean Carnival' in London in January 1959. Through this event, it was hoped to bind West Indians in the United Kingdom together as never before. In its carnival brochure, the *Gazette* said that it stood for an 'Independent United Democratic State of West Indians in the British Commonwealth' and 'For unity of West Indians and other coloured people in the United Kingdom. For friendship with the British people, based on equality and human dignity for peoples, irrespective of race, colour or origin.' Further, the *Gazette* intended to assist in the payment of fines of 'black and white' youths involved in the Notting Hill events.

During the 1950s, the need to assert the solidarity of black people in Britain had been increasingly stressed as the horizon of 'community' expanded. This was reflected in the 'Anglo–Caribbean Diary' of the *West Indian Gazette*. But with a growing influx of Asians and Africans, this feature was renamed the 'Afro-Asian-Caribbean-UK Unity Diary'.[93] Broadening the scope of the column was timely, as immigration control became, once again, the major issue in British politics.

The door is shut

After the Conservative Party won the election in 1959 with a large majority, the 'restrictionist lobby' which courted stringent control of black immigration became active. This instilled fear among immigrants who sent word to their families, relatives and friends that the door was likely to be shut. Thus, more black settlers came to Britain. This 'unarmed invasion' in which the number of West Indian immigrants jumped from 16,400 in 1959 to 49,000 in 1960, provided the anti-immigration lobby with a stronger argument.[94]

In historical perspective, the black presence has always raised fears among white racists in Britain. Deportation and repatriation of black people from Britain was, of course, nothing new. The issue of black immigration had been a constant preoccupation in Britain. By 1958 it had recurred.

The Commonwealth was essentially 'The White Man's Club'. As the conflict between the exploited labourer and his white oppressor escalated after the Second World War, the British Labour Party and the Trade Union Movement sent out their 'labour missionaries' to advise colonial governments on bringing about industrial peace. The Labour Party worked closely with the TUC in fostering the development of colonial trade unions. The concept of 'the Brotherhood of Man', strong in the Labour Party, led after Indian Independence in 1947, to the Party's anxiety to keep India within the British Commonwealth. This resulted in the British Nationality Act of 1948, which received the support of both the Labour and Conservative Parties. The Act provided citizens of a Commonwealth country with the common status of being British subjects. In effect, this meant that Indian nationals retained their status as British subjects, even when India became a republic. This constitutional change in the relationship between Britain and India and Pakistan, however, did not change British attitudes to the non-white colonies.

During the 1950s, as head of the new Commonwealth, 'a multiracial society', Britain set the pace as *moral* leader of the world. This was a time of 'high idealism'. British leaders were, on the whole, pleased with their international standing. Indeed it was felt that all Commonwealth citizens should have the opportunity to enter and leave the mother country freely. Any limitation to this right

therefore was seen as undermining the foundation of the new
Commonwealth and would thus call into question Britain's moral
leadership.

As yet, black immigration was still largely an issue contained in
London and the Midlands. While some questions were asked in the
House of Commons, the subject had not entered the national mind.
However, the 1958 race riots changed this. Public awareness was
alerted to the black migrant's presence. In effect, the black migrant
predictably became the scapegoat for deficient housing and existing
and potential unemployment. Thus, there was a 'colour problem'
in Britain. As fear was encouraged by white racists, politicians saw
the solution to the 'colour problem' in a ban or severe restriction of
black immigration from the Commonwealth countries. George
Rogers, Labour MP for North Kensington demanded early legislation to halt 'the tremendous influx', while Alec Douglas-Home,
Junior Minister for Commonwealth Relations was in no doubt that
'curbs will have to be put on the unrestricted flow of immigrants to
Britain from the West Indies'. Moreover, the Conservative Party
Conference (aware of the public mood) added its support for
control of black immigration. One public opinion poll showed that
75 per cent of those questioned were in favour of control. Thus,
immigration and race entered British politics. The ideal of free
entry of black people into Britain was called into question. On this
issue the Commonwealth Relations Office and the Colonial Office
stood opposed to the Home Office.

Moreover, the British government was faced with the problem
of administration in the event of control, since the majority of black
migrants, at the time, were from the West Indies, and as such were
citizens of 'the United Kingdom and Colonies'. Any legal redefinition of British citizenship would have courted the charge of
racialism by the affected Commonwealth countries. To further
complicate matters, the process of Federation in the West Indies
was already underway. Once federated, the British government
hoped that, like India and Pakistan, West Indian emigration would
be controlled at source.

Taken together then, these considerations led to the government's rejection of Sir Cyril Osborne's call for immigration control. The debate on Osborne's motion revealed the racist fears of
some MPs from both parties. Martin Lindsay, the Tory MP felt
that 'A question which affects the future of our own race and breed
is not one we should merely leave to chance.'[95] And Frank Tom-
ney, the Labour MP warned that 'The coloured races will exceed
the white races in a few years by no less than five to one. This will
be a formidable problem for the diminishing members of the white
races throughout the world.'[96]

Although the government and the parties had sensed the public
mood, they were content to bide their time. But not for long.
Several months later, at the General Election, the 'unpleasant and

controversial' issue of black immigration was revived in July 1960 with R. A. Butler, then Home Secretary, saying, 'It is very unlikely that this country will turn away from her traditional policy of free entry.'[97] Not surprisingly, Sir Cyril Osborne continued his campaign for control, actively supported by a few working class and lower-middle class Tory MPs. Support for them grew with the formation of the Birmingham Immigration Control Association.

To many, black immigration control was a foregone conclusion. Inevitably, the private views of the policy-makers had started to become public. A departmental committee was set up to re-examine the mechanics of immigration control.[98] The Committee recommended control on the basis of the availability of jobs in Britain. When the details were leaked to the press in January 1961 to test the temperature of the electorate, the *Birmingham Evening Mail* and *The Observer* were confident that Commonwealth immigration would be controlled.[99]

Six months later, a Gallup Poll showed 67 per cent in favour of restrictions, 6 per cent for a total ban and 21 per cent for continued free entry. The Tories were in no doubt that the time was right to take action. The Party Conference favoured immigration control which was then inserted in to the Queen's Speech. Subsequently a Bill was published on 17 November, and on 27 February 1962 the Bill was passed by 107 votes. The Act, which took effect from 1 July 1962, restricted entry to Commonwealth citizens who held current work vouchers issued by the then Ministry of Labour. The actual scheme of control was left out of the Act; thus changes could be made without the approval of Parliament.[100]

If the Tory Party policy on black immigration was predictable, how did the Labour Party with its commitment to the socialist doctrine 'The Brotherhood of Man' approach and deal with the issue? In the 1950s and the 1960s, the Labour Party consistently opposed restrictions. In the end, however, with its sights set on forming a government, the Party accepted 'public opinion'. A number of reasons have been given for this change in position. When the Party was formed in 1900 it immediately identified itself with the exploited masses in the British colonies. It took a stand on Home Rule in India. In Africa and the West Indies it sought to ameliorate the conditions of the oppressed working classes. Indeed, the new Commonwealth was the brainchild of the post-war Labour government. The Party favoured a multi-racial Commonwealth and had no doubt that the immigration problem was 'based on colour'. After the 1958 riots, it was also aware that 'any form of British legislation limiting Commonwealth immigration into this country would be disastrous to our status in the Commonwealth and to the confidence of Commonwealth people'. But some of the Labour Party's ideals, such as 'The Brotherhood of Man' became highly questionable. The electoral irrelevance of such ideals became an electoral liability as shown by the results of the 1959 General

Election and in the by-election in Birmingham which was won by the Birmingham Control Association's candidate who received twice as many votes as the Labour candidate.

Even at this stage, in spite of its electoral liability, the national leadership of the Party remained committed to the 'open door' policy. A moral principle was at stake and was admirably upheld by Hugh Gaitskell. But while the Party declined a second reading of the Commonwealth Immigrants Bill in November 1961 (because the Bill introduced control and because 'it was widely held to introduce a colour bar into the legislation', the question still remained: how long could the Labour Party disregard popular opinion? The short answer was not very long since there was a fundamental conflict within the Party between a moral ideal and practical reality. Sooner rather than later, the Party had to take a public stand. After making a passionate speech against the Immigration Bill in Parliament, Patrick Gordon Walker, the Shadow Foreign Secretary and Labour MP for Smethwick, had to face the strong disapproval of many of his white constituents. He took note of their feelings. He did not criticise the Bill when it was finally debated in February 1962. In fact, he did not vote for or against the Bill. This episode of Labour representation was the thin end of the wedge.

The Labour Party had begun to move towards the control advocates. The shift was, however, not complete. In true British tradition a compromise was reached. After saying 'We do not contest the need for control of immigration into this country', Harold Wilson offered not to vote against renewal of the Act, if the government initiated consultations with Commonwealth governments to control immigration from their end. This offer was not accepted, and the Labour Party voted against the Act.[101] By doing so Labour supporters felt estranged.

By October 1964, however, the Labour Party manifesto for the election stated: 'Labour accepts that the number of immigrants entering the United Kingdom must be limited. Until satisfactory agreement covering this can be negotiated with the Commonwealth, a Labour government will retain immigration control.'[102] By that time the pendulum had swung the other way. Some Labour candidates, during the election campaign, blamed the Tories for 'the whole wave of immigration'. In Southall, the Labour candidate said 'Labour has not been in power for thirteen years to control the flow of immigrants, and before that Southall had not been in difficulties.'[103] The Labour candidate for Wandsworth Central had issued a leaflet entitled: 'Things About Immigration the Tories Want You To Forget' which said, 'Large-scale immigration has occurred only under this Tory Government.'[104] But this dramatic change in the Party's stand on black immigrant control was not enough. For, it seemed that aligning themselves with the Blacks would ensure their come-uppance. Although the Smethick Labour

Party campaign leaflet for Gordon Walker proclaimed: 'Immigrants only arrived in Smethick in large numbers during the past ten years – while the Tory government was in power', the Smethwick voters refused to forgive him for his earlier stand against control. He lost his seat in a dramatic way. He received 5754 votes less than when he was elected and the tag of 'Nigger Lover'. [105] There was fierce opposition to people like Gordon Walker and he was made to feel the displeasure of those who disagreed with him when he contested a safe Labour seat in Leyton, London. His defeat reduced the Labour government's majority to three.

Given that another poll had showed that 95 per cent of the voters wanted 'stringent control', the Labour government was faced with the prospect of tighter immigration control. In March 1965, according to Harold Wilson, since the Act was not working as intended because of 'evasions' a fresh examination of the whole problem was necessary. Furthermore Richard Crossman criticised the 'completely ineffective controls,' of the Tories. [106] It was claimed that during 1963 and 1964, some of the 10,255 citizens from the new Commonwealth had 'evaded' immigration controls. As usual the numbers game was played. Sheila Patterson observed that, 'The so-called "evidence" has been presented selectively to create public alarm about evasion by coloured immigrants alone.' By constant repetition, she added, the government's estimates of 'evasions' had acquired the status of fact. [107] Thus racism through a Labour government was becoming more institutionalised, and would have profound consequences on the black community.

The presentation of a White Paper to Parliament in August 1965 which, among other things, authorised the immigration officer to make police registration a condition for entry if he doubted the entrant's genuineness, began a process of growing hostility between migrants long settled here and the police. The White Paper proposed work vouchers for 8500 a year. The age of entry of dependent children was lowered from 18 to 16. The British public welcomed these strictures; 88 per cent of the population supported the White Paper. At last the government was being representative of public feelings on control of black migrants, while Irish and European immigration 'continued unabated'.

While criticism of the White Paper came from the National Council for Civil Liberties, the Campaign Against Racial Discrimination and the Young Fabians, the TUC avoided the issue. At the Labour Party Conference, a motion asking the government to withdraw the White Paper was lost in spite of the block votes from the Transport and General Workers' Union. *The Economist* commented: 'The representatives of the British working man faithfully reflected his aversion to any spirit of universal brotherhood which touched him too closely.' [108]

Predictably, Harold Wilson defended the White Paper and repudiated 'the libel that government policy is based either on colour or racial prejudice'. In effect by resenting and repudiating the libel of racialism, he was doing precisely what Tory leaders had done at the time of the 1961 Commonwealth Immigrants Bill. According to William Deedes (then Minister without Portfolio) the Bill was designed to 'restrict the influx of coloured immigrants' but 'we were reluctant to say so openly'.[109] No wonder the Labour Party's White Paper received the full support of the Tories.

As the 'open door' policy on Commonwealth immigration became threatened, more attention was paid to the settlement of Blacks. But settlement was, and continued to prove, uncomfortable for the black migrant, particularly in view of Sir Cyril Osborne's statement that 'This is a white man's country, and I want it to remain so',[110] and John Hallows's (a reporter of black settlers' reactions to the 1961 Immigration Bill) finding that 'No one with a dark face is grinning anymore. . . . Now they feel the Immigration Bill controversy will make them less acceptable'.[111]

The fear of control triggered an increase in the number of migrants and their dependants when the Immigration Act took effect in July 1962. For those who had beaten the 'ban', the process of setting up homes, in short, of settlement, had begun. The semi-skilled and unskilled workers formed the nucleus of the black working class in Britain. But why immigration control? To better understand this 'control', black migrant labour must be viewed in the context of capitalism and class.

8 Capitalism, Class, Black Workers and Racial Disadvantage

After 1962, in view of the decreasing numbers of black workers allowed into Britain, black migrant labour had become part of the British working class, at least in theory. Given this broad categorisation, it is necessary to locate black workers more specifically within the class politics of British capitalism.

To get a clearer perspective of how black migrant workers came to hold their position within the working class, they must be viewed as essentially migrant labour within the economic and political framework of British capitalism. The concepts, capitalism and class then, are directly related to black migrant labour. Marx's definition of the classes in relation to production states that, in the capitalist mode of production, there are two main classes: the bourgeoisie and the working class. This formulation has come under heavy attack. However, given that Britain is a capitalist social formation, according to one writer, class relations can be understood in terms of three processes underlying the social relations of production: control of labour power, control of the physical means of production, and control of investment and resources.[1] Control of all three processes is in the hands of the capitalist class, while the working class has no control over investment or the means of production. Indeed, the worker's labour power (both mental and manual) is sold for a wage. Moreover, the worker has no control over the labour power of others.[2] Thus, the capitalist mode of production 'produces and reproduces two unambiguous classes, the bourgeoisie and the working class, and certain contradictory locations between these classes'.

In relating this class structure to Britain, Westergaard and Resler found that "The continuing predominance of capital makes for deep fissures in the social structure. The economic order draws major lines of cleavage between people whose life circumstances and share in influence contrast, however they themselves may see their position and respond to it.'[3] As it is, and ever has been (under capitalism) the ownership and control of capital remain firmly in the hands of a very small proportion of the population. The majority, who can only sell their labour power are at the mercy of the 'swings and roundabouts' inherent in capitalism. Historically, these classes have, in general, tended to reproduce themselves.

Within the working class, however, there are class fractions. Miles and Phizaclea have used the concept of fraction to refer to an objective position within a class boundary which is, in turn, determined by both economic and politico-ideological relations. Thus, the structure of class determination simultaneously defines the position of one class *vis-à-vis* another and cleavages within a class.[4] They argue that all classes are objectively fractionalised. Indeed, a class can be said to have objective interests in relation to that other class with which it shares an antagonistic relation but in any given social formation class relations are simultaneously relations between class fractions and this applies both within and between classes. Moreover, they contend that the precise nature and effect of these relations between fractions of classes (and hence between classes and classes) is a 'historical and conjunctional' question.

Since 1945 then there have been important changes in the British labour market. For example, decline in the staple heavy industries was offset by expansion in the service sector and white-collar employment.[5] By the mid-1970s, it was in these expanding sectors that half the female wage labour force was employed, compared to only a quarter in the manufacturing industries.[6] Increasingly, women were employed in industries that paid low wages. As women, they were paid women's rates so that the sexual division of labour within the family was repeated in waged work. In time, 'industrialised housework' were the types of jobs done by women in the public and private sectors of the economy. The more 'female' a job became, the more it was devalued. Clerical work, for example, became low status, low wage occupations, when compared with skilled manual work.[7]

Thus, the married woman's objective of alleviating the economic distress at home by doing wage-work was frustrated. This need to work was reflected in the fact that the number of married women in the workforce doubled in the twenty years from 1951 to 1971.[8] Moreover, always ready to exploit labour, employers (aided and abetted by the state) viewed women as playing a dual role. Their primary function was as domestic labourers, while of secondary and temporary importance, was the wage work for the employer. This duality armed their employers with a number of reasons why their opportunities for training and promotion (never mind higher wages) should be reduced. It is not surprising, therefore, that with all the demands made on their time, some two-thirds of women wage labourers were part-time workers. Thus, their already vulnerable position became even more so.

Given the low status and low pay of these women, a distinction must be made between black labour and white female labour. Before moving on, a further distinction seems necessary. One survey showed that among black workers there was a lower incidence of discrimination among black women who had applied for jobs in comparison with black men.

Of major significance in the field of female employment for those aged between 16 and 54 years, it was found that 75 per cent of West Indian women were working compared with 55 per cent of all women.[9] This is not surprising in view of the larger families among West Indians. Indeed, the difference in the proportion of West Indian, as compared to all women engaged in wage labour is highest during child-bearing years. Therefore, that dual role in production was (and is) more likely to be performed by black women in Britain taken as a whole.

Overall then, as an actual or potential domestic labourer, a woman's role was, (and is) used ideologically against her, in the form of sexism. This kind of discrimination helps to determine her subordinate position as a wage labourer. Thus, sexism, like racism, refers to a process of social categorisation. Women have therefore come to occupy a particular position in terms of economic, political and ideological relations in order to constitute a class fraction, within the working class.

Migrant labour and capitalism in Western Europe

While migrant labour is geographically mobile in order to satisfy individual advancement, it simultaneously satisfies the demands of capital where there is a shortage of labour. Historically, migrant labour has either been intranational (or internal) or international (or external). The former involves movement within a national boundary, while the latter involves movement across national boundaries. Furthermore, international migrant labour can either be colonial or

proximate in form. Whereas in both instances there is an economic
relationship between the two nations of dominant/dependent, the
nature of the related politico-ideological domination/dependence is
different. For one of the features of the process of colonisation is the
direct politico-ideological domination of the colonised social formation to the extent of direct or indirect political rule and the
development of an ideology based on the inferiority of the subjected people. An example of this form of international migration is
migration from the West Indies to Britain.

On the other hand, in international migrant labour, there is
generally no direct politico-ideological domination of the economically dependent nation. Migration from Greece and Turkey to
Germany is an example of this form of international migrant
labour.[10] Thus, there is an international exploitation of labour to
meet the demands of the capitalist mode of production. In many
Western European countries migrant labour is directly recruited to
low grade jobs. This economic subordination is accompanied by
disadvantage in housing, education and in political rights. It has
been argued that migrant workers should be seen in the context of
this common social and economic situation, and that this objective
division within the class is also accompanied by a subjective division, namely that the indigenous working class, because of its
authoritarianism, 'a product of repressive socialisation' and a fear of
competition, is highly prejudiced towards migrant workers. In
turn, this leads to division in the labour movement, giving the
advantage to the dominant class.[11] Thus, the specific economic and
social circumstances do not change the class determination of
migrant labour. Hence, migrant labour constitutes a distinct fraction of the working class.

Moreover, migrant labour as a class fraction is better understood
when set against the backdrop of post-war economic growth and
accumulation of capital. The expansion of service industries and the
emergence of new industries attracted labour away from the undesirable low wage jobs. This labour shortage, in the context of full
employment until the late 1960s, was filled by the internationalis-
ation of the labour market. In other words, by migrant labour. But,
there were alternatives to this option. For example, higher wages
could have been paid to attract labour into the low-wage jobs.[12]
However, this alternative ignores the fact that some sections of
capital depended upon migrant labour 'as a source of excess profit
necessary to compensate for their below average rate of profit'.[13]

Further, capital was able to draw on female labour. This option
however would have been cumbersome and costly in terms of child
care and other social facilities. Thus, the contract labour system was
preferred in Germany, France and Switzerland, and migrant labour
from the New Commonwealth was used in Britain. The British
case is particularly interesting in that migrant labour involved
almost no expenditure on social capital. Therefore in retrospect, it

has become abundantly clear that many of the 'problems' that arose from migration had little or nothing to do with the character of the migrants themselves, but rather to the failure of the British authorities to provide adequate housing, social and welfare facilities.[14]

The migrant labour 'solution' in Western European capitalist economies generally has a self-generating process, producing such effects as tending to occupy a specific economic position within the broader category of wage labour (for example, it is not contained within the manual working class but extended to the semi- and unskilled sectors of the working class) and occupying a distinct position in political and ideological relations. Migrant labour occupies a subordinate legal position. For example, it has effectively been denied participation in the political process. Indeed in some Western European countries migrant labour has been denied the right of permanent residence, prevented and/or discouraged from being accompanied by families, and denied access to some institutions and services.[15]

Moreover, in ideological relations, the subordinate position of migrant labour is evident in that they have become the object of agitation by right-wing and neo-Nazi political parties. Thus, the physical and cultural characteristics have been used to justify discriminatory action against migrant labour. As 'guest' workers, on contract, both capital and labour have, in certain circumstances, agreed that it is in their mutual interests to restrict migrant labour to certain sections of the labour market. And interestingly, as a consequence, both capital and labour have tended to ascribe inferior characteristics to migrant labour to justify their actions.

Black migrant labour: the British experience

In Britain, however, migrant labour differs from those of the Western European countries in a number of ways. British capitalism made good its labour shortage, beginning in the mid-1950s, through its continuing relationship with the British Empire Commonwealth. This 'legal legacy' is central to black migrant labour in Britain in that Commonwealth citizens shared with citizens of the United Kingdom and the colonies the right to live and work in Britain. Therefore, it was comparatively easier for Commonwealth citizens to sell their labour power in Britain than for Turks and Greeks, for example, who were not only 'alien', but needed work permits. Coincidental with this labour shortage were certain factors in Commonwealth countries which encouraged black migration to Britain for economic reasons. Indeed in the context of the Caribbean it has been argued powerfully that the trends in migration are governed by factors external to the West Indies?[16]

In the early 1950s then, an economic migration from the West Indies was followed by migration from the Indian sub-continent.[17] When this migration of labour to Britain is compared with migrant labour to other capitalist countries in Western Europe, certain similarities and dissimilarities emerge. There were similarities, firstly in that their countries of origin were subordinate in terms of the world capitalist economy; and secondly, at least, at the beginning of the migration process, the majority of migrant workers were considered to be 'target workers'.

But, in the context of black migrant workers and labour relations, there were important dissimilarities which refer to the politico-ideological relations. Given that most of the migrant labour to Britain came from the New Commonwealth between 1950 and 1968, it is important to note that the populations of these countries were predominantly black. And, apart from this, at least initially, migrant labour from the New Commonwealth countries were not as officially organised and recruited selectively (with perhaps the exception of the recruitment office set up by London Transport in Barbados)[18] on a contract basis as in most of the European Economic Community countries. Related to this feature is the fact that the 1962 Immigration Act effectively restricted free entry of the New Commonwealth citizen from the right to live and work in Britain. Gradually, these rights have been removed to the extent that, since the 1971 Immigration Act, Britain had a contract labour system in line with those of the EEC capitalist formations which has come into effect.[19]

This meant that migrants already here in Britain before the 1962 Act were separated from their dependants who did not have the right to live with them in Britain.[20] However, New Commonwealth migrants to Britain during the 1950s and 1960s could, and have settled in Britain. Thus, given its specificity as a fraction of the working class, it is reproducing itself as part of the working class, not as migrant labour, but as black indigenous labour.[21] Moreover, unlike migrant labour elsewhere in western capitalism, New Commonwealth migrant labour has, theoretically at least, the right of full political participation in electoral politics.

A closer look, however, is more revealing. Firstly, there has been a continuing trend of substantial discrimination against black workers in the vital and related areas of employment, housing and services. Indeed, until 1966 discriminators had no legal constraints. Thus legally disadvantaged black migrant workers were not able to change their subordinate position. There was some attempt through the 1966 and 1968 Race Relations Acts to change this situation, but it was the 1976 Act, on the other hand, which was most effective.[22] Furthermore, evidence suggests that black migrant workers and their children occupy second class status in the process of law enforcement. This refers particularly to section 4 of the Vagrancy Act 1824 under which black youths were prosecuted on 'Sus' charges. Therefore, although black migrant labour in Britain does not formally occupy a subordinate legal–political situation, it does so in a *de facto* sense.[23]

Economic aspects of black migrant labour   Among male black workers (excluding African Asians) a 1976 Political and Economic Planning study found that 42 per cent were in semi- or unskilled jobs, with a further 45 per cent in skilled manual jobs. By comparison, the figures for male white workers were 18 and 42 per cent respectively.[24] Among black women 63.5 per cent were engaged in manual work, compared with 45 per cent of white women.

Three basic economic points need to be made about black migrant labour:

First, not only were black migrants predominantly manual workers, but also more than two-fifths of them were concentrated in semi-skilled and unskilled jobs.[25]

Second, black migrant workers, apart from being disproportionately concentrated in manufacturing industries, were also in certain types of manufacturing industry. Smith found that of his sample, 47 per cent of black male migrants and 36 per cent of black women were employed in manufacturing industries, compared with 33 per cent of white males and 25 per cent of white women.[26] And within manufacturing one also found disproportionate numbers of black migrants in shipbuilding, vehicle production, textiles, construction and food manufacture.[27] An analysis of the regional data showed a substantial, disproportionate concentration of black migrants in the textile industry in Yorkshire and Lancashire and a lesser concentration in metal manufacture in the Midlands.[28] Further, where black migrants were employed in the service sector of the economy, they were disproportionately represented in transport and communications, hotels and catering and the National Health Service, precisely those sectors in which semi- and unskilled labour predominate.[29]

Third, those manufacturing industries and services where black migrants were concentrated share several (if not all) of the following characteristics: shortage of labour, shift working, unsocial hours, low pay and an unpleasant working environment.[30] This list reveals a self-perpetuating situation in that there is a shortage of labour because the work involves unsocial hours, low pay and an unpleasant environment.

Faced with a labour shortage then, employers in these sectors of the economy were willing to employ black migrant labour. Thus, in the context of full employment during the 1950s and the early 1960s, black labour served as replacement labour for socially undesirable jobs vacated by white indigenous labour. And finally, there was evidence that the concentration of black labour in the manual working class was being reproduced in part because of racial discrimination. By 1977, Smith was able to show that there was considerable discrimination in both unskilled manual and non-manual jobs and also in promotion. The prospects then, as now, are grim. Smith concluded, 'There is little evidence that racial inequalities in the employment field will be quickly corrected by upward mobility of Asians and West Indians.'[31]

To compound the problems of black workers, black children born in Britain and who have completed higher education experience considerable discrimination. In fact, black graduates tend to find jobs commensurate with their qualifications only when there are no well-qualified Whites competing with them.[32] Consequently, it is significant that with limited opportunities, the black working class include not only a substantial proportion of black migrants with degrees obtained abroad,[33] but also the black British who hold degrees from British universities. Given their economic position in Britain, the black working class, then as now, clearly constitute a class fraction.

Black migrant labour: racial categorisation   In addition to being a class fraction in political and economic relations, black migrant labour also constitutes a class fraction in ideological relations. Historically, the concept of 'race' has tended to come into use when classification of people is made in terms of their physical appearance. Nevertheless following the arrival of black workers in Britain, politicians alerted the public to the 'problem' of the 'races' relating to each other. Thus, 'race relations' has been a thriving concern since the 1950s.

Of importance is the fact that the significance attached to physical differentiation could be either positive or negative. Historically, however, the evidence shows that this significance has been negative for those groups that were the object of racial categorisation. This, in turn, leads us to 'racism' which in this context is used to refer to those negative beliefs of one group which first identify and then set apart another by attaching significance 'to some biological or other inherent characteristic(s) which it is said to possess, and which deterministically associate that characteristic(s) with some other (negatively valued) feature(s) or action(s). The possession of these supposed characteristics is then used as justification for denying that group equal access to material and other resources and/or political rights'.[34]

Although racist beliefs can be held about certain groups which are not distinguishable by colour, for example, the hostile sentiment in Britain about Irish migrant workers and Jewish refugees, one cannot ignore the significance of skin colour to racist beliefs. Indeed, the question of colour formed the basis of the racism articulated from within all classes in Britain since the 1950s. Thus, it is the question of 'race' and the articulation of racism in Britain which places black workers in a special position in ideological relations. Indeed, the evidence shows that governments, politicians, neo-fascist political organisations, the mass media, employers, institutions representing the labour movement and sections of the British working class have all acted upon and articulated racist beliefs. In doing so, they have identified black workers as an excluded racial category.[35]

Given then, that black migrant labour in Britain is a fraction of the working class, this fraction (which many argue is a sub-class) must be seen in the context that Britain is a capitalist social formation, which needed migrant labour to solve the labour shortage in certain sectors of the economy. It is against this background that black migrant workers (and their children) have been racially categorised. The first Commonwealth Immigration Act of 1962 confirmed this. Thus located, a whole range of racially-biased forces came into play in the making of the black working class community.

The black community: urban deprivation

To a large extent, then, the current size and social characteristics of Britain's black population has been structured by the British government's immigration legislation. In response to the evolution of this socially constructed community, accumulative evidence about racial discrimination and racial disadvantage has led governments to introduce not only anti-discrimination legislation, but also a number of initiatives to tackle the steadily deteriorating position of black workers bounded by the decaying urban environment where their homes are located.

Urban deprivation

Between 1961 and 1966 the Census data on employment showed that the main conurbation centres in Britain had very similar industrial structures, and that the changes that were occurring in these industrial structures were very similar. This suggests that identical forces were at work in all the conurbations. Indeed, the similarities in the changes suggests that in searching for theories and explanations, it would be correct to apply these to cities generally rather than treat each city as being unique.[36]

In their analysis, Cameron and Evans conclude that there has been a tendency in the past for each city to be treated in isolation. This has been particularly true of London. They also suggest that the same economic forces had been at work in shaping the pattern of the central area of employment in all conurbations whether they are situated in the prosperous areas of England or in the depressed areas of Scotland and the North of England. Further, the analysis showed that even over the short period of five years, employment in aggregate and in most productive sectors had been decentralising rapidly from the core of the conurbation and, to a lesser extent, from the central cities to the outer conurbation areas.

In effect, there had been a decline in the working population in all the central urban areas following a reduction in the number employed in manufacturing industry and the distributive trades. This reflected a general shift to tertiary employment nationally, as well as a decentralisation of manufacturing industry.

However, in spite of these characteristics in all urban areas, they were not of the same magnitude, nor were they moving at the same pace. In fact, of all these urban areas, London showed the most dramatic contrast. This is reflected in the largest absolute increase in employment in the inner London area in the 1950s, and the largest absolute decrease in the 1960s, while the metropolitan outer ring showed the largest absolute growth in both decades.

This decline is illustrated by the fact that between 1966 and 1974, London's total population fell by 9.4 per cent, although the decline in inner boroughs was much greater at 17.3 per cent than in the outer boroughs. During the same period there was a decline in manufacturing employment of 27 per cent.[37] It has been argued that permanent factory closure and relocation is a more explanatory factor than relocation in London's decline.

Among the reasons put forward for factory closure and relocation were lack of space for expansion, large increases in rates and rent and wage costs, a shortage of certain types of labour, the impact of the rationalisation of capital, nationally and internationally, leading to mergers and factory closures in order to maintain and improve profitability, and finally government policy which encouraged closure and relocations.[38]

This decline seriously affected patterns of unemployment, disadvantage in housing and housing relocation, education, youth service provision and social services of Blacks in the urban centres. Employment is vital to the black workers' fight for survival. Indeed, it is the very reason that the mass of black workers migrated to Britain. Comparison between the migrant and indigenous population's patterns of employment illustrate the extent of urban deprivation.[39]

The age distribution and economic activity rates of ethnic minorities compared with the rest of the population clearly reveal that the ethnic minorities from the New Commonwealth are virtually absent among the retired population of the country. While black workers were fully represented among those employed above the age of 29, in every age category, they tended to be 'overrepresented' among the unemployed.

When employment and unemployment as it affected males and females among the ethnic minority groups is compared with the indigenous population, the 1971 Census showed clearly a tendency for both sexes of the ethnic minority workforce to be more economically active than one was led to presume, through their representation in the total population.[40] However, when employment and unemployment are taken into account the over-representation of black workers is seen more clearly. For example, while both sexes were overrepresented among the employed and the unemployed, there was a clear tendency that women were more affected by unemployment than men. This position was worsened by the recession which has had dire consequences for the economy since 1975.

Whatever generalisations have been made so far must now be qualified, since the overall rates for 'ethnic minority' workers compared with indigenous workers hide variations between different ethnic groups. Indeed, after considering such variations, a number of differences emerge, reflecting both the varying composition of these groups in relation to the total population and also a tendency for some groups to be more affected by unemployment than others.

New Commonwealth-born males tend to be overrepresented among all active males in employment (except in the case of Africans and those from other countries) and West Indian females were overrepresented among all females in employment. Pakistani women, on the other hand, were underrepresented. Moreover, West Indian women were most overrepresented among all females in employment. Indeed, they were highly prone to unemployment; being twice as likely to be out of a job as to be in one. Unemployment, then, not only tended to hit the West Indians harder than any other ethnic group, it also hit the West Indian woman harder than other women workers.[41] Thus, on the question of activity rates, a clear and systematic difference emerged between ethnic minority workers as a group and the indigenous population. In effect, black workers experienced a 'systematic pattern of disadvantage' in employment in that they were (and are) significantly more likely to be unemployed than their counterparts in the indigenous population.

However, while these national figures were likely to underestimate the activity rates and the unemployment rates which ethnic minorities experience in different regions (because of uneven distribution of its population), ethnic minority workers tended to concentrate at or near the centres of employment in the urban areas. Cross observed that when this uneven pattern of ethnic minority settlement is taken into account, the impact of their activity rates and their unemployment rates is exacerbated. Consideration of the settlement patterns and activity rates in conurbations such as Tyneside, West Yorkshire, Merseyside, South East Lancashire, West Midlands, Greater London, Outer Metropolitan Area and Scotland showed that while New Commonwealth-born persons accounted for 2.1 per cent of the total population of Britain, they constituted much larger proportions in some conurbations than in others. Indeed, they constituted 6.4 per cent of the population of Greater London and only 0.6 per cent of the population of Scotland. Further, when the uneven distribution was compared to their activity rates, their unemployment rates in such conurbations (i.e. Greater London, West Midlands and West Yorkshire) contrast sharply. This suggested a pattern of disadvantage in unemployment which affects ethnic minorities in some conurbations to a greater extent than is reflected in the total populations in these areas. In fact, Greater London, West Midlands and West Yorkshire figured among the worst conurbations for unemployment among the ethnic minority groups.[42]

Disadvantage in housing and housing allocation

On the question of housing size and dependants, the size of the household is crucial in determining the kind of family dwelling. The 1971 Census showed there was a significant difference between the average household size for ethnic minority communities and that of the indigenous population. For example, the average household size for the general population in England and Wales was 2.8 people. On the other hand, the General Household Survey showed an average household size of 3.71 for ethnic minority communities. Moreover, the PEP Survey on Racial Minorities (1975) showed 'even larger average figures'. This showed that the average household size for West Indians and Asians was 4.76 but for West Indians the average household size was below this figure (at 4.31) whereas all Asian groups had an average household size of 5.19 persons.[43]

Such large families were attributable to two basic factors: firstly that the majority of the ethnic minority groups are in the reproductive phase. Consequently there were more children in each household than in the indigenous population. And secondly, these large families were due to the number of adults within them. According to the 1971 Census there were 2.25 adults in each household. This number was exceeded among Asian groups. Few of these adults, however, were over 60 years of age.

The relatively lower levels of gross earnings among ethnic minority workers reflected their marked concentration in low-paid manual jobs as opposed to the better-paid white collar jobs. In this sense, minority workers were (and are) at a clear disadvantage in competing for housing in the open market, because this competition is fundamentally dependent on their earnings.

In 1974 poor black people were in worse housing than poor white people. By 1978, it was clear that a larger proportion of Asians were borrowing money to buy their houses, and their use of council housing was only one-third of the national average, with very few owning their houses outright. In the changing situation, council renting was decreasing. In fact, the PEP report showed the proportion of West Indian households in council housing as 26 per cent and for Asians as 4 per cent, compared with the 1978 National Dwelling and Housing Survey figures of 45 and 10 per cent.[44] Indeed, contrary to the claims that black workers take up all 'our' council houses, it was clear that neither West Indians nor Asians were occupying council housing to the extent that members of the indigenous population were.

Home ownership: the financing of owner-occupation   A further disadvantage that black people face is in obtaining loans to buy their own home. Once again, their disadvantage was (and is) reflected in the fact that Blacks were generally poorer than Whites and were therefore in 'a worse position to make the best choice'. Additionally, Blacks and Whites had to face the policy of 'red-lining' practised by some building societies. In effect, this did not allow mortgages on houses in specified inner city areas, regardless of the quality of the houses or the ability to pay of the mortgage applicant. While Whites often turned to the local council for a mortgage, most Asians tended to seek a bank loan, which was quicker to get, but involved much higher interest rates. Through this process, Asians were quite often able to buy houses with cash, thus arousing complaints from Whites who were involved in a much slower process in the housing market.

Council housing   The 1975 Runnymede Trust report showed that black people were underrepresented in council housing and that black tenants of the Greater London Council were far more likely to be in pre-war flats in central London, while white tenants were more likely to be in the newer cottage estates.[45]

The GLC explained that the report's findings were not that discrimination had taken place but that the allocation procedures were working against rather than for the disadvantaged and the black tenants. In fact, today the homeless (numbering more Blacks than Whites) are in more urgent need of housing; therefore they tend to accept offers (indeed the procedures restrict the number of rejections allowed relative to other prospective tenants) forcing them to the 'more available' but 'less desirable' accommodation. Moreover, housing managers, though denying that they purposely discriminate, admit that, in the interests of speed, white people are often not offered accommodation on estates where black people predominate, on the assumption that they will refuse.[46] In effect, the report destroyed the myth that black council tenants choose to congregate by showing that only about half of GLC tenants (black or white) were allocated to the area of their choice.

Another interesting aspect was the location of housing for Britain's black population which was not evenly distributed throughout the country, but tends to be concentrated in many of the large cities in the major industrial areas. This uneven distribution of the black population was also to be found within cities. The position remains unchanged, if not worse today.

Indeed it is undesirable for any particular group to be concentrated in poor quality housing in areas lacking social amenities. A Department of Environment report showed that 10 per cent of the census enumeration districts housed 70 per cent of the black population.[47] In fact, black people concentrated in certain areas of the cities which are often the poorest ones. Why? It has been argued that some segregation of groups of people was the result of the sort of jobs they do. An illustration of this is that if a large proportion of black people are manual workers, then obviously black people will tend to live in the same areas.

In short, the economic position of Britain's black population is reflected in their housing. Given that they tend to occupy the lower end of the labour market, black migrants could only afford accommodation which was relatively inexpensive. Thus, their housing was of a poorer quality and located in less desirable 'ghetto' areas. Underpinning this situation is the economic position in which black people are placed in British society. This forces an association between them and low standards of housing.

Further, concentrations of black people in rundown areas of the major cities has the effect of heaping blame on Blacks themselves. Thus they came to be seen as a cause for the decline in these areas, rather than what in fact they were: the victims of it.[48] To say that black immigrants are the cause of inner city decay is nonsense.

A number of general programmes and policies were put forward to ameliorate these problems. One policy intended to provide help for black people through general improvements was expressed in the 1975 White Paper, 'Race Relations and Housing'.[49] Here no distinction was made on the lines of colour. In the 1977 consultative document *Housing Policy* it was hoped that black people would continue to benefit from policies designed to help those in housing need.[50] The document recognised that black people face 'extra problems' in gaining access to local authority housing, such as the inability to meet residential qualifications and the size of families not matching the available accommodation. Further, the government acknowledged that homelessness amongst black youth was a severe problem in the inner cities. Moreover, it was suggested that direct involvement of the black population (through self-help groups) would be more likely to achieve success than solutions 'imposed from above'.

Discrimination　Commenting on a number of reports that have made recommendations about how housing authorities can fulfil their obligation under the 1976 Race Relations Act, the Runnymede Trust and the Radical Statistics Race Group conclude:

> One of the more general points to be made from this is that equality cannot be guaranteed simply by treating everyone in the same manner. Unless a housing authority considers the differences in needs and circumstances of those on its housing list it will inevitably discriminate against certain groups. Thus in order to ensure equality the particular needs of black people must be taken into account together with those of other members of the community for whom the authority is responsible.[51]

One attempt in redressing the balance was made by Lambeth Council in January 1979 by announcing a target proportion of 30 per cent of the housing on new estates and modernised properties should be allocated to black people on the waiting list.

Incredibly, keeping records of the ethnic origin of council tenants, though strongly advocated, was only recently adopted. Indeed, one of the main reasons for keeping such records was to provide information on how existing housing allocation procedures do not benefit black people to the same extent as Whites. In fact, indirect discrimination means that Blacks do not benefit as much as Whites because of the characteristics of the criteria itself. The residency requirement, for example, means that unless a person has been resident in the area for a period of time, they cannot register on the housing list. Consequently, black people, particularly Indians and Pakistanis, are less likely to fulfil this requirement, and are thus less likely to get council accommodation. In effect, the rule provided the means for this kind of discrimination.

Education

Policy issues concerning ethnic minority and indigenous pupils in school have emerged gradually. Four policy issues have aroused enough concern to indicate the extent of disadvantage in education among ethnic minority groups, compared with the indigenous pupils. These were identified as (i) the issue of the numbers of ethnic minority pupils and their concentrations in schools; (ii) their language needs; (iii) their achievement patterns and ESN school placement; and (iv) the impact of the socio-economic background.

Cross found that while these issues have been significant in policy considerations on a national level, they have not all been equally significant in every local education authority area. Furthermore, in the cases where some have been significant, the degree of significance attributed to them varied with the migrant composition of the area. The issue of 'bussing', for instance, although a significant issue nationally was not significant in every local education authority because some authorities did not adopt the principle of dispersal by 'bussing'.

Cross summarises his findings to conclude that the concentration of immigrant children in inner city schools is still a significant issue among decision-makers and 'bussing' is disliked by parents because of the long journey their children have to make to schools far away from their homes. Also of particular concern to decision-makers was that contact between the home and school was inadequate. Parents did not visit the school to discuss the problems of their children with teachers.

It was also found that among decision-makers there was opposition to changes in the curriculum designed to provide instruction in mother tongues, black studies, single-sex schools and the appointment of black staff as a special consideration of the educational needs of black school children. This was in contrast to the parents' wishes, which favoured studies reflecting their cultural and religious backgrounds, and instruction in their mother tongues. They argued that teachers who shared their cultural background would be better able to provide the kinds of instruction required and would also be able to understand the children better. Of course, those who belonged to the assimilationist school would not accept this, adopting the 'when in Rome do as the Romans do' approach. Most black parents, however, were relatively satisfied (47 per cent) with their children's education, but only 10 per cent 'positively approved' of the schools attended by their children, in the main because of the neglected aspects of education in these schools. [52]

There is little evidence that government or local authorities anticipated that changes might be required in the education system, following the entry of the children of migrants into British schools. In fact, these children were entering an education system organised on the assumption of cultural homogeneity. Therefore, it was staffed by persons without any training which might prepare them to teach children either born outside Britain, or in Britain, of parents with a distinct culture.

Moreover, the education system, in terms of its staff and many of the books used, tended to reflect the racist ideology within British society which is essentially a product of Britain's colonial and imperial past. Taken together, these factors have played an important part in creating educational disadvantage amongst black children greater than that faced by white children in similar economic circumstances. On these grounds there is sufficient reason to be concerned.

The view that the entry of black children into British schools is an 'immigrant' problem is clearly redundant. Some 40 per cent of the black population in Britain are British-born. Moreover, the problem lay not with the children but with the education system's failure to react quickly and 'intelligently' to a new situation of cultural diversity which was clearly set against a background of widespread racial discrimination. In spite of the real problems arising from the fact that the British school population includes children of a different culture, recognition has been slow and little effort has been made to solve these problems.

By 1976, however, some moves were being made. Both the Report of the Select Committee on Race Relations and Immigration on the West Indian community in 1976 and the Green Paper 'Education in Schools: A Consultative Document 1977' have emphasised the need for statistical monitoring of pupils, students and teachers. Earlier in 1971, 3.3 per cent of all pupils in maintained primary and secondary schools in England and Wales were immigrant pupils. More recently, only indirect estimates have been made based on the number of births to women born in the New Commonwealth and Pakistan. Through this rough guide, the black school population was estimated at 7 per cent of all births by the end of the 1970s. Given the uneven distribution of the black population, the proportion of black births to indigenous births varied to such an extent that in some areas black children constituted a significant element in the school population. Surely, this cannot be ignored. Moreover it is essential that the authorities, as policy-makers, bear in mind that while people from the New Common-wealth and Pakistan are categorised 'black', they nonetheless have different cultural backgrounds and they also have different experi-ences and needs.

The language problem

The hope that black children would learn English through inter-action with the indigenous pupils did not materialise. Indeed, as this became increasingly apparent, extra language tuition became a necessity. Even so, the further assumption was made that only children of Indian or Pakistani descent required this tuition. West Indian children, on the other hand, were regarded as having an adequate command of the English language. Thus, the emphasis was placed on teaching English mainly to Asian children.

Although language tuition facilities were provided since the early 1960s, there was (and still is) an acute shortage of skilled teachers in English as a second language and of teaching materials. Further, the scale of provision seemed to be closely related neither to the size of the black population, nor to the extent of need. This follows a common trend in both employment and housing. The most com-mon arrangements have been the 'reception classes' recommended in the pamphlet *English for Immigrants* by the Ministry of Education. According to the Runnymede Trust, this method had the advan-tage of combining intensive training without separation from the school, so much so that in some schools the classes have grown into special English departments.

One area of real concern has been the education of West Indian children. The patois spoken by West Indians in Britain (including those born in Britain) 'varies along a patois-standard English continuum, the balance between the two being determined by the social situation'. According to Edwards (and others) an increasing proportion of West Indian children in Britain (particularly teen-agers) are using a form of Jamaican patois much more exclusively as a response to their feelings of rejection and alienation.[53] Moreover, the argument is maintained that because there is a continuum between standard English and patois, there is a constant interplay or 'interference' between the two elements. Therefore, this places West Indian children in a disadvantageous position when educated through the medium of standard English. Thus disadvantages arise because teachers are commonly unsympathetic to the problems of comprehension and production of standard English faced by West Indian children, often to the extent that use of patois is believed to indicate low academic ability. Consequently, a process of low teacher expectation leading to low pupil performance is set in motion.

Racism in schools

One effect of the entry of black children into British schools has been to expose the ethnocentric and racist bias in the curriculum and importantly in the textbooks.[54] For example, black children are taught the history and culture of a white society by a white teacher, learning little or nothing of the society and culture from which they and their parents originate. This implies an 'inferiority' or 'backwardness' of their cultural background. By favouring the teaching of British history without its black contribution, the British Empire is legitimised, thus maintaining racist stereotypes of black people.

Through such a curriculum and books, racist ideas are reinforced among white children, leading to a negative self-concept and lower self-esteem among black children.[55] To eliminate this dual effect, a curriculum change is necessary in educating both black and white children.

Teachers' attitude   Obviously most teachers in Britain are white. According to the Caribbean Teachers' Association by 1979, 0.15 per cent of all teachers were of Caribbean origin. In the mid-1970s, a study of 102 black teachers in London by the Society for Immigrant Teachers reported discrimination against black teachers. They found that black teachers were concentrated in the 'ghetto areas' and kept on the lowest pay scales.[56]

What is equally disturbing is that many educationalists believe teacher expectations can seriously affect their pupils' performance. One study found that although teachers have a positive attitude toward Asian children, they tend to see West Indian children as a problem, particularly in the way they behave in the classroom.[57] Moreover, the use of patois leads teachers to have low expectations of West Indian pupils. Further, not only do some teachers believe in racist stereotypes, they also 'incorrectly' believe that white pupils do not hold racist beliefs. Consequently, they are incapable of making an explicit effort to challenge racist beliefs at school.

Underachievement?   The issue of underachievement or 'low performance' of black children in British schools brings together the issues of language, curriculum and teachers' attitudes. 'Underachievement' has been identified and linked primarily with West Indian children which implies that Asian children are not 'underachieving'.

Apart from reading ability, there is evidence on such issues as school placement and examination results which show the disadvantage of West Indian children in the British education system. This evidence relates to the numbers and proportions of West Indian children assigned to the educationally subnormal schools. In 1972 West Indian children accounted for 1.1 per cent of all children in state schools and 4.9 per cent of all children in ESN schools.[58]

Of major importance is the fact that educational underachievement and overrepresentation in ESN schools have wider implications that vitally affect the black working class. The evidence shows that the material and emotional circumstances of family/home life which are dependent on the level of income (among other things) substantially affect the educational achievement of black children. [59] It follows then, that as the parents of black children are disadvantaged in the jobs they do and the quality of housing they occupy, there is also a tendency for their children to be disadvantaged within the educational system because of these factors. Thus, material disadvantage is compounded by the insistent effects of racism and racial discrimination.

Given that material disadvantages are also shared relatively by the rest of the British working class, West Indian families are particularly disadvantaged in terms of nursery provisions.

While the shortage of provision for the nursery and day care facilities for the under-fives has been a recurrent problem for most parents, those living in the most deprived areas are particularly affected. Working mothers and single parents are among the most needy.

All the evidence amassed and the arguments put forward led to certain government responses towards the education of black children. The first official response was educational advice in 1963 through a Ministry of Education pamphlet[60] pointing out the need for an intensive course of teaching English as a second language at primary and secondary schools, at a time when there were virtually no trained teachers in English as a second language, nor were there teaching materials.[61] Further, the pamphlet generally advised on educational arrangements for immigrant pupils.

Circular 1/65 was issued in 1965 inviting local authorities with substantial numbers of immigrant pupils to apply for increases in their teacher quota.

Another Circular (7/65, issued in June 1965) recommended that the proportion of immigrant pupils in any one school should not exceed 30 per cent of the total. Government support reflected thinking which had nothing to do with a multi-racial society. The government felt that an increase in the proportion of immigrant children in a school or class increased the problems and would become more difficult to solve, and the chances of assimilation would become more remote. In spite of the argument for 'dispersal' based on educational need, it was mainly black pupils who were dispersed, thus incurring a further disadvantage! Later that year, a White Paper *Immigration from the Commonwealth* put forward a multi-purpose policy, which it hoped would integrate immigrant children, both to prevent a fall in school standards and to assist in the organisation of special English classes.

Thus a contradiction resulted between the pamphlet *English for Immigrants* and Circular 7/65 and the White Paper *Immigration from the Commonwealth*. While the first aimed at bringing together immigrant children for English classes in one school, the White Paper suggested that although the teaching of English was a goal, 'such arrangements can more easily be made, and the integration of the immigrants more easily achieved, if the proportion of the immigrant children in a school is not allowed to rise too high'.[62] The significance of this contradiction was stressed rather than the pressing language need. Thus, it was correctly argued that the bogey had not been discrimination – less favourable treatment – but concentration. This brought condemnation not because it might lead to less favourable treatment, but more often than not because it was perceived as the development of 'foreign enclaves within British culture and society'.[63]

So, it was on the grounds of origin rather than educational need that the Department of Education and Science emphasised the policy of dispersal which led to six local authorities (Ealing, Bradford, West Bromwich, Halifax, Huddersfield and Hounslow) implementing dispersal by 'bussing' black children to other schools. Such authorities as the ILEA and Birmingham rejected it, while others, who found it impractical to keep within the suggested 30 per cent limit, abandoned the idea.

In addition to the government machinery, independent organisations and pressure groups have been set up. For example, the National Association for Multi-Racial Education (NAME) established in 1965, initially concerned with the needs of black school children, broadened its concern to include the educational needs of British children as a whole. This essential thrust of the organisation was to campaign for changes in the educational system which will facilitate the development of a multi-ethnic society.[64]

Youth Service provision

Sir John Maude defended the formal objective of the Youth Service thus:

> To offer individual young people in their leisure time opportunities of various kinds, complementary to those of home, formal education and work, to discover and develop their personal resources of body, mind and spirit and thus to better equip themselves to live the life of mature creative and responsible members of a free society.[65]

These were very high ideals. Indeed, 'to live the life of a mature, creative and responsible member of a free society' brings into sharp relief reports about the community and delinquency of young people in general, but particularly black youth. In fact, the politics of 'mugging' is the backdrop against which the disadvantages of ethnic minority adolescents in terms of youth service provision can be illustrated.

If the demand for youth facilities is partly a function of the proportions of adolescents in the country aged between 14 and 20

years, then it is necessary to consider the major disparities between
the proportions of indigenous adolescents in this age group and
those of the ethnic minority communities. These disparities
influence their relative 'need' for youth facilities, apart from the
question as to whether this need is adequately met.

The children of ethnic minority people constitute 3.0 per cent of
all those in the total population between the ages of 11–20 years.
From the evidence, these children are almost three times as likely to
fall within the age-group compared to those of UK parentage.
Having considered the figures, Cross argued that the logic would
suggest that three adolescents from ethnic minority groups should
be making use of youth facilities for every one indigenous youth
who does so, 'all things being equal'. Indeed, the proportion of
those who require such facilities and who were (statistically speaking) more likely to use them was nonetheless still large at 9.4 per
cent.[66] But, to what extent do they use them? In spite of the
difficulty with data, the indications available from a few surveys
suggests that fewer ethnic minority adolescents were involved in
youth facilities than their statistical representation in the age
categories of 14–20 years would lead one to expect. In Bradford, for
example, in 1966 relatively few adolescents from ethnic minorities
were involved in youth club activities. In fact, the few that were
members attended regularly and participated in club activities in
much the same way as other club members. Clearly, the youth
service holds little appeal for most adolescents today. In effect, it
has failed to appeal to ethnic minority groups.

One of the reasons advanced for its failure concerns the nature of
the immigrant communities themselves and their cultural patterns
of control over their adolescent children. For example, Asian
parents are not only strict about participation of girls in mixed
activities, but also impose dietary and other restrictions to both
sexes. Moreover, the strong family ties pressurise some Asian
adolescents to seek social and leisure activities within their own
group, in spite of their fluency of English.

Even among West Indians (though they are less inclined to object
to their daughters being involved in mixed youth clubs) there has
been a tendency to maintain strong discipline over the activities of
girls and the hours they spend from home. Interestingly there has
been greater success in the recruitment of ethnic minorities by such
youth organisations as the Junior Red Cross, Boy Scouts, Girl
Guides, Boys Brigade and church groups involving, in the main,
West Indian youth. This is due partly to their parents' familiarity
with these organisations before arrival in Britain, and partly
because of the appeal of the uniforms and ideologies of these
organisations. West Indian church organisations have also been
particularly successful in recruiting West Indian youth.

Another factor in explaining why adolescents from minority
groups have not used the youth service as much as their numbers

would lead one to expect concerns their changing demographic characteristics before 1966 and between 1966 and 1971. Before 1966 the proportions of ethnic minority adolescents falling into the 14–20-year-old group was smaller than it has become since. According to the Hunt report estimate, they constituted some 2 per cent of those who were between 14 and 20 years of age in 1966. As this proportion increased to 3 per cent it became a matter of some concern to policy-makers following publication of the Hunt report and the Circular 8/67 which followed it.[67]

Health and social services

According to the Runnymede Trust and the Radical Statistics Race Group there appears to be some evidence that the black population, particularly the Asian population does have special needs.[67] These are mainly concerned with diseases and conditions associated with dietary deficiencies and child health.

Additionally, the National Institute for Economic and Social Research study concluded that 'largely because of their age structure, immigrant families make smaller demands on the Health Services than other families, and this is likely to hold true for some time to come'.[68]

A number of areas of disadvantage facing black people in their relationship with the social services have been identified by the Community Relations Commission. Firstly, there is the problem of communication. Language differences and proficiency have serious implications for the dissemination of information by social services and health departments. Yet, it is argued, the language barrier has not been acknowledged constructively.[69] Secondly, there is the question of children in care. Considerable evidence supports the fact that a disproportionate number of children in care are black. A London Borough of Wandsworth survey carried out in 1973–74 showed that 48 per cent of all children received into care were of West Indian origin. Moreover, they tended to be younger than white children in care.[70] Accompanying this high number of black children in care is a shortage of foster parents, particularly black foster parents.

In dealing with this problem, nine London boroughs initiated an experimental fostering campaign in 1975–76 of black parents for black children. The campaign was aimed at playing an educative role in informing black people of the difficulties of black children in care and in helping to bridge the gap between black people and social work agencies.[71] These initiatives, however, were not the norm.

Further, elderly black people have special problems. While the number and proportion of elderly black people is gradually increasing, a report produced by *Age Concern* in 1974 found that while the needs of the black elderly were similar to those of the general population, they have additional needs resulting from racial discrimination, differences in culture, insecurity in an alien environment, remoteness from friends and relatives and a sense of isolation.[72] Further, these factors have implication for the services which local authorities provide; for example, day centres, meals on wheels and old people's homes, among others. Justifiably, the complaint is made that special provisions are rarely made. Indeed, one local authority refused to support an Urban Aid application to provide for elderly Asians, on the grounds that separate provisions were not compatible with their policy.[73]

Finally, urgent consideration needs to be given to one-parent families. The West Indian population has a particularly high incidence of one-parent families. In fact, the *General Household Survey 1972* reported that 13 per cent of West Indian households were comprised of single-parent families, compared with 9 per cent in the general population. Apart from this, the extent of full-time female employment in minority groups probably leads to a greater demand for pre-school day-care provision from the black population than from the general population.

Taken together then, it is suggested that certain groups of black people are disproportionately represented or pose new issues within the existing traditional categories of need used by the social services. Overall, the available evidence points to the fact that 'the response of social service departments to the existence of multi-racial communities has been patchy, piecemeal and lacking in strategy'.[74]

9 The Black Workers' Industrial Struggle

Industrial relations: the colonial context

By the time that British immigration control began with legislation in 1962, a number of colonial trade unions had emerged to lead the struggle for national independence. Given the violent mass demonstrations by exploited, low paid colonial workers, the colonial government found it necessary to channel labour protest into a viable and acceptable organisation which would not disrupt the continued exploitation of the agricultural, mineral and labour resources of these colonies. In the interest of capital then, British Colonial Office policy was geared towards passing legislation to legalise workers' organisations through the formation of trade unions in the colonies, based essentially on the British model. Guidelines were sought from the more developed and sophisticated parts of the Empire. Although the territories of European settlements, namely Australia and Canada, were 'far too different' from the poorer tropical territories, much attention was focused on the codes of law and administrative practices developed in India and Ceylon (Sri Lanka), which went into the making of model legislation for the dependencies.

The social tensions arising from exploitation of native colonial labour, not surprisingly, progressively gave cause for concern to the Colonial Office. It saw the need for reforms, through labour legislation, in order to forestall disruptions to the smooth flow of production in the mines, plantations and communications network, owned and controlled by the major multinational corporations. Thinking in the Colonial Office was regarded as being 'more advanced' and 'more progressive' than in colonial governments and among the local vested interests.

The view of Empire of the stalwart trade unionist and Foreign Minister, Ernest Bevin, among others was, in fact, well known. Not surprisingly, therefore, the development of trade unions in the colonies was a typical part of the process of the 'transmission of institutions'.

In varying degrees then, trade unionism was introduced to the colonies, some of which were becoming less purely agricultural and more a complex of agricultural/industrial economies. This led to a certain amount of labour displacement which became largely redundant. Given the ownership and control of the major plantations and mines, for example, by British American, Canadian and South African companies, it was imperative that a system of industrial relations should develop. Indeed, this is precisely what happened. According to one expert the evolution of industrial relations in the tropical territories was closely related to the development of the dominant form of employment. Since there was no one type of employment, in most cases different kinds of employers co-existed. Firstly, there was the government official, the settler and native farmer, hotel-keeper, tailor and craftsman, among others, who employed a number of workers. Secondly, large plantations offered employment in some territories drawing on migrant workers. And thirdly, government services offered clerical employment.[1]

Prior to the emergence of trade unions, workers expressed their discontent by producing less, through absenteeism, high turnover rates and occasionally by spontaneous, and at times, violent demonstrations of protest. Usually such demonstrations resulted in a quick and hostile colonial response to put down such protests, but did nothing to deal with the factors underlying the essential discontent.

This phase of industrial relations was experienced by all colonial territories before trade unions received recognition as providing the necessary machinery to deal with workers' grievances. Clearly, the imperial government could not ignore the spontaneous, mass demonstrations of low wage-earners labouring under deplorable conditions throughout the colonial Empire. Before trade unionism then, mass demonstrations often led to 'riots', and of course, the well-known British official response of a Royal Commission to investigate the causes and make recommendations. In effect, this was to do little or nothing to remove the fundamental causes. With the outbreak of labour unrest in the 1930s, 1940s and 1950s (prior to independence in most of these territories) generally unsympathetic employers heaped the blame of unrest on 'agitators' and 'political adventurers', carefully excluding themselves from all responsibility.

Amidst growing discontent, by 1950, attempts were made to set up consultative machinery, through joint consultation. During this decade collective bargaining was also evident in some territories in East and West Africa. Government intrusion had made industrial relations particularly 'stormy'. Security forces, deployed to maintain law and order, were more concerned with protecting the lives and property of the vested interests, namely the employers. During the 1930s, 1940s and 1950s, the West Indian, Asian and African territories were all beset by this partisanship.

A change in the crude pattern of industrial relations came with the growth in the working population, increasing urbanisation, industrial development, advancing education, the rising political consciousness of workers and an intense growth of nationalist movements. The combined effect of these factors provided the stimulus for the adoption of laws regulating industrial relations on the British model. A fundamental requirement was the statutory setting up of a Labour Department.

As employers, colonial governments were asked to (and took) the initiative by setting up Whitley Councils and where there was no collective bargaining, with advice from London, passed protective legislation, including acts to regulate recruiting, contracts of service, payments in kind, the hours of work of women and children, workmen's compensation and minimum legislation. During the Second World War, minimum wage machinery was especially necessary to counteract the steadily rising cost of living. The Labour Departments were charged with the major role of administering these policies initiated in London. Moreover, in some colonies, Joint Industrial Councils were established on the British model with the object of promoting good relations between antagonistic employers and the emergent trade unions. Further, labour advisory committees were set up.[2]

Collective bargaining was also introduced between 1950 and 1962 as part of the developing industrial relations. Although it was difficult to determine the proportion of the workforce in every territory covered by collective agreements, in some territories such as Barbados and a number of other West Indian colonies most wage-earners worked under conditions established by collective bargaining. In African territories and in Mauritius, working conditions were also determined by collective bargaining.

The scope and content of these collective agreements reflect some measure of the development of the industrial relations system in the tropical Commonwealth territories. Union recognition, initially refused by employers, gradually became a common practice as employers, albeit reluctantly, agreed to accept trade union membership as a right of the employees to be written into a collective agreement. Bargaining, however, differed from the United Kingdom experience, in that the granting of bargaining rights to one union for the entire labour force in a firm, or an industry (the normal practice in the United States) was practised in many cases.

Although agricultural workers have been difficult to organise, collective bargaining has nonetheless been in operation for many years between unions and employers on the sugar plantations in the West Indies, the rubber plantations in Malaya and the banana plantations in West Africa. Trade union rights were confined however. Indeed, the right of union officials to enter estates for the purpose of organising the workers employed had been a major point of contention. In spite of access agreements, the prerogative remained with the employer.

Employers sometimes found it expedient to agree to closed shop agreements with the union, as was the case between the Grenada Seamen and Waterfront Workers Union and Geest Industries Ltd.[3] This agreement brought the union into collaboration with the company for the appointment of the chief stevedore, whose duties included engaging labour for the loading and discharge of ships, and the organisation of this work.

Another form of departure from the British practice of trade unions (the collection of their own contributions by a branch officer) was the 'check off' system, which followed the American practice. This system entailed the deduction of union contributions from the pay packets of employees.

Redundancy agreements (predictably new to collective bargaining) had become endemic in colonial terms of employment. This facilitated the designs of the expatriate owners, the multinational barons whose cost effective criteria led to hiring and firing at will. However phased these payments were (always of course to alleviate the labourers' distress) the fact remained that the worker had become redundant.

Employers were unwilling to concede more to the trade unions than was necessary. Indeed, capital was aided by the fact that the unions were, in most cases, inefficiently organised. The divide and rule strategy created tribal, racial and political divisions among the mass of workers.

Local labour and nationalist organisations used the emergence of trade unions as a means through which they could further assert (at least legally) their demands for independence. Prior to political independence, low wages were seen as the by-product of colonial rule. With the end of crown colony government, working class expectations were unduly raised, only to be faced with the stark realities of neo-colonialism.

The growing impoverishment of the former colonial dependencies (in the neo-colonial era) has led to growing economic dependence on Britain. High unemployment provided the necessary cheap source of labour for the British economy. As a result, black workers entered the lower end of the occupational hierarchy in Britain.[4]

Racial disadvantage in employment

The popular stereotypes of black workers as being shiftless, lazy, and living off social security must be challenged. For far from being 'work shy', it was argued that minorities in Britain have been, in general, 'more industrious than white people'. In fact, apart from the single exception of Moslem women (many of whom were prevented from going to work by cultural factors) the proportion at work, by 1977, was the same or higher among all minority groups than among comparable white groups.[5]

In this comparison, the age factor is important since far more whites than the minorities are above retiring age. Moreover, there were far more black working mothers than white. In addition, full-time rather than part-time work was more the norm among Asian and West Indian women than among women generally.

On the question of black unemployment, it was found that as total unemployment rises, the minorities tend to make up a greater proportion of this total. More particularly, one survey has shown 'very high levels' of unemployment among young people and women within the Asian and West Indian communities.[6]

The job levels of Blacks were also affected with those of Asian and West Indian men being substantially lower than those of white men. In fact, the gap between Pakistanis and Whites was the widest, followed by West Indians and Indians. Indeed, Pakistanis were particularly disadvantaged.[7] Significantly, it was found that the minority groups had penetrated comparatively little into non-manual jobs such as the professional or management positions. Generally, however, all the minority groups were more concentrated than Whites in semi-skilled and unskilled manual jobs. Pakistanis were poorly placed in that 20 per cent of them were in the poorest, unskilled manual jobs, compared with 6 per cent of Whites.

Commenting on minority men with qualifications to degree standard, Smith found that 79 per cent of the white men were in professional or management positions compared to only 31 per cent of minority men, and that 21 per cent of minority men with degree-standard qualifications were doing manual jobs, whereas none of the white men with equivalent qualifications were doing manual jobs of any kind.[8] Put simply, Asians and West Indians faced the greatest difficulties in trying to enter the better non-manual jobs. The explanation that inadequate English is responsible for the low job levels of Asian men is unfounded for 'there is a very strong relationship between fluency in English and academic qualifications – so strong, in fact, that nearly all Asian men with degree-equivalent qualifications speak English fluently. Nevertheless, a substantial proportion of them are doing manual jobs'.[9] Furthermore, among West Indian, Indian and African Asian women, job levels were lower than for white women. It was also found that in regions containing the main concentrations of Pakistanis (Yorkshire, Humberside and the North-West) there were comparatively high proportions of minority men doing unskilled or semi-skilled manual jobs and comparatively low proportions doing skilled manual jobs.

Shift work and earnings

Not surprisingly, black workers had to do shift work as the only means through which low basic earnings could be supplemented. It was found that 15 per cent of white men worked shifts of ten hours or more per week, compared with 31 per cent of minority men. Shift work was most common among Pakistanis, African Asians, West Indians and Indians. In the textile industry, for example, Pakistanis were engaged in a 'very high level' of shift working. Thus, because of their economically weak position and language difficulties, employers exploited Asians to the hilt, using them particularly to do jobs involving unsocial hours.

Given that the job levels of the minority groups were (and are) substantially lower than those of the white population, how low were their earnings from those jobs? Comparing white and minority men at each job level, it was found that at the higher level, Whites earned 'substantially more' than the minorities; at the middle levels, they earned 'about the same'; and at the lower levels, the minorities earned 'more' than Whites.[10]

In sum then, the earnings of minority men were lower than those of Whites. Indeed, the use of Asians and West Indians for unskilled and semi-skilled shiftwork was a form of exploitation. Moreover, while academic qualifications were actually of little value to Blacks in enabling them to get better jobs, they were extremely valuable to Whites. Further, while the earnings of minority and white women were much the same, there was an enormous disparity between the sexes.[11]

Employment and recruitment

In relating the gap between the minorities and Whites, at the workplace, it is vital to look at the policies and practices of employers. Before examining these policies and practices, however, we should look briefly at the distribution of the minority workforce by type of industry.

Between the indigenous population and the minority groups, there were marked differences in the types of industry in which they worked. How did the minorities come to work in certain industries? Although the process is complex, a few basic assumptions can be made.

According to Smith, one of the main features by 1977, was that a relatively high proportion of the minority groups worked in manufacturing industry (47 per cent of minority men, compared with 33 per cent of white men), probably because this industry used a relatively high proportion of unskilled and semi-skilled labour and the minorities were concentrated in this kind of job. Transport and communications was the one service industry with a relatively high proportion of workers from the minority groups – some 13 per cent of minority men compared with 9 per cent of all men. Transport and communications was one of the service industries in which semi-skilled and unskilled labour was concentrated.

The minorities tended to work in those industries where there was a high demand for cheap, unskilled or semi-skilled labour. Indeed, a relatively high proportion of black workers were to be found in vehicle manufacture and transport and communications. By contrast, there were fewer black workers in agriculture and in paper and printing and publishing, where the demand for labour was relatively low.

Furthermore, there was a high concentration of Asians (particularly Pakistanis) in the textile industry, in spite of the fact that agriculture was the main area of employment in their country of origin. While Pakistanis were concentrated in the textile industry (62 per cent of Pakistanis in Yorkshire and Humberside, compared with only 6 per cent of Whites and in the North-West 52 per cent of Pakistanis compared to 5 per cent of the white population) both Indians and Pakistanis constituted a high proportion of those employed in vehicle manufacture – 12 per cent in each case, compared with 4 per cent of the white population. More particularly, Sikhs predominated, constituting 16 per cent. On the other hand, a high proportion of West Indians were working in professional and scientific services; many were employed in secretarial and other white-collar jobs in the National Health Service.

Among Asians, the facts do not bear out the popular view of them as shopkeepers. Apart from African Asians, the proportion of all the minority groups working in the distributive trades was relatively low by 1977. The African Asian accounted for 15 per cent, compared with 13 per cent of the whole workforce. Further it was found to be untrue that a high proportion of Asians were controlling small businesses of various kinds, such as shops and restaurants. While self-employed white men accounted for 12 per cent of the working population, the proportion was *lower* among the minority groups: 8 per cent of Asian working men and 6 per cent of West Indian were self-employed.[12]

Concentrations within particular plants

While it is fairly predictable that concentration of minorities will tend to be higher among plants in high concentration areas than in the low concentration areas, nevertheless, within each group of areas, there was still a wide spread of plants with different concentrations. In fact, in the high density areas, where the *average* concentration of minority workers was over 13 per cent, 19 per cent of plants employed only Whites, and a total of 38 per cent employed less than 4 per cent. Conversely, even in the low density areas, where the average concentration of minority workers was 4.36 per cent, 12 per cent of plants had workforces which accounted for at least 10 per cent from minority groups.[13]

Thus, the evidence reflected a polarisation between those plants that employed and those that did not employ minority workers. Interestingly, in the majority of cases, the plants that had employed few or no minority workers had not employed any significant number of them in the past.

In effect, then, there were many all-white plants and many with high concentration of Asians and West Indians. Given this uneven distribution of black workers across plants, what role did these plants play? And what policies and practices did they adopt?

The number of minority job applicants received by plants had been used to define this role. The basic finding showed that plants generally tended very strongly to give preference to white applicants. Moreover, it was found that Asians and West Indians had to make about twice as many applications as a white applicant before employment. Asians and West Indians fared worst at both ends of the employment scale, when applying for both non-skilled and non-manual jobs.

Racial discrimination in employment

Given that the minority groups are more vulnerable to unemployment than the white population (for a number of reasons)[14] they have to make twice as many applications as Whites before finding a job. Indeed, it was found that racial discrimination is an important factor in the situation.

The PEP Report of 1977 demonstrated very clearly the existence of 'very substantial racial discrimination against Asians and West Indians when seeking manual jobs and that discrimination is worse for non-skilled than for skilled job applicants'.[15] This discrimination was based on a 'general colour prejudice' which does not distinguish between people of different racial groups with different religions, speaking different languages and coming from different countries. They tended to be all lumped together as 'coloured people'.[16]

The results of correspondence testing showed that Asian and West Indian applicants for white-collar jobs were discriminated against in 30 per cent of cases, compared with only 10 per cent for Italian applicants.

Bearing in mind that the method employed identified discrimination only at the screening stage, a level of 30 per cent is very substantial. Smith argued that if nearly one-third of Asian and West Indian applicants failed to get an interview because of discrimination, we should expect an even higher proportion to fall by the wayside, as a result of unfair treatment by the time a selection is finally made. Indeed, the very much lower figure for Italian applicants showed that discrimination in manual jobs was based largely on colour prejudice.

The black workers' experience of discrimination

Among white working men 76 per cent thought that at least some employers discriminate unfairly against minority job applicants. Similarly, 74 per cent of West Indian men held the same view. Among Asian men, however, the proportion was markedly lower at 47 per cent. Clearly, discrimination in recruitment was (and is) widespread, pointing up the fact that awareness of discrimination generally was actually higher among white men (and West Indians) than among some of the affected Asians; while a smaller proportion of Asian women believed that some employers discriminated (31 per cent), it was found that West Indian women held similar views to their menfolk.[17] In effect, then, the 'passive or compliant' attitude among Asian women was not present among West Indian women.

On a personal level, the proportion claiming discrimination in recruitment was low among West Indians and Asian men, ranging between 14 and 16 per cent, and very low among Asian women, 3 per cent. Significantly, this reinforces the point that those who were discriminated against were not usually aware of it.

What had emerged clearly from the findings was a reflection of the general attitude and orientation of the Asian and West Indian communities (given that West Indians were no more aware of discrimination than Whites, and Asians even less aware of it) which instead of being over-sensitive to any signs of unfair treatment and resentful of their position in relation to the host community and militant for change, the minority groups were often very slow to recognise an injustice which affected them most closely.

Clearly then, the existence of racial discrimination was generally recognised by the white population. Thus, it was argued, public opinion was ready to accept the relevance of policies to doubt discrimination, in spite of the fact that people may have regarded this as either a low priority or believed that discrimination was (and is) inevitable or necessary.

People's awareness of discrimination, it was reported, was strongly influenced by their general attitudes and way of life. Indeed, the culturally enclosed Asians provided the clearest example of this in that those who do not speak English well, 'are much less aware of discrimination, and claim less personal experience of it, than the more outgoing middle-class element'. Therefore, culturally enclosed Asians were less alive to personal discrimination (since they ventured little outside their communities) and were less concerned about it because their orientation was with other Asians, rather than with Whites.

In effect then, racial discrimination reinforced this cultural confinement, by discouraging contacts outside the communities. Paradoxically, however, discrimination had the effect of encouraging a pattern of life among Asians which made them unaware of the central significance of discrimination itself.

Among both Asians and West Indian informants who had been refused a job because of race or colour, it was found that in a substantial proportion of cases, the applicant had reasonable grounds for thinking that discrimination had occurred. Interestingly, it was found that among Asians and West Indians who believed that employers discriminated, only a minority could relate a personal experience of discrimination. Indeed, although direct evidence was hard to come by, they had 'good general reasons' for believing there was discrimination.

Any comparison of awareness and experience of discrimination, must take into consideration that any change of opinion does not refer to the same set of ethnic minority people. In fact, earlier and later arrivals of immigrants have different opinions. For example, among Asian and West Indian men who arrived in Britain from 1970 onwards, only 37 per cent felt that some employers discriminated. In contrast, 63 per cent of those who came up to June 1962, believed this to be the case.[18] Both waves of immigrants reflected different experiences. Those long-settled immigrants faced 'open and accepted' discrimination, while recent arrivals (without this experience) were less likely to be aware of the true extent of discrimination.

Policies and practices of employers

A survey of employers showed that policies to combat discrimination were least common in those plants that employed few minority group workers, or none at all. Moreover, plants with 500 or more workers were twice as likely as smaller ones to have taken steps to prevent discrimination. The general feeling among employers was that there was no need for a policy because it was assumed that there was no discrimination.

The majority of management informants (64 per cent) thought the 1968 Race Relations Act had made little difference to race relations in employment, while 19 per cent felt it had good effect and 16 per cent a bad effect. Moreover, while a substantial proportion of informants (40 per cent) thought the minorities were better off as a result of the Act, only 3 per cent thought they were actually worse off. The remainder thought that the legislation made no difference.

Furthermore, only 5 per cent of plants had changed their policies and practices because of the Act, while 19 per cent of the large plants with at least 500 employees had made changes.[19] A more difficult problem concerned employee relations and the nature of white resistance. Employers may be reluctant to prevent discrimination in recruitment because they fear the consequences of a large number of Asians and West Indians in their workforce. Indeed, such factors may be based on the racial prejudices of the employers or managers themselves.

Overall, the effect on industrial relations of employing members of minority groups into the workforce was 'slight' and did not provide reasonable ground for the reluctance of employers to introduce policies of equal opportunity. Indeed, this trend was in line with the existing state of industrial relations. In fact, the fear among white employees of the employment of Asians and West Indians and equal opportunity policy was also a reason given by trade unions for not adopting more positive policies.

Moreover, it was found that a high proportion of large plants had complaints from white workers, and complaints were more often than not made where Asians rather than West Indians constituted the main minority group. This latter point is important in reflecting the cultural disparity between Asians and Whites. The general conclusion however, was that resistance from white workers to the employment of racial minorities was 'not particularly common'.[20] Nevertheless, the resistance that did occur in a substantial minority of cases most emphatically cannot be ignored. Indeed, this problem can be compounded when strong views about Asians and West Indians are expressed by some managers.

Job mobility, job satisfaction, promotion and supervision

It was found that the firms which had already employed large numbers of Asians and West Indians received more applications from these groups than other firms. This resulted in a concentration of minorities which tended to increase in those firms employing them. Significantly, also, one is reminded of the fact that minorities tended to avoid firms that did not employ people from their own group. Indeed, most Asian and West Indian men (58 per cent) had never applied for a job without prior knowledge that the firm employed Asians and West Indians.

Between white workers and minorities, the important difference in job-seeking was that Asian and West Indian manual workers, seeking semi-skilled and unskilled jobs, applied directly to the factory gate, rather than reply to an advertisement. This approach was adopted by 47 per cent of minority men, compared with only 20 per cent of white workers who found their jobs by direct application.

Given the above findings, one would suppose that Asians and West Indians would be dissatisfied with their jobs, become impatient for promotion and be constantly on the look out for a better position. On the contrary, the evidence, at the time, showed that they accepted their position with 'equanimity'.

One explanation was that this was a reflection of the informants' expectations as much as the nature of the job. The boring and repetitive nature of the jobs has had an overall depressing effect on the ethnic minorities who felt their chances of a better job were slim. Therefore, (although the desire was strong) they had no grand schemes to become Chairman of the Board or indeed, making it to one of the line manager's positions. The hard reality of their lives, under oppressive racial discrimination, had engendered this unhappy existence.

According to Smith, the minorities 'are not actively discontented, and there is no dynamic, at present, for a strong political movement'. He reasoned that it may be that most adult Asian and West Indian migrants, having achieved a substantial improvement in their standard of living since they arrived in Britain become 'satisfied' with their dead-end jobs, particularly by comparing their position in Britain with that in their country of origin. Indeed, the majority of migrants who arrived in Britain during the 1950s and early 1960s were strongly influenced by the idea of an eventual return home. We must not however assume that the immigrants were satisfied. In 1977, Smith has argued that 'the more they come into contact with the white majority, the more they will tend to see themselves as part of the mainstream; this will lead to a shift of their point of reference, to a change of attitude, and to a new kind of evaluation of their own position in Britain.' Seven years later, in 1984, this 'new kind of evaluation of their own position in Britain' has clearly led to a 'change of attitude' but certainly not 'as part of the mainstream'.

Nevertheless, the evidence showed that, of the minority groups, Pakistanis who did the least desirable jobs for the worst pay, still showed the highest level of job satisfaction. This had been attributed to them being the 'most culturally enclosed' group, adopting the 'narrowest frame of reference'.[21]

It is as well to remind ourselves at this stage, that most Asians and West Indians were satisfied with their jobs and that a majority also believed that many employers practised racial discrimination. Against this background, how did they see themselves in relation to promotion and supervision?

Among minority men 29 per cent would like to have been promoted, compared with 22 per cent of white men. But how did Asians and West Indians rate their chances of promotion? Thirty-eight per cent of minority men considered their prospects of promotion as good, compared to 42 per cent of white men.

As was the case in job satisfaction, both the desire for promotion and the expectation of getting it were least strong among Pakistanis. In fact, only 19 per cent thought their promotion prospects were good compared with 39 per cent of the other minority groups combined. More particularly Indians and African Asians were most likely not to want promotion, but also to consider their prospects as 'good'. Further, poor English speakers neither wanted nor expected to get promotion. This was in line with the thinking of Pakistanis confirming the view that culturally enclosed Asians took a narrow frame of reference.

An inhibiting factor in the promotion of Asians and West Indians was (and still is) the feeling among employers that it was dangerous to promote minority workers to positions which necessitate supervision of white workers. Put simply, although the gap between the minority and Whites was substantial, nevertheless there were minority workers in supervisory posts with responsibility for white and minority workers.

Among the few employers who appointed Asian or West Indian supervisors, there had been remarkably few difficulties. In fact, only 5 per cent said this led to any problems; 95 per cent definitely stated that it had not. While 3 per cent thought it impossible that white workers would adjust to this situation, the majority (60 per cent) thought the adjustment was immediate and the remainder said it took a few weeks (32 per cent) or a year (5 per cent). In spite of these encouraging developments, the stark fact was that the majority of plants (78 per cent) had yet to take this step. These plants were inhibited by the belief that the appointment of minority supervisors would create problems.

Overall, the evidence reflected a distinct contrast between the extent of the problems actually experienced by plants with minority group supervisors and the problems expected by those not employing them. Only 31 per cent of those with none thought that they would be resisted by white workers.[22] While these findings relate to supervision of manual workers, exactly the same conclusion was reached following a similar set of questions about supervision of white-collar workers.

Given the similarity of the job levels of those who came to Britain up to 1962 and afterwards – the earlier arrivals tended to be West Indians and to be less qualified than the more recent arrivals who tended to be Asians – it is likely that the earlier arrivals may have moved up the job scale to some extent since coming to Britain. If indeed this was the case, they are still doing substantially poorer jobs than Whites, even after a degree of token 'upward mobility'. The concentration of the minorities to 'dead-end' jobs is not a temporary phenomenon. On the contrary, those who had been in Britain for twelve years, and considerably longer, were (and still are) doing jobs substantially inferior to those of Whites.

The struggle against the employers and trade unions

Strikes

According to Knowles, 'one cannot agitate successfully without widespread grievances'.[23] For black workers in British industry during the 1960s, 1970s and early 1980s, there certainly was no shortage of grievances. These years constituted a period of rapid changes in industrial organisation. The growing size and complexity of production units and their greater interdependence (through multinational corporations) and the rate of technological change demands planning and co-ordination from the centre. Thus, the tensions generated by strikes between groups of workers, shop stewards and formal trade union machinery resulting in strikes (be they unofficial or unconstitutional); though essentially a management problem, is, in the last analysis, very much a government problem. It was within this context that black workers took action during the period. Many of these strikes revealed the entrenched positions adopted by employers, white workers and the trade unions towards black workers. In effect, black workers' grievances challenged the unrealistic containment of conflict in certain industries. Moreover they challenged (and in some cases proved) racism at all levels of the industrial structure.

The strike at Courtaulds

Some firms openly practised discrimination against black workers. Others (the more 'enlightened' managements) adopted the 'soft glove' technique. Both, however, inevitably had to face the problem of increasing productivity and profit, and the resistance of black workers who were drawn into devious schemes to achieve these targets. Prolonged exploitation led to inevitable reaction.

In May 1965 one of the first important 'immigrant' strikes took place at Courtaulds Red Scar Mill in Preston over management's decision to force Asian workers (who were crammed with a few West Indians, into one area of the labour process) to man more machines for proportionately less pay. This first skirmish has become a landmark in black labour history in Britain. The weaving firm, Red Scar, used chemical processes in making its products. Workers in the Tyre Cord Spinning Department supervised a bank of spindles on a machine. Not surprisingly, throughout 1964 Courtaulds was seeking improved productivity from its plants and in the person representing management at Red Scar duly negotiated (without consultation with the workers) a deal with the regional organiser of the Transport and General Workers' Union. Thus, a devious deal was struck. After signing an agreement, the union official told the shop stewards (only one of whom was Asian) to convene a meeting and get the workers to accept supervision of one and a half machines instead of the existing one. The financial reward for this was a ten shilling bonus a week. Incensed by this, the workers called a meeting with the union's regional organiser who was asked to explain his 'agreement' with Red Scar management. His attempt to explain his indefensible action was jeered. The workers drew his attention to the fact that the agreement meant a 50 per cent increase in output for a 3 per cent increase in their wage![24]

Needless to say, they voted against the new proposals. Consequently, the plan to increase productivity at the expense of disproportionate wages, an unviable proposition in the face of unanimous black workers' resistance, was shelved for a month.

This brief respite was ominous. The ever resourceful capitalist cunning was put into operation. Without warning, the workers on the afternoon shift were suddenly confronted with new work allocations. The line managers moved in with red paint and brushes and drew boundary lines along the machines dividing them into halves. Each worker was now allocated the supervision of 1½ machines. The men promptly refused and staged a sit-in to management's astonishment. This action resulted in machines being clogged. There was chaos for 17 hours. In their final act of solidarity that day, the black workers, most of them Indians and Pakistanis, walked out.

They went on strike for three days. Predictably, the TGWU Chairman at the factory, Richard Roberts, immediately began a campaign to get the strikers back to work, before any negotiations could begin. Clearly he was sympathetic to management's threat that they would not negotiate under duress. After all, he was the link man, the mediator, the 'responsible' trade union leader. He could not therefore be seen to be disruptive of the smooth operation of the firm's policy objectives. In short, the trade union officials had to be experts at man-management (for example, keeping workers within the established norms of productivity), an approach welcomed by the employer who saw human beings only in terms of labour cost.

Revealing his, and clearly the trade union hierarchy's position, Roberts told the press that the strike was 'unofficial' and 'racial'. He told Paul Foot, the journalist, 'I could have said it was "tribal" but that might have been a bit unfair.'[25] Playing 'unfair' then was not outside the bounds of possibility in official trade union thinking. Uncharacteristic of a 'responsible' trade unionist, one might add.

Regardless of his and the union's views, the strikers had been through a painful experience. Though disorganised (and lacking in trade union experience) they were resolute, staying out until mid-June. During this period, with no 'precept or precedent' they made attempts to organise themselves. They were further disadvantaged by the fact that they had 'no recourse to a black movement equipped to mobilise the assistance they needed to win'. In disarray, and vulnerable, the pressures were indeed great. Early in June, the 120 West Indians involved in the action returned to work after a 'pep talk' about 'responsible behaviour' by representatives of the West Indian High Commission who had called a 'strike meeting'. Ultimately, the strike failed but not before it had exposed the active collaboration of the white workers and the union with management.

The strike at Red Scar nevertheless was significant. For the first time in the industrial struggle of Asian workers, the black movement made a well publicised intervention during which Roy Sawh and Michael de Freitas (Michael X) of the Racial Adjustment Action Society (RAAS) made statements. While Sawh called for a separate union of Blacks, De Freitas later said that although he was against white people 'he was not for separate unions'. In spite of the publicity focused on the dispute because of the intervention of the two RAAS speakers, the workers listened to these two militant West Indians, applauded their spirit and laughed at their anti-white jokes, 'but couldn't take them or their organisation as serious channels of industrial struggle. It was apparent to the workers from the beginning, that Michael X would bring them publicity in the quality Sunday papers, but no more. RAAS had no experience with mobilising an independent black revolutionary force in Britain, and didn't seem to the workers as capable of analysing the issue of the strike, let alone mobilising national or international support for it.'[26]

When the Red Scar strike had ended, there was no shortage of views from reporters. John Torode advocated an educational drive by the union of their Asian workforces in order to avoid strikes.[27] But would this alone alleviate the workers plight? Paul Foot, the socialist, felt 'If the Red Scar strike shocks management and unions into greater care over communication with and promotion of immigrant workers its consequences may not be as disastrous as they once threatened to be.'[28]

What is revealing is the fact that although the strike was fought by the immigrant workers (with the crucial support of the Asian community and in particular, the Indian Workers Association) they failed to win against their oppressive employers, because of the lack of official union support.

The Imperial Typewriters strike

By 1974 a clear pattern had emerged. Indeed, the 'apotheosis of racism' and the 'resistance to it' was reached during the strike at Imperial Typewriters in Leicester. Significantly, this firm was a subsidiary of the multinational Litton Industries.[29]

The trade union's position in this strike was revealed by the TGWU negotiator, George Bromley, a JP, 'stalwart of the Leicester Labour Party', and one of the 'lieutenants of capital'.

The workers have not followed the proper disputes procedure. They have no legitimate grievances and it's difficult to know what they want. I think there are racial tensions, but they are not between the whites and coloureds. The tensions are between those Asians from the sub-continent and those from Africa. This is not an isolated incident, these things will continue for many years to come. But in a civilised society, the majority view will prevail. Some people must learn how things are done . . .[30]

In referring to the tensions between African and Indian Asians, Bromley totally ignored the racial tensions that already existed between the Whites and Blacks as a direct result of a large National Front presence in Leicester. Indeed the NF had polled 9000 votes in the previous elections. They were concerned about Communists as was Bromley who felt the strike was being led by professional agitators. He argued that they wanted a change in society, to take over and control the union machinery. But since they could not do it from outside, they were being supported by Chinese Communist money. 'I've had reports of money,' he said, 'of £5 notes changing hands on the picket line . . .'[31]

Bromley's comments reflected a greater readiness to understand management's desire to maintain exploitation of the predominantly Asian workforce at the existing level. His lame excuse that these Asian members of his union had 'no legitimate grievances and it's difficult to know what they want', was copping out of his official responsibility. Whose side was Bromley really on in this major industrial dispute involving Asian workers? Was he unaware of the ownership and control of Imperial Typewriters? A little background to this company is necessary in order to set this dispute in its proper context.

Established in 1908, Imperial Typewriters had by 1960 achieved an annual profit of £571,000. Its Leicester base was extended to premises in Hull. However, profits were not maintained at this level throughout the 1960s. In fact, there was a down-turn through the decade because of 'foreign competition'. In 1965, for example, annual profit fell to £360,000 and by 1966 it was down to £267,000. The company's shares at a book value of 23/- in 1960 dropped to 16/3 in 1966. The prosperity of the small firm throughout the 1950s was now a thing of the past. The international depredations of monopoly capital had made their impact.

The growing and expanding multinational Litton industries, based in Delaware in the United States, sought access to ever cheaper labour and new markets. The growing difficulties of the British firm made it easy for take over. Consequently Litton industries moved in on the British scene in 1961 dealing in London office machinery. By 1966, as a producer of 'Royal' typewriters in the United States, it was poised to move into the British typewriter market. During the year, Litton made a bid for Imperial Typewriters, at a share price of 16/3. Eventually, for a total price of £1.9 million, Litton bought 100 per cent control of a business whose property assets alone were valued at £1.7 million. Given a growing pool of cheap East African Asian labour there was reason to be optimistic.

At the time, Litton International was the second largest typewriter company in the world, with a controlling interest in Olympic business machines, and Triumph and Adler typewriters. In 1972, the company owned 267 major manufacturing plants and laboratories and 1393 factories in 31 countries. Its interests extended to building the navigation and control systems of the United States Army, Air Force and Navy. Also in 1972, the company's annual turnover was $2,476,623,000.

It was therefore, not surprising that Litton's control over Imperial Typewriters had wider implications. Soon much of its production was moved to Europe. Having installed new machinery and generally updated its production operations in Leicester and Hull, the number of workers employed by IT doubled, from 1,900 in 1968 to 3,800 in 1972. Interestingly, until 1968, Imperial's employees were all white. Thereafter, it was noticeable that recruitment was centred largely on Asian workers. Productivity of these migrant workers brought about a turnover which more than trebled between 1968 and 1972 from £3,346,000 to £10,762,000. The surplus value per worker during this period reached more than 50 per cent, and since 1972, although productivity 'increased enormously' bonus levels were re-negotiated downwards.[32] To further reduce labour costs, more women were employed. Black workers had made a fundamental contribution to the firm's success, yet their grievances were ignored. After all, Asian women workers were regarded by multinational employers as passive.

When the Asian workers turned to their union for help, they soon realised the true nature of the union's role. They were reminded by their union negotiator of the need to keep the company as a going concern. He wrote to the strikers: 'You are ill-led and have done nothing but harm to the company, the union and yourselves.'[33]

The strategy of using fear of unemployment was resorted to at every opportunity to keep these workers in passive servitude. Of the 1600 employed at the Leicester factory, approximately 1100 were Asians. As they became impatient with their grievances being ignored, it became clear that there was an unholy alliance between the union full-time official and the employers' representative.

As the politics of Litton International was being played out, the Asian labour force, bought on the cheap, were pawns in the game. Even so, there was a limit to depression.

The rumblings came to a head on May Day (the day of international working class solidarity) when workers from four firms in Leicester took action. The walkout involved 300 workers at the

British United Shoe Machinery; 300 at the Bentley Group, 200 at the General Electric Company factory in Whetstone, and 39 Asian workers who left section 61 of Imperial's factory. The substantial numbers engaged in the walkout action from the first three firms soon walked back to work. In spite of this psychological disadvantage the majority of those workers who walked out from Imperial's factory stayed out, and managed to bring out a further 500 workers with them. This withdrawal of labour had the desired effect: within a few days production fell to 50 per cent of normal and fell much further as the strike entered its fifth week. [34]

The Asian workers had struck because of a deep feeling; the cumulative effect over a long period of 'economic wrong doing' and racial exploitation. At the beginning of the strike, the main issues were about bonus rates and producing progressively, first 16, 18, 20 then 22 machines every day for the same wages. But, as the strike evolved, a host of related grievances became integral. Moreover, the strike was about racism reflected in the election of shop stewards and the preferential treatment for white workers who could clock in their mates, while Asians were not allowed to do so. Further, the strike was about the 'dignity of human beings, the right to go to the doctor when they were ill or to take time off to look after their children'. [35]

The strikers demanded their own shop steward to be elected by their section, who would not just negotiate on the question of production and bonuses, but also on all the important restrictions that made up their daily working lives compared to those of white workers – washing time, tea breaks, lunch breaks, toilet breaks, and so on.

In the course of their demands to Reg Weaver, the TGWU factory convenor, they found out that although they were being paid bonus on a target of 200 or more, they were in fact entitled to bonus on 168 (an agreement which dated back to 1972, and would have meant an extra £4 per week). [36] It was this discovery, heaped on top of management's oppressive organisation of production, that sparked-off their revolt.

Having walked out, the manner in which the strikers picketed and conducted themselves, and the strategies and creativity they brought to bear on the struggle were instructive. It seemed clear to them that traditional, hidebound British trade unionism could not cope with their legitimate workplace problems. As the strike escalated into a major industrial dispute, the Asian workers from East Africa brought, as one commentator put it, 'a vivacity and style to it that makes it unique'.

Between 50 to 200 workers manned the picket line continuously. [37] The women workers played a central role. They engaged in a 'fearful howling and hollering', whenever a scab or representative of management appeared. Tremendous noise (echoing down the street) was an outstanding characteristic and an effective factor in the picketing. The myth of the Asian woman's passivity was debunked as her presence was not only felt, but heard. These women showed great courage. In the midst of their isolation, the odds against them seemed even greater.

In spite of the ubiquitous presence of the police, the immovable unsupportive position of the union (in refusing to make the strike official) and the hostility of the employer and the indigenous working class, the Asian strikers on the picket line remained undaunted. As the struggle wore on, Asian youth increasingly became a part of the strike scene. Others took an intermediate position. One East African Asian served as a go-between (interpreter) between the Asian strikers and his fellow-policemen. Needless to say, he was taunted and made the target, especially of Asian youths. As the struggle gathered momentum, there were other spin-offs.

The emergence of Asian youths in the struggle worried state officials who were already faced with controlling West Indian youth. Later this would have implications on social policy. Together, these youths, with no background of employment experience and no real work prospects in the foreseeable future had little to lose by demonstrating the plight of the black working class. Their parents' struggle had, in effect become theirs, a family/communal affair.

By the third day of the strike, the strikers from section 61, who had been led by women workers announced that Hasmukh Khetani and N. C. Patel were their unofficial leaders. The women leafletted and picketed the relevant sections of the factory and were joined by 500 other workers for a meeting in Spinney Hill Park at which the original strikers demanded that 'their bonus, out of which they had been fiddled, should be backdated to January 1973, and that new rates should now be negotiated on the basis of their present position'.

As the strikers gained more support from people in the factory, their collective power and resolve grew. Thus fortified, they demanded an end to the use of racialism by management to divide workers; they called for democratic elections in the trade union and reiterated their demand for backdated bonus payments. Sensing the strikers' implacable resistance to its malpractices, the company's response was positive and predictable. The original strikers were notified that they would be sacked if they did not return to work. In the ensuing deadlock third parties intervened. Tom Bradley, the local MP and President of the Transport Salaried Staffs Association tried to get the workers back to work. He said: 'I told the strike leaders they were getting nowhere by walking the streets and urged them to adopt the proper procedure by returning to work and resuming discussions under an independent Chairman.'[38] This was trite nonsense, for after many months of complaining, their reasonable 'discussions' through the proper procedure got 'nowhere' in the factory.

Bradley, however, was not alone. He was supported by Reg Weaver, the local TGWU convenor. Predictably, these gestures were rejected by the strikers, who stood by their demands. They would not be tricked back to work. In fact, they injected a broader perspective in the struggle, by calling on 'all workers, men and women, black and white'. Indeed, all who worked at Imperial.

By the end of the first week of the strike, on 7 May, the effectiveness of the strike was evident. The factory was down to 50 per cent of its normal production, and more than 500 workers were on strike. In this unprecedented action, the workers were out on a limb. But, they were free from the bureaucratic trappings (rules and regulations which had not anticipated or considered their introduction into the British workforce) of trade union organisation. Freed from these trammels, the workers invented new ways and means of achieving a more effective strike organisation to further their cause. Thus, the 'grievance meeting', a mass meeting of the strikers came into being. Individuals expressed their grievances and the salient issues arising from these taped interviews were co-ordinated into a series of demands by the central Strike Committee. Thus, a close bond was forged between the strikers and their leadership. As the confidence of the rank and file grew, so too did the number of militants.

Nine days after the strike started, the company sacked 75 of the original strikers. In protest against this action, the workers refused their cards. Instead, they sent them back. Was this cheekiness on their part? Or was the initial act of dismissal an insult to their integrity? Moreover, they formulated a list of demands to be negotiated with the company. Although the company was 'willing to talk', Reg Weaver, feeling that his authority had been undermined, hindered the process. He said he was not ready to talk to any but the strikers' leaders. In his diligence to undermine the strikers, Bromley conveniently discovered a TGWU rule to the effect that workers could not be elected as shop stewards until they had been at the factory for two years. While this kind of shop floor democracy was later repudiated by Jack Jones, the Union's General Secretary, it never occurred to Weaver that perhaps a change in the rule (or more accurately, facing trade union racism) might be necessary.

As the mass picketings and demonstrations intensified, police were called in. But things had already gone too far. Aware of the task confronting them, the strikers appealed to workers in other factories represented by the same branch of the TGWU. Four factories with large Asian memberships aided the strikers with donations to the strike fund and pledged a 24-hour stoppage at their factories 'if and when needed'. Significantly, at that point in the struggle, 'race and a sense of community' constituted the vital power base of the strikers. Still, the rest of the Leicester white working class remained unmoved. The strikers were determined to demonstrate their commitment and sense of solidarity in the hope of winning crucial support from other workers.

On Sunday 19 May, the Strike Committee called a mass meeting and 2000 people demonstrated through Highfield. Three weeks after the strike, factory production had 'slowed to a trickle', and six workers faced fines of £315 for obstruction and assault on the police. With little positive support from the labour movement, the Race Relations Board intervened. They were invited by Benny Bunsee, a South African Asian who had helped Asian workers in an earlier strike. But although the Board's intention was to carry out a preliminary investigation, which was welcomed by the union officials and factory management, the strikers were sceptical. Given the urgency of their demands, they felt this intervention would lapse into a slow and tardy process, and more importantly, it was unlikely to meet their demands.

The Board's intervention came as no surprise. George Bromley had been a founder member of the East Midlands Conciliation Committee on the Board. According to one report, he had resigned due to pressure of work. The Board's intervention, however, was timely. By the end of May the strike had begun to take its toll. Most of the strikers were officially sacked by Imperial Typewriters and were therefore ineligible for social security. In these circumstances, a long drawn out inquiry was the last thing these courageous Asians needed. As far as they were concerned the Race Relations Board was 'a toothless Bulldog'. However, attempts at intervention to end the strike continued. At that point, David Stephens's (of the Runnymede Trust) proposal of the intervention of Michael Foot (then Minister of Employment) was also ignored.[39] Fundamentally, the strike continued. The picketing was maintained and the grievance meetings were held regularly. Individual grievances were voiced and the nuances of discontent shored up the central issues which remained in the foreground of the strikers' minds, thus maintaining the strike's momentum.

As the strike entered its tenth week, forced by the creativity and solidarity of the Asian workforce, Bromley retreated from a 'position of rational collaboration with capital into the realms of social fantasy'.

The amateurs were now regarded as 'professional agitators'. As far as Bromley was concerned, the strikers should go back to work and reach some agreement according to the rule book. For the strikers, however, having endured a wageless 10-week struggle (during which substantial hire purchase debts were defaulted) there would be no return without victory.

The preposterous idea of Chinese Communist money was regarded as a sick joke. In fact, the strikers were desperate for money. On this question of money, support came from the community and political organisations and meetings. For example, the Birmingham Sikh Temple contributed £125, the Southall IWA £50, the Birmingham Anti-Racist Committee £14, the European Immigrant Workers Action Committee £12 and the Edinburgh Women's Conference £40. While the needs of the strikers were amounting to large sums of money weekly, such contributions as were made came to them in 'dribs and drabs'.[40]

Heaped on the financial problem was the combined pressure of management manipulation, alleged union collaboration with them, and a constant barrage of racist propaganda from the Leicester branch of the National Front. In the face of all this, the strikers stayed out.

This was an extraordinary strike. Whereas an 'ordinary strike' would have collapsed within days because of an initial lack of commitment by workers or a lack of union support, or both, the strikers at Imperial Typewriters responded with a strength and creativity which would help to shape the future of the black working class struggle. Free from the unprogressive traditions of British trade union bureaucracy, and newly proletarianised after leaving East Africa, and the Indian sub-continent, the Asian strikers brought certain notable qualities to their struggle: a spirit, an approach and a willingness to try any tactic. This experience of migrant workers provided lessons, particularly for the trade unions and the wider labour movement.

The TGWU, supposedly an organisation of the working class in fighting against capital, was exposed as a vehicle for the further accumulation of capital. Indeed this had been the case in earlier disputes; for example, Woolf's and Rockware Glass in West London in 1965, Malmic Lace, E. E. Jaffe, Jones Stroud, British Celanese and Harwood Cash in 1973, Perivale Gutterman, and Coventry Art Castings.

Interestingly, the black migrant workers chose to remain within the framework of the union (in spite of alleged 'communist' infiltration) in the hope of getting union support for their demands. Instead, the union set up an inquiry to look into the conduct of Bromley and Weaver, and their role in Litton International's dealings. No strike and no ex-officio payments were forthcoming. Still hopeful the strikers welcomed the union inquiry. While the inquiry was being conducted, mindful of the role of colonial Royal Commissioners, the strikers became disenchanted. Put simply, their positive feelings were to 'Throw the bastards out'.

One of the outstanding problems to be settled was the question of strikers' leader, Benny Bunsee, the 'outsider' labelled by Bromley as an agitator. The strikers were opposed to the dumping of Bunsee. Brian Mather, one of the members of the inquiry team told a reporter, 'Its purely an industrial issue, but there are forces at work trying to escalate it such as the National Front. . . . There is a language problem of course. And George Bromley, the local officer has been personally and perhaps emotionally involved.'[41]

One of the most significant factors to emerge from the strike was the fact that in spite of the shabby treatment of these Asian workers over many weeks, they continued to defend the union. 'We have a high regard for what the union can achieve once it is determined to flex its muscles and to take up the genuine grievances of the workers. But for this to happen the trade union officials must be responsive to the genuine grievances of the members.'

This became a recurrent theme among black working class organisers. As the strike dragged on, the central power base increasingly became the independent intervention of Asian women. Of vital importance to this strike, and others (and underlying it all), was the question of the role of the union and the common experiences of the vast majority of black workers in Britain. This raises many important questions. For instance, when the IWA unionises a complete foundry and then hands over the membership to the TGWU, is that really the best way forward for black workers? And why the dichotomy between black and white members of the union and Bromley's role in it; and more fundamentally was there a racist ramp among white workers on the shop floor and elsewhere in British society?

When the Imperial Typewriter factory closed for two weeks' holiday, picketing was suspended. However, the struggle continued with the strikers maintaining contact with each other, essentially through lectures, discussion groups and two evening concerts. They persisted in seeking TGWU rank and file support nationally, sending letters to branches all over the country. Furthermore, they called for a national solidarity committee, co-ordinated by *Race Today*, 'to collect money, to circulate information, to organise pickets on Litton's branches across the globe, to support the pickets and to involve Asian workers and all workers in active support for the struggle'.

But foremost in their mind at all stages in the strike was the hope that the TGWU would make the strike official. This was a vain hope. Finally they lost their jobs as Litton industries decided to close down the factory rather than make even the minimum concession to the strikers' demands. And since the union did little to prevent this, it must be implicated as contributing to this end. Indeed, race emerged as the major divisive issue within the British working class.

In the aftermath, the strike's casualties were counted. By the end of July 1974, management issued notices sacking most of the strikers. Nine arrests were made on the picket line and the struggle was directed to London where 200 workers lobbied Transport House (the Labour Party headquarters) to make the strike official. Instead of badly needed support, they got a promise of an inquiry by Jack Jones and Moss Evans of the TGWU. In effect, the disowned strikers were left to struggle on their own. The wider trade union and labour movement remained largely deaf to the appeals of the Asian workers.

Lessons of the strike This strike showed (i) how the Imperial Typewriter factory at Leicester, a 'cog in the multinational corporation wheel', was used as a meeting point of cheap labour and access to markets; (ii) how the prevailing rate of pay for men was £14 below the national average, while the women workers' pay was £6 below; (iii) that cheaper sources of labour were sought from white female workers and Asians from both the Indian sub-continent and from East Africa; and (iv) how the union collaborated in this international scheme of things, acting as the 'lieutenants' of capital, more concerned with people 'learning how things are done in a civilised society' than mobilising sections of the class for political change.

Of fundamental importance in this strike was the move away from the trade union directives which was a source of political strength. In effect, this meant control of the action of the rank and file. Thus the 'grievance meetings' of the entire strike force became the organisational focus.

Significantly, the power of the women came not only from their being half of the strike force, but from their position as mothers and housewives in the community. Not only did they see capital giving them a low wage, they saw it snatched back by inflation. In the past, Asian women fully supported the industrial demands of their menfolk. Given low wages, they had no choice. The alternative was scabbing. This strike was unique in that the women had the collective power to make their demand for equal pay a priority. They were the latest section of the working class to fall into factory production. As younger and more recent recruits to factory employment in Britain, their acute awareness of the problems made them less willing to take the horrors. Their militancy on the picket lines, their forcefulness at the grievance meetings and their determination to fight till the end were all proof of this. Later, the Asian workforce would be tried and tested again, in the epic struggle at Grunwick.

The epic Grunwick strike

If black migrant workers had been exploited in small firms and factories because trades unions were either weak or simply not allowed to exist, then the Grunwick strike proved most revealing. It became an historic dispute. Indeed, it was a record-breaking strike; the most militant in British history, undertaken by a white-collar union, resulting in some 550 arrests, hitherto more than any dispute since the General Strike of 1926. Incredibly, this strike forced the government to set up a Court of Inquiry and made post-war history by bringing together 500 MPs in the House of Commons on a Friday afternoon.[42] Further, this dispute not only attracted national, but also international interest and support. Why? Apart from the anti-union stand taken by Managing Director, George Ward of the Grunwick Processing Laboratories Ltd, a number of related questions were raised, as 'high politics' became increasingly involved.

The firm, founded by A. Grundy, George Ward and John Hickey, which first began processing (developing and printing) black and white films for photographers in 1965, prospered and grew as more expensive colour film was being used. By 1972, new premises was required off Cobbold Road, Willesden, and in 1973, Grunwick merged with Cooper Pearson, located in Chapter Road, Willesden. Further progress, particularly in the mail-order side of the enterprise, resulted in the need for more space to accommodate the rapid expansion. Thus, in 1974 it rented the thirteenth floor of Station House in Wembley, where a computer was installed.

Predictably, hot summers meant a rapid increase in photographs and more orders for Grunwick. The increased workload in the summer was partly dealt with by employing students. There was nothing unusual about this, since Grunwick had consistently done so and found it a workable system.

In 1976, the modernised premises at Chapter Road accommodated a busy mail-order department. By August 1976, the vast majority of Grunwick's staff of 480 were at the Cobbold Road and Chapter Road sites. In fact, about 100 of the 160–170 workers were in the mail-order department. [43] This department was not only of vital importance to Grunwick, but also of central concern to the strike and strikers.

By August 1976, nearly all the workers engaged in mail-order were migrants from East Africa who spoke predominantly Gujarati. A large number of women formed this group, some wearing saris (their traditional dress); others wore European clothes. Traditionally, and in the popular mind of the British people, among others, these women were passive, always obedient and subservient to their husbands. There were a number of East African students. In fact, from a total workforce of 429 in August 1976, 140 were students, some of whom worked in the mail-order department. Together, this migrant workforce laboured to procure the increasing profits of the firm. To profit, however, is to exploit. To what degree this is done is largely dependent on the level of contentment among the workers. Grunwick was no different from other sweatshops. In spite of Managing Director Ward's complacency, the workers' grievances were more deep-seated than he cared to admit.

Among many workers, therefore, it was not surprising when a 19-year-old worker (not a student) Devshi Bhudia, unhappy with pay conditions, decided to take action on Friday 20 August 1976. That morning, as he put it, he argued with the mail order department manager, Malcolm Alden, who tried to get him to supervise the students in his work area. A 'good worker', Bhudia would only undertake this responsibility, if given more money. The strict disciplinarian, Alden, ordered Bhudia to get on with his work and promised a rise later.

That same day, Bhudia was given 13 crates of new work, a 'difficult target'.[44] Given their earlier confrontation, and the task before him, Bhudia expected the worst from the tough 'sacking manager' Alden. Past discontentment and the 'bullying tactics' of management had prepared Bhudia to expect the sack. Indeed he was ready to leave that day as an individual expression of protest. He was not alone in feeling this way.

If some were aware but cowed by gratefulness to have a job (especially at a time of high unemployment), others were more sensitive and outspoken about the grievances. One of the grievances was Alden's 'aggressive manner' by pressurising slower workers with dismissals and threats of dismissals. Some evidence of this was reflected in the high labour turnover in the mail order department which, in 1976 (albeit a time of high unemployment) was about 'one hundred per cent as an annual rate'.[45]

In time, fear of dismissal became a fundamental grievance at Grunwick. Another grievance more deeply felt was the nature of compulsory overtime. Although Ward argued that this was written into their contracts of employment, the theory bore no resemblance to working practice which entailed long hours imposed at short notice, thus disrupting the workers' private lives. One woman who had worked 65 hours per week in the summer, in evidence to the Scarman Inquiry, said she had accepted 'compulsory overtime', but not 'till 10 o'clock at night'.

Alden, an excellent enforcer of compulsory overtime at short notice, had become unpopular among workers in his department. Bhudia, for one, was particularly concerned about this grievance. Other irritants to the workers were close surveillance through glass-fronted offices and the suffocating heat. Taken together, these grievances led to a certain amount of unity of thought and action. Devshi Bhudia and three of his workmates were not thinking of trade unions when they decided that Friday afternoon to work slowly in anticipation of dismissal. They anticipated that if one of them was given the sack, the other three would walk out in protest. Surely this reasoning was a reflection of the frustration and despair of four young workers who were acutely aware of having no machinery through which they could channel their grievances. Since they could not change things through the process of negotiations within Grunwick, they were prepared to vote with their feet! As it was, the 13 crates, still unsorted, led to a row between Bhudia and Alden, following which Bhudia was sacked. His three workmates told Alden the dismissal was 'unfair', before resigning in protest.

The four workmates stood outside the Chapter Road gate arguing. Whether or not they discussed trade unions was by the by. What was important is that they stayed at the gate, instead of going home. These four young Asians standing at the Chapter Road gate was the beginning of a long and bruising presence on a picket line that would have far-reaching consequences for British industrial relations. Thus, the historic Grunwick Strike had begun.

While the four men stood outside, Jayaben Desai, a middle-aged Indian woman, four feet ten inches tall and slightly built, was packing up work to go home. Unlike most of the Grunwick employees, she was born in the Gujarat. Although physically small, passive obedience was not her pattern of behaviour. While at school during the time of Indian independence, though young, she was already independent-minded in her views. She was aware of the imprisonment of Gandhi (who was also a Gujarati) and Nehru, by the British in India, and had listened to Gandhi's lectures on philosophy which were broadcast on Indian radio, after he was assassinated in 1948. This was all a long time ago, but it was not lost on her. Her Gandhian background would serve her well during the desperate weeks of struggle in the summer weather which came and went, and in the cold and wet streets that led to and from Grunwick. This frail figure came to symbolise the determination of the strikers to win. How did she come to Britain?

Jayaben married Suryakant Desai, a Gujarati from Tanzania. She lived for many years in Tanzania where her husband managed a tyre company. Earlier, to maintain British supremacy in Africa, thousands of Gujaratis and other East Indians were imported to build railways. Although many of the original workers returned to India, after the railways were built those who stayed constituted the artisans, craftsmen and shopkeepers, the middle-class of East Africa, acting as a buffer between the Whites (landowners and administrators) and the unskilled black African masses. Needless to say, this remained a source of discontentment among Africans. The British Imperial strategy of divide and rule helped matters little. Nevertheless, when Kenya, Uganda and Tanzania gained independence early in the 1960s, the East African Asians hoped to be assimilated. But the closed Gujarati community, which had supported the white rulers so well in the past opted to keep their British passports. Thus, in the late 1960s and early 1970s, East African Asians were forced to leave.

Many of the thousands who arrived in Britain settled in the London borough of Brent and elsewhere in Britain. Moreover, they have had to accept a 'lower standard of living'. Unlike the earlier waves of migrants, the East African Asians were forced to settle in Britain. Their dilemma was that they were caught between the humiliation of expulsion (particularly during President Amin's regime) and the Conservative government's Immigration Act of 1971 and the provocative race-speeches of Enoch Powell. Animosity greeted them in Britain as the neo-fascist National Front stirred race-hatred. The Ugandan Asians came in for a particularly chilly British reception.

The East African Asians then were also unlike other black migrants in that of all the migrant groups in Britain, although they possessed better educational qualification, they received the lowest average earnings.[46] The cumulative effect of these circumstances led to great disillusionment. As it was, this middle-class group were forced to do largely semi-skilled and unskilled work. Taken together, the effect of all these factors was accentuated by the powerful impact of work-a-day slights to their dignity and self-respect at Grunwick, among other workplaces in Britain.

In dealing with racists, Mrs Desai was understanding, even forgiving to those who had 'no knowledge of history'. When she and her husband arrived in Britain in 1969, they had to start a new life. He worked for Desoutter Engineering in Wembley as an unskilled labourer, while she laboured on a sewing machine in Harlesden. Given her husband's improved earnings, she was able to attend to the affairs of the home and their two children. This period, as a full-time housewife, was, however, short-lived. The need for money forced her to seek part-time employment at Grunwick, working during the evenings between 5 and 10 pm. Rising unemployment nationally led to her accepting full-time employment at the company in September 1974.

Almost two years later (during which time she tolerated many indignities), as she was about to leave her workplace, a supervisor barked at her, 'Who told you to pack up?' This hostile approach reactivated strong feelings against management's imposition of compulsory overtime which the abrupt question inevitably implied. Although she had not objected to compulsory overtime as part of her contract, the short notice given and the 'atmosphere of fear' concerning overtime had become too much. Following the question, new work was given to her which meant working until after 7pm. She had not worked past this hour before at Chapter Road and was angry now that management was ordering her to do so. Fear of management in the mail order department seemed all-pervasive. The spectre of dismissal was the particular fear in Mrs Desai's mind. Indeed, this proved decisive. Confronted by Alden alone (and anticipating the sack) she said to him (as she explained to the Court of Inquiry): 'If you are prepared to listen to me I am prepared to listen to you as well, but if you shout like that to me I am not talking to you.' Alden's words, 'I warn you', alarmed her into making the pre-emptive statement, 'Anybody, anytime, we expect our sack . . . Look, I do not want to work for you. I do not want your warning . . . Please give me my cards straight away.'

Before leaving, she told the workers in Gujarati that hers was a voluntary decision. 'My friends', she said, 'listen to this. What is happening to me today will happen to you tomorrow. This man wouldn't speak to white workers like he speaks to us. He says he is giving me the sack but I am leaving myself. I do not want to be given his sack.' Realising her position was now beyond recall, for good measure, she addressed the workers nearest to her: 'I am asking this in front of Mr Alden and I am asking him why he is not employing any white girls in this department.'[47] This privately well-understood discrepancy was now given a bold, public airing. As hard-working people with 'small money' she felt Grunwick was 'taking hard work from us'. Once and for all, she wanted it to be understood that, 'I am leaving myself and you have to understand that I am here to clear it that I am leaving myself. Do not understand he sacked me. That is why I am asking him in front of you: "Please give me my cards"'. With her son Sunil, at her side, they both 'harangued' the workforce. According to the *Morning Star*, her final words to the 'sacking manager' Malcolm Alden were: 'What you are running here is not a factory, it is a zoo. But in a zoo there are many types of animals. Some are monkeys who dance on your finger tips, others are lions who can bite your head off. We are those lions, Mr Manager.'

At the gates, Jayaben Desai and her son Sunil found a 'picket line' of the four men who, earlier that day, had started the Grunwick Strike. Together, their discussions triggered-off forms of protest, one of which was trade unionism. This Mrs Desai pondered and discussed with her husband.[48] At that stage, it seemed, trade unionism was a means of protest against their grievances and not designed to win recognition (of the union to be formed) and reinstatement. Nevertheless, Mrs Desai grasped the trade union idea fervently, a commitment she was ready to take to its bitter end.

That weekend, the search for a trade union was initiated by Sunil Desai who prepared a petition for Grunwick management and placards 'for a strike that did not exist'. Thus prepared, that Monday morning Grunwick's directors found pickets at their gate on Chapter Road. The strikers' campaign for support for trade unionism by signing a petition resulted in the support of 'nearly every' member of the mail order department.[49]

After advice from the Citizens Advice Bureau, contact with Jack Dromey, Secretary of the Brent Trades Council, and advice from the TUC, APEX was approached as the 'appropriate' union for the strikers. Given that it was almost impossible to organise anything inside the factory without management's interference, the strikers decided to call for an immediate walkout that Monday afternoon of those in favour of joining a union. To the surprise of Alden and his line-manager Duffy, over 50 workers walked out at 3 pm from the Chapter Road site and assembled at the gate with the original 'pickets'.

As Dromey rightly stated, 'even now the Grunwick Strike was still not really off the ground. It was still only a walkout from Chapter Road.' The walkout had its own dynamic: a 'liberating effect' on the workers as all the past grievances were voiced and publicly endorsed by their assembly and placards, a show of solidarity.

The strikers who had remained more or less at Chapter Road were joined by 'seven or eight' from Cobbold Road. Thus strengthened, the revolt gathered momentum. The seed of trade unionism had been truly planted. That day Alden was told his offer of reinstatement would only be accepted if they could have a trade union. Alden was firm: he would only have them back as 'individuals' (the great cornerstone of the firm), not as a union. The idea of a combination of individuals – a union – was anathema, even at that embryonic stage.

The next day, the strikers leafleted the Chapter Road and Cobbold Road buildings calling for a mass meeting of the Grunwick workforce to be held that lunchtime in the car park of the White Hart pub. By now, professional help was to hand in the form of Jack Dromey and local APEX members. Increasingly, Dromey became involved. These developments aroused deep concern among the directors of Grunwick. Indeed, that Tuesday, John Hickey, a 38-year-old founder-director (in the absence of George Ward, Managing Director of Grunwick) used fear again to prevent an exodus of his labour force to join the strikers on the picket line. He warned that any walkout by those then employed was futile, since a trade union would never be accepted by Grunwick. The message, reflecting Grunwick's philosophy, was clear.

The company was so anti-union that it emphasised it would rather close down than recognise a trade union. So dismissive of trade unionism (and indeed of industrial relations) was Grunwick's management that when cross-examined at the Court of Inquiry, Hickey could not define 'collective bargaining'. The fact that they did not care for industrial relations might have been forgivable, but this was a British firm, operating at a sophisticated level in the twentieth century. But this, as the Judges argued, was no grounds to victimise the freedom of a small, committed anti-union employer who instilled fear among his workforce. At least he should be allowed the freedom to exploit that!

That Tuesday, whatever chances there might have been of a compromise between the company and the strikers vanished. After it was formally decided to join a union through Dromey and an APEX representative on the Brent Trades Council, 60 strikers who met at the Brent Trades Hall, joined the union and elected a delegation to meet Len Gristey, an APEX official. The formation of a union was welcomed by many members of the workforce at Cobbold Road who began walking out at about 11 o'clock on Wednesday morning. Noorali Valliani (a Pakistani technician with some trade union experience) and Vipin Magdani (who had none) led the walkout.

At this stage, management was still interested in getting the strikers back to work. George Ward, still holidaying in Ireland, reiterated that on no account would he allow a trade union in his company. What was he afraid of? Many workers began to question their position *vis-à-vis* a union. Increasingly, workers drifted out of the factory to join the strike. By Friday the number of strikers was 137 out of a total workforce of 480, and a total weekly paid workforce of 430 (176 male, 254 female). Of the 137 on strike, 46 were students. Clearly, this was not a student-led revolt.

Representing this solid, militant backing, the first letter from APEX was sent to the Grunwick management on Friday 27 August. The company directors acted promptly by seeking legal advice. Although these directors (largely ignorant of industrial relations procedures) did not know it at the time, it was to be their saving grace.

On the same day that the Grunwick board of directors met, APEX made the strike official by announcing that strike pay would be given to the strikers. The emphasis of this decision was, however, lessened as Grunwick hit back hard. The company despatched dismissal notices to the strikers. Not only were the 137 workers who walked out sacked (for breach of contract) Hickey also rejected APEX's claim for recognition. In fact, dismissal had become inevitable once the workers had joined the union.[50] From this point onwards, it was argued that the labour movement rallied to the cause of the strikers as a 'recognition issue', bearing in mind that the strike was not started by trade unionists. Frustration, built up over a long period, because they could not give vent to their grievances for 'fear', found full and liberating expression in the spontaneous demand for a trade union. As immigrant workers, they were at a particularly severe disadvantage. Indeed, the PEP report found East African Asians to be greatly disadvantaged in terms of employment. Having come from middle-class backgrounds and having been occupationally downgraded, their self-respect was at stake in view of Grunwick's disregard for the human sensibilities of their workers. In fact, the company regarded its workforce simply as cost in a balance sheet that *must* show a profit. This was, indeed, the *raison d'être* of the company. There was no need for human values. Len Murray, General Secretary of the Trades Union Congress, caught the stikers' mood accurately when he told them that trade unionism meant self-respect, 'the right to answer the gaffer back'. Clearly such self-respect had no place in George Ward's 'Fort Grunwick'. And, as he was to prove, the Judges' law was on his side.

Grunwick had grown and expanded continuously. Its mail order business had prospered so much that, although strike-bound, it was still the 'most efficient' and 'least expensive' of all film-processing companies. Just before the walkout in August 1976, the prospects looked distinctly good for Grunwick; its pre-tax profits rose from £13,500 in 1969 to £126,719 in 1973–74 and then to £210,687 in 1975–76. Ward was cock-a-hoop that his 'sweatshop' was one 'happy family'. In fact, with his relatives, he controlled 51 per cent of 'GP Combined'.[51] Moreover, the firm was fortunate in not having experienced labour unrest since 1973. His profits rose rapidly because, to a large extent, his company was strike-free. He was able to maintain this strike-free position by instilling fear among a vulnerable immigrant workforce, who knew little or nothing about trade unionism. The question remained: what were the causes of the walkout and strike in August 1976?

While low pay, racism and the oppression of women were contributory factors, the main cause of the Grunwick strike was the 'conditions of work'. Of these conditions, compulsory overtime was of primary concern. Even the concession of leaving work (during the slack period in winter) a half hour or an hour earlier was not enough to compensate for the long extra hours worked during the summer.

Holiday entitlement was another source of discontentment. After 1974, as Grunwick increased its immigrant labour force it decreased its holiday entitlement. Though honourable by Ward's standards, the intention here was clear, particularly since the two-week holiday entitlement, if requested in the summer, could only be granted at management's discretion. This was insufferable for people from the tropics to take their holiday (except in few cases) annually during the winter. Given low pay, saving for a holiday abroad during the winter months was unrealistic. And furthermore, for those who had managed to save enough to visit relatives or friends abroad, two weeks was much too short a time to make such a journey (holiday) worthwhile. Naturally then, these 'sweatshop' conditions either had to change or lead to inevitable rebellion.

Underpinning these conditions were the insistent dictates of bad management. Although management varied from department to department, in the mail order department, management was somehow able to create an atmosphere of real fear among those who were 'expecting our sack'. Management's failure was reflected in the fact that labour turnover was 100 per cent; bonuses and rises were given at the discretion of the manager; and most significantly Grunwick's directors like Hickey and Alden (self-made men) had read little and understood little about the art of management and, in particular, industrial relations.

Although there was a works committee, there was a distinct lack of any mechanism for dealing with workers' grievances which were significantly numerous and specific to immigrant workers. As for the works committee, many workers such as Devshi Bhudia and his friends were not aware of it. George Ward, however, argued that there had been an elected works committee at Grunwick since 1973, which was 'not designed as an alternative to direct contact between workers and management, but as a supplement to it'.[52] The only direct contact between workers and management it seemed was when managers such as Alden, with an arrogant and severe tone, barked orders of work.

It seems that the manager of the mail order department, Malcolm Alden, was particularly hard on his workers. Whatever personality traits he had brought to bear (such as his bullying tactics) in getting the work done, they were never publicly disowned by Ward. Efficiency in both Alden and Ward's mind meant getting the job done. Those who back-pedalled under the pressure would be sacked. In the East African Asians, Ward picked on the wrong group of migrants. Unlike earlier black migrants they did not come to Britain for 'economic' reasons. Therefore, their treatment by their employer was high on their list of priorities for a good management.

Grunwick's problems were a reflection of similar problems of small firms elsewhere in Britain. Though they were small, their workers' problems were no less real or significant. In fact, at the time of the Grunwick strike there was an estimated 800,000 small and medium firms in Britain, employing 3.2 million workers.[53] Indeed, the publicity received by Grunwick workers led to a growing demand for information about trade unions from the Brent Trades Hall.

An important aspect which went into the taking of this initial step to walk out and join a union was the sense of community of those who went on strike. Increasingly, some myths were shattered in that the 'passive' Asian women at Grunwick proved to be as militant, if not more militant than the men. They came out to challenge their oppressive employer, at a time when the trade union movement was in retreat.

Support for the strike from sections of the British labour movement was quick and widespread. As it happened, about two weeks after the walkout on Monday 6 September 1976, the Trades Union Congress met. Encouraged by the strong commitment of the strikers for trade union recognition, both APEX and the local Brent Trades Council became involved.

APEX, a 'right-wing', white-collar union, was founded in 1890, and by 1976 had a membership of 142,000 half of whom were women. The union's positive response to the Grunwick strikers' call for help was exemplary in that within three days it accepted the strikers as members of the union and within only eight days on 17 September, they began to receive strike pay of £8 per week backdated to 31 August. Moreover, this strike pay was increased to £12 per week supplemented by payments of between £2.50 and £6 to individual strikers. This benefit had the effect of welding the strikers firmly together as winter approached.

The General Secretary of APEX, Roy Grantham, was a shrewd and extremely capable trade unionist. Whatever else Ward might have thought of him for coming to the strikers' aid so quickly and positively, Grantham was no radical. Indeed, he was a moderate trade unionist whose union supported entry into the European Common Market, the government's Social Contract and insisted that candidates for office should declare their political affiliations.[54]

The need of the strikers and the attitude of Grunwick's management towards trade unions had touched-off his own deep commitment to trade unionism. In this spirit, he mounted the rostrum of the TUC on 7 September to deliver a powerful speech on behalf of his new Grunwick members. He maintained that the Grunwick management had gone over the top in exploiting black immigrant workers. His impassioned plea met the approval of Tom Jackson, General Secretary of the Union of Post Office Workers, which promised help. In the meantime, the company was silent. Anticipating resistance from the Grunwick management, after writing to Jackson for the official support of the post office workers, Grantham also wrote to Len Murray calling for the support of the TUC.

Grantham's strategy was first to seek the reinstatement of the 137 sacked members. As Dromey put it, Grantham's argument was based upon custom: 'It was not without precedent in Britain for strike action to precede union membership but it was unusual for workers on strike to be sacked and stay sacked. Most peace settlements where strikers had been sacked started with the reinstatement of those dismissed. Recognition and the tackling of the grievances of the strikers came second in the list of objectives.'[55]

In effect, the Grunwick members became part of the Hythe Road branch of APEX in Brent of which Gristey was in charge. Gristey, 'a hearty individual', was faced with the task of organising the Grunwick members who were 'as green as cooking apples'. After an earlier attempt in August, he tried again to open negotiations with Grunwick management on 8 September. He was rejected. Grunwick remained ominously silent. Gristey and Grantham, having drawn a blank thus far (unusual for them), had begun to consider the prospect of a hard battle for which, at that stage, they seemed to be prepared. In spite of his charms, as the front-man during the dispute, at the beginning he found it difficult to communicate with the workers. However, unlike so many trade union officials, he tried smiling through. But smiles from a trade union official representing black workers in Britain was clearly not enough. By November 1976, when asked by a striker at a mass meeting if there was really any hope of victory, Gristey assured the strikers, 'I promise you that no power in Christendom will defeat you.'[56]

Apart from APEX union officials, the strikers were in close contact with Dromey and the local Trades Council. His role in the dispute cannot be denied. As the local representative of the TUC in Brent, he was in close liaison with the strikers. Not surprisingly, therefore, the Council generously made available its Labour Hall which was used as the strikers 'headquarters'.

Gristey and the Council advised the strikers who elected a Strike Committee which started issuing strike bulletins. The first Secretary of the Committee was Sunil Desai and the Treasurer was his mother, Mrs Desai. Noorali Valliani was elected Chairman (later replaced by Kamlesh Gandhi) and Mahmood Ahmed succeeded Sunil who had to continue his studies. The Strike Committee of 15 members, with Gristey and Dromey as non-voting members, was the cultural focus of the strikers, and their bulletins reflected the progression of their feelings, hopes and fears as the strike developed into national (and international) proportions. During the first months, the Strike Committee was highly effective holding committee and mass meetings in the Trades Hall daily for the first six weeks.

George Ward was no friend of the Trades Council. Predictably, therefore, as the Council actively supported the strikers, Ward singled out Dromey (Secretary of the Council) as 'the key adviser'[57] to the strikers, one of the prime 'stirrers' in the Brent area, the 'moving spirit' behind the Strike Committee as fabricating the strike. While the 'virgin' strikers knew little about trade unions, like 'chickens out of a coop',[58] Ward denied the strikers their individuality and the ability to determine what they wanted. Their walkout was not proof enough. Rather he saw the strikers (a reflection of his attitude towards them as an employer) as putty in the hands of Jack Dromey. It was clear he personally disliked Dromey, who was trying to use his position to get a 'political platform'. Indeed, he was reported as saying, 'I'll make him a political eunuch before I'm finished', and wrote that Dromey said to him during picketing, 'We're going to close you, Ward.' 'I am not an aggressive man', said Ward, 'but I could not refrain from replying, "I think you're going to be a failed revolutionary – we're going to trim your beard."'[59] Further, in his personal battle with Dromey, he stated that Dromey's 'propaganda served to stiffen our resolve',[60] and later boasted that Dromey 'continually underestimated our determination to resist and our resourcefulness. We were able to outmanoeuvre him at every turn.'[61]

From these statements, it seemed that the focus of the dispute had shifted to Dromey and his left-wing politics, relegating the strikers' demands (for the time being at least) as being of secondary importance. This personal conflict would lead Ward, the supreme egoist, to go to any lengths to reinforce his commitment against trade unionism at Grunwick.

Another leading figure, Tom Durkin, Chairman of the Brent Trades Council, a staunch supporter of trade union rights (who was involved in an earlier dispute with Grunwick in 1973), only confirmed Ward's do or die approach. It had become clear by the autumn of 1976 that polar opposites faced each other in a war of attrition. Necessarily, therefore, both sides had to prepare for the struggle. Thus, the 'virgin' migrant strikers were thrown into the maelstrom of trade unionism, industrial relations and into the essential nature of British politics of the hard Left and the hard Right. In the middle, there were the Liberals and moderate Labour leaders with high ideals and the rhetoric of the 'brotherhood of man'. Increasingly strong words and positive action in support of the strikers gave no indication as to the outcome when faced with the acid test: a full-scale confrontation.

Already by the autumn, Dromey was complaining that the

Grunwick Strike, 'increasingly consumed the energies of the Trades Council'.[62] The people of Brent, however, responded magnificently with donations from Mulliner Park Wards/Rolls Royce Works Committee, Express Dairies, Associated Automation (GEC), TGWU, the UPW Cricklewood Office Branch and a Miners Lodge in South Wales.[63]

Through the Trades Council's initiating efforts, the Strike Committee's weekly bulletins were published. This proved to be a vital communication link in arousing widespread support for the strike. They were, with the help of the Liaison Committee for the Defence of Trades Unions, distributed throughout the country. Paul Vig and Sunil Desai, the first writers of the bulletin, now put forward their case to a wide audience. Regular socials and meetings canvassed further support. Each day, each week, the strikers found new supporters, but they also spent less time with their close knit families. 'Sari Power' and marches meant less time with, and disruptions to family life. Anticipating this the strikers and the Trades Council called an unprecedented meeting of husbands and relatives of the Asian women strikers. This highly imaginative and practical development was absolutely necessary to reassure families and thus sustain the effects of the struggle they were in. British trade unionism had known little or nothing of this strategy before. Now it was being proved that, in spite of a different social and cultural pattern, militant migrant workers can be accommodated within the system of industrial relations if some of the trade unions employing black workers were not so hidebound by tradition and racism. In fact, if industrial relations was a changing system, then 'Sari Power' should be accepted as part of this framework and indeed of the industrial scene. After a march of 400 people from Grunwick's Cobbold Road to its Chapter Road site on 1 October 1976, it was observed that,

> . . . outside the factory gates of Willesden the High Road suddenly exploded into a blaze of colour. Down the road, banners flying, swept hundreds of demonstrators, led by Indian workers. In the vanguard, saris swirling, were the Indian women. Not submissive housebound women but Grunwick strikers – fists raised in anger. Not the inarticulate immigrant women we are often told about. Hardly. For at every building they passed, they shouted their one resounding slogan: 'Union! Union! We want union!'[64]

The Indian women involved shouted 'Union!' with the full support of their husbands. By early October 1976, together the Strike Committee, APEX and the Trades Council brought pressure to bear on Grunwick to enter negotiations. In addition, individuals and organisations within the Indian community and local MPs were asked for support. Ward stated that several people, claiming membership of the Brent Indian Workers' Association, had put pressure on the relatives of one of his workers, and that his small company was subjected to a 'tremendous propaganda barrage, sniped at by MPs and union chiefs who had never set foot inside the firm'. In spite of the growing pressure to negotiate and conclude a peaceful settlement, he dug his heels in. Having sunk 'our life savings' and 'many years of our lives' in the company, since Grunwick had always 'led from the front' to secure the jobs of its workers, Ward wrote, 'We were determined to guarantee their livelihoods, whatever the cost.'[65]

Whatever the pressure then Ward had shifted the anti-union emphasis to show his magnanimity in putting the interest of his workforce first. Unfortunately, the favourable image of a caring and good employer was contradicted by a statement he made at the outset of his book which revealed the real basis of his stand. He wrote that he had grown fairly thick-skinned about being tagged a 'reactionary employer' and an 'inflexible, hardline, anti-trade unionist'. He then made it abundantly clear, 'I don't much care what people think of me; I care what *I* think of me.'[66] Bearing this in mind, he explained his position *vis-à-vis* the trade unions thus:

> The pickets have said that they are besieging Grunwick because we will not permit our workers to join a trade union. This is a complete fabrication . . . I have never dismissed an employee for joining a union, and there are a number of union members still working in the company. But this is different from granting an official status to the union by 'recognition', giving it the contractual right to negotiate with the company.[67]

He feared that in practice this would mean that the union was likely to seek to negotiate not just for its own members but for the whole workforce and eventually try to impose a 'closed shop', excluding from employment all those who refused to join. Moreover, he was not prepared to accept APEX's other major demand, reinstatement of the strikers who were lawfully dismissed for 'breach of contract and industrial misconduct'. Indeed, given the impasse between the company and APEX, the directors were not prepared 'to let Grunwick move one inch in the direction of the closed shop'.[68] The gap between the two sides was clear. And during the autumn months of 1976 there was no reasonable grounds for compromise. Ward was prepared for all or nothing. Indeed, he was prepared to 'close down the business' rather than agree to conduct it on the terms of 'organised bullies'.[69]

The strikers, APEX and Brent Trades Council, did not know of these entrenched views of them held by Ward and his associates. In fact, in October 1976 they were optimistic, hoping for a speedy settlement. Early in the month, in view of Ward's intransigence, Grantham led a delegation of strikers to press the Secretary of State for Employment, Albert Booth, for a Court of Inquiry into the dispute. This was not granted. Instead Booth referred to the Employment Protection Act (1975) which provided machinery for the resolution of the dispute. Under section 11 of the Act, ACAS was allowed to investigate the union's claim for recognition.

ACAS was the outcome of the Report of the Royal Commission on Trade Unions, known as the Donovan Commission Report. ACAS, constituted by the Conservative government of 1970–74, had its terms of reference enlarged by the Labour government of 1974. With the dismantling of the National Industrial Relations Court, a 'consensus approach' to the resolution of problems was embodied in ACAS. The Service's governing Council comprised three TUC representatives, three Confederation of British Industries representatives and three academics. Charged with the duty 'of encouraging the extension of collective bargaining', ACAS is 'independent' of the government. However, ACAS had no powers to enforce its decisions. The whole object of this tripartite exercise was to persuade the parties involved, not to compel them.

Given these limited powers and Ward's continuing refusal to negotiate, according to Dromey, Grantham reluctantly referred the deadlock to ACAS. On 1 November when the Union of Post Office Workers blacked Grunwick's mail, the police arrested nine pickets. The blacking action cheered the strikers, their families and their supporters. Indeed, they felt victory would be theirs. On the other hand, Ward, alarmed by the blacking, 'a threat to our jugular',[70] turned to John Gorst, the Conservative MP for Barnet and Hendon North, for advice. This led to Ward's agreement to meet ACAS. He was not impressed. 'It seemed to me', he said, 'that the rules [of ACAS] were made up as you went along.' He insisted that the proper subject for any ACAS inquiry was 'the opinion of our workers'. ACAS, on the other hand, insisted that views of the sacked workers had to be taken into account. Resisting outside interferences in 'his business', Ward made perhaps the most important move that had far-reaching consequences, beyond a local dispute, and ultimately affecting the outcome of the dispute: he turned to the lawyers. From here on Ward's reluctance to negotiate, incited intense and widespread feelings among trade unionists, left-wing groups, labour leaders and politicians. The strike at Grunwick was national news daily as the strikers' action received unprecedented publicity. Given the proportions which the dispute assumed, the political implications necessarily came into focus.

On 4 November 1976, Grunwick was debated in Parliament. Earlier, Ward had enlisted the support of John Gouriet and the right-wing National Association for Freedom (NAFF) which brought pressure to bear on the blacking of Grunwick. During the debate, Albert Booth announced that the UPW had agreed to suspend its blacking of Grunwick on receiving an assurance that the company would co–operate with ACAS. On the face of it, it seemed only a matter of time before the dispute was settled. But encouraged by the lifting of the blacking, Ward was boastful. He felt that the UPW blacking was called off because of the combined effect of the threat of legal action and Parliamentary pressure.[71] Increasingly, law and order and politics would enter the debate on the central issues of union recognition and reinstatement of the strikers.

Given the possibility of a ballot of his existing workforce, Ward and company increased the wages of their workforce by 15 per cent towards the end of November. This incentive had the desired effect of getting the workforce to back the company in the event of a ballot. The strikers, faced with wintry weather, had the support of Len Murray who spoke to them and their supporters at Brent Trades Hall. Towards the end of December, ACAS had become wary of its attempts to win Grunwick's co-operation for a ballot of its workers. Delaying tactics was Grunwick's strategy. Efforts to get Grunwick to another meeting with ACAS had failed by Christmas. At this point, ACAS felt justified in sending out 110 questionnaires on 29 December to a list of Grunwick's employees (supplied in the absence of the company's co-operation) by APEX. Of these questionnaires, the 93 that were returned all voted 'yes' to trade union recognition at Grunwick.

By the turn of the year (in fact, several weeks into the New Year) in February 1977, Grunwick, with enough time to respond to the outcome of the ballot, countered with its own ballot. The company employed the Market Opinion Research Insitute (MORI) which found that the weekly-paid staff of 153 workers voted against having a trade union and 21 voted for. APEX felt that the 137 workers who walked out should have been included in this poll. Moreover, the vote was undertaken in conditions of duress – both the recent pay rise and the 'fear' of losing their jobs were coercive elements in the 'yes' vote. Indeed, the truth in this statement was reflected in the fact that a few months later in June and July, more workers joined the strike.[72]

While Ward was jubilant following the MORI result of his workforce, ACAS was not impressed by his image of being a good employer and decided to produce a preliminary report which would be sent to APEX and Grunwick for comment. Later, a full report would be made. Needless to say, if Ward did not look forward to the report, the battle-weary strikers were eagerly hoping for a favourable one, particularly since February and March brought no victory, only 'setbacks and defeats' which had begun to take their toll.

NAFF's continuing anti-union strategy in getting an injunction preventing the blacking of Grunwick mail, which was contained in the High Court and upheld on appeal, momentarily dealt a real blow to the strikers' morale. The victory they had expected to come quickly was still elusive. On 10 March 1977, however, the final ACAS report was published. NAFF and Grunwick fared badly. ACAS's recommendation of recognition of APEX also received the support of James Prior, the Shadow Minister for

Employment in the Conservative Party. As far as the strikers were concerned, this was a victory. But how real was it in terms of meeting their demands? NAFF's 'legal' strategy, having caused havoc in the past, was to do so again: Grunwick's threat to take ACAS to court to have its report declared invalid became a fact when on 19 April Grunwick served a High Court writ on ACAS which asked that the report be invalidated because it was limited to Grunwick's 'former employees' – the strikers. In effect, Ward had taken NAFF's advice and acted. This 'insolence' angered the trade union movement. Dromey commented, 'Grunwick was taking ACAS to court for not carrying out a survey which Grunwick itself had refused to allow.'[73]

In doing so, Ward felt confident that he had secured the support of his existing workforce which was awarded another pay increase of 10 per cent on 1 April.[74] A week before this, on 23 March, the General Council of the TUC had turned down APEX's request for the blacking of essential services. And on the same day, an Industrial Tribunal ruled it had 'no jurisdiction' to say whether the strikers were sacked fairly or unfairly.

If the spring had brought setbacks, defeats and despair to the strikers, the summer of 1977 called forth a dramatic increase in support from trade unionists and sympathisers on the one hand, and a quick response of a massive police presence on the other. On 27 April, over 1400 people marched through Willesden in support of the strike. Police harassment of the Grunwick pickets through the winter months of 1976–77 had become a matter of serious concern as some chanted 'Company police'.[75] Indeed on 3 May the Middlesex Crown Court found arrested pickets innocent. Moreover, the Willesden police were vigorously condemned and ordered to pay costs.[76] Dromey, arrested for chanting 'Company police', was acquitted. As the police presence grew, the relationship between them and the pickets became an important issue, particularly because of the use of violence. The experience of Kantilal Patel, who was, in a rare moment, left alone on the picket line during a change of duty, was cause for serious concern. When his colleagues returned, they found him 'beaten up and bleeding from the lip and cheek, his face badly bruised'. Although there were no witnesses to prove who actually committed the act, when the police were called in, it was alleged, although they were stationed less than a mile away, 'they did not hurry'. When they eventually arrived, 'One large policeman towered over Kanti and told him that he deserved what he got.'[77] The relationship between the police and the immigrant community had deteriorated so much that Brent Community Relations Council suspended all its formal links with the police.

Although no arrests were made in the month of May, on the 19th three government ministers had joined the picket line. This, however, was the calm before the storm. On 1 June, Mrs Jayaben Desai was arrested for 'assault' and 'exchanges' with George Ward and Malcolm Alden her former bosses. Later, following an appeal, she won her case.

So far the strikers had no reason to believe that they would get justice from the police. They felt they were 'up against the police', and on this basis, they called on the trade union movement to support a mass picket, for one week only, from 13 to 17 June.[78] The strikers had experienced many moments of disappointment particularly in that the trade union movement did not act swiftly and decisively to confront Grunwick when it flouted the ACAS report. Now in June 1977, over ten months since the strike began, they felt an urgent need for support, for the kind of solidarity reflected in Tom Durkin's words to the Brent Trades Council earlier in the year: 'there has been no struggle in Brent more glorious, none more courageous, than that of the Grunwick strikers since the General Strike of 1926. The trade union movement cannot afford their defeat.'[79]

If May was a relatively calm and trouble-free month, in terms of police harassment and violence on the picket line, it also had the effect of arousing suspicions and doubts as to the outcome of their struggle. Two of the strikers made their feelings abundantly clear. Reflecting creeping bitterness, on 3 April, Mahmood Ahmed, Chairman of the Strike Committee, told 2000 trade unionists at the British Leyland Convenors' Conference in Birmingham Town Hall that TUC promises could not compensate for effective action. Indeed, the TUC should approach the strikers, asking how they could help rather than the other way round. He added finally, what many felt, 'If the British trade union movement wants to recruit Asian workers, then it has to do better than this.'[80] Already real fears had set in, but the struggle continued.

The mass picket was to bring home via television screens, the unforgettable scenes of the Grunwick Strike. Given the foregoing developments in the dispute by June 1977, the Strike had already become widely known in Britain. The Strike Committee's bulletins put forward this summary of the issues involved:

IF THE STRIKE IS LOST
1. The right to organise will have been made a mockery of.
2. ACAS will have been discredited and the Employment Protection Act.
3. Millions of unorganised workers at other Grunwicks will be discouraged from joining a union.
4. The confidence of Asian and West Indian workers in our movement will be severely affected.
5. 'Sweat Shop' employers up and down the country will take heart.[81]

Moreover, both the union and the strikers saw the necessity of a mass picket to stem the blows dealt to the working-class movement. For the pattern of counter-attack had become clear in that whenever normal trade union pressures such as blacking and picketing were applied 'some upper class twit' appeared on television 'with a court writ in his hand'. Some felt the NAFF was making a nonsense of British industrial relations, and getting away with it.

Another important reason for calling a mass picket in June was because some two-thirds of Grunwick's business was carried out between June and September. A mass picket during this period was expected to cause disruption to this trade. One of the aims of the mass picket was to win support from the blacklegs. The summer months then were crucial in the joint strategy of the union, the Strike Committee and the Trades Council to bring about a speedy and peaceful settlement to the dispute. The language used by both sides during the dispute conjures up the image of battle lines being drawn for an inevitable confrontation. Indeed 'Blockading' 'Fort Grunwick' were common expressions. Clearly they were not 'playing cricket'. There was genuine anger and outrage among members of the labour movement. Equally, in the company and its advisers and NAFF, there was animosity and contempt for the strikers, the idea of trade unionism and their supporters on the picket line. Yet 'peaceful picketing' was the intention.

The original and main aim of the mass picket was to get the maximum publicity for the strikers' cause. According to Dromey, the idea of a mass picket was that 'two hundred people would man the gates daily throughout the week from Monday 13 June, in a show of strength to demand action, particularly on essential services'.[82]

The employer and the forces of law and order saw the intimidation of the blacklegs as a declaration of war by the presence of a mass picket. Fort Grunwick had to be fortified, before the siege! As both sides made preparations, on the basis of past experience, they were surprised by the size of the escalation that began on Monday 13 June, the first day of the mass picket. A number of organisations (including women's groups) sent representatives to join the pickets which started at 6am at Chapter Road. Half an hour later, there were 60 people. These movements were closely monitored.

In no nonsense 'mood' and in defence of the 'Fort', police chief Sadler demanded that the pickets be reduced to six only.[83] This had no basis in law, the strikers argued. Once again, the police were denying the strikers their rights.

The police moved in, 'whiplashing into the pickets on the pavement' and arrested 84 pickets on that first day. According to one observer, there was 'no resistance' from the pickets. However, the police allegedly pulled, 'prodded their victims on with kicks and punches, irrespective of age or sex'. Some policemen used this as the ideal opportunity to vent their racism and sexism.

On Tuesday a bus was used to drive the 'loyal workers' through the picket line. By the end of the day 11 of the 'loyal workers' had joined the strikers. Even two pay increases in six months and the might of the law to protect them could not maintain their loyalty to George Ward and his company. That same day, the Special Patrol Group entered, for the first time in British labour relations history, a picket line. This heavy squad further reinforced protection of the 'Fort'. Predictably, it called forth deep questioning among pickets. As one trade unionist put it: 'We're not bloody terrorists.'[84]

On Wednesday that week, the Cricklewood sorters launched the unofficial blacking of Grunwick mail on the advice of the UPW's London District Council. Support for the strikers came from some TGWU drivers, working for the police on contract (they refused to drive them to Chapter Road), and from the National Union of Bank Employees. And significantly, more 'loyal' Grunwick workers joined the strike. The next day, Grantham ready to seize any opportunity for negotiation with Grunwick agreed to meet Ward at Grunwick to 'exchange views'. This afternoon meeting turned out to be a meeting with the 'loyal workers' with whom Grantham tried to reason. He was abused and his presence at the meeting was filmed.[85] According to one of the workers who later joined the strikers in July, Ward had plied his staff with alcoholic drinks.[86]

On Friday morning 17 June, the last day of the mass picket, outraged trade unionists came out in full force. Some 1500 had gathered near the Chapter Road site. The picketing grew to outnumber, for the first time, the 700-strong police force. It was, perhaps, opportune that Dromey, on behalf of the Strike Committee, announced to the crowd that mass picketing would be extended for another week. The crowd approved.

The strikers had come through a battering from the police but were nevertheless in buoyant mood. Mrs Desai's soreness and sadness gave way to optimism as she beheld the trade union banners behind which a solid mass of British working men and women marched in support of the strikers' struggle. 'When they talked of the power of the trade union movement', she said, 'I listened but I didn't really believe. Now I see that power.' What Mrs Desai did not know is that only very rarely has the British trade union movement come out *en masse* to demonstrate solidarity for a cause. This turnout made the Grunwick dispute special; an important event in British labour history. For the ruling class who predictably had to believe in law and order to protect their property, this massive crowd (a powerful statement in opposition to an oppressive employer and police violence) represented a real threat to the status quo. 'Fort Grunwick', symbolic of vested interests, had to be protected. Given this perspective, one begins to understand the presence of the SPG that Friday morning which sliced through the crowds 'like a knife through butter'.[87] Their ferocious charges seemed unbelievable to eyewitnesses. Noticeably, as was the case on Monday, the first day of the mass picket, the SPG seemed to single out only women, 'rushing us like animals', as one

woman put it. Although Grunwick had made even bolder headlines, the media played down this attack on women. The next day,
another 40 arrests were made.

The 'war' resumed on Monday 20 June, at the beginning of the
second week with 1200 pickets at Grunwick's gates. This encouragement to the strikers was accentuated by a miners' vote to join
the picket line, later in the week. Monday passed with relative
calm. But, on Tuesday, there was violence again. There to witness
the 'most violent scenes on the picket line so far', were Tribune
MPs led by Ian Mikardo. After the bus delivering the 'loyal
workers' had entered and left, a policeman allegedly laid hands on a
black man. According to Mikardo who witnessed the incident, it
was likely that the man's colour made him an easy and identifiable
target. Whatever the provocation, this man was viciously attacked
by three policemen. Soon more policemen charged into the crowd
and a full-scale confrontation ensued. Comparing this with the
Cable Street battle in the 1930s, Mikardo said, 'At no one time
during the course of the morning did we [the MPs] see anybody
offer violence to the police of any sort. Nor did we see anything
that could be called provocation other than vocal provocation.'[88] It
seemed what constituted 'vocal provocation' was left to the discretion of individual police officers, as indeed, were matters to do with
the 'loyal workers' decided at the discretion of Grunwick's managers. Thus, MP Audrey Wise's comment to a policeman who was
dragging a woman picket, was interpreted as an arrestable offence.

Apart from the recklessness of the police, the high speed at which
the workers' bus was driven through the factory gates, aroused
concern. On Wednesday, two leading Communists, Mick
McGahey (leader of the Scottish miners) and Gordon McLennan,
General Secretary of the Communist Party in Britain, were present
on the picket line. McLennan presented Mrs Desai with a £288
cheque, and McGahey, after an enthusiastic welcome, addressed
the 'smallest' crowd of the week with a 'powerful speech'. George
Ward was irked by McGahey's call to 'close the place [Grunwick]
up and stop that industrial hooligan Mr Ward in his tracks'.[89] He
went on to assure the courageous strikers: 'You will win as night
follows day . . . the whole of the Scottish miners will come here if
necessary.' Conscious of the escalation of the dispute into high
politics, and the silence of certain organisations, he voiced a widespread feeling, 'I want to see marching down Chapter Road the
General Council of the TUC. Behind them I want to see the
National Executive Committee of the Labour Party. And behind
them, the Parliamentary Labour Party led by the Prime Minister.'
The crowd applauded. Confrontation involving the people was one
thing, but confrontation involving those with power was another.
McGahey had put his finger on it: what was vitally necessary in the
dispute, given all that had gone before, was confrontation; *action*
from the strikers' supporters, no more words.

The next day the Yorkshire miners led by Arthur Scargill responded. They came to Cooper Road and joined the 2000 pickets which was also the estimated number on the picket line on the following day. In anticipation of the miners, the 'toughest' and 'most militant' section of the British working class, the police and SPG forces were ready for confrontation. In spite of the outrage at their behaviour during the first three days, the SPG charged into the crowd again. Scargill and many of his colleagues were arrested. The miners were taken by surprise. As one of them put it, 'This is not traditional British policemen we have here. These here are thugs in uniform.'[90]

During the day's violence, PC Trevor Wilson was hit by a bottle. This, in spite of the Strike Committee's sympathy (Mrs Desai visited the injured policeman) and its condemnation of violence on both sides, was a major setback for the strikers as the media and right-wingers, advising and supporting Ward blamed 'red fascists' and painted a picture of an all-powerful trade union movement which had driven poor George Ward to a secret destination, because he was 'suffering from exhaustion'.[91]

Not all journalists were caught up in 'union-bashing'. Although much damage was done, one journalist wrote: 'As usual it was not until there was violence that the BBC or ITN or most newspapers bothered to report the issue.'[92]

On Friday of the second week of the mass picket, there were an estimated 1,521 police. During this week, it had become clear to many that there was more 'calculation and premeditation' behind this presence. What was this 'force' designed to achieve? Roy Edwards, Assistant General Secretary of APEX, a 'moderate', offered his view. He felt that the violence was caused by the police who waded into the crowd with their fists, knees and boots and used their helmets and truncheons. '. . . I have seen action on picket lines many many times but I have never seen such brutality. It was unprovoked and I think it was planned in advance to discredit the pickets.'[93]

The two weeks of mass picketing provided the politicians with two pegs on which they hung their arguments – picketing and law and order. Merlyn Rees, who had earlier said, 'this kind of activity [violence against police] I know, has no place in responsible trade unionism', after visiting the scene on Monday 27 June, defended this policy of policing which led to the violence thus: 'I learnt this in Northern Ireland: operational control must be in the hands of the police.'[94]

As far as the strikers were concerned, neither the Strike Committee, the Trades Council nor APEX could have predicted the massive support they received or what had happened on the picket lines. Neither were they to be blamed. 'The union, we are satisfied', the Scarman Court of Inquiry stated, 'had no intention of provoking violence and disorder by calling for the mass picket.'[95] It was on the last day of that historic month that Albert Booth announced this Court of Inquiry.

What did the mass picket in June achieve? Firstly, the mass support mobilised helped to get more of Grunwick's 'loyal workers' to join the strikers; secondly, it brought about an unselfish act of solidarity amongst postal workers to boycott Grunwick's mail; and thirdly, it helped to bring into being the Scarman Court of Inquiry into the dispute.

With the support of NAFF, Ward was able to mount 'Operation Pony Express' and get round the blacking of the company's mail by the Cricklewood sorters who continued their action, in spite of suspension by their union. Significantly, since the strike started, this small group of postal workers had done more in directly affecting the Grunwick business than the 20,000 pickets at the gate.

The 'Operation' (a classic strike-breaking exercise) consisted of a strange little convoy of a 40-foot container lorry, two cars, a large box lorry and a mini-bus with about 25 volunteers on board. An hour after they arrived at 1am on Saturday 9 July, Grunwick's backlog of mail was safely out of its premises. Proudly, Ward quoted one of his supporters saying, 'It was the best thing since Entebbe.'[96]

Given the mounting support and interest in their cause, in order to maintain the momentum, the Strike Committee called for a 'day of action' on 11 July. That day a 'super-picket' of 20,000 people had assembled to demonstrate against the company. And significantly, seven more 'loyal workers' joined the strikers. The 'day of action' was supported by the Yorkshire miners. Again in a gesture of solidarity they joined the strikers. As Scargill said, 'We haven't fought for trade union rights for two centuries to give them away in the back streets of Willesden.'[97] The spectacular march with brilliant trade union banners and the meeting that followed in Roundwood Park, involved relatively little or no violence. However, there was a mood of anger among many in the crowd that the speakers who addressed them did not include members of the Strike Committee, the Trades Council or the Union of Post Office Workers. Only after shouts for Desai, Dromey and Durkin did Dromey tell the thousands 'The mass picket must go on'.[98]

The media was again disappointed by this extraordinary demonstration against a small company. They attacked the pickets as 'mobsters' inciting 'mob rule' and singled out 'megalomaniacal Mr Scargill'.[99]

The following day, Lord Widgery gave the High Court judgement in favour of ACAS against Grunwick. Widgery felt that ACAS was correct in regarding the strikers as workers whose views should have been taken into account on the issue of union recognition and that ACAS had sought through every means possible to get the views of Grunwick's employees, but this was frustrated by refusal to provide their names and addresses. In the light of this judgement, the Prime Minister asked both sides to accept the High Court ruling. George Ward might have been down, but not out. He replied, 'We shall go to the Court of Appeal and on legal advice if necessary to the Lords.'[100]

Friday 29 July was indeed 'Black Friday'. Firstly, the postal workers voted to end their blacking, secondly the Grunwick strikers voted to call off their 8 August mass picket, and thirdly, Lord Denning ruled that the Appeal Court should allow Grunwick's appeal against the earlier High Court ruling of 12 July, thus invalidating the ACAS report.[101]

The long, hard struggle of the migrant trade unionists had begun to take its toll. The earlier support of the two unions, APEX and the UPW, was faltering. Jayaben Desai wept outside the Brent Trades Hall. After '49 weeks, rain and snow', and being dragged by her hair by a policeman, she asked, 'was it for this?' She commented on Grantham, the lapsed 'moderate' who after the euphoria of the earlier weeks, became again a true catholic: he threatened to 'cut off our strike pay'. There was also bitter disappointment from members of the UPW Cricklewood Branch whose Chairman, Colin Maloney said, 'our union leadership has done something that George Ward, John Gorst and the NAFF failed to do. They forced us back.'

At the beginning of August, the Brent Trades Council responded to this clear slackening of support for the strikers. They accused the government and trade union leadership of forcing a retreat on the Strike Committee and the Cricklewood postmen. The rank and file was being dictated to by their executive and the gap was widening between the Strike Committee and APEX. When the postmen unwillingly returned to work the next day, ACAS announced that they would challenge the High Court decision in the Lords. And in the continuing unpredictability of official trade union support, the following week, the TUC adopted a resolution calling for increased financial and political aid for the strikers.

Already the strikers' disillusionment was becoming evident. Hitherto they had fought and lost many battles, yet, they were hopeful. On 25 August, the Scarman Report was published. The report called for union recognition and reinstatement while criticising the mass picket and the postal blacking. This was seen as a victory by APEX who had listed five background issues to the strike: (i) low pay; (ii) long hours with compulsory overtime; (iii) petty restrictions on workers; (iv) management's attitude towards supervision; and (v) frequent dismissals.

In essence, the report emphasised belief in the British tradition of compromise through collective bargaining and the need for workers and employers to act reasonably. Scarman commented on the vulnerable immigrant workforce who were 'particularly at risk' in that they were employed in fiercely competitive businesses where low prices and rapid service brought great rewards.[102] He also felt

the genuine sense of discontent and grievances could not be dealt
with since there was no effective machinery through which this
could be done. Grunwick's Works Committee was woefully inadequate for dealing with these grievances. He felt that Malcolm
Alden's attitude towards workers was a real source of discontent in
the mail order department. Indeed, in this context, he became, as
Dromey put it, 'advocate, judge, jury and hangman in his own
cause'. Grunwick according to Scarman,

> by dismissing all the strikers, refusing to reconsider the reinstate-
> ment of any of them, refusing to seek a negotiated settlement to the
> strike and rejecting ACAS offers of conciliation, has acted within the
> letter but outside the spirit of the law. Further, such action on the
> part of the company was unreasonable when judged by the norms of
> good industrial relations practice. The company has thus added to
> the bitterness of the dispute, and contributed to its development into
> a threat of civil disorder.[103]

In his balancing act, on the other hand, Scarman also criticised
the mass picketing and the unofficial boycott. Overall then, the
Scarman Report findings, broadly in favour of the union, were
welcomed by APEX, but a harder line was taken by the Strike
Committee and the Trades Council. Indeed, it was hoped it would
provide the basis for a negotiated settlement, that the question of
recognition would not be allowed to drag on.[104] Ahmed, Desai,
Gandhi and Dromey were all pleased at the vindication of their
stand, but were acutely aware that the strike was not yet over.
Furthermore they were concerned that Scarman's recommendation
concerning a government review of the law on picketing might
lead to further legal restriction on the right to picket. At that
moment, Ward was the only real threat to a quick and peaceful
settlement. Wary of the NAFF and Ward's response, the strikers in
a letter to the union Executive Committee warned: 'We are firmly
convinced that it would be a major mistake to lose this golden
opportunity and to allow Ward to think that, in our anxiety for a
negotiated settlement, we might be weakening.'[105] Dromey supported this view.

As many had predicted on 31 August, Grunwick rejected the
Scarman Report. The NAFF dismissed it as having 'no legal force'
and after APEX's 'olive branch' Ward responded on 1 September
with his 'Counter Scarman Report' which was published in *The
Times* and the *Telegraph*.

> Never under any circumstances will the company reinstate those
> who were, very properly, dismissed. The suggestion is completely
> impracticable as the existing reinstatement would be a surrender to
> rampant illegality, brute force, and the coercive power of a mighty
> vested interest that seeks not to reason but to compel.[106]

Hours later, he received the support of Sir Keith Joseph who
condemned the Scarman Report.

Time was running out, and the strikers felt the moment had come to have a showdown with their union officials. Indeed, when they met Grantham and Deputy General Secretary, Tudor Thomas, 'bitter exchanges' marked a long meeting. The strikers argued for a motion on the question of action in essential services to be moved at the TUC Conference, a few days later. The strikers' optimism of the result of such a meeting came to grief as Grantham announced that the motion had already been sent to the TUC General Secretary in Blackpool. In effect, it was now much too late to discuss essential services and of course (conveniently or not) he did not have a copy with him. He assured the Strike Committee, however, that in lieu of reference to essential services the unions would be asked to increase their 'financial and practical support'. Grantham, the 'moderate' trade unionist was behaving true to form and in doing so, had effectively denied the strikers any degree of real success in the strike. According to Dromey, a leading TUC General Council member, who could not 'understand' Grantham, said: 'The motion is as weak as piss. He could have asked for the moon and Congress would have given it to him.' Instead, he assured the strikers that action would be taken *after* Congress had met, to affect essential services to the company. [107]

What could explain this incredible behaviour of Grantham following the Scarman Report. Dromey was accurate in stating that 'the Court of Inquiry did precisely what the Government set it up to achieve and what suited the majority of the TUC General Council: the battle was moved off the streets, the mass picketing was brought under control and the "illegal" blacking of Grunwick's mail was ended'. [108]

Indeed, neither Tom Jackson (UPW) or Frank Chapple of the EETPU were interested in taking action on essential services. In fact, one observer wrote: 'The mood among trade unionists at Blackpool was of embarrassment at getting dragged into battle. . . . The principal pre-occupation in TUC minds now is how to get out of the affair gracefully and with the minimum loss of face. The same is true of Ministers and Labour MPs, who have become noticeably reluctant to comment or get involved in the past few weeks.' [109]

In a last desperate attempt to win TUC support, the strikers leafletted delegates at the 109th Annual Congress in September 1977. After the TUC General Council's failure to act on essential services, the strikers, not relishing the prospect of returning to the streets and the impact on local residents, unanimously agreed to a resumption of the mass picketing on Monday 17 October. It was hoped that the mass picket would put pressure on the company and arouse interest and support for action on essential services. On Monday 17 October some 5000 pickets assembled outside Grunwick. In mounting its last desperate battle, the Strike Committee called for another day of action on Monday, 7 November. After 14 months their energy had not flagged: they believed in trade unionism and were guided in this belief by left-wing trade unionists. As the Strike Committee saw it, they had two choices: to sit it out until the Lords' decision or to pursue action on essential services.[110]

Three days before the 'Day of Reckoning' seven MPs, Neil Kinnock, Audrey Wise, Ron Thomas, Jo Richardson, Martin Flannery, Ian Mikardo and Dennis Skinner, joined the pickets at Chapter Road. As the interest and support for the strikers intensified during the weekend prior to the 'day of action', Mahmood Ahmad said 'even in the event of winning, there is no legal way of getting our jobs back'.[111]

By the afternoon of the 'Day of Reckoning' 8000 pickets had assembled to demonstrate their support for the strikers' cause; a 'magnificent tribute' to the trade union movement after 63 weeks, said the Strike Committee. The day was marred, however, by 'one of the worst attacks upon pickets in living memory.' Two hundred and forty-three pickets received injuries inflicted by the police and 113 were arrested.[112] Police brutality was 'organised and indiscriminate'. This policy of 'unbridled savagery' involved an attack 'from behind by several hundred policemen'.[113]

The Strike Committee wondered how much more violence was necessary before the TUC and the unions providing essential services would take action to force recognition and reinstatement. Winter had come again and another Day of Action was called for early December. The Strike Committee appealed to APEX for support. But APEX had grown weary of the long battle and the strikers had failed to win the support of their own union and the EEPTU, GMWU and the UPW.

The frail Mrs Desai had not bargained for this physically, mentally and spiritually demanding struggle when she walked out of Grunwick's mail order department on 20 August 1976. After a tortuous 15-month picket in all weathers, facing police hatred and violence, victory seemed as far away as ever.

On 21 November, as a final act of protest in line with the Gandhian technique, she was joined by Vipin Magdani, Johnny Patel and Yasu Patel on hunger strike on the steps of TUC Headquarters on Great Russell Street. This hunger strike met the displeasure of APEX and the TUC, not the support they had hoped for. And for good measure, Mahmood and Gandhi who had joined the hunger strikers, had their membership in APEX and strike pay withdrawn. In effect, they were, at that stage, non-union members powerless to act. Suddenly their struggle for trade union recognition had become a bitterly disappointing exercise; they were disciplined by their employer, the police, and now incredibly by their own union!

For the strikers, more disappointment was on the way. On 14 December, the House of Lords supported Denning's defence of Grunwick in the ACAS appeal. Christmas 1977 was not a happy time. The winter and the turn of the New Year were bleak. An attempt by the Strike Committee to renew mass picketing in April 1978 failed. Moreover, the strikers were bitterly disappointed that the union's annual conference held in May 1978 refused to take industrial action. Instead, it was agreed to call-off the dispute if ACAS did not within five weeks again recommend recognition. The strikers and their union had drifted further apart. After George Ward had dismissed ACAS as the 'Association for the Advancement of Socialism', in May, on 14 July, the Strike Committee, nearly two years after it began, announced the bitter end of the Grunwick Strike.

The bitter lessons

The lessons of the earlier strikes (fundamentally that black workers needed to rally the community behind them and from that base force the unions to their side) had been unlearnt by workers who had not had the benefit of that tradition. On the other hand, the persistence and courageousness of Asian women in maintaining the picket lines, month after month, against the pressure of some members of their community, the deception of the union and attacks of the SPG, with support from the white women's group, had established the strength of the emerging black women's movement.

The Grunwick Strike, viewed as part of the history of Asian workers' struggles in Britain, had some significant distinguishing features. Earlier struggles by these workers came to fruition in this strike in that hitherto, it showed the determination to abolish the relationship between sweated labour and sweatshop owners; a cause which had been spotlighted nationally. The dispute was historic in that the small Asian workforce on strike was able to win massive support from various sections of the white working class.

But, in spite of the massive publicity and trade union support throughout Britain, the Grunwick Strike demonstrated that a victory (for example, a path out of the deadlock between the strikers, the union and management) was only possible if the lessons of the earlier struggles by black workers in the previous ten years was unlearnt. Given the circumstances, this could only be effected through the emergence of an 'autonomous leadership', capable of an international appeal, free from the 'traps inherent in unionism'. Thus the celebrated Grunwick Strike taught the black working class bitter lessons.

It is therefore necessary to focus on the central question in the dispute, 'The right to join a union', and the strategy adopted by the Strike Committee. The newly proletarianised East African Asians, eager to redress their workplace grievances, wanted to be unionised. They sought the help of experienced trade unionists. Indeed, from the first day of the walkout, the strategies adopted by the strikers were led and dominated by Jack Dromey and the Brent Trades Council. Dromey was from the Left of the trade union movement. He believed the trade unions could be used as vehicles for positive action. Thus placing the Asian workers' trust in the union, a Strike Committee was formed and an attack on three fronts was launched. But why did these attacks fail?

Firstly, although widespread support was received through the appeal of the 'fundamental right of unionisation' the leadership of the strike chose to use this support on the picket line as a publicity weapon rather than as a force to stop the bus carrying blacklegs into the factory. In effect, while mass confrontation took place between the police and the pickets outside the factory, inside it there was business as usual for Grunwick Film Processing Laboratories. Secondly, the Strike Committee's strategy of seeking support from the rank and file and particularly of trade unionists in other trades, left much to be desired. And thirdly, the Strike Committee agreed to use the machinery of state to settle their dispute with George Ward of the Grunwick Company.[114]

On reflection, the strike revealed that the power of Asian workers, accumulated through years of shopfloor battles against opposition from the white union power structure and management treachery, had been defused in the potentially explosive Grunwick confrontation. The Grunwick workers, like their predecessors in sweatshops elsewhere in Britain did not walk out of the job primarily on the issue of union entry. Indeed, they walked out because they were prepared to tolerate no longer the abuse, the exploitation, low wages and unbearable conditions (heavily overlaid with fear) at their workplace.

In 1974 workers at Imperial Typewriters were fighting 'the slavery of it all'. One of the leading lights among the Grunwick strikers, Jayaben Desai, said, 'The treatment we got was worse than the slaves in *Roots*.' These workers were echoing a common historical experience. Moreover, the Grunwick strike clearly showed that this rank and file militancy was at cross-purposes with the trade union spokesmen. As *Race Today* commented: 'What we are witnessing is a takeover bid for the independent movement of Asian workers by the left-wing of the labour movement, whose immediate interest is to keep the union kite flying.'[115]

Trade union activists such as Arthur Scargill and Jack Dromey saw the Grunwick struggle as being symbolic of the fundamental right of a worker to belong to a trade union. In this respect, the Grunwick strikers have been likened to the Tolpuddle Martyrs and the East End Match Girls. But, of course, this was not the tradition from which the Grunwick workers came. The emotional appeal to defend unionism succeeded in getting the support of thousands of white workers to the Grunwick picket lines. However, this did not mean that the white workers were there to support a strike by black workers. Indeed given the experience of black workers in earlier strikes, this had yet to happen. The white workers were there simply on the issue of 'defending the trade union movement'.

In effect then, the strategy that the Grunwick strikers had subsumed themselves to was a complete denial of their own history.
From the outset of the Grunwick walkout, the strikers had been led
to believe that mobilising white workers had to be their prime
purpose. Fourteen months later, with no victory in sight, the
strikers appealed to black workers in other parts of the country for
support by issuing a leaflet as part of its mobilisation for the 'Day of
Reckoning' on 7 November. This appeal to all Asian workers
stated that the dispute was of vital importance 'for our community
and the whole trades union movement. If Ward and the National
Association for "Freedom" defeat us, then immigrant workers will
have been denied the right to join a trade union.'[116]

Not surprisingly, this appeal was ignored. The history of black
workers and their experience of trade unions in Britian have forced
them to create their own methods and means of struggle. As all
previous black movements had done, at one point or another (and
certainly within the 10 years preceding the strike), the movement of
Blacks internally and the activities of young Blacks and black
workers in Britain had thrown up *race* into the forefront of the
struggle (as a daily lived experience) and thus laid the basis for a
powerful national and international linkage of black struggles. This
source remained untapped during the Grunwick dispute.

The central lesson of the Grunwick dispute then was that in spite
of years of demonstrated strength to sections of the white working
class, trade unionism was found inadequate to deal with their wider
and special problems. The issue was not simply 'trade union
recognition'; in fact, it was an issue based on race and class. The
absence of a trade union or even a modicum of grievance machinery
in the Grunwick factory was a reflection of this. Also of crucial
significance to the black community was the fact that both the
Grunwick, Imperial Typewriters and earlier strikes had smashed
forever the myth of the passive Asian woman.

The foregoing strikes involved mainly Asian workers. Simultaneously their 'sisters' from the Caribbean were also waging a hard
struggle against the National Health Service and other employers.

Black Caribbean women: nurses and ancillary workers

To many black Caribbean women, migration to Britain meant
some change in terms of status. Among rural Jamaican women
who had migrated to Britain, of particular importance to the
changes in their lives were the patterns of work and the control
of economic resources. In fact, work has in many cases played the
positive role of providing the economic support for women's
independence. In London, for example, isolation from relatives,
loneliness and boredom at home is alleviated at work, which

provides the opportunity to meet other people, to socialise and perhaps to learn new skills. Moreover, this economic underpinning, it was argued could disrupt close-knit networks, thus engendering a greater sense of independence. [117]

In 1974 for the first time nurses came out on strike in support of their demands for more money. Earlier, in 1972, auxiliary workers were among the first in bringing the strike weapon to the hospital. In doing so, they had acted in opposition to the myth that women administering to the sick, the young and the old should not behave in this 'unprofessional' way. Seen in historical perspective, this strike was but a manifestation of a long struggle.

Nursing, the 'caring profession' nurtured in the traditions of the family and in waged employment in Britain and her former colonies, brought generations of black women conditioned to think in this way into British hospitals. There is then a historical connection between nationalisation of the British Health Service in 1948 and the migration of hospital workers with this tradition. [118]

A health service covering the whole working class (and not just those who could afford it) meant a massive recruitment of low-wage workers whose conditions of service could not seriously be challenged. But in the 20 years leading up to this first nurses' strike, the *class* composition of nursing had changed. In 1874, this was said of nurses: 'Many gentlewomen were recruited because it is the belief that this type of nursing required the highest type of women who were well educated.' One hundred years later, this was clearly not the case, and clearly did not reflect the recruiting policy of the National Health Service. In fact, what used to be a vocation for women of the middle class in the nineteenth century was now a *job* for women of the working class, particularly for black and other migrant women. Black women were responsive to the idea of service, regardless of the circumstances. Interestingly unlike the high-brow status which nursing had enjoyed in the nineteenth century, in recent years, black nurses found it to be a job that few Englishwomen wanted.

Overseas student nurses had been a major source of cheap labour for the British Health Service. The number of these nurses increased rapidly each year. In 1959 some 6000 arrived; by 1970 there were 19,000. [119] They came mainly from the Caribbean, Hong Kong, Mauritius, Malaysia (and Ireland). Their desire to train as nurses was not always the paramount reason for their decision to come to Britain. However, once here they were contracted to work for the NHS for at least five years. In a new country and hopeful, they were willing to work hard and tolerate initial exploitation and harassment in the hope that things would get better. Indeed (unknown to them) many were deliberately directed to take the (SEN) State Enrolled Nurse training and qualification, instead of the SRN, the State Registered Nurse qualification. As it was, the SEN qualification was of no use to them outside Britain.

At best, however, it guaranteed a trained, low-paid workforce on the ward floor. One way in which women from overseas were directed into SEN training was by demanding educational qualifications for the SRN which they were not likely to possess.

Moreover, during their stay in Britain, they had to renew their permits through the hospital every six months. In addition they undertook to stay in Britain for a stipulated period of time after their training, so that Britain could benefit from 'the training she has paid for'. Throughout her training, it was abundantly clear that the SEN pupil nurse repaid for her training 'a million times over by the cheap labour she provided'. Understandably, there was no deviation from this policy which was fully implemented and reflected by the fact that in 1972 only 120 qualified nurses were allowed into Britain.

But how was this labour allocated (stratified) in the National Health Service? Labour in the hospital was divided according to sex, race and age. Different jobs were done by people in different uniforms, getting different wages and having different degrees of power. Significantly, though (as black workers have come to expect), those who worked hardest had the least status and the least wages. During training as an SEN, a pupil nurse aged 21 during the first year of training, received an allowance of £1065 out of which a lodging charge of £120 was deducted. The salary scales for qualified SENs were: Enrolled Nurse, £1203–1455 with a lodging charge of £162; a Senior Enrolled Nurse, £1380–£1755 with a lodging charge of £192. The next and lowest grade was the unqualified nursing staff, the nursing auxiliaries. These workers at the age of 21 received a yearly income of £1053–£1293 and had to pay a lodging charge of £120.[120] Given that the prospects for promotion for these two grades were virtually nil, the exploitation becomes even more oppressive.

These divisions within the hierarchy were reinforced by the division between the 'professionals' and those who were not. While in theory every one had a chance of promotion, in practice very few got one promotion and fewer still more than one. There were two types of training. There was a two-year course leading to an SEN qualification which, in effect, could not lead to promotion. A large number of Asians, Irish and West Indians were deliberately directed to become SENs.

For the unsuspecting new trainee, the trap was carefully laid. 'When you are interviewed', said one nurse, 'they ask you if you want to do the course in two years or three, and all of us said we would like to do the two year course. It's only when you get here that you realise that if you do two years, you will be an SEN.'[121] The SRN, on the other hand, goes through a three-year training and it is this qualification that gives a nurse the potential for promotion.

Black women are predominantly employed in the lower grades,

serving doctors, 'professional' nurses and patients. Indeed, so discouraging were their promotion chances that few black nurses entered the NHS as a vocation in the hope of becoming a matron. For the ever hopefuls who did, it very soon became clear that 'this is not what they have been recruited for'. For black women nursing is essentially a job, nothing more. By refusing to treat it as a vocation they were not only exposing the real nature of nursing in the health services, but were undermining the hierarchy which is so dependent on their 'wanting to be part of it'. For many nurses, the stark realism has led to despair.

Together, black nurses and ancillary workers have laboured in the NHS in large numbers for more than a generation. Their cumulative experiences led to justified resentment and the dire need for change.

Agency nurses

Given low pay, bad working conditions and unsociable hours of work, the disgruntled black nurses sought alternatives. Thus, agency nursing became an attractive proposition and 'a force for change in the National Health Service'. The switch to agency nursing was dramatic. Between 1972 and 1974, the number of nursing agencies and nurses 'mushroomed'. For those who were married, agency work provided a flexible alternative to working in the Health Service. Agency work was especially concentrated in London where the teaching hospitals' demand relied heavily on agency supply to ease their labour problems. The DHSS figures showed that on 30 September 1971 'the equivalent of 2720 agency nurses and midwives working the whole time were being employed in the area of central London and the four Metropolitan Regional Hospital Boards . . . 54 per cent were employed in the teaching hospitals which employed only 11 per cent of NHS nursing and midwifery staff'.[122]

Having found an alternative to the deplorable conditions and treatment of the NHS, agency nurses were made a focus for attack. According to one report this attack came from within the 'profession'. For example, from the union executive of COHSE, and from 'so-called revolutionary organisations'. They were all united that NHS nurses should refuse to work with agency nurses. By August 1974 COHSE was adamant that its ban on working with agency nurses should remain permanent. Further support was given by the National Rank and File Organising Committee whose journal *Hospital Worker* also called for a complete end to the use of agency nurses. In addition, *Women's Voice* (paper of International Socialist Women) said: 'At our first meeting we decided that the best action would be to ban working with agency nurses. There's 300 in King's [Hospital] and £12,500 a week is spent on them – the hospital would collapse without them. Of course it's hard on them, but if they're bothered about the state of nursing they should be in the NHS fighting with us.'[123]

Fortunately the black nurses would not be drawn by this facile catch-all argument of workers' solidarity within the NHS. In their experience, the 'labour aristocracy' within the labour movement worked against the lower grades. Without a complete separation, in other words an autonomous organisation of black workers, they realised their case could not be fully represented. A break from the NHS by black nurses was predictably not appreciated by those who were dependent on them. Indeed those who called on black agency nurses to fight with them within the NHS failed to appreciate the black nurses' dilemma.

By 1971, the reality was that the National Health Service wage rose with seniority from grade to grade. If a nurse broke her service, for example, by having children, she lost all seniority and the wage that went with it. When she rejoined she had to begin again working her way up the scale. Because this kind of penalisation excluded almost all black nurses from rejoining, increasingly they turned to agency work since they had no choice. Furthermore, black nurses with children, because of inadequate child care facilities at a price which they could afford, were forced in many cases to work the night-shift in order to care for their children and get through their housework during daytime.

The money earned by black agency nurses aroused wild exaggeration. In fact, even in this kind of nursing there was colour discrimination. Some agencies operated a pay scale for white nurses and a lower one for black nurses. A black nurse, told never to discuss her wages, said, 'I did and I discovered that Australian nurses were getting more.' Yet, black nurses found agency work more acceptable than employment in the NHS. A Jamaican nurse who started as a nursing auxiliary and later trained as an SEN explained why she was doing agency work:

> Most of the night staff are black. Night nurses are black because they have children and it's more convenient for them to be at home in the days to see after the children. If you work days you're not there to send them off to school, you're not there to receive them when they come back, and you have to get somebody to look after them. With nights, you can actually put them off to bed before going to work. I support the strike wholeheartedly. Nurses are saying they won't work with agency nurses and I think they're being silly, because number one, they should find out why nurses have to go to the agency, because in my case it's not because I wanted to but because I was forced to . . . I can't do without working . . .

On the question of the money earned by black agency nurses there had been wild exaggeration by the NHS lobby. In fact, as many have complained, there was colour discrimination in this kind of nursing. The divide and rule strategy was nothing new to black workers. Interestingly, among women workers, a black/white distinction was made. Racism and sexism were brought into play in creating schisms and outright divisions to maintain the profitability of capital. The Black Women's Group saw the struggle of black members as related to the NHS and agency nursing thus:

> The nursing workforce *appears* to be divided by different unions and professional bodies, but they are not. In this case the divisions between unions need not divide workers, and may even be helpful since nurses are getting together across trade union barriers. Non-trade union workers (and that includes Agency nurses) are therefore not excluded by the workers' own way of organising. The divisions that are dangerous are between first, nursing and non-nursing staff, and second, NHS and agency nurses – divisions among hospital workers. They must come together and refuse these divisions that the government, unions and the Left are trying to deepen. Racism and sexism are not about whether you take position with black women, agency or non-agency, auxiliary, SRN or SEN.[124]

They argued that the agency nurse was the first to refuse being tied to the hospital hierarchy, thereby confronting the blackmail that faced all nurses. For example, that they were caring 'professionals' and not workers; that the issues, which created the agency nurse were fundamental to all nurses and in fact, to all women. Here the unity necessary to make a fight was expected to come only when NHS nurses joined with agency nurses to raise these issues. Moreover, they stated that black nurses had been accused of not participating militantly in the struggle. Indeed, accusations against agency nurses were based on the racism inherent in the hospital hierarchy.

Black women and the black community

In 1971 for the first time, the night cleaners came out on strike. In their protracted struggle they demanded more money, shorter hours of work, modern equipment and the right to have their *own* union. Of major importance, this workforce comprised a large number of immigrant women of whom West Indians formed a large percentage. According to the 1971 Census, in the West Indian community women outnumbered men (130,300 to 127,300),[125] yet by 1975, little had been said about the quality of their lives in relation to British capital and their resistance to it.

In 1975 five black women auxiliaries (hospital ancillary workers) were elected by their fellow workers to represent them on the negotiating team which had talks with the government during the 'pay-beds' dispute at Westminster Hospital, London. Racist elements in British society were quick to respond with hundreds of abusive letters and a bomb.[126]

This representation marked a new stage in the struggle of West

Indian women in Britain. Indeed, it smashed the myth (a gross over-simplification) that West Indian women of that generation were non-participants in militant action. One of five women on the negotiating team had this to say about the dispute:

> The dispute arose when, because of a shortage of staff, management decided to close 48 beds in NHS wards while all the private wards remained open. We auxiliaries went on a work to rule in protest against that decision. . . . My first experience of strike action was in 1972. We did not stay out very long. We wanted more money. At that time we worked in the hospital scrubbing and cleaning. You came to work at 7.00am and went home at midday, back again at 2.00pm and left at 7.00pm and at the end of the week you had £10 in your hand.
>
> It was a wonderful experience striking. We marched and shouted. From 1972 to today we have had to fight for everything we have since won. Now we no longer work the split shift but we work harder than before because after 1974 they introduced the bonus system – where before there were four of us to a ward now there are only two. [127]

One of her major complaints concerned the problems black workers faced with patients and doctors alike.

These women were representatives of that section of West Indians who came to Britain during the early years of immigration. As part of a 'defeated and demoralised' section of the Caribbean working class, they arrived in a 'hostile' country, to be employed in the worst jobs with the lowest wage. They were crucial in laying the foundations of the black community as we know it today. They showed patience and also a capacity to fight which 'is not a phenomenon new to their presence in Britain'. In fact, it was a continuation of their struggle in the Caribbean. For many years their rebellion in the British workforce (particularly in the NHS) has been muted, underplayed and ignored. This tendency was rooted in the past.

In the anti-colonial struggles in the Caribbean, women threw themselves into the Independence movements whose leaders promised a brighter future for everyone, if they were voted into power. In defeating British colonialism, the activities of women helped to bring working class leaders to power: for example, Bustamante in Jamaica and Eric Gairy in Grenada. Indeed, women were the 'organisational backbone' of the political parties, forming their own sections within them and shouldering a considerable amount of administrative work. Furthermore women were used as spokespersons to win the support of other sections. In Trinidad, for example, in the early 1950s the women's auxiliary of the Oilfields Workers' Trade Union was formed, and women took advantage of the fact that they were free to speak out against employers on behalf of the workers who could not. [128]

After the British were driven out and local leaders took power, their true 'political complexion' became clear. Many of these leaders formed British and American alliances to further exploit their national resources of bauxite, oil, sugar, asphalt and local labour. Thus, neo-colonialism brought with it large-scale unemployment and exploitation. None felt this betrayal as much as the women. The administrative jobs after the departure of the British were filled by middle class men and a few women. Those new industries, primarily assembly and clothing, that sprung up were woefully inadequate. They were never on a scale large enough to absorb the mass of women who were the main source of labour for this kind of work. For those who were employed, wages were kept very low because of intense competition. Significantly though, service work was familiar to almost every black woman. Thus the migration of working class women and men was an extension of the work they did as domestics in the kitchens of the colonial white and black middle class. Thousands arrived in Britain, with nothing but their labour to offer in the hope that they would be able to help their families left behind. They brought, however, the tradition of 'rebellion and resistance'. For most women it was their first experience of wage labour in a modern industrial economy, and it turned out to be a bitter one. Dirty, boring, low pay, low status jobs was their common experience. They received an average wage of about £6 per week which was used to maintain themselves (and the children with them) and also their children and relatives in the Caribbean. An estimated 98 per cent of children of Jamaican women were left behind when they came to England. During 1961–3 approximately £22 million was sent back to Jamaica. By 1965, a survey taken in Nottingham showed that 85 per cent of West Indian women were sending money back home.

The 'second generation'

Young black women upheld the tradition of resistance and rebellion of their colonial forebears. During the late 1960s hundreds of young women participated in the Black Power organisations in Britain. This rebellion burst forth irrevocably. It was characterised by open confrontation with the police, against school authorities and employers, and also within their own families, all of whom were unable to restrain them. The bitterness of a sense of defeat, a common experience, rankled giving rise to their boldness.

Inevitably, within the black community, violent clashes between mothers and daughters occurred as the push for independence pointed up the conflict between the conservatism of parents and the aspirations of their children. Consequently, hundreds of young black women were accommodated in hostels provided by the state. Sociologists, psychologists, the police and community relations workers were quick to blame black mothers for 'not caring' enough. This was a superficial and unwarranted attack for it was a denial of the essential fact that the black mother 'has always had to carry the burden of the black family' from slavery, through colonialism and the racism and sexism inherent in wage slavery in Britain.

However, what distinguishes this rebellion of young black women from their mothers is the fact that they know what is available now in Britain and want it 'without having to be wage slaves'. They demand better jobs and in general a better deal.

The question at issue is not simply concern over young people refusing to do the work their parents were forced to do. Rather they oppose the alternative activity practised by the youth because it makes them vulnerable to the police. However, what parents failed to see was that the refusal to do traditional immigrant jobs meant that there was less competition for the jobs they were doing and, therefore, they had the power to demand a better wage and negotiate better working conditions. To undermine this situation, the ever vigilant hospitals began recruiting cheap labour from southern Europe and the Philippines. The weakness of young black women stems from the fact that they lack a regular wage and the discipline that goes with getting one. To compound their problems the fact that many of these women had young children meant they suffered also from the powerlessness of being a housewife. Not surprisingly, many became desperate, and, it was argued, occasionally getting involved in mugging and shoplifting – manifestations of their powerlessness.

The transition from receiving no wage at all in the West Indies (or at best a woefully inadequate and irregular one) to receiving a regular wage under the discipline of a modern industrial economy in the metropolis had given to older West Indian women 'an access to power previously denied to them'.

And although by 1975 the West Indian community was still relatively new, about a generation old, the black women on the National Union of Public Employees negotiating team had shown they were ready to have a say in exercising that power.

Health workers after the strike

In the remaining years of the 1970s the 'power and significance' of black women since their arrival some 30 years before had grown. By the early 1980s, their circumstances had changed dramatically, for the worse, of course. Norman Fowler, Secretary of State for the Social Services announced the government's proposals that ancillary work in the NHS should be taken over by private companies. This directly affected an estimated 70,000 black workers (mainly women) 'a third of the total workforce' in catering, portering, washing up, cleaning jobs and laundry jobs.[129] Doing the 'unwanted' jobs was in itself no guarantee that these jobs were safe. In fact, the threat to them had come. Black women had had enough. It was time to act.

For nine months these women were on strike. They picketed and voiced their opinions forcefully. Their tenacious struggle won them support from thousands of workers, black and white. Some powerful unions showed concern and even the TUC gave its backing. But what at one point seemed like certain victory ended in defeat.

Three months after the strike, some black women ancillary workers at Dulwich and St Giles hospitals spoke out. At Dulwich 60 out of 774 NUPE members were black women and at St Giles hospital half the workforce were black women. During the 33-week dispute they demanded a 12 per cent wage rise, against wages assessed at half the 'average wage' and below the 'poverty line'. Their struggle was crucial since in many cases black women were the only wage-earners in their families. One worker complained bitterly. 'How can someone live on £45/47 a week. Rent is £30 and you have three children to look after, its disgusting.'[130]

This situation was particularly trying for those one-parent families which relied on a take-home pay of £72 after working a six-day week. The situation was so deplorable that when the strike happened these women were optimistic. They all believed that they would win the 12 per cent pay rise.[131] In this belief, they stayed out on strike, picketed and demonstrated for months. This protracted struggle had called forth all their reserves. For many of them, it was the first time they had ever been involved in such action. Indeed, it was the first time they had directly confronted the public with their plight or taken action with their fellow workers, black and white. They were positive, readily taking part in any union decision for action, thus dispelling the myth of the passive black woman.

With solidarity among health workers and widespread support as the strike raged on, it was not surprising that these ancillary workers showed optimism. Indeed it seemed impossible that they would lose. The workforce was united, morale was high, public opinion and moral authority were on their side. As the strike gathered momentum, more nurses joined the strike. Of crucial importance was the militant support of sections of workers with national stoppages by, among others, miners and print workers. And on 22 September 1982 when over 120,000 workers marched through London, the interests of the nurses and ancillary workers appeared to be the same. Solidarity was evident. The *Financial Times* commented 'NHS unions would resist attempts to split nurses from other health workers.' But, in spite of this massive following, all was not as well as it seemed. By November, the Royal College of Nursing had accepted the government's two-year settlement and agreed to call off the dispute. The result was 7.5 per cent for the nurses, 6 per cent for ancillary workers with 4 per cent in 1984. The TUC which had assumed the leadership of the strike then gave in. For the hopeful black women, it was all over. Once again, in their representation of black workers, the unions took a tangential course, revealing their true intentions and serious limitations. Confederation of Health Service Employees, aware of its members' mood, offered militant gestures (role playing) by refusing to accept the deal. Needless to say, the ancillary workers were furious. The moral authority and public support at the height of the strike was allowed to be dissipated by the leadership. For historic reasons there were devious elements at work behind the facade of solidarity between the ancillary workers and nurses. The ancillary workers felt betrayed by the TUC and the nurses.[132]

In the aftermath, the ancillary workers showed their anger over the TUC's and the union's handling of the dispute. In short, they were disgusted with the way they were sold out.

The defeat was measured in terms of a 'meagre increase'. Moreover, the employers demanded their pound of flesh. The ancillary workers were unanimous that they had to work harder when they returned to work after the strike. As one worker put it, 'The two of you have to do three people's work.'[133] The philosophical comments, 'we'll just have to cope with it' and 'you just have to carry on', acknowledged the fact that the combined pressure of the NHS hierarchy, the government and the anything-for-an-easy-life unions, had had the desired effect of bludgeoning (at least temporarily) the ancillary workers into acceptance of an inadequate pay offer and to bearing the brunt of the NHS. The exploitation of black Caribbean women engendered and reflected a rising militancy and solidarity with other sections of Britain's black workforce, caught in struggles in the motor and textile industries.

The struggle at Ford's in the early 1980s

In Ford's assembly plants, a major area of industrial production in the British economy, both Asian and West Indian workers came together as an act of solidarity in the shopfloor struggle. Ford workers have earned a reputation for militancy. In 1981, there were unprecedented uprisings in the streets of Britain's inner cities as black and white youths rebelled against their oppressors. Given their militancy, Ford workers were able to channel into their industry, the momentum of the uprisings in the streets of Brixton, Southall and Moss Side during the spring and summer of 1981. Indeed three Ford plant locations had connections with the troubled areas: Halewood with Toxteth, the Langley truck plant with Southall (where many Asian workers live) and the Dagenham plant whose many workers came from Brixton and other London areas affected by the summer revolt.

The uprisings were directly related to these workers. In this unprecedented action, 'there were Ford workers who played their part'.

Following the uprisings the question of pay once again came into contention. Nationally, workers at British Leyland, in the coal mines and public sector, were opposed to the government. Ford workers took the initiative. They demanded a £20 pay increase, a 35-hour working week and better pensions. [134] The central figure in drawing up this claim was the union's chief negotiator Ron Todd, then the National Organiser of the Transport and General Workers' Union. By the time the first meeting with Ford management was held (on 30 October 1981) workers at British Leyland had struck over the government's pay ceiling. Anticipating a low offer from Ford's, it seemed likely that Ford workers would join Leyland workers on strike. But when the offer of a 4.5 per cent bonus to be paid only when each factory achieved 'satisfactory' efficiency was announced, Ron Todd went on television and condemned the idea that Ford workers might join Leyland workers on strike. This, however, was not the end of the story. Negotiations were still in progress. By December the company yielded some ground, offering a miserable 7.4 per cent together with the introduction of a 39-hour week in 1983. Moreover, they continued to insist on 'efficiency measures' to be monitored by none other than a panel of full-time union officials.

Aware of the militant mood of the workers, Todd rejected this proposition. Again he appeared on television to explain to the public the implications of the efficiency measures advocated by Ford management. The union membership was leafletted. Todd wrote: 'The trade unions were not prepared to enter into an agreement that would make Ford workers poorer and worsen their working conditions.' Ultimately the deal was overwhelmingly rejected in all but three of Ford's 23 factories. Strike action was scheduled to take effect after Christmas. The two crucial issues in this dispute were the inadequate pay offer (which meant yet another real fall in living standards) and the 'efficiencies'.

No one wanted a long strike during the recession, particularly the Ford company and the government. Amidst rising unemployment, the government was concerned that the strike at Ford's might spread among miners and railwaymen. Political risks had to be minimised. And so for the 'first time' government arbitrators intervened in a Ford dispute. Pressure was brought to bear on the workers through their union. Almost suddenly, the pay question, central to the strike, seemed secondary. On 30 December 1981, Todd listed the union's priorities: 'All we're saying to the company is give us a good deal on pensions, give us a good deal on shorter hours and we'll meet all your requirements on efficiency.'

Thus the sell-out began. Furthermore, Todd was quoted as saying that he would accept the pay offer and efficiencies. All he really wanted was 'more radical movement' on hours of work and pensions. But, the *pièce de résistance* was yet to come.

On the day before the strike began, Todd called an emergency meeting of London convenors and delivered his bombshell. He told them that Ford's had improved their offer: better pensions in August, a 39-hour week in June, but no more money and no concession on efficiencies. In view of this, he added, the union would not support strike action and there would be no strike pay. There was uproar at the meeting. The union's decision to call off the strike brought anger and confusion in the factories. Although workers at Halewood walked out immediately and those at Swansea the next day, after mass meetings, it was decided by a vote of 29,000 for and 25,000 against to accept the offer. Thus the militant workers at Halewood and Swansea reluctantly called off their strike. The turning point in this sell-out has been attributed to the defeat of the Leyland strike. The fact that the right-wing union leaders of the Engineering Union had withdrawn their support for the Leyland strike brought a lack of confidence to many moderates at Ford's. Thereafter Todd was in 'full control'. Again, the defeat at Leyland's had organisational repercussions bringing changes in the motor industry. The most important change was that from piece-work to the Measured Day Work system of payment. The effect of this change on shopfloor organisation (and on social and political life in Britain) has been dramatic.

The piecework system had established a real understanding between the shop stewards and the workers in their section, resulting in strong shopfloor organisation. Under this system it was the steward who bargained the rate for the job for each worker. Together with overtime, earnings were 'pushed up'. Of course this gain in wage levels meant less profits. The solution to this intolerable trend was a shift to the MDW system. Under this system a set amount of work was allocated to each worker. This left no scope for greater earnings. The real significance of this shift was to reduce the power of the local shop stewards. As it was, under the MDW, the hourly rate for each grade of the five or six grades of manual workers was negotiated by national union leaders who it seemed were far removed from the shopfloor realities. Indeed it had a beneficial effect to trade union officialdom in that it was accompanied by strict disciplinary agreements between union and management. Thus the shop steward no longer had an important role in wage bargaining under the MDW. His relationship to his section was therefore weaker and so too was shopfloor organisation. These fundamental changes in the motor industry had the effect of reinforcing the MDW system at Ford's where, according to one worker, 'the workers had never been on piecework'. Consequently, wages at Ford's were the 'lowest' in the motor industry until the mid-1970s. [135] Furthermore, their factories were located in areas of high unemployment (for example, Halewood and Swansea) and significantly they employed large numbers of black, immigrant workers, a source of cheap labour. Indeed the large majority of Asian and West Indian workers occupied the lowest unskilled grades. Few black workers achieved Grade C status.

Divisions also existed within sections on the assembly lines where in the 'bottom section', the majority of workers were Asians with 'only the occasional white and West Indian worker'. The 'middle section' (involving slightly more skilled work) was less arduous. Here there were fewer Blacks and more Whites. Finally, in the 'top section' (the repair area) where the pace of work is slower and the 'most overtime' worked, white workers predominated. [136]

In recent years, at the southern plants, the Ford method of discipline and control has met with strong working class resistance. These were 'hidden' struggles, not well documented or publicly known. The most potent of these, especially in the mid-70s, was the workers' refusal to tolerate low pay and intolerable working conditions. Indeed, the turnover of workers on the assembly lines was estimated at over 65 per cent as late as 1978. For most of the 1970s, lineworkers were involved in daily disputes on such issues as 'grading and wash up time; time to prepare for work, wash before meal breaks, and time to wash and change in the evening before clocking off'. [137]

Simultaneously there was a general insubordination on the shopfloor. Foremen's orders were disregarded, cars and machinery were, at times, sabotaged, and there were 'slowdowns' and disputes. At the time, the situation at Ford's was verging on an almost 'total disintegration of the workforce'. Ford's retaliated with lay-offs which resulted in two big riots in August and September 1973, which were repeated in 1976.

Partly because of the recession and because of the concerted attempt by the unions to assert their authority on the shopfloor, these struggles have subsided. The unions have been accused of allowing militants to be sacked and in 1977, for smashing a major strike and occupation at Dagenham, against unpaid lay-offs. In spite of the pressures, the 'hidden' struggles continued mainly in the form of 'sabotage'.

Internal union conflict

Although these struggles were (and are) kept from the full glare of publicity their cumulative effect was reflected in the growing conflict with the unions. For example, under MDW, the unions were largely involved in the process of discipline and control. Furthermore, there is strong pressure on convenors and senior stewards from national union leaders to ensure that 'members carry out their side of the agreements we enter into with the Company'. The message to the rank and file was accept Ford's discipline. This does not reflect the interest of 'lineworkers' and thus makes redundant the 'representative' role of convenors and senior stewards. Moreover, although more than half of the workforce in Ford's southern plants were by mid-1982 Asian or West Indian, there were only four West Indian stewards and one Asian out of a total workforce of 138 senior stewards. The Asian steward was a token gesture.

Nevertheless the force for change from below was insistent. As a result of these struggles there has been an increase in the number of

Asian and West Indian stewards representing lineworkers. Given the nature of their tasks and their position in the union hierarchy, their voice will no doubt be heard at the workplace. But their effect is still ultimately largely dependent on their union's structure. For many this was clearly unacceptable.

The textile industry

Into the 1980s with rising unemployment among black youth, black workers were still largely employed to do 'shit work'. Inevitably, their struggles were many. Of particular interest was their struggle in the textile industry where thousands of Asians were employed: 'dirty jobs' and bad working conditions prevailed. In the wool textile industry in Bradford, they provided cheap labour. According to Yusuf Ahmat, the racist attitudes of the union ensured a divided and malleable workforce as a whole. Given that the financial structure of the industry was changing throughout the period, many small firms were driven out of business, unable or unwilling (because of profitable alternatives) to keep up with the pace of technological change required of them to survive the competition. A lot of smaller firms either closed or amalgamated with the larger firms. In addition chemical multinationals such as Imperial Chemical Industries and Courtaulds, wishing to exploit the potential of mixing wool with synthetic fibres, moved into the industry.

In spite of these strategies, few jobs were saved. Jobs were clearly being lost as a result of changes in the level of productivity in a situation of falling consumer demand. In just two years between 1970 and 1972 output per head rose by 50 per cent. This figure is no doubt much higher now as a result of more recent changes in technology.[138] With government assistance, firms have been encouraged to implement programmes of drastic closures and amalgamations resulting in massive redundancies. Rationalisation, amalgamation and new technology have not provided any answer to the employment problems of the wool textile industry. It was argued that 'Demands for increased productivity are being made in those firms where no new technology has been introduced, meaning a constant pressure on those who are still at work.'

In effect, technology meant more work but fewer workers. The massive decline in jobs throughout the late 1970s increased dramatically into the 1980s. The introduction of new machinery and techniques have resulted not only in speeding up processes. Those who continue to be employed are under the pressure of increased workloads, implemented by and largely because of the threat of redundancies and lack of effective union resistance. The implications of new technology were essentially permanent job losses, brought about by increased productivity. The apparent ease with which redundancies have been accepted is symptomatic of the

nature of worker organisation in the factory. The unions involved
were the textiles section of the General Municipal Workers' Union
and what used to be the National Union of Dyers and Bleachers,
recently absorbed by the Transport and General Workers' Union.
Significant proportions of the workforce, however, are non-
unionised. It was argued that traditionally, these 'bosses' unions'
were more interested in representing particular craft sections to the
detriment of all others. The bureaucratic structure of these unions
was therefore in conflict with the participation of any workers –
black or white. Their leadership has tended to be self-perpetuating
oligarchies who have not exactly been known to represent the
interests of their membership, and have often worked against their
interest, particularly that of the Asian members. [139]

The experience of the Asian workers involved in the unions has
been an unfortunate story of betrayal and sell-outs. Asian workers
have repeatedly had to defend themselves at work, without help
from either the unions or their white co-workers. In spite of all this,
the number of disputes (unofficial) that involved Asian workers had
increased by the turn of the 1980s.

Overall, as the confidence of black workers grew, through
struggles both at the workplace and in the black communities,
many of them were (and are) moving towards independent organisation. Their experience points logically in this direction.

Black workers and the trade unions

Colonial background: the emergence of trade unionism

Colonial Office policy decisions and Colonial Office advice were
often the strongest of the many pressures to which a colonial
government was subjected. Labour developments in colonial territories was a vital consideration for metropolitan investment.
Thus, a knowledge of the raw material and labour resources
inevitably meant an exchange of information and ideas between the
governors of the dependent territories and the British government.
This was most important in formulating policy and in reaching
agreement on changes in the territories themselves.

In general, British colonial administration was, in certain
respects, one of flexibility and diversity, reflecting the differences in
social and economic conditions in the various colonies, the different
views and personalities of the Governors and the different historical
developments and stages of constitutional advance. However, there
was some unity on policy matters concerning human rights and
social policy, a unity co-ordinated by the Colonial Office.

Labour policies then, and especially the policies concerning trade
unions and industrial relations, must also be viewed in relation to
the Colonial Office.

Before the First World War, the Colonial Office had no general labour policy. In fact, it played no role in formulating or implementing general policy on any question during that period. In effect, this meant that considerable powers on these matters were invested in the Governor and his advisers.

Despite mounting agitation for constitutional advance to full suffrage and local representation in the colonies, the colonial legislatures remained unrepresentative, did not reflect a full range of opinion and often tended to be reactionary and against social progress.

It was only with the loss of some of their power to political parties and elected bodies that the traditional local leaders had to change their attitude towards the activities of trade unions. For example, the owners of mines, plantation managers and settlers who fiercely protected what they considered to be their right to a steady supply of cheap labour were strong supporters of traditional authority and firmly opposed to any manifestation of trade unionism. When the First World War broke out the scarcity of labour and the need to improve and control the system of recruitment, contracting and discipline of labour were already emergent issues. The war itself stimulated interest in the colonies and brought new responsibilities to the Colonial Office. More particularly, it focused attention on labour problems. After the war, the International Labour Organisation was created (in 1919) and labour standards in the non-self-governing territories for which ILO member states were responsible began to receive increasingly more attention. [140]

Emergence of Colonial Office labour policy

In the 1920s labour problems in the colonies received growing attention from the Colonial Office. Early in the decade, labour conditions in East Africa were discussed in Parliament, petitions were presented to the government and several despatches were sent to the Governor of Kenya. During these years, there was a rapid growth of trade unions in India, accompanied by an increase in the number of strikes. This rising militancy was largely attributable to the activity of Indian and British Communists, who saw the development of Indian trade unions as an opportunity for the promotion of revolutionary political doctrines.

As a result of monitoring events in India and other parts of the Colonial Empire, the Labour Party, on its return to power in 1924 and 1929, quite naturally devoted more attention to labour matters than previous governments, concentrating on changes in policy. Consequently, when the East African Royal Commission was appointed to visit Northern Rhodesia, Nyasaland, Kenya, Uganda and Tanganyika in July 1924, it was asked, among other things, to report on: (i) the action necessary to ameliorate the social conditions of the natives of East Africa, including improvement of health and economic development; and (ii) the economic relations between natives and non-natives with special reference to labour contracts, care of labourers, certificates of identification and the employment of women and children.

The Commission's report, however, concentrated on constitutional matters, rather than on labour and social matters. Subsequently, communication between the British government and colonial administrations grew in importance.

The Labour government that took office in 1929 attached much importance to colonial problems. The Labour Party and the TUC favoured the formation of trade unions in the colonies. In 1930 the Colonial Office Labour Committee was established to deal, over a projected 12-year period, with the basic formulation of Colonial Office labour policy, the drafting of model laws and the effects on dependencies of some of the international labour conventions of the period.

Colonial Office policy was designed to direct the colonised peoples away from economic and political discontent and to provide some opportunities for 'progress'. Apparently, it was easier for a government to deal with an organised body such as a trade union than with a number of 'irresponsible' individuals. In this context, the success of co-operative societies augured well for the future success of trade unions. This, then, was a clear statement of policy by the new Labour government.

The Colonial Office was now prepared to begin formulating a policy for the improvement of labour and social conditions. While this move was recognised, there remained considerable doubts about the readiness of the colonial governments to accept such institutional developments as trade unions. However, the Secretary of State was in little doubt as to the need for more positive action. Consequently, the Colonial Office conference was followed by a circular despatch in September 1930 to all colonial governments advocating the passage of trade union legislation. The despatch portrayed the formation of trade unions as being a natural and legitimate development in the colonial territories as social and industrial progress took place. It also suggested that where no unions had yet been established simple legislation should be passed incorporating the principles of the 1871 British Trade Union Act which exempted trade unions from liability to prosecution and to civil action on the grounds that their objects or activities were in restraint of trade. Further, the despatch recommended the compulsory registration of all trade unions. The justification for this was that the idea of combining together for economic purposes (because of its novelty in most territories) meant that 'sympathetic supervision and guidance' would be necessary.

As far as Colonial Office policy was concerned, the despatch reflected and formalised a change that had been pending since the end of the First World War. On the other hand, to the majority of colonial governments, the effect of the despatch was minimal. It met with much resistance and apathy in the various territories, and little or no action was taken for more than ten years in certain cases.

After a further despatch two years later in which model work-men's compensation provisions were circulated to African colonies, again little or no immediate action resulted. In effect, the financial difficulties of the decade meant that labour conditions in the colonies were neglected. Meanwhile the deterioriating conditions increased working–class discontent and brought mounting tension. In 1935, a strike in the copper mines of Northern Rhodesia ended in death for some workers when the police opened fire. About this time, Malcolm MacDonald was appointed Secretary of State for the Colonies. And, in November 1935, a despatch was sent to all colonial governments, asking for a revision of their arrangemen_s for the supervision of employment conditions. The despatch, hav-ing set out the duties of a Labour Department emphasised the function of enforcing legislation, thus forestalling complaints, rather than taking action on them as they happened.[141]

The impact of colonial industrial unrest was to lead to the MacDonald despatch of 1935. And it was the colonial industrial unrest during 1937 (particularly in the Caribbean) which led to some concentration on labour matters in Parliamentary colonial debates in which the above factors were cited. Following these developments the Colonial Secretary was encouraged to send yet another circular despatch in August 1937. Urgent action was stressed and colonial governments were reminded of the terms of the MacDonald despatch of 1935. While the despatch reiterated that the establishment of labour departments should be the 'ultimate aim' in the larger dependencies, it again left a wide margin of discretion to each government. In effect, this 1937 despatch had a greater impact than earlier Colonial Office communications. It evoked a more favourable response from the colonial governments because of a growing realisation (forcefully brought about by events) that labour unrest would continue if the changes advocated by the Colonial Office were not followed.[142]

Black workers and the trade unions: the British experience

A black worker when asked whether he had taken his case of alleged discrimination to the union, said, 'The union? Man, that's for white people.'[143] The vast majority of black workers in Britain will agree with this.

On the other hand, the unions, essentially defensive working class organisations, used their full official powers to defend them-selves against criticism from black workers. But having put in perspective the general struggle of black workers, how do the essentially white unions and black workers see each other? There are no straightforward answers in the complex interrelationship between the various groups of black workers and their unions. Pakistani workers, for example, posed special difficulties. Questions as to what their attitude to unions were and their reasons for joining or not joining were put to 187 Pakistanis, the majority of whom were employed in the textile industry, with a smaller number in transport and engineering.

The result of the interviews taken during a survey conducted by the Runnymede Trust (1970) showed that Pakistanis joined unions less frequently than their English counterparts. Of the 187 employed only 27 were union members. It is necessary to look behind these figures at the work situation of those involved and their behaviour over a long period.

When asked what they thought of British trade unions, only 14 per cent of the Pakistanis were convinced enough to join. By comparison, the overall figure for all immigrants was 6.2 per cent, while that for English workers was 46 per cent. Furthermore, just over half the Pakistani workers (96) thought that trade unions were helpful. The other 91 thought the unions were not. Provoked into further response, 30 out of the 96 explained firstly that the unions were helpful 'but we don't take any interest – we should make them realise our presence – we do not co-operate'. Secondly, 40 out of the 96 were of the view that 'We can get experience from them and secure better working conditions, religious holidays, etc'; and thirdly, out of the 91 that took a negative view of the unions, 23 said 'They don't do anything to help us', while 11 felt that 'They don't want to include us – they are prejudiced and seek to exploit us.'

In sum then, a large number believed in the power of the unions. For example, in their ability to get things done. They were hopeful that the unions would get things done for them. Indeed, many of these immigrants blamed themselves for the lack of success of their unions. But the statement also showed that some Pakistanis held out little hope of being helped by the unions. They spoke of 'prejudice and discrimination'.[144]

Did these workers expect special treatment from the unions? When asked to explain in what ways they thought a trade union or shop steward could be helpful to them, 76 out of the 187 pointed to their needs as industrial workers, while only 12 referred to cultural needs, for example, religious holidays, prayer time, etc.

Moreover, out of the 76 the majority called for direct representation through officials who happen to be immigrants but elected in the 'normal way' rather than through special liaison officials or 'go-betweens'. Indeed, the Pakistanis felt they had the same needs as their English colleagues. Of the 36 who could think of no way in which the union could help, one thought that 'they are English trade unions . . . they must represent us instead of sowing seeds of disunity among us'. Another immigrant referred to the unions as 'frauds' which only 'confuse us'. 'They are English', he added, 'and unless they give us representation it is useless to expect anything sensible from them.' The alienation reflected here was abundantly clear. Significantly the majority of migrants in this group spoke little or no English. Equally important was the fact that generally, speaking ability in English appeared to have had little connection with whether immigrants thought of unions as helpful or not.

Finally the question of the role of these Pakistani workers in union affairs was posed. Like the majority of trade unionists in Britain, after paying the union subscriptions, the Pakistani worker played little part in the union. Of the 27 union members, 22 had never been to a union meeting, and 'only 5 attended some time over the period of the previous year'.

At times what the Pakistani worker believed to be the union's obligation remained unfulfilled. In one case involving an accident, a Pakistani worker left the union when the union failed to get him compensation. Wrongful dismissal was another bone of contention between the immigrant worker and the union's desire or ability to help. The frequent occurrence of accidents and wrongful dismissals had a cumulative effect of disenchantment. However, one reason advanced for the low union membership among Pakistani workers in the textile industry was the fact that only about 40 per cent knew that a union existed! In the case of the engineering industry, the figure was 50 per cent. Matters were helped little by the fact that 'weak' unions saw their role as keeping things as they were, maintaining the customary wage differentials and not going out of their way to recruit new members. This attitude on the part of the union led to inevitable misunderstandings.

Another factor which determined whether men and women joined a union was the union's 'image'. This was crucial to the alienated Pakistanis who said they would be unwilling to join a union which they perceived to be 'too much with management'.[145]

In general, the problems of the Pakistani workers were symptomatic of the relations of immigrant workers as a whole. These non-white workers posed a challenge to the predominantly white trade unionists. This raised many questions. Firstly, why was the immigrant worker under-represented? The percentage between immigrants and English workers in such industries as textiles, printing, building, engineering, service industries, transport and the public service showed that white workers were more likely to be union members than immigrants. The evidence also revealed that the degree of union membership among immigrants in one particular industry follows the same pattern as that of the white workers in that industry. This meant that in a weaker union both immigrant and English union members will be relatively few. But the fact that large numbers of immigrant workers were concentrated in such unions (in the textile industry, for instance, which had traditionally had weak unions) the misleading impression was created that they were not really interested in the unions. A major factor in organising immigrant workers was that they came from different countries with different backgrounds. One study showed that, on the whole,

West Indian workers were more highly organised than Pakistanis. West Indians did not have English language problems which the Indians and Pakistanis were faced with when they came to England. Indians, however, were helped by the Indian Workers Association which was well organised by Sikhs in Bradford.

Taken as a group, among immigrants as a whole, in 1970, union membership in the printing, engineering and transport industries respectively, were: Pakistanis – 100%, 41% and 89.8%; Indians – 100%, 44% and 100%; while West Indians – 0%, 66.6% and 87.5%.[146] Given these membership concentrations, why did immigrant members not play a more active part in the unions? Clearly they were under-represented as a group. In fact only in a few cases (before 1970) were they active members in the trade unions. One argument advanced for this was the fact that immigrants who knew little English were not in a position to become union officials. But why since there were many who spoke and wrote English well, were they so under-represented?

Before 1970 there were only 13 immigrant part-time union officials. Two of these were branch committee members in the transport sector; three were shop stewards and eight were collectors in the textile industry. They were chiefly concerned with immigrant workers in the unions, especially where there were language problems. But 'language' problems was obviously much too limited an area of trade union involvement, especially where there was blatant discrimination in pay and working conditions and promotion.

Another question of vital importance in the relationship between black workers and the trade unions was: were they 'workers' or 'immigrants'? This question was posed particularly because union officials tended to stress the differences (cultural and otherwise) between immigrant workers and the others. Union officials said the difficulties were caused by the language barrier; immigrants joining and then becoming disillusioned by the lack of effectiveness of the union, immigrants' distrust of the union, and frequent job changes, lack of understanding of the purpose of unions, apathy and objections to political levy.

These 'causes', as the union officials saw them, were flawed. In fact, a number of these reasons were based on misinformation as in the case of 'frequent job changes, lack of understanding of the purpose of unions, apathy and objections to a political levy'. On this point, there was 'little to show that immigrants do in fact change jobs frequently'. Further, taken together, the reasons advanced by the officials heaped all the blame on the immigrants themselves. Were the unions themselves that blameless?

One could not escape the all-pervasive prejudices which understandably existed. Indeed there was a widespread belief (shared by a few union officials) that Pakistani workers in Bradford – as other immigrants elsewhere–worked long hours and enjoyed doing so.

In fact, by far the largest proportion worked 'no overtime at all'. Many of the Pakistanis interviewed said that they preferred not to work long hours, for health reasons. Thus, immigrant union membership became confused with the question of overtime and long hours. Indeed, these matters reflected the union's failure to improve adequately its members' standard of living.

In explaining low membership and under-representation, it might also be easily misconstrued that because it was assumed that the immigrants were 'already earning good money' they did not feel union membership was necessary. In fact, the average weekly wage of those interviewed was £16.16s. By comparison the national average around that time (1967) was £20.12s. for men over 21. [147] Moreover, there was little evidence to support the generally held view that the longer time a job was held the more likely a man was to become unionised.

More importantly, when asked how they were recruited, it was found that immigrant workers had usually been asked to join by their friends, and not by the shop steward. It is clear then that the question of communication played some part in whether immigrants held a favourable opinion of the unions or not.

According to the figures, however, it must not be assumed that simply improving communication between immigrants and unions would solve all problems. The rhetoric of trade union officialdom tended to project this view. In fact, the Bradford study showed that immigrants faced much the same difficulties as English workers when at work.

There is also the question of the union's failure to act on the immigrant's behalf. The implication of this failure was that immigrant workers on the shopfloor were likely to act collectively themselves. In one case, a group of Pakistani workers involved in a dispute with management over bonus payments sent one of their number to put forward as spokesman their problem to the management. When the 'spokesman' was sacked, the group of 25 walked out of the shift in protest against what they considered an act of victimisation. They made a powerful statement as to their lack of trade union involvement and under-representation and untended grievances. Indeed, when they walked out in protest at the dismissal of their representative they were, of course, using trade union methods but this was outside the accepted union framework.

The conclusions of the study carried out in Bradford revealed clearly that trade union officials knew and cared very little about immigrant workers. In particular, they often stressed, sometimes unwittingly, cultural differences rather than the similarities in the work situation of all trade union members. For example, some officials said that few immigrants join unions, while others expressed their belief that immigrants join unions as readily as English workers. Significantly, few of those questioned appeared to distinguish between the various nationalities of immigrants; Pakistanis, Indians and West Indians tended to get 'lumped together'.

Moreover, although some immigrants mentioned cultural and linguistic differences, on the whole they saw themselves as workers who wanted to improve their industrial position like other workers. Further, the study showed that some unions made little effort to encourage immigrants to join. [148] Thus, even when they joined, they rarely played an active part in their union. Emphasis was placed in the disillusionment of many immigrants, and showed how discrimination (real or apparent) by a trade union could give rise to mistrust. Finally in the extreme circumstances (a not unusual situation for immigrants) unilateral action by immigrants themselves acting outside the trade union framework was always a real possibility.

On the question of economic status and occupations, despite high economic activity rates, recent studies and surveys showed that unemployment among young West Indians, in particular, was a problem causing mounting concern. The 1971 Census showed that 16.2 per cent of persons aged 16–20 born in the West Indies were unemployed, compared with 8.1 per cent of all youth aged 16–20 in Great Britain, and other researchers had suggested even higher proportions. [149] Alienation from the culture of the host society and low educational attainment were only two of the factors creating this problem. Additional factors such as unequal opportunity and discrimination on the basis of colour had been highlighted by two PEP reports, *The Extent of Racial Discrimination* (October 1974) and *Racial Disadvantage in Employment* (June 1974). The findings of the latter report supplement and reinforce the findings of the former which states that a substantial level of discrimination was found even at the level of recruitment for unskilled manual jobs (46 per cent met discrimination): and that 30 per cent of Indian and West Indian applicants were discriminated against at the earliest stage of recruitment (the written application stage) in a broad range of white collar jobs. [150] The authors of this carefully designed research stated that the findings in all the tests strengthened the conclusion that it was prejudice over colour which underlay most of the discrimination shown.

There was one area in which it was possible to reach reasonably firm conclusions, and that was in the net cost to the economy of the social services absorbed by immigrants. Here it seemed clear that immigrant workers, a predominantly working age population with (originally) a relatively low number of children and dependants and a relatively small population of retirement age, made a substantial once-for-all net contribution to the economy. A careful study by members of the National Institute of Economic and Social Research, concluded that taking 'all social security expenditure and public expenditure on health and welfare benefits together, the average immigrant received about 80 per cent as much as the average member of the indigenous population in 1961 and the figure seems likely to be 85 to 90 per cent by 1981'. [151]

Trade union membership and participation

By 1975, apart from the 'Bradford Study', there was unfortunately very little research material available on the extent of trade union membership among black and other migrant workers. What there was suggests firstly, that overall trade union membership was proportionately lower for black migrant workers, and secondly, that in well-organised factories and industries there was no significant difference in the level of trade union membership of the two groups.

The major reason for lower proportionate membership was that black and immigrant workers were over-represented both in industries and service where trade union organisation was low (for example, catering and hotels, building and textiles) and in plants, factories and workshops employing relatively few workers in which it was in general more difficult to organise and maintain membership. Other factors cited, though relatively less important, included the failure of the movement to develop recruitment techniques which take account of both language and cultural differences.

With regard to participation, the evidence by 1975 was even scantier and measuring criteria was difficult to establish. There were forces at work which made it difficult for Blacks to play their full part in the movement. These included such factors as language differences, shift working, ethnic work groups, and lack of trade union experience. To involve rank and file workers was a general problem, though not one peculiar to black workers. But where there were special difficulties for these workers, there was the need for flexibility in approach regarding, for example, communication and time and place of meetings. It was clear, however, that black workers were under-represented at every level of trade union activity. This was so whether it be full-time official level, attendance as delegates to policy-making bodies, at branch or at shop floor level.

One kind of solution, so far as appointed officials were concerned, might be the deliberate adoption of targets for the appointment of certain numbers of people, from ethnic minority groups, particularly in the unions with a substantial black membership (actual or potential). According to the Runnymede Trust, a different kind of solution would be to seek, through traditional trade union democracy in the labour movement, the removal of all barriers to participation, so that immigrant workers were offered every assistance and encouragement in their trade union activity. [152]

One barrier to participation exists in some relatively undemocratic union structures. In spite of a very healthy movement in recent years towards greater shopfloor participation and the development of much improved shop steward representation (both in quality and quantity), it was no surprise that this development had been uneven and that there were still large areas of 'backwaters'. In the two most bitter disputes involving black workers (up to that time) the question of democratic rights and representation in the union was a major issue, as for example, in the Mansfield Hosiery Mills dispute and at Imperial Typewriters. Where union rules and practices effectively discriminated against newcomers (as at Imperial Typewriters, or against the unskilled, as at Mansfield Hosiery Mills) they had a particularly powerful impact on immigrant workers.

Special services for black immigrant workers

There has often been resistance to the development of special services for particular groups of trade union members; for example, women, youths and most recently, migrant workers. It has been argued that such practices perpetuate divisions, draw attention to differences and therefore hinder unity. On the other hand, where workers had specific problems and needs, it was the job of the movement to develop ways and means of dealing with them. It was this latter argument which gained ground in recent years, and which had in the case of both women and young workers been largely accepted.

The creation of conditions for greater unity was emphasised. Indeed, it was recognised that language and cultural differences could create misunderstandings; it was argued, for example, that some migrant workers could not play a full part in the movement because their command of English was rudimentary or non-existent. Lack of knowledge of trade union procedures and the context of collective agreements also led to misunderstandings and frustration. Some groups with strong religious or cultural traditions, said the Runnymede Trust, may want some changes in holiday arrangements, or canteen diets, to represent what could be seen as a normal union function. To cope with the difficulties, it was further argued that provision should be made to make available a much needed trade union service to a group of members such as will assist greater unity of action. [153]

While language remained a problem, in one area at least, a trade union was directly involved in language training for its members. The Southall District Committee of the TGWU provided specialist language classes for Asian union members. But perhaps the most interesting development, at the time, was the formation of the TGWU International Workers' Branch. Indeed, developments within the TGWU's London region was regarded as constituting the most creative attempt to overcome some of the many problems outlined above. For example, hotel and catering workers of many nationalities were organised into a Catering Workers Branch, which, at the time, was open to all workers in the industry and the area. Unfortunately, even while these encouraging developments were taking place, discrimination against black workers was being widely practised.

The general problem

Two factors were present in the Imperial Typewriters case which have characterised *all* the disputes mentioned above: the tremendous unity and solidarity of the black workers during long and bitter struggles and the failure to build unity of all workers, black and white, around the strikers' demands.

It might be tempting, despite isolated though important disputes involving black workers during the 1960s such as Courtaulds, Woolf's and Birmid Qualcast, to conclude that it was the Mansfield Hosiery Mills dispute which in 1972 really convinced black workers of the value of militant action. But other factors were almost certainly involved. Firstly, there was the general increase in trade union militancy which, as we have seen, had involved many black workers; secondly, black workers themselves had settled in, became accustomed to the stresses and strains of industrial life, and reconciled themselves to the idea that instead of going back home to start a new life, they were here to stay. In this climate they had become a lot less tolerant of the injustices of race discrimination. In fact, they had begun to think of their future in Britain and they looked both for support and ways of improving their position in Britain. As workers they looked to the trade union movement for support and chose traditional trade union methods of struggle. The outstanding victory of the Asian workers at Mansfield Hosiery, in the teeth of opposition from their union, employer and white workmates, gave force and confidence to a developing movement.

Apart from the rise in militancy among black workers, there had been the continuing discrimination against black people in Britain; discrimination which rests on a strong current of racialist ideas. In this environment it is perhaps not surprising that disputes such as those mentioned above should lead to the bitterness and frustration exemplified in the events at Imperial Typewriters.

The union inquiry report was clear that the strength of emotional feeling on both sides created disharmony to a point where the industrial issues were submerged. Moreover, in both the Mansfield and Imperial disputes, management was able to exploit racial divisions and win support from local trade union leaders for agreements which were against the interests of black workers (indeed all workers) and their trade unions. At Loughborough, for example, a productivity deal which had been successfully resisted for two years, was negotiated during the strike by skilled white workers. And at Imperial the Union Branch and the District Committee backed management's attempts to victimise the strike leaders.

The crucial problem facing the strike leaders, shopfloor and national union leaders had been that of uniting the workforce. Strikes are difficult to win without solidarity; where workers are divided, the situation becomes almost impossible. In all these disputes the strike leaders and the factory leadership were at loggerheads. Moreover, the task of uniting them was dependent upon top union officials who were far removed from the black workers' problems. Where divisions were wide and bedevilled by race prejudice this was no easy task.

While there was harmony in some workplaces, black workers' demands for greater participation in union affairs, at all levels, were generally a direct challenge to some of the relatively undemocratic structures that existed. Given that the trade union movement exists to protect and advance the interests of all working people, it was argued that in this role it cannot tolerate discriminatory practices which were based on criteria such as race and colour. Indeed, in cases where the movement had failed to apply such basic trade union principles, a price had been paid, not only by those discriminated against, but by those who had been party to the discrimination. While race prejudice remains widespread, trade union actions to end discrimination will be that much more difficult. This highlights the need for 'race relations' education within the trade union movement which could play a central role in undermining blatant prejudice.

In a case study of a Midlands building site, a black worker was discriminated against; a case in which, once again, the question of colour was significant. Generally, the white workers did not mind working with black workers, who they thought were not as good as white workers. Amidst mounting tension on the building site, a West Indian carpenter was dismissed. It was said he told the foreman to f*** off when asked to move a ladder. The West Indian denied this was the real reason for his dismissal. While admitting that the incident may have occurred, he said the real problem arose from the bad relationship which had developed between himself and the foreman. He attributed this to the foreman's willingness to talk about the sexual behaviour of black people. He concluded that from his experience people who wanted to know about the sex lives of black people were usually racialist. Consequently, he told the foreman that the only conversation he wanted was strictly about work. It was after this that he had been dismissed.[154]

Race, sex discrimination and the British trade unions

One researcher found that when black workers first entered the labour force in large numbers in the early 1980s, many trade unionists were afraid that they would act as a source of cheap labour and, as competitors, force down the wages of white workers. The stoppage of labour into Britain during the past decade has meant, however, that most black migrants were receiving the 'same' wage for a job as would a white man.[155] Moreover, the researcher concluded: 'Where some had expected me to discover a picture drawn in black and white, my investigation of six weeks indicates a scene painted with a most varied palette. Instances of overt discrimination are to be found in the labour movement. But for the national trade unions, local branches and the colonial immigrant, the problems of communication seem to be greater.'[156]

In spite of these findings, a few years later, interest in racial discrimination had grown. In December 1970 a Conference on 'The Trade Union Movement and Discrimination' was convened by Ruskin College, Oxford. The Conference grappled with two problems: 'how far is there a special problem? and 'how far should things be left to look after themselves?' Further, the Conference was not concerned simply with race relations in isolation, but with the wider issues and implications of discrimination in general. While the academic institutions were conscious of the problems, there was a general feeling among trade unionists that if the problems were left alone, they would in time, solve themselves. 'But', as H. D. Hughes, Principal of Ruskin College put it, 'the emergence of Powellism means that the problems can no longer be left to solve themselves.' He added, 'The trade unions have tended to take the view that a worker is a worker is a worker; all workers should be treated equally. When trade unions were asked how far immigrant workers participated in education programmes, most unions replied that they could not say because as a matter of principle, they took no steps to find out.'[157]

Trade unions were concerned with the capacities of individuals and with their needs, and neither needs nor capacities depend essentially on sex, colour, race or religion. Furthermore, as experience has shown the trade union movement can be weakened if workers are divided as instanced in the dichotomy between white workers who isolated themselves from black workers. Employers, of course, would not hesitate to exploit such divisions. Also to be borne in mind, is the fact that the history of trade unionism in Britain shows that there had been a constant need to overcome difficulties which arose from prejudice and shortsightedness and to extend the boundaries of trade unionism effectively to include groups which initially had not been within them. In this context, it was essential to bring into full participation groups which had linguistic and cultural differences.

Comparative trade union membership

By 1976, there were significant findings on the relationship between black workers and the trade unions. Asians and West Indians arrived in Britain from countries with a different structure of industrial relations, but they nonetheless readily joined the British trade union movement. Significantly, by the mid-1970s, trade union membership among these black workers was 'higher' among the minority groups than the white population.

Among male members of these groups in employment, 61 per cent were trade union members compared with 47 per cent of white males. There were however some differences between minority groups, with African and Asians being the group with the 'lowest' membership. For them, the Grunwick strike was both an historic beginning and a bitter failure of trade unionism. Taken together, however, these minority groups still had a higher level of union membership among each group taken separately than among Whites. Disadvantaged women (except Moslem working women, comparatively low with an 18 per cent membership) reflected a different picture in that about one in three working women from the minority groups were union members, which was about the 'same level' as the union membership of white women.

Whether or not Asians and West Indians made a positive choice to join unions, or just happened to be working in certain kinds of jobs in certain types of industries or plants which were unionised, their high membership needs further explanation. A study of the job level analysis showed that among non-manual and skilled manual workers, the levels of union membership were about the same for the Whites and the minorities. Among the semi-skilled and un-skilled manual workers, however, membership was 'distinctly higher' for Asians and West Indians than for Whites. [158]

Although there was a tendency for the minorities to work in unionised industries, as Smith points out, this only partially explained the differences between the minorities and Whites. In fact, even confinement of an analysis to unionised plants still revealed that in these plants both Asian and West Indian men at each job level (including non-manual and skilled levels) were more likely to join a trade union than was the case with white men. Even so, contrary to the expectations that an 'incompletely adapted minority' group would show a low level of union membership, the findings showed the opposite to be true.

Clearly then, black workers had not been reluctant to become trade union members. This must have surprised white working class trade unionists who, while arguing that cultural and language factors would pose problems of integration, found Asians who did not (at least during the early years of immigration) speak fluent English (and who were isolated from the mainstream of British life) but had joined unions in large numbers. In fact, it was found that among Asian men who spoke no English at all 60 per cent were union members. Moreover, while those who had arrived in Britain earlier were considered to be the most likely candidates for union membership, it was also found that among the most recent arrivals (for example, those who came to Britain from 1970 onwards) the level of union membership was no lower than it was among Whites. In fact, at 47 per cent it was 'exactly the same'. [159]

Union policy The foregoing findings clearly show then that Asians and West Indians who came to Britain (essentially for economic reasons) had a marked degree of confidence in trade unions to uphold their rights and privileges and to protect theirs and the interests of all workers. Undoubtedly, this was the acid test of the British working class movement to implement its 'brotherhood of man' ideal. Indeed, historically the attempts of distressed colonial workers to form trade unions have received support through resolutions and letters of encouragement from individual unions and trades councils in Britain. Now that the ravages of colonial poverty led colonial workers to seek jobs in Britain, it seemed natural that they should join the trade union movement. Thus, the British trade union movement was faced with practising what it had for so long been preaching. The common purpose of mixed workforces was clear to trade unionists. Thus, the framework within which black workers were to be accommodated was encapsulated at the Trades Union Congress in 1955 in the following resolution condemning racial discrimination:

> This Congress condemns all manifestations of racial discrimination or colour prejudices whether by Governments, employers or workers. It urges the General Council to lose no opportunity to make the trade union attitude on this issue perfectly clear and to give special attention to the problems emerging in this country from the influx of fellow workers of other races with a view to removing causes of friction.

The problem of such worthy policy is its practical result. Were the unions desirous of being seen to be doing something or were they genuine initiators of change among union officials? Further, was it indeed another instance of official trade union rhetoric? The General Secretary of one of the largest unions had no doubt: 'It's the same with this as with so many other union matters', he said, 'the bullshit beats the brains everytime.'

This failure to confront the problem squarely at the outset would cause havoc within the movement in years to come. But how did the unions deal in practice with the TUC resolution? The condemnation of discrimination implied four kinds of action: (i) steps to deal with any cases that come to light where trade unionists were discriminating; (ii) energetic representation of any workers from minority groups who were being discriminated against by management; (iii) steps to ensure that union grievance procedures were adopted to take care of complaints with a racial element, that the racial minorities understand the procedures and that they use them to the full; and (iv) that steps be taken to ensure a rapid feed-back of information to higher union levels about cases of alleged discrimination and situations where it might be likely to develop.[160]

Furthermore, in response to giving 'special problems' emerging in the hope of 'removing causes of friction and preventing exploitation', the PEP report recommended further action such as: arrangements for the induction of new members from the minority groups into the theory and practice of trade unions, the inclusion of information and discussion on race relations in training courses for shop stewards and other union officials, active encouragement to members of the minority groups to take part in the movement as shop stewards, convenors and full-time officials, and discussions with management and joint policies to improve race relations in industry.

Contact with management   Following the TUC resolution, contact between the unions and management on racial issues was necessary. Among the employers asked whether they had had any contact with trade unions on race relations policy, only 8 per cent said they had and even the plants with at least 5 per cent from minority groups said this figure was only 10 per cent. There was also evidence that formal opposition from the union to the employment of racial minorities was rare. Indeed only 3 per cent of the plants surveyed said that a union had any disagreement with their policy. Moreover, the percentage was no higher among plants with high concentrations of minorities. Further, generally managers did not feel the trade unions tended to resist the introduction of minority workers. In fact, only 3 per cent of plants thought they did so. On the other hand, 5 per cent felt that they supported it and 52 per cent thought that they just accepted it. The balance of 40 per cent had no opinion. However, 25 per cent of plants said that there were complaints from white workers when minority workers were employed, complaints rarely formalised by the trade unions. The two conclusions drawn from these findings were that although there were notable cases of formal confrontation between unions and management over racial issues, this was an unusual situation; and secondly, that unions at local level were reluctant to make representations to management on behalf of minority workers on racial matters or to suggest positive policies.

The survey also found that there was very little evidence of any contact between senior management and trade union representatives on racial issues. The exceptions were situations where racial conflicts had been serious enough to force some attention from Board members. Even in these cases, however, generally discussions were conducted with union officers at local or district level, thus forestalling a top-level meeting between senior management and the union leaders.[161]

Overall then, on race issues, there was little contact between management and unions. In effect, while the unions have rarely made formal representations against racial minorities, they had seldom made positive representations.

The situation at the plant   According to the PEP report, there were situations which fell into two groups where the trade union at local level was not acting within the framework of official TUC policy. Firstly, there were instances where the local union was encouraging discrimination rather than counteracting it; and secondly, while the union was not directly involved in discriminatory practices, nevertheless situations had developed partly because of inadequate representation.[162] The first case of union involvement in discriminatory practices, implicated a district official of the TGWU. According to the Asian Branch Secretary of the union there was collusion between the management and the district official to prevent Asians from being promoted to bus inspector. The PEP report stated that there were 'strong reasons' for thinking that the allegation was justified, and that 'While this particular case could not be proved in law, the general reasons which we have given for thinking that discrimination is occurring are powerful ones.'

In another case of union involvement the plant management admitted that while they had previously excluded minority workers altogether, they had first decided to change this policy before the 1968 Race Relations Act. The union, however, argued that it was the Act which brought about the change. Nonetheless, once the decision was taken management had meetings with trade union representatives to get their reactions to the introduction of racial minorities. The union representatives told management that there would be 'strong opposition'.[163] When asked if they themselves had any objection, they said they were expressing the views of their membership. Lucky for them, there was no real disagreement with the white 'brothers and sisters' in the union.

Whatever the opposition of the white workforce to the employment of Blacks, the shortage of labour prompted the employment of a small number of black workers, mainly Asians. By the time they had accounted for 5 per cent of the workforce, conflict emerged. Both the AUEW shop steward and the TGWU convenor agreed that white workers resented the Asian workers and that social contact between them was minimal. Basically, the white workers feared that the plant would, in time, become Asian dominated. Thus they resisted Asian entry strongly. Whatever prior feelings management had for their Asian workers, pressure from the white workforce aroused little enthusiasm for employing more black workers. But, of course, there was the essential pressure of a labour shortage to consider. How they wished there was no such shortage. Eventually, the fear of white resistance won through, although there had been 'no formal discussions' between the two sides. Indeed there had been no intra-union discussion because the shop steward and convenor were 'too embarrassed' to raise the matter at union meetings.

In one case the attitudes of both union representatives were most revealing. The AUEW shop steward was frank. He regarded 'coloured' people as 'dirt'. Although he was barely tolerant of an Italian or Pole living next door, he said if a Pakistani came to live next door, 'I would spit'.[164] On the other hand, the TGWU convenor was 'liberal-minded' and 'conciliatory' in his approach.

Thus, by not discussing and raising racial issues at higher union levels, the union's negative attitudes helped to justify any racially discriminatory policy adopted by management. More damning than the attitude of the local union representation is the fact that there were cases where the full-time union officials had not acted because the workers were Asians. In this kind of situation, the union would normally be expected to deal with the situation as a matter of course, if the workers were white. But they chose to act differently by ignoring black workers and not making any 'special efforts', 'with a view to preventing exploitation' in line with the TUC resolution.

Apart from showing that the unions at local level have sometimes been involved in discriminatory practices, the above examples more importantly question whether the minority workers have fully entered into the mainstream of the trade union movement, and whether (given their faith and confidence as union members) they are able to contribute to, or benefit from it to the same extent as white workers. Of course, there were the rare cases where things were marginally better, as in the case of a plant which had a workforce of which over 90 per cent belonged to minority groups. Predictably (and the clue was 'little' white labour) the work was repetitive, mostly unskilled and was done in 'very bad conditions'. The TGWU membership was high. This was entirely due to the efforts of a West Indian convenor. As representative of a predominantly black workforce, it was not surprising that his complaints and accusations against management were 'comprehensive'. Most of his specific complaints, however, were found to be unjustified because his arguments, it seemed, were based on 'anti-White' prejudice. Nonetheless, the downright bad physical working conditions in the plant were only improved because of union pressure. As the PEP report stated: 'This is a case where the benefits of trade unionism are being felt by a largely West Indian workforce, and where a West Indian has been able to channel his energies through the movement, but without special encouragement from higher levels in the union.'[165]

On balance, the cases where individual union officials have represented the cause of racial minorities are far outweighed by the cases where the trade union has failed to give adequate representation or where it was directly involved in discriminatory practices.

Action from the centre   Interviews with eight of the largest unions at head office level showed that there was little evidence of any definite action taken by the centre. Indeed, most unions avoided matters that were likely to lead to specific action because they feared that white members might think that minorities were being given special treatment. Moreover, this approach was sometimes justified by stating that the action specifically on behalf of minority groups would be discriminatory.

Furthermore, none of the eight unions knew how many of their members belonged to minority groups, and none could give more than a rough estimate of the number of part-time officers from these groups. In fact, (at the time of the PEP report) there were virtually no full-time officers from minority groups. Although the unions were aware of this, none of them proposed to do anything about it.

While there were an unspecified (indeed they recorded just about everything else) number of shop stewards from minority groups elected by mixed workforces, senior trade unionists felt that the minorities representation was woefully inadequate. Given that 'you have to be a nut case' to want to be a shop steward, and that no special encouragement had been given, it is surprising that a number of black shop stewards have emerged. Justifying their passive, non-caring attitude, trade union leaders insisted that it would be wrong to interfere with the democratic process; an attitude that was dangerously close to saying that any show of initiative from the leadership would be undemocratic![166]

Although the TGWU took on its first black full-time official the minority groups remained well outside the higher levels of the trade unions. In this, as in other major unions with a large black membership, there was no systematic policy of inducting part-time officials in race relations problems. In open discussion of the issues in this vital area of day-to-day relationships, the unions remained unmoved. They did little to educate minority groups in the history, purposes and practices of the trade union movement. And in spite of grievance procedures, head office either did not care or did not want to know of complaints of racial discrimination within the union.

In sum, the evidence showed that few positive initiatives called for in the TUC resolution had been taken from the centre; and that in the known cases, there had been no action to combat discrimination. The main argument used by trade union leaders for not taking positive action was that they had to take account of the views of the membership and could not go too far ahead of them. More explicitly, this argument is that the unions are democratic, that they could therefore only act in accordance with the wishes of the majority of their members and that the membership was not ready to accept specific policies of equal opportunity.

In principle: TUC policy and resolutions

The TUC, black workers and immigration (1955–73)

Before 1955, there was no reference either in the General Council report to Congress or during the Conference proceedings, to 'race relations', racial discrimination or immigration in relation to Britain. As the TUC saw it, the arrival of New Commonwealth immigrants (particularly West Indians) was not cause for undue concern. This period, however, did see the emergence of an 'attitude' to immigration.

In 1954 the General Council was consulted by the Minister of Labour about a code to be signed by members of the Organisation for European Economic Co-operation which would deal with the admission of citizens of other countries for employment purposes. According to the Council, 'the policies underlying the code were in conformity with current British practice, namely that full regard must be taken of the interests of British workers before permits are granted to workers from the OEEC countries. Permits were not given if this would result in displacing British workers. There must be no under-cutting of British standards and the views of trade unions and employers organisations in the industry must be respected.'[167]

This argument of 'economic nationalism' (relevant to the mass unemployment of the 1930s, in the 1970s and now in the 1980s) was by the mid-1960s, not the 'main plank' of opposition to New Commonwealth immigration. The Council's opposition was based on the immigrant's failure to 'integrate' rather than the argument that they were taking the jobs of British workers. In 1955, however, the latter view was an implicit concern on occasions. By 1955, 'Immigration from the Commonwealth amounted to no more than a paragraph in the report to the 1955 TUC which referred to the withdrawal of a resolution by the Ministry of Labour Staff Association from the 1954 Agenda, so that the General Council might consider the subject.' After this decision, the MLSA submitted a memorandum to the Council concerning black workers and immigration.[168]

In response to this memorandum, the General Council requested a meeting with the Minister of Labour. They stressed two points: (i) the need for the government to formulate an immigration policy for people from the Commonwealth and that 'colour' should be excluded from this policy; and (ii) that since it was the reponsibility of the government to maintain full employment it should necessarily have a policy to ensure immigration control. This was explicit enough. In effect, the TUC was calling for immigration control as far back as 1955. Thus the TUC 'implicitly defined' New Commonwealth immigration as a problem.[169]

In the context of this general 'problem', the following motion was moved by T. J. O'Dea at the 1955 Congress by the Civil Service Clerical Association:

> This Congress condemns all manifestations of racial discrimination or colour prejudice whether by governments, employers or workers. It urges the General Council to lose no opportunity to make the trade union attitude on this issue perfectly clear and to give special

attention to the problems emerging in this country from the influx of fellow workers of other races with the view to removing causes of friction and preventing exploitation.[170]

This motion was strengthened by a similar motion on 'racial discrimination' from the Association of Cinematograph and Allied Technicians.[171] Both motions were formally seconded and carried. It was well-known among General Council members that employers were practising discrimination. In his speech, although he suggested that the Council had certain responsibilities, the mover of the CSCA motion did not see the need for action by affiliated trade union leaders or rank and file members. The mover of the CSCA motion, aware of working class prejudice and friction, did not feel that the TUC and the trade unions should oppose the reactions of white workers. Instead, he was concerned that black workers might become a pool of cheap labour.

The 1955 Congress was therefore instructive. While in principle, it condemned racial discrimination or colour prejudice, it nevertheless 'implicitly accepted' that the 'problem' was not the expression of prejudice or discriminatory practice by white employers and workers, but was attributable to the very presence of immigrants from the West Indies. This was reflected by the General Council's view of immigration control and the failure of Congress even to consider (never mind taking positive action) against the prejudice and discrimination practised by white workers.

Between 1956 and 1957, there seemed to have been little interest in immigration and race relations at the Congress. However, in the General Council's report to the 1956 Congress there was a paragraph on 'Immigration from the Commonwealth'. This suggested that Commonwealth immigration had taken precedence over the issues of prejudice and discrimination, issues on which the TUC continued to pay lip service and little else. Of course, no one can deny their good intentions and broad statements of principle.

The National Union of Railwaymen had contacted the General Council and declared its support for some form of immigration control. It was therefore not surprising that in reporting the suggestion that conflict between black and white workers should be monitored by the General Council in tandem with the National Union of Railwaymen's demand for immigration control, the Council was yet again, 'indirectly linking the negative reaction of white workers to the arrival of West Indian workers and suggesting that this would be best dealt with by immigration control'.[172]

By the end of 1957 then, there was no clear and positive response from the TUC to the claim that black workers were subjected to the prejudice and discrimination of white workers. Furthermore the monitoring of 'instances of friction' seemed to have been shelved.

During 1958, the year of the race riots in Nottingham and

Notting Hill, the TUC General Council still viewed immigration as 'the problem'. On the other hand, they did not see racism as part of their responsibility. In the cases where racism was admitted to exist, trade unionists were not among those to be blamed. Instead attention was deflected to the resurgence of fascist and racist political organisations. What they forgot to take into consideration in such calculations was the fact that trade unionists were also political activists. Given these self-imposed limitations, the area of action to be taken by the TUC was narrowed. Thus the view prevailed that it was the responsibility of the New Commonwealth immigrants themselves to take action. In effect, it was up to them to adjust, as best they could, to their new and hostile environment.

The effect of the 1958 race riots was to highlight the problems of black people in Britain. As a national body, the TUC, concerned with the 'brotherhood of man' was forced to respond. When the 1958 Congress met after the riots, a delegate from the Clerical and Administrative Workers Union reflected a new-found sense of urgency. He stated that 'the problem' of racial discrimination was now 'on our doorsteps' and argued that it was not only a matter for the police and the magistrates: 'As one of the most powerful organisations in the community we should undertake our responsibilities and give what leadership and guidance we can in order to try to help.'[173]

He concluded that trade unionists should take every opportunity to oppose cases of prejudice. Moreover, they should assist in the process of 'integration' and that the General Council should consider positive action in order to prevent a recurrence of violence. These statements were historic. Not only was it the first open recognition at Congress that there was racial prejudice in Britain, it was also the first time an argument was put forward to suggest that because the trade unions had a direct responsibility to deal with racial prejudice they should adopt a programme of action.

The question of immigration in fact appeared in the General Council's report to the 1958 Congress. Concern was expressed over the lack of control of immigration from the Commonwealth (with the permit system to regulate foreign workers) and on the distinction between Commonwealth immigrants who were passport-holders and those who were not, particularly in relation to Pakistani immigrants. Finally, the Report, leaving no room for ambiguity, concluded:

> It was suggested to the Minister of Labour that controls adopted by other self-governing Commonwealth countries should be studied and that it would be suitable for Britain to adopt some measures of control over would-be immigrants for whom no job is waiting or is likely to be available. It was also suggested that a medical examination should be included within these immigration controls.

Here then we have a turn up for the books. The so-called pro-labour movement people were demanding immigration control while the Conservative Minister of Labour stated that the government was 'unwilling to contemplate a departure from the traditional readiness of this country to receive citizens of British status'. [174]

On reflection, therefore, in his speech, TUC General Secretary, Vincent Tewson, was not so much expressing a personal opinion on immigration control, as also reiterating the General Council's position. The Tories could not have been happier. Indeed these views assisted the Conservative government in preserving the 'traditional readiness of this country to receive citizens of British status', while controlling 'coloured' immigration. A year later, in 1959, the Council was pleased with the 'overwhelming support' it had received from the trade union movement on immigration control. Exuding self-satisfaction, the General Council also included in its report to Congress, discussions with West Indian government officials about the problems of housing and the question of 'learning to live together' in Britain. The rhetoric continued with the Council determined to keep 'the problem' under continuous review. [175]

But although 'the anything for an easy life' approach won through, the thorn in their side (the Clerical and Administrative Workers Union) had its say. This union's position was clearly at variance with that adopted by the General Council. Referring to this section of the report, the CAWU delegate Ms J. Mellors reminded delegates of the gap between the passage of Conference resolutions and the actual day-to-day practice on the shopfloor. Surely there was more to be done in dealing with racial prejudice. [176]

This direct demand for urgent action on the shopfloor was counteracted and, as it were, floored by a more 'acceptable' (and typically rhetorical evasion by shifting the emphasis from the present to some future time) motion moved by the Chemical Workers' Union. This tactical motion deplored 'the racial violence' of the race riots and in calling for legislation to prevent racial discrimination, qualified this legal measure by stating that the law had only limited usefulness, and as such, 'the hope for racial tolerance lies with the younger generation'. [177] Although the motion was carried, strong dissent was expressed by the Transport Salaried Staff Association who called for immediate action, the mover adding 'I say that nobody has any greater responsibility at the present time than our great Trade Union Movement.' [178] In spite of the arguments put forward, the Trade Union Movement was still not clear what action could be taken. As it was, the situation prevailed for the next sixteen years.

The issues of immigration and race relations were not debated at

Congress for the next five years. The relevance of the race riots to the TUC 'faded away' after reference to it in the 1960 Congress Report.[179] During this period, however, there was a change in emphasis regarding black workers. The General Council began to campaign for a policy of 'integration' and opposition to any special provision for black workers. In other words, they were hoping to achieve parity regardless of racial disadvantage.

Between 1960 and 1964 the Council's main preoccupation was the Commonwealth Immigration Bill which it decided to oppose in a statement.[180] The statement itself, however, did not oppose immigration control in principle. In fact, the statement implied that immigration should be limited by the country of origin, reflecting the view expressed by Tewson at the 1958 Congress. In essence, there was no real contradiction between the General Council's position on immigration as stated in 1955 and 1958, and that expressed in opposing the Commonwealth Immigration Bill in 1962. Interestingly there was also no debate at Congress of the Council's Report in 1964.[181]

The themes of 'integration' and opposition to any special provision for black workers became a fundamental part of the TUC's discussions and representations. They remained silent on racial prejudice and discrimination, which was spreading and becoming more entrenched as reflected in disputes at the workplace. The problem was much too pervasive and hit at the very root of the trade union movement. Thus, not surprisingly, the above themes provided the rationale for the TUC's failure to act.

It was clear, then, that the trade union movement had no special obligations towards black workers. Learning 'British ways' and joining the trade unions were all the black worker needed to do, as it were, to put right the wrongs. In fact, doing these things was precisely 'the problem' for the black migrants. Indeed, except for the token gesture, it has been shown that those who suffered most from racial discrimination were those most integrated. In effect, for so long as the immigrants toed the TUC line, there was no necessity to make special provision.

The TUC's vague position became somewhat more positive between 1965 and 1966 following the Labour government's line by supporting legislative control of immigration. As far as the majority of trade unionists were concerned, racial discrimination was not a reality and urgent trade union action to eliminate it was therefore not necessary.

But why did the General Council come out in the open for immigration control? According to the 1965 Congress Report, two changed circumstances led to a reappraisal of its opposition to immigration as expressed in 1961. The first of these changes was 'the growth of the proportion of Commonwealth immigrants lacking an adequate knowledge of English and of British customs'; the second was the arrival of the wives and children of earlier immigrants which put into perspective the fact that whereas many immigrants were becoming settled with their families in sufficient numbers to require access to the full range of opportunity at every level of British life, progress towards their integration was in some aspects being reversed as the numbers became large enough to constitute an extension of their previous environments. Moreover, it was feared this would lead towards their settlement 'as a series of communities, differentiated from themselves as from the main body of the population'. [182]

One of the General Council's particular concerns, among others, was that the existing system handed over considerable control of immigration policy to immigration officials at the expense of 'interested bodies such as the TUC', which was not invited to comment. Again in the General Council's 1966 Report to Congress, the TUC showed concern over being consulted about immigration control. To this effect, they had corresponded with the Home Secretary and the Minister of Labour. In the latter case, they felt 'it was desirable to recruit workers who would adapt themselves'. [183] They were also concerned about the position the Commonwealth immigrant was placed in concerning the possibility of permanent residence in Britain compared to the alien. As it was the black immigrant worker was already a victim of increasing alienation. The message was clear enough; adaptability was the pre-requisite for permanent residence.

Indeed the General Council's change of policy was shaped most significantly by the increasing number of immigrants from the Indian sub-continent who were strict adherents to their social and cultural backgrounds. In fact they did not follow 'British ways' and intended to maintain their distinctive life style. This was precisely what the General Council was afraid of. To 'integrate' and 'adapt' were the dominant themes. Consequently, they supported immigration control so long as it did not distinguish between alien and Commonwealth immigrants. To surrender one's racial characteristics in a racist society was to commit double-suicide, something most immigrants were unwilling to do. Many members of the British working class regarded themselves as tolerant. By implication they were not prejudiced and did not discriminate. They were therefore not part of 'the problem'. Thus the blame was shifted, and 'the problem' became the beliefs and behaviour of the immigrants themselves. Thus, controlling the numbers was imperative. It was necessary that the number of immigrants should not 'become large enough to constitute an extension of their previous environments'. The consequence of this was that immigration from these countries with undesirable 'social and cultural norms and values' should either be reduced or stopped altogether. This policy of integration by the TUC must be related to the Labour government's approach to immigration from the Commonwealth. With the 1965 White Paper, 'integration began to assume the proportions of a philosophy'.[184] The Labour government's strategy was to bring together (and they knew the problems of racial discrimination very well) the worsening problem of race relations with immigration control. Thus, it was hoped that by introducing legislation in the form of the Race Relations Act 1965, the problems arising from black immigration could be dealt with, thus reinforcing the argument for control.

The influence of the Labour Party on the General Council was evident by the time of the 1966 Congress. During the Congress the TUC and the Labour Party were agreed on policy. This was the 'top down' perspective with the black workers' experience being totally ignored. Thereafter, the TUC became increasingly 'integrated' in the process of government. TUC representatives sat on various statutory bodies set up by the Labour government. Trade union approval was of course important in carrying through Labour Party policies while in government. However, the TUC did oppose both Labour and Conservative government policy on the question of the extent of anti-discriminatory legislation, until 1973.

At the 98th Congress, in a motion moved by the National Union of Journalists, the TUC re-affirmed its opposition to all forms of racial discrimination.[185]

The period 1967–8 was significant. In 1967 the PEP report on the extent of racial discrimination was published and the government had plans to include employment within the new Race Relations Act. The General Council argued that the report dealing with discrimination only at one given point in time failed to establish the 'extent or speed' of 'integration' and as a consequence, did not draw a 'clear distinction between problems arising with new immigrants and those which might be characteristic of a fully settled population, nor could the report relate changes in the situation to the extent of union organisation or action'.[186] The TUC's 'integration' argument was beginning to assume a hidebound quality. The General Council was not pleased with the findings of the PEP report; thus it became irrelevant.

The General Council came round to thinking that the existing voluntary procedures might not be sufficient. It was able to convince the Confederation of British Industry of this and together they issued a joint statement in June 1967, calling for 'a new central body with an independent Chairman which would receive complaints and refer them to the appropriate industrial machinery or deal directly with them if there was no absence of voluntary arbitration at the local level'. This modification of the General Council's view led it to reluctantly agree that legislation might have a role to play, after all. Thereafter, the Council was more preoccupied with details of the legislation rather than the principle and practical use of the law in industrial relations.

The 1968 Race Relations Act did not get the full support of the

Council. However, during the 1968 Congress, the activities among the rank and file delegates were yet again (the Council's views were 'seriously challenged' in 1967) to put the General Council to the test. Racial discrimination was emphasised, not 'integration'. The British Actor's Equity Association delegate moved this motion:

This Congress notes with concern that there are social and Working Men's Clubs which practise racial discrimination in regard both to admission to the clubs and to the engagement of performers. Congress endorses the action taken by the performer's unions in instructing their members to refuse engagements in such clubs and asks the General Council to call upon all affiliated unions to support the performers' unions in this matter by any means open to them. [187]

The motion seconded by the Amalgamated Union of Engineering and Foundry Workers received the support of the delegates from the National Union of Dyers, Bleachers and Textile Workers and the Musicians' Union. During the debate reference was made to discrimination in working men's clubs and the double-standards of the trade union movement. Then the Musicians' Union delegate delved deeper. He argued, it was time 'to get past the concern stage and on to the support stage'. In short, he felt the motion demanded strike action. He spoke of 'direct action' and demanded that each union should commit itself by making a clear statement to its members; and that it should consider the extent to which it could act in concert with, or even initiate, industrial action. These were more than militant gestures. They were a rallying cry to take a stand. The Congress delegates responded. The motion was carried. The General Council now faced the challenge of taking positive action against racial discrimination crucially within the trade union movement itself. Clearly, top-heavy, authoritarian directives were no longer viable. How then would the TUC act?

The years 1969–73 marked the General Council's involvement in established government machinery dealing with race relations. By all accounts, the General Council was more concerned with integration and immigration. Therefore, except in cases of racial discrimination in working men's clubs, it did not initiate any 'racial discrimination' moves. Instead, the Council clung to its integration position stubbornly, until 1973 when delegates from the floor of Congress organised another attack on its position.

Opposition came from the Civil and Public Services Association which moved a lengthy motion criticising the government 'for refusing to allow an amnesty for illegal immigrants subject to the retroactive provisions of the 1971 Act and for use of the officers of the Department of Health and Social Security as part of the law enforcement process'. Finally, the motion requested that the next Labour government repeal the Act. The motion was supported by the AEUW delegate who believed that 'the basic cause of insecurity in the black and immigrant communities is the Act itself'. [188]

Significantly, no delegate spoke against the motion. The General Council was stunned into awkward silence. The motion was carried. This was a historic victory for the rank and file. It was, in fact, the first time that a motion from the floor during a Congress had changed the General Council's policy on either race relations or immigration. More importantly, it marked the turning point in the TUC's policy toward black workers in Britain.

The TUC and black workers: the 1970s and 1980s

After reaping the benefits of the Keynesian theory of full employment, trade union power, in the wake of the 'wild-cat' strikes during the 1960s first threatened the government (a Labour government at the time) through its inquiry into the unions and industrial relations in the document 'In Place of Strife'. This was followed soon after by the Conservative Party study 'A Fair Deal At Work'.

Since 1944 governments of both parties had consulted and sought the advice of the TUC in formulating economic policy. The growing shop steward militancy had however brought criticism and needed to be stemmed. Thus, 'In Place of Strife' was the first attempt to restore trade union control back to the national union leadership. Further, the 'formal' and 'informal' systems of industrial relations revealed a major weakness in the TUC's ability to exercise control within the movement.[189] Faced with this dilemma, the TUC's advice, support and consultation in the formulation of national policy could not be relied upon if government was to carry out its policies.

As it was, economic recession had brought economic paralysis to the British economy and a further weakening of the trade union movement. After the 'winter of discontent' (1978–9) and the advent of the Thatcher government (and its monetarist policies which dramatically increased the number unemployed) the trade union movement was further weakened, to the dismay of trade union leaders. This weakness was reflected in the lack of TUC influence on government policy-making into the 1980s.

The Select Committee on Race Relations and Immigration stated: 'The record of the TUC is similar to that of the CBI, in that both organisations have declared their opposition to racial discrimination but have taken wholly inadequate steps to ensure that their members work effectively to eradicate it.' Criticism was also directed to the TUC from within its constituent unions: 'The evidence shows that positive initiatives of the kind called for in the TUC resolution have not been taken to combat discrimination that is known to occur.'[190]

In spite of these condemnations, no attempt was made to consider the policy and practice of the TUC over the entire period of New Commonwealth immigration. The conflict between the General Council and sections of Congress on the link between the question of immigration with that of the relations between black and white workers during the period of New Commonwealth immigration showed that New Commonwealth immigration and race relations had been 'consistently muddled together' by the General Council as a consequence of which it eventually came to hold the position that black immigrants were a 'problem' and their arrival in Britain should therefore be controlled. [191]

In fact, the period 1954–73 showed that the TUC's failure to act was consistent with the way in which it had chosen to perceive the situation in Britain. This period included the main period of New Commonwealth immigration to Britain and the latter date marks the time when a change in TUC policy began to become evident.

The written reports of the TUC were revealing. Firstly, they indicated that the General Council failed to acknowledge that there was 'considerable hostility' towards black workers among white trade unionists, and increasingly came to adopt the position that the problems arose from the immigrants' refusal to integrate; secondly, that although the TUC stated its opposition to racial discrimination on several occasions, those manual unions which organised the vast majority of black workers had failed to speak openly in favour of such motions; and thirdly, the reports indicated that, in spite of its 'principled' opposition to racial discrimination, the TUC between 1968 and 1973, 'eventually came to accept at least implicitly that immigration should be controlled on a racial basis'.

Miles and Phizacklea have argued that

> given the structural position of trade unions in the present stage of British capitalist development, the most probable reaction of the trade unions to immigration and immigrant workers is one of hostility. In contrast to earlier immigrations, TUC hostility to immigration from the New Commonwealth was principally on social rather than economic grounds because in the 1950s and 1960s immigrant workers posed no direct threat to the jobs of British workers and 'integration', which had become the hallowed philosophy of successive governments, was in turn uncritically adopted by the TUC. [192]

As we have seen, the policy and practice of the TUC between 1954 and 1973 showed that the TUC failed to act positively because of the way in which it chose to define the position of black workers in Britain, and perhaps more particularly because of constraints placed on its initiatives by individual unions. They perceived a more serious problem in the unwillingness of black immigrants to 'integrate', thus transferring the onus for action on black workers. (In fact, black workers with no alternative and no real trade union support, struck in several intolerable workplaces.) Moreover, the largest unions representing manual workers (the TGWU, for example) made no contributions to debates on 'race' and failed consistently to make a contribution to anti–discrimination motions.

Further, the General Council was especially concerned with immigration from the New Commonwealth. However, although they consistently declared themselves opposed to any form of racially based immigration control, they did not oppose the 1971 Immigration Act on these grounds until 1973.

Since 1974, however, new TUC policy and initiatives have emerged. Events, both internal and external to the trade union movement, had forced the TUC to re-evaluate its past policy and practice. Three developments had forced this re-evaluation. Firstly, a number of industrial disputes in the early 1970s were distinguished by (amongst other grievances) complaints by black workers of discrimination practised by trade union officials. Consequently, there was public criticism of both the trade unions involved and TUC policy and practice. Secondly, since the 1950s, the hidebound values of trade unionism in the face of a grievance-ridden black workforce had brought mounting criticism at Annual TUC Congresses which received added thrust following these 'disputes'. And thirdly the growing support for the National Front heightened trade union concern. [193]

TUC policy 1974–76

In 1974 the TUC General Council reported to Congress[194] the submission of a memorandum and oral evidence to the Select Committee on Race Relations and Immigration. To see the TUC memorandum in perspective, it should be related to the oral evidence presented to the Select Committee by representatives of the General Council. [195] The two dominant themes were firstly, responding to a specific question, the TUC representative replied that, although white workers might refuse to work with black workers, such action was never sanctioned by the national and regional officials. [196] This meant, after all, a recognition that white trade unionists do engage in discriminatory practice. And secondly, in response to a question concerning the TUC's view of the need for an equal opportunity policy in union agreements, the TUC representative said that this indicated their belief that the situation was serious.

The Select Committee Report marked a 'watershed' in the history of the TUC's policy and practice concerning black workers. The arguments from the floor of the 1958 Congress (echoed by an official House of Commons Committee) were raised yet again at the 1974 Congress. In response to the General Council's report on its memorandum to the Select Committee, the Association of Scientific Technical and Managerial Staff's delegate, S. Jefferson, welcomed 'an important shift in the General Council's approach to the struggle against racial discrimination'. He believed, however, the statement did not go far enough: 'What is needed is a determined attack by the trade union movement on racial discrimination, the development of anti-discrimination trade union education and the development of specialist trade union services to the section of our black and immigrant membership who have problems such as language difficulties.'[197] At the same Congress there was also concern about the General Council's attitude to the 1971 Immigration Act. On reflection, the ASTMS delegate argued that since the Council had not seriously pressed the government to remove the Act from the statute book, it should now do so on the grounds that it was racist and anti-union.

Unfortunately, the great expectations of such delegates were not satisfied at the 1975 Congress. The Report of this Congress did not indicate that any further consideration of policy was being undertaken concerning black workers.[198] However, the TUC seemed proud to report that a model clause on equal opportunities had been drawn up and circulated to union officials and representatives involved in negotiations at all levels.

By October 1974, following the House of Lords decision that Preston Dockers' Labour Club were not guilty of unlawful discrimination, the General Council sent a letter to the Home Secretary stating their opposition to discrimination in working men's clubs on the grounds of colour, race or origin. So concerned was the TUC on this issue that a meeting was held with the Executive Committee of the Club and Institute Union to explore ways of ensuring the non-practice of discrimination in clubs.

Although the report of the 1975 Congress did not hold out much hope as far as policy-making related to black workers was concerned, unusually, things happened quickly thereafter. In October of that year, 'a major initiative' was taken by the General Council.[199] In effect, this meant a re-organisation of existing arrangements to accommodate this new development. Race relations and discrimination, the responsibility of the International Committee was reallocated to become part of the Organisational and Industrial Relations Department. This change meant that the TUC felt the need to monitor these questions more effectively. To this end, it also proposed the setting-up of a new sub-committee of the General Council, the Equal Rights Committee. In December 1975, the ERC's terms of reference were put before the General Council for ratification. The focus of the Committee's work was on 'those fields where special and cumulative advantage exists, for particular groups linked with discrimination on arbitrary grounds (such as race, sex or religion) and generally to develop 'positive policies to promote equal opportunities'. In so doing, the ERC's task was to press for government legislation against arbitrary discrimination to monitor the results of such legislation. The Committee also had to examine and monitor the policies of the TUC and affiliated unions on the question of equal opportunity and to approach the government and other relevant bodies to act in accordance with the special needs of disadvantaged groups.

On the question of 'race relations' the General Council acknowledged the need for special consideration and accordingly set up, in December 1975, the Race Relations Advisory Committee. The ERC and RRAC were both expected to complement each other. The RRAC was composed of 13 members: 4 General Council members and 9 trade union representatives, some of whom were also members of minority groups. Tom Jackson, General Secretary of the Union of Post Office Workers acted as Chairman of both the ERC and the RRAC.[200]

After setting up these two Committees, the General Council issued a press release in July 1976 endorsing the work of these bodies. The Council stated: 'Much needs to be done to eliminate the discrimination and disadvantage facing ethnic minorities and for their part the General Council are advising affiliated unions about steps they should take to strengthen trade union organisation among immigrant and black workers and unity between work people.' The press release having deplored the racialist activities of the National Front, and attempts to blame unemployment on black workers, also made its 'first mention' of a proposed campaign against racialism; a campaign that would also involve the Labour Party.

As it was, the press release foreshadowed what was to happen at the 1976 Congress. The TUC's procrastination during earlier years now seemed irrelevant as it put forward a clear denunciation of racialism and the racist activities of the National Front and the National Party. Overall, the mood was one of optimism. A motion on racialism, moved by Bill Keys, General Secretary of the Society of Graphic and Allied Trades, condemned racist propaganda and called for a government ban on the National Front and the National Party. He also pointed to the danger posed by racialism to working class unity which detracted from the provision of equal opportunities for black and white workers and called upon the General Council to 'organise and invite' a national campaign against racialism.

Moreover, referring to the National Front, Keys argued that 'These people who peddle race hatred are no different from the people who peddled the hatred in Germany in the 1920s and 1930s which led to the last war.'[201]

Notable support came from Maurice Styles of the UPW who argued that the roots of racialism were buried in everyone and as a consequence it should be recognised that 'earlier' immigrants were becoming today's citizens. David Basnett (GMWU) denounced racialism as abhorrent on moral, ethical and trade union grounds; and Jarvis Mahoney (British Actors Equity Association), one of the few black delegates at Congress, and interestingly one of the few to speak during this debate, called for action to stem rising unemployment and the alienation of black youth and argued in favour of 'integrated acting' in the media. Other speakers included the delegate from NALGO and the National Union of Teachers, the latter arguing for positive discrimination in favour of ethnic minority members for full-time and elected posts.[202] The debate reflected a widespread feeling. The resolution was carried unanimously.

Thus between the Congresses of 1975 and 1976 the General Council and TUC policy and practice changed. Firstly, the General Council openly admitted that black workers faced disadvantage and discrimination, and that the serious problem of racialism should be strenuously opposed. Secondly, it was clearly recognised that the trade unions should actively oppose racialism within their own ranks (racialism within the British workforce) and should openly oppose racialist and fascist organisations. Thirdly (and reflecting a clear shift in emphasis), the stated issues requiring action were not 'integration' of the immigrants, but racialism and the activities of the National Front and the National Party; fourthly the General Council was in favour of giving special attention to 'race relations' through new organisational arrangements and by actively working towards equal opportunity; and fifthly, apart from the General Council's willingness to speak out over the problems and dangers of racialism, it was also concerned with mobilising the labour movement in a campaign against it.

On reflection, by 1976, the General Council had come a 'long way' since its policy and Memorandum to the Select Committee in 1974 and dramatically since its policy and debates in the 1950s and 1960s. How did this change come about? Three developments have been cited: black workers and industrial conflict; the General Council critics, and the National Front.

Black workers and industrial conflict

During the early 1970s, black workers were involved in a number of industrial disputes in which allegations of discrimination practised by white trade unionists were made.[203] As Miles and Phizacklea have argued elsewhere, the General Council was, at least up until 1973, unwilling to accept publicly that white trade unionists engaged in discriminatory practices. In fact, this position had been flatly contradicted by Mansfield Hosiery Mills and Imperial Typewriters disputes, among others. The weakness of the TUC's policy was therefore revealed and criticism came not only from black workers and a group of trade unionists opposed to the General Council's position, but also from official bodies.

Thus, both disputes were characterised by conflict on the one hand, between Asian workers and management, and between Asian union members and union officials, on the other. Although such three-cornered disputes were not uncommon occurrences in the black workers' industrial experience in Britain, in the cases cited above, there was the added dimension of allegations of racial discrimination by Asian workers on strike, against both employer and union. And although the 'media led bias' had had some effect, what was abundantly clear in these two disputes was the fact that rank-and-file trade unionists and trade union officials 'could be guilty of discriminatory practice'.

Apart from the media criticism of the union's practice, the government-sponsored CIR was, as already shown, seriously concerned about the union's role *vis-à-vis* black workers. The CIR's view, publicly aired, flew in the face of the General Council's earlier argument that the problem was one of integration ('them' adopting 'our' ways) and immigration, and not that of the extent of discriminatory practice amongst white workers. Understandably, the Council was careful not to refer to these disputes at the Annual Congress.

In relating these disputes to the trade union movement and in particular to the TUC, it is necessary to consider the responses of senior trade union leaders. There was consensus on two points. Firstly, that the disputes had no immediate or direct effect on the General Council of the TUC; and secondly, by contrast, that they did have a significant effect on the national leadership of the unions involved, and particularly, the TGWU. This reflected the divide between the unions and the TUC. It was argued that because trade union officials were extremely busy, and in the absence of specific events to jolt their consciousness 'there was little reason for considering the position and problems of black workers'.

The General Council critics

The General Council's 'internally contradictory' policy since the mid-1950s has often been challenged by delegates at Congress, most significantly at the 1967 Congress by a motion moved by the Association of Cinematograph Television and Allied Technicians in response to the General Council's report on its opposition to the government's intention of extending the legislative control of racial discrimination to the field of employment. While re-affirming the TUC's condemnation of racial discrimination, the motion expressing concern about the extent of racial discrimination as revealed by the 1967 PEP study, called for trade union action to prevent discrimination, and endorsed the government's intentions to make racial discrimination in employment an offence.[204] In effect, the motion attempted to reverse the Council's policy. This 'most significant challenge' to the Council's policy (though not the only one) indicated that a 'substantial proportion' of trade unionists were of the view that the TUC should take positive action against racial discrimination.

Further evidence of the existence of opposition to the General Council policy was contained in the memorandum submitted to the Select Committee in 1974 by the Midland Region Trade Union Conference to Combat Racial Discrimination. The memorandum's argument was that white workers were prejudiced against black workers on the grounds of colour, and feared that it would continue to exist in future generations. It was particularly concerned that widespread discrimination was encouraged by the passive role adopted by Parliament, employers and trade unions. Moreover, it pointed out that no employer or trade union had established a special department to assist the black worker to overcome disadvantage in employment.[205] This Committee had organised a Conference attended by over 100 delegates from the Midlands in January 1974. A resolution was passed calling for an active campaign against racist ideology and racial discrimination. Moreover, it urged the TUC to appoint a full-time officer with responsibility for 'advising affiliated unions on all aspects of race relations'.[206]

Further, other locally-based committees were set up by trade unionists in London, the Midlands and in the North of England in the 1970s to combat discrimination and to attempt to change their respective unions and TUC policy. In addition, Trades Councils organised conferences and campaigns, expressing concern about racist ideology and racial discrimination within the labour movement and in British society generally. For example, the Black Coventry Trades Council Conference of 1974 passed a resolution which called on its members to bring pressure to bear on union district committees to appoint a delegate essentially concerned with 'racialist problems', to initiate recruiting campaigns among immigrant workers (using literature which was printed in their own languages) to demand an end to police harassment of black workers and ensuring that known racialists did not hold trade union office. A year later, in 1975, following a trade union conference on the problems of racialism; a delegation from Warley Trades Council met local councillors, after which Warley Council agreed that a person of 'immigrant origin' should be employed to deal with such matters as language, form filling and other problems relating to the Council, and to make representations to constituency bodies to discuss the repeal of the 'patrial clauses' in the 1971 Immigration Act which were 'racial in intent and effect'.[207]

It is not easy to assess the meaning or effect of the resolutions passed by, and the actions of, these locally-based committees and conferences in the early 1970s. Some of the trade unionists who initiated or took part in them were members of political organisations to the left of the Labour Party, but far from all participants were politically committed in this way. Nevertheless, these forums indicated a current of opposition at the local level to the official TUC policy and were able to pose as representing the trade union principles on racism and discrimination in their areas of influence.

Opposition to the TUC policy has not been confined to the floor of Congress or the grass-roots level. Interviews with trade union officials have revealed that many full-time officials tried to develop a more positive policy. To them, the many industrial disputes during the early 1970s were evidence of the weakness of TUC policy. But, even if the TUC leadership wanted to, it was hamstrung by its obligation to listen increasingly and act upon the dictates of its member unions whose representatives sat on the General Council.

By the mid-1970s, then, the situation within the TUC was one in which certain trade union leaders, as a result of particular events, were re-evaluating TUC policy. Moreover, within the trade union movement there were a few trade unionists who wanted the adoption of a more positive policy by the TUC. And what seemed also necessary was 'a broadening of the concern' in the General Council and the TUC, as a result of the racial abuse and attacks (and increasing public awareness) of the National Front.

Union officials interviewed were asked about the reasons for the re-evaluation of TUC policy and about National Front activity amongst their own members. All of them said that the Front was active and had some support amongst their members. Four of them specifically referred to it as a fascist organisation; two officials drew parallels between the NF and the rise of National Socialism in Germany, pointing to the current economic crisis and high level of unemployment. Although two officials also pointed out that the current influence of the National Front should not be overstated, there was concern about its activity and future potential amongst all union officials interviewed. Three of the five officials, including a member of the TUC General Council, also stated that the emergence of the National Front had necessitated a new policy from the TUC. The General Council member, Tom Jackson, referred to the 'casual attitude of the TUC to the "race question" prior to 1975', saying that the members of the General Council believed that there was no real cause for concern or felt that they 'did not want to lift the stone'. However, when the NF intervened in 'a big way' by putting up a large number of candidates, he and one or two Council members, including Jack Jones (TGWU) and David Basnett (GMWU), made calls for action.

A further dimension to this was that Jackson also claimed that the National Front's intervention in 1974 gave the Left in the trade union movement a good reason to act on the 'race issue'. In presenting their interpretation to this, Miles and Phizacklea argued that trade unionists who had wanted a more positive policy towards the issues posed by black immigrant workers have had to contend with the racism of white trade unionists, but after 1974 it became possible for them to argue that the National Front as a neo-fascist party, was the 'enemy' of the trade union movement. Thus identifying the NF, they were now prepared openly to demand support for a policy of opposition to racialism. Therefore it seemed that the effect of the NF's activities was to force the General Council and the TUC to act in relation to the 'race issue' between 1970 and 1973.

By comparison, little had been done through the combined activities of the internal critics at the annual Congresses and the left-wing organisations and rank-and-file trade union groupings over the preceding 25 years. Although the latter served to needle the General Council continually with the exception of the motion passed at the 1973 Congress opposing the 1971 Immigration Act, it had no fundamental and decisive impact.

By the end of the 1970s, however, there was no doubt as to the NF's provocative racist marches. The murder of a young Asian, in 1976, the growing concern over racist policemen at the Grunwick picket lines (and within the black communities) and violence on Blacks in several parts of the country, highlighted the need for anti-racist support in fighting NF-led racism.

Conclusion

The focus then of TUC action and speeches by General Council members since 1974 had been to combat racism and racialist practices within the white working class. If, however, Maurice Styles was correct in arguing that the roots of racialism are buried deep in everyone and are derived from Britain's imperial depredations then in the absence of evidence to the contrary, one must doubt whether a propaganda campaign lasting a few months, and of very uneven intensity, was adequate to the task. Certainly, some of the trade union officials interviewed were cynical about the extent of the influence of the campaign on shopfloor practice, although all believed that union representatives at all levels were fully aware of union policy and were likely to act in opposition to it.

The General Council had, by comparison, placed less emphasis upon dealing with the material disadvantage of black workers. Instead, it followed a two-pronged policy: first, to press all affiliated unions to negotiate acceptance by employers, of equal opportunity clauses and, secondly, to press both government and the CBI to pursue equal opportunity policies. This strategy achieved little.

Between 1976 and 1979 although race relations, equal rights, the Grunwick dispute and racialism had consistently been on the Annual Congress agenda, polarisation between the black and white sections of the British working class had increased. The ASTMS delegate's words in moving his motion on the 'Select Committee on Race Relations' at the 106th Annual Congress had a particularly hard ring: 'If racialism is to be checked and then eradicated, if black workers are not to be tempted by separationist solutions or simply opt out of the Movement then solidarity must be forthcoming. There have been too many instances recently when black workers have had to struggle alone. They must be given the support of the whole trade union movement.'[208]

Indeed, into the 1980s with the passage of the Nationality Bill, that 'support' was clearly not forthcoming. Thus, 'separationist solutions' and opting out of the movement seemed the only alternative as the TUC, in desperation, took initiatives to fight rampant racism.

TUC initiatives: workbook on racism

By the end of 1983, faced with high unemployment and a determination by the Thatcher regime to crush the trade unions, the TUC, aware of the divisiveness of the government's policies, felt the need to stem the racism among rank-and-file trade unionists. Of course, they had all along known of the racist attacks on black workers both at the workplace and in the black communities. Thus, the TUC took the step (following the earlier TUC Black Workers' Charter) of stating its position in the *TUC Workbook on Racism*.

No longer could the TUC ignore the evidence of racism which had at last filtered up to the General Council. Given that attacks on black workers has taken such forms as verbal abuse and physical violence, to unfair treatment in pay and working conditions, the TUC felt that if these attacks (which came from employers, government and fellow trade unionists) are not opposed, all workers will suffer. Indeed, racism will continue to be used to divide worker against worker. Hence the value of their *Workbook* to all trade unionists. This statement on racism was intended to help build confidence and skills in four main ways: to understand racism and its effects on working people; to present the arguments against racism; to improve organisation to overcome divisions at work and in the union; and to develop bargaining aims to win equality at work.[209]

It was hoped that this instructive *Workbook* (covering such work-related aspects as 'the issues', roots of racism, racism at work, the law and union action, among others) would be used on trade union and TUC courses.

For its part (given that in 1977, 61 per cent of the employed black males belonged to trade unions but only 47 per cent of employed white males), the TUC posed the question: why tackle racism? After years of Annual Conference debates, the TUC was now able to admit that because black workers experience discrimination it was the unions' job to do something about it. Indeed they could no longer afford to ignore the issues raised by racism stating: 'Once trade unionists start picking and choosing between different groups of workers, segregating one from another, we are on a slippery slope towards our own destruction.'[210]

The TUC pointed out that black workers have been hit harder by the economic crisis than the majority of white workers and reiterated what earlier reports had found, that the black community experiences high levels of unemployment and are employed in low paid, unskilled work with few or no real opportunities for promotion. And, remarkably, the TUC unlike its earlier phase of reluctance and ambiguity (to put it mildly) in dealing with race and immigration was now, in response to repeated government attacks, ready to state boldly that the background to these problems lies in Britain's colonial past and the willingness of governments and employers to see black workers as a source of cheap labour.

Moreover, the TUC admitted (in self-criticism) that trade union-ists have also tended to side-step the issues raised by racism because they have often been concerned not to upset white members by challenging racist attitudes. Indeed, it was felt that in the changing situation forced by a recession, racism was most likely to be used to destroy union organisation, particularly at a time when trade union unity was most needed to defend jobs and services.

In practice: the disillusionment of black workers (alternative organisations)

In spite of the TUC's directives, black workers were (and are) wholly dissatisfied. In effect, no real progress was made. After the miners' strike in the early 1970s dealt the Conservative government a crushing blow and inflation rose rapidly, wage restraint in the form of a 'Social Contract' became the Labour government's policy. At the back of the pay queue were black workers, women and pensioners. By 1973, there was strong resentment and disillu-sionment among black workers. In their relationship with, and experience of, the trade unions, two basic questions were asked: Are the British trade unions in their relations with black workers 'too much part of the problem to be any part of the solution?' Or should black workers, whatever their criticisms of the unions, act in the belief that there is no prospect for success if they wage their fight for justice outside the union structure? Of the 24 million people at work in Britain it was estimated that only 9 million belonged to a trade union.[211] When asked what their policy and practice on race relations was some of the major unions' answers varied widely. Although the NUR, NUPE, USDAW, TGWU, ASLEF, GMWU and the AEUW were opposed to racism, few of them signed the 'TRJ' letter to *The Times*, and more importantly, none of them (certainly during the early 1970s) had black full-time officials. Furthermore, the GMWU felt that 'race relations are another dimension of industrial activity and that the problems of black workers are those of workers in general'. Therefore they were opposed to any organisation that set itself up in opposition to the official trade union movement. More specifically, they felt the idea of a black caucus within the trade union movement should be viewed with suspicion. Apart from three black trade unionists (Bill Morris, National Secretary of the Transport and General Passenger Transport Group, Robert Walker, the first West Indian to be elected to the posts of Branch Secretary and Chairman of a group within ASLEF, and the author who was the first secretary of the Whitley Council elected from the trade union side when the British Library was formed in 1973), the odds were clearly stacked against black trade unionists achieving positions of prominence within their unions. The democratic principle of majority rule militated against it. Not surprisingly, there was deep disillusionment with the quality of black workers' representation in the trades union movement. As one commentator put it: 'There is a cold, hard logic in the unions' democratically proper refusal to let the interests of a minority override those of the majority. But this short-sighted easy option has contributed much to the deeply ingrained, seemingly insoluble problems of today.'[212]

When at the height of their wealth and power during the 1950s and 1960s the unions had enormous potential for effecting radical change for the benefit of Britain's working class as a whole, they failed to accept the challenge on behalf of their black members. While it was understandable, it was nonetheless unforgiveable.

Capitalism and curbs on discrimination

Concern for the ending of racial discrimination at work is not always disinterested argued Ian Macdonald, 'sometimes the motive is simply profit, or a desire to buy social peace at the expense of justice'.[213] Indeed, the recent strikes of black workers sounded a warning that they were no longer prepared to tolerate the discrimination practised against them in the form of low wages, bad working conditions and no promotion opportunities. They could not be left to form separate organisations. Macdonald concludes, 'It is their action which has created liberal sentiment among important sections of industry, trade unions and government, and has forced them to develop further strategies for dealing with discrimination. It has also, I suggest, been responsible for the wave of liberal sentiment over the deportation of illegal immigrants and the calls for an amnesty.'[214]

Yet in spite of the liberal slogan 'White labour can't be free while black labour is in chains', the black working class has remained firmly shackled under the pressure exerted from all sides within the British capitalist system.

The black workers' response

In spite of the real problems they face, some militant black trade unionists have concentrated on workplace oriented organisations. Forging links with black fellow workers had become a necessity. To wage their own struggle (given the trade unions' racism and back-pedalling tactics) black workers formed their own combinations. For example, the Black Workers Co-ordinating Committee, Black Unity and Freedom Party and the Croydon Collective.

Links were indeed forged with the Black Workers' Alliance in an effort to agitate and struggle against racism at all levels. It was argued that the alliance must incorporate those organisations in our black communities that are equipped to participate in the struggle at the highest level. Together they must strive to develop the right political ideology among the black working class, so that it can be applied to black workers' problems, and subsequently arrive at the right conclusions and the right tactical methods with which to tackle the stranglehold of state-instituted poverty and oppression. It was therefore necessary to understand the methods of the race-ridden capitalist state machinery, as all forms of oppression are interrelated.

Finally, it was argued that the only alternative was the seizing of state power by the working class and the establishment of scientific socialism, not only on a national level but internationally. Their recommendations to the Conference on Trade Unions and Racism were:

1. The formation of a Black Workers' Alliance to co-ordinate our struggle with the trade union movement.
2. The re-introduction of the periodical issuing leaflets that point out to workers the importance of a trade union that truly represents the interests of workers.
3. For the Black Workers' Alliance to help black workers outside the organised industrial framework to organise themselves in protection of their interests.
4. To take the Black people's case, in relation to racism, as one of priority.
5. The Alliance must further develop the working class ideology of revolutionary and scientific socialism amongst all workers especially black workers.

(FORMULATED BY: Black Workers Co-ordinating Committee (BWCC), Black Unity and Freedom Party (BUFP) and Croydon Collective.)[215]

One is reminded of what Vic Feather (a former General Secretary of the TUC) said in the Westminster Trinity Lecture in 1970: 'The trade union movement is concerned with a man or a woman as a worker. The colour of a man's skin has no relevance whatever to his work.'[216] If only this were true!

Another black workers' organisation, the 'Black Workers' Movement' distributed a paper at the Conference on Trade unions and Racism called by the Mansfield Hosiery Strike Committee. The Movement posed the question: How can we translate our experience into unity of the whole black working class to make our demands?' In answer, it stated,

Our experience has indicated the forms of strategy around which we can organise to make our demands.

1. Mobilising the strength of the whole black class in the community and in the factory

2. Seeking to talk directly to the white workers and demanding they
   support our struggles (as we give ours) in their own class interest.
   But refusing to concede to racist hostility if they refuse.
3. Internationalising our struggle wherever possible. [217]

The aim was to show how black workers organising themselves
can bridge the gap between the fight in industry and the struggle of
communities. It is this diversion that black workers have brought
to the working class movement in Britain.

The Black Workers' Movement (BWM) believed that in order to
formulate demands within industry, black workers needed a co-
ordinating front which could be called 'Black Workers Against
Racism in Industry'. The BWM pointed out that this was not a call
for a new black organisation. Indeed, the struggle in Britain had given
birth to many such groups, including the Black Peoples' National
Action Collective of which the BWM was a part. The primary task
was to document a thorough investigation into the situation of
black workers firstly, in industry generally, and secondly, in the
trade unions. Out of this investigation, demands were to be made
on the government, on their unions and on employers. Moreover,
they believed that such an investigation must deal with apprentice-
ships, a minimum wage for all workers, employed and unemployed, equal pay for all, including equal pay for women workers
inside the home and in the factory, an end to classification of skills,
and the effects of the Immigration Act on black workers.

Finally the BWM believed that the platform of demands that
emerged must speak for the needs of the whole black working
class. They believed that within the black community there was
ample experience and willingness to make a front of Black Workers
Against Racism in Industry a serious political force for unity and
struggle within the black working class.

The organisation called the Black People's Freedom Movement
(and the BWM) both belonged to the Black Peoples' National
Action Collective. Their statements do not differ greatly in
analysis. However, under the heading 'Mobilising Our Community' the BPFM made the following demands:

> pressure should be put on unions to recognise racism, as opposed to
> sweeping it under the carpet. Steps should be taken by the unions to
> see that black workers have the same rights as white ones. *Black
> caucuses*. We see the formation of black caucuses, especially in
> subsidiaries of the same firm, as a necessity. Black workers must
> recognise the failings of the trade unions and seek to be self-sufficient
> within them – organising and creating conditions whereby they ally
> themselves to the white progressive workers to make the necessary
> demands. Moreover, it was necessary to forge links with our fellow
> workers, wherever they may be employed with the aim of forming a
> broad politically-based 'Black Workers' Alliance', which would ally

itself with the just struggle of black working class people everywhere.[218]

Furthermore, the IWA Southall declared that the trade unions were the only avenues open to black workers through which they can fight against racial prejudice. They did not dispute the fact that there was considerable racial discrimination even in the trade union movement but felt it was the duty of the leaders of the trade unions to inform the members of their unions about the sinister policies of the ruling classes to divide and rule. Conscious of their own disunity, they commented that the 'present split' was only beneficial to the bosses who could exploit it for their own ends. Moreover they argued that 'by active participation of the immigrant community in the Trade Union Movement we can reduce the prevailing racial prejudice among the workers. Finally, Trade Unions should employ more full time immigrant officials in order to win the confidence of the immigrant community.'[219]

These were the themes being emphasised by the leading black organisations. Although they were disenchanted with the white trade unions, towards the end of the 1970s the immediacy of black workers' problems, in spite of Sivanandan's call, 'Put Politics in Command' drew them closer to the workplace where at the end of the day, it really mattered.

In December 1981, a group of black trade union activists (Asians and West Indians) founded the Black Trade Unionists Solidarity Movement. They came together 'to begin a united movement of all black people in Britain, to pressurise the existing institutions, and fight for our rights'. Membership was open to people of Asian, African and Caribbean descent, employed or unemployed. The BTUSM founders declared that as Black Trade Unionists they were concerned at the extent of racism in British society and particularly in the trades unions and labour movement.

The disturbances in Brixton, Southall and other parts of London showed that black people are no longer prepared to accept unemployment, bad housing, police provocation and the institutional and individual racism inherent in British society.

BTUSM was strongly opposed to continuing political trends in the area of race relations, e.g. the Nationality Bill, the Circular issued by the Department of Health and Social Security (DHSS) on overseas patients, the refusal of the DHSS to pay benefits to people who do not speak English, passport checks and immigration 'fishing raids', and calls for the repatriation of Blacks, among others. These measures, they argued are an exacerbation of previous racist policies and practices.

As trade unionists, they felt the day-to-day racism at the workplace must be of primary concern. Moreover, they were aware that unemployment, short time working, redundancy and other forms of direct and indirect discrimination affect black people more than any other section within British society. Indeed, their duty was to organise black workers within the trade unions and labour movement to combat racism in such a way that they could promote and protect the interests of black people in the trade unions and labour movement.

Thus they pledged themselves to: firstly, organise a London-based Conference of Black Trade Unionists to discuss a programme of action; secondly, make links with other black workers' organisations with a view to launching a National Black Trade Unionists Solidarity Movement; thirdly, work to improve the increasing participation of black people at all levels within the trade unions and labour movement and, fourthly, to work for changes within the trade union and labour movement to restore the confidence of black people. [220]

In its first factsheet issued at the price of 10p, the focus was on such articles as 'We Are Our Own Liberators', 'Racism in NALGO Exposed', and 'Why We Need BTUSM?'. Furthermore, under the heading 'Norman Tebbit Rides on Grunwick's Grave' it was argued that the foundation for Tebbitt's anti-union laws can be traced back to the unheeded lessons of Grunwick. The BTUSM writers criticised the present Conservative government which was reaping the benefit of the TUC's lack of courage in not going the whole way. They argued that the TUC's lack of leadership in opposing secondary picketing and the closed shop, for example, allowed Tebbitt to tighten the noose round the trade unions. Disillusionment, widespread among black workers, was increasingly being channelled into organisation and action. Moreover, the factsheet quoted Mrs Jayaben Desai who, having started a hunger strike outside Congress House, said to Len Murray, TUC General Secretary, 'I will not remove my hunger strike from your doorstep. The problem is you, and I want to expose you to the world.'[221]

After several months of advertising its aims and objectives, BTUSM called its first Conference, in accordance with its first pledge, which was held on 4–5 June 1983 at County Hall, London. Notably, the Conference organisers had made arrangements for the accommodation of the disabled among the delegates and guests, and facilities for those with children. This Conference was a decisive move by black trade unionists; disenchantment and anger had given way to organisation and putting together a programme of action. Significantly, BTUSM has made it abundantly clear that they would work for changes *within* the trade union movement.

The interesting thing about this development is that many militant black trade unionists see clearly the link between their workplace struggle and their community struggle. Thus, they have clearly stated their intention to organise and work within the trade union movement. In other words, they want white workers to recognise and act on the real, day-to-day problems of racism and sexism, so that together they can work effectively. So far however, the black initiative has met with only marginal response. Historically, the vast majority of trade unionists have been complacent about black workers and slow to act. The annual reports of the Trades Union Congress confirm this.

10 Organisers and Organisations

Black Power and its advocates

From Pan Africanism to Black Power

Over a long period stretching back to the late eighteenth century, a few members of the small black community in Britain had initiated and, with the sympathy and co-operation of indigenous liberals and radicals, gradually developed an ideology on which to build its organisations in the face of racism and overt hostility in an alien land – the home of their rulers.

The departure of the radical Pan African leaders from Britain, following the Fifth Pan African Congress, to lead the nationalist movements in Africa and the West Indies, left a vacuum of black militant leadership, in Britain, during the 1950s and for most of the 1960s.

In the main, apart from Claudia Jones and Amanyu Manchanda, such leadership as there was during these decades, was middle-class and conservative. Not only did this contrast sharply to the radical Pan Africanists, it essentially misled black migrants, at least for the first decade and a half, into believing that multi-racial organisation and integrationist arguments were the best means for improving their disadvantaged positions. In short, as the black migrant's status as 'second-class' citizens deteriorated (and the prospects for their children appeared particularly depressing) they sought a way out of their dilemma.

Unlike the Pan Africanists, potential and actual black leaders had to wrestle with the problems of a permanent and growing black community. Indeed (as racial discrimination ran 'riot') such leaders faced the task of confronting the racists, the fascists, the trade unions and government, or settle for going through the motions of leadership and do nothing about the root of the problem: white racism. Although some were willing to delude themselves, others had no illusions: they were acutely conscious of representing a minority in a racist society, and the oppression and suffering emanating from the depredations of individual and institutionalised racism.

Nonetheless, many attempts to organise and integrate black migrants were made, but time and again, they were refused entry into many areas of British social life. Increasingly, they paid attention to the decaying inner city environment, as they witnessed on television screens and read in the newspapers of a different historical, but parallel experience of Blacks in the inner city ghettoes of the United States of America. Black nationalism, which the Pan Africanists had preached to end colonialism abroad, had evolved into Black Power, a cry from the 'colonised' American ghettoes, which had strong echoes among Blacks in Britain by the close of the 1960s. Black Power and black autonomy were increasingly being applied to the struggle of the black community 'colonised' in the metropole.

Generally, black organisations from 1950 to 1984 can be divided into two periods. Firstly, between 1950 and the mid-1960s, they were tolerant and accommodationist, reflecting to a large extent, their leaders' attitudes; and secondly, from the mid-1960s, the 'wind of change' had introduced greater militancy as reflected in the industrial struggles (resulting in the formation of strike committees, for example) and community-oriented social and cultural organisations created to fight racism and fascism during the 1970s and 1980s. In fact racism had reached a disturbing level during the 1970s and 1980s, as the black community mounted many campaigns in response to repeated attacks by racists and fascists. As it was, 1980 saw the return to Britain of the extraordinary radical Pan Africanist and Marxist historian, C. L. R. James. To commemorate his eightieth birthday he gave a series of lectures. Since 1938 he had been one of the chief black advocates of autonomous organisation. Soon after these lectures, many of James's writings were republished, including his famous book *Black Jacobins*. A new militant readership was now able to either re-read or be initiated into Jamesiana. As it was, the very year that he delivered his lectures, 'spontaneous crowd violence' erupted in Bristol. This change from

'integrationist' to greater emphasis on 'independent' black organisation can be directly related to the acceptance of Black Power by
Britain's enlarged post-war black community.

The ideology of Black Power: 'from Black Power back to Pan Africanism'

Gold Coast Independence in 1957 was the first example of 'Black
Power' in Africa. This was an example of the black man's right and
ability to govern himself. In effect, he was, at least politically, free
of foreign occupation.

When Kwame Nkrumah (the first Black African Prime Minister)
assumed the leadership of the Gold Coast, black Americans, 'colonised' for some 400 years, took note. Pan Africanism had brought
organisation in the black colonies and Black Power in the United
States. Indeed, the foremost Black Power advocate by the mid-
1960s, Stokely Carmichael (who was born under the British colonial system in Trinidad), had caught the essence of a two-way flow
of ideas and identity when he wrote in 1965, *Black Power Back to Pan
Africanism*.

Marcus Garvey who had taught the black man to see 'beauty in
himself' had been in contact with many Pan Africanists, although
there were differences between them. The phenomenal growth in
membership of his Universal Negro Improvement Association in
the United States spread the idea and real possibility of this 'Black
Moses' leading oppressed black people out of American back to
their African fatherland. This vision struck deep responses among
his disciples. One such disciple was Earl Little, the father of
Malcolm X. Little's black radicalism led to him being lynched by
white racists.[1] Malcolm could not and did not want to forget his
father's commitment and the manner of his death. In turn, he also
committed himself to the cause of Blacks in America by joining the
Black Muslims. His forceful messages of black separation and black
autonomy exceeded the limits imposed by the black Muslims'
leader Elijah Muhammad. Differences of opinion led to Malcolm
X's suspension. Nonetheless he continued to preach black separation.[2] Later, in 1965, he was shot dead.

By the time of his death, he had become a figure of national and
international importance. His passing, which raised a number of
questions, stunned thousands of black people and created a vacuum
of black militant leadership. Urban deprivation, in terms of unemployment, housing, education and welfare, to some extent, reflected
parallels in British cities. Clearly, radicalism was most appealing in
these circumstances.

In 1966, after the famous Meredith Mississippi March, Stokely
Carmichael and the concept of Black Power (as we understand it
today) affected the lives of thousands of black people throughout
the United States. In line with the black leaders who had preceded

him, he too was most conscious of Africa. On the subject of 'Power and Racism' he wrote: 'This is one reason Africa has such importance: the reality of black men ruling their own nations gives blacks elsewhere a sense of possibility, of power, which they do not now have.'[3]

Between 1965 and 1971, a crucial period for black struggle, both in the United States and in Britain, Carmichael's articles and speeches record his consistent growth and development as a revolutionary activist and theoretician. He saw the civil rights movement of Dr Martin Luther King as a sort of 'buffer zone' between the liberal Whites and angry young Blacks. Predictably, the words Black Power were met with decided white hostility. Conscious of this, Carmichael explained that an organisation such as the Student Nonviolent Co-ordinating Committee which claimed to speak for the needs of a community must speak in the tone of that community, not as somebody else's buffer zone. This is the significance of Black Power as a slogan, he argued. Applying this to the situation in Britain, how right he was about the crop of accommodationist black leaders at that time. He added that such an organisation as the SNCC 'must work to provide that community with a position of strength from which to make its voice heard. This is the significance of Black Power beyond the slogan.'[4]

Carmichael felt that the economic foundations of the United States had to be shaken if black people were to take control of their lives. He had no doubt that the colonies, 'the black ghettoes' in the United States, had to be liberated. For racism to die, a totally different America must be born.

On the question of integration, Carmichael said that 'integration speaks not at all to the problem of poverty – only to the problem of blackness'.[5] Recognising his radical responses, he stated that the reconstruction of American society, 'if at all possible, is basically the responsibility of whites – not blacks'.[6] He saw as one of the major tasks of Black Power, the necessity of reclaiming black history and black identity from the 'cultural terrorism and depredation of self-justifying white guilt'.[7]

Moreover, he was careful to emphasise the concept of independent organisation within the Black Power programme. For it is only when the black community is able to control local offices, and negotiate with other groups from a position of strength that the possibility of meaningful political alliances on specific issues will be increased.[8] He warned that the 'inner city' in most urban areas was already predominantly 'Negro' and that these areas

can become concentration camps with a bitter and volatile population, whose only power is the power to destroy, or organised and powerful communities able to make constructive contributions to the total society. Without the power to control their lives and their communities, without effective political institutions through which to relate to the total society, these communities will exist in a constant state of insurrection. This is a choice that the country will have to make.[9]

Speaking to students at Berkeley in 1966, Carmichael said, 'What we have in SNCC is anti-racist racism. We are against racists. If everybody who's white sees himself as racist and sees us against him, he's speaking from his own guilt.'[10] And at Morgan State College he said the trouble with black students is that they do not read enough. 'If we could get books like we could boogaloo we would be uptight.'[11] Later in his speech he said only by eradicating the cause could rebellion be stopped. 'It is time for you to stop running away from being black', he said, and urged the college students, to think, to begin to understand that, 'as the growing intellectuals, the black intellectuals in this country, must begin to define beauty for black people.'[12] He was re-stating Garvey's message. Further, he criticised 'individualism' as being unviable; indeed, it was time to think as a people and as a group and work towards the advance of that group.

Speaking on the Dialectics of Liberation in London on 18 July 1967, he said he had 'something against England' because of all the rot he read as a young man about how good England was to Trinidad. He expressed amazement to read that England had decided to give independence to the West Indies. 'You cannot grant anybody independence', he argued, 'they just take it; and that is what white America is going to learn. No white liberal can give me anything. The only thing a white liberal can do for me is to help civilise the whites, because they need to be civilised.'[13] Moreover, he argued, given that capitalism and racism 'go hand in hand' it is necessary to understand that the SNCC's analysis of United States and international capitalism begins in race. Indeed colour and culture were, and are, the key to black oppression; therefore the SNCC's historical and economic analysis is necessarily rooted in these concepts.

He also argued that the glorious American Constitution guaranteed 'life, liberty, and the pursuit of happiness', for white men only. In fact, the black person was counted only as *three-fifths* of a person. The enslavement and colonisation of black people abroad and in the United States had laid the base and framework of institutionalised racism in America. Thus the cheap labour of Third World workers benefit the American working class. Given the double-exploitation of black people at home and abroad, the SNCC was committed to increase the revolutionary consciousness of black people in America to join with the Third World. 'We are fighting a political warfare', said Carmichael. 'Politics is war without violence. War is politics with violence.'[14] He was careful to point out that Black Power must be seen (and understood by Blacks) as a part of a new force, sometimes called the Third World. Thus, the black struggle in the

United States was closely related to the liberation struggles around the world. He pointed to the fact that American cities (and indeed British cities) are populated by people from the Third World. Although these cities were the heart of commercial trade, black people who lived there had no control over their resources. In fact, they did not control the land, the houses, or the stores. All these were owned by Whites who lived outside the community. Thus, the cry of rebellions since 1966 has been Black Power; a cry rooted in an ideology which the masses identify with instinctively. Because Blacks are powerless, they are oppressed. In effect, Black Power was an attack on racism and exploitation.

Carmichael argued that because colour has been used to oppress black people, they must now use colour (as other people have used nationality) as a weapon of liberation. But, he warned, even if racism was destroyed, exploitation would not necessarily mean the end of racism. They must both be destroyed. [15]

In a speech given at the birthday benefit party for Brother Huey P. Newton (Minister of Defence of the Black Panther Party for Self Defence) in Oakland California, on 7 February 1968, Carmichael said it was most important to understand that 'for black people the question of community is not a question of geography, it is a question of colour. . . . We have brothers in Latin America, we have brothers all over the world. And once we begin to understand that the concept of "community" is simply one of "our people", it makes no difference where we are – we are with our people and therefore we are home.' He also pointed out that while poor Whites have their culture, their values and their institutions, 'ours have been completely destroyed'. Therefore, it was necessary for Blacks in America to form alliances with people who are trying to rebuild their culture, history, dignity and honour. [16]

Further, he focused on the ideologies of Communism and socialism which concerned the class structure and its endemic oppression. He pointed out that much more than exploitation was at stake. Indeed Blacks were the victims of racism. And underlining Padmore's argument, he felt, given their 'present form', neither Communism nor socialism spoke to the problem of racism. He elaborated: 'If you were exploited by other black people, it would be a question of how we divide the profits. It is not that for us. It is a question of how we regain our humanity and begin to live as a people. We do not do that because of the effects of racism in this country. We must therefore consciously strive for an ideology which deals with racism first, and if we do that we recognize the necessity of hooking up with the 900 million black people in the world today.' [17]

Again, he reminded his audience (including Rap Brown, Jim Forman, Chico Neblett, Bobby Seale, Eldridge Cleaver, Alprentice Carter and Ron Williams) of the black diaspora, and that the Black Power struggle was an international political struggle not a national one. He said the world was heading for a 'colour clash' and the only means of survival for the black community was by organising them and orienting them towards an African ideology that speaks 'to our blackness – nothing else.'[18] Thus, black youth must be organised with a revolutionary prospectus, stating that Blacks were fighting a war of liberation.

But to do so, an ideology of nationalism was necessary. Although he specified that black nationalism 'must be our ideology', he argued that while blackness was necessary, it was not sufficient. Therefore, there must be a conscious move to organise the black communities.[19]

In true revolutionary fashion, Carmichael stated in 'The Pitfalls of Liberalism':

> So whether the liberal likes it or not, he finds himself being lumped, by the oppressed, with the oppressor – of course he is part of that group. The final confrontation, when it does come about, will of course include the liberal on the side of the oppressor. Therefore if the oppressed really wants a revolutionary change, he has no choice but to rid himself of those liberals in his rank.[20]

Carmichael had left the United States, taking the Black Power message far and wide. At the opening of the Malcolm X Liberation University in October 1969, his 'Message from Guinea' was delivered, in his absence, by Howard Fuller. He regarded the MXLU as 'one of the most fruitful and promising institutions' in the United States and fully supported the underlying concepts that had guided and directed such efforts. Ultimately, he felt that all African people must work toward the unification of Africa – in other words, the concept of Pan Africanism.[21]

From Africa, he reflected on the ten years of struggle from civil rights to Black Power, such as sit-ins, freedom rides, freedom schools, freedom organisations and community control just to develop political consciousness in black people and to point up the contradictions in American society.

For Carmichael 'Back to Africa' was not to be 'just a dream' but 'it will be a reality'. Indeed for him this became true. He now lives in Africa. Having formed the first Black Panther Party in 1965, and later resigned, Carmichael had learned the lesson of the study of history from Malcolm X, of confrontation, and the mobilisation of the masses taught by Dr Martin Luther King. In April 1970 he reminded his audience in Atlanta, Georgia, that when Malcolm X got 'offed', 'we did nothing'. But when Dr King was 'offed', 'we tore up the country'. This change he interpreted as an historical development of the people; from inaction to confrontation and armed struggle.[22] What was vitally important in bringing black people together was a common ideology.

Carmichael was aware that although many people had accepted the slogan Black Power there were others who 'tried to make it mean what they want it to mean'. Further, he argued that the highest political expression of Black Power is Pan Africanism. In effect 'Black Power meant that all Black people should come together, organise themselves and form a power base to fight for their liberation. That's Black Power.' For Carmichael then, since it was necessary to have a land base in a revolution, black people must move logically to Pan Africanism. [23]

Given Lenin's view that imperialism is the highest stage of capitalism and Nkrumah's view that neo-colonialism is the last stage of imperialism, Carmichael regarded Nkrumahism as the 'highest political expression of Pan Africanism'. Finally, Carmichael argued in 'Back to Pan Africanism' that although advocates of Pan Africanism have assured Africans in the diaspora that Pan Africanism does not mean returning to Africa, 'I refuse to do so.' [24]

Given the conditions (social, political and economic problems) that create dynamite to set ablaze the ghettoes of American cities, the goal of black self-determination and black self-identity – Black Power – is full participation in the decision-making process affecting the lives of black people. In searching for 'New Forms' Carmichael regarded a political party that sought only to 'manage conflict' as being hopelessly inadequate to the needs of a growing body of alienated black people. Uppermost in his mind, at that time, was an educational system which crippled, each year, hundreds of thousands of black children. New mechanisms of control and management were urgently necessary. In fact, it was clear to the Black Power advocates that the initiative for such changes could only come from the black community. Carmichael argued that black people should not expect white Americans to move forcefully on these problems, unless and until black Americans begin to move.

In effect, this meant that black people had to organise themselves in new ways because the traditional approaches had failed. Black Power would not be realised until black people organised independently to exert power; they should concentrate on forming independent political parties and not waste time trying to reform or convert the racist parties. Moreover, he emphasised that black visibility (token Blacks in office) was not Black Power.

Overall then, what was necessary was a new consciousness among black people. Growing disillusionment in the American government, particularly among educated Blacks in the inner cities bred a new militancy.

Liverpool: 'Negro' associations

The 'Negro' settlement in 1952

The estimated 'Negro' population in Liverpool of 4000–5000 in 1919 had increased to 5550 adult male 'Negroes' by 1950. [25] Although the Chinese, Indians, Arabs and Malays were not included in this estimate, they made up a large proportion of the total non-European population.

Since there were no reliable figures available concerning the volume of African migration during 1951 and 1952, it must be admitted that no one really knew how many 'Negroes' lived in Liverpool at this time. However, in 1952–3 the numbers of 'colonials' were 'unlikely to be greatly in excess of 1500'.[26]

This section of the black population settled in a district near the south end docks, the 'coloured quarter', from which one could walk to the docks in about half an hour. Adjacent to this quarter was a settlement of Chinese. Arabs and Indians lived interspersed among the 'Negroes', but tended to congregate closer to the docks.

This typical urban 'slum' close to the commercial and business centres and in a zone of deteriorating houses, attracted seamen of all races. They arrived at the port with food, margarine and 'ganja', and engaged in an illicit trade which gave the district a shady reputation in the public mind. While the great majority of the white and coloured residents had no connection with these rackets, one 'Negro' complained, 'we all get classed together'. Nevertheless, the alarming rate of anti-social behaviour was attributed to high rates of unemployment and sub-standard living conditions which had existed in the district for a very long time. Thus, the 'Negro' colony or the 'coloured quarter' possessed a distinct identity of its own, generally recognised by both Whites and Blacks.

The 'Negro' population's position in the economic life of Merseyside can be best seen by comparing its occupational distribution with that of Merseyside as a whole. In the following categories, the percentages for coloured workers and the populations as a whole are set out respectively: professional and administrative, 1 and 2 per cent; intermediate (owners, managers, professionals), 6 and 13 per cent; skilled workers, 18 and 52 per cent; and semi-skilled and unskilled workers, 75 and 33 per cent.[27]

'Negroes' were therefore largely engaged in unskilled work, while the majority of Whites were employed in some skilled occupation. This concentration of black workers at the bottom of the economic scale 'must have been greater before the last war brought numbers of skilled black workers into Merseyside'. Moreover, according to Maddox, the Anglo-coloured were also mainly engaged in semi-skilled and unskilled work. A few 'Negroes', however, were clerks in public transport, particularly on the railway; a number of women did clerical work for Littlewoods Football Pool Company and a few were nurses.[28] D. R. Manley, who was in Liverpool in 1952 said, as far as he knew there were 'no Negroes employed in secretarial work, no shop assistants and no professional people such as lawyers, doctors, teachers or accountants', although Maddox mentioned one doctor.

The exceptional cases were a number of 'Negroes' who owned property in the form of houses. Some of these property-owners ran 'shebeens'. Nevertheless, most Blacks lived in cramped conditions, impoverished. Unemployment and general deprivation led to dope-peddling in marijuana and prostitution. On the whole, the West Indian and West African immigrants, as wage earners, were concentrated at the bottom of the socio-economic scale.

Unemployment

Although it was difficult to estimate the rate of unemployment among the Liverpool 'Negro' population (and even more so in the case of the Africans since even less is known about immigration from Africa than was known about the inflow from the Caribbean) if one assumed that the 1953 adult population was approximately 1500, about 15 per cent was unemployed. If, however, the population had remained stationary since the 1951 Census, then the rate would be about 41 per cent. It was suggested that unemployment among Africans 'may be even higher than among West Indians'. Furthermore, unemployment rates appeared to be lower among black women than among black men. In July 1953, for example, there were no unemployed 'Anglo coloured' women in contrast to 31 men. It must however be borne in mind that not all West Indian women were seeking work; some were students or housewives, while others managed their husbands' lodging houses.

The large difference between the figures for Anglo-coloured males and females suggested very powerfully the differences in the employment opportunities between the two sexes. Most of the 'coloured' women were employed in Littlewoods Pools, in the Dunlop Rubber factory and in clothing factories. This sex difference was attributed to the structure of Liverpool's economy, in which there were 'greater employment opportunities for girls than boys'. It was also, in part, due to the fact that immigrant women encountered less resistance than did the men. [29]

The greater unemployment among 'Negroes' than among Whites was due to the former's lack of skill and to discrimination against them. The socio-economic position of the 'Negro' group was, therefore, one of low status, relatively little skill and high unemployment.

Sub-groups within the 'Negro' population: regional and tribal groups

Within the 'Negro' population there were many sub-divisions. Yet the white attitude to this population was to treat all 'Negro' groups in more or less the same way. Needless to say, this had important influences upon 'Negro' social organisation. The 'Negro' population was extremely heterogeneous in cultural background. The Census showed three main groups: West African, West Indian and locally-born Anglo-coloured. There was also a much smaller group of East African Somalis.

The West African migrants from all four British West African territories could be further subdivided into a number of tribal sub-groups, such as Tiv, Ibo, Ijaw, Yoruba, Ga, Ewo, Fanti, Asante, Kru, Mende and a number of Freetown creoles amongst others. This West African community was therefore composed of a large number of small, distinct ethnic sub-groups loosely linked by racial feeling.

On the other hand, the West Indian group was composed of immigrants from various territories in the British Caribbean with Jamaicans forming the largest single group. Finally, the Anglo-coloureds were originally the offspring of 'Negro' migrants and local white women. In 1952 there was a fairly large adult population of locally-born 'coloured' people who inter-married among themselves. The numbers increased as the group reproduced itself and received the children of 'Negro-White' and immigrant 'Anglo-coloured' children as well.

The distinction between West Africans and West Indians was not difficult to understand. Although racially allied they were however culturally 'very different'. As far as the West Indians were concerned, slavery had disrupted the culture of the West African slaves. What remained of this culture was heavily overlaid by the customs of Western Europe. Consequently, the culture of the West Indians became closely identified with Europe rather than Africa.

For the Anglo-coloured, their physical appearance served to prevent their acceptance by Whites on the one hand, while on the other, cultural differences distinguished them from the immigrants. The result was the distinct locally-born group usually called 'the half-caste'.

These three divisions among the 'Negro' population was of great importance in understanding the group's social structure. The first important consequence arising out of these culturally determined divisions could be seen in the formation of informal cliques of friends and in the organisation of various voluntary associations within the 'Negro' community. The immigrants may have rejected many aspects of their traditional culture, but had not necessarily rejected the whole of their background. Indeed, they still thought of themselves as primarily Fanti or Gold Coasters, as Ibo or Nigerians, as Jamaicans or West Indians. Thus, the newcomers firstly identified themselves with their own tribal or home group.

The West African Eru tribe occupied a special position. This group from Liberia had 'offshoots' in Sierra Leone and several West African ports. More often than not, they were employed as seamen along the West African coast. Most other Africans regarded them with some hostility because they were prepared to do the dirtiest work for the lowest wages, thus undercutting everybody else. In purely cultural terms then, the most noticeable characteristic of the 'Negro' community in general, was its highly segmented character.

Intergroup relations

Relations between these various sub-groups of the 'Negro' community were characterised by a certain amount of friction. This was clearly expressed between the three main sections of the group – the West Africans, West Indians and Anglo-coloured. The West Africans frequently complained that the West Indians 'think they are better than us'; that they were aggressive and inclined to throw their weight around. The Anglo-coloured complained that West Indians would never give money to support anything, they never worked but lived 'on women and the dole' and would 'come to the party and eat up everything'. Interestingly, West Indians themselves occasionally made similar statements about their compatriots.[30] Such statements were made by ambitious 'upward mobile' West Indians who feared that the group was 'getting a bad name'.

However, it must not be assumed that these two groups were imbued with a sense of hostility towards each other. They could not afford such hostility, since the indigenous white population did not make many distinctions between West Indians and Africans. Nevertheless, West Indians and Africans faced common problems in housing, employment and social life. In these circumstances they had no alternative but to co-operate with each other. Consequently, a feeling that all 'Negroes' should unite began to emerge. Race consciousness among politically active West Indians made them critical of Africans on the grounds that anything tending to perpetuate the division between the two groups should be eliminated. A 'race-conscious' West Indian analysed African–West Indian relations in Liverpool thus: 'The West Indian is ashamed of the African because he is backward, but at the same time he is filled with a burning desire that this were not so. So he will admire and put on a pedestal an African who can achieve a lot. Look how many people admire Nkrumah.'[31]

Two sets of factors influenced this rising 'race feeling'. Firstly, there was the sense of hostility to Whites which many immigrants seemed to have brought to Britain, in either overt or latent form, and which had increased as a result of experiences in Britain; and secondly, the fact that 'Negroes' had penetrated to some extent into the social and economic life of the community. In 1952 there was a strong feeling that all 'Negro' groups must co-operate'.

Formal associations

The formal associations organised by African and West Indians in Liverpool can be broadly classified in terms of cultural and national differences. Six associations were identified: tribal associations, national associations, racial associations, inter-racial associations, religious associations, and defunct and abortive associations. Of primary importance were the Tribal and National Associations.

Among the defunct and abortive associations in 1952 were the Colonial Defence Committee, the Anglo-Coloured Association, the Convention People's Party and the Central Council of Social Services. [32]

A reasonable average membership for these associations was 40–50. [33] All, including the tribal associations, were organised with a chairman, secretary and executive committee. Attendance at meetings of these 'Negro' associations was irregular and few people came except on special occasions. It was therefore left to those who attended regularly to run things.

Tribal and National associations The proceedings of the meetings of the tribal associations were conducted in the tribal language. In this 'closed' organisation, outsiders seeking information could only acquire it at second-hand from members of these groups. Broadly speaking, the tribal unions functioned as mutual benefit societies. They provided members with help when difficulties arose and assisted newcomers to Liverpool in finding lodgings and in registering at the Employment Exchange. Moreover, they occasionally opposed cases of racial discrimination involving one of their members and held socials and lectures. Among them there was a great desire for educational self-improvement. The fundamental activity of these tribal unions was the administration of a benevolent fund to help members in times of crisis such as sickness or a funeral.

These African tribal associations varied considerably in their ability to carry out their activities. Generally, however, the insurance and mutual aid functions predominated and were likely to be most successful among groups with a continuous culture (little disrupted by western influences) in which in-group feeling was strong. In an emergency, these groups called upon each other for assistance.

There were, at the time, four National Associations in existence: Nigerian, Sierra Leone, Somali and West Indian.

At the outset, it must be pointed out that the activities and goals of the national associations were very different from those of the tribal unions. Apart from the usual social activities and lectures, there was strong interest in political activities at home. In particular, these activities were associated with the Independence movement. Further, the mutual aid schemes (unlike the tribal associations' insurance schemes) were protest activities oriented to fight racial discrimination in Britain.

The development of 'Negro' associations until 1953 Among the major Negro associations existing in Liverpool at the time were the Merseyside West Indian Association, the Colonial Peoples Defence Association, the African Social and Technical Society, The Convention People's Party, Stanley House (the community centre), the

African Churches Mission, the Inter-racial Committee, and the Colonial Defence Committee. [34]

The Merseyside West Indian Association   In 1951 a small group of skilled workers in an ordinance factory founded the Merseyside West Indian Association. They were motivated by a deep sense of insecurity and the real fear of redundancy. They were distrustful of the English workers in the factory and felt they could not rely on the trade union or on 'working class solidarity'. The dismissal of several West Indians had moved them to organise.

In essence, these men organised themselves as representing a 'special interest' group of workers because they had no confidence in the trade union leadership. The group became a National Association with the following main objectives:

1. To foster closer co-operation among West Indians in Merseyside;
2. To promote the political and economic welfare of the West Indies;
3. To work with all existing organisations in the West Indies and Britain that are fighting on similar issues;
4. To create facilities for the furthering of the cultural development of the West Indies;
5. To tackle local issues affecting West Indians. [35]

In July 1952, the MWIA sent a representative to a conference (organised by a local clergyman with the assistance of another black organisation the Colonial Peoples' Defence Association, CPDA) on the colour question and sent delegates to a conference on race problems in Kenya. It was represented at a meeting in London to organise a British delegation to a Peace Festival in Budapest, and to the Manchester Peace Conference in 1953. [36] Also in 1952, it supported the Caribbean Labour Congress (London Branch) in a dispute with the Union of Post Office Workers over the question of promotion for 'Negro' postal workers in London. In this matter, support was confined to passing a resolution endorsing the stand taken by the CLC and sending it a copy.

The Association was particularly concerned with progressive organisations in the West Indies. The Association protested to the Colonial Office against the Trinidad and Tobago government's refusal to permit a Jamaican representative of the CLC entering the country. It was alleged that this 'representative' was endeavouring to win popular support for Seretse Khama, the African leader.

More directly, the Association attempted to establish contact with various organisations in the West Indies.

These activities showed that 'pseudo-political protest' was an important part of the Association's programme. It was clear therefore that purely local problems were only part of the Association's concerns. Equally obvious was the fact that the Association had virtually no contact with white political institutions.

Little practical benefit accrued from their activities. The leadership was primarily concerned with bringing the grievances to the attention of the authorities, and left them to take whatever action they saw fit. Needless to say, the Association was never able to influence the authorities one way or the other.

White participation and conflict   General interest, stimulated by the increase in social activity, had the effect of changing the Association's structure. The membership was broadened to include women, some of whom sat on the Social Committee. Many of these women were the white wives of West Indian members.

Nearly all the active members were 'newcomers' and the majority were Jamaicans. Moreover, a large proportion of this membership were skilled workers. While there was unity at certain levels within the Association there was also considerable rivalry arising from differences in outlook between them on questions of policy and on the most appropriate way certain issues ought to be handled.

In spite of their opposing views, the radicals and moderate factions within the MWIA did not operate as rival groups in any formal organised sense. Instead they reflected differences in temperament and outlook. Clearly there was a fear, either real or imagined, among the moderate leaders of 'progressive' elements (for example, the radicals in the Association). To them progressive was synonymous with communist. Indeed, following the attempt to make contact with the CLC in the West Indies, a few moderates including the chairman, felt that the choice of the left-wing Congress was unfortunate, 'but could not raise the issue of Communism for fear of provoking an open clash with the Radicals and perhaps splitting the Association'.[37] While this seemed admirable and responsible, the moderates went on to criticise the radicals' 'emotional attack' on the Colonial Office. Thus, the moderates revealed their primary allegiance to the status quo in a racially divided society.

The Colonial People's Defence Association   The Colonial People's Defence Association founded in October 1950 was the 'heir' of an earlier organisation, the Colonial Defence Committee which had come into being following the inter-racial disturbances of 1948. Following the disturbances, arrangements had to be made for the legal defence of the arrested 'Negroes'. Contributing towards this were two notable black organisations outside Liverpool, namely the League of Coloured Peoples and the Pan African League with headquarters in Manchester. Both organisations helped to raise funds for the men's defence. In addition, public meetings and conferences were held bringing together black leaders and 'sympathetic whites'. The links forged through these meetings led to the formation of the CDC. Although the most immediate objective was the legal defence of the arrested men none of these organisers wanted a repeat performance. Therefore, they had intended that after the trials the Committee should continue to function by promoting better race relations in the city. After the prisoners were defended and the Committee was formed it seemed the organisers were either too busy to care, or at a loss as to what to do next.

Formation of the CPDA   After the war, unemployment was the only reward for the black men who had risked their lives by serving in British and Allied ships. In peacetime these men had become a 'problem'. It was hoped that they would be employed ashore. However, many of those in their forties and fifties, did not relish the type of work that might be available.

In 1947, the Colonial Office set up an Advisory Committee to deal with migrant unemployment in Liverpool. Three years later, the Committee expressed regret that there were in Liverpool about 250 unestablished colonial seamen ashore. More significantly, they feared the possibility of large numbers being discharged from the merchant navy establishment. Were they concerned with the unemployment problem or with the prospect of a growing black presence in the city?

Before taking action to deal with these men, a case against them had to be carefully constructed and so the Committee requested what seemed like a harmless inquiry. The recommendations emphasised that a restricted number of black men be employed in accordance with merchant navy requirements and more importantly, repatriation. Further, the inquiry recommended that 'To be effective repatriation arrangements should be completed with a minimum of delay.'[38] Only about 200 men chose repatriation instead of shore work. They had earlier sensed the repatriation designs of the inquiry and now that it became explicit, between 75 and 100 men were prepared to accept offers of shore work instead. In short, the repatriation idea had outraged the black seamen. And justifiably, they feared its compulsory enforcement. Only prompt action they believed could forestall the real and impending threat to their position in the city. Unlike the CDC in which a large black group was led by a racially mixed group of leaders a new black group was formed under an all black leadership. They wanted to succeed the CDC and therefore wished to be linked with it, if only, partially, in name. Consequently, the Colonial People's Defence Association was formed:

To foster unity among the various sections of the coloured race;
To protect individual and collective interests of the coloured race;
To bring about the abolition of all forms of social discrimination;
To provide better understanding between Negro and other races in the city;

> To provide facilities for mental and racial recreation among members. [39]

All 'coloured' people including the Anglo-coloured were eligible for membership. Soon after its formation, the Association's representatives met members of the Advisory Committee and petitioned the Colonial Office, requesting that the recommendations of the Advisory Committee be rejected.

The Colonial Office assured the CPDA that no seaman would be repatriated against his will. Subsequently, two ships were manned by colonial crews. Was this result due to CPDA opposition? Clearly, CPDA members felt that their organised protest activities had exerted some influence upon the trend of events.

In March 1951 when the Labour Councillors on the City Council proposed that the City Corporations should accept black workers as municipal workers, the CPDA welcomed the proposals. Members of the Association were informed that the two trade union representatives on the Council (from the GMWU and the TGWU) were mounting strong opposition to the scheme, on the grounds that they feared an unfavourable reaction on the part of the union membership.

Later, in August that same year, the CPDA was invited to attend a meeting of the sub-committee of the Labour Party to discuss problems affecting black people. The sub-committee promised to recommend that some of the existing vacancies in the nationalised industries should be allocated to black workers; that the City Council should be further pressed to employ black workers; and that a serious attempt should be made to make it an offence to refuse employment because of racial origin. [40]

The effect of this Labour Party initiative had some influence. After the meeting, the Trades Council wrote to all the trade unions in Merseyside, informing them that they should report to the Council any case of an employer who refused employment to black workers. This monitoring of racial discrimination in employment, crucially important to the black community, was clearly an act of solidarity. For this, the CPDA was grateful. Indeed, they regarded the Trades Council's action as 'very significant', particularly because it was an admission that racial discrimination was being practised by employers, to the extent that it had seriously affected the rate of employment among black workers. This encouraged the CPDA application for affiliation to the Trades Council. Unfortunately affiliation was only open to national associations. Nevertheless, the CPDA had achieved recognition by the Labour Party and the local Trades Council.

Having gained in confidence, the Association sought the co-operation of other organisations to further the interests of its members. It established contact with the local Co-operative Party in 1952 and with the Communist Party. [41]

In addition to these two political parties, the CPDA also had contact (of an 'informal nature') with specific trade unions. A number of Association members, themselves active trade unionists, performed the role of 'informal liaison officers'. They drew the unions' attention to cases of colour discrimination and appealed for their active support of the CPDA. Here then was an example, however fleeting, of inter-racial working class co-operation.

Moreover, between 1952 and 1953, the Association dealt with a number of individual cases involving colour prejudice. And significantly, it co-operated with the MWIA in protesting against the closing of the Liverpool Branch of the Colonial Office, and in passing resolutions endorsing the CLC's stand in the Postal Workers Union dispute. Other activities included finding jobs for the unemployed, accommodation for newcomers to the city, and providing legal advice for those in need of it. Moreover, the CPDA helped to organise a Conference in 1952. The need for closer co-operation between the black and white communities was high-lighted. The CPDA's representatives argued that the 'most sensible course of action' was in reorganisation of the Executive Committee to include representatives from other Negro associations. Thus, it should be recognised as the 'official agency' representing the black population.

Having embarked on an educational programme, the CPDA's most loyal social workers were women who were integrated in an *ad hoc* way. This practice was stopped and all its social activities were organised by a special committee, the 'General Council of Women'.

This Council had far-reaching consequences for the CPDA. The entirely male-oriented organisation was broken in March 1952, when the GCW was formed. In effect, membership was open to 'all coloured women' and to the white wives of black men. Three women, two of them white, sat on the Executive Committee and an 'Anglo-coloured' woman held the post of Vice-Chairman of the CPDA.[42] The introduction of women was fully accepted. Indeed, they had 'enriched' the institutional life of the Association, essen-tially by their ability to organise 'social activities'. Significantly, no white men became members.

The African Social and Technical Society   The press reports in 1952 of large-scale economic development in Africa, particularly the Gold Coast Volta River Project, aroused great interest among Blacks in Liverpool. The skilled workers among them were most keen and hopeful of employment.

Amidst the rumour in September 1952, a small group of 'Negroes' formed an Association with the object of finding em-ployment for skilled black workers in the Gold Coast and else-where in Africa. The aims of the African Social and Technical Society were

1. To promote cultural, educational and technical knowledge;
2. To foster and promote liaison between all governments that may show interest in our aims;
3. To encourage all Africans and peoples of African descent in Merseyside and United Kingdom in general into various Civil Services of any Government that shows interest;
4. To cultivate and promote friendliness among all nations and in particular the British Commonwealth where possible and to seek such aids for technical skill and other vital occupations as may be needed;
5. To assist all charitable organisations where and when possible;
6. To exhibit from time to time and where permissible the old African plays, dances and other forms of physical education;
7. To give moral support to members and where possible render financial aid;
8. To express sympathy with all such organisations or bodies that are keenly interested in helping Africa;
9. To do all such things which are permissible by law and which will bring honour and glory to our race. [43]

The ASTS's Constitution allowed it to carry out a wide range of activities, except taking part in political protest activities. Moreover, the Society became increasingly mutual aid oriented.

On the question of white participation, the Society's Constitution expressly provided that anyone irrespective of race, colour or creed could be enrolled as an associate member. Accordingly, a dozen white women were accepted as 'associate members'. [44] They consisted of wives and women friends of members. As was the case with the MWIA, no white man ever became a member.

Although there was provision in the Constitution, some men could not overcome their suspicion of Whites. African critics were equally divided: some were willing to accept the membership of white women, while some believed that their kind of Society was 'not women's business'; therefore they should be excluded. Fortunately this was a minority view reflecting a deep prejudice against women.

In spite of the fact that 'associate member' was not precisely defined, generally these white women expected to participate in the running of social activities and 'not interfere in other matters'. In practice, however, some of them attended general meetings and voted on any motion that happened to come before a meeting. Indeed, their main activity was the organisation of socials.

The ASTS like the MWIA, sought to establish contacts with organisations in the British colonies. Their petition to the Gold Coast for example, had served to make known the Society's existence. Consequently, a list of organisations, prepared by the Executive Committee, showed that most of these organisations were in the West Indies.

In addition to personal conflicts, initially between the Chairman and various members of the Association, there were also serious differences of opinion with the Secretary and both men had to be restrained from coming to blows. Thereafter, confidence in the organisation as a whole, was shaken.

Once the Chairman's leadership was challenged and defeated, the whole structure collapsed. It was no wonder then, that the community identified the society with the personality of its leader. The inevitable consequence of his disgrace was its collapse.

The Community Centre The Community Centre (or Stanley House) founded in 1946 was situated in an area of 'heavy "Negro" settlement'. The interesting thing about this organisation is that it was first launched in 1943 by a group of prominent Whites.[45]

The membership (reaching 285 in 1954)[46] made the Centre the largest 'Negro' Association in the city. In an effort to attract more members the management relaxed its regulations. This resulted in a larger number of non-members patronising the Centre than members. The consensus within the community was that the Centre, instead of being segregated (thus running the risk of becoming a 'Little Harlem'), should be run on general inter-racial lines. But how did the Centre relate to other 'Negro' groups in the community? In fact, it had had little contact with other 'Negro' groups.

The African Churches Mission The African Churches Mission was the only church in the city, at the time, being run by 'Negroes'. Located near the docks, in 1930 it was described as containing a larger proportion of Negroes than any other part of the city. The Mission occupied a building which was in a state of 'extreme disrepair', and the Pastor and his close associates gave the general impression of 'extreme poverty'. Sunday services were usually attended by a small congregation of about twelve people which included members from all three black groups – the MWIA, ASTS and the Community Centre. West Africans were its main supporters.

Like the previous leaders mentioned, the Pastor too was subjected to severe criticism. Two things worked against him: firstly, due to advanced age and a reputation for being difficult to work with, the Pastor no longer took an active part in the various protest activities of the 'Negro' groups; secondly, he did not have much prestige among the younger better educated men who led the protest action.

The allegation that black people had been discouraged from attending white churches raised real doubts as to the value of Christianity in the minds of black people. Recalling their upbringing in the Christian churches in their respective colonial homelands, many continued to maintain a more or less conventional life-style with an emotion-charged content, particularly in view of their economic, social and political deprivation. By contrast, in Britain, the approach to religion was tinged with doubt; they were sceptical and restrained. Many became disillusioned. Most West Africans in the city had been educated in Mission schools through which they formulated their initial conceptions of life in Britain. However, they quickly realised that Christianity was associated with the ruling class. Therefore, it was not easy for them to reconcile the doctrine of 'love thy neighbour' with their hard experiences of life in a modern British industrial slum. For another thing, they did not fail to observe the fact that most white people did not attend church services, and for many of those who did, attendance was irregular. Many Blacks interpreted this as a lack of faith.

To add to their scepticism, the newcomers especially were not attracted to the image of the poverty-stricken Mission with its aged, poorly educated Pastor. Generally then, it seemed that most of these 'colonised' newcomers with strong religious beliefs attended a white church in preference to the Mission. Most of the rest attended church erratically, and some not at all. In effect, the black/white schism, revealed in both secular and religious organisations, remained a complex pattern.

The People's Convention Party   The idea of forming a branch of the Gold Coast Convention People's Party was given expression in 1952 by a man (a former law student who failed to qualify) reputed to be 'a relative of Kwame Nkrumah.'[47] This individual, 'considerably better educated' than the great majority of black people was unpopular with another section of the African community which accused him of 'living on his wits' and exploiting the people who turned to him for advice and help. Some were so distrustful of him that he was even regarded as a 'police informer'.

When he returned to Liverpool in 1952 after a trip to the Gold Coast, he announced that the leaders of the CPP had commissioned him to organise a branch of the Party in Liverpool. In spite of opposition, he began organising activities. After a few weeks of regular meetings, there were serious disagreements. Quarrels, and his 'dubious reputation' had a harmful effect on the organisation.[48] As the situation deteriorated, the CPP itself gave no assistance to its new British branch. This lack of support did not go unremarked among the leader's enemies who said that he had not really been given a mandate to organise the branch of the Party, but was simply 'working on his own'. Since he had no real proof, this remained the fundamental issue of contention. Clearly the organisation had failed to attract and hold the loyalty of the majority of members although a 'small nucleus' continued to hold occasional meetings which were largely directed to the organisation's nationalistic aspirations.

Other Organisations   Among the more important of the other 'Negro' organisations in Liverpool in 1952 were the Inter-racial

Committee and the Anglo-Coloured Association. The main result of the Conference held in July 1952 was the proposal to set up a special Committee to represent the 'coloured population'. Although by 1953, no such Committee was created, the proposal resulted in a great deal of activity, which not surprisingly was disrupted by disagreements among the various groups.

The main differences of opinion were in respect to the structure of the new Committee. Eventually, the Blacks, impatient of waiting for white approval, went ahead with their own discussions and efforts to organise the Committee.

The wide differences of opinion concerning the structure of the Committee reflected the differences inherent in the structure of the black community. It was clear that some people wished to retain their tribal and national identities, while others advocated group representation merely because they believed that co-operation would be difficult to achieve on any other basis. Others, impatient with internal divisions within the community, wished to ignore them and to organise on a purely 'racial' basis. Although several meetings were held, no synthesis of the various viewpoints was ever achieved. Consequently, the project of an Inter-racial Committee was abandoned.

The other organisation, the Anglo-Coloured Association (founded in Liverpool by a black American) was designed to provide employment for the membership by developing 'Negro'-operated shops and other undertakings. When the founder, obviously the leading light, left Liverpool, the ACA disintegrated without having achieved any of its objectives.

Associations in Africa and the West Indies   Regarding associations in Africa and the West Indies, one is mainly concerned with their development in the urban areas of these territories, since they were relevant to the essential urban conditions in which most 'Negroes' lived in Liverpool and the rest of Britain. Indeed, one was concerned with associations such as the major political parties or the larger colonial trade unions to a limited degree, since 'Negroes' in Britain during the early 1950s lacked the numbers to organise and run successfully organisations of this type. As it was, in Liverpool at least, they had not attempted to do so.

Among the African associations there is an abundance of evidence that the urbanisation of Africa had been accompanied by the formation of a large number of voluntary associations of very varied character such as tribal unions, friendly societies, occupational associations and recreational associations. Perhaps the most notable feature of these associations was the great variety of their functions, but there is some evidence that many of the new types of associations (for example, those identified as 'non-traditional') were frequently unstable and in some areas even tribal groupings had not long survived the impact of modern life.

It seemed therefore that the background of West African immigrants to Liverpool was rich in associational activities. However, a high proportion of these organisations were themselves the result of urban living and were not established in the sense of having a long history and traditions of their own.

In the West Indian context, one is particularly concerned with associations which recruited members largely from the lower class. These have been divided into two broad categories: (i) associations composed mainly of lower class members with a proportion of members of higher status levels, who hold most of the offices and run the organisation; and (ii) exclusively lower class associations. The large and influential professional and social organisations such as the Jamaican Union of Teachers or the Kingston Club, related to status and did not on the whole contribute to the West Indian population of Liverpool. Associations functioning in the urban areas were the churches of the major religious denominations, political and trade union groups, friendly societies and ratepayers' associations. Friendly societies were particularly interesting in that they appeared both in urban and rural areas and were widespread through the Caribbean. In 1946 there were 161 in Barbados and 317 in Trinidad with a total membership of over 97,000 in the former and 121,000 in the latter.

In general aim and details of structure, these societies resembled the English Friendly Societies. For example, they provided benefits at death, in sickness and in old age, and made loans. Moreover, in some cases they owned property and profits were distributed to members. In spite of these secular matters, the activities of many of these societies had a strong religious flavour.

Most of these associations were to be found in towns. In the rural areas, most group activities involving economic objectives or mutual aid, tended to be organised informally between relatives, friends and neighbours. 'Lower class' organisations had much bearing on the West Indian working class. The most characteristic type of associations created by them were the religious cults such as Pocomania (and other revivalist sects in Jamaica), Shouters in the Eastern Caribbean, and Shango in Trinidad. In addition to their religious activities, some of these groups performed functions of mutual aid. Some go much further. The Ras Tafari cult in Jamaica must be considered politico-religious for the members believe that Haile Selassie was the living God who would one day arrange their return to Africa, and that one day 'Negroes' will dominate Whites. While the Pocomania and Ras Tafari cults have been in existence for years and continue to flourish, specific groups of both types dissolved and coalesced with great rapidity. It is clear then that West Indian migrants to Britain came from a background less rich in associational structures than do West Africans. There is an accent on informality which does appear to be characteristic of Africans.

Characteristics of the 'Negro' group One of the main characteristics of the 'Negro' group as a whole was its 'highly segmented structure'. The sub-groups were further divided in terms of status and 'style of life' regarding length of residence in the city.

Within the 'Negro' community there was no basic homogeneity in outlook, manner of thought and personal habits to develop an integrated community life of their own. In fact, the concept of a 'Negro community' was misleading. Indeed, one was better able to understand the social structure of the so-called 'Liverpool Negro Community' if one regarded it as consisting initially of an agglomeration of small groups which increased in numbers as a result of immigration. Basically, these small groups had little in common, other than an awareness of their racial similarity, as distinct from the members of the host society. By 1952 the 'Negro' community in Liverpool could only be considered for historical reasons, as a community only in a very crude sense. Most 'Negroes' had closer relations with each other than with other ethnic groups. The closest relationships of an individual however were likely to be within his own tribal or national group. The 'Negro' population as a whole lacked the organisation of the institutions which were usually associated with a highly developed community life. Thus the 'Negro' population comprised a number of sub-groups. In Liverpool, they had not reached a stage where they felt as 'one people'. Indeed, the ties linking the various tribes and national organisations were tenuous and mutual jealousy was still strong. The racial feeling upon which 'Negro' (as distinct from tribal or national identifications) group feeling partly rests, was neither a new nor a local phenomenon, but merely one manifestation of a more widespread development which resulted in the organisation of conferences to discuss the problems of the 'Negro'. There was also the attempt to build a permanent organisation dedicated to the ideals of 'Negro' unity and co-operation. In 1952 co-operation between 'Negro' groups was achieved only with great difficulty. It was, however, even more difficult to maintain, never mind increase, that co-operation. Once a crisis was over, the old divisions reappeared and co-operation petered out, leaving in some cases, the group leaders without followers.

Among those factors that contributed to the formation of associations and which determined their main characteristics were traditional forms, feelings of insecurity and the need to emphasise group solidarity, assimilative drives, the degree of concentration of the group, and incidents which precipitate activity. The associations themselves fell into categories which had been described as tribal and national, for example. They could also be classified in terms of the main orientation towards the members' country of origin or towards life in Liverpool. The two types of orientation were labelled 'traditionalist' and 'modern'. [49]

As it was, the 'Negro' migrants lacked the formation of institutions which were culturally uniform groups. But it was evident that traditional tribal divisions were still an important element in the total social situation since many of them were largely tribal in composition. Indeed, the largest and most successful associations appeared to be purely tribal in character. But what was the 'Negro' associations' role in the context of inter-group relations?

The voluntary associations of all important minority groups tended to have certain basic functions, but in addition they were likely to acquire special characteristics resulting from the contact situation. Thus, the adjustment of Liverpool 'Negro' migrants and the role of their voluntary associations in the total contact situation forms a part of the wider pattern of race relations in Britain. Associations with similar characteristics occurred in other parts of the country such as the League of Coloured Peoples in London, and the Pan African League in Manchester. Similarly, there were the tribal organisations in East London, [50] the defunct Afro-West Indian Friendly Society in dockland and, since the volume of West Indian migration increased, similar associations had been formed in the 'Negro' communities of the Midlands. The League of Coloured Peoples was the only association which could be said to have had more than purely local influence and it is noteworthy that in this case, much of the leadership was of a 'traditional' West Indian type in the sense that the founder and leader of the organisation possessed personal attributes and the status to play a role which the West Indian migrants regarded, to some degree, as appropriate. Thus 'Negro' associational activities in Liverpool were similar in most aspects to their counterparts in other parts of Britain. The chief difference was that in 1952 there were more voluntary associations in Liverpool than in most other communities.

On the question of leadership, it was pointed out that immigrant groups adjusted most successfully and were likely to assimilate most rapidly if traditional and accepted leaders were present, provided the goals of the leaders were compatible with the demands of the host society. There was no traditional elite in Liverpool and in any case the ethnic composition of the 'Negro' population was so complex that the presence of a number of leaders of the traditional type might have exerted a divisive influence. A new elite had not as yet arisen in a form that was acceptable to the group as a whole, or to a major part of it, and the contact situation tended to increase difficulties of leadership on this level. The chief effect of this situation was that individuals who presented themselves as leaders tended to be regarded as self-seeking upstarts.

In general, Liverpool 'Negro' associations were similar to equivalent organisations among other ethnic groups in Britain at the time, in that they sought to maintain group solidarity, maintain contact with the past, and aid in the adjustment to new conditions.

Asian workers' associations

Pre-1969 developments

Immigrants from the Indian sub-continent living in Britain formed various associations which fell within two broad categories. First, there were those who sought to provide the cultural activities of the regional society in India, and secondly, those associations which were organised to deal directly with problems arising out of the new relationship with British society. Moreover, the first was concerned with the immigrants who operated as part of the internal structure of the immigrant community. In effect, it existed to make cultural activities possible. On the other hand, the second type of association was primarily political in that it sought to represent the immigrant community as a whole in its relations to the host society. Both types of associations provided opportunities for leadership and the exercise of authority – 'activities which are denied to, and refused by, Indian immigrants in the social organis-ation of the host society'.[51]

In October 1959 the *Bharatiya Mandala* (the Indian Association) was founded in Bradford by a student immigrant, formerly a high-school teacher in Gujarat. He and his friends began by organising a meeting to celebrate Divali (the most important festival in the Gujarat Calendar). A cultural programme was arranged and all Gujaratis in the area were invited to attend. The aim was to form a permanent cultural association which would, among other things, provide a library with Gujarati books, period-icals and newspapers, a recreational club where local Gujarati families could meet and an educational centre for children to learn to read and write Gujarati and for adults to learn the English language. Significantly, the Association had no 'political' aims.

In contrast to this organisation, there was the Indian Society of Great Britain, established in Birmingham. This organisation was a failure. Its primary object of uniting the Indian community in the area was frustrated by prolonged wrangles arising from factional loyalty.[52] In short, the difference between the Bradford and Birmingham Associations was the basic unity in the former and its absence in the latter. However, it must be remembered that unity, to some degree, existed in Bradford before the Association, and indeed, independently of it.

Film societies In towns in the Midlands and elsewhere in the United Kingdom where the Indo-Pakistanis resided in sufficient numbers (before videos became popular) local cinemas showed Indian and Pakistani films at weekends and on holidays. These shows, usually run by film societies, were also run by private enterprises and sometimes by cultural associations. The film societies were regarded as friendly societies. In fact, many film societies (in spite of legal impediments) were private business concerns. A privately-owned film society could not obtain tax exemption and other benefits if it did not register as a friendly society. Hence all film societies appeared to be democratically organised and managed friendly societies.

The Eastern Film Society was founded in January 1956 in the West Midlands where approximately 10,000 Indo-Pakistani immigrants lived.[53] The founders and members of the first Executive were Punjabi-speaking Sikhs from the Jullundur district in India, most of whom knew each other. The Society hired films from the Indian Film Society in London which, apart from showing films in London also rented its films to provincial film societies.

In promoting one of its aims of fostering education in English, the Society made donations to the Commonwealth Centre and to the West Bromwich Education Department 'for equipment for Indian and Pakistani children classes' and bought linguaphone records in English and Hindustani. Understandably, the ability to speak and write English fluently, was a major preoccupation among members of the Asian community.

By 1961, business had grown. There were four film societies in the Birmingham area. Competition for more or less the same audience led to conflict. To sum up, film societies brought together, in an essentially cultural context, Indians and Pakistanis from the various immigrant communities. The formal structure of the film societies reflected in their executive body, linguistic and regional isolation. On the other hand, the political association differed from others in that one expressed purpose was to regulate relationships between Indian immigrants and the host society.

The Indian Workers' Association: leaders and their supporters For the vast majority of immigrants from India and Pakistan, their inability to speak or write the English language posed a difficult problem in their daily life in dealing with the British bureaucratic machine. For those who could, they felt duty-bound to help their fellow villagers in the tasks of letter writing and form-filling, endemic in British life.

In the early 1950s there were not many immigrants capable of helping themselves, never mind assisting their compatriots in such time-consuming assistance.

Manmohan Singh Basra, who had come to Britain in 1953 felt the full impact of this need among his fellow-immigrants to the extent that 'he hardly had a moment to relax'. The size of the problem required the assistance of a formal organisation working systematically. Basra and a few 'socially active' Indians decided to establish such an organisation. Thus, in 1956, they founded the Indian Workers' Association in South Staffordshire. Soon after they were able to claim 150 members.[54] This name was derived from an earlier organisation.

In 1938 three Indian workers, Udham Singh (a trade union activist in the Electrical Trade union, and a delegate to the local Trades Council), Ujjager Singh, and Akbar Ali Khan formed the Indian Workers' Association in Coventry.[55] This name was carefully chosen in order to avoid confusion with the middle-class India League (formed in 1929 and primarily concerned with Indian Independence) and the Birmingham Indian Association, with a student and doctor membership. The IWA's members were Punjabi pedlars from the Midlands and factory workers in Coventry. A similar group was organised in London. Middle-class Indians, such as Gujarati doctors, who were scattered all over the country, joined local India Leagues which included many English sympathisers with the cause of Independence. Both organisations worked for the cause and co-operated with Indian students and intellectuals in London. Quite often these intellectuals provided leadership for both the Leagues and the IWA. However, the IWA was essentially trade union-oriented while the India League concentrated on politics. After playing a significant role, following Indian Independence in 1947, these Associations declined.

In effect, the IWAs were essentially voluntary associations concerned both with Indians in Britain and with the continuing ties which immigrants have with India. However, the IWAs were primarily welfare and social organisations. Membership was open to any Indian in Britain. Although they did not, in practice, represent all Indians in Britain they had the support of most Punjabis. Until about 1967, the exceptions were a few pedlars.

There were signs between 1966 and 1967 that the IWAs were weakening. New organisations had been formed. Moreover, some Punjabis won posts in prominent British organisations, and the IWAs in many areas were split. Furthermore, some IWAs found new roles while others declined in prominence.

Nevertheless by 1965 the IWAs were the most important organisations in the Punjabi communities. Interest had been intense at election time. Every two years each Punjabi community held local IWA elections. The campaigns of these Indian 'politicians' were elaborate.

Ilaqa groupings   Among the Indians in Britain during the 1950s and 1960s, village and kinship ties were all-important. Usually, IWAs consisted of immigrants from a group of adjacent villages called a 'village-kin group' because they were linked by a combination of village and kin ties. Some IWAs, however, were coalitions of two or more village-kin groups.[56]

Ilaqa (or area) ties were therefore of importance for two reasons: firstly, the pattern of friendship among the immigrants and secondly, the rules of behaviour towards those to whom one was indebted, and with whom one lived. Within each Ilaqa group a few men were influential. Family influence back in the Punjab was important. However, most leaders won popularity within their *Ilaqa* group through their activities in Britain. Many immigrants saved a great deal of money, some of which they sent home to support their families. Others invested in shops and/or houses in Britain. A man who owned many houses was able to win control over the votes of a large number of migrants who were his tenants. Thus a politically-oriented landlord was assured of support during the IWA elections.

Another kind of influence was derived through friendly relations with English foremen in factories. Those who spoke English fluently were among those who got jobs for their friends and had, in some cases, influence in the allocation of overtime. In addition, some men found a shorter road to positions of influence. They began as political activists. Such men spent much time forming friendships in public houses and engaged in speaking at public meetings and generally made themselves known by collecting IWA memberships and organising social functions, or classes to teach English to immigrants. These 'activists' however, were under enormous pressure to compromise with the influential men from their *Ilaqas* and from others.[57]

Within the IWAs there were groups and quasi-groups. While social activities brought Indian migrants from the various *Ilaqas* together there were other more important forces at work to break down the unity of these groups. One such force was the rise of men who did 'large numbers of favours' for immigrants. These 'social workers' were at a premium since few migrants had the time to do social work.

Doing social work was a recognised means of winning influence within one's *Ilaqa* group. In time, these social workers had a growing influence on migrants to the extent that they began doing favours for men outside their *Ilaqa* group. Thus a few men with no *Ilaqa* support were able to build a following based on their social work. Two such types whose jobs allowed them to spend a great deal of time doing social work were insurance agents and shop-keepers. Moreover, those who organised Indian film shows often became outstanding social workers.

Gradually, *Ilaqa* groups began to lose their political unity as the activities of social workers forged new ties which cut across *Ilaqa* lines. Simultaneously, many *Ilaqa* groups were losing their social cohesiveness. Hitherto, there were few women in Punjabi settlements. Consequently, the men lived in lodging houses. The arrival of wives and other women in the early 1960s shifted the social life in the Punjabi communities from lodging houses and pubs to private homes.[58] Thus, the shift from lodging houses to family homes not only increased but coincided with the decline of social groups composed largely of men from nearby villages.

Nevertheless, some *Ilaqas* maintained their social unity since in each Punjabi settlement there were a few *Ilaqas* which were represented by a few closely related families. The kinship ties cemented relations between these families. However, in their new environment, the pattern began to change and the larger groups of village-mates could only maintain their social unity when they were able to find a social focus. In many cases, where men from adjacent villages lived in the same Punjabi settlement, they were referred to as a 'quasi-group'. The simple distinction between the 'group' and the 'quasi-group' was made because it was becoming increasingly clear that the village-mates were no longer acting together in IWA politics. Indeed, their support was not influenced by any consideration of loyalty to the group. Nonetheless, the leader's role remained crucial. He would often mobilise his village-mates' support on the basis of personal loyalties to him for without his guidance, the villagers tended to back different candidates.

Another element in the IWA political scene was the 'action-set' used for specific occasions. The action-set was the complex of ties, individual or family, clique or work-group, and quasi-group, which surrounded an IWA politician. Moreover, action-sets were not confined to politicians.[59] Other men were able to set themselves up as opinion leaders. However, the changing pattern of association had become clear-cut – the village-mates were no longer a social or political group. Some were likely to become quasi-groups.[60] Although some questioned village loyalties as not being 'progressive', on balance the great majority of migrants remained loyal to their *Ilaqa* politicians.

Overall, in the relationship between the leaders and their followers, essentially, the ordinary Indian immigrants joined the IWAs and voted in elections because the leaders asked them to do so. Group solidarity in terms of kinship and obligation was very much in evidence.[61]

Leaders and elections in IWA politics   Within the Punjabi communities, it was clear that many leaders had independent power bases. And although loyalties based on personal obligation were rooted in kinship ties and past favours, it is equally clear that a leader could change his position (forging alliances and breaking them) 'without losing very many of his followers'. Until 1965, at least, it was particularly noticeable that almost all these 'independent' leaders in the Punjabi communities participated in the same local IWA.

Two main reasons had been advanced for the involvement of all influential Punjabis in IWA politics. Firstly, there was a strong feeling among the migrants that the Punjabi community should be united. Unity came naturally to the proud Sikhs who placed a high value on it. Secondly, their common appearance and uniform ensured easy recognition. One can easily spot a true Sikh in a crowd. Lastly a common uniform fosters brotherhood and a sense of unity in the community. Historically, the rituals of the Sikhs were prescribed not only to preserve the corporate life of the community, but also to remind the Sikh to play his part as a unit of the Panth (Community of Sikhs).[62]

Religious devotion was fused with loyalty to the community. Proud of their community, the bond of brotherhood unites them.

The second reason for the involvement of Punjabis in IWA politics was the homogeneity of the Punjabi immigrant community. According to one estimate, an overwhelming majority, some 90 per cent were of the same caste.[63] In addition, they came from a small area, having done similar work which they left for similar reasons. In Britain, they found similar jobs, and earned more or less the same wages. In effect, they faced common problems. It followed that this homogeneity of experience could best be understood, and a campaign mobilised to tackle their problems in Britain, through one organisation. Hence their united front within the culturally based IWA.

The high value of unity demanded organisation and, it seemed, the one reinforced the other. Thus it was usual to find in Punjabi communities an organised group of members working towards unity. This group was composed of Indian members of the Communist Party in Great Britain. For Indians so inclined, this was a real opportunity not to be missed, given the fact that few of those immigrants had been Party members in India where joining the Communist Party was very difficult. According to the migrants, it involved a great deal of party work and a probationary period of about two years before admission. By comparison, as one immigrant put it, 'You can join the Party in this country just by filling in a blank in the *Morning Star*', whereas in the Punjab it was 'easier to get into the IAS (India's elite Civil Service Corps) than into the Communist Party.[64]

Once in the CPGB though, there were other problems. For example, they could not speak English to the extent of participating in the party meetings. Therefore with the blessings of the CPGB they were allowed to meet separately. Thus, until 1966, in the large Punjabi communities there were two separate branches of the CPGB. In the main, these Indian CPGB branches ignored British politics. Indeed, until recently, they had few ideas about what should be done on race relations in Britain. On the other hand, the CPGB seemed too preoccupied to offer much guidance. Inevitably, the Indian Communists were more involved in the politics of India.

Apart from these pursuits, these Communists worked towards unity, organising Indian migrant associations on the basis of class interests. In time, they established a strong foothold in the IWAs. As social workers, they were particularly active. The Communist branches included both men of influence within large *Ilaqa* groups and quasi-groups which cut across *Ilaqa* lines. The Communists' willingness to work with influential non-Communists meant a large IWA membership, whenever the Communists and other allies were in power. In effect then, whether in or out of power the Communists were assured of wide-based support which contributed towards uniting the Punjabi community.

As mentioned earlier many influential migrants in the Punjabi communities became politicians while others, equally drawn into leadership positions, were either powers behind the scenes or opinion leaders. Thus, the competition for influence and prestige became structured in terms of IWA policies.

The IWA group structure   During membership drives and the first weeks of an election campaign, two alliances or 'groups' tended to emerge. The Indian branch of the local Communist Party formed the core of one group. The other alliance was known by the name of the Presidential candidate. This candidate was rarely a man of great influence within the alliance since the men wielding real power did not want any challenge from that office.

Internal dissensions within both alliances led to divisions into rival cliques. Nevertheless both groups struggled to achieve cohesiveness. In the Communist group there were ideological and personal conflicts. The basic flaw in the non-Communist groups was their *ad hoc* nature. Not surprisingly, between elections they lacked unity, essentially because they were composed of several 'cliques of politicians' who were not interested in an alliance with the Communist Party.

In a few communities the core of the non-Communist alliance was the office-holders of the local *gurdwaras* which were administered by a *Granthi* (priest).

The position that officers of a *gurdwara* held within a non-Communist alliance was not unlike the position of the Communists' branch within the Communist alliance. The bond that held *gurdwara* officers was not formal discipline but friendship resulting from working together within the *gurdwara*.

Gurdwaras were an integral part of IWA politics. Indeed it was rare for them to stay aloof or withdraw. Where the *gurdwara* was large and economically viable (indeed few achieved this) their internal politics tended to be an extension of IWA politics. *Gurdwara* elections were open to all Sikhs (by birth at least) who lived in the local community. Not surprisingly, in many instances the same politicians fought both *gurdwara* and IWA elections.

The most important features of IWA politics – the *Ilaqa* groupings, the 'social workers' and the continuous struggles for prestige – had parallels in the experience of other migrant groups. But among the Punjabis each of these institutions had a character which was quite unique.

Between 1965 and 1967 however, IWA politics including these essential features, had begun to change significantly reflecting, in part, political trends in India. They also reflected the impact of life in Britain on immigrants. There were four aspects of this influence which were very important for IWA politics: (i), the immigrant settlements were becoming permanent communities composed largely of families; (ii), individual migrants were learning how to get along in daily life without their comrades' help; (iii), the Punjabi communities were becoming differentiated along caste, religious, class and educational lines; and (iv), the migrants were increasingly aware of their low status in British society. [65]

Punjabi immigrant politics The political situations in Southall, Coventry and Birmingham were dissimilar. At one time, the Coventry Punjabis were the only community without a splinter IWA. This unity, however, was shattered and by the summer of 1967, there were two IWAs in Coventry and there seemed little hope of reconciliation. Both organisations continued with such activities as social work, campaigning during Indian elections and holding celebrations. [66]

In Birmingham, there were indications that the Punjabi communities would develop organisations which were essentially concerned with combating racial discrimination in Britain. In Birmingham also there was a split which put one of the IWAs out of action for several months. The other IWA, the IWA–GB–Birmingham remained active. This group had 'sophisticated leaders' who took a militant stand on race relations. The branch condemned the Labour government's policy on immigration as 'racialist' and refused to participate in the National Committee for Commonwealth Immigrants. These leaders wanted a concerted effort to build support for their position among the Punjabis in the Midlands. In doing so, they organised protest meetings and marches. This last method was radical – a clear shift from traditional methods.

The situation in Southall was, however, different. The alliances there had, by 1968, split into at least eight small cliques, all competing for control of the same IWA. [67] In addition, the minority castes and religious groups formed their own associations. Their officials, however, competed in IWA elections as new 'groups'. Furthermore, in Southall there were other formal organisations including a literary society and a number of *gurdwaras*, and caste associations. Apart from one very large *gurdwara*, almost all of the activists in Southall were involved in IWA politics in one way or another. It was not difficult to see why. The Southall Punjabi community was one of the largest in the country, and it was more concentrated in terms of area than the other large Punjabi communities. For many years the IWA Southall was alone in running Indian film shows in Southall, shows which were profitable. Indeed, at that time, the Southall IWA was the only IWA which owned an office as well as a cinema. In effect, the IWA-Southall towered over the rival associations, reducing them to playing a supporting role in terms of power and influence.

Generally, in towns where the IWA had no control over a cinema or church, the local associations were likely to go the way of the Coventry IWA. A few were also likely to follow in the militant footsteps of the Birmingham IWA–GB. Looking ahead, the number that were likely to follow the Birmingham pattern was dependent on the extent of racial discrimination and the course this was likely to follow.

Relations with British organisations During the sixties, the IWA leaders faced many difficulties when they became involved in trade unions, constituency Labour Parties, or inter-racial committees such as the Voluntary Liaison Committees supported by the NCCI.

As a result of the British government's concern with black immigrants (and immigration) by giving financial support to the Voluntary Liaison Committees (VLCs), Punjabi leaders had more opportunities to serve on such bodies. The willingness of these immigrant leaders to participate, reflected the growing pressure and concern over racial discrimination in the immigrant community. Their participation, however, was effectively contained by these British-dominated organisations. This was the dilemma facing the IWA leaders who were involved in three kinds of associations, namely the trade unions, constituency Labour Parties and inter-racial committees.

The IWAs and trade unions The trade unions had, above all British institutions, the closest contacts with the largest number of adult Punjabis. As workers, the Punjabis came face to face with British working class values and patterns of behaviour. In the uneasy relationship between the unions and the immigrants the occasional Indian shop steward was pivotal; a double-liaison. He not only had to be a workmate and leader within his work group, but he also had to come to terms with white trade union officials and foremen and with his role as shop steward. Inevitably, there were conflicts, and the IWA had a role to play in relating to its members as workers and shop stewards, and with white trade unionists.

Punjabi workers were engaged in two kinds of work situation: working with Whites as bus drivers, conductors and factory workers and working in shops which included only migrants. Some of these shops employed only Punjabis. Most of these all-immigrant shops fell into one of two further classes. The workers were either members of the TGWU or were left at the mercy of a *padrone* system.[68] Under this system the foreman exacted bribes with the co-operation of the informal leaders of the workers.

A commonly held view at the time was that IWAs had organised trade unions in shops where there were none, thus resisting the *padrone* system. But, according to De Witt, 'These claims must be taken with a grain of salt.' Clearly, an attempt at union organisation could only be successful if the workers were united and willing to take strike action. This unity of action could not be achieved without the support of the workers' informal leaders.

IWA politicians were particularly hampered in trying to organise unions, since a move in this direction was likely to be viewed as a leader trying to gain prestige within the community. Naturally, a rival would block such an attempt. Ultimately, a pro-union organiser was laid open to the charge that he was not interested in the union itself but in making a personal challenge to the *padrones*.

Race relations and IWA politics In the summer of 1967, a debate within the Punjabi communities led, on the one hand, by the officers of the IWA–GB Birmingham and, on the other, by the officers of the IWA–Southall, resulted in disagreement on two related questions: who were the enemies of the migrants? and what role should the IWAs play in the process of acceptance?

The leaders of the two IWAs agreed that the migrants were threatened by 'racialists' who were to be found not only in extremist movements but also in the Labour and Conservative Parties. They also agreed that many 'respectable politicians' had not done enough to oppose the racialists and cited the Commonwealth Immigration Acts and the Labour government's White Paper on immigration as examples. They regarded both as racialist documents. While both groups of leaders recognised that they were also white sympathisers, in the trade union movement and in the VLCs, and felt that the Punjabis should co-operate with them, they disagreed over the fundamental attitude of the Labour government, and over the stand taken towards the Government, the NCCI and the Labour Party.

The IWA–Southall, though critical of the Labour government, had given loyal support to Labour candidates in elections. In 1966, for example, its officers advised Punjabis in Southall to vote for the Labour Party candidate but cautioned: 'We ask you (to vote for Labour) despite the deeply critical feelings most migrants hold, and which we share, of some of the Labour government's legislation. This is particularly so in regards to the White Paper which is racially biased, and which we will fight to get withdrawn.'[69]

Moreover, the Southall leaders supported the NCCI and CARD (Campaign Against Racial Discrimination). In the summer of 1967, members of the Southall Executive Committee had begun to serve on Committees of both these organisations, and the IWA–Southall was finally affiliated to CARD. Earlier in the summer of 1966, the IWA–Southall and CARD were co-sponsors of a project which brought several university students to the Southall Punjabi community for several weeks. (More of this kind of movement towards the grass-roots was sadly lacking in the CARD organisation.)

By contrast, the leaders of the IWA–GB Birmingham Branch,

condemned both the Labour government's anti-immigration policy and racialist foreign policy, stating:

> In July 1962, the Government enacted legislation known as the Commonwealth Immigrants Act as a measure supposedly designed to control immigration, but which in fact laid the blame for the government's failing housing and employment policies at the door of coloured immigrants.
>
> Since the racialist Commonwealth Immigrant's Act had been enforced race relations in Britain have deteriorated. Racial discrimination has been intensified and racialist organisations have been encouraged. Racialism has been used to attract the voters in local and the last two General Elections and coloured immigrants have been made the scapegoats. . . .
>
> The attempts made to improve race relations in Britain were in fact aimed at whitewashing the Government's anti-colour policy. Under pressure the Race Relations Act was watered down and the freedom to discriminate still remained.
>
> The setting up of the NCCI was an attempt to misdirect the activities of many well meaning people. It has attempted to pacify the national minorities 'and their allies' resistance to racialism.

From a leaflet announcing a protest march and rally against the Commonwealth Immigrants Act in Birmingham on 2 July 1967, the sponsors of the rally were listed as: 'IWA–GB (Birmingham, Coventry and Leamington branches), Akali Party JK; CCARD; CND West Midlands Region; Association of Indian Communists GB; Pakistani Workers Association; Pakistani Welfare Association; West Indian WA.'

The meeting was chaired by the Secretary of the IWA–GB, Birmingham branch and most of the audience was Punjabi.[70]

Pursuing this militant line, the General Secretary of the Birmingham branch refused an invitation to serve on a panel (subcommittee) of the NCCI. Further, the Branch refused to endorse two Labour candidates in the 1966 General Elections and moreover the IWA publicly stated that in the last general election they supported the Labour Party in the belief that, if elected, they would remove the racial basis of the Commonwealth Immigrants Act of 1962. But all such hopes had been dashed. However, they had met two local Labour MPs and questioned them on their present positions vis-à-vis the assurances they gave before the last election. They were particularly concerned that Roy Hattersley was honest about completely 'changing his mind' and that Brian Walden was honest in admitting the desertion of principles by his Party, but was not prepared to vote against his government.[71]

The main area of disagreement then between the IWA–Southall and the IWA–GB, Birmingham was on how best to influence the British to accept the migrants and to eliminate racial discrimination. At least until the end of 1967, the Southall leaders trusted the

NCCI and CARD to bring pressure to bear on the government to pass anti-discrimination legislation. But the Birmingham leaders had foreseen the difficulty in this, since by introducing such legislation the Labour Party would run the electoral risk of seeming to favour the migrants. Black migrants and immigration control were the key issues in British politics at the time. In this political climate all parties were likely to shift the blame (as indeed some were actively doing) for Britain's economic difficulties to black migrants. Thus, sympathetic British organisations and individuals paled into insignificance as the migrants intensified their own efforts to deal with racial discrimination. In so doing, there were internal problems to overcome.

The Southall leaders criticised this approach of the IWA–GB Birmingham for two reasons: that it ignored the real possibility of influencing the Labour government through the NCCI and CARD and that by insisting on militancy it alienated many prominent Punjabis and thus split the Punjabi communities.

In reply, the Birmingham leaders interpreted the Southall leaders' arguments as the excuses of opportunists concerned with securing prestigious posts for themselves on inter-racial committees. By doing this, they were ignoring the real interests of the migrants and thereby dividing the Punjabis.

Since both groups were concerned with Punjabi unity, perhaps the best way to reflect their differences was to categorise them as 'militants' and 'moderates'. Not surprisingly, this neat division was contested by some of the Southall leaders who argued that there was no difference between their militancy and that of the Birmingham leaders, but that theirs was not directed towards friendly Whites. While clear-cut militant and moderate positions had developed, there was as yet no national polarisation along these lines.

By the end of 1967, it was obvious that the IWA–GB, Birmingham was the only IWA in Britain to have taken all these militant positions. One reason advanced for this militancy was the possibility that race relations was worse in the Birmingham area than anywhere else in Britain. [72]

Given the stage of development reached between 1967 and 1968, it was not clear whether the Birmingham leaders would be able to build a national militant movement. While most Punjabis recognised that racial discrimination existed (indeed they were the victims) they had managed to ignore it. The cumulative effect of unexpressed resentment was building into a highly combustible element in British industrial relations, as racial disadvantage at work became increasingly unbearable. Thus, much of the attention of Asian workers shifted to their common problems (as a group), from the *gurdwaras* and the IWAs as the major organisations of Punjabi workers until 1967, to the struggles of the Asian workers' experience which brought about a greater degree of militancy among Asian workers as the 1960s ended and the 1970s began. Generally, the IWAs retained their insular role of 'social work' and personal influences were being superseded as young militant workers became the vanguard of the struggle; a struggle focused on the workplace where Indian, Pakistani and African Asian workers took an unprecedented and militant stand.

The Asian workers' struggle and the IWAs, 1968–1981

New perspectives on the Asian struggle: the 1970s

It is an established fact that the migrants from India and Pakistan who came to Britain in the late 1950s and early 1960s laboured where the work was tedious, dangerous, low paid and quite hopeless for any person with initiative or talent. For example, at the Courtaulds Red Scar Mills in Preston, a rayon spinning mill, Asians first sought and got jobs in 1956. By 1964, a third of all the workers at the mill were Asians. In fact, two departments were manned entirely by immigrants organised in ethnic work teams under white supervisors.

In Southall, West London, the 350 Asians in 1951 had increased by the mid-1960s to 12 per cent of the area's population. This Asian workforce was in the main employed in four factories. By 1965, 90 per cent of all unskilled labour at Woolfs' factory was Punjabi Sikh.[73] The introduction of Asian workers in these factories had far-reaching consequences for British industrial relations. At Courtaulds in Preston, and at Woolfs in Southall, the confrontations between workers and employers became significant in the history of immigrant labour in Britain. The battles fought in these factories were repeated elsewhere. In time, the pattern of industrial struggle of the Asian workforce was clear. The arrival of Asian immigrants from Africa, during the second phase of immigration in the early 1970s inevitably intensified the industrial conflict at these flashpoints. At the Mansfield Hosiery Mills in Loughborough in 1972, at Imperial Typewriters in Leicester in 1974, and at Grunwick in 1978, Asian workers, largely from African backgrounds (Kenya and Uganda) came out in open rebellion. In effect, they organised against their oppressive employers.

Predictably, profits depended upon long working hours, overtime, low wages, and on constant strategies to step-up production. While profits have always been made from surplus labour value, in the Asian workers' case, this surplus of profits was extracted with a ruthlessness which the white labour force would not tolerate. In fact, the Asians went where there was a shortage of white labour willing to accept unduly long hours of work.

This separation of black workers into the lower paid and more demanding jobs was an integral part of the 'colonial relationship' which British industry had established with its new workforce. Because of this strategy, in many factories Asian workers had to contend with a lack of promotion. In the 1960s, very few Asians found promotion to supervisory posts. In many factories they worked in gangs under the control of one white charge-hand who allocated work, dispensed overtime, recommended the hire and fire of migrant workers and, in many cases, he was prone to take bribes. It is therefore not difficult to imagine the real power he had in playing off one migrant worker against another. This 'ghettoisation' of labour also led to lumping all Asian workers together regardless of their qualifications or background.

It was after the first wave of industrial unrest that the distinctions were created. A separation was made between the 'militants' and the 'moderates'. (Note the separation of the militants in the Birmingham/Midlands area, and the moderates in Southall, and between the political activists and their followers.) This was being clearly reflected in the IWAs' politics of the late 1960s. Indeed, it was in the industrial struggle that management realised that Pakistanis and Indians had political allegiances which may keep one section working while the other was on strike.

The IWAs in the 1970s and 1980s

During the 1960s, the IWAs played an instrumental part especially in the early years of the struggle. In many instances, it supported shopfloor revolts, and pronounced and demonstrated on issues affecting the immigrant Asian population. However, its intervention as a positive force in the newly emerging independent movement of black workers was severely restricted in that its mass base was confined to Punjabi workers. Moreover, the inherent splits in its political allegiances, along lines of fracture in the Indian political scene, made it an unacceptable vehicle for the struggles of Asians from the African continent who had entered the British industrial scene in the 1970s. Furthermore, it was unacceptable to the young Asians who were born or were growing up in Britain.

The IWA had been unable to accommodate the demands of Asian youth in Britain. As a political and industrial force, the IWAs peaked in the mid- and late 1960s. In the 1970s, it inevitably began to degenerate into the position of mediator and into 'downright conservative leadership – seeking reaction'.[74] Because of the essential nature of its activities, there was hardly any need to apply foresight to establishing an independent Asian struggle in Britain. Instead, the main associations tended to hark back to India, ignoring the immediate problems of Asian workers in Britain.

As the number of strikes in the Birmingham area increased, the IWA (Marxist–Leninists) led by Jagmohan Joshi were called upon to provide leadership in the industrial struggle. In doing so, these radicals 'out of courage, vision and necessity' were able to incorporate the emerging Black Power ideology that was generating militant revolutionary organisation among young West Indians and Africans.[75] For some of the IWA activists, Black Power was somewhat difficult to accept. This was surprising since their leadership seemed to champion it. There were, however, connections between the IWA and the Black Panther Movement, the Black Unity and Freedom Party and other black groups.

In 1971 when the Black Panther Movement called a National Conference on the Rights of Black People at Alexandra Palace in London, the IWA sent a 'grudging delegation' which arrived in a coach from Birmingham.

The disappointed delegation returned to Birmingham. As an essentially Asian organisation, they were willing to co-operate with West Indians under the political label 'black', but since there was no analysis of imperialism and no ideological denunciation of the Soviet Union, they could not participate. Indeed, they had the confidence of having organised a conference of militants from the factories in the Midlands who had been on strike during the previous two years. After this, they did not make common cause with the West Indian organisations for some time except when delegations from both communities met to demonstrate against the anti-immigration legislations in London in 1968 and in 1970. By the end of the 1970s and the beginning of the 1980s, however, Afro-Asian solidarity was much in evidence. On these occasions the solidarity was impressive: coaches came from Birmingham and contingents set out from Brixton and Notting Hill to denounce the Wilson government as racist. The most massive of these demonstrations was against the Kenyan Asian Bill which was passed by the Labour government in record time.

Elsewhere, in Leicester 4000 marched against Callaghan's Bill. Indeed, the IWA (predominantly the CP Marxist wing) was the motive force mobilising the Asian community and bringing together the student and organised left-wing sections of white society. The Whites marched under the banners of the Communist Party, the International Socialists and as trade union officials, obviously not reflecting rank and file feeling. The West Indians, in a minority, followed the Black Power groups. Finally, in the demonstrations, the Asians forming the largest community groupings from Birmingham, Southall, Leamington Spa, Derby, Coventry and Leicester, followed the banners of the IWA.

Historically, the IWA (in spite of supportive action) was never the prime moving militant force in any industrial struggle. For example, in the 1960s only after workers had initiated action to confront management by joining their trade unions (and demanding representation) did the IWA offer assistance. By the 1970s, with the settlement of the African Asians, on whose behalf the IWA had demonstrated and agitated, a new force confronted and challenged them. In fact, the IWA gave this new workforce minimal support, and in a few cases, 'blundered into opposing the impatience and independence of this new battalion on the Asian industrial front'.[76]

The struggle of African Asians

Most African Asians who arrived in Britain became labourers in British factories and in a few years of militant action changed the course of the Asian workers' struggle. Although new to the discipline of factory shift work, through their heightened awareness of exploitation and racial injustice, they carried through the industrial struggles of Mansfield Hosiery Mills in Loughborough in 1973, the Imperial Typewriters strike in Leicester in 1974 and the Grunwick strike in Willesden during 1976–1977.

A significant feature of these struggles was that large numbers of women who had not previously done a day's paid labour outside the home were forced by economic necessity to seek employment in factories. They filled the labour-vacuum created in jobs abandoned by white workers. In these struggles, the Asian workers initiated the action and then approached their unions for official help. Their causes posed many challenges to British working class solidarity.

The Standing Conference of West Indian Organisations

The West Indian Standing Conference (hereafter referred to as Standing Conference or Conference) was formed as a result of the impetus of the race 'riots' in Nottingham and in Notting Hill in 1958. These disturbances brought to the fore the fact that race relations in Britain were deteriorating and prejudice and discrimination were widespread. This had repercussions on the High Commission of the newly Federated Government of the West Indies. The Migrant Services Division of the Commission, through its Community Development Section felt that West Indians in London and throughout Britain, faced general problems requiring collective action. Accordingly, two Community Development officers (Edward Burke and Ms Gregory) came to London from the West Indies. They worked in conjunction with officers of the Migrant Services Division to bring together leaders of West Indian social, religious and cultural groups, to start 'Standing Conference'.[77]

In 1959 Standing Conference under the control of High Commission officers met. Thereafter, its work was 'inspired' by the help of the Community Development officers. By the end of that year, a constitution was prepared and representatives from the constituent unions elected their leaders.

The aims and objects as provided in the constitution were that Conference was established to be a channel of communication between the existing West Indian organisations in the London region and between these organisations and the High Commission; to develop leadership among the West Indian community and to help these leaders with organisational problems, and to foster integration and improve relations between the races. [78]

Each organisation affiliated to Standing Conference had its own constitution, functions, executive committee and sources of revenue. By the middle of 1961, eighteen organisations had affiliated to Standing Conference. [79]

During the early years, however, some tension had existed between the leaders of Standing Conference and the members of the High Commission. The fact that Burke and Gregory no longer worked with Standing Conference led to misunderstandings between the civil servants in the MSD and the Conference officers. A feeling of unease arose from a lack of recognition of the 'independence' of Standing Conference as the High Commission tried to exercise control over the member groups. This factor would continue to preoccupy Conference leaders.

Two events in 1962 caused a significant shift in Conference's position. They were the break-up of the West Indies Federation (after the September 1961 referendum in Jamaica resulting in a move to seek Independence), which made redundant the High Commission and its subordinate bodies, and the passage of the Commonwealth Immigration Act which severely reduced West Indian immigration to Britain. Confronted with these developments, Conference was forced to adopt a new programme of independent action to unite the West Indian community in London.

Whatever belief there was among Standing Conference members in the goodwill of British society was weakened by both the passage of the Commonwealth Immigration Bill and attacks by racialist spokesmen Oswald Mosley and Cyril Osborne. Prejudice and discrimination had to be counteracted, and if 'integration' was to take place it had to be on terms of 'equal partnership'.

This change of mood came after 1962. A few Conference leaders were suspicious, distrustful and angry. This generated increased pride among some of Conference's officers, especially Laidlow, Crawford and Maxwell. [80]

These leaders were committed to making Conference an independent organisation, free of white participation on the Executive Committee. Historically, in 1959, two out of six EC members were white. This had increased to three out of nine in 1960 when more positions were created; and to four out of nine in 1961 and 1962. The white members had come from the multi-racial organisations affiliated to Conference, during its early life. At that time, the inter-racial aspect of Conference was considered important. However, given the changed mood of Conference, white members on the EC thought it best to leave, and after 1963, no 'European' members sat on the Executive Committee.

Furthermore, in this mood of independence, although the new

constitution (rewritten after the collapse of the West Indian Federation) urged co-operation with the MSDs of all the various West Indian governments, in practice, contact was irregular.

Research work on West Indian immigrants (a thriving industry) aroused suspicion and distrust. Standing Conference fought shy of such observers as those working on the Institute of Race Relations 'Survey of Race Relations' and sharply criticised Sheila Patterson's study of Brixton. [81]

Together, the new mood, the different approach to the High Commission and the antipathy towards research formed the background for approaching 'integration' differently. After Notting Hill, the 'tea and bun' approach was no longer viable. Inter-racial gatherings were no substitute for 'real opportunities'. For Maxwell 'Integration must of necessity be a game for two . . . each respecting the other's dignity as a human being and recognising merit where it exists – with no reservations'. [82]

In achieving 'equal partnership', as a basis for 'integration' it was important that the West Indian community should develop its self-respect and self-sufficiency. Tolerance and goodwill, so far as these went, were woefully inadequate. Economic development was vital. Towards this end, Maxwell suggested that credit unions, consumer co-operatives, investment societies, housing and business associations should be developed. Politically, he urged West Indians to exert their group influence. And culturally, development of a sense of 'negritude' was the pre-condition for 'cultural independence'.

One of the major problems facing Standing Conference was inherent in its structure: its dependence upon the affiliated groups for support and active participation. In effect, this placed constraint on decisive action by the 'new breed' of Standing Conference officers. These mixed groups had black and white members and also engaged in a range of activity. In the spring of 1967, six of the fifteen affiliated organisations in 1966 had multi-racial membership. [83] Four were regarded as having a mixed membership ranging between 'middle class' and 'working class'; one was 'middle class'; and the rest as 'working class'.

Many of the leading officers were also active in the churches. Indeed, Christian fellowship and worship constituted an integral part of the West Indian community. Thus, informal welfare work was accepted as part of their leadership role. They made representations on behalf of individuals, to authorities, landlords and employers. Politics, however, was kept at a safe distance. Although there was a good deal of political discussion, significantly, there was no involvement in voter registration or canvassing.

In spite of the pronouncements of Conference leaders, by 1967, there was little community development or the desired cohesion of organisations for co-operative action. For example, the development of economic goals was attempted by only three groups, and co-operation through anti-discrimination work at regional level was yet to be established. Moreover, these groups showed no interest in local council and parliamentary elections, and made little or no effort to register voters or lobby Parliament. They did, however, press for extension of the Race Relations Act.

Given the increasing incidence of police harassment and widespread discrimination in housing, it was not surprising that Conference leaders devoted much time attending to individual cases involving the police and landlords. While their representations were useful, Conference could perform only limited functions; it lacked a strong organisation with premises of its own, money and a secretariat. Consequently, internal development of the organisation and crucial anti-discrimination work evolved haphazardly.

Problems of organisation and leadership

A few of Standing Conference's leaders were acutely aware of the organisational problems, due to the federal structure of the organisation which undermined the group. The lack of commitment to advance Conference activities was pronounced and meant that the predominant groups, essentially 'social in nature', were reluctant to follow the Conference leaders. Many group leaders were reluctant to re-orient their leadership and their groups to problems common to all West Indians.

The dilemma for the Standing Conference leadership was the fact that these leaders were invested with the ultimate authority of Conference. Given the multiplicity of interests of the constituent groups, when Conference was faced with taking action on an important issue such as the union with the Birmingham Conference, it was difficult to reach unanimity.

Apart from organising the constituent groups, Conference faced the more general problem of organising West Indians in Britain. Reluctant to admit the problem to non-West Indians, nevertheless among themselves they were critical of West Indian apathy. Regional and island conflicts, class and status orientations were especially divisive. [84] In general, these explanations for West Indian organisational difficulties suggested the patterns which frustrated the leaders of Standing Conference. In spite of the historical difficulties that Conference faced, the more politically-oriented officers were deeply concerned. A number of traits had to be combatted.

Maxwell cited 'The Problems of Individualism'. He argued that it was necessary to voluntarily surrender 'a little part of one's freedom and resources for the preservation and progress of the whole'. Standing Conference represented in embryo the making of a truly great organisation, but needed the participation of the whole community. [85] On 'apathy and leadership' he pinpointed a rejection of leadership and a refusal to support those who were willing to lead.

Maxwell, especially concerned about the 'general low level of organisation among West Indians', put forward several reasons for 'this woeful disorganisation'. Firstly, he felt that 'bread and butter issues' took precedence over people's lives. Consequently, they had little time for group work; secondly, there was a 'lack of awareness of the benefits that can be derived from an organised community'. He attributed this, in part, to the narrow vision and the complacent attitude that (despite the difficulties in Britain) the standard of living might still be slightly higher than in the West Indies. Far more serious, however, was the 'individualism' or selfishness with which the West Indian was richly endowed. He made the important observation that this 'individualism' had been due to cynicism about the value of leaders and groups. [86] Moreover, there was a lack of national consciousness.

These traits, fully understood by a few of Conference leaders, became a source of frustration. Clearly these leaders had to overcome formidable obstacles: to encourage self-pride in an oppressed people and develop economic and social strengths. According to Maxwell, leadership of the West Indian community (and particularly 'Negro leadership') at both national and local levels required such qualities as 'foresight, enterprise, tact, patience, the art of persuading others and an absolute dedication to Negritude'. [87] More importantly, he added, leaders needed two special qualities: independence of thought and action and the ability to identify completely with rank and file West Indians.

The trend of disorganisation had become a central theme consistent with the theme of 'Independence' which was always seen by Conference as a desirable state, though its implications remained unexplored. The message was clear: not only would West Indians as immigrants have to adjust as strangers to a new society, but at the same time they would have to preserve their self-respect and develop a complex configuration of attitudes, values and beliefs by which they could preserve their own individuality. Yet the problem for Conference leaders was to reach a large number of West Indians. However, while 'Negritude' and 'Africanism' suggested a general orientation, it did not directly relate to all West Indians in Britain. Moreover, achieving 'cultural' independence underlined the obvious difficulties of eventual 'assimilation' through integration. A major factor which inhibited West Indian organisational development in Britain was the duality of West Indian attitudes; that is, should they take part in separate or 'joint' integrated organisations? [88]

The problem for Conference was whether West Indians would gain an 'equal place in society' through independence or co-operation with British organisations. This remained unresolved, reflecting an ambivalence or seriously conflicting views among the officers of Conference. Undoubtedly, it seemed that most of Standing Conference executive committee, from the most active and political to the more conservative, wanted their organisation to be recognised by Englishmen. More than that they wanted to be independent. Their isolation and powerlessness led to frustration and anger. Thus what seemed like extreme behaviour was counteracted by some. The less active Conference members allied themselves to British organisations, hoping to gain acceptance. This dual approach split the ranks and leadership of the Conference. The debilitating effect of this became evident when the more active leaders of Conference joined the other immigrant groups to oppose the NCCI while both the Conference executive and the delegates' meeting voted to recognise the NCCI. Therein lay the paradox of the powerlessness of Standing Conference.

Organisation from the top: CARD

'The organisation of organisations'

In December 1964 the Campaign Against Racial Discrimination was founded 'to speak for a social and political movement that did not exist'.[89] It was designed to bring together disparate black migrant groups in order to press for changes in national policy. Furthermore, CARD was expected to persuade those in power to act in such a way that would benefit those who were powerless. CARD's predecessor, The League of Coloured Peoples, had attempted to unify 'coloured' citizens in Britain before and after the Second World War. Indeed, it was largely concerned with fighting the colour bar and altering the colonial system.

The one million black immigrant population in Britain by the mid-1960s was divided into three main nationality groups: Indian, Pakistani and West Indian. Their lives were commonly affected by racial discrimination. Many individuals (journalists, academics and MPs) showed concern, but no political organisation or pressure group existed to represent the three main nationalities to those in power. The commonality of experience, and all-pervasive discrimination, the founders of CARD hoped would draw together Indians, Pakistanis and West Indians to form a strong organisation. CARD would try to change the pattern of public policy at both national and local levels by

> eliminating discriminatory legislation (regarding immigration controls); insuring equal opportunity in vital areas like employment and housing through passage of an anti-discrimination legislation; pressing for broad social and economic policies that would promote social equality for all people in lower income classes; policing the administration of existing social and economic programmes to make sure that immigrants were not adversely affected by them.

Moreover, CARD tried to mobilise, organise and represent immigrants and their children. Thus, CARD had two broad sets of relationships; with those in the immigrant communities and within the immigrant organisations that it wanted to mobilise and with those who had the power necessary for the alteration of public policy. In a sense, CARD attempted to become a 'pressure group'.

Given that immigrants suffered from problems of race and class, CARD's aims were to defend the interest of black immigrants and their children against discrimination and to promote the cause of 'general social reconstruction and social equality in Britain by emphasising the need for the public and private sectors to provide better housing, jobs, education, medical care, and other social services for a number of British citizens; not just immigrants'. It was hoped that by advancing the cause of greater social equality CARD would be able at least to counter some of the causes of discrimination, if not remove them.

In trying both to promote a cause and to represent an interest, CARD was to be a coalition, a union of nationalities, races, classes, languages, cultures, religions, and political beliefs. They faced many difficulties. In the formative period, the outline of the organisation was by no means clear. However, two things were obvious: legislation against discrimination was necessary and organising and involving the immigrant in the CARD structure were imperative. These were the guidelines for the Campaign Against Racial Discrimination.

Origins

Powerless, Blacks in Britain continued to seek, through organisation, redress for their basic grievances. The arrival of Dr Martin Luther King, Jnr. in London on 5 December 1964 was a significant event. On his way to Stockholm to receive the Nobel Peace Prize for leadership of the Civil Rights movement in the United States, King preached at St Paul's cathedral and was widely quoted in the British press. At a meeting organised by Canon John Collins of Christian Action, he spoke on American race relations. He warned of Britain's racial problems becoming 'tragic and intractable' if they were not publicised and dealt with.

While in London, he also met 30 Commonwealth immigrants and a few white sympathisers. Encouraged, following his departure, this immigrant group decided to form an organisation to speak on behalf of all coloured people in Britain. Incidentally, the League of Coloured Peoples founded by the middle-class doctor, Harold Moody in 1933 also had this aim, but it did not have a mass rank and file following. This was its weakness. Would CARD learn from this mistake? In fact, many of the founder members of CARD were of middle class backgrounds whose commitment to the black working class was undoubted. It was understood that the setting up of CARD had to be initially a job for professionals and intellectuals; those socially and politically committed to the cause of redressing inequality inherent in the structured racism of British society.

Clearly, King's visit acted as a catalyst, but the impetus for the then unnamed organisation did not emanate from King. In fact, this came from a West Indian, Ms Marion Glean, who was not only a member of the Society of Friends Race Relations Committee, and warden of William Penn House, but also founder of Multi-Racial Britain.

As a Quaker, Glean believed in non-violent direct action. Yet she was not passive. Indeed, she was active in the Campaign for Nuclear Disarmament and the Committee of 100 and was also concerned with aspects of British race relations, and the need to build a strong immigrant organisation to combat racial prejudice and discrimination.[90] In this she had the support of the editor of *Peace News*.

After the General Election, Glean saw Patrick Walker's defeat in Smethwick as a body blow for good race relations and decided to act. She contacted Alan Lovell and Michael Randle (both pacifists and also firmly involved in the Committee of 100) who were interested in helping to found an exclusive organisation. She then contacted several friends: Ranjana Ash (an active member of the Movement for Colonial Freedom), C. L. R. James (the distinguished West Indian historian) and Barry Reckord (the West Indian playwright and actor). Together, Blacks and Whites, they constituted the informal group called Multi-Racial Britain.

Of crucial significance to MRB was the fact that none of the members were directly connected with the rank and file of the immigrant communities, through immigrant organisations. However, Glean, Ash and James were on friendly terms with many immigrant leaders. In effect, MRB was essentially a 'forum of debate'. Indeed, discussions at meetings and seminars were regular. It was not all talk however. MRB was active through a 'hurriedly organised' lobby of Parliament to oppose the extension of the Commonwealth Immigrants Act of 1962. This failure was instructive to the black members of MRB who felt that contacts made by Lovell and Randle with the CND and the Committee of 100 were not transferable to another group. In fact, it was abundantly clear that Blacks had to organise and act for themselves; self-determination within the black immigrant community was the most potent way of influencing British politics.

Against this background, Bayard Rustin the black American arrived in London in November 1964 to help plan King's visit. Through Michael Randle of the British Peace Movement, Rustin was able to meet Marion Glean. They agreed on the need for a broad-based British anti-discrimination organisation and that King should be used to meet with 'black faces' in promoting this end. Rustin, Glean, Randle and Roszak agreed that the 'new movement' should be in the hands of immigrants with, of course, the necessary support of Whites.

Unfortunately, plans for the meeting were not put into motion because it was not clear who was responsible for inviting immigrants. Thus, when King arrived in London on 5 December, it was Glean's responsibility to get a group of people together for a Monday morning discussion. In spite of the short notice given, MRB was able to call together several organisations to attend its first 'mass' meeting. The organisations represented were CND, the Committee of 100, the Movement for Colonial Freedom, the Indian Workers' Association (Southall), the Standing Conference of West Indian Organisations (London Region), the West Indian Students' Union, the British Caribbean Association, Anti-Apartheid, the National Federation of Pakistani Associations, and the Council of African Organisations. Also present was a 'prominent immigrant' Dr David Pitt.

At the meeting, held at the Hilton Hotel, King and Rustin urged the assembled group to fight discriminatory legislation and to bring pressure to bear on the government by uniting in protest. In a BBC interview, the next day, King said:

> I think it is necessary for the coloured population in Great Britain to organise and work through meaningful non-violent direct action approaches to bring these issues to the forefront of the conscience of the nation wherever they exist. You can never get rid of a problem as long as you hide the problem, as long as you complacently adjust yourself to it. [91]

King's evangelical style during the meeting had the desired crusading effect as far as Marion Glean was concerned. Thereafter, an *ad hoc* committee was set up to serve as a 'nucleus' for an 'umbrella' organisation to co-ordinate the anti-discrimination efforts of immigrant organisations representing their communities. This 'nucleus' avoided organisations on the militant civil rights model. The militancy alluded to was in the context of a group willing to protest through direct action.

A second formal meeting of the CARD 'nucleus' was held on 20 December at Glean's house. Of the eighteen people attending, Michael Randle was the only white person – a non-immigrant. The meeting established two sub-committees for policy finances and the legislative campaign. In view of the need for legislation and because the government was planning to introduce a Bill of its own, the task of the legislative sub-committee was vital.

At another meeting, held on 10 January 1965, attended by 33 people (about one-third representing immigrant groups) the name 'Campaign Against Racial Discrimination' was officially adopted. There was a dominant London presence among those attending the meeting. One estimate put the number of Whites at 'about a sixth', among whom was the Englishman Anthony Lester, a young barrister. His expertise and experience was invaluable. Fortuitously he sat on a Society of Labour Lawyers sub-committee concerned with drafting anti-discrimination legislation for the Labour Party's National Executive.

One of the meeting's main tasks was to formulate and adopt the aims and objects of CARD and to choose an Executive Committee *pro tem*. After the votes for the Executive Committee were counted, David Pitt and Marion Glean emerged at the top. During this crucial meeting, the sharp debate was on the fundamental question of how far the new organisation should co-operate with existing organisations and institutions in Britain. What emerged was 'general distrust' of the Labour Party because it failed to clarify the need for strong anti-discriminatory legislation. Marion Glean argued strongly against 'working closely' with the Labour Party and the trade unions. And David Pitt (a staunch Labour Party supporter) asked for the 'enlistment of allies among the more sympathetic elements of British society'. Following this debate, a set of aims and objects were adopted. [92]

It was proposed that a national founding Convention should be held in July 1965. The idea was that CARD 'must prove itself through activities before seeking formal recognition from Commonwealth immigrants and British sympathisers'. During the early days CARD developed haphazardly around the idea of opposition to racial discrimination in Great Britain. Clearly, CARD had to learn from similar organisations and civil rights groups, both in Britain and the United States. While there were many disagreements among those involved, CARD lacked a clear programme.

Working towards an organisation

The Executive Committee's role was crucial in the history of CARD. Those elected were David Pitt as chairman; Victor Page (a West Indian dentist who had been co-opted) as treasurer; Ranjana Ash, recording secretary; Selma James, organising secretary; Richard Small, press officer; Anthony Lester, chairman of the legal sub-committee.

In the following weeks, the Executive Committee was increased by seven members: a place reserved for the Standing Conference of West Indian Organisations was taken by the group's vice-chairman, Mrs Frances Ezzreco; another, reserved for a Pakistani representative Alam Ir Kabir. In addition, there were five co-options. Page, Hamza Alavi (a businessman and member of the National Federation of Pakistani Associations) and Kojo Amoo-Gottfried (past president of the Council of African Organisations) were immigrants. In an attempt to broaden CARD's appeal to liberal Englishmen, at Pitt's suggestion, Nicholas Deakin (then Director of the 'Survey of Race Relations' and Roy Shaw (business executive and former manager of Pitt's Hampstead election campaign) were also included. [93]

After CARD became operational, the legal sub-committee (which included Lester) and two West Indian law students, Small and Fitzroy Bryant, formulated legislative proposals. These proposals were met with 'sharp disagreement' among members of the

Executive. Ultimately the question was put to the full CARD membership. During this time, CARD held a series of monthly meetings at Conway Hall, London. At the membership meeting of 27 June, of the 95 in attendance 90 were from the London area. Clearly at this stage, CARD was essentially a London-based organisation. This imbalance did not detract from the focus of the debate.

In February 1965, it was resolved that 'CARD is opposed to all forms of racial discrimination and calls for legislation as one means of fighting it'.[94] Later, a public meeting held on 20 February called for support for broad anti-discrimination laws and to launch CARD into British politics. The main formal record of the developing conception of organisation was found in a series of 'Statements of Future Work' prepared in April by Selma James, Marion Glean, Ranjana Ash and Nicholas Deakin; also in three different drafts of a 'Summary of Future Work' statement which was distributed at the Founding Convention in July, and an essay on the CARD constitution prepared by Hamza Alavi.

According to Heineman, each of the various memoranda was characterised by an awareness of the need for conceptual clarity and stressed the lack of information. And each mentioned the need for careful planning and careful thought to deal with complex problems and many-faceted communities.

Marion Glean emphasised that CARD should not become so concerned with legal problems that it lost sight of creating a strong organisation. Citing the experience of Blacks in the United States she argued:

> CORE [the Congress of Racial Equality] and SNICK [sic] [The Student Non-Violent Co-ordinating Committee] were revolts against the old coloured, legalistic bourgeoisie of the NAACP [the National Association for the Advancement of Coloured People] . . .
> It would be a pity if CARD became the NAACP equivalent in Britain.[95]

Most of these writers of various memoranda, clearly outraged by discrimination in Britain, were not experienced rank-and-file organisers. They were aware of the distance between themselves and immigrant workers, the local communities and many immigrant organisations. There were, however, two exceptions. Ranjana Ash and Selma James were closely in touch with the Indian Workers' Association–Great Britain and with Standing Conference, London Region, respectively. They both wanted these organisations to join CARD. However, the elitists among the Executive Committee (feeling a shade threatened) came out in the open. Hamza Alavi felt that it was perhaps 'too early to hope that an organisation can be brought into existence in which the entire rank and file of the immigrant communities take part directly'. The multiplicity of 'images' that were conjured up did not systematically develop into strategies for 'joining the immigrants or gaining power'. Indeed, none were used as a premise from which a coherent conception of CARD could be developed. In this imprecise way the organisation limped on.

Among the activities engaged in was the Parliamentary lobby. The concurrent discussions about the development of CARD and about its activities were both characterised by an uneasy consensus. Significantly, between the adoption of the name CARD on 10 January 1965 and the Founding Convention in late July, CARD was active in two areas only: lobbying for amendments to the Race Relations Bill and building up the organisation. The Bill was not introduced until 7 April, but CARD members had correctly predicted that it would not be adequate in two important respects: scope and means of enforcement. The proposals approved by CARD urged extension of the law to housing, employment, insurance and credit facilities and asked for a change in the method of enforcement so that criminal sanctions would be based only as a last resort following conciliation efforts, a civil action, and a contempt order from the final court.

Throughout the founding period, Pitt and Lester, the legal Committee members and Small as press officer, spent much time in putting CARD's views to the government and the public. In addition, a petition campaign was started to 'muster enough support to convince the government to amend their proposals to our requirements'. Accordingly, 20,000 forms were printed and a target of one million signatures was set. The petition was essentially Pitt's idea. He felt it would serve two functions: it would be palpable pressure in support of CARD's legislative proposals and it would allow CARD to canvass at local level and make itself known to immigrants.

The petition, a failure, was never presented to the government, as intended. This failure was attributable in part, to the 'lukewarm' CARD leadership and partly, because the CARD office was not efficient in co-ordinating the efforts of the inherently weak immigrant organisations. This unfruitful relationship between CARD and the immigrant groups it was intended to help, was a portent of things to come.

CARD's other activities did not require major policy decisions. Money was raised and the membership drive continued sporadically. By June 1965, 400 people had joined and 28 organisations had affiliated and agreed to support CARD's aims and objects. CARD also supported striking Indian and Pakistani workers at Courtaulds Preston plant, submitted a memorandum on 'Racial Discrimination in Great Britain' specially for the Commonwealth Prime Ministers' Conference in June, laid plans for the July Founding Convention, and had written and discussed CARD's constitution.[96] Significantly, there was little concern over the allocation of CARD's inadequate resources.

A verbal war ensued concerning the 'issues'. The first six months from January to June 1965 developed into a 'nightmare situation' with meetings and discussions marked by severe factionalism and bitter in-fighting. Personal attacks hampered the Executive Committee, while mass meetings often resulted in 'embarrassing acrimony' between Executive Committee members. There were endless doctrinal battles as accusations and counter-accusations were made. So much so that a month before the Founding Convention, the organisation was stationary. The tensions revealed a clear picture: the organisation was split into two factions, the effective working majority and the dissidents. The working majority included Pitt, Lester, Deakin, Shaw, Singh, Alavi and Page. The dissidents were Small, Ash, James, Glean and Ezzreco. Glean had left CARD in February 1965 to work in Paris for the United Nations. Except for Small, the core of the dissident group were women. As the working majority saw it, CARD was divided into 'realists' and 'romantics', while the dissidents saw this division as one between 'militants' and 'moderates'. Thus, there was an ongoing conflict between the left-wing and those in the left of centre of British politics. On balance, both groups had little to do with the reality of organising immigrants. In effect, they used some of the arguments in CARD to grind their own axes.

Paradoxically, although there were deep divisions within CARD in terms of style, rhetoric and political beliefs, 'these differences were never directly manifested in divisions over specific, explicit proposals for action'. However, both factions were agreed on establishing CARD in the immigrant communities and to amend the proposed Race Relations Bill. Each faction became identified with one of these issues. The dissidents concentrated on developing CARD as a group, while the working majority was associated with the government's proposed legislation. There was, however, a 'fundamental confusion' in both groups as to what type of power CARD should have and how it would go about gaining that power.

Although they were essentially middle class in terms of occupation and education, the dissidents were emphatic in establishing an essentially rank and file organisation of immigrants which would be 'strong and independent' and in control without the domination of Whites or by middle class. On the other hand, the working majority had more immediate concerns. They wanted a strong CARD organisation, but were conscious of their lack of power and the need for allies. To them, amending the Race Relations Bill was a first step in shaping race relations in Britain.

Moreover, the two groups were separated by other issues such as whether immigrants should not politely show they were for equality, but angrily oppose discrimination. In addition, there was bitter debate during the early days as to whether CARD's first aim and object should express opposition to prejudice and discrimination directed at all minority groups or just prejudice and discrimination practised on the basis of colour. This was an extremely important issue for the dissidents who feared that Whites and moderates would play down the need to combat colour discrimination for fear of alienating liberal opinion.

Another issue disputed by the two factions was the Commonwealth Immigrants Act 1962. The two issues involved on this question were firstly, whether CARD should state its aims and objects in opposition to the Act and express a desire for its repeal; and secondly, whether a resolution should also be approved criticising the 1962 Act. The left-wing group felt that CARD, as an organisation founded to combat racial discrimination should publicly oppose this discriminatory Act and demand its repeal. In striking contrast, Pitt, Lester, and Deakin felt opposition to the Act in January 1965 was pointless. They had a point, for race was not a flexible issue in British politics. Indeed it had become an entrenched part of the British state control and would so reveal itself as time wore on. Therefore the government was unlikely to change its policy on immigration lightly. Thus, the three moderates felt that CARD should press for anti-discrimination legislation instead.

The division between the militants and moderates in CARD was a distinction relevant only in terms of the desire of one group to appear militant, and of the other group to appear moderate or, more accurately, reasonable, technically proficient, knowledgeable, responsible. [97] These differences were based on differing immediate goals (for example, to organise and to amend legislation) and on the expectations that each group had about people who were central to the achievement of these objectives.

To compound CARD's problems there was no individual leader who could command individual respect. Moreover, the debate on how to organise never really developed, and foundered on the stark fact that neither group had much, if any, experience in organising at grass-roots level or in building a strong organisation among the people. Clearly, CARD's formative period was bedevilled by division, polarisation and paralysis which had particularly destructive effects. The period of sharp disagreement demonstrated that in a multi-racial, multi-nationality coalition, debilitating factionalism could obstruct the work of the organisation even before such work began to reveal divisions based on real choices about the present. But as the 'verbal war' raged, drawing the energies and concentration of the participants, attention was deflected from the main issue facing CARD. Thus the central question of power was avoided in a confusion of promotional and sectional roles. In their frustration, attacking each other forcefully was easier for both factions than tackling the essential problems of developing influence and facing the reality of powerlessness. [98]

Constitution and convention

Not surprisingly, the constitution was symbolic of the confusions and contradictions with which CARD struggled during the formative period. In essence, the constitution's authors attempted to combine provisions for a federal structure ('an organisation of organisations') with a role for individual mass membership, not necessarily based on the membership of immigrant organisations. It also tried to reconcile the idea of central control with the need for membership participation in the organisation, and hoped that a large measure of support would come from organisations that were themselves directly involved in the same field of work.

The Annual Conference was to have two types of delegate: representatives from affiliated organisations (the number depending on the size of the organisation); and individual members. The Annual Delegates Conference was presumably the highest policy-making body in CARD. The Conference's main functions were to elect a Chairman and a National Council.

The CARD chairman was head of the National Council, the members of which elected a vice-chairman, secretary and treasurer, all of whom sat with the chairman on the Executive Committee. It also selected the Executive Committee's other 10 members from within its own ranks.

To function properly CARD had to have an elaborate bureaucracy. The Executive Committee would effectively run the organisation, since the National Council would meet only four times a year. Significantly, the participation of individual members of the immigrant communities was made 'extremely difficult'. The structure was such that it would be cumbersome to call area conferences and send delegates to the Annual Conference. The number of such delegates was limited. Individual delegates were eligible for election only to 15 of the 45 National Council seats.

While the dissidents had shown their displeasure, they themselves were unclear as to how 'immigrants were going to be mobilised on their own behalf'. Thus, given their commitment to the existing immigrant organisations and the active participation of individual immigrants, they were unhappy about the constitution, but sadly they did not know how to amend or reconstruct it. Thus, when the National Founding Convention was held in Conway Hall on 24–25 July 1965, there was very little attempt to change the tentative structure suggested by the constitution committee and approved by the Executive Committee. The Convention was attended by 230 individual CARD members and 100 delegates or observers from affiliated organisations. After six months in existence, CARD claimed 400 individual members and 31 affiliated organisations. Any paid member was eligible to vote. Attendance at the two-day Convention fluctuated between 200 and 300. And while there were no precise figures, it was estimated that roughly half of those present were black and half white. The constitutional structure was accepted without much trouble and a number of resolutions were passed.

After the Convention the dissidents departed and Pitt, the Chairman supreme, was unrivalled as the leading immigrant in

CARD. He had become the leading black spokesman in Britain. There was a sense of relief with the election of a New National Council and a new Executive Committee that was less divided.[99] On balance, the general description of CARD's Executive Committee as 'middle class', 'intellectual' and 'professional' held as well with the second EC as with the first. The main change was that divisions did not arise in discussions with the frequency that characterised the meetings during the formative period. It seemed that the work of the organisation would be able to continue without the bitter feuding, and that the essential anti-discrimination work and organisation-building was about to begin.

Was CARD a parliamentary pressure group? Soon after the Founding Convention in August 1965, the Labour government introduced its policy statement, a White Paper on immigration from the Commonwealth. This White Paper discussed future immigration control policy. In essence, it proposed a tightening of the existing discriminatory measures written into the Commonwealth Immigration Act 1962. Predictably, this was bitterly attacked for continuing and strengthening the existing measures and for introducing new powers of detainment and deportation. This was seen as giving the government dangerous arbitrary authority.[100] The government gave its blessings on the work of the Commonwealth Immigrants Advisory Council and the NCCI; bodies which could not be said to have helped the process of better race relations. Like the Royal Commissions which were set up to look into colonial matters (usually after working class unrest in the colonies) these official bodies were essentially concerned with enquiry. Whereas the Royal Commissions reported on the workers in the colonies, the CIAC now reported on them as immigrants, 'colonised' in Britain.

The White Paper posed two problems for CARD. Firstly, because CARD had failed to amend the Race Relations Bill and was anxious to work towards a further extension of anti-discrimination laws, it was forced to turn its attention to preventing the proposed tightening of immigration controls. Secondly, the setting up of the NCCI meant a broadening of its membership base; thus CARD had to decide whether or not to co-operate with this semi-official body. Not surprisingly therefore, before there was any discussion, a decision was taken for CARD. David Pitt and Hamza Alavi announced their acceptance of invitations from the Prime Minister to become members of the NCCI. The result was renewed 'recriminations and disputes' within CARD. The organisation was confronted with two crucial issues: should members of CARD co-operate with and participate in a committee established by a document which approved (and proposed to extend) discriminatory immigration policy? Moreover, should CARD Executive Committee members make such important decisions without referring back to the National Council for advice?

In defence Pitt and Alavi argued that although the NCCI was reconstituted in a document which perpetuated a discriminatory government policy, nonetheless the Committee's functions were geared towards improving race relations and formulating a more enlightened internal policy. Both men argued that they were join-ing the NCCI in their 'personal capacities'; therefore there was no need to consult the National Council. One might well ask: would they have been invited to sit on the National Committee if they were not influential members of CARD? The fears of the dissidents were realised.

Unfortunately, a new and bitter argument engulfed CARD as new dissidents and new alliances emerged. Although the debate lasted for several months, CARD's final position towards the NCCI was postponed. Given this breathing space, Pitt and Alavi began attending meetings; and a number of CARD Executive Committee members joined specialist panels of the NCCI. Thus drawn into government machinery, CARD's subsequent role was predictable. CARD's fight for 'independence' had ended with the dissidents in disarray. The organisation was now increasingly concerned with the formation of public policy, within government guidelines.

Thus, the formative period had ended, and CARD began routine operations under its new constitution. In a promotional sense, the 'national pressure group' idea took precedence.

The collapse of CARD

The withdrawal of Standing Conference

The decision taken by Pitt and Alavi to join the NCCI had profound effects not only within CARD's Executive but also resulting in the withdrawal of Standing Conference of West Indian Organisations from the CARD structure. (Hereafter, Standing Conference would refer to the London regional organisation, not the Standing Conference for the Birmingham region.)

In October, the Standing Conference Executive Committee decided that either Pitt and Alavi should resign from the NCCI or Standing Conference would disaffiliate from CARD. Given CARD's public commitment to the NCCI, Conference's stand was an effective announcement of disaffiliation. This formal step was confirmed in Feburary 1966 in a vote of the general monthly meeting of Standing Conference. [101]

The withdrawal of the West Indian organisation, symbolised the failure of the 'organisation of organisations' idea (cherished by Pitt) to be binding and to exist as a successful strategy through which CARD could unite those groups in a campaign against racial discrimination. This dual focus of the idea was to bring in all British organisations sympathetically disposed to the immigrants' cause, and to bring in all existing immigrant organisations. This second function, considered by far the most important task by many CARD members, had failed from the start.

The organisation of organisations idea envisioned that CARD would have three types of relationship with the existing groups. Firstly, it would co-ordinate efforts already launched against discrimination; secondly, it would act as a clearing house for information; and thirdly, it would participate in organising and initiating further efforts to eradicate discrimination.

Clearly, both at national and local level CARD needed to mobilise and develop organised power. Members of the CARD Executive Committee were aware that the immigrant communities were not particularly well organised and, more importantly, that immigrants were not involved in groups dedicated to improving their life in Britain.

To achieve cohesion, it was hoped that the 'consent and participation' of the Pakistanis, Indian and West Indian national group structures (for example, the IWA, the NFPA and Standing Conference) would help local development and increase participation and organisation building at that level. Thus, through these developments, CARD would amalgamate and strengthen the concentration of immigrant organisations.

This strategy failed both to indicate the kinds of difficulty that CARD had in developing as an organisation and to explain the nature of the internal constraints which hindered CARD's effective operation as a force against discrimination.

CARD's relationship with Standing Conference and the difficulties in establishing relations with the Indian Workers' Association–Great Britain and the National Federation of Pakistani Associations during the period 1965–7 was revealing.

CARD and the Standing Conference of West Indian Organisations

Although the Standing Conference of West Indian Organisations' London Region was among the first groups to affiliate with CARD, it did so reluctantly. There was deep concern among members of the Conference Executive (Vernon Laidlow, chairman; Mrs Frances Ezzreco, vice-chairman; Jeff Crawford, secretary; and Neville Maxwell, welfare officer) about the implications of joining the newly formed anti-discrimination group. They were, however, keenly interested in the possibilities of CARD. Members of Standing Conference attended all CARD meetings after King's visit to London. At the 10 January 1965 organisational meeting, Crawford was asked to serve on the CARD Executive *pro tem*. He declined this offer not only because he lacked the time but also because he had serious doubts about CARD. So concerned was Crawford that he and other members of Conference discussed these matters with

Pitt at a special meeting held in February at Pitt's surgery in Gower Street, London. [102]

The Standing Conference delegation wanted assurances from Pitt that individual membership would not be allowed to outweigh (for example, outvote) the membership of the affiliated organisations. Further, Conference needed assurances that CARD would not be 'white-dominated'. Indeed they could only accept a CARD run and controlled by immigrants. Pitt did not concede this, but explained that Whites had a useful role to play in the organisation. Eventually, after discussing the nature of white involvement, Standing Conference and Pitt agreed that, in general, Whites would not run the organisation but should play a supporting role in the fight against discrimination. Finally, Ezzreco, Crawford, Maxwell and Laidlow asked that CARD be 'militant' in publicly opposing discriminatory practices and in its efforts to counter them. They also insisted that CARD should in no way be tied to the Labour Party.

For some eight months, Standing Conference was formally associated with CARD, but interestingly it had little involvement in the activities of the organisation. Of the two places offered to Conference on the Executive Committee, only one was filled by Frances Ezzreco, whose attendance at Executive meetings was irregular. Nevertheless, Standing Conference supported CARD's proposals to amend the Race Relations Bill and attended conferences before and after the National Founding Convention to discuss the aims and objects of CARD. In spite of this show of concern, a place for it on the committee drafting the constitution remained vacant. Standing Conference was not particularly interested in helping CARD. In this sense, the Conference members, Crawford, Maxwell, Laidlow and Ezzreco, were fundamentally different from their colleagues in CARD, namely the 'dissidents', Small, Glean, Ash, and Selma James. For a number of reasons, some of which they shared with the dissidents, Conference members were extremely suspicious of CARD. Given that they were uncertain of their role within CARD, this wariness was understandable.

Bitter personal attacks at pre-Founding Convention meetings on the dissidents led to a strong dislike of CARD among Conference members so that by the time of the National Founding Convention this bitterness within CARD was already well-known among Conference leadership who saw the new organisations as being 'middle class, white-dominated, moderate and controlled by the Labour Party'. This was in line with the thinking of the CARD dissidents.

One of the most outspoken dissidents, Selma James, was the Conference's closest ally. When she failed to be elected to the Executive Committee by the National Council, following the Convention, Conference became suspicious and thus further alienated. They felt that David Pitt was wheeling and dealing behind the scenes. For them, the last straw was Pitt's and Alavi's acceptance of positions on the NCCI. Standing Conference then decided to leave the 'organisation of organisations'.

In effect, the withdrawal of Standing Conference was much more than a militant black working-class organisation leaving one which was moderate, middle class, white-run and gradualist.[103]

The Standing Conference had made its mind up about CARD fairly quickly. Indeed Conference members made no forceful attempts to push CARD in any direction. While personal tensions existed, their meetings were not frequent enough to parallel the personal breakdown which had occurred in the CARD Executive Committee. Perhaps the most significant aspect of Conference's ambivalence (or confusion) was reflected in the fact that it could have made a significant contribution to CARD's development. Attesting to this, members of both the dissident group and the working majority agreed that if Standing Conference had wanted to, given that the constitution was weighted in favour of organisations, it could have 'effectively controlled CARD'. Selma James regretted their lack of commitment. She said, 'They would not come in and say "Conference wants A, B, and C" and insist on getting it. I think they would have won.'[104]

So unsure was Conference of its direction that soon after it disaffiliated from CARD, it decided to affiliate to the NCCI, thus trivialising criticism of Pitt and Alavi. This 'peculiar shift' in image seemed at variance with a 'militant' black organisation. Yet the Standing Conference of West Indian Organisations during the first years of CARD's existence was both a 'militant' black organisation and a talking shop. More fundamental, and the essential reason for its withdrawal from CARD, was its quest for 'independence' as an essentially working-class and middle-class organisation.

The richness of African culture and colour consciousness was a part of this independence. Although for men like Maxwell and Crawford, negritude and a distrust of multi-racialism were contributory factors towards the development of a militant posture, they were not militant or isolationist enough. Thus, apart from being a form of gaining recognition, this posture also reflected discontentment over their powerlessness.

David Pitt and Standing Conference

Central to the CARD–Standing Conference split was the personality and career of the CARD Chairman, David Pitt. As a West Indian of unusual achievement in British public life (and, indeed, what he represented to Standing Conference leaders) Pitt must be regarded as a key figure. To many, he was one of the most prominent spokesmen for West Indians in Britain. His view of himself was quite different, however. According to one commentator, he thought of himself as an Englishman and regarded his birthplace as irrelevant. His renunciation of the West Indies, and willingness to embrace English norms, alienated Conference spokesmen. They were angry and resentful that a member of their own more representative organisation was not regarded as presenting a truer picture of West Indians in Britain.

If the Conference leaders were little known in Britain, Pitt, in contrast was well established. His middle-class origins in the West Indies had served him in good stead. In Britain, he became a man of many parts – a medical doctor, a Greater London Councillor and a Labour Party candidate for Parliament. More recently, he has become a member of the House of Lords. A well-educated, professional man, he moved easily in British society. Why was Pitt so acceptable? One observer commented: 'He had conventional status in British terms that many members of the Conference leadership structure did not have.'[105] What apparently differentiated him most clearly from Conference leaders was the fact that he did not identify with the rank-and-file West Indian.

Pitt was involved in a number of British organisations, and what was particularly galling to politically conscious West Indians was the fact that he took no special interest in working with Standing Conference. More than that, he was at times 'positively contemptuous of its efforts'. He was more concerned with mobilising white opinion in support of anti-discrimination work and to this end he made contact with many people in British party politics. He was no novice. Indeed, he knew conventional political techniques from his experience in West Indian politics. Born in Grenada, he became active in politics in Trinidad, helping to found the West Indian National Party there. Both he and Conference members were in favour of a united West Indies.

As a politician, he urged West Indians in Britain to join political parties – especially the Labour Party, even though the Labour Party persisted in extending the discriminatory immigration policy of the Conservatives. This action convinced Conference leaders of the futility of attempts to influence the party structure by working within it. Thus, when Pitt joined the NCCI and made 'no protest' against the White Paper, this was interpreted by Conference as acceptance of the government's immigration policy by Pitt.

Whatever personal rivalry there had been (although some advanced this as a cause for the CARD–Conference split) it was clear that Crawford had never attempted to challenge Pitt for the CARD leadership. However, both Crawford and Maxwell would have welcomed recognition as *the* spokesman for West Indians in Britain.

CARD and the National Federation of Pakistani Associations

CARD's efforts to co-ordinate effectively the work of the Indians and Pakistani groups in Britain were no more successful than the attempts to attract the West Indians. The Indian Workers' Association, Great Britain was never formally affiliated to CARD, while the National Federation of Pakistani Associations in Great Britain was barely functioning in 1967. Moreover, it had little contact with CARD.

The NFPA, representing local Pakistani societies and welfare associations, decided to affiliate to CARD in March 1965, a few months before the National Founding Convention. Tussaduq Ahmed, a London restauranteur and leader of London's Pakistani community, played a central role in the formation of the Federation in 1963 and also in the move to join CARD. Ahmed's aim was to bring the Pakistani community out from its isolation and orient it to participate in British life. Equal respect and equal status were important and desired goals.

Breaking out into the wider society is always a tentative and difficult process for immigrants. Not surprisingly therefore the Federation's leaders were reluctant to join the embryonic CARD organisation. They felt that Pakistani immigrants should co-operate with sympathetic members of the host society in order to establish channels of communication. They felt that CARD might become an 'all coloured' organisation, thus realising their fear of immigrant isolation.

Significantly in November 1965, the Federation had joined with Standing Conference and the Indian Workers' Association, Great Britain, to oppose the government's White Paper. A boycott was promised.[106] In early October, a letter signed by Nurul Islam was sent on behalf of the Executive Committee of the Federation asking for the resignations of Pitt and Alavi; Alavi, they said did not in 'any capacity' represent the Pakistani community.

The militancy of the Federation's leadership had led to a deterioration in its relations with CARD. By early 1967, there was little communication between the organisations. In fact, the Pakistani community in Britain as a whole had no real links with CARD. By June 1967, there was no Pakistani representative on the CARD Executive and the places reserved for Pakistani organisations on CARD's National Council were unfilled. Tussaduq Ahmed, the original Pakistani supporter of CARD remained on the National Council as a co-opted member.

This lack of involvement of the NFPA with CARD reflected internal disorganisation. The NFPA was founded in April 1963 by the leaders of the various Pakistani associations in Britain. Twenty-three organisations formally launched the Federation on 14 April 1963. They represented 21 localities and an estimated 15,000 members.[107] The Federation also adopted several aims and objects among which were to try to inculcate the spirit of organised and disciplined life among the overseas Pakistani community in general, and their organisations in particular; to provide a national platform for the Pakistani Associations in Great Britain, and in this regard the Federation was to be the national spokesman of all the affiliated associations; and to be responsible for directing and executing all measures aimed at prompting on a national level, the social, cultural, economic and religious interests of the overseas Pakistani community. [108]

The constituent organisations came together in the Federation to deal with the specific problem of getting the best value for foreign currency (pounds for example) that immigrants were remitting to Pakistan. They were also concerned with the security of life, property and jobs. More specifically, the Federation's leaders who felt that it was more profitable for Pakistanis in Britain to convert their earnings on the black market than to send them through government channels, wanted the Pakistani High Commission to press their government to either alter the exchange rate or provide bonuses for people sending money home. After resolving this problem, the Federation (a 'proper organisation' which had only provided a base for an 'assiduous lobby' of the High Commission) suffered a series of factional disputes as various Association leaders jostled for positions of influence.

In essence, the associations which constituted the Federation had developed over a period of 15 years. Their activities were centred around issues that related to Pakistanis as a nationality group and not as 'coloured' immigrants in a foreign country. These groups were broadly concerned with social, cultural, religious and welfare issues relating to Pakistan.

In general terms, the Pakistani community, in a given area in 1967, was considered to be divided in three parts: students of middle class origin who planned to return to academic, business, political or professional life in Pakistan; middle-class multi-occupational entrepreneurs who ran the internal economies of the communities; and workers (many of them unmarried) who were in Britain temporarily and who lived in dwellings with other Pakistanis. [109]

At factory level, there was leadership within the working class, but this was subsumed by organisation at a more communal level by those with higher economic status; for example, the owners of grocery shops, restaurants, travel agencies and other property. Thus workers seeking social contact out of loneliness and isolation joined the local association. Moreover, through their village or regional links in Pakistan and through the voluntary help they offered, the leaders gained the workers' support.

Often there were keen contests for positions within the associations, as rival leaders fought not so much to fulfil a desire to help the working people in the community, but essentially to satisfy a personal need for power and prestige. Thus, they mobilised people not on the issues but because of 'obligations and territorial alliances'. It was clear then that while few workers took an active part in the associations, fewer still aspired to leadership positions. A prerequisite for leadership was 'free time and a good education'. Students and businessmen were the front-runners constituting the main groups engaged in the power contest.

Given this power structure, reflecting the divide between the rank and file workers and the Federation's leadership, it was clear that CARD would not use the Federation to co-ordinate the efforts of the local associations against discrimination. Furthermore CARD as a multi-racial organisation could not effectively bring together the various associations for either concerted action or common statements. Indeed, if anti-discrimination work was to be done locally, the fact remained that a 'difficult reorientation' was necessary among the associations and among Pakistani workers whose isolation was bounded by attitudes of religion, language and culture.

The Indian Workers' Association, Great Britain and CARD

The politics and factional divisions which characterised the IWA during 1965–7 were complex and problematic. [110] Since the first IWA was founded in the 1930s to support the Indian Independence movement and to establish solidarity with British workers, the waves of Indian immigrants which came in the 1950s altered the nature, function and aims of the groups. In 1965, they claimed to be more concerned with anti-discrimination activities ranging from lobbying to demonstrations. Even as far back as 1958, the IWA was explicitly in opposition to discrimination on colour, creed or sex.

They were willing to co-operate with other organisations for the same ends: equal human rights and social and economic opportunities. This was in contrast to the vague more generalised aim of Standing Conference which called for understanding between the races and for integration.

The two foremost leaders of the IWA–GB in 1967, were Rattan Singh, President, and Jagmohan Joshi, General Secretary, who were regarded by those involved in British race relations as pro-Peking communists. IWA leaders in Birmingham were divided into three categories: those who held prestige within their village-kin group; entrepreneurs who ran the internal economy of the community and the university educated members with experience and/or understanding of Indian politics. Moreover, 'Most members of the third group hold left-wing political views and some of them were members of left-wing parties in India.' [111]

However, in 1963, as the Commonwealth Immigrants Act was being debated, Joshi helped to found the Co-ordinating Committee Against Racial Discrimination (CCARD), a federation of immigrant organisations and sympathetic British groups in Birmingham which was to oppose discrimination from a broader base.

At about the same time, complex strains were developing between the IWA–GB and the Southall Indian community. For example, different political approaches and ideologies; rivalry between Singh (President of the London IWA branch) and H. S. Ruprah, a leader of the IWA, Southall; a factional struggle for control of the Sikh temple in Shepherds Bush, resulting in Southall breaking away from the IWA–GB and establishing itself as an independent Indian Workers' Association.

The IWA–GB had no formal contact with CARD during its formative stage in the spring of 1965 and refused to affiliate. Southall IWA, on the other hand, agreed to support CARD. The reluctance of the national IWA to work with CARD was more clearly based on sharp differences in ideology than in the case of CARD and Standing Conference or the Federation of Pakistani Association. Approaches by Ranjana Ash, whose political sympathies were close to Joshi's, to persuade the IWA–GB to join CARD did not materialise. Fundamental political differences persisted. CARD was characterised by IWA–GB leaders as a front organisation for the Labour Party, a platform for careerists and as being dominated by the middle class.

Here again, a comparison could be made with Standing Conference. The dislike of CARD as an organisation associated with the Labour Party was different for the IWA–GB than it was for Standing Conference. For whereas Conference disliked the Labour Party because it had gone back on its word and had perpetuated discriminatory policies, the IWA–GB's critique, while including the Conference viewpoint, was also based on a broad conception of the proper nature of a 'Labour' Party.

The leaders of the IWA–GB, generally committed to the development of a strong, exclusively working class movement united on colour, were not opposed to the concept of a multi-racial organisation. Indeed, they were far less concerned about the influence of Whites than the West Indians. In fact, they were obviously sensitive to the 'strategic' value of British citizens in their attempts to counteract discrimination, as the formation of CARD demonstrated. They felt that the CARD leadership did not have enough contact with black workers and therefore could not possibly provide the leadership against discrimination which they envisaged.

Apart from its relations with the Southall IWA, CARD's contacts with local Indian associations were rare and weak. There were branches of the IWA in Birmingham, Bradford, Coventry, Derby, Erith, Glasgow, Gravesend, Huddersfield, Leamington Spa, Leeds, Leicester, Nottingham, Southampton and Wolverhampton. However, only the IWAs in Bradford, Glasgow, Leamington Spa and Leeds were in touch with the local CARD groups at various times.[112] In fact, the Southall IWA was 'the only immigrant group of a single nationality which had close relations with the national CARD structure.'

Reaching for the grass roots

The WISC, IWAs and the NFPA were far removed from the representations of the CARD leadership. By June 1967, the 'organisation of organisations' idea had become untenable. In effect,

CARD had failed to co-ordinate the efforts of other groups active in anti-discrimination work, to act as a 'clearing house' for information and to help other interested organisations to campaign against discrimination.

Of the local groups affiliated to Standing Conference, only one (the multi-racial, all-party British Caribbean Association) was formally involved with CARD. And of the local groups affiliated to the Federation of Pakistan Associations none were affiliated to CARD. Finally, none of the local branches of the IWA–GB had formal contact with CARD. Moreover, of the sympathetic British organisations, only the National Council of Civil Liberties was affiliated to CARD. And of the multi-racial organisations there were two sub-categories, namely the voluntary liaison committees and the local anti-discrimination groups. Of these committees, which by June 1967 had increased to over 30, only the Oxford Committee for Racial Integration was an affiliate of CARD. Further, of the multi-racial local anti-discrimination groups two were affiliated – the Cardiff Inter-racial Council and the Leicester Campaign for Racial Equality.

Clearly, CARD had failed to involve the existing immigrant organisations. The reasons involved the usual problems that beset voluntary organisations – the lack of time, money and personnel. While there was some truth in this, it might be more precise to state that the weaknesses of the CARD organisations were reinforcing in that an organisation cannot be built because there is no money; there is no money because there is no organisation. Obviously, given greater support for CARD, a self-generating process was likely to bring about an efficient and strong organisation. The lack of organisation was therefore both a cause and effect of CARD's failure to involve immigrants either individually or in groups.

The percentage of groups that could have been affiliated and in fact did so was extremely small, no matter how one calculates 'immigrant' and 'sympathetic' organisations. The fact that no Pakistani organisations, only one Indian group, just two West Indian organisations, and no local trade unions had affiliated indicates the low order of magnitude. Given that local association leaders, at least in the case of Standing Conference organisations in the London area, and possibly the Pakistani associations, tended not to be actively engaged in 'political' matters, there was little enthusiasm about supporting a national umbrella organisation.

Thus there was no communication flow between these local groups and CARD whereby, for example, CARD could ask that a local branch of a national firm be tested for practising discrimination, or the immigrant organisation could ask national CARD to intercede on its behalf with the government in London.

By 1967, among those members of the CARD executive who were most interested in organising locally, there was a general wariness of the immigrant associations and a belief that, as Ahmed suggested about Pakistanis, it was necessary to go directly to the individual immigrant to build up an organisation. And for such factors as the immigrants' status, their patterns of behaviour as conditioned by life in their homeland, and their reasons for coming to Britain, they could not generally be oriented towards a multi-racial group (at either national or local level) engaged in British politics. Obviously, CARD had to organise the communities if it was to gain the support.

Thus, many of the assumptions held by the founders of CARD in 1965 were proven wrong within two years. Individual immigrants did not come willingly into CARD assuming that they were reached. The organisation did not develop as planned since the fundamental problems of motivating and uniting newcomers of three different nationalities proved more complicated and difficult than had been envisaged. In 1967, aware of immigrants' problems, CARD approached Jack Jones, General Secretary of the TGWU to ask if the union would put out a pamphlet in conjunction with CARD on discrimination in employment and affiliate formally with CARD. Significantly, the reply to both questions was negative. [113]

The enigma of how to develop political consciousness among immigrants and how to secure their active participation in an organisation to oppose racial discrimination eluded and perplexed CARD officials at every step of the way during the two years of the organisation's existence.

The factional battles within CARD raged on, steadily weakening it before the organisation finally lost all credibility. It was abundantly evident by spring 1967 that CARD was in a state of limbo, detached from the political structure and from the immigrant communities. While the so-called 'Nandyites' within the EC hoped for the passage of an extended anti-discrimination law during the summer of 1967, simultaneously a different group within the EC was laying plans for a different future. The immediate goal was not pressure for legislation, but rather a take-over of the CARD organisation.

Thus, before CARD finally collapsed, a new mood of militancy had stirred race relations in the summer. On 26 July, Roy Jenkins had announced the government's intention to extend the Race Relations Act of 1965 in housing, employment, insurance and credit facilities. Yet, on the same day, he banned American Black Power leader Stokely Carmichael from Britain. While in London, however, Carmichael had made speeches at rallies in Notting Hill and Brixton, appeared on BBC television and attended meetings of Islington CARD and the Standing Conference of West Indian Organisations.

In Britain, Carmichael preached the tenets of the Black Power movement initiated in the United States. Prominent coverage of rioting in several cities in the United States was given by the British press. In Britain, where only 2 per cent of the population was black, 'race relations' again surfaced as an explosive and fundamental issue.

Furthermore, in July 1967, Michael Abdul Malik (known also as Michael X or Michael de Freitas), the leader of the separatist Racial Action Adjustment Society, was arrested on charges of violating the public order provisions of the Race Relations Act 1965. Malik's arrest aroused deep resentment among black immigrants who felt that Duncan Sandys should be indicted for stating the day after Malik's arrest that race riots in Britain were inevitable if black immigration was not stopped. Sandys suggested that the government pay the fares of all those immigrants who wished to return to their homelands. He also deplored the growing number of mixed marriages: 'The breeding of half-caste children', he said, 'would merely produce a generation of misfits and create increased tension.'[114] No public censure of Sandys was made by the government.

Moreover, as Black Power activity increased, Nigerian playwright and poet, Obi Egbuna founded Britain's first Black Power group, the Universal Coloured People's Association. Thus violence, colour consciousness, Black Power with all its connotations in the context of a world-wide black struggle, emerged from the fringes of Britain's racial minorities in the inner cities, to counteract and challenge 'the concepts of integration, multi-racialism and anti-discriminatory legalisms upon which CARD had been built'.

Moreover, implicit criticism of CARD came from the Joint Council for the Welfare of Immigrants. The limited aims of the organisation were: to help immigrants entering Britain by providing case-workers and establishing liaison with government officials at the ports and airports. In effect, those refused entry could approach the organisation for help. Although the scope of the JCWI was 'relatively narrow', it received widespread support. By September 1967, more than 100 people representing 74 voluntary organisations met at the Dominion cinema ('bailiwick of the IWA Southall') and agreed to accept the constitution of the JCWI. Within a few weeks, 115 immigrant organisations, from the 'militant' IWA–GB to the 'mildest' West Indian cultural and social club, had become part of the JCWI. Thus, the formation of the JCWI invalidated the government excuse that there was no spokesman for the immigrant interest, at least on immigration procedures. Given these developments during the months leading up to the 1967 Convention, tensions within CARD were mounting. The National Council had ceased to function and the Executive Committee was made impotent not by inertia, but by division. In the developing schism, the West Indians became increasingly isolated and opposed what was referred to as the 'Anglo-Asian axis'.

Thus, three years after Martin Luther King had met immigrant leaders in London and served as a catalyst for a new organisation, the need for strong, outspoken leadership, remained to be tackled realistically. Essentially, immigrants were still without power. CARD, as a potentially united front for all immigrants, had split and finally collapsed. The immigrant community was left to devise new forms of organisation and leadership. Some had already begun; others would make transitional adjustments where their predecessors had failed.

West Indian organisations in Moss Side and Easton

In June 1965, there were nine formal West Indian organisations in existence in Moss Side (Manchester) or its immediate vicinity. They were: The Colonial Sports Club, The Caribbean Federal Association, The Jamaican Circle, The Trinidad and Tobago Society, The Jamaican Association, The Leeward Islands Peoples' Association, The British Coloured Association, The West Indian National Association, and The British Society for Coloured Welfare.

By themselves, these associations (as their leaders were well aware) could only perform limited functions. An umbrella organisation, a real necessity, was first suggested in June 1965 in a letter addressed to the various West Indian associations' leaders, by a Tobago economist doing research at Manchester University. He emphasised that the proposed organisation was not intended to replace associations, but rather to serve as a point of contact between them.

When the leaders of the associations eventually met on 8 July, an *ad hoc* committee was set up. A list of recommendations was drawn up when the Committee met on 20 August. Indeed, it was suggested that the proposed organisation should take the form of a co-ordinating committee of *bona fide* organisations, each being given equal representation by an official who would act on its behalf. Moreover, it was suggested that the Committee should co-opt a limited number of persons who could make important contributions to the Committee's work. Furthermore, it was suggested that the Committee should have three purposes: (i) to co-ordinate the activities of member organisations and to bring about closer relationships between them; (ii) to help the member organisations to strengthen themselves and to broaden the base of their activities; and (iii) to channel opinions between the West Indian population and English society on social and communal matters. When the *ad hoc* Committee met again on 26 September, it was unanimously agreed to set up the Co-ordinating Committee for Caribbean organisations. This body was later re-named the West Indian Co-ordinating Committee.

The WICC (hereafter referred to as the Committee) represented

10 organisations – (the nine mentioned above, excluding the British Society for Coloured Welfare) and two new organisations, the West Indian Students' Association and the Bolton West Indian Sports Club. By 17 October when the Committee next met, the number of organisations it represented was reduced to six and then to five (the Colonial Sports Club; The Jamaican Association, The Caribbean Federal Association; The Leeward Islands Peoples' Association and Cheetham Hill Social Club) at the meeting held on 7 November. Thereafter, the 'backbone' of the Committee was made up of representatives from five associations: the CSP, CFA, JA, LIA, the Trinidad and Tobago Association and three co-opted members.[115]

Aims and objectives

The five constituent associations of the Committee promoted social activities (dances and socials) for their members. All, except the CSC, included educational and commercial activities and stressed the importance of co-operation with other West Indian organisations, primarily within the framework of the Committee.

A comparison of the activities of the five associations showed an important distinction between the Jamaican and non-Jamaican organisations. The Trinidad and Tobago Society and Leeward Islands Peoples' Association, both engaged in activities other than social, attempted to reach West Indians in other associations to attend a debate or public lecture. The three Jamaican associations, on the other hand, did very little other than hold dances and routine meetings.

One reason suggested for the difference (between the T&TS, the LIA and the Jamaican associations) was the quality of leadership in the T&TS and the LIA, which was young, professional and had not been long in England, and the middle-aged, long-established and lower status in terms of jobs, of the Jamaican leaders. This distinction, it was argued, may indicate a division of the West Indian population in Moss Side along socio-economic lines.[116] The fact that no Jamaican students or professional individuals took an active interest partly explained the lack of harmony within the Jamaican Associations.

Nevertheless, in times of need, these associations also performed a function for non-members. For instance, towards the end of 1967 and the early part of 1968, as the police intensified their campaign against West Indian cellar parties or shebeens (characterised by loud 'bluebeat' music and the sale of liquor) a number of cases of alleged police brutality had to be investigated.[117] The associations were helpful in directing the defendants to lawyers and solicitors. In a sense, this adversity (a rapid deterioriation of the racial situation) brought a semblance of solidarity to an essentially disorganised community. In fact, unlike the Pentacostalists, most of the ordinary

members of the associations experienced all their social relationships with their fellow members.

The Co-ordinating Committee

Since its formation, the leaders of the Co-ordinating Committee
were dominated by younger West Indians (in their early thirties)
from the T&TS and the LIA. They were in direct contrast to the
Jamaican Association leaders.[118] Their authority was based more
on personal charisma than was the case with the Jamaican leaders,
and they were also more administratively capable.

Not surprisingly, friction within the Committee sometimes
exploded into bitter quarrels which developed between the 'lower
class' and 'middle class' Jamaican representatives, and as a result of
the ethnic and class differences that existed between the leadership
and the majority of the West Indian population.[119]

A major cause of conflict within the Committee was the socio-
economic gap and the difference in ethnic origin which existed
between the leadership and the West Indian population. Given
growing concern that the executive of the Committee was not
representing the real interests of the black man in Moss Side, the
issue reached a head during the 'police brutality phase'.

The Committee's first two years of existence was a time of
relative calm *vis-à-vis* the racial situation in Manchester, with
multi-racial organisations establishing themselves and incorporating the West Indian leaders of the different organisations.[120] In
September 1967, however, race and colour became major issues
following intensification of the police campaign against illicit drink-
ing and all-night cellar parties. Any hope of racial harmony vanished with a spate of arrests. The police were accused of brutality.
The rapid deterioriation of the racial situation had repercussions
within the Committee, reflected in a polarisation of attitudes.
Inevitably, there were calls for greater militancy.

Significantly, the situation threw up a new, radical working class
association, the West Indian United Association (WIUA) formed
by young Jamaicans in Moss Side who suffered at the hands of the
police. The Association's leaders were the 'informal leaders' of the
'bluebeat society' namely those who patronised the cellar parties,
the cafes and the betting-shops. These leaders, aged under 40, who
lived in Moss Side and worked in the factories (or were unemployed) and had large families with young children, were in direct
contrast to the suburb-based leaders of the Jamaican Associations.[121] These rank-and-file leaders knew the problems of West
Indians at first hand and were able to command the support of large
numbers of West Indians, for short periods, at least. Indeed, having
been directly affected by the police, they carried through their vigil
outside Manchester Town Hall and advocated protest and radical
action against the police. The Committee members, on the other
hand, who were not directly affected by the actions of the police,

favoured 'reasoned consultations' between themselves as 'mouth-piece' for West Indians and the police.

CARD also became involved during the police campaign against the cellar parties, by organising a protest march against police brutality. The Dean of Manchester (Chairman of the Manchester Council for Community Relations) and the Chairman of CARD managed to get the organisers to call off the march because the Chief Constable promised to appoint a police liaison officer! This deal aroused the wrath of the few CARD radicals who felt that it would do nothing to reduce tension or cases of alleged police brutality since the liaison officer was powerless to intervene once an arrest was made.

Interestingly, this group of radicals was predominantly of white students who were members of the Manchester International Socialist group. There was only one West Indian involved. He was an informal leader who had attended Committee meetings and was a member of the WIUA. Through his concern and efforts, the police brutality issue became a major issue in the Committee. Indeed, much of the criticism of the Committee's leaders came from him and his supporters.

A split within the West Indian community was evident. The CARD radicals had exerted a strong influence over the informal leaders of the WIUA. These leaders opposed the Committee, who gave overwhelming support to the Dean and the Chairman of CARD. For a time, Committee meetings were exercises in confrontation between the informal leaders of the WIUA and the Committee's Executive.

Before the confrontation, the working-class Jamaicans, non-joiners and their informal leaders were inactive in inter-racial activity which was dominated by the Committee and the Manchester Council for Community Relations. However, the 'police brutality phase' forced the Committee to come to grips with the real problem reflected in the rank-and-file activity of an essentially Jamaican population which was clearly antagonistic towards their leadership; a leadership which was seen to be ethnically and socially separated from the grass roots. Indeed, the police issue showed a divergence of attitudes between the various social groupings represented in the Committee, with the non-Jamaican and 'middle-class' Jamaican leaders adopting an accommodative approach, while the informal leaders of the WIUA and the Colonial Sports Club advocated a radical approach. In effect, there was, at the time, open conflict between young Jamaican activists and the accommodative leaders of the Committee. [122]

The police raids on black working-class social activity in Moss Side had engendered a new mood of hostility towards the host society, as a whole. This hostility reflected an accumulation of disappointments, the result of the discrepancy between the West Indians' expectations and the extent to which they were realised.

For example, the expectations of being accepted as a social equal and gaining well-paid employment to facilitate a return to the West Indies economically secure were unrealised. Thus, the migrant's perception of rejection compounded by police harassment, resulted in hostility and bitterness towards Whites. Simultaneously, there was an increasing commitment to settlement in Britain, through mortgage debts and the education of their children. Significantly, there was no change in personal acceptance by members of the host society.

The new militant mood was conditioned by two 'external imperatives': the emergence of Black Power in the United States of America and Enoch Powell's speeches on immigration. The Black Power influence was best seen during and after the 'police brutality phase'. Police brutality in Moss Side had attuned the West Indian working class to a new militancy which was encouraged by reports of the American racial situation.

Moreover, Powell's inflammatory speeches on black immigration aroused considerable anti-white feelings. The majority of West Indians felt that Powell more or less reflected the views of the majority of British society. Furthermore, and significantly, they did not expect the racial situation to improve. More importantly, unsatisfactory inter-racial relationships were exacerbated by the nature of the employment market. As manual workers, West Indians were particularly vulnerable in times of economic recession; the prospects for their children were a deeply disturbing cause for concern.

Black youth

Teenage West Indians faced problems not only with the host society but also with their parents and older West Indians. There was, for example, considerable inter-generational discontinuity between the immigrant teenagers and their parents.

The adults who adopted a disciplinarian approach tended to relate to youths simply in terms of superordination and subordination, displaying an unwillingness to get to know the young people. For the black youth who formed an essential part of the 'bluebeat society', many in lieu of employment, resorted to 'hustling'. In fact, the militant WIUA leaders came from this 'bluebeat society'.

The West Indian teenager was 'very West Indian'. The working-class Jamaican, for example, was drawn closely to Jamaican heritage, preferring to speak patois and listen to bluebeat music, and think of himself as Jamaican. Indeed, in spite of the fact that the ethnic isolation of social relationships appeared to be less prevalent among West Indian teenagers than among adults there was a considerable reinforcing of West Indian, and particularly Jamaican, distinctiveness. Moreover, there was a marked racial 'encapsulation' of leisure-time social relationships in the institutional and informal spheres. While at school there was a considerable amount of inter-racial mixing, up to about 13 years old: after this contact was much less. In fact, only in few cases were these relationships, developed at school, continued after leaving.

Nevertheless black youths showed a greater willingness than their parents to make and develop contacts outside the West Indian community.[123] It was, however, left to be seen whether this tendency towards inter-racial mixing among teenagers would continue as teenagers assumed the roles of adults.

Easton

In Easton, as elsewhere in Britain, a variety of West Indian communal associations sprang up in the face of the host society's rejection. But attempts to organise formal associations were characterised by ephemerality and fragmentation arising from, amongst other factors, internal conflicts, island parochialism, class status, and respectability.

The distinctions of class, status and colour, engendered by the colonial history of West Indian societies, are generally reproduced, albeit in a modified form, in British settlements. In Easton, however, both colour and physical attributes had diminished as important status features as the colour scheme of the West Indian societies gave way to a 'colour code' in Britain which sharply distinguished between Black and White.

Moreover, in religious membership, West Indians adhering to 'denominational beliefs' were accorded a higher status than members of the local black pentecostalist churches. The latter was seen as less respectable than the former.

Together, these distinctions had significant consequences for potential and actual leadership of the West Indian population. In measuring status, for example, upwardly mobile West Indians had to decide in terms of their own island community and the local West Indian population or the host community. For many, the safe option was retreat.

Needless to say, this withdrawal of higher status West Indians who were seen as potential local leaders falls in line with the avoidance of the middle class Jamaicans from working class oriented associations in Moss Side. Thus, West Indian political mobilisation in Easton in mid-1970s, and earlier in Moss Side, was lacking in leadership with a broader perspective. This lack of consistency in organisation was accentuated by the stronger local Indian and Pakistani associations. In time, white racism would have a more consolidating effect on black organisations generally.[124]

Black churches

By 1970, almost a generation after the first major group of post-war West Indian and African settlers came to Britain, they found that their last refuge of hope (the Christian religion) had also been infected with racism. This realisation was surprising, even shocking, to most black Christians, given the missionary zeal with which British missionaries had carried the word of God to the black, uncivilised heathens in the colonies. At once, it was clear the white Christians were not practising what they had for centuries been preaching.

Rejection by the English Christians, during this formative period of black working-class life in Britain, led increasingly to West Indians and Africans setting up their own forms of worship, in spite of the fact that they had previously and regularly attended British churches in their respective colonial homelands. As white Christians stayed away from their places of worship, a 'quiet revolution' was taking place among black Christians.

This 'urban evangelical explosion', contrary to the trend in religious belief in Britain, resulting in the rapid growth of West Indian and African churches was, as Clifford Hill put it, 'a movement of the proletariat', which sprang from the grass roots. He added, 'It is led by no solid middle-class trend-setters. It has no ruling intelligentsia. It has not been produced by (neither has it produced) any outstanding charismatic leaders.'[125] Indeed, the leader and founder of the largest of the sects in Britain, the New Testament Church of God, the Revd O. A. Lyseight exercised an effective but spectacular behind-the-scenes leadership over his nation-wide organisation.[126]

An interesting feature of the development of these black working-class churches was its spontaneity among people seeking through religion, satisfaction of their spiritual and emotional needs. Confronted with earlier forms of oppression (as in slavery and colonialism) religion performed a similar function. Clearly, the problems of worship could only be tackled with satisfaction, given the rejection of white churches', by rank-and-file black migrants.

These were the circumstances in which there was a rapid increase in the formation of all-black congregations in migrant areas. The earlier local 'house-meetings' gave way to larger congregations in disused white churches. While many of these local congregations had affiliated to a few larger sects which originated in the West Indies, Africa or in the United States of America, many remained autonomous. These black church groups began to appear in the early 1950s.

West Indian sects

Many of the West Indian sects met as home groups. Interestingly, even within these small (enlarged family prayer meetings) there were constant leadership battles, which brought 'fission and fusion'. In spite of the difficulties of gathering reliable figures, the rapid growth rate can be measured from earlier estimates. In 1962, there was an estimated total of 77 West Indian sect congregations of all types in Britain. This increased to well over one hundred twelve months later, reaching an estimated 390 in January 1966. Since the mid-1960s a clearer pattern emerged with many small independent groups forming national organisations. Their establishment reflected a degree of independence: occupying their own premises and being run by full-time pastors and administrators.

The largest West Indian sects were The New Testament Church of God; The Church of God Prophecy; and The Apostolic Church of Jesus Christ. [127] The NTCG, formed in 1953 held its first group meeting in a rented YMCA hall in Wolverhampton. Four years later, eleven other groups had sprung up in the Midlands and London area. The NTCG bought a small hall in Hammersmith, London and with the rapid increase of its membership to 23 congregations, they were able to set up a national organisation with its base in Birmingham. Through this national network they were able to further increase their membership.

The NTCG received the support of the Church of God in Cleveland, in America, to which it was affiliated. Through 'great personal sacrifices' the organisation was able to purchase other buildings for worship. In fact, by 1966 the organisation had grown to 61 congregations (total membership 10,500) administered by 15 full-time ministers. In addition, 20 students were in training for the ministry at a theological college and the 8 provinces across the country were each administered by a full-time overseer.

Given these rapid strides in organisation, the total sect membership increased from 10,500 in 1966 to 15,800 in 1968 to 20,600 in 1970. Among the West Indian congregations most, though often similar in their type of worship, differed in emphasis on certain points of doctrine. There was, however, a large body of common characteristics in terms of preaching and life-styles. [128]

Life styles Like the African Church of the Cherubim and Seraphim, the West Indian sects, 'strongly authoritarian' and 'hierarchical', demanded high standards of personal morality with strict taboos on tobacco, alcohol, obscene language and extra-marital sex relationships. Women could not wear cosmetics or too much jewelry, and hairstyles and dress had to be conservative. Moreover, members were expected to give a tithing of 10 per cent. [129]

In terms of social class, the membership of the West Indian sects varied. The evidence shows that in the NTCG, the majority of members were not from the 'lowest classes' but from the migrant 'new middle class'. [130] Indeed, many sect members had become home-owners and landlords, who owned cars and enjoyed a 'good standard of economic prosperity.' [131] But by 1970 the NTCG population was 20,600, a small proportion of the vast majority of working class West Indians in Britain, who were far-removed from a 'good standard of living and economic prosperity'. How truly representative then have the West Indian and African sects been of the black working class in Britain?

African sects

Given a smaller African population, although there were fewer African congregations, nevertheless they were 'equally fast-growing'. The Africans concerned, who came mainly from Nigeria, had settled mainly in South, North and East London. Through affiliation many of the small independent local congregations formed the Church of the Lord in South London – a Nigerian Yoruba sect. The Church of the Cherubim and Seraphim, the largest of the affiliated African groups (also a Yoruba sect) had established congregations in the West Midlands and London. The CCS's largest congregation was in Newham, East London where it met in a former co-operative hall. The membership was predominantly male students.

Although the CCS was not Pentecostal in its form of worship it bore many similarities to the West Indian sects. Music was important. Singing (very expressive) was 'loud and rhythmical'. Moreover, at certain stages in the worship individuals lapsed (as did Pentecostalists) into 'speaking with tongues'.[132] Their worship services were of long duration, lasting some four or five hours on Sundays.

In terms of lifestyles, unlike the West Indian NTCG whose members followed the European Protestant culture in a fusion of religious and moral precepts, such an ideology was alien to the African. This has been the difficulty of Christian missionaries who saw their evangelical task as one of replacing African culture with a European-oriented culture. As one observer put it, 'Their practice of the Christian faith enables members to overcome the evil forces that surround them. It does not require them to practise a particular form of morality or to change social customs that are indigenous to an African way of life.'[133]

In answering the question, why the sects have grown, Hill saw the rejection of English churches as a major factor. Given that there was no single solution for this rejection by the English churches, in seeking an answer one had to transcend the bonds of religion and enter the field of race relations in Britain. He cited five reasons for this rejection, including 'culture shock', racial discrimination and its attendant disillusionment with the English; the conformity to English culture in that the English working classes are largely absent from churches; the basic failure of Christian mission; and the failure to satisfy the religious needs of black people in Britain,[134] due to differences in their pattern of worship in comparison with the churches of the New Commonwealth.

While these differences in worship and doctrine may account for some of the all-black congregations, it was argued that the importance of these differences as formative factors should not be exag-

gerated, firstly because many West Indian Pentecostal assemblies
would never have come into existence if their founders had been
welcomed into local English Pentecostal communities; and secondly, no amount of stress upon doctrinal or other differences can
account for the phenomenal growth rate of the all-black congregations.[135]

Moreover, the fact remains that if the membership of the West
Indian Pentecostal Assemblies were entirely composed of those
who had been Pentecostalists in their home countries, or if the
African churches in Britain were only attended by former members
of those same sects in Africa one could give credence to such an
argument, but this was not so. Indeed, a growing number of
disaffected members of all major branches of the Christian church
who felt alienated from the English churches or rejected by white
Christians found ready acceptance in the congregations of the black
churches.[136]

Social deprivation

Another factor related to the rapid growth of all-black churches in
Britain, particularly between 1960 and 1970 was the role of social
deprivation. In fact, it has been argued that there is a relationship
between the growth of the West Indian NTCG, the African CCS
sects and the experience of deprivation due to social rejection.[137]
Indeed, the ethnic and status deprivation of New Commonwealth
migrants had the effect of social solidarity among members of the
'pariah' group.

Social deprivation seems to be crucial. In the 1964 General
Election race first became a political issue in a British election;[138]
thereafter 'race relationships' received increasing attention from the
mass media and from the MP Enoch Powell and other race-
conscious politicians. In time, they managed to make 'hard line'
attitudes and racism 'respectable'. Naturally, black people were
conscious of the fact that more black men were prosecuted than
white men under the Race Relations Act 1965 which was designed
to protect Blacks from racial discrimination. What Powell and
Duncan Sandys were saying conveniently escaped the prosecutors'
notice. According to one observer, the beginning of the hardening
of racial attitudes in 1964 marked the point after which the immigrant black churches received their high growth rate.[139] It is clear
then that the degree of felt deprivation increased the sects' membership.

The creative role of West Indian and African sects, it was hoped,
would 'one day break through into the local white population'. The
black sects could radically affect the course of church history as well
as race relations. Hill, who had testified how much he had gained
from worshipping in West Indian congregations and under West
Indian leadership, expressed this optimism and urgency:

If the English churches are to benefit from the vision and spiritual gifts of the Africans and West Indians, then the first step is the recognition of their ministry and the admission of their representatives, on a fully equal-status basis, into ecumenical church councils. There are indications that this is beginning to happen, but much more needs to be done, and much more quickly. [140]

Given that black churches have played a central role in demanding equal rights for black people in the nineteenth century and in the development of Pan Africanism, by the end of the 1960s in Britain they had responded positively to racism in 'the house of God' by forming autonomous organisations.

Black organisations: the 1970s and 1980s

The workplace

To combat the problems of black workers, strike committees were formed and conferences were called to highlight the problem of racism at the workplace. Arising from this struggle, the Black Trade Unionists Solidarity Movement was formed. In fact, by 1980 there were some 59 projects and groups involved in the industrial aspects of race relations. [141] More specifically, in the Midlands and Wales area there were 29 ethnic minority organisations concerned with employment in 1982. [142] These groups indicate to a large extent that traditional trade unionism could not deal effectively with the special problems of black workers. Self-help and autonomous organisation was the only response to racial discrimination among employers and trade unions.

The black community

The 1970s and early 1980s have been crucial for the black community in terms of organisation. The cumulative effects of racial disadvantage in all aspects of the black community's life such as police harassment, particularly against black youth; provocation from extremist fascist organisations, and the overall racist (both individual and institutional) violence had served to reinforce black resistance. Throughout the 1970s the harassed black community offered strong resistance. Rebellion, after a long gestation period, eventually came in the early 1980s.

While member organisations within the Black Peoples' Alliance (BPA) were allowed local autonomy in terms of the particular communities and problems, moves at national level and co-ordination of the various campaigns against racism were the task of the BPA. In 1969, the Alliance took to the streets leading a march of over 7000 people to Downing Street to demand the repeal of the Immigration Acts. Feelings ran high as the Black Panther Movement warned: 'Unless something is done to ensure the protection of our people . . . we will have no alternative but to rise to their defence. And once we are driven to that position, redress will be too late, Detroit and Newark will inevitably become part of the British scene and the Thames foam with blood sooner than Enoch Powell envisaged'.[143] Thus, the racial ball was thrown back into Powell's and his followers' court.

The 1971 Immigration Act was no less damaging in its effects on the black community. This was one more stage in the deepening of state racism. Another strand of continuing associational concern was the serious question of the education of West Indian children. The North London West Indian Association which was set up by West Indian parents and teachers in Haringey, North London, in the 1960s, under the leadership of Jeff Crawford, had aroused interest among black parents in many other areas and became an integral part of the programmes of black political organisations. Clearly the question of ESN schools could not be left to the British authorities. The Caribbean Education Association held a conference on the ESN schools, and soon after, Bernard Coard clarified the problem in his work *How the West Indian Child is made Educationally Subnormal*.

In the wake of this exposé, a number of black militants and organisations took the initiative by setting up supplementary schools. In London, the activity was particularly intense. Among the schools set up were the Kwame Nkrumah school (Hackney Black Teachers), the Malcolm X Montessori Programme (Ahoy Ghose), the George Padmore School (John La Rose, leader of the Black Parents Movement), the South East London Summer School (BUFP: Black Unity and Freedom Party), Headstart (BLF:Black Liberation Front) and the Marcus Garvey school (BLF and others).[144]

Moreover, there was an impressive development of projects to teach skills to black youth. For example, the Mkutano Project, started by the BUFP in 1972, taught typing, photography and Swahili; the Melting Pot set up by Ashton Gibson (formerly of RAAS) organised a workshop for clothes-making; and the Keskidee was organised by Oscar Abrams (formerly of CARD) who taught art and sculpture and encouraged black poets and playwrights.

For older students, Roy Sawh supervised the Free University for Black Studies; for the unemployed and homeless black youth, there were hostels, such as Brother Herman's Harambee and Vince Hines' (formerly active in RANS) Dashiki and youth centres and clubs. Furthermore there were bookshop-cum-advice centres, namely the black peoples' information centre; BLF's Grassroots Storefront and BWM's (Black Workers' Movement was the Black Panther's new name in the 1970s) Unity Bookshop. Among the publications, weekly and monthly newspapers, were *Black Voice* (BUFP), *Grassroots* (BLF), *Freedom News* (Black Panthers), *Frontline* (Brixton and Croydon Collective), *Uhuru* (Black Peoples Freedom Movement), *BPFM Weekly*, the *BWAC Weekly* (Black Work-ers' Action Committee) and the less frequent but more theoretical journal *Black Liberator*, among a number of other more ephemeral publications.

The question of black women was taken up by some of these publications and the BUFP (following on the UCPA's Black Women's Liberation Movement) had a black women's action com-mittee. Interestingly, after RAAS's Black House was raided by police and closed down, many of its members helped to organise various self-help projects as mentioned above.

By 1971 the repressiveness of the system had also led to the break-up of the UCPA. The hard core of the membership went on to form the BUFP. In the previous two years, the UCPA, RAAS, the Black Panthers and other black organisations had been increas-ingly concerned with police brutality and fascist violence. But as Sivanandan argued:

> The success of Black Power had brought down on its head the wrath of the system. Its leaders were persecuted, its meetings disrupted, its places of work destroyed. But it had gone on gaining momentum and strength: it was not a party, but a movement, gathering to its concerns all the strands of capitalist oppression, gathering to its programme all the problems of oppressed peoples. There was hardly a black in the country that did not identify with it and, through it, to all the non-whites of the world, in one way or another. And as for the British-born youth, who had been schooled in white racism, the movement was the cradle of their consciousness. Vietnam, Guinea-Bissau, Zimbabwe, Azania were all their battle lines, China and Cuba were exemplars. The establishment was scared. The media voiced its fears. There were rumours that Black Power was about to take over Manchester City Council. [145]

Blacks had to fight simultaneously both as a people and as a class (for instance as Blacks and as workers, their struggle against racism was a struggle for the class). They were engaged in a number of strikes in the early 1970s in the textile and allied industries of the East Midlands and in factories in London.

In the 1972 strike at Crepe Sizes in Nottingham involving Pakistani workers, with no support from the TGWU, they formed a Solidarity Committee composed of wives and the families of the strikers, of other Asian workers, community organisations and the Nottingham-based BPFM, which put pressure on the union to act.

Time and again, black workers confronted trade union racism. The NCTUAR called on trade unions and trade unionists to back workers' official strike action against racial discrimination. Moreover, they leafletted the TUC Annual Conference in Black-pool. A clear pattern had again emerged: all the black political organisations (the London-based BUFP, BCC, BWCC and the BWM, and the East Midlands-based BWAC and the BPFM) gave support to the strikers. Further, the BWAC informed the Non-Aligned Conference in Algiers of the international operations of ITT, the multinational company involved.

By the time of the Imperial Typewriters strike in 1974, there was virtually a standing conference of black strike committees in the Midlands, a network of community associations and groups, and a number of black political organisations, all in support of the strikers. In fact, financial support came from a number of sources such as the Southall IWA, the Birmingham Sikh temple, a Women's Conference in Edinburgh, the Birmingham Anti-Racist Committee and the European Workers' Action Committee.

The Community Relations Commissions (CRC) which emerged as the successor to the NCCI under the Race Relations Act of 1968 was merged (through the 1976 Race Relations Act) with the Race Relations Board to form the new Commission for Racial Equality. The CRE, armed with a few more powers to deal with discrimination, was to develop 'a class of collaborators who would manage racism and its social and political fall-out. At the same time, it would hand out massive sums of money from its Urban Aid programme to key black self-help groups and so stamp out the breeding-grounds of resistance'. [146]

The murder on 4 June 1976 of an Asian youth in Southall stunned the community. The old-style traditional forms of organisation proved inadequate in the circumstances; new radical forces in the community emerged in the form of the Southall Youth Movement. This initiative led to the formation of a number of other Asian Youth movements; organisations which were largely concerned with defence in the face of fascist attacks. As racist attacks and murders increased, Asian youth organisations and defence committees were formed in London (Brick Lane, Hackney and Newham), Manchester, Leicester and Bradford. And in the same community spirit of the strike committees, formed earlier, these youth groups, supported each other and joined and worked together with West Indian youth groups, occasionally on an organisational basis (SYM and Peoples Unite, Bradford Blacks and Bradford Asian Youth Movement) and, at times, as individuals participating in political groups, such as the Hackney Black Peoples' Defence Organisation and Bradford's United Black Youth League. [147]

Political groups were also formed involving radical Afro-Caribbeans, Asians and Africans disenchanted by the white left because they neglected the black experience. And characteristically, as all black political organisations have historically done (beginning with the Pan Africanists), they focused not only on the black condition in Britain, but also on Blacks internationally. In belief and approach they were anti-racist and anti-imperialist; both were acted out as a lived experience in their communities. Their concern to politicise black people was reflected in their publications: *Samaj in 'a Babylon* (in Urdu and English), *Black Struggle* and *Mukti*.

Following these organisational developments, the Black Socialist Alliance moved on to 'campaigning material'. Blacks Against State Harassment concentrated on state racism. Many other papers, journals, news sheets and newsletters were published, but short-lived. Indeed, they represented various stages of black struggle. Nevertheless, the movement was always in one direction: against the police, the government and racism.

Flexibility within the black movement was vital. There had been a qualitative change in the relationship between the organisers and organisations. In 1969, the educated middle-class leadership in Moss Side, for example, and later in Easton, either evaded leadership positions or did so as authoritarian figures. By the mid-1970s, however, after consecutive struggles, at various levels, some organisers who had hitherto led as charismatic accommodationist, liberal individuals, could no longer do so.

State racism and racial discrimination increasingly engendered black community demands for representation that reflected these basic issues. Indeed the stage was reached when 'the educated gave of their skills to the community and the community grounded them in the realities of political struggle'. [148]

The black women's movement in the 1970s

The strikes involving black workers in the 1970s saw a new phenomenon on the British industrial relations scene: Asian women 'womanning' the picket lines, with an unusual commitment. In their various industrial struggles, they were consistently supported by women's groups. As their experience deepened and their particular problems loomed large, a 'black women' movement emerged. [149]

Black feminist groups   Between 1977 and 1980, the provocative daubings, meetings and marches of the National Front in areas of large black communities heightened black resistance which led to new types of struggles and new leaderships in the form of a black women's movement; a movement encompassing all the struggles and adding its own perspective to the black resistance in the late 1970s. For at least a decade previously a few Afro-Caribbean women's groups, pursuing legitimate issues, germane to black women, were isolated in their efforts since neither the black political groups nor the white women's liberation movement showed real concern.

Through contact at the point of common industrial struggles, Asian women began to support their Afro-Caribbean sisters at Grunwick and at Heathrow Airport. By 1978, awareness of their social, economic and political position, in the black community and in white society generally, increased dramatically. A number of black women's groups came into being and formed a national body, the Organisation of Women of Asian and African Descent.

OWAAD published its own paper FOWAAD. And recognising the organisational complexities, to be effective it allowed its constituent groups local autonomy. Moreover, it held national conferences and significantly worked in conjunction with other black national groups. This crucial development, long overdue, was able to highlight and orchestrate the different experiences of Asian and Afro-Caribbean women. In developing particular strands of struggles, they supported each other's campaigns and, through this process, benefited and strengthened the black community as a whole.

Their struggles relating to households and children's welfare reflected the very essence of black community life. Thus, this new leadership confronted simultaneously the issues of discrimination against class, race and gender. Asian and Afro-Caribbean women combined forces to tackle a number of on-going problems specific to the black community. Moreover, Asian women joined the campaigns against 'Sin-bins' (special 'adjustment units' which replaced ESN schooling for West Indian children) and the Brixton Black Women's Group organised the first black women's centre in 1979.[150]

Black women as a whole recognised their problem as a common racism, as endemic in the social, educational and welfare services of the entire community. Health care was particularly germane: in Brent there were campaigns against sickle-cell anaemia (among West Indians) and vitamin D deficiencies causing rickets (among Asians). The fertility and mental health of black women were also matters of serious concern to both communities.

Certain aspects of immigration had disturbing effects on Asian women which the male-oriented IWA had neglected, woefully. Asian women began to put this right as AWAZ and Southall Black Sisters (formed after the police violence on 23 April 1979) led the protest against the virginity testing and X-raying of immigrants. The IWA followed this lead. Following Asian youth groups, these women joined the community campaigns over specific immigration cases.

By the end of the 1970s and the beginning of the 1980s, black women were again actively involved in industrial struggles at Futters (March–May 1979) and at Chix (1979–80). They also worked in local self-defence groups and in the BSA and BASH national campaigns. Significantly, in June 1979, their work jointly with IWA and BASH, resulted in the first black national demonstration against state brutality. During this march, Jagmohan Joshi, one of the longest serving, militant black organisers in Britain, died of a heart attack. This was a fitting epitaph for a man who had not only initiated black working class and community movements in the early years of struggle, but also 'clarified for us all the lines of race/class struggle'.[151]

Historically then, the black working-class organisers and organisations spent much time resisting the British government's ideology of racism and repression. Consistently, their practices and policies have been anti-working class, anti-women, and anti-youth. In pursuit of the ideology of repression, the state relied heavily on the police and policing. Increasingly (particularly during the 1970s) police brutality and police harassment of black youth and the black community came to a head as an 'accumulation of blunders' resulted in the Bristol 'riot' in 1980 and the national summer 'riots' of 1981.

During these riots the police resorted to 'dispensing justice on the streets, to arbitrary arrests and in some cases mass arrest'. By Tuesday 14 July, according to the press, 1000 people had been arrested. This figure, according to the Home Office, had risen to 3000 by 20 August 1981. After the 'riots', committees were set up to defend and campaign for those arrested, and to expose the official version of events. In Brixton, the black community organisations were headed by the Brixton Defence Campaign.

The BDC called for a total boycott of the state's inquiry into the Brixton Uprising of 10–13 April 1981, set up under Lord Scarman's chairmanship, with the terms of reference: 'To inquire urgently into the serious disorders in Brixton on 10–12 April and to report, with the power to make recommendations.'

The BDC argued that there was no escaping the fact that the Scarman inquiry (particularly Phase I) 'very seriously prejudices the legal position and therefore endangers the liberty of all defendants yet to be tried'. The three main arguments against this Phase were firstly, that Scarman himself had positively to agree that Phase I will 'prejudice the rights of fair trial to those who have yet to come before the courts'; secondly, the question that must be asked was: what were the 'immediate causes' into which Scarman was going to investigate so urgently in Phase I. (They argued that the immediate causes of what happened in Brixton were already well understood); and thirdly, instead of looking at the real 'immediate cause' of the uprising, they feared that Scarman would 'give subtle legitimacy to the totally racist view (so dramatically put by Margaret Thatcher) that the Brixton uprising was simply a confrontation between, on the one hand, fundamentally blameless forces of law and order and, on the other, mainly black criminals!'

Thus, the BDC was satisfied that Lord Scarman was disposed to be used by the state to provide it with a basis for re-writing the Riot Act and to provide justification for dramatically increasing repressiveness in policing methods which were already massively racist, lawless and brutal as well as substantially uncontrolled. Why, the BDC asked, was there no response by the state to the repeated requests for a public inquiry into police brutality and malpractice during the previous five years.

On Phase II of the Scarman inquiry, it argued that for the black community there were no benefits to be derived for three reasons.

Firstly, it was not aware that Scarman had any expertise in the field of social policy and was not satisfied that even were he to have both the necessary expertise and sympathy that these would be sufficient, given the other factors which apply. Secondly, that there were no good reasons to hold that ignorance on the part of the state was a major cause/force determining the present direction of its policies in the field of housing, employment, education, etc. Thirdly, that the BDC was satisfied particularly that where the black communities' grievances over the racist, brutal, lawless and uncontrolled policing methods used against them were concerned, the state had no basis for even claiming to be ignorant. 'A mountain of evidence', the Campaign argued, had been 'submitted and ignored'. [152]

The Liverpool 8 Defence Committee, the Liverpool Black Organisation and the Liverpool Trades Council, called for the dismissal of the Chief Constable of Merseyside, Kenneth Oxford. All three organisations were firmly convinced that he was the prime obstacle in the way of any constructive dialogue between the police and the community. The Committee's specific reasons were, given that the responsibility for the fair and proper policing of any community was the responsibility of the Chief Constable, Oxford's own racism, combined with his belief that tough and repressive policing methods were the best way of establishing order, had resulted in excessive police harassment, especially of black people which stretched back many years; that Oxford was well-known for making racist remarks about the Liverpool 8 Community; that Oxford had shown himself to be incompetent; that the treatment of those arrested during and since the 'riots' was appalling; that three weeks after the 'riots' young people had been stopped and searched for no reason at all, racially abused and frequently questioned about their movements during the weekend of the riots; and that Oxford had, as a last ditch attempt to gain credibility within the community, invited representatives of the community groups to meet with him.

The Liverpool 8 Defence Committee wondered why Oxford had waited to engage in dialogue with a community which had been harassed by his police for many years, and towards which he had shown himself to be racist. Thus, the Liverpool 8 Defence Committee, the Liverpool Black Organisation and the Charles Wootton Centre declared that they would boycott the meeting and called upon other community organisations to do the same. Also caught in the struggle were the outspoken Hackney Legal Defence Committee and the United Black Youth League in Bradford.

Indeed in the aftermath of the 'riots', black organisers and organisations in the various black communities nationally had rallied round to support their victimised youths, as they alerted each other to their common need and common oppression. Before the 1980 and 1981 'riots', the black working class fought in isolation. Now through an historical progression of struggle (having shifted and reformed, through new types of struggles and new leaderships) they have attained a hard-won national black class consciousness. And in this process, they were joined, if only fleetingly, by white youth, militant white women and gays. But how did this black consciousness develop?

11 Black Working Class Consciousness

Black youth: the oppressed seen as a social problem

Social policy and black youth

Gradually, during the late 1960s and early 1970s it was realised that the education system had been failing the black second generation 'achievement-wise'.[1] If education was a major 'problem' among black youth, then the high and disproportionate incidence of unemployment[2] amongst black school-leavers in conjunction with the 'alarming levels' of homelessness among West Indians[3] were also cause for concern. The black 'second generation' had become the 'central yardstick' to measure race relations and immigration policies.

Given these circumstances, throughout the 1970s, young Blacks were increasingly being linked with criminality. Blacks, as far as the police in the London area were concerned, were usually found to be over-represented in every main category of crime. 'Mugging' was liberally used in relation to the criminality of black youth living in the multi-deprived, inner city areas. The media accentuated mugging very often by depicting the victims as 'white and helpless', when the truly victimised were the Blacks in the decaying inner city areas. Thus, mugging introduced 'racially directed' crime. Black youth had become a social problem and as far as the state was concerned, control was necessary. Therefore, heavier sentences were imposed by the courts and the 'sus' law was vigorously enforced by the police.

Relations between the police and black youth and, in general, the black community had deteriorated considerably throughout the 1960s and 1970s, so that by the beginning of the 1980s the situation had become one of serious concern. This entire period was frequently punctuated by incidents of police harassment of black youth. The oppressor and the oppressed were confronted with each other, for example, at the explosive Notting Hill carnival.

The Notting Hill explosion had served, at least for those who knew, as a public warning of the crisis of black youth. In its 1980 study entitled 'The Fire Next Time', the Community Relations Commission warned of the total alienation of black youth from society. The state, however, had already begun to draw a clear link between race and law and order. Surrounded by the system, and particularly in the persons of the law-enforcers, black youth had to find a way out.

During the 1970s the stark fact remained that black youth as under-achievers at school were unemployed and disillusioned with their prospects in British society. As part of the black working class, they were alienated, the direct result of the precise and cumulative effect of British policy-makers. Black youths understood through hard experience that colour was the major determinant of their alienation. Their parents' culture had been subsumed by the state, through an integrative policy employing various controlling agencies.

Educationally, while the struggle for O levels and CSEs continues, few West Indian youths make it through the system. The selective systems which operate within schools appear to operate systematically against Blacks. Predictably, the upholders of the system have attempted to explain such selection as due to the hereditary qualities of the Blacks. However, on the question of the process of socialisation and acculturation, other factors come up for consideration. The fact remains that in using English culture at all, let alone in trying to do well in it, the West Indian child (unlike the Punjabi child) faces unique difficulties in that there is no alternative culture to turn to at home. Indeed, both the culture of his home and school devalue black people and their achievements. Thus, starting with a low self-image, the child faces selective processes which present a further sense of inadequacy. If such tests are difficult enough for the white working class child to cope with, imagine how much more difficult it could be for the West Indian child.

Thus, more often than not, the West Indian child ends up in remedial or disciplinary class situations and once there, it is likely that the process becomes cumulative because teachers' stereotypes of West Indian children have tended to become the basis for further processes of selection. For many West Indian children, therefore, it appears that the system is loaded against them, and they take refuge in a culture which urges them to take pride in their own black culture, while treating school as a process which one endures. Given this negative low self-image, Rastafarianism, among other things, has tended to uplift and restore the self-esteem of black school children tagged as 'remedials' and 'low streamers'.

Moreover, rejection in the selective process is only one of many breaches with society that the West Indian child experiences. The others may be with the family and later, with the world of work, if they were fortunate to get it. Unlike the Asian family which makes a break between even young adults and their parents virtually impossible (although there is evidence of growing conflict between them) the link between a young West Indian male and his parents is relatively weak.

Significantly, whether or not young Blacks succeed education-ally, they are likely to suffer a similar experience of rejection when they seek employment. Discrimination against young working-class Blacks is widespread at all levels of employment. The altern-atives to employment are joining the 'hustlers' or turning to the political/religious teaching of Rastafarianism.

Young men and women do not normally turn to religious movements for explanations of their rejection and their deviance. If they are to be affected by ideas such as Rastafarianism, there must be some medium through which ideas reach them. That medium is reggae music. Apart from its rhythms and its themes, they also receive a political message which relates to their oppression. The word 'Babylon' conveys the powerful message of 'four hundred years of slavery', as well as the immediate injustices of the selective system to which they are subjected. In effect, it approximates the function which the slogan Black Power performed for young Blacks in Britain and the United States in the 1960s.

Before the 1970s, the Rastafarian movement was relatively unknown in Britain. A deepening of Third World impoverishment and black 'colonisation' in Britain led inevitably to self-examination and black history. Marcus Garvey, the founder and leader of the Universal Negro Improvement Association sought the return of all black people to Africa. But Garvey never publicly acknowledged the legitimacy of the Rastafarian enterprise nor the divinity of the Emperor Haile Selassie I, Ras Tafari, King of Kings, Lord of Lords, the all-conquering Lion of the Tribe of Judah. In fact, after the invasion of Abyssinia, Garvey described Haile Selassie as 'a great coward' who ran away from his country and of playing white.[4] He also castigated the Emperor for being the ruler of a country where black men were chained and flogged. However, Garvey who taught the black man to see beauty in himself, saw in his message a lingering influence. He said, 'Be assured I planted well the seed of Negro or black nationalism.'

This separation in education has led to strong social solidarity among working-class school children. They expressed themselves strongly in the popular arts and in popular sports. Outside the schools, the police assumed, almost as their fundamental activity, the control and at times harassment of the young who demonstrated their support for football teams and pop music stars. In time, they came to be called hooligans and vandals. If white working-class youth experiencing a popular culture appear as a threat, young West Indian Blacks seem even more threatening to the authorities and to white working-class people.

Black youth in Babylon

As Garveyism spread in Jamaica, Garvey was cast in the role of prophet by early Rastafarian leaders who utilised his 'Back to Africa' movement. Thus, thousands of Rastafarians prepared to journey back to the African 'fatherland', an act expected to free the Rastas from the white man's domination, referred to as Babylon. As yet, this exodus to Africa has not materialised and Babylon remains oppressive and intact. By the late 1970s, the vision of a redeemed Africa had spread to the inner city areas of Britain, as thousands of black youths adopted new modes of defiance. Through this life style, they widened the gap between the first and second generation Blacks in Britain.

Unlike their parents, black youths were drawn by a 'messianic consummation of history', through a new style: wearing 'dreadlocks' and the Tam in the national colours of Ethiopia – red, green and black. Their rejection of British society draws them closer to Africa and the Jamaican patois (witness the life style of the Moss Side 'bluebeat' society of the late 1960s). Symbolically, it engendered a feeling of brotherhood for all Blacks. Already alienated, they resisted the influence of Babylon. Thus, the Rastafarian movement reflected the qualitatively different life experiences of the black immigrants, particularly Jamaicans and their children.

Significantly, however, the black youths' indulgence was (and is) no escapist fantasy. Indeed, it became a lived experience. Their commitment was real, an open rejection of British society. The contrasting life styles and beliefs of first and second generation West Indians was a reflection of profound changes in consciousness. But how did black youths become progressively involved in the movement immersing themselves in the Rasta system to the point where they accepted the divinity of Jah Ras Tafari and, by implication, the inevitability of a return to Africa. According to one writer, black youths who engage in the process of becoming a Rastaman go through four broad phases: first, the apprehension of racial disadvantage; secondly, the loss of plausibility of parents' beliefs; thirdly, the drift to Ras Tafari; and fourthly, the acceptance of Haile Selassie. In spite of a few 'road blocks', since the early 1970s, there was an increase in the number of black youths who (with varying interests) were able to carry through this journey.[5]

Along the road to Jah, the black school-leaver gets the full devastating blast of racialism in employment. For the West Indian youth, it is argued that the process of alienation begins during the later stages of secondary-school education. For it is during these years that they come to realise that their colour is a liability in the eyes of the society and that it is often used as a basis for exclusion and rejection. Thus, the experiences of other black people, relations, friends and indeed, members of their own family leave a deep and lasting impression.

One major experience of racism is related to confrontations with the police in their day-to-day whereabouts in their communities, and also at the annual Notting Hill carnival. Police harassment and brutality were recurring experiences for black youths. Consequently, the apprehension of racial disadvantage sparked off a pattern of events which gave the necessary credibility to a British Rastafarian movement.

Both parents and children realised that there was no entry into positions of authority and prestige, for example, because of skin colour. In their 'exile' in Britain, blackness has become their common identity; their separateness was clear.

Although their parents' beliefs and religion began to lose its significance, there was no outright rejection of them. Nonetheless, their readiness to accept an alternative resulted in an increasing importance of the Rastafarian-inspired reggae music, through which the Rastas built their beliefs and through which they constructed a world view. Rastafarianism made sense to black youths particularly because it put into perspective their parents' views.

Pervasive racialism in all aspects of British society pushed more and more black youths to the acceptance of Rastafarianism and opposition to Babylon. In the 1970s, Bob Marley's reggae music made a powerful impact on black youths in Britain. This music was an important starting point in that it brought insight on several broad issues. Thus a process of learning was set in motion. The acquisition of knowledge bred further questioning and a movement away from their parents' British-based culture. Helping them along on their journey to Jah was their music. From their communities in Britain, Africa beckoned.

Their parents' lack of pride in their African ancestry was in contrast to the total acceptance of Africa by these youths. The quest for the 'true self' the 'I and I' and their 'African roots' were paramount concerns. In effect, membership of the Rastafarian movement directed the black youth, alienated from the host society, closer to the acceptance of Selassie I as God Almighty. For the deprived young Black, the brotherhood of Rastafarianism was a 'morally uplifting experience'. Given that there was simply no alternative, enslavement in Babylon had to be resisted. In accepting Rastafarianism then, the Rastaman acknowledged the unity of Rastas through the bond of God, with an unshakeable conviction that the white man's domination was at an end, that Babylon will be destroyed.

The decade of the 1970s then led to a phenomenal growth of the Rastafarian movement, with the acceptance of Haile Selassie becoming perhaps the most important feature of the young West Indians beginning their journey to Jah. In effect, Rastafarianism had instilled in the young Black a sense of real brotherhood. Moreover, acceptance of Selassie has led to marked changes in consciousness, widening the gap over a period of one generation between the original immigrants and the young Rastas who perceived the racism inherent in the social, economic and political structures of British society, and took a tangential course to Jah instead. To the Rastaman, integration was, and is, unworkable.

Having accepted Jah, the actual life and practice of the young Rastas is 'complex', particularly to those who do not care to understand. For example, young Rastas may live in squats and smoke ganga, but they also read the Bible. The Rasta life style has its own meanings and its own religious significance, as is the case with the mainstream Rastafarian Church or the Pentecostal and Holiness Churches. But, unlike these churches which can be co-opted into mainstream life, the Rastas of the streets remain stubbornly separated.

Racism and sexism

The young black female's predicament and struggle

For young black females, the relationship between education, paid employment and power is important. Their parents' view was put into context by the Organisation of Women of Asian and African Descent thus:

> The dream of a good education for their children has always had a particular significance for black people. White colonialists fed generations of Asians, Africans and West Indians the myth that the reason they were being savagely economically exploited was not because of race or class but because they were backward, under-developed, uneducated. The old colonialist equation of education power explains why so many black parents passionately wanted for their children the education they never had.

In linking education with future earning power, Prescod-Roberts suggested why 'girls' in the Caribbean may be supported by their family to pursue educational qualifications. She took the view that the sexual division of labour and responsibility within the family binds women more strongly and permanently into family responsibilities than it does men, thus making women the better migrants from the perspective of those left behind. It is clear therefore that such power as women obtain is directly channelled into one institution in which women's power is sanctioned – the family. Their positive identity is female but a belief that in Britain and the Caribbean women were often accorded less than their due meant that girls were angry at the foreclosing of options available to them. Instead of engendering apathy and despair, the girls remained persistent and resourceful. Indeed, the struggle of black women had become one of persistence and resourcefulness. These have been common themes. Furthermore, this is a statement of a continuing double-subordination of black women.

Regardless of the girls' undeniable strength and perseverance, even if their ambitions are realised, they are not about to become part of a privileged elite. A labour market which is largely sex-segregated and which operates differential rates of pay for women and men, means that the only edge which the black girls may have over black boys is that their paper qualifications may give them the option of obtaining their lower wages through shorter hours of work and in possibly more congenial working conditions.

Commenting on the fact that matrifocality can and does exist within essentially patriarchial social formations, Fuller argues that 'black women in Britain and the USA are faced with just such a situation. Matrifocality may allow women to develop with a definition of femininity that includes strength, competence and so on which enables them to challenge patriarchal relations of sexual dominations but it does not thereby do away with patriarchy.'[6]

Asian (Pakistani and Indian) 'girls'

Asian girls (like Asian boys) not only face the language problem at school, but are also made to feel that being an Asian is a 'disadvantage'. Given that the structure of primary education in Britain is implicitly racist, for example, in the books used, the curriculum and the teachers' attitudes, this serves to reinforce this disadvantage. While some school teachers take a strong anti-racist line, they remain very much the exceptions waging an unsuccessful fight against the racism of the school system.

Asian children in schools, surrounded by white figures of authority, quickly realise their disadvantaged position. Indeed, they are made to feel embarrassed when their parents, who are unable to express themselves adequately in English, try to talk to teachers. The laughter and derision aroused among pupils, both black and white, pushes the Asian child into a sense of isolation. In this predicament, as one observer put it, 'what the child faces is a kind of colonial experience which they are far too young to fight against. The children under eleven I spoke to almost invariably had a sense of inferiority similar to that of colonised people. They were ashamed of anything Indian. They disowned their food and their language and in some cases even their Indian first names. A few tried to make even their skin as inconspicuous as possible – as white as possible.'

Yet as Indian children grow older, these 'racist opinions' are altered dramatically by their experiences. Remarks about food, curry for example, lacerate their tender sensibilities. They receive broadsides from several fronts – for their colour, their food and their religion. And what is more they begin to see themselves as inferior.

According to Amrit Wilson, an Indian writer,

> Children between eight and twelve seem too young to fight against cultural racism in school; it is as though they are almost stunned into accepting the inferiority with which white society has labelled them. But at twelve their feelings seem to change. It is not that racism vanishes – in fact it intensifies and violence increases, but most children start to face up to it at this point, and their 'inferiority' usually clears away. After all, when racism takes the form of violence, they can't fail to recognise it as an attack on themselves and part of a value system they cannot go along with. [7]

In schools in the Harlesden area, there were three social groups: West Indian, English and Irish, and Asian. One girl said, 'There is hostility between West Indians and English ... they don't mix much, they keep apart, though sometimes there are fights. But attacks on Asian girls are much more common.' According to these girls, apart from the violence, it was difficult to be friendly with white girls. [8]

Some East African Asian girls felt that West Indians sometimes behaved as though they are superior to Asians, 'because Asians are religious or because Asians can't speak English well'. A counter-argument was that 'Indian children are only reacting to the insufferable cultural superiority that Asians feel. Indian culture is a big barrier and they make it more so by always thinking they are superior.' While there is truth in both opinions, it was also argued that it was a 'matter of style'. As a white secondary school teacher put it, 'In the eyes of children, West Indians have it and Asians don't. When a West Indian boy walks in, the girls look up; they don't do that for an Asian. In our school there is no doubt there is a hierarchy. The West Indians are at the top and the Asians are at the bottom.'

Be that as it may, the overriding reason for conflict must be the British education system itself, 'with its essentially ethnocentric curriculum, its apathy, its built in attitude that Western culture is the only culture and its pervasive mockery of people who are "different"'. [9]

Asian girls are faced with a real dilemma. At school they have (with no one to turn to except each other) to endure bullying and racism. When they get home nothing is said about racism. As one girl put it, 'everyone is tired in the evenings and we don't like to talk about it.' More tellingly though, many girls from orthodox Muslim and Sikh families feel that even if they did tell their parents, they would not understand. Thus criticism of the school system in these circumstances would be 'not only pointless but risky'.

Asian girls also have to face their parents' attitudes to education which 'vary tremendously with religion, background in Pakistan or India, and, of course, with the people involved'. Without consultation some parents tend to map out the careers of their daughters, pressuring these girls in almost impossible situations. One Gujarati girl said: 'My parents, and most Asian parents, they live for their children. Everything they do is for their children. They have so many hopes and dreams for their children's future. When it doesn't come out the way they want it to, that is when they get most hurt I think. . . .'[10]

In extreme cases, the daughter's education is irrelevant. Between these two extremes, most parents do not show much interest in their daughters' school life. Indeed they discourage them from entering higher education. In the case of Muslim girls, the demands of Islam conflict with the requirements of the school system. For example, the Koran's teaching that arms and legs must always be covered makes the wearing of school uniform a difficult problem. This raises the questions of nakedness which some girls were brought up to think of as 'undesirable, even immoral', and of course, sex education in school. Most Pakistani mothers were against sex education.[11]

Torn in a conflict between their parents' culture, language and religion, and the host country, on the one hand, and the inherent racism of the British school system, on the other, Indian and Pakistani girls, whatever education they manage to achieve, prepare for the post-school threat or prospect of marriage which begins 'to loom over her, casting a blight over her chances of further education'.[12] While Hindu girls from an urban background are most likely to study or at least to continue their courses after marriage, for Muslim or Sikh girls higher education can rarely be achieved without struggle.' Indeed, many families feel that marriage is preferable to a college career and that higher education is 'dangerous', 'destructive' and 'potentially immoral'.[13]

The struggle for freedom in the school rooms, in many cases, pales into insignificance when compared with the restrictions placed upon them during adolescence and eventually in marriage. The potential for revolt among these Asian girls and women is great. For in spite of their differences in life style, Wilson's findings show (i) that although they come from so many different parts of the Indian sub-continent and have so many different religions, it is clear that as women they face a special kind of oppression; (ii) that they are also united by racism in Britain; and (iii) that because of their exploitation as a class, most of them, even those who were middle class before had become working class. Wilson concludes:

> What struck me was that all these three things together affected the outlook of these women and it wasn't possible to separate them. You might think of yourself as just a person, maybe with a husband or parents or children, but when you step out of your door you know that you will be looked at by other people as just an Asian woman – a black woman. As for class – immigrants come basically because of jobs, of money; so all the women, even those who don't go out to work, are conscious of their class. They are conscious of their families being working class. One could put it this way – they may feel that when oppressed as women they are being oppressed as individuals, but racism is an attack on them as part of their family and community, and these things cannot be separated in the identity of a woman. [14]

Black feminist responses

Given the government's apparent concern over the discriminatory practices and the disadvantages of the black working class, particularly as it related to black youth by the 1970s, the issue of race had become a major topic of debate within sections of the black working class in Britain.

In raising the level of black consciousness, black feminists, for long ignored by the Women's Liberation Movement, addressed white feminists as to the boundaries of sisterhood in the struggle. In response to the white feminists' emphasis of patriarchy as being the main source of oppression, black feminists feel the need for a redefinition of the term since 'Racism ensures that black men do not have the same relations to patriarchal capitalist hierarchies as white men.' The Combahee River Collective argue:

> We believe that sexual politics under patriarchy is as pervasive in black women's lives as are the politics of class and race. We also often find it difficult to separate race from class and from sex oppression because in our lives they are most often experienced simultaneously. We know that there is such a thing as racial–sexual oppression which is neither solely racial nor solely sexual, e.g. the history of rape of black women by white men as a weapon of political oppression.

As feminists and lesbians, they feel solidarity with progressive black men and do not advocate the factionalisation that white women who are separatists demand. Black people, they argued, necessitated solidarity around the fact of race, which white women of course do not need to have with white men, unless it concerned their negative solidarity as racial oppressors. Therefore, 'We struggle together with black men against racism, while we also struggle with black men about sexism.' [15]

Black feminists, alienated by the non-recognition of their 'herstories' in the WLM, are demanding that racism be acknowledged as a 'restructuring feature' of their relationships with white women. They argue that in theory and practice, the white feminist must recognise that white women stand in a power relation as oppressors of black women. Given this 'theory and practice' simple equality was out of the question.

The three concepts central to the feminist theory which posed problems when applied to black women's lives are the family, patriarchy and reproduction. Too often they have been placed in the context of white (middle-class) women, thus becoming contradictory to the lives and experiences of black women.

While accepting that the family can be a source of oppression for black women, the black family has also been a prime source of resistance to oppression. The need to recognise the historical dimensions of the struggle was necessary. During slavery and periods of colonialism the black family was the basis of political and cultural resistance to racism. Further, it was argued that 'Ideologies of black female sexuality do not stem primarily from the black family. The way the gender of black women is constructed differs from constructions of white femininity because it is also subject to racism.'[16]

Day to day, black women in Britain have been, and are, constantly challenging the racist ideologies of black female sexuality. For example, Asian schoolgirls are resisting the racist mythology of their femininity. The belief that Asian girls will be forced into marriage immediately after leaving school perpetuates the racist attitude that Asian women in career jobs are a waste of time. Consequently, careers officers do not offer them the same interviews and job opportunities as white girls. The struggle against the racism of the careers service is but only one aspect of the Asian girls' struggle in schools.[17]

The concept of dependency is also a problem for black feminists. If this concept provides the link between the 'material organisation of the household, and the ideology of femininity' how can the situations be explained in which black women, as heads of households are not financially dependent upon a black man? This has been the case in both colonial and metropolitan situations. The historical legacy reveals that systems of slavery, colonialism and imperialism have denied black men positions in the white male hierarchy. Moreover, black men have been oppressed by the terror employed in these systems.[18]

Black feminists also sought to clarify the concept of 'reproduction' and how it relates to two basic questions: how the black woman's role in rural, industrial or domestic labour affects the construction of ideologies of black female sexuality which are different from, and often constructed in opposition to, white female sexuality and how this role relates to the black woman's struggle for control over her own sexuality.

The 'herstory' of black women in post-war Britain points to an interesting contradiction between 'home-making as a career' and the campaign to recruit women into the labour force during post-war reconstruction. The recruitment of black women remains unmentioned. The tendency was not to separate male and female black workers. Instead a list was given of the industries and services where labour was most urgently required. The boot and shoe industry, clothing, textiles, iron and steel, all required female workers, as did hospitals, domestic service, transport and the women's land army. There was also a shortage of shorthand typists, and a dire shortage of nurses and midwives. [19]

This bald statement shed no light as to why black women were concentrated in certain work areas more than in others. However, as temporary workers in a period of crisis they did not threaten the traditional division of labour industry along 'sex lines'. Indeed, the survey (the economic survey of 1947) reflected the dominant view that married women 'would not naturally wish to work'.

But, not all black women were subject to this process. Ideologically Afro-Caribbean women were 'naturally' suited for the lowest-paid, most menial jobs. These black women bridged the division between the alternatives 'work and marriage' and of being two kinds of women, a wife and a mother. Rather than being perceived as involved in a desperate struggle to protect and preserve the black family in Britain, black women were seen to fail as mothers precisely because of their position as workers. [20]

Furthermore, there was the problem of the black woman's struggle to gain control over her own sexuality when faced with the racist experiment of enforced sterilisation. Black feminists have criticised white feminists for ignoring their experiences and struggles both before and after they came to Britain. This was not surprising since the black woman's experience, steeped in racism and sexism, was necessarily different from those of white women.

Carby argues that the spoils of economic exploitation of the colonies not only benefited the plantation mistresses, but, in various degrees, all white women in Britain. Moreover, the pro-imperialist attitudes of many nineteenth century and early twentieth century feminists and suffragists have yet to be acknowledged for their racist implications and so to the exploration of contemporary racism within the white feminist movement in Britain.

In constructing alternatives, Hazel Carby adds that it should be imperative for feminist 'herstory' and theory to avoid reproducing the structural inequalities which exist between the 'metropoles' and the 'peripheries', and within the metropoles between black and white women, in the form of inappropriate polarisations between the 'First' and 'Third World', developed–underdeveloped or advanced–backward.

Moreover, it is very important that white women in the women's movement examine the ways in which racism excludes many black women and prevents them from unconditionally aligning themselves with white women. Instead of taking black women as the objects of their research, white feminist researchers are directed to uncover the gender-specific mechanisms of racism amongst white women since 'this more than any other factor disrupts the recognition of common interests of sisterhood'.[21]

Indeed, there have been many instances of racial oppression at work from white women. Asian women, for example, 'are paid low salaries and everything is worse for them, they have to face the insults of supervisors. These supervisors are all English women. The trouble is that in Britain our women are expected to behave like servants and we are not used to behaving like servants and we can't. But if we behave normally . . . the supervisors start shouting and harassing us . . . They complain about us Indians to the Manager.'[22]

Black women resist being grafted onto feminism in a tokenistic manner. They argue that feminism has to be transformed if it is to address them. Neither do they wish their words to be misused in generalities as if what each one of them utters represents the total experience of all black women.

Gender, race and class

In the debate on the unhappy marriage between Marxism and feminism, Gloria Joseph has pointed out that:

> the feminist question has never truly embraced 'Black women' and that 'incestuous child of patriarchy and capitalism', namely racism, is not acknowledged. [Given this serious omission, it is necessary that] in discussion of Marxism and the woman question, to speak to women, all women categorically, is to perpetuate white supremacy – white female supremacy – because it is white women to whom the comments are addressed and to whom the comments are most appropriate.[23]

In short, the WLM has failed to recognise the specificity of black women's experiences of racism, structured by racially constructed gender roles. In this respect, the Asian woman's experience in relation to waged work is of particular interest.

Migration and gender

Fundamentally 'the state takes on new tasks; first of all economically by regulating the ebb and flow of foreign labour power and then also politically by finding and carrying out new means of direct and indirect political oppression, and finally ideologically by trying to integrate, on a non-political basis, the immigrant workers selected to stay'.[24]

The fact that migrant workers play an important economic role in advanced capitalist economies has led to massive research into this 'role' and on the political and social effects of large immigrant settlements in the major urban centres in most European countries. In Britain, the field of 'race relations' has been reponsible for several studies on housing, employment and education as large numbers of black workers came to Britain during the 1950s and 1960s. [25] Not surprisingly there has been an absence of gender-specific studies dealing with migrant women who constituted an integral part of this population.

Migration and the state

The extent of immigration and the strategic role of immigration in the European economy have to be explained, not in terms of the technical demands of production but by the specific interests of capital in a particular phase of its development. Given that primary immigration was declining without the aid of controls:

> the threat of controls caused a wave of 'panic immigration' to 'beat the ban' [in 1962]. . . . many Pakistani and Indian women and children came to Britain to join their husbands and fathers. In contrast to West Indian women, the majority of Asian women came to Britain as the dependants of male workers. In fact, Asian women were never drawn into the metropolis as wage labourers. They were not recruited directly as cheap labourers as were Asian men, whose migration to Britain from the subcontinent was closely linked to the post-war economic boom . . .
>
> The forces and motivations behind Asian women's migration to Britain were different and their entry was circumscribed by different state policies and strategies. On the other hand, the East African Asian men and women who came to Britain in 1967 were nearly all British passport holders who were forced out of East Africa when the former British colonies gained independence. In 1968 the British Government moved in very quickly to try and control this new source of immigration to Britain by altering their legal rights of entry. A voucher system was introduced whereby vouchers were issued to heads of households, normally males, for themselves and certain categories of dependants. Here, the dependent status of women was clear. Women holding British passports had great difficulty in proving they were heads of households; though widowed, divorced and deserted women as well as those with dependent husbands, came into this category. Thus from the very beginning Asian women have been discriminated against not only because they are black but also as women in terms of their legal rights of entry and settlement. [26]

Both 'black labour' and 'female labour' are regarded as cheap. Indeed, the value of domestic labour carried out by women in Western industrialised countries has been reckoned to be approximately one-third of the gross national product. Parmar states:

When looking at the advantages to Metropolitan capital of importing exclusively male labour power (whereby there is a saving on the cost of reproduction) it is important to assess the role played by the wives and children of male migrants in the maintenance and renewal of their families. . . . Without doubt the domestic labour of women in Third World countries greatly subsidises the cost of reproducing male labour in the cities, mines and other centres of production.[27]

Thus, Asian families and Asian women have been particularly affected by the repressive effects of 'racist and patriarchical immigration legislation'. Indeed, state racism had grown. In Britain the Asian community has been subjected to abuse and humiliation by the process whereby Asian women before arriving in Britain are exposed to British racism by having to undergo 'long and vigorous' interviews in the British embassies in London, Pakistan and Bangladesh, and the ordeal of answering intimate questions. In 1978, for example, 'there was an expose of the vaginal examinations carried out on Asian women to determine whether they were married or not, and to determine whether they were fiancees of men already settled in England ... Examinations to "prove" whether a woman is a virgin can only be seen as acts of violence and intimidation against black women by the British state.'

This 'testing' is based, according to Parmar, on the racist and sexist assumption that Asian women from the sub-continent are always virgins before they get married and that it is 'not in their culture for women to engage in sexual activity before marriage'.[28] This kind of absurd generalisation, she argues, is based on the same stereotype of the submissive, weak and tradition-bound Asian woman. The fact that the immigration officers administer them quite haphazardly on pregnant Asian women is only one example of the racism not only of individual officers but also the structural and institutional racism of the British state. Such practices also indicate the direct control the state intended to have on Asian women's sexuality.

One of the effects of the 1971 Immigration Act and subsequent legislation has been to break up Asian families. The 1981 Nationality Act put further constraints on the right of dependants to join their families in Britain. One of the most obvious threats posed by this was to the future of black families and black culture. This trend can be traced back to the 1978 parliamentary select committee. One of its recommendations was that children aged over 12 born abroad to those settled in Britain would not be allowed in to join their parents.

Parmar concludes:

The ways in which capital, patriarchy and race structure Asian women's oppression and exploitation, does not make it possible or desirable to separate out the primary cause of oppression; all three factors are intrinsic to the day-to-day experiences of Asian women.

The stereotypes and myths that exist about Asian women are being constantly challenged through the militant actions that many of them have taken in the past and will continue to take in the future. The collective actions that they have taken have sometimes been alongside their white sisters and at other times they have struggled alongside their black brothers. They have learnt that while it is necessary for them as black women to struggle with white women on issues of mutual concern and with black men against their common oppression as black people, they have to do this from a position of strength and power as organised black women. As black women they are successfully defining their own experiences of oppression and developing their own framework for struggling against it. [29]

The oppressor: Blacks and the police

The debate on 'sus'

On 28 August 1981, the Criminal Attempts Act came into force and created a new offence of 'vehicle interference'. The use by the police of the 'being a suspected person' or 'sus' charge, has resulted in a great deal of bitterness among black people against the police. Moreover, it has become part of a wider controversy regarding civil liberties and the extent of police powers. [30]

From the figures on 'sus', it is clear that proportionately more Blacks are arrested than Whites. Mindful of this and in their own defence, the police took the view that the figures do not represent a bias against black youth but that the arrests for 'sus' reflect the relative involvement of various groups in that category of street crime. Roberts argued, 'Presumably, if the number of Blacks arrested for "sus" begins to decline (and in proportion to other groups) this merely shows their declining involvement rather than any change in police discretion or policy.' The Haringey Community Relations Council has noted that the proportion of black people arrested for 'sus' declined from 47 per cent in 1977 to 10 per cent in 1978 of total arrests. [31]

These figures will, however, bring us nowhere nearer a full understanding unless 'sus' is seen in the context of the history of Black–police relations. For one thing, this charge by the police has created bitterness and resentment in the black community. Incidents of malpractice have exacerbated relations with the police. Examples given by the Institute of Race Relations include disregard of the Judges Rules, the inadequate investigation of racial attacks, the abuse of the power to enter homes, harassment of juveniles to accept guilt, and the swamping by the Special Patrol Group of areas where black people are concentrated.

The black community's hostility and resentment towards the police today must be seen in historical perspective. During the

1960s and 1970s there had been a steady increase in the number of complaints against the police. In view of this, in 1971 a Select Committee of the House of Commons was set up to look into these complaints and the general concern regarding police–Black relations. Clearly, from the evidence given by both the black community and the police organisations, relations between black youths and the police were very bad.

In their use of the 'sus' charge, the police have denied any bias against black people. Yet they persist in linking black youths with crime. For example, David McNee, the Commander of the Metropolitan Police, stated that 'law and order in the capital . . . are now firmly linked to matters of race'.[32]

The police against the people

In September 1981, as unemployment approached 3 million there were no signs that the economic recession would 'bottom out' into better times. For the jobless the forecast was gloomy. In order to get registered unemployment back down to one million (as it was in 1970) it was estimated that 5 million extra jobs had to be created in the next three years. And this was regarded as an 'optimistic' forecast.[33]

In the aftermath of the introduction of the microprocessor there was an assumption of 'almost a third of the potential of the working population being permanently unemployed', and to cope with this a highly authoritarian regime was necessary. This mass unemployment had been anticipated during the 1970s. By the end of the decade the police force was ready to put down any potential trouble as tension mounted particularly in the inner city areas. The police were invested with increased powers as their numbers increased. In 1980 the police force in England and Wales reached a record of 117,423. This was not surprising since Britain had 'proportionately the largest prison population in Western Europe, about 44,000 in 1982.[34] Moreover, Britain had been contending with 'civil war' in Northern Ireland, for over 12 years. As it was, this would prove good training for controlling and disciplining Britain's black communities. This growing social and political problem marked the transition from 'liberal democracy' to 'authoritarian democracy'.[35]

National security

By 1970 the emphasis was on national security. Unemployment already stood at one million and the post-war social 'peace' was quickly shattered when the Heath government took on the trade union movement and defined the limits of trade union activity in the Industrial Relations Act 1971. The miners' 1972 strike was in defiance of the government. More than 30,000 miners and other workers had gathered to block the entrance to the coal depot at Saltley in Birmingham. The police, outnumbered, decided to retreat. The government, the state and the ruling class saw this mass defiance of 'law and order' not only as a challenge to their authority and the power structure, but also as a major defeat in trying to curb the power of trade unionists. This victory for the labour movement led to the state totally revising its 'contingency plans'. The Home Secretary set up the National Security Committee to review all aspects of maintaining order. Indeed, evidence of this tightening up process was apparent in the unprecedented police presence in the mining communities during the 1984–85 miners' strike. (During the strike the author was informed by a black NUM officer that there were approximately 3,000 black members in the National Union of Mineworkers.)

After the Labour Party was returned in 1974, under the aegis of a Social Contract, the working class was weakened and demoralised. In 1978, E. P. Thompson wrote:

> [once] the libertarian response of the British people has been brought under sedation, then the reasons for the invisibility of the state within the state began to lose their force. And so we see the evidence, in the past decade of the police, the army, the security services . . . becoming more public, engaging in active 'public relations', lobbying for new curbs on civil rights and for a 'simplified' legal process and attempting to familiarise the public with their intrusive presence. [36]

As Bunyan put it, this feature marked the transition from the 'old' order to the 'new', from the 'liberal–democratic' system in which the coercive state agencies played a key role to an 'authoritarian–democratic' system where these agencies move to the forefront.

After Saltley, two steps were taken: first, to strengthen the police in the community, thus altering their role and image. As a second step, the Security Services were strengthened. Techniques of surveillance were introduced, to reinforce the Security Services. Given the experience in Northern Ireland (and the technological advances applied there), computerised record-keeping systems were developed.

The 'most secret' change, however, involved the military, in order to deal with public order situations, beyond 'Bobby capability' and to intervene in strikes. This was done in the winter of 1977–78 when the army was brought in during the national firemen's strike. More than 20,000 troops were used. It was the first time that the army replaced a workforce in Britain, and achieved the desired end – the defeat of the strike. Another element in the new 'contingency' planning was the setting up of the Civil Contingency Unit in the Cabinet Office.

Largely hidden from public view, these moves, legitimised through the media, marked the emergence of 'authoritarian democracy'. The police force was at the forefront of the move towards authoritarianism. Gone was the post-war image of the 'friendly Bobby'. Towards the end of the 1970s, the police had acquired a new image. In 1977 riot shields were introduced for the first time on mainland Britain, for example, at Lewisham in London during battles between the police and anti-fascists at a National Front march, and later at the Notting Hill Carnival. Yet the police have continued to present themselves as a neutral force.

Amidst the general circumstances of recession, the police regarded the maintenance of public order as their ongoing, primary task. In 1980, James Anderton, the Chief Constable of Greater Manchester said:

> I think that from the police point of view . . . my task in the future, in the ten to fifteen years from now . . . that basic crime such as theft, burglary, even violent crime will not be the predominant police feature. What will be the matter of greater concern to me will be the covert and ultimately overt attempts to overthrow democracy, to subvert the authority of the state, and to in fact involve themselves in acts of sedition designed to destroy our parliamentary system and the democratic government of this country.[37]

Characteristic of the 'fire-brigade' strategy of policing was a tendency to 'over-react' and 'over-police' in a 'blatantly aggressive manner.' Moreover, consideration was given to a 'third force', a para-military police. In fact, they were tooling-up to face their biggest enemies, the disadvantaged, harassed and impoverished black communities. Such a force not only have sophisticated riot-control equipment (for example, water cannon, CS gas and armoured personnel carriers) but have in their ranks specially trained experienced, armed marksmen to deal with riots, demonstrations and strikes. Earlier attempts to create such a force in Britain had been opposed. However, deliberation over the idea continued. The main argument in favour of a third force was that the aggressive role in conventional policing would be removed in dealing with public order, and thus help the police to maintain friendly relations with the public. But, the experience of some European countries showed that more hatred and counter-violence was directed at riot police than the ordinary police. 'Unlike the policemen on the beat, they have little chance to mend their fences by being seen as friends and protectors because they seldom meet people until they become rioters.'[38]

There was agreement, however, that it was the responsibility of the police to maintain public order generally. Riot training, however, considered to be necessary, led to 'joint military exercises' being undertaken.

At least, in theory, the separate roles of the army and the police were to be maintained. In practice, however, from this time on, the role of the 'ordinary policemen' would change. One approach was the creation of Special Patrol Groups (SPGs) in the major cities.

Like the London SPG, they were to be trained in riot control techniques. But why retraining? Clearly the state was worried about the effects of the deepening recession on the black communities. From here on police tactics assumed a war-like approach as in Northern Ireland. Robert Mark, impressed by the techniques used by the Royal Ulster Constabulary had his 200 strong SPG trained in 'snatch squad' methods (to arrest ring leaders), 'flying wedges' (to break up crowds) and random stop-and-search and roadblock techniques, 'based on the army's experience in Ulster'.[39] In 1981, there were about 28 SPG-type groups in the 52 local police forces in the United Kingdom. In effect, in almost every major city the SPG played the 'dual role of anti-crime and paramilitary units'.

Notorious examples of the style of such 'third force' policing could be seen at the Red Lion Square demonstration in June 1974 when one of the protesters was killed. And in April 1979, at the anti-National Front demonstration in Southall, where a member of the SPG allegedly murdered Blair Peach.[40] But, it seemed local SPGs alone were unlikely to contain riots on the streets. Thus, Police Support Units were also created.

Already before the 'riots' in Bristol in April 1980, in Brixton in April 1981 and nationally in July 1981, the contradiction between policing the community and simultaneously forming a 'hidden' third force in the event of major trouble in the streets, was evident. The police were faced with two 'incompatible and irreconcilable demands placed on them – to police the community in the normal everyday sense and to act as Britain's third force'.[41]

But, in view of this development, what of community policing? John Alderson, Chief Police Constable of Devon and Cornwall, given such overtly oppressive policing stated, 'The era of preventive policing is phasing out in favour of a responsive or reactive police.' According to him, the trust and confidence the community places in the police becomes the main casualty with the police and the people likely to meet only in conflict situations. This 'fire-brigade' policing in Britain's major cities, was likely to lead, Alderson argued, to policing 'more akin to that of an occupying army'.[42]

The other aspect of community policing of concern is the role of the police officer on the beat. The fact that part of their training is to gather intelligence on the people within their area and feed it through to their local police station, in effect, community policing could also be used 'to penetrate the community through other professional agencies and by spying on the community, under the guise of offering a protective, friendly approach. "Consent" is thus to be "engineered" and, in case this fails, intelligence is gathered in an attempt to pre-empt dissent.'

The police and the community

Insensitivity in their relations with the black community has led to calls for a systematic programme of police education on ethnic minorities and for a departure from the wilful use of 'strong-arm' tactics which arouse hostility to police presence as at Southall. Indeed, the outside intervention of the SPG has, so far, not inspired any feelings of mutual trust and co-operation between local groups and the police.

Although there has been much criticism of the specialist police units, McNee, Anderton and Jardine have singled out such units for praise. McNee in particular made his feelings for the SPG abundantly clear. He told a black reporter, following references to the group in connection with Blair Peach's death (during the NF protest) 'If you keep off the streets of London and behave yourselves you won't have the SPG to worry about. I understand the concern of your people. But if you don't get into trouble you won't come into confrontation with the police.'[43] By contrast, the Institute of Race Relations stated:

> The SPG . . . has been increasingly deployed in so-called 'high-crime' areas (Brixton, Peckham, Lewisham, Tooting, Stoke Newington, Kentish Town, Hackney and Notting Hill) which are in reality decaying inner city areas of substandard housing, low amenities and high unemployment where the white working class and the majority of black people live. Evidence of its operations in these areas clearly demonstrates that black people have been a prime target of the SPG, especially in Lewisham and Lambeth. The tactics used by the SPG officers when 'doing over' a 'highcrime' area are aggressive (because of their training in riot-control) result in a high proportion of arrests for assault or obstruction as a consequence of this and, because of what appears to be an in-built prejudice, result in a high number of arrests of black people, especially young blacks.[44]

Moreover, the Institute argues that the SPG's essential function had changed from being a 'support anti-crime unit' to a 'police command unit', actively involved in 'indiscriminate stop-and-search activities'.

Lambeth, with a major concentration of black people, was given special attention from the SPG. 'Swamp 81' was the latest in a long line of 'attacks' in the area. Between 1975 and 1979 there were six such 'attacks' by the SPG, characterised by road blocks, early morning raids and random street checks. The SPG operation was concentrated around four housing estates, all with large black populations. The police felt these methods were essential to general crime prevention and particularly effective in combating 'crime waves' such as 'muggings'.

Growing interest in 'sus' aroused wider discussion of police powers and practice as it relates to civil rights and criminal procedure. The controllers of the state machinery, however, felt that tighter control of law and order was necessary. For example, the Home Office, the Director of Public Prosecutions, the Magistrates Association and police organisations were demanding changes in criminal procedure to make prosecution easier and to enlarge police powers.

Blacks and the British police

Given this historical development of police strategy and their proposed increased powers (the Police Bill) what was the relationship between the police and the black community? The Metropolitan Police campaign to recruit Blacks into the force, supported by an editorial in the *West Indian World* was yet another case of 'come and join us and we will help you'. In response, *Race Today* ('The voice of the Black Community in Britain') advocated the opposite: 'the mass organisation of unemployed youth, students and parents to fight this particular issue. We will continue, as we have been doing, to commit all our resources in this direction.'[45]

This stand was hardly surprising. Armed with wide powers and the security of full backing from the state, police harassment during the 1960s and particularly in the 1970s had hit a new low in 1976. Between November 1975 and June 1976, there were several clashes between the police and black youths.

It was clear that the black community, under attack on an ever-increasing scale, would not be bullied in their 'home ground'. They strongly resisted the actions of police officers, one of whom reported it to the Parliamentary Select Committee on Race Relations:

> Recently there has been a growth in the tendency for members of London's West Indian communities to combine against police by interfering with police officers who are effecting the arrest of a black person or who are in some other way enforcing the law in situations which involve black people. In the last 12 months 40 such incidents have been recorded. Each carries a potential for large scale disorder.[46]

Repeated clashes with the police, in many black communities, brought a heightened awareness of this repressive force, nationally. Unemployed youth and students were the usual targets. With growing unemployment among school-leavers a mass of young wageless persons emerged within the community. Financed by Urban Aid, youth projects were set up in the black communities where black youths congregated daily to 'while away the hours'. In these 'haunts' confrontation with police officers led to resistance from these young Blacks. The view that as unemployed workers, they were supposed to be demoralised victims ready to move anywhere, cap in hand, imploring employers for jobs, was based on the traditional view of unemployed workers. Although their parents might have taken this line, in 1976, this attitude towards work was dead among young Blacks. Clearly, they were not prepared to be isolated or demoralised. Energetic and resourceful they hoped that society would respond positively to meet their needs. Anything less would be resisted. Indeed, theirs was a movement of resistance, one which police officers instinctively attack. This was the basis for the on-going war between young Blacks and the police.

How did the police operate? Their general strategy to groups of young Blacks has been to 'harass, attack and disperse', as was the case at Chapeltown, Leeds. In the 'war against the unemployed', individuals became the target. Here is an account of how it happens: two or three youths are walking down the street or standing at a bus stop. The police swoop and arrest them. The charges are loitering with intent to steal or attempting to steal from person or persons unknown. There is, in most cases, some resistance which leads to an additional charge of assault on police.

The police make up their notes in the canteen. The attempted or intended theft is in all cases from a woman's handbag. Although the woman is described in detail, more often than not the police were unable to bring her to court. She always eludes them at that crucial moment. Nonetheless, a conviction is guaranteed in the magistrate's court. Hundreds of cases of this kind have been reported against black youths.

Race, class and autonomy

According to Stuart Hall, in contemporary Britain, 'The class relations which inscribe the black fractions of the working class function as race relations. The two are inseparable. Race is the modality in which class relations are experienced.'[47]

On the question of 'Race, Struggle and Class Formation' one writer has argued that confronting a class struggle in and through 'race', the move from 'race' to class becomes crucial at this point because 'The division of humanity into social classes explains its history infinitely better than its division into races or peoples.' However, he adds, 'it cannot be accomplished without reconceptualising class in opposition to a Marxist orthodoxy which views the working class as a continuous historical subject.'

In opposition to theorists who reduce race to custom or ethnicity as part of their own parochial battle to maintain the sociology of ethnic relations it is necessary to locate racist and anti-racist ideology as well as the struggle for black liberation in a perspective on culture as an area of class conflicts.[48] Richard Johnson's contribution to the theorisation of working class culture directs us that although working class culture cannot be seen as having a simple function to workers' need, capital has a stake in the forms of working class culture. Given that the mass of black people who arrived in Britain recently, the casualties of colonial underdevelopment, brought with them legacies of their political, ideological and economic struggles in Africa, the Caribbean and the Indian subcontinent, instead of being inflexible, their accumulated histories of resistance have brought new dimensions to struggle at the cultural level.

Sivanandan has argued that:

> . . . it is cultural resistance which takes on new forms . . . in order to fully contest foreign domination. But culture in the periphery is not equally developed in all sections of society . . . it does have a mass character . . . at the economic level different exploitations in the different modes confuse the formal lines of class struggle but the common denominators of political oppression make for a mass movement. Hence the resolutions in these countries are not necessarily class, socialist resolutions – they do not begin as such anyway. They are not even nationalist resolutions as we know them. They are mass movements with national and revolutionary components – sometimes religious, sometimes secular, often both but always against the repressive state and its imperial backers. [49]

Given the political traditions which Blacks have brought with them, they and their British-born children have preserved organic links with their transplanted political consciousness, 'in their kitchens and temples – in their *communities*. Though their new struggles at the centre are diffused throughout a different structure . . . the lingering bile of slavery, indenture and colonialism remains in the forms of struggle, political philosophy, and revolutionary perspectives of non-European radical traditions.'

On the questions of such localised struggles over education, racial violence and police practices, black people have used the community 'to provide the axis along which to organise themselves'. Thus, in this context, 'the concept of community is central to the view of class struggle' which 'links distinct cultural and political traditions with a territorial dimension, to collective actions and consciousness within the relation of 'economic patterns, political authority and the uses of space'. [50]

It has been argued that the history of working-class communities is an integral part of the processes of industrialisation and social discipline which established the city as a site of unique political conflicts. The form and relevance of community have responded to the changing social character of capitalist production which allocated black labour to a specific place, highlighting the means by which 'the dissociation of the upper and lower classes achieves form in the city itself'.

Moreover, Gareth Stedman-Jones has directed our attention to a growing separation of the workplace from the domestic scene as having a major bearing on the cultural and political patterns of urban workers in late nineteenth-century London. Gilroy adds crucially that this description of community 'illustrates how the concept can be useful in the connection of waged and domestic labour space. It is valuable not only where leisure practices impinge on the labour process, but also where political organisation forged outside the immediate processes of production (for blacks, with juridico-political apparatuses, organised racists or profiteering ghetto landlords) has effects on the struggle at work, and vice versa'.[51]

It is therefore vital to our understanding, that 'the political traditions of black people, expressed in the solidarity and political strength of their communities, have determined a specific *territorialisation* of social control'.

The integration of Blacks into the political apparatuses of the social democratic state requires consideration of the ideology of self-help which fused political representation and state intervention, disorganising black discontent and channelling it into 'quasi-colonial institutional structures . . . [which would] deal with the issue of race outside traditional political arenas'.[52] Thus, it was argued:

> If the political consensus over containing the black problem owed something to the colonial period the black organisations which struggled with it on the terrain of community made this connection increasingly explicit . . . In a nationalist framework which could do little more than present an inverted image of the oppressor's power, the issue of black control of self-help projects sometimes obscured the nature of the schemes themselves. By restricting their analysis to racial parameters, the nationalist self-help groups become easy prey for state institutions already placing a premium on self help 'as a response to the threat posed by alienated black youth'. The Community Relations Commission's self-help report of 1976 spells out the limits of their approach: 'Some of the leaders of self-help groups have strong political views particularly with regard to the struggles for freedom for blacks in the USA and Africa. These do not however appear to have any significant effect on the work of these organisations'.[53]

Indeed the generational conflict in the black communities reflects conflicts both of organisation and ideology. This is clearly expressed in the debates concerning political responses between the Asian Youth Movements and the IWAs, illustrating 'a distinction between composite and autonomous modes of class struggle in complex fashion, overdetermined by the peasant political traditions from which both have sprouted'.[54]

In Britain, black people are involved in political and ideological struggles through their collective experience of racism and refusal of racial domination. Hence the politics of black liberation is necessarily cultural politics in that Coons, Pakis, nig-nogs, sambos and wogs are social constructions *in culture*. Indeed central to the

cultural politics of Blacks in Britain is the 'profound negation of
Race'. It has been argued that 'the key to understanding the
relatively recent supercession of nationalist politics by an international revolutionary movement of black people, the most visible
manifestations of which are organised popular currents in the
Caribbean, America and Britain which have been identified by the
dominant ideology as 'Ethiopianism' or 'Rastafarianism' . . . is no
recent development.'[55]

Historically, 'Rastafarian culture remains an indelible link be-
tween the resistance of the maroons, the Pan Africanist appeal of
Marcus Garvey, the materialist and historical analysis of Walter
Rodney and the defiance of reggae.'[56]

The influence of Afro-Caribbean culture in general, and through
reggae, Rastafarianism in particular, on the lives and politics of
white working-class youth is much overlooked.

Given the central importance of the cultural offensive of reggae
music to the political development of the mass movement, Rasta
women engaged in their own distinctive feminist struggle. On this
struggle and the Rastas cultural development, it has been argued
that Judy Mowatt:

> had made 'the queen' the starting point for a redefinition of the Rasta
> women, establishing her in an activist role waging struggles distinct
> from but complementary to those of her brethren . . . Her songs
> *Strength To Go Through*, *Slave Queen* and *Black Woman* were the
> basis of the record's great popularity at grassroots level, but it was in
> *Sisters Chant* that Mowatt made her straightforward demand for the
> validity of 'feminist' Rastafari in language which recalled the
> nineteenth-century feminists who distinguished between 'man' and
> 'god' . . . The breadth of the Rastas' cultural intervention is also
> important. Like the 'Bop' players of the 1960s who absorbed black
> nationalism and Elijah Mohammed alike, reggae musicians have
> been converted to Rasta in such numbers that it has become impos-
> sible to discuss one without the other. Though there are certain styles
> which appeal more to older people, the universal popularity of Bob
> Marley is a good illustration of how these different preferences have
> been spanned . . . The popularity of communalist ideology and its
> implicit politics may also be gauged by the widespread use of Rasta
> concepts and speech patterns by those who do not wish to express
> their affiliation or interests more overtly. Such language is able to
> convey commitment in a selective or intermittent manner, and its
> racially exclusive mode invites speakers to appropriate the ideas
> which appeal to them without being pigeon-holed by the oppres-
> sor.[57]

Significantly, the most theological amongst Rastas see the primary struggle for black liberation here and now. Indeed, religion
has consistently formed a basis of struggle for the colonised and
enslaved, reinforcing their resistance to servitude rather than wait-

ing for deliverance in a state of passive obedience. To this extent it must be understood that 'the radical potential of religious ideology is not the sole property of African and Asian traditions'.[58]

Thus, those who tend to see 'religion' as detracting from the development of political consciousness have yet to explain the Rastas' 'disinterest in the New Testament gospels, or their predilection for Psalms, Revelation, and the history of the children of Israel'.

In the politics of the Rasta, the effect of music is pervasive. Essentially, in Britain it has been argued that in the realm of 'leisure no less than that of work has hosted the extraordinary encounter between the political traditions of disorganic development in the periphery and the urban working class at the centre. Youth culture has also created an important space for dialogue between black youth from the different communities. Asian youth movements have been inspired by the combativity of Afro-Caribbean young people which has received spectacular press coverage while their own equally tenacious deference of their communities remains concealed behind a stereotype of passivity.'

Thus the change in post-war British politics – particularly the introduction of the welfare state and changes in production – informed consequent changes in political organisation and struggle. Given the 'ultimate direction' of the popular struggle of white youth, it has been argued that:

> its form has been prefigured in the resistances of the black com-
> munities, in much the same way that the movement of black
> Americans in the 1960s determined the patterns of autonomous
> protest which followed it . . . The mechanisms of white youth
> culture provided the means to popularise oppositional ideas forged in
> the powerlessness of youth. Since the incorporation of reggae into
> the subcultural repertoire in the late 1960s, political themes have
> begun to displace moral and generational conflict as the raw material
> of young peoples' cultural expression.

In spite of the short-lived alliance between punk and reggae muscians, reggae continued to have a steady appeal to white youths. The emergence of local radio with minority appeal music programming during 1970–2 made the music available to white youths. Of course with this widening appeal and potential market, entrepreneurial business was not slow to act. Indeed, 'the link between the multinational entertainment corporation and the purveyors of reggae to the ghettoes of Britain was secured by a Jamaican exile who owned the company Island Records . . . an appendage of EMI.' Through Jimmy Cliff, Island took black music to the white pop fan. The release of the film *The Harder They Come* in 1972 marked the 'beginning of the mass movement of black British Youth towards Rastafari'.

According to Cashmore, the expression of discontent in reggae, 'acted to slough off any latent militancy in the black working class by translating the hostility into musical form rather than converting it into programmatic proposals'.[59]

Barry Troyna believes that the social and political orientations of young Blacks may be read off from their musical preferences.[60] He explains that 'The Rastafarian-inspired lyrics inform and help structure their particular perspectives and provide them with their own distinctive and impenetrable group argot.'

It was also argued that:

> While reggae music may be subdivided into 'lovers' and 'roots' styles which echo Troyna's categories, this distinction *does not apply at the level of lyrics*. The contrast relates to the different dance styles and the overlapping social relations in which they appear . . . the dominant form of reggae.
>
> Dub is not a style of music as such. It is 'a process of enrichment in which music is deconstructed and the meaning of its lyrics transformed and expanded . . . Though they may introduce an analytic coherence, political lyrics must be regarded as secondary to the issues implicit in the form of reggae and its consequent exploration in Dub . . . Dubbing is a feature of overtly committed and apparently unpolitical recordings alike. Dub is a bridge between them rooted in their form[61]

Thus, reggae music is instructive and should remind the Eurocentric sociologist that, 'Acquiring and developing class consciousness does not mean obligatory boredom. It is a question of transforming what used to be used exclusively for pleasure and leisure into a means of instruction.'[62]

Given that reggae music is much more than the 'lullaby of a beleaguered population' Gilroy argues 'the Dub movement avoids a trap set for all singers of political songs forced to contend with their art being packaged and sold as commodities.'[63] On the question of automonous class struggle, Rastafari is regarded as an expression of the critical consciousness which informs those black struggles (which are 'not merely political in the broadest sense but approach the task of social transformation) . . . commenting on society and state, and extending into an analysis of the post-colonial scene as a whole'.

In 'Steppin' Out of Babylon', Gilroy argues further:

> Though for the social analyst 'race' and class are necessarily abstractions at different levels, black consciousness of race and class cannot be empirically separated. The class character of black struggles is not a result of the fact that blacks are predominantly proletarian, though this is true. It is established in the fact that their struggles for civil rights, freedom from state harassment, or as waged workers, are instances of the process by which the working class is constituted politically, organised in politics.' We have distanced ourselves from

the view of classes as continuous subjects of history, they are made and remade in a continual struggle. We must also reject the ancient heresy of economistic Marxism which stipulates that the relations of community production alone determine class relations. The Marxist concept of class refers primarily but not exclusively to the location of groups in production relations . . . The political organisation of surplus population is particularly salient to class segmentation, and therefore to racial politics in the era of structural unemployment. It serves to remind us that the privileged place of economic classes in the Marxist theory of history is not to be equated with an a priori assertion of their primacy in every historical moment. [64]

As Prezworski wrote: 'Classes must be viewed as the effects of struggles structured by objective conditions, that are simultaneously economic, political and ideological.'[65] However, given the change in these objective conditions and the fact that the unity between the 'economic movement and political action' of the working class was different in 1981 from what it had been in 1971, it was argued that:

The indeterminacy introduced by a view of class formation is an effect of heterogeneous struggles perhaps premised on different communalities – linguistic, sexual, regional, ecological and 'racial' – is a useful tool against reductionism. It is also a place at which a historical and non-essentialist theory of human needs can be worked into the practice of class politics. [66]

According to Alan Touraine, 'The politics of need is to the fore in movements for black liberation, as in many of the other autonomous political forces in the ascendant during the last 15 years.'[67] Thus, on the question of class formation, it was argued that,

in our view of class formation, the racist ideologies and practices of the white working class and the consequent differentiation of 'the Blacks' are ways in which the class as a whole is disorganised. The struggles of black people to refuse and transform their subjugation are no simple antidote to class segmentation, but they are processes which attempt to constitute the class politically across racial divisions – 'that is which represent it against capitalism against racism. [68]

Furthermore, it appears that 'autonomous organisation has enabled Blacks and women to "leap frog" over their fellow workers into direct confrontations with the state in the interest of the class as a whole.' The struggle for abortion rights, and campaigns by black organisations against state harassment are examples of this.

Indeed, both movements have long struggled to transform society. Concluding his exploration of 'Race, Class and Autonomy' Gilroy wrote:

black political traditions fall outside the 'contradictory unity' of corporatism/parliamentarism. There is also overwhelming evidence to support the view that the institutions of the white working class have failed to represent the interests of black workers abroad and at home, where black rank-and-file organisation has challenged local and national union bureaucracy . . . these institutions (do not) represent the class *as a class* at all. Nor are Blacks alone in the marginalisation they suffer. The experiences of female, young, unemployed or even unskilled workers present parallel examples, while the growth of rank-and-file organisation, and of conflict between shop stewards and their higher echelons of union bureaucracy only hint at the complexity of workplace struggle. The failures of these institutions must be compared to the rapid growth of new movements with an autonomy from capitalist command as well as from the constricting political repertoire of the 'labour movement'. [69]

Black consciousness: spontaneous crowd violence

Violence against black people in the British colonies had its counterpart in Britain. The ideology of racism, rooted in capitalism, having spread through the exploitation of black people inherent in colonialism and imperialism, had become a part of black repression in the modern metropole.

The settlement of Blacks in the dockland areas of Britain, in spite of their impoverishment in these 'decaying' areas, had been a convenient target for the 'ills' of the government, the employers and the white working class. Like earlier disadvantaged powerless groups in society, they were conscious of their oppression and responded appropriately through collective action.

Collective violence, however, is not seen as a mere 'side effect' of social strains, but as a consequence of the impact of structural changes on the arrangements of groups in contention for power. Such violence, seemingly disorganised and meaningless, underscores a group and class cohesion, and the mobilisation of violence to 'complement and extend organised, peaceful attempts . . . to accomplish . . . objectives'. [70]

Given these arguments, the findings of the National Advisory Commission on Civil Disorders (The Kerner Commission) is relevant. Using the disorganisation approach to the 1967 ghetto uprisings in the United States, the Commission viewed typical riot participants as '. . . criminal types, over-active social deviants, or riff-raff – recent migrant members of an uneducated underclass – alienated from responsible negroes and without broad social or political concerns'. It was found, however, that the 'typical rioter' was male, between 15 and 24 years of age, resident of the city (not a newly arrived migrant) who was (most interestingly) likely to be of the same economic status as his neighbour who did not riot, but 'better educated, informed about politics, and more likely to have been a "political activist"'. [71] Moreover, the report also based on the 1967 riots, in the context of black involvement and support for the riots found:

> First that a substantial minority of the Negro population, ranging from roughly 10 to 20 per cent, actively participated in the riots. Second, that the rioters, far from being primarily of the riff-raff and outside agitators, were fairly representative of the ghetto communities. And third, that a sizeable minority (or, in some cases a majority) of the negroes who did not riot sympathised with the rioters.[72]

In Britain, strong support for these findings are to be found in the works of E. J. Hobsbawm, George Rude and E. P. Thompson referring to violent crowds in eighteenth-century England and France. They approached collective violence as political struggle and the protest of ordinary people for a common cause. In the eighteenth century disturbances, in Paris and London, Rude found a 'representative cross-section' of the working classes involved in well-planned and 'ritualised' protest informed by coherent, if not fully developed ideologies. Commenting on these disturbances and the crowd's importance in history between 1730 and 1848, he argued that:

> in general, it is perhaps not unreasonable to see these earlier, immature, and often crude, trials of strength . . . as forerunners of later movements whose results and successes have been both significant and enduring.[73]

In support, Hobsbawm saw such 'Primitive Rebels' as participants in 'collective bargaining by riot'; riots which affected the political process and were significantly maintained. He argued:

> The classical mob did not merely riot as protest, but because it expected to achieve somehing by its riots. It assumed that the authorities would be sensitive to its movements, and probably also that they would make some sort of immediate concession. For the mob was not simply a casual collection of people united for some ad hoc purpose, but in a recognised sense a permanent entity even though rarely permanently organised as such.[74]

Commenting on the ideas and beliefs behind crowd action, E. P. Thompson refers to a 'moral economy'. He wrote:

> It is possible to detect in almost every eighteenth century crowd action some legitimising action. By the notion of legitimation I mean that the men and women in the crowd were informed by the belief that they were defending traditional rights and customs; and in general that they were supported by the wider concensus of the community.[75]

This focus on collective violence as political protest, opposition or dissent to some extent has been directly related to instances of collective racial violence where black communities confront the repressive forces of the state. Martin Luther King described riots as 'the voice of the unheard'.[76] Indeed, according to Rude, the black uprisings in America in the 1960s were seen as having a 'distinct flavour' of the 'pre-industrial riot' during the eighteenth and nineteenth centuries in Europe.[77] Moreover, given the various social groupings 'jockeying' for power, this approach to collective violence is also relevant to instances of inter-racial communal violence.

Given this orientation, historically, collective racial violence in twentieth-century Britain covers two major phases: the period from 1900 to 1948, a time when inter-racial violence took largely communal form and the period from 1948 to the 'Bristol Riot' and later, when violence was the outcome of confrontation between the police and black communities. Of course, there is no clear demarcation line between the two periods.

The first period can be seen as one in which collective racial violence is but a part of wider changing conflicts and contradictions between social groups and interests. Indeed, it has been argued that 'The conflicts and contradictions which are racial, within class and between classes, all incorporate a power and political dimension; but in the formal sense this dimension is also evident in the role of the state'; and in the second phase, race is shifted to the centre of the political stage, achieving a 'greater complexity and significance' within the state. Significantly, it is in the location of the state's disposition on race, in the post-war social changes in Britain, that one must seek an explanation of declining collective white racial violence.[78]

The historical background

Between 1900 and 1948 white violence was met with black resistance. From the 1880s until the Second World War, and after, white seamen were opposed to the use of colonial labour. The pattern of British race relations during this period was reflected in the labour relations in the shipping industry.

A growing number of black seamen had settled in Cardiff. This black population was a matter of great concern to people of local eminence. Commenting on life 'In Nigger Town', George R. Sims, the socialist reformer wrote in 1907:

> The conditions which prevail in this unpleasant quarter are responsible for a grave scandal. It is a scandal which would not be tolerated for one moment in say America. . . . The district has of course, a number of respectable inhabitants, honest and decent people, black and white, who toil and trade and are superior to their environment. But it has certain features which make it one of the most repellent places in which a Briton, blest with pride of race, can spend a morning, afternoon or an evening.[79]

Given this background, the Chinese community in Cardiff was attacked on 20 April 1911. The trouble arose when a national strike was called by the National Seamen and Firemen's Union to win higher wages. Weak unionisation, endemic in this industry, was the real problem in the way of the seamen realising their demands, not the numerically small group of Chinese seamen whose permanent domicile in Cardiff presented no real threat to the strike. Nevertheless, when the shipowners threatened to use Chinese labour to break the strike, the whole Chinese community came under attack.

This attack must be seen as a continuing process of animosity against the Chinese, engendered by the Seamen's Union and the middle-class Christian pressure groups concerned with 'moral order' in Cardiff. In its propaganda, the union resorted to racism against the 'yellowman' and his community.

Particular hostility was directed against the dreaded mixing of the races – the association of Chinese men with white women, either as wives or employees. [80] In fact, when the employers did use Chinese labour to break the strike, the strikers and their supporters were enraged. Thereafter, the Chinese community was faced with the full blast of the white community, including the Trades and Labour Council whose earlier reluctance gave way to condemnation of the shipowners for using Chinese blacklegs, and called upon the Cardiff working class to boycott the Chinese laundries. [81]

Race relations had not improved by 1919. Black-bashing in the United States struck familiar responses in Britain. From the 'yellow' (and the earlier anti-Jewish riots in Cardiff) the focus shifted to black seamen, the rock-bottom of the social scale. Between April and August 1919 the black population in most of Britain's major seaports experienced racial violence. Unlike the 1911 'riots' which arose out of a trade dispute and were directed at one group of colonial workers, these instances of violence were 'race riots' involving white crowds attacking local black communities.

The street violence had started in Liverpool on the night of 4 June when a fight between a group of Blacks and Norwegian seamen dramatically turned into a 'siege' of black boarding houses.

The violence, which continued for more than a week, revealed something of the relationship between the police and the black community. Significantly, the police, unable to protect the black community from the marauding white crowds, did an interesting thing: they took whole black families into 'protective custody'. Seven days after the riots began, the police held over 700 black people. [82]

From Liverpool the violence spread simultaneously to Newport, and then to Cardiff. But although the violence had petered out, the Cardiff area continued to be heavily policed. One wonders whether the police were protecting or provoking the black community at a time when 'Negro Hunting' as the South Wales *Daily News* put it, 'had developed into something like a fever'.

Why were the Whites so resentful of Blacks? The dominant theme explaining this resentment (a major media preoccupation) was relations between black men and white women. Indeed, sexual relations between them aroused deep racial tension. Given that the black man's 'chief failing' was his 'fondness for white women', the solution to the immorality inherent in the racial situation in British ports, was to 'Deport or Colonise'. The *Liverpool Courier* suggested racial segregation. [83] It would seem that the press were dissatisfied with their objective of enlightening public opinion by turning it against black seamen. They argued that if the public had been 'more vigilant' (could it have reacted more violently?), as in the United States, there would have been no 'evil'! [84]

There were violent clashes during the inter-war years and in 1948 in Liverpool. During these years, black seamen and the emergent black 'second-generation' underwent severe economic and social hardship. They became a subject for social investigation. The most significant violent racial clashes during the inter-war years were in Cardiff in 1923 and 1929 and in South Shields in 1930. [85] These incidents arose from industrial disputes. Later in 1948, racial violence erupted in Liverpool for three nights during the August Bank Holiday. Even more than in 1919, the behaviour of the police was a major issue in these clashes. One observer reported:

> the police appear to have retaliated with a singular lack of discrimination with the result that a number of men who had not been involved in the affair received unwarranted injuries and were arrested . . . The general impression appears to be that the police took action which they thought could bring the disturbances to a close as quickly as possible – which, in their view meant removing the coloured community, rather than attempting to arrest the body of irresponsible whites who were involved. [86]

In effect, the police strategy during these violent clashes, and their use of excessive violence in indiscriminate arrests of Blacks, engendered solidarity within a beleaguered black community. Positive organisation led to the setting up of a defence fund to help towards the legal expenses of 60 Blacks (as opposed to only 10 Whites) arrested. Once again, through selective arrests, the police was propagandising against the black community.

In the inter-racial violence, the state had its role to play. By the time of the 1919 disturbances, it was apparent that the state was ready to confirm and legitimise racial practices within the shipping industry, which was powerfully influential in the 'City' and well represented in Parliament. [87] Indeed, the convenient increase in colonial labour during the first settlement, already in the air in 1911, was greater in 1919 with the growth of popular nationalism during the war. Interestingly, this nationalism excluded Blacks from post-war benefits, although thousands of black men had risked their lives in the cause of the war.

To add insult to injury, repatriation became a major issue soon after the 1919 riots. The South Wales press pulled out all the stops on this issue: 'The government ought to declare it to be part of National Policy that this country is not to be regarded as an immigration field, that no more immigrants can be admitted, and that immigrants must be returned whence they came. This must apply to black men from the British West Indies as well as from the United States.'[88] The trade unions and ex-soldiers also gave their support to this policy.

What emerged after the 1919 violence was the fact that the black population was the primary responsibility of the government. In fact, both the Cardiff and Liverpool local authorities approached the Home Office, the Colonial Office, the Ministry of Shipping and the Ministry of Labour to repatriate the Blacks.[89] The persuasion tactic, left in the hands of the police both in Cardiff and Liverpool, in spite of some success in registering Blacks, was strongly resisted. In Liverpool of the 200 black seamen and ex-soldiers who had registered, only 43 were actually repatriated.[90] In Cardiff, only 30 black seamen accepted.

These departures of Blacks from Britain had the effect of increasing the importance of immigration control and repatriation in state manoeuvres. Legislation was necessary. Thus, the 1925 Special Restriction (Coloured Alien Seamen) Order drawn up by the Conservative government of 1924, came into being. Blacks found themselves trying to prove that they were British colonial subjects. In the witch-hunt the black community was harassed by the police, local alien departments and immigration officers. Representatives of the black seamen called on the assistance of the League of Coloured Peoples who found that the registration process was a police 'campaign'.

The LCP investigation and report showed that where 'persuasion' failed, the threats of arrest and imprisonment were used. It was not until 1932, largely through the political agitation of the black community that the Home Office formulated a procedure through which registration under the 1925 Order could be reversed. When, however, the procedure was applied in 1935, in relation to a provision made under the Shipping Assistance Act 1935, virtually debarring aliens from employment in British ships eligible for government aid within the terms of the Act, hundreds of 'coloured alien seamen' were thrown out of work.[91]

During the inter-war years, the 1925 Order had an all-pervasive effect on the black community, dominating their lives and political struggles. When finally, it was repealed, just before the Second World War, Britain again called on the services not only of black seamen, but of hundreds of thousands of other black colonials.

Black revolt

Race, class and power relations determined the form of collective racial violence during the 1911, 1919, and 1948 riots which were initiated by white crowds. Black seamen posed both an economic and political threat to white organised labour. The discriminatory wage levels applied to black seamen pointed up the contradiction within organised labour. In fact, organised labour had collaborated with capital to effect racial strictures within the shipping industry. Thus, in defending its sectional interest, organised white labour used its collective bargaining power to restrict the employment of black labour.

The economic threat was followed by the political. Because most black workers in the industry were outside the union, in ensuring the structured power relations between capital and organised labour, it weakened the union's bargaining power to win wage increases and better working conditions, thus giving the advantage to capital to effectively resist labour's demands.

Another area of concern to the white crowds was competition with black workers for housing and residential space. This segregation and isolation in Cardiff of the black working class (a result of local official politics) also reflected a racial and imperialist ideology, strongly advocated by the middle class moralists, the local media, religious associations, police officials and other local administrators.

Although they were clearly disadvantaged, Blacks were not willing victims. In 1919 there was determined black resistance in defence of the black community in Cardiff. Unemployment among Blacks in British seaports after the war was compounded when the Shipping Federation decided to give preference to white seamen in British ports. Given that there were no real prospects of alternative employment, their war efforts showed up a deep sense of injustice, which white racial attack did little to assuage.

Moreover, the police were active in the suppression of black cafes and in enforcing the 1925 Special Restriction (Coloured Alien Seamen's) Order. For the black community which had survived the violent confrontations of 1919 and 1948, the message was clear: harassed black crowds had sound reasons for resisting police aggression in their communities. Indeed the police were increasingly being perceived as one form of institutionalised racism. Consequently, during this period the black community, in need of support for its resistance, relied essentially on black organisations such as the Cardiff-based Coloured Seamen's Union, the League for Colonial Freedom and the London-based League of Coloured Peoples – organisations which played the leading role in Cardiff's black political struggle during the inter-war years.

Between 1948 and 1980, the patterns of racial violence showed a number of trends. There was firstly, a decline in collective white violence. Nottingham and Notting Hill in 1958 and Dudley in 1962 were the most noteworthy instances, though small in scale in comparison to 1919 and 1948. Secondly, there was the growth of individualised white racist attacks from the late 1960s. Thirdly, from the mid-1970s, there was the growth of 'race related' collective political violence. As in Lewisham in 1976 and Southall in 1979, there was public protest by the anti-racist movement, and violence which occurred between the crowd and the police. Finally, dating from the early 1970s there was an increasing incidence of violent collective conflict between Blacks and the police. Such confrontations were of two kinds: clashes occasioned by black political demonstrations and other kinds of black street assembly; for example, the Mangrove demonstration in 1971, the carnivals in Chapeltown, Leeds in 1975 and in Notting Hill in 1976 and clashes resulting from specific police actions within the black community, such as the Metro Youth Club incident in 1971, or the Four Aces Club, Dalston in 1975 and the collective violence that occurred in Bristol in 1980, and elsewhere in 1981.

The increasing incidence of violent conflict between Blacks and the police is perhaps the most significant development in the pattern of collective racial violence in post-war Britain, culminating in the 'Bristol Riot'.

These conflicts and contradictions between Blacks and the state are of course central in the structuring of race in the post-war period. The fundamental questions to be asked at this stage are: why and how this came to be so? And how does inter-communal collective violence come to be replaced by the mobilisation of black violence against the state?

In responding to these questions, it has been argued that race in the post-war era had been situated 'within two related processes: the distinctive subordination of black workers in the new phase of immigration and the nature of the state's involvement in that subordinating process, with special reference to the politicisation of race within the state'.[92]

From black resistance to black revolt

During the early period of post-war reconstruction, racialism in employment, housing and schooling was a fact of life for the black community. At first, both Afro-Caribbeans and Asians found it difficult to cope with British prejudices. In alien territory, they were forced back into their own communities. While the West Indians organised their own churches, clubs and welfare organisations and congregated in barber shops, cafes or street corners, if the weather was fine, Indians and Pakistanis took naturally to their temples, mosques and cultural associations.

At the workplace, resistance to racialism often comprised individualistic and unco-ordinated responses. Given that Asians were generally employed in textile mills, foundries and factories, while

Afro-Carribbeans were concentrated in the service sector, the racial division of labour (the practice of the divide and rule strategy in the colonies, now a fact of life in post-war Britain) kept the Asian, Afro-Caribbean, Asian-Caribbean workers apart. Moreover, the 'ethnic jobs' and 'ethnic shifts' distinctions detracted from providing common ground for a common struggle of the black community as a whole. Further, during these early years of immigration, the black population was small, with fewer Asians and more West Indians. At this time, resistance to racial discrimination at work was largely spontaneous. There were, however, more 'organised', collective efforts in the form of petitions calling for improvements in working conditions, facilities and more pay. Generally white workers showed no interest in these collective actions. Undeterred, black workers persisted in forming associations on the shopfloor, as was the case in 1951 in a Merseyside factory. In their resistance to racial abuse and discrimination several organisations were formed.

Gradually the post-war black community through traditional cultural and welfare associations engendered black self-reliance and independent organisation. They recognised the immediate realities confronting them in Britain as having their roots in the past. Some – particularly the organisers – were aware of the connections between colonialism and racialism, and were reminded of an earlier black radical tradition in Britain by such writers, activists and organisers as George Padmore, C. L. R. James, Ras Makonnen, I. T. A. Wallace-Johnson and Jomo Kenyatta. This radical group had helped to bring to fruition the struggles of earlier Pan Africanists who had resided during their periods of agitations in Britain, on and off, since Equiano and Cugoano. Black nationalism for Africa and the colonies, then, sustained black organisations in Britain.

Indian Independence in 1947 and Kwame Nkrumah's leadership of Ghana to Independence in 1957, followed by independence for other colonies in Africa, Asia and in the West Indies, strengthened the resolve of black British associations to resist racialism. Thus the anti-racial and anti-colonial struggle of the early post-war immigrants had begun to reflect strong community bases.

Colonial freedom and black settlement was followed by state action to institutionalise racial discrimination, thus encouraging fascism. In the face of the gathering forces, black struggle and black unity were engaged in a continuous process of meeting the challenge. Already by the mid-1950s, black immigration, though small in scale, had aroused strong feelings. Racialism had once again entered the political arena when moves were being made to bring about immigration control.

As Britain released her 'burdensome' colonies, the imperialist ideology of racial superiority was adopted by extreme right-wing groups with Hitlerian fervour. So much so, that one was left to wonder to what purpose was the war fought against Germany and her allies. Indeed, it was a time when fascism achieved a real sense of respectability by taking part in electoral politics. Racial superiority was preached by various groups. The race-hate they stirred led to racial attacks on black people. Thus 'nigger-hunting' and 'paki-bashing' became an aspect of the everyday experience of the black working class in Britain. In the repeated instances of collective crowd violence the victims were portrayed as the aggressors and the 'cause' of the riots. Thus, they were the 'problem'.

As in the case of India, attempts to get West Indian governments to restrict immigration to the United Kingdom failed. Nonetheless, the 1962 Commonwealth Immigration Act was passed.

In the face of this act of institutionalised racism, the black community, which had increased dramatically by those trying to 'beat the ban', were even more conscious of their status as second-class citizens. Before 1958, a few black activists who saw the growing wall of racial prejudice worked towards bringing both the West Indian and growing Asian communities together to resist their common oppression. A campaigning paper was vitally necessary in linking the struggles of the various sections of the black community. Thus, in 1958 Claudia Jones, a Trinidadian Communist and Amy Garvey (widow of Marcus Garvey) launched the first issue of an Afro-Caribbean journal in Britain, *The West Indian Gazette*. And as if to convince the sceptics who believed that Blacks did not read, other publications followed such as *Link*, *Carib*, *Anglo-Caribbean News*, *Tropic*, *Flamingo*, *Daylight International*, *West Indies Observer* and *Magnet*. [93] Black consciousness, having reached a high point after the riots and Cochrane's death, moved Claudia Jones and Frances Ezzrecco to found the Coloured Peoples Progressive Association which, with the support of other West Indian organisations, sent representatives to see the Home Secretary. Several other events helped to maintain the level of black resistance.

Concern in the former colonies was reflected in representations made in Britain by leading politicians. Norman Manley, the Prime Minister of Jamaica and Jawaharlal Nehru, Prime Minister of India, both advised their respective communities in Britain. This international support helped to place clearly the ideology of racism in its historical and international context. The struggles on the periphery were directly related to the metropole.

After the 1962 Immigration Act, a number of issues directly relating to the black community left a lasting impression. Through its nationalisation, racialism had become necessarily a part of the state machinery. Other British institutions such as the Employers' Association and the trade unions, essentially capitalist organisations, were expected to, and began to conform to the standards set by the state. Not surprisingly, racial discrimination became even more widespread during the 1960s and 1970s, than in the 1950s. As agents of the state, 'the police felt liberated too'.

The 'bussing' of black schoolchildren, 'nigger-hunting' and 'paki-bashing' became the butt of popular jokes. Racial discrimination was rampant. The hard experience of the black communities had informed them to close ranks, to build a stronger community base. At home, and particularly at work, they were faced with major struggles.

By the mid-1960s, the mass of black immigrants had become settlers. Whether or not they entertained ideas about returning 'home' (and there's every reason to believe that a large number of them did) the stark reality of racial discrimination in all walks of their daily lives in Britain commanded their immediate attention. Gradually during the 1960s and even more so in the 1970s and 1980s, their industrial struggles, compounded by many instances of trade union racism, intensified. Black working class and political activists were finding common ground during different stages of the struggles.

After Malcolm X's visit in 1965, Black Power groups led by the activists Michael X, Obi Egbuna and Roy Sawh came to the aid of black workers who had courageously taken strike action. From this period onwards the workplace would be a battleground on which the struggles against racial discrimination practised by employers, on the one hand, and trade union racism, on the other, steeled black workers into bitter resistance.

If the racism had been 'hidden' before, by the mid-1960s it was more in the open. The inter-racial tension and Black Power struggles in the United States during this period were paralleled in Britain by a growing sense of injustice and black working-class consciousness. The British strategy of divide and rule in the colonies (by separating the African and Afro-Caribbean from the Asians and Asian-Caribbeans) was replicated in post-war Britain. Such Black Power activists as Roy Sawh (the East Indian from Guyana) and Michael X (the Afro-Caribbean), operating in the British context, recognised this division of labour and were determined not to have it repeated in Britain.

In addition to the state's involvement in race via the 1962 Immigration Act, race became an issue in the 1964 General Election. Perhaps the most galling, and, to some, surprising aspect of racial politics, at this time, was the hypocritical attitude of the Labour Party which had sufficiently aligned itself with Blacks to warrant Peter Griffiths's (the Tory candidate for Smethwick) comment: 'If you want a nigger neighbour, Vote Labour'. [94]

As it happened, the Labour Party won the election and Prime Minister Wilson went on to introduce his White Paper in August 1965. In effect, this was intended to restrict 'coloured immigration'. Later in the year, the Race Relations Act (September 1965) was passed under which Michael X was prosecuted for inciting racial hatred. Two other statutory bodies (the National Committee for Commonwealth Immigrants and the Race Relations Board) were set up in the hope of minimising the impact of racial discrimination and racism on the black community. The thinking behind these bodies was to weaken the rising militancy in the black community by integrating the 'leading lights' in CARD within the state's designs. No wonder the militants and moderates in CARD were at each other's throats and CARD collapsed as grass roots militancy surged forward towards the latter part of the 1960s. The state, however, was more concerned, if not obsessed, with putting a stop to Blacks coming to Britain rather than tackling the real and serious problems of the black community.

Moreover, the press, no friend of the black community, gave its calculated support to the government. In a well orchestrated strategy the newspaper influenced the mood of its readership, warning of 'The Dark Million' before the government's White Paper. Further, any hint of a black positive response was quickly discouraged and deflected. Black Muslims, Black Panthers or Black Power were interpreted as having negative value. Those who suffered gladly, relying on the benevolence of changes coming from above, such as the black middle class leaders of CARD, were, of course, acceptable. Predictably then, the collapse of CARD was lamented by *The Times* news team who, given the black uprisings abroad, stated 'that the mixture of pro-Chinese communism and American style Black Power on the immigrant scene can be devastating'. Clearly, they were more concerned with what 'can be' devastating about black people, completely ignoring what in fact is the devastating black reality that constitutes black resistance.

Time was racing and one could not put the clock back, though some tried. Racial attacks and race-hatred was stirred up by the Ku Klux Klan. British fascists with grassroots support were encouraged. In February 1967, the National Front was formed. Since 1919, the position of the black community had not changed. Gradually, they were becoming isolated, 'colonised' in the metropole. Indeed, the black community faced a most formidable opposition in the state which, not content, was intent on further tightening its control over the black 'mob'.

In the ensuing years, repression grew as state racism provoked black militancy. There were signs that hitherto separate struggles on the shopfloor and in the black community were sporadically bringing Asians, Afro-Caribbeans and Asian-Caribbeans together.[95] The goal of black resistance was (still is) to achieve Black Power as systematically set out by its chief advocate, Stokely Carmichael. It was no surprise therefore that the Black Power organisation, UCPA, was formed. Already, the Black Power struggle in America had inspired and influenced many activists in Britain so that Carmichael's visit to London in 1967 confirmed their actions and strengthened their resolve.

Egbuna and Sawh were particularly strident in denouncing the oppression of black people. Through the UCPA, Black Power rhetoric, meetings and study groups helped to raise black consciousness; its ideology was to politicise the black community. In line with the black radical tradition of the Pan Africanists in Britain, while RAAS stressed black nationalism, the UCPA focused on the working class struggles abroad.

Confrontations with management involving Asian workers in April 1967 and 1968 at the Conegre Foundry (Tipton) and in 1968 at Midland Motor Cylinder Company and at the Newby Foundry (West Bromwich) in 1969, given no support or outright opposition from their trade unions, had to rely on the support of their communities and community organisations such as the IWAs, the Pakistani Welfare Associations and other black organisations. The community support was especially crucial since some of the workers' grievances involved 'cultural' questions which affected the whole community. Thus through the lived experience in Britain, the politics and political organisations of the 'home' countries had a bearing on the life and politics of Indian and Pakistani settlers in Britain. Authoritarianism in India was resisted by settlers in Britain. [96] In turn, growing racism in Britain was a source of reciprocal concern to those at 'home'.

By 1968 black class consciousness had become evident. This was the year of the 'Kenyan Asian Act' when Enoch Powell, 'man of the people', alerted the nation (once again on the immigration issue) that 'hundreds of thousands' of Kenyans who held British passports regarded themselves as British. Earlier in the year, in February, Powell had the support of other politicians and the *Daily Mirror* scare of an 'uncontrolled flood of Asian migrants from Kenya'. [97]

When the Bill was passed on 1 March 1968, the black community resisted. A sequence of events triggered off black anger. In response, Jagmohan Joshi, Secretary of the Birmingham IWA, called on black organisations to unite against the Act. Moreover, the assassination of Dr Martin Luther King on 4 April aroused deep emotions which were compounded a few days later by Powell's 'nightmare' of swarming, black migrants. Although state control of black immigration had tightened, Powell was not content; the emphasis on the numbers coming in was now being shifted to those already settled in Britain.

The passage of this racist Act gave Powell political leverage and his supporters licence to abuse Asians and West Indians; thus fascists went 'paki-bashing'. Attacked time and again, the black community responded when representatives from over 50 organisations met in Leamington Spa and formed 'a militant front for Black Consciousness and against racialism' – the BPA. [98]

Significantly, on the same day, while the black working class was constituting itself into a national body, a section of the white working class, the London dockers and porters (supporters of Powell) marched and demanded an end to black immigration. The heightened black consciousness and militancy was reflected in exclusion from BPA membership of immigrant organisations that

were involved with the government urban aid programme or
sought the assistance of the Labour Party.

The acceptance of Black Power by the black community was
given a boost by the racist 1968 Immigration Act and Powell's
incitement to racial hatred speeches. Several black militant organisations, black newspapers and journals came into being. Interestingly, the issues they discussed and were concerned with were not
purely British – and fittingly so, since more British capital was
invested abroad than at home. For the militant leadership of the
black British working class then, the issues were clearly international. The ban on the works of Carmichael and Malcolm X led
to a march of Jamaican organisations on their High Commission in
London and a sit-in in protest against Walter Rodney's ban from
returning to the University of the West Indies. Moreover, black
entertainers and Michael X appeared in a Third World Benefit at
the Round House for the imprisoned playwrights Wole Soyinka in
Nigeria, Le Roi Jones in America and Obi Egbuna in Britain. At
this time, the words of the Black Panther Movement were prophe-
tic. On 3 October 1968, they warned: 'Unless something is done to
ensure the protection of our people . . . we will have no alternative
but to rise to their defence. And once we are driven to that position,
redress will be too late, Detroit and Newark will inevitably become
part of the British scene.'[99]

Powell, an historical agent of British racism, having cornered the
black community, now wanted to eliminate it. He called, in the
best British administrative tradition, not for a Commission of
Inquiry, but for a 'Ministry of Repatriation'. For those who did not
understand what he meant, the media obliged by giving Powell
ample opportunity to explain his 'Ministry'. Edward Heath, the
Tory leader, went further calling a halt to all immigration. Callaghan showed his willingness to move in their direction. Finally
the Heath government passed the 1971 Immigration Act. The
dependants of black people already in Britain were particularly
affected. The Act reinforced existing practices of bans and entry
certificates, stop and search arrests and 'sus', detentions and depor-
tations, intensifying police harassment of the black community. If
life became intolerable for Blacks, they could now, of course, be
assisted to go 'home'!

Given that cheap black labour in Britain was being made redundant because of technological change, the Act, it was argued, must
be seen in conjunction with the Industrial Relations Act, also passed
in 1971.[100]

The struggles on the shopfloor and in the community were
beginning to merge more effectively and became politicised
through the Black Power movement and black political groups.
This autonomous organisation, in part, reflected the failure of
white radicals to recognise the special problems of the black work-

ing class. Thus, the black political groups directed their essential attention to black struggle in the factories, schools and to the disturbing harassment by the police. Apart from the workplace, black resistance was conducted at different levels, in different places and often with different priorities.

The Asian community, for example, more concerned with the entry of families and dependants were involved in legal fights, largely through the JCWI, through petitioning and lobbying. Later, from 1972, Asian leaders also had to contend with the problems of resettlement of refugees from Uganda. Particularly disturbing was the subjection of Asian women to vaginal examination. The Afro-Caribbean community, on the other hand, was concerned with the ESN schools in which their children were dumped.

With no assistance from the Race Relations Board (1970) black self-help was set in motion, spawning a multiplicity of black militant organisations. These projects received spontaneous and widespread support from the black community. It was a movement, gathering all the strands of capitalist oppression.

Police violence within the black community was nothing new. By the summer of 1969, however, black organisations had begun to monitor police violence against black people. Both the UCPA and the Pakistan Progressive Party protested against 'paki-bashing' in London's East End and elsewhere. Police attacks on the black communities in London, Liverpool, Manchester, Bristol, Birmingham and Leeds 'put whole communities under siege'.

In the fight against racism, a black class interest emerged, linking Indians, Pakistanis and West Indians. Their fight was a two-pronged one: as Blacks and as workers. In perspective, their fight was as a people and a class. This however did not mean 'subsuming the race struggle to the class struggle but by deepening and broadening class struggle through its black and anti-colonial, anti-imperialist dimension'.[101]

Essentially, black strike committees, a new phenomenon in British industrial relations, appeared to co-ordinate their struggles against intransigent employers. In four major instances, they were not given the support of their unions, which chose to oppose them instead. In fact, the activities of these strike committees, reflected a courageous and militant stand which highlighted the racism in the trade union movement.

By the end of the 1970s, black youth, after a long tradition of racist violence directed at their forebears now moved forward to accept the challenge of resisting white racism. Already 'marginalised' by the education system (in fact, dumped in ESN schools) they stepped outside of Babylon and into the popular politics of Rastafarianism. This development, compounded by the deepening recession and no job prospects, given high technology and rising unemployment, left them out of the reckoning. Thus, through the deliberate designs of the state, they became social outcasts. The police, geared up, would try to intimidate them, as they had done their parents and other black people before. Thus, black youth became the vanguard of the new resistance.

Unlike their parents, this generation of black youth having experienced racism at an early age (in fact 'schooled' in racism) did not intend to suffer gladly. When the Asian youth Gurdip Singh Chaggar was stabbed to death by a gang of white youths in June 1976 in Southall, the elders of the Asian community continued to respond in the old way of passing resolutions. The youths, however, had organised a march to the local police station. Subsequently, they formed the radical Southall Youth Movement.

The race-hatred and provocation engendered by the NF led to racial attacks and death to many black people. Black youth moved quickly to form youth movements and defence committees in London, Manchester, Leicester, Bradford and elsewhere. In addition, anti-racist, anti-imperialist political groups were formed by Asians, Afro-Caribbeans and Africans. Their agitations were comprehensive; the aim was to politicise the whole black community. Thus black consciousness was heightened in the 1970s through the publications of *Samaj in a Babylon* (in Urdu and English – published after the racial attacks during 1976 involving Chaggar's death), and in the wake of the Notting Hill riots and events in Soweto. This was followed by the publications *Black Struggle* and *Mukti*.[102] Indeed, Blacks were united against state and police harassment and were anti-racist and anti-imperialist. The black community, nurtured and nursed after each battering by the state and the police, relied heavily on the support and leadership of black women. Oppressed as mothers and as wives, nonetheless having absorbed the pain and suffering of their communities, they came to add a voice of their own, when the odds were really stacked against them, at the workplace and elsewhere. Their unprecedented struggles at Mansfield Hosiery Mills, Imperial Typewriters, Grunwick, Futters and Chix and the National Health Service, among others, has shattered the myth of the passive Asian woman. During the Grunwick strike, through sheer commitment to their cause of 'racist exploitation' they were able as 'green' trade unionists to get the whole labour movement behind them. In a marathon stint of picketing they weathered the kicks and punches of the defenders of law and order – the police. Thereafter, the 'friendly Bobby' image was being questioned by British liberals as though they had not already known of past police brutality.

If the police had displayed violence at the Grunwick picket lines, then the Thatcher warning about immigrants 'swamping' the country gave licence for greater latitude. Media attention helped matters little. In fact, it served to exacerbate the race situation. Powell, the opportunist, was again up to his 'induced repatriation' tricks. And in London three Asians were murdered in three months. The NF

marches, given wide publicity, received incredible police protection. Yet when Blacks asked for police protection from white racist
attacks (in the Tower Hamlets area, for example) they were denied
it. The historical pattern had not changed since 1919. And in 1978
there was absolutely no reason for black people to believe that it
was going to change without struggle.

In 1979, the NF, refused permission by Ealing Council, was
granted permission to hold meetings in Southall Town Hall where
one of the largest Asian communities resided. In response, the
Southall community protested peacefully, to avoid this deliberate
provocation. But this was not to be: again the black community
was involved when 2756 police, including SPG units, moved in to
put down the protest. [103] Suddenly because of the law-abiding NF,
the local residents could not enter the town centre. The massive
police presence prevented the people from moving back home or to
the Town Hall. They were trapped. The police went 'berserk'
allegedly beating one man to death, and seriously injuring hundreds. The police damage to the offices of Black People Unite was
symbolic of their disregard for black people. Bruised and battered,
the Southall Asian community, unprepared, had learnt a vital
lesson.

The sense of outrage among black people was compounded by
the introduction of Thatcher's Nationality Bill which aroused
strong feelings of resistance significantly among black women. By
the late 1970s, the cumulative effect of the mounting police harassment gave rise to new types of struggles and 'new leaderships'. The
black women's movement now gave a lead. Following Grunwick,
a major development had taken place as black women's groups
came into being. Together, these Asian and Afro-Caribbean groups
through their national body – the Organisation of Women of Asian
and African Descent (OWAAD), brought to the struggle an
urgency to issues hitherto neglected, such as class, race and gender,
from a black viewpoint. Indeed, they brought to the forefront the
issues at the heart of the black community, such as households,
children's welfare, child-care, Depo-Provera and abortion law and
black prisoner's rights. In 1979, the Brixton Black Women's Group
set up the first Black Women's Centre and Asian women joined the
campaigns initiated by the United Black Women's Action
Group. [104] The Asian and Afro-Caribbean women 'herstories' sig-
nalled a vital stage in the black community's struggle.

Overall then, by June 1979, under the leadership of the IWA and
Blacks Against State Harassment the black community, keyed up
to act, embarked on their first national demonstration. In spite of
these protests, however, black youth remained the real target.
Deprived, defenceless and disoriented, they were open to police
abuse, charges and violence. 'Sus' and 'mugging' followed them
everywhere. None, it seemed, was innocent in the eyes of the
police on the beat; every one was suspected. Given police methods,

the relation between the police and the black community had deteriorated markedly. Many black people were kicked into the ground; they had no choice but to resist. They had nothing to lose, except their 'fears'.

Links between crowd violence, the current economic crisis and inner city deprivation, disadvantage and decay were denied by government ministers. Moreover, and in the teeth of hard evidence, government spokesmen misleadingly insisted that police/black relations were good. In effect, the state refused to defuse or prevent crowd violence. Instead, it tried to repress it. [105]

Given the changing patterns of collective racial violence in Britain, violence was integral to the political struggles of the groups concerned. Moreover, it is important to see those struggles in the context of race and class in British society, historically. Seen against this background, the 'riot' in Bristol on 2 April 1980 could have happened at any time during the heightened racism, exploitation, repression and police harassment that confronted the black community in the previous decade, a time of increasing state authoritarianism. [106] Thus, with a larger black presence than ever before in Britain, the state through its policies and practices, engendered black resistance which, none too soon, exploded into open rebellion in the old slave port of Bristol.

The 'Bristol Riot', a significant juncture between race in the 1970s and race in the 1980s, shocked the state, the police and the media and alerted the British public of all shades of opinion to the deep malaise of race and class in British society. Television pictures of the violence in the St Paul's area of Bristol informed the public. This was big news. Hitherto, the festering problems of black people were ignored. Now, the newspapers moved in with alacrity to apportion blame, thus revealing their bias. For example, the crowd violence which occurred was labelled 'The Bristol riot' by the press. On 3 April 1980 some newspaper headlines were:

Pull-out ordered as shops burn
19 police hurt in black riot
Hundreds rampage after swoop on Bristol club. [107]

The Guardian reported that hundreds of angry youths went on the rampage after a raid on a black cafe in Bristol: '19 police hurt as rioters burn, loot city streets'. [108] The *Daily Mirror* stated, 'Gang of Looters Go On Rampage' [109] while *The Times* told its readers that 'Hundreds of black youths battle with police in Bristol riot'. [110] The emphasis, highly emotive – 'police hurt', 'black riot', 'black youths', 'burn', 'loot', 'mob fury' – was clearly directed to solicit public outrage against the 'black mob', and sympathy for the forces of law and order in performing their legitimate duty. In Bristol, the local papers were even more alarmist. The *Western Daily Press* reported, 'Gangs of coloured youths ran wild; looting, stoning police and starting fires', [111] while *The Evening Post* from their correspondent in enemy territory, the 'riot zone', reported on the 'war on the streets', involving 1000 rioters on the rampage.[112]

This sample of images was used by the press to get the 'riot' across. The black identity of the 'mob' was established and the 'riot' was set in the context of the background of the St Paul's area, described in *The Guardian* as a 'poverty-stricken black ghetto'[113] in which 30 per cent of the population was black. Given this tit-bit about a hostile black environment, what the press had made abundantly clear was their concern for the '19 police hurt', rather than the 'twenty-five people injured'. Further, *The Guardian* reported: 'When they [the police] entered the club . . . a large crowd quickly gathered. As the police left they faced a barrage of bricks, stones and bottles. Several officers fell to the ground with head wounds.' And communicating what seemed like extraordinary bravery on the part of the police, the Deputy Chief Constable told the newspaper:

> Every time we went in we increased what was a volatile situation and I feared for the lives of the policemen. It was a very, very dangerous situation, and in the interests of the safety of the policemen, and due to the inadequate number I had available, I felt it necessary to withdraw and establish law and order.[114]

The police retreat from the St Paul's area, was portrayed by the press as a withdrawal to 'cool down' the situation and 'avoid further confrontation'.

In the same way that Blacks have been linked with crime, so too they are linked with prostitution and loose morals. As the *Daily Mirror* put it: 'Bristol's crime rate is one of the highest among provincial cities. St Paul's is Bristol's poorest area. It is known as a red-light district, with prostitutes openly soliciting on the streets. The area has the city's highest proportion of Blacks.'[115] Interestingly, such public commentators had turned a blind eye on that part of Bristol as an area of 'endless pressure' for Blacks.

Newspaper editorials became more cautious as the days passed. The *Daily Mail* commented: 'This was not a 'race riot',[116] while *The Guardian* warned of the 'appalling tensions which now exist between black youths and the police'.[117] *The Daily Telegraph* saw West Indian youth as 'the most serious problem' confronting the police. It added, their sub-culture had a 'substantial criminal fringe . . . we are dealing not with black migrants, but with the irresponsible worst group of those migrants'.[118]

Significantly, none of the newspapers mentioned explained why socio-economic differences exist between Blacks and Whites, or how black communities came into being in the inner city. In fact, these questions could only be adequately answered by reference to the roles of racist ideologies and practices. Comments about law and order occupied much space in the press. Indeed, it seemed to be the cure for all social ills. *The Guardian* was aware of this when it pointed out the disproportionate effect of government policies on the inner city, by calling for a programme to improve housing, job opportunity and education for the black population. [119] Declaring its concern, the local *Western Daily Press* editorial stated: 'The future of St Paul's is now Bristol's No. 1 problem. To say it is insoluble is to be defeatist; to say that it is a difficult problem with many complexities, is to be realistic.'[120]

Overall, the nature of the press reporting of the crowd violence in Bristol was 'instrumental not only in the reproduction of racial stereotypes amongst large sections of the white population, but in the alienated sections of the black population'. Unfortunately, in calling for government action most of them meant an increased police presence – the very action that had triggered off crowd violence before.

Clearly in the case of Bristol those Acts of Parliament, structures and agencies designed to lessen the effect of discrimination and racism failed showing a callous disregard for the past confrontations and the urgent demands of the black community for help.

Summer 1981

In the aftermath of the 'Bristol Riot', between April 1980 and summer 1981, the cumulative effect of racist attacks centred in London (the death of 'Cartoon' Campbell in Brixton prison in March 1980, and the murder of Akhtar Ali Baig in Newham in July 1980) and the burning to death of 13 young West Indians in New Cross in January 1981 brought increased distress to the black community. The crowd violence in Bristol had echoed a wave of deep-seated resentment among black people across Britain.

The violence against Blacks in London reached crisis point following the New Cross fire. According to one writer, the fire had been started by fascists. The police, however, would have none of it. Before the investigation was over, the police felt that it was (in descending order) the work of a disaffected black partygoer, or a prank which went wrong or maybe an accident. Finally, they 'proved' through forensic expertise that the fire had been self-inflicted one way or another. Notably, there was no mention that white, anti-black hooligans (who had been known to terrorise black neighbourhoods) might have been responsible.

The deaths of the black youths and others that took place in the months after the 'Bristol riot' activated black consciousness into top gear. Meetings held in New Cross were attended by people from all over Britain. They came as an act of solidarity. A day of action was organised by the New Cross Massacre Action Committee and the Race Today Collective, under the leadership of Darcus Howe and John La Rose. On 2 March, 10,000 people marched through London in a public demonstration of black solidarity. [121] It was a long march and the few skirmishes led to several arrests. Nine months after Bristol, this kind of news, it seemed, was to be expected. The press, once again, attacked the black community for lawlessness and put forward their pet formula of law and order. The banner headlines were 'mob violence' and 'Blacks on the rampage'. As if police/black relations had only broken down that day, the press showed its concern and thanks for the 'Bobby'. Indeed, since the confrontation in Bristol, the police had received nothing but encouragement. Not surprisingly, then, cock-a-hoop, (and no wonder they were, with might on their side) the police antagonised black people in Brixton while fascists baited Southall.

The period after the New Cross Massacre demonstration in March 1981 was a troubled one in terms of police/Blacks relations. There were clashes with the police over the Deptford demonstration in Coventry in May, Thornton Heath in June and on two separate occasions in July in Southall. The 'massacre' struck deep responses within the black communities. The tinder was there, it needed only a spark. That spark was lit (after a long period of intense police harassment) in Brixton on Friday 10 April 1981. Brixton was set ablaze as violence continued for three days. In terms of intensity, Bristol was dwarfed. Petrol bombs were used setting many buildings alight; a fire symbolic of a burning desire for human dignity among a shamefully oppressed people. For the record, the police made 200 arrests. [122]

The estimated £10 million damage to property in Brixton had deeper political significance. Lord Scarman was called upon to provide an explanation (as though the government did not already know the causes of this black revolt in the heart of the metropole). Brixton, like Bristol, was not regarded as a 'race riot' and saturation policing as a possible cause was dismissed. More plausible was the 'outside agitator' theory. This was another example of a dishonest approach to a grave social problem. The idea of extraneous forces then, was given credibility by the police and press. The Assistant Commissioner of Police said that a number of people were 'seen to be in an organising position with black youths'. [123] The *Daily Express* aware of the social tinder, asked 'Who lit the fuse of fury?[124]

The following weekend, 17–20 April, Blacks and police clashed again in Finsbury Park and Ealing Common in London. And in the seaside resorts Brighton, Scarborough and Margate, violence broke out between skinheads, punks and rockers. In May a protest march against violent racial attacks in Coventry, organised by the Asian community and anti-racist groups, led to confrontations in Thornton Heath and in parts of London.

By the end of June, the violence continued in London with little action elsewhere. July proved to be an historic month. The 'July riots' marked a turning point in British politics. Black youth, no longer able to contain their feelings of bitterness and frustration, acted together on the streets against the police. And for the sceptics who were prone to dismiss the Blacks as 'hot-heads', it was significant that white youths also joined the violent protests; in effect, race and class had become the battle cry. In Liverpool and other cities, black and white youths, faced with an oppressive and tangible force, in desperation, petrol-bombed the police, police stations and police vehicles. If there was any doubt that the violent racial attacks were the source of animosity against the police and against organised fascist groups and could lead to more generalised violence, the evidence was clear in the violence in Southall 3–5 July.

As the fires burned in Southall, collective racial violence (an integral part of the history of race, and black settlement in Britain during the twentieth century) erupted, almost simultaneously, in some 29 cities and towns in the summer of 1981.

British immigration legislation which has clearly indicated that 'blacks are not wanted here' is a fact known intimately by all black people in Britain. Racial discrimination and racial disadvantage, and the sub-class position of the black working class *vis-à-vis* the white working class has led black cultural and political organisations across the country, to achieve and acknowledge (at various levels), for the first time, a national black working-class consciousness – the inevitable outcome of race and class oppression.

According to E. P. Thompson, the English working class 'made itself as much as it was made'. He adds crucially:

> Class consciousness is the way in which the experiences are handled in cultural terms: embodied in traditions, value-systems, ideas and institutional forms. If the experience appears as determined, class consciousness does not . . . class is defined by men as they live their own history, and, in the end, this is its only definition. [125]

Indeed, an integral part of these 'cultural terms' was racialism. Thus historically, the practices and policies of British capital that have made the English working class, ironically, in turn, received the general endorsement of the white working class in the making of the black working class in Britain.

Conclusion

At the Centenary Conference held in Winnipeg, Canada, in March 1983 to mark Karl Marx's death, Ralph Miliband, reflecting the spirit of the Conference said: 'Today Marxism is full of contradictions, full of holes. . . . But just as Marx was inspired throughout by a magnificent optimism, in due course we can reach ever closer to fulfil Marxism's potential and we share in that optimism. For peace and socialism, let us advance together.' A truly worthy vision.

Nevertheless, black working-class autonomous organisation is today's reality, necessitated and conditioned by institutionalised racism. Historically, the trade unions, the Labour Party and the British working class generally (in spite of their hollow, hypocritical pronouncements of 'the brotherhood of man') have actively helped to make and maintain this fracture within the class. They must know, more than ever before, that it is incumbent on them to listen and *act* on the representations of black autonomous organis- ations. The disadvantages are too glaring to legitimise mere reforms.

At the outset, as a 'class', black workers were deliberately made: policies and practices determined their colonial backgrounds and created the conditions for their emigration to Britain; made them live and work in the decaying inner city environments; made them accept low pay, bad housing, unemployment, sub-standard educa- tion; made them feel guilty when receiving state welfare benefits; and made them the subjects of humiliating public repatriation debates.

Indeed, the black working class have been socially, economically and politically pushed to eking out an existence (and a precarious one at that!) on the fringe of British society. Thus made, they have been criticised for being a 'society' apart, alien. While much politi- cal capital has been made from this, their alienation brought deepening impoverishment and desperation. Wherever and whenever their exploitation had become unbearable, they fought courageously for redress, particularly at the workplace. In so doing, they consistently campaigned for solidarity with white workers, significantly, without success.

It is evident, however, that the black British will not suffer gladly while they wait (as their forebears on the colonial plantations and mines were asked to) for a 'dispensation from above' to be free from the trammels of their 'makers'. Thus, through a painful process of heightened social, economic and political awareness, the lessons of the past have been learnt, at every turn of the authoritarian screw. Their intentions are clear. In the face of oppression, they will do as black, oppressed people (under slavery, indentureship, imperialism, colonialism, neo-colonialism and, today, as secondclass citizens in Britain) have always done, wage a struggle for their freedom, for their civil rights in the teeth of the forces ranged against them.

Their history of struggle against racism and harassment has evolved from resistance to open rebellion. Indeed, the black work- ing class in Britain have taken the initiative in the class struggle. While they may hope for a positive response from the white 'labour aristocracy' and the white working class generally, their autono- mous struggle (the direct result of British racism) will continue as their urgent, insistent demands extend to every aspect of their essential deprivation.

I Aims and Objects of the IWA–GB

The full text of Article iii, 'Aims and Objects of the IWA–GB' read:

To organise Indians to:

(1) safeguard and improve their conditions of life and work;
(2) seek co-operation of the Indian High Commission in UK towards the fulfilment of its aims and objects;
(3) promote co-operation and unity with the trade union and labour movement of Great Britain;
(4) strengthen friendship with the British and all other peoples in Great Britain and co-operate with their organisations to this end;
(5) fight against all forms of discrimination based on race, colour, creed or sex, for equal human rights and social and economic opportunities, and co-operate with other organisations to this end;
(6) promote the cause of friendship, peace and freedom of all countries and co-operate with other organisations, national and international, striving for the same;
(7) keep its members in particular, and the people of Great Britain generally, informed of political, economic and social developments in India; and

(8)   undertake social welfare and cultural activities towards the fulfilment of the above aims.

II Organisations Affiliated to the West Indian Standing Conference in 1966

British Caribbean Association (White–Black ratio approx. 50–50, predominantly middle-class); Caribbean Co-operative League (black, middle and working-class-economic); Clapham Inter-racial Club (Black–White ratio approx. 50–50, middle and working-class, social and welfare); Coloured People's Progressive Association (black, working-class, social and welfare); Croydon Commonwealth Citizens Association (black, working-class, social and welfare); Ferme Park International Association (White–Black ratio approx. 50–50, middle and working-class, social and welfare); Hornsey Co-operative Credit Union (black, working-class, economic); North London West Indian Association (black, tiny percentage of Whites, working-class, social and welfare); St John's Inter-Racial and Social Club (White–Black ratio approx. 30–70, working-class, social and welfare); West Indian Students' Union (White–Black ratio approx. 20–80, middle-class social); Willesden International Unity Association (black, tiny percentage of Whites, working-class, social and welfare); Caribbean United Nationals Association (black working-class, economic); and the Paddington

Overseas Club (black, middle and working-class, social and welfare).

III The Aims and Objects of the Campaign Against Racial Discrimination

To struggle for the elimination of all racial discrimination against coloured people in the United Kingdom.

To struggle for the elimination of all forms of discrimination against all other minority groups in the United Kingdom.

To be concerned about the struggle of oppressed people everywhere.

To seek to co-ordinate the work of organisations already in the field and to act as a clearing house for information about the fight against discrimination in Britain.

To oppose all racially discriminatory legislation or that inspired by racial prejudice, for example, the Commonwealth Immigrants Act of 1962.

To work for the ratification of the United Nations Bill of Human Rights by the Government of Great Britain.

IV Organisations that Sent Delegates or Observers to the National Founding Convention of CARD in July 1965

Caribbean Association; Cardiff Inter-racial Council; Committee for Tamil Action; National Federation of Pakistani Associations; Indian National Association (Leamington); Indian Workers Association (Southall); Islington International Friendship Council; Labour Worker; London School of Economics West Indies Society; Manchester Coloured Sports Club; Oxford Committee for Racial Integration; Society of Friends Race Relations Sub-committee; Standing Conference of West Indian Organisations; Student Conference on Racial Equality; Simon Community Trust; Pakistan Immigrant Socialist Group; Sheffield Coloured Workers Association; Council of African Organisations; United Social Club; West Indian Student Union; East Pakistan House; and London Majlis.

Those organisations sending observers were Student Campaign

Against Racial Discrimination; Co-ordinating Campaign Against Racial Discrimination; National Council for Civil Liberties; Pakistan Friends League; Wood Green Young Socialists; Amnesty International; Wood Green Commonwealth Citizens Consultative Committee; Pakistan Welfare Association; and Campaign for Social Justice.

V Black Women's Groups and Organisations

ASHA Co-op; Asian Female Umbrella Organisation; Asian Women's Aid; Asian Women Community Workers; Asian Women's Forum; Asian Women's Group; Asian Women's Project; Battersea Black Women's Group; Behno Ki Milan; Birmingham Black Sisters; Black Female Prisoners Scheme; Black Health Workers and Patients Group; Black Women and Legal Rights; Black Women's Creativity Project; Black Women's Health Action Project; Black Women's Radio Group; Brent Asian Women's Centre; Camden and Isslington BWG; Camur Chilean Women's Group; Caribbean Educational Project; Carila; East London Black Women's Organisation; Eritrean Women's Association; The Foundation for Black Bereaved Families, Single Parents and Individuals; Hackney Black Women's Centre; Harringey Black Women's Centre; Lambeth Asian Women's Asha Co-operative Refuge, Young Women's Hostel; Leeds Asian Women Refuge; Leicester Black Women's Group; Liverpool Black Women's Centre; Manchester 'Abasindia' Co-op; Manchester Asian Women's Aid; Newham Rights Centre (Asian Women); Nigerian Organisation of Women; North Paddington Black Women's Group; Nottingham Black Women's Group; Peckham BWG; Sahara Leeds Asian Women's Refuge; Sheffield Black Women's Group; Shepherd's

Bush BWG; Somali Women's Group; Southall Black Sisters; Southall Black Women's Centre; Tamil Women's League; Theatre of Black Women; West Indian Women's Organisation.

VI

James Townsend: Pioneering Black Politician

James Townsend was born in 1737 and baptised on 8 February at St Christopher-le-Stocks in London. He was the son of Chauncy Townsend, a Member of Parliament, and Bridget, the daughter of James Phipps of Wiltshire. James Townsend's African ancestry can be traced on his mother's side to his grandmother. His grandfather was James Phipps, who had served as Governor General of the Royal African Company at Cape Coast Castle. After being deposed from his top position, Phipps stayed in Africa; and overall he worked and lived on the Gold Coast for twenty years. During this time he met and married an African woman named Catherina. She was a mulatto, a person of mixed-race. Known locally as a 'Consa' (the African wife of a European), Catherina bore Phipps five children, four of whom (Bridget, Susanna, Henrietta and Thomas) survived to become adults. According to one account, they were of 'fair complexion'. Catherina was a woman of strong character, a 'Strict Adherer to the Negrish Customs', John Atkins, a Navy surgeon, wrote. Surprised by Phipps's behaviour, Atkins added that he 'was a gentleman of good sense, yet could not help yielding to the silly customs created by our Fears … He cannot persuade this woman to leave the country tho' he has stole or forced her consent for all the children in regard to their education'. He doted on this woman who was 'always barefoot and fetished with chains and objects of gold at her ankles, her wrists and her hair'.

Being married to an African woman was one thing, but insisting that she accompany him to England was quite unusual. Though Phipps seldom mentioned her in his correspondence, according to his will his intention was that Catherina should come to England as his legal wife. Such a move, however, was likely to have its downside. Phipps's close friend Seth Grosvenor expressed his concern. He wrote:

> As to your intentions of bringing Catherina with you to England ... in my opinion it would be much more agreeable to her to remaine in the Country than to bring her heare among Strangers where she would most certainly be uneasy and Slighted, and then put to [the] Trouble and Experience of sending her back againe. There I think it more prudent ... and ... it would be to her satisfaction to leave her handsome allowances.

When Bridget and Susanna arrived in London, sometime between 1714 and 1715, Phipps's brother Thomas was taken by surprise. 'Grosvenor disclosed to me yesterday', he wrote on 24 June 1715, 'of some issue of yours he brought over with him, two you thought not fit to disclose to me, yet on his discovery I offered to put them out to School which I shall do on Monday.' Later, Henrietta and Thomas followed. In his will, James Phipps left money to cover the cost of his children's 'Boarding, Schooling, Clothing and other necessaries'.

In May 1770 Bridget married Chauncy Townsend and had ten children with him, including James Townsend, who was the eldest son. He studied at Hertford College, Oxford, but left in 1756 without taking a degree. Instead, he was keen to enter politics. Fortuitously, through his marriage on 3 May 1763 to Rosa Peregrima du Plessis, 'the illegitimate daughter of Henry Hare, third and last Baron of Coleraine, James secured possession of Hare's estate in Tottenham, Middlesex', he gained 'financial independence'. This prepared the way for his chosen career.

He was ambitious and aimed high. Soon he formed an association with the highly respected and influential Lord Shelburne who, as Secretary of State in the Chatham Ministry, helped Townsend to enter parliament as the representative for the Cornish borough of West Looe following a by-election in 1767. Thus he became the first Black Member of Parliament. At the general election the following year, he was re-elected. The young politician learned fast and acted positively. He became a founder member of the Society of Supporters of the Bill of Rights, formed in February 1769; and in June 1769 he was elected as a 'lifetime Alderman and annual Sheriff in the City of London'.

Determined to follow the radical path he chose, he joined others in support of a new Constitutional Society. This move had serious consequences for City of London politicians. For one thing, the split leading to the existence of two societies enabled a government supporter to be elected lord mayor in 1771. To prevent this happening again, for the following year's election John Wilkes and Townsend stood 'on a joint ticket for the office of Mayor which was chosen by Aldermen from the top candidates'. In this contest, if Wilkes was the front runner, what was Townsend's role? If, as Wilkes thought, it was just to help him to win the Mayoralty, Townsend was ready to spring a surprise. Instead of supporting Wilkes, Townsend changed his mind; and in the 'fierce struggle' that followed, with the support of a 'Coalition of Hornites and Courtiers', James Townsend was elected Lord Mayor of London in November 1772. This was another big achievement, the first Black man to hold this office. Predictably, there was great animosity between Wilkes and Townsend; and on Lord Mayor's Day, Townsend's 'treachery' resulted in a riot. So unpopular had he become that when he appeared on the campaign trail for the General Election in 1774 'vehement abuse forced his withdrawal'. Nonetheless, Townsend's portrait as Lord Mayor was painted by Joshua Reynolds in March 1773. As Mayoress, his wife also sat for Reynolds.

For his part as a public figure, Townsend showed radical tendencies and spoke forcefully for parliamentary reforms and annual parliaments. Until 1787, he continued to make strong representations, including opposition to the impeachment of Warren Hastings. According to the diarist Nathaniel Wraxall, though he 'seldom mingled in debate, he manifested whenever he spoke a manly mind, great facility of expression, strong sense combined with upright principles of action.' Much of these sterling qualities were, it seemed, inherited from the character of his maternal African grandmother Catherina. James Townsend died at Bruce Castle, Tottenham, on 1 July 1787. His wife died on 8 November 1785.

From all that I have read, James Townsend MP, was clearly of light complexion, so much so that none of the official pre-2016 biographical accounts of him as a public figure – in places such as *Notes and Queries*, the *Oxford Dictionary of National Biography* or *The History of Parliaments, Commons* – mentions either his colour or his African lineage. Nonetheless, his mother, Bridget, his siblings, and children were all descendants of the African woman from the Gold Coast. In addition to these official profiles, the recently published article in *Notes and Queries* by Wolfram Latsch sheds much light on James Townsend's dark past. My thanks to Professor David Skilton for his query about Latsch's article. This led to further research at the National Archives and the British Library, which is presented here. Hopefully the little known contribution of this pioneering radical Black politician, like much of the 'hidden' histories in *The Making of the Black Working Class in Britain*, will now become more widely known.

See: The National Archives: NA: C. 113/272; John Atkins, *A Voyage to Guinea, Brasil and the West Indies*, London: Ward and Chandler, 1737, pp. 94–5; National Archives: NA C113/71–73, Letter to James Phipps from Seth Grosvenor, January 1721; NA: C.113/28/82–83, pp. 20–46, 15 May 1723–11 January 1724, pp. 20–46; NA: 38/436; W. P.Courtney, *Notes and Queries*, New Series, Vol. 5, January 6, 1912, pp. 2–4; Peter D.G. Thomas, *Oxford Dictionary of National Biography*, Vol. 55 (2004), pp. 122–3; *History of Parliaments, Commons, 1754–1790*, pp. 537–8; Wolfram Latsch, *Notes and Queries*, Vol. 63, Issue 4, October 2016, pp. 615–17.

Ron Ramdin
The British Library, London
22 May 2017

List of Abbreviations

AACP	Association for the Advancement of Coloured People
ACA	Anglo-Coloured Association
ACAS	Advisory Conciliation and Arbitration Service
AEUW	Amalgamated Engineering Workers' Union
AITUC	All India Trade Union Congress
AOR	African and Orient Review
APEX	Association of Professional Executive Clerical and Computer Staff
APU	African Progress Union
ASLEF	Amalgamated Society of Locomotive Engineers and Footplatemen
ASTMS	Association of Scientific Technical and Managerial Staffs
ASTS	African Social and Technical Society
ASW	Amalgamated Society of Woodworkers
ATOR	African Times and Orient Review
AWAZ	Asian Women's Organisation
BASH	Blacks Against State Harassment
BCC	Brixton and Croydon Collective
BDC	Brixton Defence Campaign
BLF	Black Liberation Front
BPA	Black Peoples' Alliance

BPFM	Black People's Freedom Movement
BPM	Black Parents Movement
BSA	Black Socialist Alliance
BSM	Black Students' Movement
BTUSM	Black Trade Unionists' Solidarity Movement
BUFP	Black Unity and Freedom Party
BWA	Black Workers' Alliance
BWAC	Black Workers' Action Committee
BWCC	Black Workers' Co-ordinating Committee
BWM	Black Workers' Movement
CARD	Campaign Against Racial Discrimination
CAWU	Clerical and Administrative Workers' Union
CBI	Confederation of British Industry
CCARD	Co-ordinating Committee Against Racial Discrimination
CCS	Church of the Cherubim and Seraphim
CCSU	Coloured and Colonial Seamen's Union
CDA	Colonial Defence Association
CDC	Colonial Defence Committee
CFA	Caribbean Federal Association
CIAC	Coloured International Athletic Club
CIAC	Commonwealth Immigrants Advisory Council
CID	Criminal Investigation Department
CIR	Commission on Industrial Relations
CLC	Caribbean Labour Congress
CMS	Church Missionary Society
CND	Campaign for Nuclear Disarmament
CO	Colonial Office
COHSE	Confederation of Health Service Employees
CORE	Congress of Racial Equality
CPDA	Coloured Peoples Defence Association
CPGB	Communist Party of Great Britain
CPP	Convention Peoples Party
CRC	Community Relations Commission
CRE	Commission for Racial Equality
CSC	Colonial Sports Club
CSE	Certificate of Secondary Education
CSU	Colonial Seamen's Union
DES	Department of Education and Science
DHSS	Department of Health and Social Security
EC	Executive Committee
EEC	European Economic Community
ERC	Equal Rights Committee
ESN	Educationally Sub-Normal
ETU	Electrical Trades Union
'FOWAAD'	The newsletter of OWAAD
GLC	Greater London Council
GMWU	General and Municipal Workers' Union
HLDC	Hackney Legal Defence Committee

IAFE	International African Friends of Ethiopia
IAO	International African Opinion
IASB	International African Service Bureau
ILEA	Inner London Education Authority
ILO	International Labour Office
ILP	Independent Labour Party
INC	Indian National Congress
IO	India Office
IRR	Institute of Race Relations
IT	Imperial Typewriters
ITT	International Telephone and Telegraph [Corporation]
ITUC–NW	International Trade Union Committee of Negro Workers
IWA	Indian Workers' Association
JA	Jamaica Association
JCWI	Joint Council for the Welfare of Immigrants
JP	Justice of the Peace
J and P	Judicial and Public [Department]
KC	King's Counsel
KKK	Ku-Klux-Klan
LAI	League Against Imperialism
LCP	League of Coloured Peoples
LCS	London Corresponding Society
LIA	Leeward Islands Association
LMS	London Missionary Society
LRCP	Licentiate of the Royal College of Physicians
LSE	London School of Economics
MD	Medical Doctor
MORI	Market and Opinion Research Institute
MPD	Metropolitan Police District
MRB	Multi-Racial Britain
MRCS	Member of the Royal College of Surgeons
MSD	Migrant Services Division
MWD	Measured Day Work
MWIA	Merseyside West Indian Association
MXLU	Malcolm X Liberation University
NA	Negro Association
NAACP	National Association for the Advancement of Coloured People
NAFF	National Association For Freedom
NALGO	National Association of Local Government Officers
NAME	National Association for Multi-racial Education
NCCI	National Committee for Commonwealth Immigrants
NCCL	National Council for Civil Liberties
NCNC	National Council of Nigeria and Cameroons

NCTUAR	National Committee for Trade Unions Against Racism
NEC	National Executive Committee
NF	National Front
NFPA	National Federation of Pakistani Associations
NHS	National Health Service
NIESR	National Institute for Economic and Social Research
NIRC	National Industrial Relations Court
NLP	National Labour Party
NSP	National Society of Painters
NTCG	New Testament Church of God
NUGMW	National Union of Government and Municipal Workers
NUKHM	National Union of Knitwear and Hosiery Makers
NUM	National Union of Mineworkers
NUPE	National Union of Public Employees
NUPGDE	National Union of Plumbers, Glaziers and Domestic Engineers
NUR	National Union of Railwaymen
NUS	National Union of Seamen
NUSMWB	National Union of Sheet Metal Workers and Braziers
NUT	National Union of Teachers
NWA	Negro Welfare Association
OWAAD	Organisation of Women of Asian and African Descent
PAF	Pan African Federation
PAC	Pan African Congress
P and J	Public and Judicial [Department]
PEP	Political and Economic Planning
RAAS	Racial Action Adjustment Society
RRB	Race Relations Board
RILU	Red International of Labour Unions
RRAC	Race Relations Advisory Committee
SEN	State Enrolled Nurse
SNCC	Student Non-violent Co-ordinating Committee
SPG	Special Patrol Group
SRCASO	Special Restriction Coloured Alien Seamen Order
SRN	State Registered Nurse
SYM	Southall Youth Movement
TGWU	Transport and General Workers' Union
TUC	Trades Union Congress
TUUL	Trade Union Unity League
UBISS	United Society of Boiler Makers and Iron and Steel Shipbuilders
UCPA	Universal Coloured Peoples' Association
UN	United Nations
UNIA	Universal Negro Improvement Association

UPW	Union of Post Office Workers
USDAW	Union of Shop Distributive and Allied Workers
VLC	Voluntary Liaison Committee
WANS	West African National Secretariat
WASU	West African Students' Union
WDL	White Defence League
WINA	West Indian National Association
WISC	West Indian Standing Conference
WIUA	West Indian United Association
WLM	Women's Liberation Movement
WPM	Words Per Minute
WWL	Workers Welfare League
YMCA	Young Men's Christian Association

References

Part One   The 'Blackamoores'' Presence (1555-1900)

Chapter 1
1. Williams, E., *Capitalism and Slavery* (University of North Carolina, Chapel Hill, 1944).
2. Ibid., p. 4.
3. Ibid., p. 5.
4. Ibid., p. 7.
5. Ibid., p. 9.
6. MacInnes, C. M., *Bristol, a Gateway of Empire* (Bristol, 1939), pp. 158-9.
7. Ragatz, L., *The Fall of the Planter Class in the British Caribbean, 1763-1833* (New York, 1928), p. 3.
8. Williams, op. cit., p. 16.
9. Harlow, V. T., *A History of Barbados, 1625-1685* (Oxford, 1926), p. 307.
10. Calendar of State Papers, Colonial Series, IX, 15 August 1676, p. 445.
11. Cumberland, R., *The West Indian: A Comedy* (London, 1775 edn.).
12. Ragatz, L., *Absentee Landlordism in the British Caribbean, 1750-1833*.
13. Williams, op. cit., p. 87.

14. Ibid.
15. House of Commons, Sessional Papers, 1837–38, Vol. 48, pp. 20, 22, 46, 52, 67, 79.
16. Howard, R. M. (ed.), *Records and Letters of the Family of the Longs of Longville, Jamaica and Hampton Lodge, Surrey* (London, 1925), Vol. 1, pp. 67, 71; Cundall, F, *The Governors of Jamaica in the Seventeenth Century* (London, 1936), p. 26.
17. Namier, L. B., *The Structure of Politics at the Accession of George III* (London, 1929), Vol. 1, p. 210.
18. Latimer, J., *Annals of Bristol in the Nineteenth Century* (Bristol, 1887), pp. 137–8.
19. Williams, op. cit., p. 93.
20. Hansard, Third Series, Vol, XVIII, 30 May 1833.
21. Ragatz, L. (1928), op. cit., p. 53.
22. Williams, op. cit., p. 95.
23. Williams, op. cit., p. 96.
24. Penson, L. M., *The Colonial Agents of the British West Indies* (London, 1924), p. 228.
25. Ragatz, L. (1928), op. cit., p. 50.
26. James, C. L. R., *The Black Jacobins* (New York, Vantage Books, 1963), second edition, pp. 53–4.
27. Williams, op. cit.
28. Walvin, James, *Black and White: The Negro in English Society 1555–1945* (Allen Lane and Penguin Press, London, 1973), p. 1.
29. Ibid., p.10.
30. Walvin, J. (ed.), *Slavery and British Society, 1776–1846* (London, Macmillan, 1982), p. 39.
31. Walvin, J., op. cit., p. 10.
32. Shyllon, F. O., *Black Slaves in Britain* (London, Oxford University Press, 1974), p. 230.
33. Walvin, op. cit., p. 7.
34. Ibid.
35. Leonard, E. M., *The Early History of English Poor Relief* (Cambridge 1906), p. 297; Walvin, op. cit. p. 7.
36. *Acts of the Privy Council*, Vol. XXVI, 1596–7, p. 16.
37. Ibid.
38. Ibid., pp. 20–1.
39. Hughes, J. L. and Larkin, J. F. (eds), *Tudor Royal Proclamations 1588–1603*, 'Licensing Casper Van Senden to deport Negroes' (1601) (Yale University Press, 1969), Vol. 3, p. 221.
40. Walvin, op. cit., p. 112.
41. Shyllon, op. cit., p. 230.
42. Walvin, op. cit., p. 84.
43. Walvin. J., *The Black Presence: A Documentary History of the Negro in England, 1555–1860* (London, Orbach and Chambers, 1971), pp. 83–6.
44. Ibid., p. 84.

45. Equiano, Olaudah, *The Interesting Narrative of the Life of Olaudah Equiano or Gustavas Vassa, the African Written by Himself*, 2 vols (London, 1789).
46. Equiano, O., Vol. 2, op. cit., p. 120.
47. Ibid., p. 121.
48. Long, E., *The History of Jamaica* (London, T. Lowndnes, 1774), Vol. 2, pp. 364–5.
49. Ibid., p. 383.
50. Edwards, B., *The History of the British Colonies in the West Indies*, 2 Vols (Dublin, Luke White, 1793), Vol. 2, p. 75.
51. Carlyle, T., *Occasional Discourse on the Nigger Question* (London, Thomas Bosworth, 1853), p. 4.
52. Ibid., p. 8.
53. Trollope, A., *The West Indies and Spanish Main* (London, Chapman Hall, 1839), p. 57.
54. Wordsworth, W., *Poetical Works* (Oxford Edition, London, 1904), p. 305.
55. Ibid., pp. 312–13.
56. Walvin, op. cit., p. 197.
57. Mill, J. S., *Fraser's Magazine*, January 1850, pp. 30–1.
58. Walvin, J. 'The Propaganda of Anti-Slavery', in *Slavery and British Society, 1776–1846*, J. Walvin (ed.), (London, Macmillan, 1982), p. 68.
59. Fryer, P., *Staying Power: The History of Black People in Britain* (Pluto Press, 1982), p. 230.
60. Banton, M., *The Coloured Quarter* (London, Jonathan Cape, 1955), p. 26.
61. First Report of the Society established in London for the Suppression of Mendicity (1819), p. 33, Second Report . . . 1820, pp. 29–30, 32.
62. Egan, P., *Life in London* (Sherwood Neely and Jones, 1821), p. 347; Fryer, op. cit., p. 231.
63. Smith, J. T., *Vagabondia, or Anecdotes of Mendicant Wanderers through the Streets of London* (1817), pp. 33–5; Grant, J., *Sketches of London* (London, S. Orr, 1838), pp. 26–7.
64. Wilberforce, R. I. and S., *The Life of William Wilberforce* (London, John Murray, 1838), Vol. 4, p. 154.
65. Fryer, op. cit., p. 232.
66. Ibid.
67. Wilberforce, R. I. and S., op. cit., Vol. 4, pp. 154–5.
68. Fryer, op. cit., p. 233.
69. Marryat, J., *More Thoughts Occasioned by Two Publications* (J. W. Richardson, 1816), pp. 99–100.
70. Law, I. and Loy, L., 'A History of Racism and Resistance in Liverpool, 1760–1960', paper presented to the International Conference on the History of Blacks in Britain, London, 28–30 September 1981; Law, I., and Henfrey, J., *A History of Racism in Liverpool, 1660–1950* (Liverpool, Merseyside Community Relations Council, 1981); Fryer, op. cit., p. 236.

Chapter 2

1. Drescher, S., 'Public Opinion and the Destruction of Colonial Slavery' in James Walvin (ed.) *Slavery and British Society, 1776–1846* (1982), p. 24.
2. Thompson, E. P., *The Making of the English Working Class* (London, Victor Gollancz, 1963), p. 162.
3. Parsinnen, T. M., 'The Revolutionary Party in London', *Bulletin of the Institute of Historical Research*, Vol XLV, p. 267.
4. Thompson, op. cit, p. 156.
5. Prothero, I. J., *Artisans and Politics in Early Nineteenth Century London* (Dawson, 1979), p. 88.
6. *The Horrors of Slavery: exemplified in the Life and History of the Rev. R. Wedderburn* (R. Wedderburn, 1824), p. 5.
7. Ibid, p. 4.
8. Ibid, pp. 10–11.
9. Wedderburn, R., *The Axe Laid to the Root, or a Fatal Blow to Oppressors*, being an address to the Planters and Negroes of the Island of Jamaica, No. 1 (1817), cols. 12–13.
10. Report of John Eshelby on meetings at Hopkins Street Chapel, 16 August 1819, PRO HO 42/192; Fryer, op. cit., p. 223.
11. Thompson, E. P., op. cit. (Penguin edition, 1968), pp. 750–68.
12. Handbill, PRO HO 42/194; Report of Informer BC, 15 September 1819, PRO HO 42/194.
13. Prothero, op. cit., p. 87.
14. Wilkinson, G. T., *An Authentic History of the Cato Street Conspiracy, with the Trials at large of the Conspirators for High Treason and Murder* (London, Thomas Kelly, 1820), p. 14.
15. PRO HO 44/5/426.
16. Fryer, op. cit., p. 216. The author is grateful to Peter Fryer for allowing him to see a draft of the section on Robert Wedderburn in *Staying Power*.
17. *The Republican*, 11/7 (3 March 1820), p. 219.
18. Fryer, op. cit., p. 218.
19. Beresford Ellis, P., and Seumas Mac a'Ghobhainn, *The Scottish Insurrection of 1820* (London, Victor Gollancz, 1970), pp. 166–78. The author is grateful to Peter Fryer for referring him to this book.
20. Wilkinson, op. cit., pp. 312–13.
21. Ibid.
22. PRO HO 44/5/202.
23. *Reynolds Political Instructor*, 13 April 1850.
24. Goodway, D., *London Chartism 1838–1848*, (Cambridge University Press, 1982), p. 35.
25. Prothero, op. cit., pp. 80, 98.
26. Saville, J., *Dictionary of Labour Biography*, Joyce Bellamy and John Saville (eds), Vol. VI, (Macmillan, 1982), p. 77.

27. *Northern Star*, V/256, 8 October 1842, p. 3; Prothero, op. cit., p. 97; Bellamy, J. and Saville, J., op. cit., p. 78.
28. Saville, J. and Bellamy, J., op. cit.
29. *Weekly Dispatch*, 16 April 1848 (Third Edition, 181); Fryer, op. cit., p. 239.
30. Saville, op. cit., p. 78.
31. *Hansard, Parliamentary Debates*, 3rd Series, Vol. 74 (1844), col. 518.
32. Saville, J. and Bellamy, J., op. cit., p. 78.
33. Gammage, R. G., *The History of the Chartist Movement* (Holyoake & Co., London, 1854), p. 330.
34. Fryer, op. cit., p. 241.
35. *Morning Chronicle*, 11 April 1848.
36. Ibid.
37. Goodway, D., op. cit., p. 94.
38. Ibid., p. 93.
39. Frost, T., *Forty Years' Recollections: Literary and Political* (1880), pp. 162–5; Saville, J. and Bellamy, J., op. cit., p. 78.
40. *The Times*, No. 19,983 (2 October 1848), p. 4.
41. Saville, J. and Bellamy, J., op. cit., p. 79.
42. Seacole, M., *Wonderful Adventures of Mrs. Seacole in Many Lands*, W.J.S. (ed.) (London, James Blackwood, 1853), pp. 2–3.
43. Ibid., p. 5.
44. Ibid., p. 14.
45. Ibid., p. 73.
46. Ibid., p. 79.
47. Ibid., p. 81.
48. Ibid., pp. 88–9.
49. Ibid., pp. 90–91.
50. Ibid., p. 91.
51. Elise Gordon, J., 'Mary Seacole – A Forgotten Nurse Heroine of the Crimea', *Midwife, Health Visitor & Community Nurse*, February 1975, Vol. 11, p. 50.
52. Ibid.

Chapter 3

1. Tinker, H., *A New System of Slavery: The Export of Indian Labour Overseas* (Oxford University Press, 1974), p. 17.
2. Ibid., p. 18.
3. Ibid., p. 24.
4. Ibid., p. 25.
5. Ibid., p. 26.
6. Anderson, J., *A Descriptive Account of Mauritius, its Scenery, Statistics, etc.* (Calcutta, 1858), pp. 99–104.
7. Long, J. (ed.), *Selections from Unpublished Records of Government, 1748–1767 relating mainly to the Social Condition of Bengal* (Calcutta, 1869), p. 54.

8. Tinker, op. cit., p. 44.
9. Tinker, op. cit., p. 49.
10. Ibid., p. 53.
11. Ibid., p. 56.
12. Ibid., pp. 113–15.
13. Klass, M., *East Indians in Trinidad, A Study of Cultural Persistence* (New York and London, 1961), p. 10.
14. Knighton, W., *Forest Life in Ceylon* (London, Hurst and Blackett, 1854), Vol. 1, p. 281.
15. Tinker, op. cit., p. 201.
16. Harvey, T. and Brewin, W., *Jamaica in 1866: A Narrative of a tour through the Island* (London, 1867), p. 117; S. Copland, *Black and White; or the Jamaica Question* (London, 1866), p. 46.
17. Tinker, op. cit., p. 218.
18. Ibid., p. 219.
19. Ibid., p. 221.
20. Ibid., p. 227.
21. Mathurin, O. C., *Henry Sylvester Williams and the Origins of the Pan African Movement, 1869–1911* (Greenwood Press, Westport and London, 1976), p. 68.
22. Allen, R. V., 'Celestine Edwards: His Life, Work and Death', in *Lux*, 29 September 1894, p. 140.
23. Duffield, I., *The Dilemma of Pan Africanism for Blacks in Britain, 1760–1950*, Paper presented to the International Conference on the History of Blacks in Britain, London, 28–30 September 1981.
24. Hill, R. A., 'Zion on the Zambesi, Dr J. Albert Thorne, A Descendant of Africa, of Barbados and the African Colonial Enterprise: the "Preliminary Stage" 1894–97', Paper presented at the International Conference on the History of Blacks in Britain, London, 28–30 September 1981, p. 4.
25. Ibid., p. 8.
26. Hill, op. cit., p. 19.
27. Ibid., p. 26.
28. 'Distinguished Correspondent Hon. J. Albert Thorne, M.B.C.M., Discusses the Race Question and Repatriation – Race Unity the World Over', *Voice of Missions*, 1 August 1897; Hill, op. cit., p. 28.
29. Mathurin, op. cit., p. 9.
30. Ibid., pp. 29–30.
31. Ibid., pp. 32–3.
32. *Review of Reviews* (January 1897), p. 4.
33. Mathurin, op. cit., p. 41.
34. *Anti-Slavery Reporter*, March–May 1899, p. 112.
35. Mathurin, op. cit., p. 50.
36. *The Times*, 7 July 1900.
37. Mathurin, op. cit., p. 60.
38. Ibid., pp. 63–4.

39. Ibid., p. 68.
40. Ibid.
41. Ibid., pp. 72–3.
42. Ibid., p. 77.
43. Ibid., p. 81.
44. *The Mirror*, 1 June 1901.
45. Mathurin, op. cit., p. 104.
46. *Pan African* (October 1901), p. 4.
47. Mathurin, op. cit., p. 107.
48. *Pall Mall Gazette*, 2 November 1906.
49. Hooker, J. R., *Henry Sylvester Williams: Imperial Pan Africanist* (Rex Collings, London, 1975), p. 119.
50. Ibid., p. 121.

Part Two   The Black Man's Burden (1900–1962)

Chapter 4

1. Palme Dutt, R., *Britain's Crisis of Empire* (Lawrence and Wishart, London, 1949), p. 12.
2. Marx, K., *Capital: A Critical Analysis of Capitalist Production*, translated from the third German edition by Samuel Moore and Edward Aveling and edited by Frederich Engels (Swan Sonnerschein & Co. Ltd, London, 1896), Chapter, XXXI, p. 778.
3. Palme Dutt, op. cit., p. 19.
4. Lenin, V. I., *British Labour and British Imperialism*, a compilation of writings by Lenin on Britain, (London, Lawrence and Wishart, 1969), p. 63.
5. Tinker, op. cit., p. 308.
6. Ibid., p. 329.
7. Ibid., p. 330.
8. Ibid., pp. 335, 347.
9. Ibid., pp. 365–6.
10. Churchill, W., *Budget Speech*, 15 April 1929; Dutt, op. cit., pp. 22–3.
11. Bevin, E., *House of Commons*, 21 February 1946; Dutt, op. cit., p. 23.
12. Dutt, op. cit., pp. 23–4.
13. Burnham, T. H. and Hoskins, G. O., *Iron and Steel in Britain* (George Allen and Unwin Ltd, London, 1943), p. 70.
14. Dutt, op. cit., p. 25.
15. *The Economist*, 20 November 1937, p. 359.
16. Lenin, V. I., *Imperialism* (New York, Vanguard Press, 1926), p. 89.
17. Henderson, I., *The Attitude and Policy of the Main Sections of the British Labour Movement to Imperial Issues, 1899–1924* (B.Litt., Oxford, 1965), p. 191.

18. Ibid., pp. 193–5.
19. *Parliamentary Debates*, 21 February 1946, col. 1365.
20. *Daily Herald*, 15 October 1948.
21. Dutt, op. cit., pp. 120–1.
22. Little, Kenneth L., *Negroes in Britain* (London, Kegan Paul, 1947), pp. 34–5.
23. Ibid., pp. 35–6.
24. Tupper, E., *The Life Story of Capt. Edward Tupper* (London, Hutchinson and Co., 1938), p. 40; Little, op. cit., p. 36.
25. Thornton, R. H., *British Shipping* (Cambridge University Press, 1939), pp. 219–20.
26. Ibid., p. 215.
27. Tupper, op. cit., p. 20.
28. Little, op. cit., p. 56.
29. Tupper, op. cit., p. 242.
30. Little, op. cit., p. 57.
31. Tupper, op. cit., pp. 50–1.
32. *Western Mail*, 12 June 1919, p. 5.
33. Little, op. cit., p. 59.
34. Ibid.
35. Marquand, H. A., *An Industrial Survey of South Wales*, 3 vols.; Little, op. cit., p. 61.
36. Thornton, op. cit., p. 219.
37. Little, op. cit., p. 61.
38. *Hansard*, Vol. 295, December 1934, col. 1532.
39. Ibid., p. 66.
40. Ibid.
41. Margery, P., *Industrial South Wales* (1940), p. 122; Little, op. cit., p. 67.
42. *Hansard*, Vol. 344; Little, op. cit., p. 69.
43. *Report of Cardiff Special Watch Committee*, 1 January 1929 (Resolution); Little, op. cit., p. 69.
44. Ibid.
45. Little, op. cit., p. 69.
46. *City of Cardiff Education Committee, 14th Report of the Juvenile Employment Committee*, 31 July 1929, pp. 14–16; Little, op. cit., p. 70.
47. Fletcher, M. E., *Report on an Investigation into the Colour Problem in Liverpool and Other Ports, 1930* (issued by the Liverpool Association for the Welfare of Half Caste Children, Liverpool, 1930); Little, op. cit., p. 70.
48. Little, op. cit., pp. 70–1.
49. Ibid., p. 73.
50. Ibid., p. 74.
51. Little, op. cit., pp. 74–5.
52. *Seaman*, 1 May 1935, p. 1.
53. Little, op. cit., pp. 79–80.
54. *Western Mail and South Wales Echo*, 8 July 1935.

55. *Western Mail*, 7 July 1935.
56. Little, op. cit., p. 83.
57. Ibid., p. 84.
58. Richmond, A. H. *Colour Prejudice in Britain* (London, Routledge and Kegan Paul, 1954), p. 20.
59. Fletcher, op. cit., p. 38.
60. Richmond, op. cit., p. 21.
61. Stockdale, Sir Frank, *Development and Welfare in the West Indies*, p. 2, para. 7 (London, HMSO, 1945).
62. Richmond, op. cit., p. 24.
63. Richmond, op. cit., pp. 67–8.
64. Ibid., p. 37.
65. Ibid., pp. 38–9.
66. Ibid., pp. 40–1.
67. Ibid., p. 41.
68. Ibid., p. 42.
69. Ibid., p. 44.
70. Ibid., p. 47.
71. Ibid., p. 57.
72. Ibid., p. 58.
73. Ibid., p. 59.
74. Ibid., p. 64.
75. Ibid., p. 65.
76. See *Report of the West India Royal Commission, 1939*, Cmd 6607, HMSO, London 1946; Major G. St. J. Orde Browne, *Labour Conditions in the West Indies*, Cmd 6070, HMSO London, 1939; and *Report of the 1937 Disturbances in Trinidad*, Cmd 5641, 1938.
77. Citrine, W., *Men and Work: An Autobiography* (London, Hutchinson, 1964), p. 337.
78. Richmond, op. cit., pp. 67–8.
79. Ibid., pp. 133–4.
80. Ibid., p. 135.
81. Ibid., p. 139.
82. Stockdale, Sir Frank, *Development and Welfare in the West Indies, 1943–44* (HMSO, London, 1947), p. 2.
83. MacPherson, Sir J. *Development and Welfare in the West Indies, 1945–6* (HMSO, London, 1947), p. 123.
84. Richmond, op. cit., pp. 143–4.
85. Banton, M., 'Immigration from the British Colonies to the United Kingdom', *Population Studies*, Vol. VII, no. 1, July 1953.

Chapter 5

1. Macdonald, R. J., 'Dr. Harold Arundel Moody and the League of Coloured Peoples, 1931–1947: A Restrospective View', *Race*, XIV, 3 (1973), p. 291; for further details see J. A.

Langley, *West African Aspects of Pan African Movements* (Ph.D. Thesis, Edinburgh University, 1968).

2. Vaughan, D. A., *Negro Victory: The Life Story of Dr. Harold Moody* (Independent Press Ltd, London, 1950), p. 55; also LCP *Newsletter, Annual Reports* and *The Keys*.
3. Morris, S., 'Moody – the forgotten visionary', *New Community*, Vol. 3, spring 1972, p. 194.
4. Makonnen, R., *Pan Africanism from Within*, Kenneth King (ed.) (London, Oxford University Press, 1973), p. 126.
5. *The Keys*, Vol. 1., July 1933.
6. *The Keys*, Vol. IV, no. 3., January–March 1937; Tenth Annual Report of the League of Coloured Peoples (1940–41).
7. *The Keys*, Vol. 1, no. 1, July 1933.
8. *The Keys*, Vol. 1 nos. 1 and 2, July and October 1933.
9. Vaughan, D., op. cit., p. 77.
10. Ibid., p. 78.
11. Ibid., p. 9.
12. Ibid., p. 14.
13. Ibid., p. 21.
14. Ibid., p. 25.
15. Ibid., p. 41.
16. Ibid., p. 46.
17. Ibid., p. 50.
18. Ibid., p. 54.
19. Ibid., p. 55.
20. *The Keys*, Vol. 1, no. 1, July 1933, p. 3.
21. Vaughan, op. cit., p. 60.
22. Makonnen, op. cit., p. 127.
23. Vaughan, op. cit. pp. 63–4.
24. Morris, op. cit., p. 196.
25. Bush, B., 'Blacks in Britain', *History Today*, Vol. 31, September 1981.
26. Vaughan, op. cit., p. 65.
27. *The Keys*, Vol. 2, no. 4, April–June 1935, p. 66.
28. *The Keys*, Vol. 2, no. 4, April–June 1935, pp. 66–7.
29. Macdonald, op. cit., p. 297; Vaughan, op. cit., p. 75.
30. Duffield, I., 'Review of reprints of *The Keys* and *The Black Man*', *Journal of African History*, XIX (1978), pp. 475–6.
31. Macdonald, op. cit., p. 298; Drake, J. G. St. Clair, *Value Systems, Social Structure and Race Relations in the British Isles*, Ph.D. Thesis (University of Chicago, 1954), p. 106.
32. Vaughan, op. cit., p. 79.
33. Sharpe. N., 'Cardiff's Coloured Population', *The Keys*, Vol. 1, no. 3, October 1933, p. 44.
34. Vaughan, op. cit., pp. 81–82.
35. Makonnen, op. cit., pp. 132–3.
36. *Report of the West India Royal Commission*, 1939, Cmd 6607, HMSO London 1946; Report of Major G. St. J. Orde

Browne, *Labour Conditions in the West Indies*, Cmd 6070, HMSO, London 1939; Report of the 1937 Disturbances in Trinidad, Cmd 5641, HMSO London 1938.

37. Vaughan, op. cit., p. 83.
38. Ibid., pp. 89–90.
39. Ibid., p. 91.
40. *News Notes*, October 1939.
41. Vaughan, op. cit., p. 96.
42. Vaughan, op. cit., p. 107.
43. Ibid., p. 111.
44. Ibid., p. 125.
45. Ibid., pp. 130–1.
46. Ibid., pp. 131–2.
47. Ibid., p. 153.
48. Ibid., p. 130.
49. Drake, op. cit.
50. Saha, P. *Shapurji Saklatvala: A Short Biography* (People's Publishing House, Delhi, 1970); Nield, B. and Saville, J., *Dictionary of Labour Biography*, Joyce Bellamy and John Saville (eds), Vol. VI.
51. Drake, op. cit., p. 85.
52. Ibid.
53. *The Keys*, April–July 1935; Drake, op cit.
54. *The Keys*, Vol. I, no. 5, 1934, p. 2.
55. *The Keys*, July–September 1935.
56. *The Keys*, April–June 1934; also other issues.
57. Vaughan, op. cit., p. 65.
58. *The Keys*, April–June 1934, p. 66.
59. *The Keys*, July–September 1934, p. 16.
60. Drake, op. cit., pp. 94–7.
61. Vaughan, op. cit., p. 133.
62. Drake, op. cit., pp. 97–8.
63. *The Keys*, January–March 1935, p. 46.
64. Drake, op. cit., pp. 103–4.
65. Little, op. cit., pp. 71–8; Drake, op. cit., p. 104. Little mentions the 'Colonial Seamen's Unions' while Drake wrote of the Colonial Defence Association. If indeed they were separate organisations, it would seem certain that they were united in the cause of the black seamen.
66. *The Keys*, 'Presidential Message', January–March 1935, p. 47.
67. Drake, op. cit., pp. 104–9.
68. Garvey, Amy Jacques, *Philosophy and Opinions of Marcus Garvey* (Universal Publishing House, New York), pp. 68–72.
69. Drake, op. cit., pp. 109–10.
70. Vaughan, op. cit., pp. 88–92; *The Keys*, Vol. 5, no. 2.
71. See Drake, op. cit.
72. Drake, op. cit., pp. 395–6.
73. Ibid., p. 403.

74. Ibid., p. 410.
75. Ibid., p. 415.
76. Ibid., p. 421.
77. Ibid, pp. 429–30.
78. Ibid., p. 431.
79. Makonnen, op. cit., p. 127.
80. Makonnen, op. cit., pp. 127–8.
81. Ibid., p. 128.
82. PRO CO 295/599, file 70297; CO 295/606, file 703078; *International African Opinion*, Vol. 1, no. 1, July 1938, pp. 9, 13, 16; see Macdonald, op. cit.
83. Vaughan, op. cit., pp. 89–92.
84. Macdonald, op. cit., p. 300.
85. *The Keys*, Vol. 6, no. 2, October–December 1938, p. 2.
86. Ibid., pp. 12–15.
87. LCP *Newsletter*, no. 10, July 1940, pp. 63–4; Macdonald, op. cit., p. 301.
88. *Newsletter*, no. 23, August 1941, p. 119; Macdonald, op. cit, p. 303.
89. Drake, op. cit., pp. 114, 116.
90. *Fourteenth Annual Report of the League of Coloured Peoples,* 1944–45, pp. 15–16.
91. Drake, op. cit., p. 117.
92. Morris, op. cit., p. 196.
93. Coleridge Taylor, Avril, *The Heritage of Samuel Coleridge Taylor* (London, Dennis Dobson, 1979), p. 54.
94. Duffield, Ian, *Duse Mohamed Ali and the Development of Pan Africanism, 1866–1945* (University of Edinburgh, Ph.D. Thesis, 1971, 2 vols).
95. Duffield, op. cit., pp. 98–99.
96. Duffield, I., *The Dilemma of Pan Africanism for Blacks in Britain, 1760–1950*, Paper presented to International Conference on the History of Blacks in Britain, London, September 1981, pp. 7–8. The author is grateful to Bill Elkins for access to the papers of this conference.
97. Ibid; see also Robert A. Hill, 'The First England Years and After, 1912–1916', in John Henrik Clarke (ed.) with the assistance of Amy Jacques Garvey, *Marcus Garvey and the Vision of Africa* (New York, 1974), pp. 50–51; Duffield, op. cit., p. 9.
98. Langley, J. Adoyele, *Pan Africanism and Nationalism in West Africa, 1900–1945* (Oxford, Clarendon Press, 1973), pp. 71, 86.
99. Duffield, op. cit., p. 9.
100. Padmore, George (ed.), *Colonial and Coloured Unity: History of the Pan African Congress* (London and Hammersmith Bookshop Ltd, 1963), p. 17.

101. Padmore, George, *Pan Africanism or Communism? The Coming Struggle for Africa* (London, Dennis Dobson, 1956), p. 105.
102. Padmore (1956), op. cit., p. 139.
103. Ibid., p. 140.
104. Ibid., p. 151.

Chapter 6
  1. Robinson, Cedric J., 'Black Intellectuals at the British Core: 1920s–1930s'; Paper presented at the International Conference on the History of Blacks in Britain, London, 1981, p. 7.
  2. See Geiss, I., *The Pan African Movement* (Methuen & Co. Ltd, London, 1974), p. 359; Vaughan, op. cit.; Padmore (1956), op. cit.
  3. Makonnen, op. cit., Introduction, p. XVII.
  4. Ibid., pp. 145–6.
  5. James, C. L. R., *Beyond a Boundary* (London, Hutchinson 1963), p. 151.
  6. Robinson, op. cit., p. 12.
  7. Ibid., p. 13.
  8. Padmore (1956), op. cit.
  9. La Guerre, J. *The Social and Political Thought of the Colonial Intelligentsia* (Institute of Social and Economic Research, University of the West Indies, Mona, Jamaica, 1982), p. 51. The author is grateful to Carole Holden for showing him this publication.
 10. Ibid., p. 52.
 11. Padmore, G., *The Life and Struggles of Negro Toilers* (London, Red International of Labour Unions, 1931), pp. 53–4.
 12. Ibid., p. 57.
 13. Hooker, J. R., *Black Revolutionary: George Padmore's Path from Communism to Pan Africanism* (London, Pall Mall Press, 1967), p. 31.
 14. Macdonald, R. J. (1981), op. cit.
 15. Shirsat, K. R., *Kaka Joseph Baptista* (Bombay, Popular Prakashan, 1974), p. 1; Rothermund, D., *The Phases of Indian Nationalism* (Bombay, Nachiketa Publications Ltd, 1970), p. 17. The author is grateful to Jude de Lima for mentioning this book.
 16. Argov, D., *Moderates and Extremists in the Indian Nationalist Movement 1883–1920* (London, Asia Publishing House, 1967), Introduction, p. XII.
 17. Ibid., p. XI.
 18. Shirsat, op. cit., p. 3.
 19. Argov, op. cit., p. 159.
 20. Suda, J. P., *The Indian National Movement* (Meerut City, Jai Prakash Nath & Co. 1969), p. 3; Shirsat, op. cit., p. 4.
 21. *The Mahratta*, 18 July 1920; Shirsat, op. cit., p. 13.

22. Shirsat, op. cit., p. 61.
23. Ibid., pp. 62–3.
24. Ibid., p. 67.
25. Ibid., p. 56.
26. Ibid., p. 16.
27. Saha, P., *Shapurji Saklatvala: A Short Biography* (Delhi, Asia Publishing House, 1970).
28. Ibid., Introduction.
29. Ibid., p. 3.
30. *Daily Worker*, 20 January 1936.
31. Saha, op. cit., p. 6.
32. Ibid., pp. 6–7.
33. Saha, op. cit., p. 7.
34. *Daily Worker*, 18 January 1936.
35. Saha, op. cit., p. 9.
36. Nield, B. and Saville, J., 'Saklatvala' in Joyce Bellamy and John Saville (eds) *Dictionary of Labour Biography*, Vol. VI, (London, Macmillan Press Ltd, 1982), p. 237.
37. Klugmann, J., *History of the Communist Party of Great Britain*, 2 vols. 1968–69, p. 166; Saha, op. cit., p. 18.
38. *Daily Worker*, 18 January 1936.
39. Saha, op. cit., p. 20.
40. Morris, M., *The General Strike* (Penguin Books, 1976), p. 380.
41. Nield and Saville, op. cit., p. 239.
42. Hooker, J. R., op. cit., p. 6.
43. Ibid., pp. 7–8.
44. *Report of the Fourth Congress of the Red International of Labour Unions* (London, RILU Minority Movement, July 1928), p. 187.
45. Hooker, op. cit., p. 10.
46. Ibid., p. 11.
47. Geiss, op. cit., p. 325; Brockway, F. *Inside the Left* (London, Allen & Unwin, 1942).
48. Hooker, op. cit., pp. 12–13.
49. Ibid., pp. 14–15.
50. Report of the Commission on the Trinidad and Tobago Disturbances, Cmd 5641, 1938, para 171; Ramdin, Ron, *From Chattel Slave to Wage Earner* (London, Martin Brian & O'Keeffe), pp. 88–9.
51. Brockway, op. cit., p. 261; Hooker, op. cit.
52. *New Leader*, 13 September 1941; Hooker, op. cit., p. 22.
53. Hooker, op. cit., pp. 31–2.
54. Hooker, op. cit., p. 33.
55. Ibid., p. 35.
56. Ibid., pp. 39–40.
57. Ibid., pp. 40–1.
58. Ibid., p. 42.

59. Ibid., p. 43.
60. Reynolds, R., *My Life and Crimes* (London, Jarrolds, 1956), pp. 116–20.
61. Hooker, op. cit., p. 44.
62. Ibid., p. 46.
63. *New Leader*, 20 May 1938.
64. Hooker, op. cit., p. 47.
65. Ibid., p. 49.
66. Ibid., p. 50.
67. *New Leader*, 23 September 1938.
68. Hooker, op. cit., p. 54.
69. Ibid., p. 55.
70. *New Leader*, 2 June 1939.
71. Hooker, op. cit., p. 59.
72. LCP *Newsletter*, no. 9; Hooker, op. cit., p. 60.
73. *New Leader*, 29 March 1941.
74. *New Leader*, 17 October 1940.
75. Hooker, op. cit., pp. 70–1.
76. Hooker, op. cit., p. 71.
77. *Tribune*, 1 September 1944; Hooker, op. cit., p. 72.
78. *Left*, February 1940.
79. Hooker, op. cit., p. 73.
80. Ibid., p. 80.
81. *New Leader*, 12 December 1944.
82. Hooker, op. cit., p. 81.
83. Ibid., p. 82.
84. *Defender*, 29 August 1942; Hooker, op. cit., p. 82.
85. *Courier*, 25 November 1944; Hooker, op. cit., p. 83.
86. Padmore (1956), op. cit., p. 149.
87. Hooker, op. cit., pp. 84–6.
88. Ibid., p. 87.
89. *Defender*, 26 May 1945.
90. Hooker, op. cit., p. 90.
91. Ibid., p. 91.
92. Phillips, J., *Kwame Nkrumah and the Future of Africa* (London, Faber and Faber, 1960), p. 82.
93. Geiss, op. cit., pp. 388, 398.
94. Hooker, op. cit., pp. 93–4.
95. Ibid., p. 95.
96. Ibid., pp. 53–4.
97. Padmore, G. (ed.), *Colonial and Coloured Unity*, op. cit., pp. 6–7.
98. Hooker, op. cit., p. 97.
99. Ibid., p. 100.
100. Nkrumah, *Autobiography*, op. cit., p. 61.
101. Hooker, op. cit., p. 101.
102. *Defender*, 16 February 1946.
103. Hooker, op. cit., p. 106.

104. Ibid., pp. 107–8.
105. Ibid., p. 114.
106. Ibid., p. 116.
107. Ibid., p. 125.
108. Ibid., p. 131.
109. Ibid., p. 132.
110. Padmore (1956), op. cit., Preface, p. 11.
111. Hooker, op. cit., pp. 139–40.
112. Geiss, op. cit., p. 426.
113. Ibid., p. 428.
114. Ibid., p. 432.
115. James, C. L. R., *A History of Pan African Revolt* (Washington D.C., Drum and Spear Press, 1969), p. 143.

Chapter 7
 1. Glass, R. and Pollins, H. *Newcomers* (London, Centre for Urban Studies and George Allen and Unwin Ltd, 1960), pp. 6–7.
 2. *Parliamentary Debates, House of Commons*, 5 December 1958, cols. 1580–1.
 3. Glass, op. cit., pp. 37–8.
 4. Ibid., p. 41.
 5. Ibid., pp. 45–6.
 6. Eggington, J. *They Seek a Living* (London, Hutchinson, 1957), pp. 65–6.
 7. Glass, op. cit., pp. 48–9.
 8. Ibid., pp. 50–1.
 9. Gladstone, F. M., *Notting Hill in Bygone Days* (London, 1924), p. 202.
10. Glass, op. cit., p. 52.
11. Ibid., p. 54.
12. *The Times*, 20 May 1959.
13. *Manchester Guardian*, 3 July 1959.
14. *The Times*, 29 May 1959.
15. *The Times*, 29 May 1959.
16. Glass, op. cit., p. 67.
17. Ibid., p. 6.
18. Ibid.
19. Ibid., p. 68.
20. Ibid., p. 72.
21. *Report of the Proceedings of the 90th Annual Trades Union Congress*, September 1958, p. 459.
22. Glass, op. cit., p. 76.
23. Ibid., pp. 77–8.
24. *The Times*, 25 February 1955.
25. Glass, op. cit., p. 80.
26. *The Times*, 1 September 1955.
27. Glass, op. cit., p. 80.

28. Ibid., p. 85.
29. *The Senior and Manley Report* (1955).
30. *West Indian Gazette*, September 1959.
31. Glass, op. cit., p. 90.
32. Ibid., p. 131.
33. *The Times*, 26 August 1958.
34. Glass, op. cit., p. 132.
35. *Manchester Guardian* and *The Times*, 1 September 1958.
36. *The Times*, 16 September 1958.
37. *The Times*, 1 September 1958.
38. *Manchester Guardian*, 27 August 1958.
39. *The Times*, 1 September 1958.
40. Ibid.
41. *Manchester Guardian*, 1 September 1958.
42. *The Times*, 2 September 1958.
43. *Manchester Guardian*, 17 September 1958.
44. *The Times*, 3 September 1958.
45. Glass, op. cit., p. 141.
46. *Manchester Guardian*, 9 September 1958.
47. Glass, op. cit., p. 142.
48. *Parliamentary Debates*, House of Commons, 23 February 1960, cols. 331–339.
49. *The Times*, 16 September 1958.
50. *Manchester Guardian*, 11 September 1958.
51. Glass, op. cit., p. 146.
52. Labour Party Statement on 'Racial Discrimination', September 1958.
53. Glass, op. cit., p. 148.
54. *Manchester Guardian*, 4 September 1958.
55. *Parliamentary Debates*, House of Commons, 3 April 1958, cols. 1426, 1430.
56. *Manchester Guardian*, 28 August 1958.
57. *The Times*, 4 September 1958.
58. Cabinet Papers 1954; *The Times*, 12 October 1958; *The Times*, 2 January 1985.
59. *Parliamentary Debates*, House of Commons, 5 December 1958, col. 1588.
60. Labour Party Statement on *Racial Discrimination*, op. cit., p. 4; Glass, op. cit., p. 154.
61. Glass, op. cit., p. 154.
62. *Parliamentary Debates*, House of Lords, 19 November 1958, col. 659.
63. *Parliamentary Debates*, House of Commons, 21 November 1949, cols. 2–3.
64. Labour Party Statement on Racial Discrimination, op. cit., p. 4; Glass, op. cit., p. 159.
65. Race Discrimination Bill (Bill 105, 6 & 7, Eliz, 2), 30 April 1958.

66. Glass, op. cit., p. 162.
67. *News Chronicle*, 18 May 1959.
68. *Daily Telegraph*, 25 May 1959.
69. *The Times*, 19 May 1959.
70. *Manchester Guardian*, 22 May 1959.
71. *New Statesman*, 9 May 1959.
72. *West Indian Gazette*, June 1959; Glass, op. cit., p. 169.
73. *Report of the Proceedings at the 90th Annual Trades Union Congress*, September 1958, op. cit., p. 458.
74. Glass, op. cit., p. 173.
75. *Combat*, no. 1, Autumn 1958; Glass, op. cit., p. 174.
76. *Black and White News*, no. 1 (1st Reprint, November 1958).
77. *Daily Herald*, 15 June 1959.
78. *Action*, 14 March 1959; Glass, op. cit., p. 176.
79. Glass, op. cit., p. 176.
80. *Combat*, no. 2, January–March 1959; Glass, op. cit., p. 177.
81. *Daily Herald*, 16 June 1959.
82. Letter published in *West Indian Gazette*, Vol. 1., no. 6, September 1958.
83. *Kensington Post*, 2 October 1959.
84. *The Times*, 6 October 1959.
85. Glass, op. cit., p. 194.
86. Ibid., pp. 195–6.
87. *The Kensington News*, 30 October 1959.
88. Glass, op. cit., p. 197.
89. *Manchester Guardian*, 10 September 1958.
90. Glass, op. cit., p. 206.
91. Ibid., p. 207.
92. Ibid., p. 209.
93. Ibid., pp. 210–11.
94. Hiro, D., *Black British White British* (London, Eyre & Spottiswoode, 1971), p. 48.
95. Foot, P., *Immigration and Race in British Politics* (London, Penguin Books, 1965), p. 130.
96. Ibid., p. 190.
97. Hiro, op. cit., p. 47.
98. Rose, E. J. B., *et. al.*, *Colour and Citizenship* (London, Institute of Race Relations, Oxford University Press, 1969), p. 218.
99. Hiro, op. cit., p. 48.
100. Ibid., p. 208.
101. Ibid., p. 212.
102. Ibid., p. 213.
103. Ibid.; *The Middlesex County Times*, 5 October 1964.
104. Foot, op. cit., p. 181.
105. Hiro, op. cit., p. 213.
106. Foot, op. cit., p. 183.

107. Patterson, S., *Immigration and Race Relations in Britain 1960–1967* (London, Oxford University Press, 1969), p. 34.
108. *The Economist*, 2 October 1965.
109. Hiro, op. cit., p. 216.
110. Foot, op. cit., p. 129.
111. Hiro, op. cit., p. 47.

Part Three   The Black Working Class (1962–1986)

Chapter 8

1. Wright, E. O., 'Class Boundaries in Advanced Capitalist Societies', *New Left Review*, no. 98, July–August 1976, p. 31.
2. Ibid., pp. 20–3, 32–5.
3. Westergaard, J. and Resler, H., *Class in a Capitalist Society: A Study of Contemporary Britain* (London, Pelican Books, 1976), p. 346.
4. Phizacklea, A. and Miles, R., *Labour and Racism* (London, Routledge & Kegan Paul, 1980), p. 6.
5. Hobsbawm, E. J., *Industry and Empire* (London, Pelican Books, 1969), pp. 285–6.
6. Mackie, L. and Pattullo, P., *Women and Work* (London, Tavistock Publications, 1977), p. 40.
7. Counter Information Services (1976) *Crisis: Women Under Attack* (London, CIS), p. 10; Phizacklea and Miles, op. cit., p. 8.
8. Phizacklea, A. and Miles, R., op. cit., p. 8.
9. Smith, D. J. *Racial Disadvantage in Britain: The PEP Report* (Penguin Books, 1977), p. 65.
10. Phizacklea and Miles, op. cit., p. 11; see also Suzanne Paine, *Exporting Workers: The Turkish Case* (Cambridge University Press, 1974).
11. Castles, S. and Kosack, C., *Immigrant Workers and Class Structure in Western Europe* (London, Oxford University Press, 1973), pp. 430–82.
12. Bohning, W. R., *The Migration of Workers in the United Kingdom and the European Community* (London, Oxford University Press, 1972), pp. 55–7.
13. Castells, M., 'Immigrant Workers and Class Struggles in advanced capitalism: the Western European experience', *Politics and Society*, 1975, Vol. 5, no. 1, pp. 33–66; Cohen, B. G. and Jenner, P. J., 'The employment of immigrants: a case study within the wool industry', *Race*, 1968, Vol. 10, p. 55.
14. Phizacklea and Miles, op. cit., p. 13.
15. Castles and Kosack, op. cit., pp. 430–81.
16. Peach, C., *West Indian Migration to Britain: a social geography* (London, Oxford University Press, 1968), pp. 23–36.

17. Deakin, N., *Colour, Citizenship and British Society* (London, Panther Modern Society, 1970), pp. 35–40.
18. Brooks, D., *Race and Labour in London Transport* (London, Oxford University Press, 1975), p. 256.
19. Sivanandan, A., 'Race, Class and the State: the Black Experience in Britain', *Race and Class*, Vol. XVII, Spring, no. 4, 1976, pp. 347–68.
20. Moore, R. and Wallace, T., *Slamming the Door: The Administration of Immigration Control* (London, Martin Robertson, 1975).
21. Phizacklea and Miles, op. cit., p. 16.
22. Ibid.
23. Ibid, p. 17.
24. Smith, D. J., *The Facts of Racial Disadvantage* (London, Political and Economic Planning, 1976), p. 64; Phizacklea and Miles, op. cit., p. 18.
25. Phizacklea and Miles, op. cit., p. 18.
26. Smith, op. cit., p. 73.
27. Ibid., pp. 74, 219.
28. Smith, op. cit., p. 75.
29. Ibid., p. 73.
30. Phizacklea and Miles, op. cit., p. 19; Smith, op. cit., pp. 64–81.
31. Phizacklea and Miles, op. cit., p. 19.
32. Ballard, R. and Holden, B., 'The Employment of Coloured Graduates in Britain', *New Community*, Vol. IV, no. 3, Autumn 1975, p. 334.
33. Smith (1977), op. cit., pp. 75–6.
34. Phizacklea and Miles, op. cit., p. 22.
35. Ibid., p. 23.
36. Cameron, G. and Evans, A., 'The British Conurbation Centres', *Regional Studies*, Vol. 7 (London, Pergamon Press, 1973), pp. 47–55.
37. Dennis, R., 'The Decline of Manufacturing Employment in Greater London: 1966–74', *Urban Studies*, Vol. 15, no. 1 (University of Glasgow, 1978), pp. 63–73.
38. Phizacklea and Miles, op. cit., p. 51.
39. Cross, C., *Ethnic Minorities in the Inner City: The Ethnic Dimension in Urban Deprivation in England* (London, Commission for Racial Equality, 1978), p. 37.
40. Cross, op. cit., p. 34.
41. Cross, op. cit., p. 36.
42. Ibid., p. 37.
43. *PEP Survey on Racial Minorities*, op. cit., p. 55.
44. *Britain's Black Population*, The Runnymede Trust and Radical Race Group (London, Heinemann Educational Books, 1980), p. 76; Smith, D. J. op. cit.
45. *Britain's Black Population*, op. cit., p. 80.

46. Ibid., p. 82.
47. *Britain's Black Population*, op. cit., p. 83.
48. Phizacklea, A. and Miles, R., 'Working Class Racist Beliefs in the Inner City' in R. Miles and A. Phizacklea (eds), *Racism and Political Action in Britain* (London, Routledge & Kegan Paul, 1979), pp. 93–122.
49. *Race Relations and Housing*, Cmnd 6232 (London, HMSO, 1975).
50. *Housing Policy: a Consultative Document*, Cmnd 6851 (London, HMSO 1977).
51. *Britain's Black Population*, op. cit., p. 89.
52. Cross, op. cit., p. 98.
53. Edwards, V. K., *The West Indian Language Issue in British Schools: challenges and responses* (London, Routledge & Kegan Paul, 1979); R. Miles, *Between Two Cultures? The Case for Rastafarianism*, SSRC Research Unit on Ethnic Relations Library, Paper no. 10, 1978.
54. Hatch, S., 'Coloured People in School Textbooks', *Race* 1962, Vol. 4. no. 1, pp. 63–72.
55. Milner, D., *Children and Race* (Penguin Books, 1975); *Britain's Black Population*, p. 97.
56. *Britain's Black Population*, op. cit., p. 99.
57. Townsend, H. E. R. and Brittan, E. M., *Organisation in Multiracial Schools* (National Foundation for Educational Research in England and Wales, 1972).
58. Tomlinson, Sally, 'West Indian Children and ESN Schooling', *New Community* Vol. VI, no. 3, Summer 1978, pp. 235–42; Coard, B., *How the West Indian Child is Made Educationally Sub-normal by the British School System* (New Beacon Books, 1971).
59. Douglas, J. W. B., *The Home and School: A Study of Ability and Attainment in the Primary School* (London, Panther, 1964); Raynor, J. and Harden, J. (eds), *Equality and City Schools*, Readings in Urban Education, Vol. 2 (edited by Raynor and Harden) (London, Routledge & Kegan Paul, 1973).
60. Ministry of Education, *English for Immigrants*, Pamphlet No. 43 (London, HMSO, 1963).
61. *Britain's Black Population*, op. cit., p. 103.
62. Ibid., p. 104.
63. McNeal, Julia, 'Education', in S. Abbott (ed.), *The Prevention of Racial Discrimination in Britain* (London, Oxford University Press, 1971), p. 111.
64. *Britain's Black Population*, op. cit., p. 106.
65. *Immigrants and the Youth Service* (London, HMSO, 1969), p. 8.
66. Cross, op. cit., pp. 100–1.
67. *Britain's Black Population*, op. cit., p. 112.
68. Jones, K., *Immigrants and Social Services* (London, National Institute of Economic Review, 1967), p. 3.

69. *Britain's Black Population*, op. cit., p. 113.
70. London Borough of Wandsworth, *Statistics of the Social Service Department*, 1974; *Britain's Black Population*, op. cit., p. 115.
71. *The Soul Kids Campaign* (London, The Association of British Adoption and Fostering Agencies, 1977).
72. *Britain's Black Population*, op. cit., p. 115.
73. Ibid.; *CRC: Evidence to the Royal Commission on National Health Service 1977*.
74. *Britain's Black Population*, op. cit., p. 118.

Chapter 9
1. Roberts, B. C., *Labour in the Tropical Territories of the Commonwealth* (London, G. Bell and Sons Ltd, 1964), p. 382.
2. Ibid., p. 390.
3. Ibid., p. 395.
4. See Clegg, H., *The Changing System of Industrial Relations in Britain* (Oxford, Basil Blackwell, 1979).
5. Smith, D. J., *Racial Disadvantage in Britain* (London, Political and Economic Report, 1977), p. 64.
6. Ibid., pp. 71–2.
7. Ibid., pp. 72–3.
8. Ibid., p. 75.
9. Ibid., pp. 76–7.
10. Ibid., p. 84.
11. Ibid., pp. 85–8.
12. Ibid., pp. 90–2.
13. Ibid., pp. 96–7.
14. Ibid., p. 104.
15. Ibid., p. 109.
16. Ibid., p. 111.
17. Ibid., p. 128.
18. Ibid., p. 142.
19. Ibid., p. 170.
20. Ibid., pp. 173–4.
21. Ibid., pp. 182–4.
22. Ibid., pp. 186–8.
23. Knowles, K. G. J. C., *Strikes – A Study in Industrial Conflict* (Oxford, Basil Blackwell, 1952) p. XII.
24. Foot, P., 'The Strike at Courtaulds, Preston', *IRR*, July 1965; *New Society*, 17 June, 1965.
25. Ibid.
26. *The Struggle of Asian Workers in Britain* (The Race Today Collective, 1983), p. 16.
27. Torode, J., 'Race Moves in on the Unions', *New Society*, 17 June 1965.
28. Foot, P., op. cit.
29. Dhondy, M., 'The Strike at Imperial Typewriters', *Race Today*, July 1974.

30. Ibid.
31. *Race Today*, August 1974.
32. 'Who are Imperial Typewriters', *Race Today*, July 1974.
33. Ibid., p. 201.
34. Ibid.
35. *Race Today*, August 1974, p. 223.
36. *Race Today*, July 1974, p. 202.
37. Ibid., p. 201.
38. Ibid., p. 202.
39. Ibid., p. 204.
40. *Race Today*, August 1974, p. 223.
41. Ibid., p. 224.
42. Dromey, J. and Taylor, G., *Grunwick: The Workers' Story* (London, Lawrence and Wishart, 1978), p. 13.
43. Ibid., p. 14.
44. Ibid., p. 15.
45. Ibid., p. 16.
46. Ibid., p. 24; PEP Report 1974.
47. Ibid., p. 28.
48. Ibid., p. 29.
49. Ibid., p. 31.
50. Ibid., pp. 34–5.
51. Ibid., p. 37.
52. Ward, George, *Fort Grunwick* (London, Temple Smith, 1977), p. 31.
53. Dromey and Taylor, op. cit., p. 48.
54. Ibid., p. 50.
55. Ibid., pp. 51–2.
56. Ibid., p. 53.
57. Ward, op. cit., p. 46.
58. Ibid., p. 48.
59. Ibid., p. 69.
60. Ibid., p. 51.
61. Ibid., p. 77.
62. Dromey and Taylor, op. cit., p. 57.
63. Ibid., p. 58.
64. Ibid., p. 59.
65. Ward, op. cit., p. 52.
66. Ibid., pp. 2–3.
67. Ibid., p. 1.
68. Ibid., p. 2.
69. Ibid., p. 4.
70. Ibid., p. 54.
71. Ibid., p. 56.
72. Dromey and Taylor, op. cit., pp. 79–80.
73. Ibid., p. 84.
74. Ibid., p. 10.
75. Ibid., p. 85.

76. Ibid., p. 10.
77. Ibid., p. 90.
78. Ibid., p. 10.
79. Ibid., p. 94.
80. Ibid., p. 102.
81. Ibid., p. 105.
82. Ibid., p. 107.
83. Ibid., p. 110.
84. Ibid., p. 114.
85. Ibid., p. 117.
86. Ibid., p. 118.
87. Ibid., p. 119.
88. Ibid., p. 122.
89. Ward, op. cit., p. 72.
90. Dromey and Taylor, op. cit., p. 123.
91. Ibid., p. 127.
92. Ibid., p. 128.
93. Ibid., p. 132.
94. Ibid., p. 138.
95. Ibid., p. 107.
96. Ward, op. cit., p. 89.
97. Dromey and Taylor, op. cit., p. 141.
98. Ibid., p. 148.
99. Ibid., p. 149.
100. Phizacklea, A. and Miles, R., 'The Strike at Grunwick', *New Community*, Vol. VI, no. 3, 1978, p. 273.
101. Dromey and Taylor, op. cit., p. 11; see also Rogaly, J., *Grunwick* (Harmondsworth, Penguin, 1977).
102. Dromey and Taylor, op. cit., p. 155.
103. The Scarman Report, Cmnd 6922 (London, HMSO, 1977); Dromey and Taylor, op. cit., p. 156.
104. *The Guardian*, 26 August 1977.
105. Dromey and Taylor, op. cit., p. 161.
106. *The Guardian*, 1 September 1977.
107. Dromey and Taylor, op. cit., p. 163.
108. Ibid., p. 165.
109. *Sunday Telegraph*, 11 September 1977.
110. Dromey and Taylor, op. cit., p. 174.
111. Ibid., p. 177.
112. Ibid.
113. Ibid., p. 178.
114. 'The Grunwick Strike: the Bitter Lessons', *Race Today*, November/December 1977.
115. Ibid., p. 154.
116. Ibid.
117. Foner, N., *Jamaica Farewell* (London, Routledge and Kegan Paul, 1977), pp. 224–5.

118. 'Black Women and Nursing: A Job Like Any Other', *Race Today*, August 1974.
119. Ibid., p. 226.
120. Ibid., p. 227.
121. Ibid.
122. Ibid., p. 228.
123. Ibid., pp. 228–9.
124. Ibid., p. 230.
125. 'Black Women and the Wage', *Race Today*, May 1975.
126. 'Caribbean Women and the Black Community', *Race Today*, May 1975.
127. Ibid., p. 108.
128. Ibid., p. 109.
129. Hassan, L. and Dick, P., 'Health Workers After the Strike', *Race Today*, March/April 1983.
130. Ibid., p. 209.
131. Ibid., p. 210.
132. Ibid.
133. Ibid., p. 211.
134. 'The State of Play at Fords', *Race Today*, May/June 1982.
135. Ibid., p. 95.
136. Ibid., p. 96.
137. Ibid., p. 97.
138. Ahmat, Yusuf *et al.*, 'The Textile Industry and Asian Workers In Bradford', *Race Today*, March/April 1983.
139. Ibid., p. 218.
140. Ramdin, R., op. cit., p. 113.
141. Ibid., pp. 120–4.
142. Ibid., pp. 124–5.
143. Ali, A. (ed.), *Third World Impact*, Formerly West Indians in Britain, (London, Hansib Publications, 5th Edition, 1982), p. 36.
144. Allen, S., and Bornat, J., *Unions and Immigrant Workers: How They See Each Other* (Runnymede Trust Industrial Unit, 1970), p. 1.
145. Ibid., p. 2.
146. Ibid., p. 3.
147. Ibid., p. 4.
148. Ibid., p. 5.
149. 'Trade Unions and Immigrant Workers', (Runnymede Trust) *New Community*, Vol. IV, no. 1, 1974–75, p. 21.
150. See PEP Report, *The Extent of Racial Discrimination* (October 1974); PEP Report, *Racial Disadvantage in Employment* (June 1974).
151. Jones, K. and Smith, A. D., *The Economic Impact of Commonwealth Immigration* (Cambridge, The National Institute of Economic and Social Research, 1970), p. 107.

152. Runnymede Trust, *New Community*, Vol. IV, no. 1, 1974–75, p. 25.
153. Ibid., p. 25.
154. Harrison, R. A., *Union Policy and Workplace Practice: A Black Worker Alleges Discrimination* (Runnymede Industrial Trust Unit, December 1970).
155. Radin, B., 'Coloured Workers and British Trade Unions', *Race*, Vol, VIII, no. 2, 1966, pp. 171–73.
156. Ibid., p. 173.
157. 'Introduction', *The Trade Union Movement and Discrimination: A Collection of Essays* based on papers given at a conference convened by Ruskin College (Oxford, December 1970).
158. Smith, D. J., *Racial Disadvantage in Britain*, The PEP Report (Penguin Books, 1977), p. 191.
159. Ibid., p. 192.
160. Ibid., pp. 193–4.
161. Ibid., pp. 194–5.
162. Ibid., p. 196.
163. Ibid., p. 197.
164. Ibid., p. 198.
165. Ibid., p. 201.
166. Ibid., pp. 202–3.
167. *Report of the Proceedings of the 86th Annual Trades Union Congress* (London, 1954), p. 238.
168. *Report of the Proceedings of the 87th Annual Trades Union Congress* (London, 1955), pp. 145–6.
169. Miles, R. and Phizacklea, A., *The TUC, Black Workers and New Commonwealth Immigration 1954–1973* (Bristol, SSRC Research Unit on Ethnic Relations, 1977), p. 6.
170. *Report of the Proceedings of the 87th Annual Trades Union Congress*, 1955, p. 456.
171. Ibid., p. 473.
172. Miles and Phizacklea (1977), op. cit., p. 8.
173. *Report of the Proceedings at the 90th Annual Trades Union Congress*, 1958, p. 378.
174. Ibid., p. 125.
175. *Report of the Proceedings at the 91st Annual Trades Union Congress*, 1959, p. 253.
176. Ibid., pp. 425–6.
177. Ibid., p. 426.
178. Ibid., p. 428.
179. *Report of the Proceedings at the 92nd Annual Trades Union Congress*, 1960, pp. 203–4.
180. *Report of the Proceedings at the 94th Annual Trades Union Congress*, 1962, pp. 215–16.
181. *Report of the Proceedings at the 96th Annual Trades Union Congress*, 1964, pp. 273–4.

182. *Report of the Proceedings at the 97th Annual Trades Union Congress*, 1965, p. 260.
183. *Report of the Proceedings at the 98th Annual Trades Union Congress*, 1966, p. 271.
184. Sivanandan, A., 'Race, Class and the State: the black experience in Britain', *Race and Class*, 1976, Vol. 17 (4), p. 359.
185. *Report of the Proceedings at the 98th Annual Trades Union Congress*, 1966 pp. 514–16.
186. *Report of the Proceedings at the 99th Annual Trades Union Congress*, 1967, p. 272.
187. *Report of the Proceedings at the 100th Annual Trades Union Congress*, 1968, p. 583.
188. *Report of the Proceedings at the 105th Annual Trades Union Congress*, 1973, pp. 585–7.
189. Royal Commission Report on Trade Unions and Employers' Associations 1965–1968, Cmnd 3623; Clegg, op. cit., pp. 232–57; see also Allan Flanders, *Industrial Relations: What is wrong with the System? An Essay on its Theory and Future* (London, Faber, 1965); W. E. J. McCarthy, *The Role of Shop Stewards in British Industrial Relations: A Survey of Existing Information and Research* (London, HMSO, 1966: Donovan Commission Research Paper 1); Allan Fox, *Industrial Sociology and Industrial Relations* (London, HMSO, 1966, Donovan Commission Research Paper 3).
190. Select Committee on Race Relations and Immigration, *Employment*, Vol. 1 Report (HMSO, 1974), p. XXII.
191. Miles and Phizacklea (1977), op. cit., p. 2.
192. Ibid., p. 4.
193. Miles, R. and Phizacklea, A., 'The TUC and Black Workers 1974–1976', *British Journal of Industrial Relations*, Vol. XVI, July 1978, no. 2, pp. 195–207.
194. *Report of the Proceedings at the 106th Annual Trades Union Congress*, 1974, pp. 212–13.
195. Select Committee on Race Relations and Immigration, *Employment*, Vol. 11, Evidence and Appendices, HMSO, 1975, pp. 457–69.
196. Ibid., p. 459.
197. *Report of the Proceedings at the 106th Annual Trades Union Congress*, 1974, p. 536.
198. *Report of the Proceedings at the 107th Annual Trades Union Congress*, 1975, pp. 73–5.
199. Miles and Phizacklea (1978), op. cit., p. 198.
200. Ibid.
201. Ibid., p. 199.
202. Ibid.
203. For commentary on these disputes, see Miles, R. and Phizacklea, A., 'Class Race, Ethnicity and Political Action', *Political*

Studies, Vol. XXV, no. 4, pp. 491–507; see also S. Bentley, 'Industrial Conflict, Strikes and Black Workers: Problems of Research and Methodology', *New Community*, 1976, Vol. 5 (1/2), pp. 127–38.

204. *Report of the Proceedings at the 99th Annual Trades Union Congress*, 1967, pp. 582–5.

205. Select Committee on Race Relations and Immigration, *Employment*, Vol. 2, pp. 469–71 (1974).

206. Miles and Phizacklea (1978), op. cit., p. 202.

207. Ibid., p. 203.

208. *Report of the Proceedings at the 106th Annual Trades Union Congress*, 1974, p. 536.

209. *TUC Workbook on Racism* (London, TUC Education Department, 1983).

210. *Race Relations at Work*, TUC; *TUC Workbook on Racism*, 1983.

211. 'Black Workers and the Trade Unions', *Race Today*, August 1973, p. 236.

212. *Third World Impact*, op. cit., p. 36.

213. Macdonald, I., 'The Capitalist Way to Curb Discrimination', *Race Today*, August 1973, p. 240.

214. Ibid., p. 242.

215. *Race Today*, August 1973, p. 243.

216. Ibid.

217. Ibid., p. 246.

218. Ibid.

219. Ibid.

220. 'Declaration', *Black Trade Unionists Solidarity Movement*, Issue No. 1 and Declaration (London, BTUSM, December 1981).

221. BTUSM Issue no. 1, p. 7.

Chapter 10

1. Epps, A. (ed.), *The Speeches of Malcolm X* (London, Peter Owen, 1969), p. 19.

2. See *The Speeches of Malcolm X*.

3. Carmichael, S., *Stokely Speaks: Black Power Back to Pan Africanism* (New York, Random House, 1971), p. 27.

4. Ibid., p. 18.

5. Ibid., p. 23.

6. Ibid., p. 30.

7. Ibid., p. 32.

8. Ibid., p. 42.

9. Ibid., p. 43.

10. Ibid., p. 52.

11. Ibid., p. 67.

12. Ibid., p. 72.

13. Ibid., pp. 85–6.

14. Ibid., p. 93.

15. Ibid., p. 107.

16. Ibid., p. 120.
17. Ibid., pp. 121–2.
18. Ibid., p. 124.
19. Ibid., p. 125.
20. Ibid., p. 173.
21. Ibid., p. 176.
22. Ibid., p. 191.
23. Ibid., p. 201.
24. Ibid., pp. 224–5.
25. Manley, D. R., 'The Social Structure of the Liverpool Negro Community with Special Reference to the Formation of Formal Associations' (Ph.D. Thesis, University of Liverpool, 1958–59), p. 85; Richmond, *Colour Prejudice in Britain* (London, Routledge & Kegan Paul, 1954), p. 17.
26. Manley, op. cit., p. 87.
27. Ibid., p. 95.
28. Ibid., p. 96.
29. Ibid., pp. 103–4.
30. Ibid., p. 161.
31. Ibid., p. 163.
32. Ibid., p. 189.
33. Ibid., p. 191.
34. Ibid., p. 203.
35. Ibid., p. 205.
36. Ibid., p. 208.
37. Ibid., pp. 223–4.
38. Ibid., p. 229.
39. Ibid., p. 230.
40. Ibid., p. 231.
41. Ibid., p. 232.
42. Ibid., p. 235.
43. Ibid., p. 247.
44. Ibid., p. 252.
45. Ibid., p. 267.
46. Ibid., p. 268.
47. Ibid., p. 284.
48. Ibid., pp. 284–5.
49. Little, K., 'The Role of Voluntary Associations in West African Urbanisation', *American Anthropologist*, vol. 59, No. 4 1957, p. 589.
50. Banton, M., *The Coloured Quarter* (London, Jonathan Cape, 1955), pp. 217–21.
51. Desai, R., *Indian Immigrants in Britain* (London, Oxford University Press, 1963), p. 88.
52. Ibid., p. 92.
53. Ibid., p. 97.
54. Hiro, D., *Black British White British* (London, Eyre and Spottiswoode, 1971), p. 156.

55. Ibid., p. 157.
56. De Witt, John, *Indian Workers Associations in Britain* (London, Oxford University Press, 1969), p. 49.
57. Ibid., p. 52.
58. Ibid., p. 55.
59. Ibid., pp. 56–60.
60. Ibid.
61. Ibid., pp. 60–3.
62. Mansukani, Gobind Singh, *The Quintessence of Sikhism* (Amritsar, Shiromani Gurdwara Parbandhak Committee, 1965), p. 204.
63. De Witt, op. cit., p. 66.
64. Ibid.
65. Ibid., p. 110.
66. Ibid., p. 126.
67. Ibid., p. 128.
68. Ibid., pp. 136–7.
69. Ibid., pp. 159–60.
70. Ibid., p. 161.
71. Ibid., p. 162.
72. Ibid., p. 165.
73. 'The Struggle of Afro-Asian Workers in Britain' (*Race Today Collective*, 1983), p. 8.
74. Ibid., p. 17.
75. Ibid., p. 19.
76. Ibid., p. 20.
77. Heineman, B., *The Politics of the Powerless: A Study of the Campaign Against Racial Discrimination* (London, Oxford University Press, 1972), p. 65.
78. Ibid., pp. 66, 103.
79. Ibid., p. 67.
80. Ibid., pp. 67–8.
81. Ibid., pp. 69, 104; see Patterson, S., *Dark Strangers* (London, Tavistock Publications, 1963).
82. Maxwell, N., *The Power of Negro Action* (London, 1965), p. 19.
83. Heineman, op. cit., pp. 72–104.
84. Pearson, D. G., 'West Indian Communal Associations in Britain: some observations', *New Community*, Vol. 5, pp. 371–9.
85. Heineman, op. cit., pp. 77–8.
86. Maxwell, op. cit., pp. 39–40.
87. Ibid., p. 37.
88. Glass, op. cit., p. 200.
89. Heineman, op. cit., p. 1.
90. Ibid., p. 16.
91. *Peace News*, 11 December 1964; Heineman, op. cit., p. 19.
92. Heineman, op. cit., p. 21.

93. Ibid., p. 23.
94. Ibid., p. 24.
95. Ibid., p. 28.
96. Ibid., p. 33.
97. Ibid., p. 40.
98. Ibid., p. 44.
99. Ibid., p. 56.
100. *Immigration from the Commonwealth*, Cmnd 2739 (London, HMSO, 1965), pp. 6–7; (see also IRR, *Newsletter*, September, 1965 for reactions to the White Paper.
101. *The Guardian*, 28 February 1966.
102. Heineman, op. cit., p. 62.
103. Ibid., p. 63.
104. Ibid., p. 102.
105. Ibid., p. 87.
106. Ibid., p. 108.
107. Ibid.
108. Ibid., p. 109.
109. Ibid., p. 94.
110. See De Witt (1969), op. cit.
111. Desai, op. cit., p. 105.
112. Heineman, op. cit., p. 110.
113. Ibid., p. 160.
114. Ibid., p. 207.
115. Kinder, C., *West Indians in Moss Side: The Effectiveness of Voluntary Organisations in Integrating West Indians* (B.Litt. Thesis, Oxford University, 1966), p. 161.
116. Ibid., p. 166.
117. Ibid., p. 182.
118. Ibid., p. 196.
119. Ibid., p. 197.
120. Ibid., p. 200.
121. Ibid., p. 201.
122. Ibid., p. 206.
123. Ibid., pp. 215–18.
124. See Pearson, D. G., 'West Indian Communal Associations: some observations', *New Community*, Vol. 5.
125. Hill, C., *Black Churches: West Indian and African Sects in Britain* (Community and Race Relations Unit of the British Council of Churches, 1971), p. 3.
126. Ibid., pp. 16, 21.
127. Ibid., p. 4.
128. Ibid., p. 5.
129. Ibid., p. 9.
130. Hill, Clifford, *Immigration and Integration* (Oxford, Pergamon Press, 1976), p. 50.
131. Hill (1971), op. cit., p. 9.
132. Ibid., p. 10.

133. Ibid., p. 12.
134. Ibid., pp. 13–15.
135. Ibid., p. 16.
136. See Hill. C., *Black Churches* (1971) op. cit; *Immigration and Integration* (1976) op. cit.
137. Hill, C., *Black Churches*, op. cit.
138. See Paul Foot, *Immigration and Race in British Politics* (London, Penguin, 1965); Nicholas Deakin, *Colour and the British Electorate* (London, Oxford University Press, 1965).
139. Hill, C. (1970), op. cit., Chapter 1.
140. Hill (1971), op. cit., p. 20.
141. *Who's Doing What: A Directory of Projects & Groups Involved in Race Relations* (Commission for Racial Equality, 1980).
142. *Directory of Ethnic Minority Organisations: Midlands & Wales* (Commission for Racial Equality, 1982).
143. Sivanandan, A., 'From Resistance to Rebellion: Asian and Afro-Caribbean Struggles in Britain', *Race and Class*, XXIII, 2/3, 1981–82, p. 130.
144. Ibid., p. 134.
145. Ibid., p. 135.
146. Ibid., p. 141.
147. Ibid., p. 142.
148. Ibid., p. 143.
149. For more on black women organising see *Race and Class*, Summer 1985.
150. Sivanandan, op. cit., p. 147.
151. Ibid., p. 148.
152. 'Notes and Documents', *Race and Class*, Vol. XXIII, nos. 2/3. (1981–2), pp. 229–30.

Chapter 11
   1. See Plowden Report (1967), *Children in Their Primary Schools* (London, HMSO, 1967); Coard, B., *How the West Indian Child is Made Educationally Sub-Normal in the British School System* (London, New Beacon Books, 1971); Fisher, G. and Joshua, H., 'Social Policy and Black Youth' in *Black Youth in Crisis*, p. 129.
   2. Stevenson, D. and Wallis, P., 'Second Generation West Indians: A Study in Alienation', *Race Today*, August 1970; see also Smith, D. J., *Racial Disadvantage in Britain* (Penguin, 1977).
   3. Community Relations Commission, *Unemployment and Homelessness* (London, CRC, 1974), p. 10.
   4. Cronon, E. D., *Black Moses* (Madison, The University of Wisconsin Press, 1955), p. 162.
   5. Casmore, E. and Troyna, B., 'Growing Up in Babylon', in *Black Youth in Crisis*, op. cit., p. 77.
   6. Fuller, M., 'Young, Female and Black', in E. Cashmore and

B. Troyna (eds), *Black Youth in Crisis* (London, George Allen & Unwin, 1982), p. 98.

7. Wilson, A., *Finding A Voice: Asian Women in Britain* (London, Virago, 1978), p. 93.

8. Ibid., p. 94.

9. Ibid., p. 96.

10. Ibid., p. 97.

11. Ibid., p. 99.

12. Ibid., p. 100.

13. Ibid., p. 101.

14. Ibid., pp. 168–9.

15. *The Empire Strikes Back: Race and Racism in 70s Britain* (Centre for Contemporary Cultural Studies, London, Hutchinson, 1982), p. 213.

16. Ibid., p. 214.

17. Parmar, P. and Mirza, N., 'Growing angry, Growing strong', *Spare Rib*, No. 111 (October 1981); *The Empire Strikes Back*, op. cit., p. 215.

18. Carby, H., 'White Women Listen! Black Feminism and the Boundaries of Sisterhood' in *The Empire Strikes Back*, op. cit., p. 215.

19. Wilson, E., *Only Halfway to Paradise: Women in Post-War Britain 1945–1968* (Tavistock, 1980), pp. 43–44; Carby, op. cit., p. 218.

20. Carby, op. cit., p. 219.

21. Ibid., p. 232.

22. Wilson, A., op. cit., pp. 122–3.

23. Joseph, G., 'The Incompatible Ménage à trois: Marxism, feminism and racism', in Lydia Sargent (ed.), *Women and Revolution: A Discussion of the Unhappy Marriage of Marxism and Feminism – A Debate on Class and Patriarchy* (Pluto Press, 1981), p. 95.

24. Garchedi, G., 'Authority and Foreign labour: some notes on a late capitalist form of capital accumulation and state intervention', *Studies in Political Economy*, no. 2 (1979), p. 48; Pratiba Parmar, 'Gender, race and class: Asian women in resistance', in *The Empire Strikes Back*, op. cit., p. 237.

25. Bourne, J., 'Cheerleaders and Ombudsmen: the sociology of race relations in Britain', *Race and Class*, Vol. XXI, no. 4.

26. Parmar, op. cit., p. 241.

27. Ibid., p. 244.

28. Ibid., p. 245.

29. Ibid., p. 269.

30. Roberts, B., 'The Debate on Sus' in Cashmore and Troyna, op. cit., pp. 101–2; Clare Demuth, *Sus: A Report on the Vagrancy Act 1824* (London, Runnymede Trust, 1978), pp. 22–3.

31. Roberts, op. cit., p. 103.

32. *Daily Mirror*, 19 June 1979; Roberts, op. cit., p. 105.
33. *New Statesman*, 3 July 1981; Tony Bunyan, 'The Police Against the People', *Race and Class*, Vol. XXIII, nos. 2/3, Autumn/Winter 1981–82, p. 154.
34. Ibid., p. 154.
35. Ibid., pp. 159–69.
36. Thompson, E. P., *Review of Security and the State 1978*; Bunyan, op. cit., p. 162.
37. Ibid., p. 164.
38. Ibid., p. 165; Major General Clutterbuck, *Army Quarterly*, October 1973.
39. *Sunday Times*, 3 February 1974; Bunyan, op. cit., p. 165.
40. Bunyan, op. cit., p. 166.
41. Ibid., p. 167.
42. Ibid., p. 168.
43. *The Guardian*, 15 June 1979.
44. Institute of Race Relations (1979), *Police Against Black People*, p. 10.
45. *Race Today*, Editorial, July/August 1976.
46. Ibid., p. 149.
47. Hall, S. *et al.*, *Policing the Crisis* (Macmillan, 1978), p. 394; Gilroy, P., 'Steppin' Out of Babylon: Race, Class and Autonomy', in *The Empire Strikes Back*, op. cit., p. 277.
48. Gilroy, op. cit., p. 283.
49. Sivanandan, A., 'Imperialism and disorganic development in the silicone age', *Race and Class*, Vol. XXI, no. 2, 1979.
50. Gilroy, op. cit., p. 286.
51. Ibid.; Mumford, Lewis, *The City in History* (London, Secker and Warburg, 1961), p. 370.
52. Katznelson, I., *Black Men, White Cities* (London, Oxford University Press, 1973), p. 178.
53. Gilroy, op. cit., p. 288.
54. Ibid., p. 289.
55. Campbell, H., 'Rastafari: Culture of resistance', *Race and Class*, Vol. XXII, no. 1, 1980; Clarke, S., *Jah Music* (Heinemann, 1980).
56. Campbell, op. cit., p. 2.
57. Gilroy, op. cit., pp. 291, 292, 294.
58. Ibid., p. 295.
59. Cashmore, E., *Rastaman* (London, Allen & Unwin, 1979), p. 104.
60. Troyna, B., 'Differential Commitment to ethnic identity by black youths in Britain', *New Community*, Vol. VII, no. 3, 1979.
61. Gilroy, op. cit., pp. 299–301.
62. Mattelart, A., *Mass Media, Ideologies and the Revolutionary Movement* (Harvester Press, 1980), p. 54.
63. Gilroy, op. cit., p. 301.

64. Ibid., pp. 302–3.
65. Prezworski, A. (1977), pp. 343–401;
66. Gilroy, op. cit., pp. 303–4.
67. Touraine, A., *The Voice and the Eye: an Analysis of Social Movements* (Cambridge University Press, 1981); Gilroy, op. cit., p. 304.
68. Gilroy, op. cit., p. 304; Hall (1978), op. cit., p. 395.
69. Gilroy, op. cit., pp. 304–6.
70. Joshua, H. and Wallace, T., *To Ride the Storm* (London, Heinemann Educational Books, 1983), p. 11.
71. *The Kerner Commission*, 1968, Part III, pp. 73–7.
72. *Supplemental Studies for The National Advisory Commission on Civil Disorders* (New York, F. Praeger, 1968), p. 223.
73. Rude, G., *The Crowd in History: A Study of Popular Disturbances in France and England, 1730–1848* (London, Lawrence & Wishart, 1981), p. 268.
74. Hobsbawm, E. J., *Primitive Rebels: Studies in Archaic Forms of Social Movement in the Nineteenth and Twentieth Centuries* (Manchester University Press, 1959), p. 111.
75. Thompson, E. P., 'The Moral Economy of the English Crowd in the Eighteenth Century', *Past and Present*, Vol. 50, p. 78.
76. 'Black and Blue: Race and Violence in Britain', *Third Way*, Vol. 8, no. 5, 1985, pp. 20–3.
77. Rude, op. cit., p. 34.
78. Joshua and Wallace, op. cit., p. 13.
79. *Western Mail*, 19 July 1907; ibid., p. 17.
80. Joshua and Wallace, op. cit., p. 18.
81. *Western Mail*, 7 April 1911.
82. May, R. and Cohen, R., 'The Interaction Between Race and Colonialism: A Case Study of the Liverpool Race Riots of 1919', *Race and Class*, Vol. XVI, no. 2, 1974, p. 114.
83. *Liverpool Courier*, 9 June 1919.
84. Joshua and Wallace, op. cit., p. 27.
85. Byrne, D., 'The 1930 "Arab Riot" in South Shields: A Race Riot that Never Was', *Race and Class*, Vol. XVIII, no. 3, 1977, pp. 261–76.
86. Richmond (1954), op. cit., p. 103.
87. Joshua and Wallace, op. cit., p. 29.
88. *Western Mail*, 13 June 1919.
89. *South Wales Echo*, 13 June 1919.
90. *Liverpool Courier*, 19 June 1919.
91. Joshua and Wallace, op. cit., p. 35.
92. Ibid., pp. 42–3.
93. Sivanandan, A., *Race and Class*, Vol. XXIII, nos. 2/3, 1981–2, p. 117.
94. Ibid., p. 122.
95. Ibid., p. 125.

96. Ibid., p. 127.
97. Ibid., p. 129.
98. Ibid., p. 129.
99. Ibid., p. 130.
100. Ibid., p. 132.
101. Ibid., pp. 137–8.
102. Ibid., p. 143.
103. Ibid., p. 146.
104. Ibid., p. 147.
105. Joshua and Wallace, p. 190.
106. Ibid., p. 188.
107. *Daily Telegraph*, 3 April 1980.
108. *The Guardian*, 3 April 1980.
109. *Daily Mirror*, 3 April 1980.
110. *The Times*, 3 April 1980.
111. *Western Daily Press*, 3 April 1980.
112. *Evening Post*, 3 April 1980.
113. *The Guardian*, 3 April 1980.
114. Ibid.
115. *Daily Mirror*, 3 April 1980.
116. *Daily Mail*, 5 April 1980.
117. *The Guardian*, 5 April 1980.
118. *Daily Telegraph*, 3 April 1980; Joshua and Wallace, op. cit., p. 113.
119. *The Guardian*, 5 April 1980.
120. *Western Daily Press*, 5 April 1980.
121. Sivanandan (1981–2), *Race and Class*, Vol. XXIII, nos. 2/3, p. 149.
122. Joshua and Wallace, op. cit., p. 193.
123. *The Guardian*, 13 April 1980.
124. *Daily Express*, 13 April 1980.
125. Thompson, E. P., *The Making of the English Working Class* (Harmondsworth, Penguin, 1968), pp. 10–11; Robinson, C. J., *Black Marxism* (London, Zed Press, 1983), p. 38.

Bibliography

Primary sources: manuscripts and printed

British Library Manuscripts

Liverpool Papers
Minute Books of the Committee for the Abolition of the Slave Trade
Auckland Papers
Huskisson Papers
Place Papers (BL Add. MS. 27,808)
Clarkson's Haitian Papers (BL Add. MS. 41266)

Public Records Office

The following Home Office records covering the years 1817–1820 relate to Informers' reports on the black radicals, William Davidson and particularly on Robert Wedderburn's writings, statements and trial.

HO 40/7 (3)/(1)–(4)	HO 42/195	HO 44/4/74
June 1817–1818	HO 42/196	HO 44/4/100
HO 40/7 (3)	HO 42/197	HO 44/4/291
HO 40/7 (3)/190	HO 42/198	HO 44/4/317
HO 42/192	HO 42/199	HO 44/4/318
HO 42/193	HO 42/202	HO 44/4/322
HO 42/194	HO 44/4/29	HO 44/5/38

HO 44/5/51	HO 44/5/289	HO 44/6/31–6
HO 44/5/202	HO 44/5/391	HO 44/6/206–7
HO 44/5/278	HO 44/5/426	
HO 44/5/279	HO 44/5/494–5	

The following files relate to questions arising from labour, trade union, social and political matters essentially in Trinidad and Tobago during the 1930s – a period of widespread labour unrest in the West Indies and throughout the British Colonies.

CO 295/153: Lord Harris to Earl Grey 1846

CO 295/576/95781: Letter from East Indians to Messrs. Cipriani, Johnson and Hamel Smith on Divorce Bill, 1932

CO 295/597/70121: Governor to Secretary of State, July 1937

CO 295/597/70125: Fletcher to Ormsby Gore, November 1937

CO 295/597/70125: Governor to Secretary of State (Telegram), October 1937

CO 295/599/70285: FWTU Resolution to Secretary of State, 5 November 1937

CO 295/599/70297: Telegram from Governor to H. Beckett, 25 June 1937

CO 295/599/70297: All the correspondence in this file (and those listed below) reveal much about Colonial Office policy to local labour in relation to the profitability of the oil and sugar industries

CO 295/600/70305

CO 295/601/70307

CO 295/606/703078

For the British TUC's role in the development of Colonial Trade Unions see: TUC Private and Confidential Files, held at Congress House, London.

India Office Library and Records: papers relating to Indian indentured labour

The Curzon Papers

The Hardinge Papers

Public and Judicial Department Papers:

IO:L/P&J/6/File, 'J and P' 3779, 1914: 'Indentured Labour in the Colonies'

IO:L/P&J/6/1321/File, 'J and P' 2929, 1914: 'Confidential British Guiana'

IO:L/P&J/6/1179/File, 'J and P' 2643, 1912: 'Deputation of McNeill (sic) and Chimmanlal to visit the colonies'

IO:L/P&J/6/1412/File, 'J and P' 4522, 1915: 'Indentured Emigration for India – Discontinuance'

IO:L/P&J/6/1571/File, 'J and P' 1285; 1919: Indentured Emigration'

IO:L/P&J/6/1744/File, 'J and P' 2396, 1921: 'Indian Emigration Act 1922'

See also: Papers of the Anti-Slavery Society and Aborigines Protection Society (Rhodes House, Oxford)

Parliamentary Papers, 1840. Vol. XVI (45 and 427) Evidence given to 1838 Calcutta Committee

Parliamentary Papers, 1841. Vol. X (43) for Minutes on Emigration

Parliamentary Papers, 1842. Vol. XXX for correspondence on Emigration

Emigration from India: the Export of Coolies and Other labourers to Mauritius (British and Foreign Anti-Slavery Society, London 1842)

Parliamentary Papers, 1874. Vol. XLVII (314) for note on emigration from India

Parliamentary Papers, 1847–8, Vol. XLVI for correspondence between Secretary of State and Governors of the sugar growing colonies as to the distress existing in the colonies

Parliamentary Papers (Walker to Grey), 18 July 1848

Report on the Mortality of Emigrant Coolies on the Voyages to the West Indies in 1856–7 by F. J. Mouat

Parliamentary Papers, 1859, Vol. XVI. Papers relating to Immigration to the West Indian Colonies, presented to Parliament, August 1857

Parliamentary Papers, 1959, Vol. XVI relating to fixed female quotas of labourers

Parliamentary Papers, 1859, Vol. XVI, C2452, Emigration Commissioners to Herman Merivale, Colonial Office (10 March 1858)

Parliamentary Papers, 1878–9, Vol. LI, C2473, 'Correspondence relative to the financial arrangements for Indian Coolie Immigration into Jamaica'

Parliamentary Papers, 1878–9, C2249, 'Papers relating to the Condition of Indian immigrants in Grenada'

Indentured labour: further reports and correspondence

Annual Report on Immigration Department (Mauritius 1882)

Annual Report, Protector of Immigrants (St Lucia 1882)

Commission on the Trinidad and Tobago Disturbances 1937, Cmd 5641

Committee Appointed to Inquire Respecting the Exportation of Hill Coolies (and other papers) 1841, Vol. XVI

Convention between Her Majesty and the King of the Netherlands relating to the emigration of labourers from India to the Dutch Colony of Surinam, Parliamentary Papers (C473, 1872)

Convention between Her Majesty and the Emperor of the French relative to the emigration of labourers from India to the French Colonies (Command Papers, First Series 2887) 1861

Correspondence respecting the recent Coolie Disturbances in

Trinidad at the Mohurrum Festival, with the Report thereon by
Sir H. W. Norman, 1885

Correspondence relating to the Royal Commission of Inquiry into
the Condition of the Indian immigrants in Mauritius (C1188,
1875)

Correspondence between the Government of Mauritius and the
Indian Authorities, 1837–38, Vol. LII

Correspondence between India and the British Government
Regarding the Resumption of Coolie Emigration, Vol. XXX,
1842

Correspondence Relative to the West Indies and Mauritius from the
West Coast of Africa, the East Indies and China, Vol. XXXV,
1844

Correspondence between the Secretary of State and the Governors
of the sugar growing colonies as to the Distress now existing in
those colonies, Vol. XLVI, 1847–8

Evidence of O. W. Warner, Emigration Agent for Trinidad,
Sanderson Report, Part II.

Immigration Ordinance of Trinidad and British Guiana (1899) Cd
1989 presented to Parliament in April 1904

Labour Conditions in Ceylon, Mauritius and Malaya, Report by
Major G. St. J. Orde Browne, Labour Adviser to the Secretary of
State for the Colonies (Cmd 6423, 1942)

Labourers from India to the French Colonies, 1861, Command
Papers, First Series 2887

Minutes of the Proceedings and Papers laid before the Imperial War
Conference, Cd. 9177, 1918

Papers relative to the condition of Indian Immigrants in Grenada,
1878–9, C2248

Papers Relative to the Laws and Regulations in Force in the colonies
under responsible Government respecting the admission of
immigrants, Cd. 2105, 1904

Papers Relative to Immigration to the West Indies presented to
Parliament, August 1857, First Series 2452, 1859

Proceedings of a Conference between the Secretary of State for the
Colonies and the Premiers of the Self-Governing Colonies
(C8596, 1897)

The Present Position and Future Prospects of British Guiana; being
the second letter from Revd H. Whitfield to the colonists thereof
(London 1872)

Recent Coolie Disturbances in Trinidad, C4366, 1884–5

Report of Commissioners on Conditions in Mauritius, 1840, Vol.
XXVII

Report of the Commissioners Appointed to Enquire into the
Treatment of Immigrants in Mauritius (with accompanying evidence) 1875, C1115

Report of the Commissioners Appointed to Enquire into the

Treatment of Immigrants in British Guiana (with accompanying evidence, etc) 1871, C393

Report of the Commission of Enquiry into the Riots in Mauritius in January 1911 (Mauritius 1911)

Report of the Committee on Emigration from India to the Crown Colonies and Protectorates Cd 5192, London 1910 (cited as *Sanderson Report*)

Report of the Government of India on the Conditions of Indian Immigrants in Four British Colonies and Surinam by James McNeill and Chimman Lal, Part 1, 1914–1916, Cd 7744

Report on the Condition of Indian Immigrants in the Four British Colonies of Trinidad, British Guiana (or Demerara) Jamaica and Fiji, and in the Dutch Colony of Surinam (or Dutch Guiana) Simla 1914

Report by Kumar Maharaj Singh on his Deputation to Mauritius (Delhi 1925)

West India Committee Circular, Nos. 687 and 688, 'British Guiana and Indian Immigration'

State papers, official reports and documents

Acts of the Privy Council, Vol. XXVI, 1596–97

Calendar of State Papers, Colonial Series, IX, 15 August 1676

City of Cardiff Education Committee, Fourteenth Report of the Juvenile Employment Committee, 31 July 1929

Commission on Distressed Colonial and Indian Subjects: Minutes of Evidence and Appendices (London, HMSO, 1910, Cd 5134)

Commission on Industrial Relations, Mansfield Hosiery Mills Ltd (HMSO, 1974)

Commission for Racial Equality: Submission to Lord Scarman's Inquiry into the Brixton Disorders (London, CRE, 1981)

Commonwealth Immigrants Advisory Council: Second Report, Cmnd 2266 (London, HMSO, 1964)

Community Relations Commission: Between Two Cultures: A Study between generations in the Asian Community in Britain (London, 1978)

Community Relations Commission: Evidence to the Royal Commission on the National Health Service 1977

CRC: The Employment of non-English Speaking Workers: What Industry Must Do (London, 1974)

CRC: Religious Education in a Multi-religious Society (London, CRC, July 1969)

CRC: Unemployment and Homelessness (London, HMSO, 1974)

CRC: Urban Deprivation, Racial Inequality and Social Policy: A Report (London, HMSO, 1977)

Department of Employment Gazette, September 1975

Directory of Ethnic Minority Organisations: Midlands and Wales (CRE, 1982)

First Report from the Committee on the State of the Police of the Metropolis 1817.

First Report of the Society Established in London for the Suppression of Mendicity 1819; Second Report, 1820

Fourteenth Annual Report of the League of Coloured Peoples 1944–5

Hansard, Third Series 1833

Hansard, August 1923; December 1934

Home Affairs Committee (1981) Racial Disadvantage, Fifth Session 1980–81 (London, HMSO, HC 424)

Great Britain: Home Office: Reports of Her Majesty's Chief Inspector of Constabulary (London, HMSO, 1948–81)

Home Office: Acts and Bills

Home Office: Commonwealth Immigrants Act, 1962: Instructions to Immigration Officers (London, HMSO, May 1962, Cmnd 1716)

Home Office: Commonwealth Immigrants Act, 1962: Instructions to Immigration Officers (London, HMSO, August 1966, Cmnd 3064)

Home Office: Commonwealth Immigrants Act, 1962: Instructions to Immigration Officers (London, HMSO, November 1967, Cmnd 3064)

Home Office: Commonwealth Immigrants Bill: Draft Instructions to Immigration Officers (London, HMSO, 1962, Cmnd 1640)

Home Office: Commonwealth Immigrants Bill, 1968: Draft Instructions to Immigration Officers (London, HMSO, February 1968, Cmnd 3552)

Home Office: Immigration Appeals Bill: Commonwealth Citizens, Controls After Entry: Draft Immigration Rules (London, HMSO, March 1969, Cmnd 3951)

Home Office: Immigration Appeals Bill, 1968, Aliens: Draft Instructions to Immigration Officers (London, HMSO, November 1968)

Home Office: Commonwealth Immigrants Act 1968 (London, HMSO, 1968)

Home Office: Commonwealth Immigrants Bill 1968 (London, HMSO, February 1968)

Home Office: Immigration (No. 2) Bill (London, HMSO, July 1968)

Home Office: Immigration Appeals Bill (London, HMSO, November 1968)

Home Office: Race Relations Act 1965 (London, HMSO, 1965)

Home Office: Race Relations Act 1965 (London, HMSO, June 1966)

Home Office: Race Relations Bill (London, HMSO, 1968)

Home Office: Admission of Commonwealth Citizens to the United Kingdom (London, HMSO, February 1967)

Home Secretary: Statement on the Disturbances in Bristol, 2 April 1980

House of Commons, Sessional Papers 1837–8

Housing Policy: A Consultative Document, (London, HMSO, 1977, Cmnd 6851)

Immigration from the Commonwealth, Cmnd 2739, HMSO, 1965

Immigrants and the Youth Service (London, HMSO, 1969)

The Kerner Commission 1968, Part III

Labour Administration in the Colonial Territories, 1944–50

Labour Conditions in the West Indies, Report by Major Orde Browne, July 1939, Cmd 6070

Labour in the UK Dependencies, London 1957

Labour Supervision in the Colonial Empire, London 1951

Labour Party: Report of the Working Party on Race Relations (London, Labour Party, 1967)

Labour Party Statement on Racial Discrimination, September 1958

Labour Policies in the West Indies, ILO, 1952

London Borough of Lambeth: Final Report of the Working Party into the Community/Police Relations in Lambeth (London, London Borough of Lambeth, 1981)

London Borough of Wandsworth: Statistics of the Social Service Department, 1974

Ministry of Education, English for Immigrants, Pamphlet No. 43 (London, HMSO, 1963)

National Council for Civil Liberties: Southall, 23 April 1979: The Report of the unofficial Committee of Enquiry (London, NCCL, 1980)

NCCL: The Death of Blair Peach; the supplementary report of the unofficial Committee of Enquiry (London, NCCL, 1980)

NCCL: Civil Disorder and Civil Liberties – Evidence to the Scarman Enquiry (London, NCCL, 1981)

NCCL: Cause for Concern (Nottingham, NCCL, 1982)

Ninth Report of the Directors of the African Institution (1815)

Parliamentary Debates: House of Commons, 21 November 1949; 3 April 1958; 5 December 1958, 23 February 1960

Parliamentary Debates: House of Lords, 19 November 1958

Plowden Report: Children in their Primary Schools (1967)

Report of the Cardiff Special Watch Committee, January 1929

Report of the First British Commonwealth Labour Conference (London, 1925)

Report of the First British Guiana and West Indies Labour Conference (Georgetown, British Guiana, 1926)

Report of the Fourth Congress on the Red International of Labour Unions (London, RILU Minority Movement, July 1928)

Report of the Proceedings of the 86th Annual Trades Union Congress 1954

Report of the Proceedings of the 87th Annual Trades Union Congress 1955

Report of the Proceedings of the 90th Annual Trades Union Congress 1958

Report of the Proceedings of the 91st Annual Trades Union Congress 1959

Report of the Proceedings of the 92nd Annual Trades Union Congress 1960

Report of the Proceedings of the 94th Annual Trades Union Congress 1962

Report of the Proceedings of the 96th Annual Trades Union Congress 1964

Report of the Proceedings of the 97th Annual Trades Union Congress 1965

Report of the Proceedings of the 98th Annual Trades Union Congress 1966

Report of the Proceedings of the 99th Annual Trades Union Congress 1967

Report of the Proceedings of the 100th Annual Trades Union Congress 1968

Report of the Proceedings of the 105th Annual Trades Union Congress 1973

Report of the West India Royal Commission, 1939 (London, HMSO, 1946, Cmd 6607)

Report of the West India Sugar Commission, Cmd 3517, 1930

Royal Commission on Criminal Procedure, 1981: Report (London, HMSO, Cmnd 8092)

Royal Commission on the Police, 1960: Interim Report (London, HMSO, Cmnd 1222)

Royal Commission on the Police 1962: Final Report (London, HMSO, Cmnd 1728)

Royal Commission Report on Trade Unions and Employers' Associations 1965–8, Cmnd 3623

The Sanderson Report, Part III

The Scarman Report of a Court of Inquiry into a dispute between Grunwick Processing Laboratories Ltd and members of the Association of Professional, Executive, Clerical and Computer Staff (HMSO, 1977, Cmnd 6922)

Secretary of State for the Home Department: Serious Disturbances in St Pauls Bristol (Memorandum 1980)

Select Committee on Race Relations and Immigration, The West Indian Community (London, HMSO, 1977)

Select Committee on Race Relations and Immigration 1972: Police/Immigrant Relations (London, HMSO, 1972)

Select Committee on Race Relations and Immigration, Employment, Vol. I, HMSO, 1974

Select Committee on Race Relations and Immigration, Employment, Vol. II, Evidence and Appendices, HMSO, 1975)

Select Committee on Race Relations and Immigration 1971–72, Police/Immigrant Relations, Vol. I

The Soul Kids Campaign (London, The Association of British
Adoption & Fostering Agencies, 1977)
Supplemental Studies for the National Advisory Commission on
Civil Disorders (New York, F. Praeger, 1968)
The Senior/Manley Report 1955
White Paper 1965: Immigration from the Commonwealth
(London, HMSO, Cmnd 2739)
Who's Doing What (CRE, 1980)

Secondary sources: books, monographs, articles and pamphlets

Abbott, S., 'The UK Commonwealth Immigration Act, 1968:
right or wrong', *Migration Today*, no. 10, April 1968
Adair, A., 'Immigration: control and integration', *Contemporary
Review*, Vol. 208, April 1966
Adam, C., 'Government by frontier guard', *New Statesman*,
September 1968
Adler, D., 'Voyage to the Promised Land', *Sunday Times
Magazine*, 30 June 1968
Adler, M., 'Race relations in Britain, 1965', *Wiener Library Bulletin*,
Vol. 20, no. 3, New Series, no. 4, 1966
Ahmat, Yusuf, *et al.*, 'The Textile Industry and Asian Workers in
Bradford', *Race Today*, March/April 1983
Alavi, H., *The Pakistanis in London*, Institute of Race Relations
Newsletter, July 1963
Alderson, John, *Policing Freedom* (Macdonald and Evans, 1979)
Alexander, Z. and Dewjee, A., *Mary Seacole: Jamaican National
Heroine and 'Doctress' in the Crimea* (Brent Library Service 1984)
Ali, Arif (ed.), *Third World Impact* (formerly West Indians in
Britain), London, Hansib Publications, 5th Edition, 1982
Allen, R. V., 'Celestine Edwards: His Life, Work and Death', *Lux*,
19 September 1894
Allen, S., 'Discrimination of Race and of Sex and the Union'
(Conference paper presented at Ruskin College, Oxford,
December 1970)
Allen, S., *New Minorities, Old Conflicts* (New York, Random
House, 1971)
Allen, S. and Bornat, J., *Unions and Immigrant Workers: How They
See Each Other* (Runnymede Trust Industrial Unit, 1970)
Allen, S. *et al.*, *Work, Race and Immigration* (University of Bradford,
1977)
Anand, V. S. and Ridley, F., *The Emergence of Enoch Powell*
(London, Medusa Press, 1969)
Anderson, John, *A Descriptive Account of Mauritius, its Scenery,
Statistics, etc.* (Calcutta 1858)

Anstey, R., *The Atlantic Slave Trade and British Abolition 1760–1810* (London, Macmillan, 1975)

Aptheker, H., *American Negro Slave Revolts* (New York, Columbia University Press, 1944)

Aronsfield, C. C., 'Challenge to socialist brotherhood: British dockers and coloured immigrants', *Patterns of Prejudice*, Vol. 2, no. 4, July/August 1968

Argov, Daniel, *Moderates and Extremists in the Indian Nationalist Movement 1883–1920* (London, Asia Publishing House, 1967)

Athalye, D. V., *The Life of Lokmanya Tilak* (Poona, Jagaddhitecchir Press, 1921)

Aurora, G. S., *Indian Workers in England*, M.Sc. (Econ) Thesis, University of London, 1960

Aurora, G. S., *The New Frontiersman* (Bombay, Popular Prakashan, 1967)

Baker, P., *Glasgow's Pakistani Community*, Undergraduate dissertation, University of Strathclyde, 1967

Ballard, R. and Holden B., 'The Employment of Coloured Graduates in Britain', *New Community*, Vol. IV, no. 3, 1975

Banaji, D. R., *Slavery in British India* (Bombay, D. B. Taraporevala, Sons & Co., 1933)

Banton. M., 'Negro workers in Britain', *Twentieth Century*, Vol. 51, January 1952

Banton, M., 'The changing position of the Negro in Britain', *Phylon*, Vol. 14, no. 1, 1953

Banton, M., 'Immigration from the British Colonies to the United Kingdom', *Population Studies*, Vol. VII, no. 1, July 1953

Banton, M., 'Recent migration from West Africa and the West Indies to the United Kingdom', *Population Studies*, Vol. 8, no. 1, July 1953

Banton, M., 'The social grouping of some West African workers in Britain', *Man*, Vol. 53, September 1953

Banton M., *The Coloured Quarter* (London, Jonathan Cape, 1955)

Banton, M., *White and Coloured* (London, Jonathan Cape, 1959)

Banton, M., *The Idea of Race* (London, Tavistock, 1977)

Banton, M. and Harwood, G., *The Race Concept* (Newton Abbott, David and Charles, 1975)

Barlow, Nora (ed.), *Charles Darwin's Diary of the Voyage of the H.M.S. Beagle* (Cambridge University Press, 1933)

Barrett, M., *Women's Oppression* (London, Verso Editions and NLB, 1980)

Baylen, J. O. and Gossman, V. J. (eds), *Biographical Dictionary of Modern British Radicals* (Sussex, Hassocks, Harvester Press, 1979)

Bayliss, F. J. and Coates, J. B., 'West Indians at Work in Nottingham', *Race*, Vol. 7, no. 2, October 1965

Beaumont, J., *The New Slavery: An Account of Indian and Chinese Immigrants in British Guiana* (London, W. Ridgway, 1871)

Beetham, D., *Immigrant School Leavers and the Youth Employment*

Service in Birmingham (London, Institute of Race Relations, 1967, Special Series)

Beloff, M., *Imperial Sunset* (London, Methuen, 1969)

Bennett, A., 'Training and selection of nurses from Commonwealth countries', *Midwife and Health Visitor*, Vol. 2, no. 8, August 1966

Bennett, A. G., *Because They Know Not* (London, Phoenix Press, 1959)

Bentley, S., 'Industrial conflict, strikes and black workers: problems of research and methodology', *New Community*, Vol. 5, 1/2, 1976

Beresford Ellis, P. and Mac a'Ghobhainn, S., *The Scottish Insurrection of 1820* (London, Victor Gollancz, 1970)

Berger, J. and Mohr, J., *A Seventh Man* (Penguin Books, 1975)

Bibby, C., *Race, Prejudice and Education* (London, Heinemann, 1959)

Bidwell, S., 'Coloured Workers and Unions . . .', *Race Today*, Vol. 1. no. 1, May 1969

Blackett, R., 'Martin R. Delany and Robert Campbell: Black Americans in Search of an African Colony', *Journal of Negro History*, Vol. LXII, 1977

Bohning, W. R., *The Migration of Workers in the United Kingdom and the European Community* (London, Oxford University Press, 1972)

Bolt, C., *Victorian Attitudes to Race* (London, Routledge & Kegan Paul, 1971)

Bone, M., *The Youth Service and Similar Provision for Young People* (London, HMSO, 1972)

Bonfield, A. E., 'The role of legislation in eliminating racial prejudice', *Race*, Vol. 7, no. 2, October 1965

Bonham Carter, M., 'Legislation and the Race Relations Board', *IRR Newsletter*, April 1967

Booth, Charles, *Life and Labour of the People of London* (London, 1902)

Bosanquet, N. and Doeringer, P. B., 'Is there a dual labour market in Britain?' *Economic Journal*, Vol. 83, 1973

Boston, R., 'How the immigrants Act was passed', *New Society*, Vol. 11, 28 March 1968

Boston, S., *Women Workers and the Trade Unions* (London, Davis-Poynter, 1980)

Bourne, H., 'Smethwick – a warning and a call to action', *Labour Monthly*, December 1964

Bourne, J., 'Cheerleaders and Ombudsmen: the sociology of race relations in Britain', *Race and Class*, Vol. XXI, no. 4

Bourret, F. M., *Ghana. The Road to Independence, 1919–1957* (London, Oxford University Press, 1960)

Bowes, S., *The Police and Civil Liberties* (London, Lawrence & Wishart, 1966)

Boyle, Sir E., 'Race relations: the limits of voluntary action', *Race*, Vol. 9, no. 3, January 1968

Braham, P. *et al.*, *Discrimination and Disadvantage in Employment: The Experience of Black Workers* (London, Harper & Row, 1981)

Braidwood, S. J., 'Initiatives and organisation of the Black Poor, 1786–1787'. Paper presented at Black History Conference in London, September 1981

Breitman, G. (ed.), *Leon Trotsky On Black Nationalism And Self-Determination* (New York, Merit Publishers, 1967)

Brennan, J., 'Journalists condemn discrimination', *IRR Newsletter*, March 1966

Briggs, A., *The Age of Improvement* (London, Longmans Green & Co., 1959)

Briggs, A., 'Chartists in Tasmania: A Note', *Bulletin of the Society for the Study of Labour History*, no. 3, Autumn 1961

Briggs, A., *Victorian Cities* (London, Pelican, 1963)

Brittan, E., 'Teacher Opinion on Aspects of school life, pupils and teachers', *Educational Research*, Vol. 8, no. 3

Brockway, F., *Inside The Left* (London, Allen and Unwin, 1942)

'Brockway's Bill and Iremonger's Amendment', *Venture*, Vol. 15, no. 1, January 1963

Brooks, D., 'Who Will Go Back', *Race Today* Vol. 1, no. 5, September 1969

Brooks, D., *Race and Labour in London Transport* (London, Oxford University Press, 1975)

Brooks, D., *Black Employment in the Black Country: A Study of Walsall* (London, Runnymede Trust, 1975)

Brown, C., *Black and White: The Third PSI Survey* (London, Heinemann, 1984)

Brown, W., 'We Come from another field', in M. Prescod-Roberts and N. Steele (eds), *Black Women: Bringing It All Back Home* (Bristol, Falling Wall Press, 1980)

Brown, W. G. 'Investigation of Coloured Seamen in Cardiff, April 13–20 1935', *The Keys*, Vol. III, pp. 20–1

Bugler, J., 'The invaders of Islington', *New Society*, Vol. 12, 15 August 1968

Bullock, A., *The Life and Times of Ernest Bevin* (London, Heinemann, 1983)

Bunyan, T., 'The Police Against the People', *Race and Class*, Vol. XXIII, nos. 2/3, 1981–2

Burney, E., 'Who Comes Under Clause One?', *IRR Newsletter*, March 1968

Burnham, T. H. and Hoskins, G. O., *Iron and Steel in Britain* (London, Allen & Unwin, 1943)

Burt, R. A., *Colour Prejudice in Great Britain* (Princeton, N.J., The Author, 1960)

Bush, B., 'Blacks in Britain', *History Today*, September 1981

Busia, K. A., *Report on a Social Survey of Sekondi Takoradi* (Accra, 1950)

Butterworth, E., 'The 1962 smallpox outbreak and the British Press', *Race*, Vol. 7, no. 4, April 1966

Butterworth, E., 'Kenya Asians in Britain', *Venture*, Vol. 20, no. 4, April 1968

Byrne, D., 'The 1930 "Arab Riot" in South Shields: A Race Riot that Never Was', *Race and Class*, 1977, Vol. XVIII

Cable, V., *Whither Kenyan Emigrants* (London, Fabian Society, July 1969)

Cabral, A., *Return to the Source* (New York & London, Monthly Review Press, 1973)

Cain, P. J., *Economic Foundations of British Overseas Expansion 1815–1914* (London, Macmillan Press, 1980)

Calley, M. J. C., 'Pentecostal Sects among West Indian migrants', *Race*, Vol. 3, no. 2, May 1962

Calley, M. J. C., *God's People: West Indian Pentecostal Sects in England* (London, OUP for the IRR, 1965)

Cameron, G. and Evans, A., 'The British Conurbations Centres', *Regional Studies*, Vol. 7 (London, Pergamon Press, 1973)

Campaign Against Racial Discrimination: *How to Expose Discrimination* (London, CARD, 1960)

Campaign Against Racial Discrimination: *Memorandum of Racial Discrimination in Britain* (London, CARD, 1966)

Campaign Against Racial Discrimination: *Report on Racial Discrimination* (London, CARD, 1967)

Campaign Against Racial Discrimination: *Evidence concerning the procedures governing control of immigration from the Commonwealth submitted to the Committee of Enquiry into immigration* (London, CARD, 1966)

Campaign Against Racism and Fascism: 'Racism and Criminal Statistics', *Searchlight*, no. 83, 1982

Campbell, H., 'Rastafari: Culture of Resistance', *Race and Class* Vol. XXII, no. 1, 1980

Carby, H., 'White Women Listen! Black Feminism and the Boundaries of Sisterhood', in *The Empire Strikes Back* (Hutchinson, 1982)

Carlile, J. (ed.), *Journal of a Voyage with Coolie Emigrants from Calcutta to Trinidad* (London, Alfred W. Bennett, 1859)

Carlyle, T., *Occasional Discourse on the Nigger Question* (London, Thomas Bosworth, 1853)

Carmichael, S., *Stokely Speaks: Black Power Back to Pan Africanism* (New York, Random House, 1971)

Carmichael, S. and Hamilton, C., *Black Power: The Politics of Liberation in America* (London, Jonathan Cape, 1968)

Carpenter, M., *The Last Days in England of Rajah Rammohun Roy* (London, Trubner & Co, 1866)

Casely-Hayford, J. E., *Gold Coast Native Institutions* . . . (London, Sweet & Maxwell, 1903)

Casely-Hayford, J. E., *Ethiopia Unbound: Studies in Race Emancipation* (London, C. M. Phillips, 1911)

Cashmore, E., *Rastaman* (London, Allen & Unwin, 1979)

Cashmore, E. and Troyna, B., *Black Youth in Crisis* (London, Allen & Unwin, 1982)

Cashmore, E. and Troyna, B., 'Growing Up in Babylon', in *Black Youth in Crisis*

Castells, M., 'Immigrant Workers and Class Struggles in Advanced Capitalism: The Western European Experience', *Politics and Society*, 1975

Castles, S. and Kosack, G., *Immigrant Workers and Class Structure in Western Europe* (London, Oxford University Press, 1973)

Castles, S. *et al.*, *Here For Good: Western Europe's New Ethnic Minorities* (London, Pluto Press 1984)

Catholic Institute for International Relations, *Race and Religion* (London, CIIR, 1965)

Catholic Institute for International Relations, *Conscience and Colour* (London, CIIR, 1967)

Centre for Contemporary Cultural Studies, *The Empire Strikes Back* (London, Hutchinson, 1982)

Chansarkar, B. A., 'Skilled Indian immigrants', *IRR Newsletter*, July 1968

Chater, A., *Race Relations in Britain* (London, Lawrence & Wishart, 1966)

Checkland, S. G., 'Finance for the West Indies, 1780–1815', *Economic History Review*, 2nd series, Vol. X, 1957–58

Checkland, S. G., *The Gladstones: A Family Biography 1764–1851* (Cambridge University Press, 1971)

Chirol, V., *Indian Unrest* (London Macmillan, 1910)

Church Information Office, *Police: A Social Study* (London, CIO, April 1967)

Churchill, Winston, Budget Speech, 15 April 1929

Citrine, W., *Men and Work: An Autobiography* (London, Hutchinson, 1964)

Clapham, J. H., *Economic History of Modern Britain* (Cambridge University Press, 1926–38)

Clarke, S., *Jah Music* (London, Heinemann, 1980)

Clarkson, T., *The History of the Rise, Progress and Accomplishment of the Abolition of the African Slave Trade* (London, Longman, 1808)

Clegg, H., *The Changing System of Industrial Relations in Great Britain* (Oxford, Basil Blackwell, 1979)

Cliff, T., *The Crisis – Social Contract or Socialism* (London, Pluto Press, 1975)

Coard, B., *How the West Indian Child is made Educationally Subnormal in the British School System* (London, New Beacon Books, 1971)

Coates, K. and Topham, T., *The New Unionism* (London, Peter Owen, 1972)

Cohen, B. G. and Jenner, P. J., 'The Employment of Immigrants: A Case Study within the Wool Industry', *Race*, Vol. 10, 1968

Cole, G. D. H., *Labour in the Commonwealth* (London, Headley Bros, 1918)

Cole, G. D. H. and Filson, A. W., *British Working Class Movements, Select Documents 1789–1875* (London, Macmillan, 1951)

Coleridge-Taylor, A., *The Heritage of Samuel Coleridge Taylor* (London, Dennis Dobson, 1979)

Collins, H. and Abramsky, C., *Karl Marx and the British Labour Movement* (London, Macmillan, 1965)

Collins, S., 'The social position of white and "half-caste" women in coloured grouping in Britain', *American Sociological Review*, Vol. 16, no. 6, December 1951

Collins, S., 'The British-born Coloured', *Sociological Review*, Vol. 3, no. 1, July 1955

Collins, S., *Coloured Minorities in Britain* (London, Lutterworth, 1957)

Collison, P., 'Immigrants' varieties of experience', *New Society*, Vol. 13, June 1969

Comins, D. W. D., *Note on Emigration from the East Indies to British Guiana* (Calcutta, 1893)

Comins, D. W. D., *Note on Emigration from the East Indies to Jamaica* (Calcutta, 1893)

Constantine, L., *Colour Bar* (London, Stanley Paul, 1964)

Copland, S., *Black and White: or the Jamaican Question* (London, 1866)

Corfield, T., 'Racial Discrimination in Industry', Conference paper presented at Ruskin College, Oxford, December 1970

Counter Information Services, *Crisis: Women Under Attack* (London, 1976)

Coxon, T., *Second Class Citizens* (London, Independent Labour Party, 1965)

Craft, E. and W., *Running a Thousand Miles for Freedom* (London, William Tweedie, 1860)

Craton, M., *Sinews of Empire* (London, Temple Smith, 1974)

Craton, M., *Testing The Chains: Resistance to Slavery in the British West Indies* (London, Longman, 1976)

Craton, M., Walvin, J. and Wright, D., *Slavery, Abolition and Emancipation* (London, Longman, 1976)

Craven, A., 'West Africans in Britain', *West Africa*, September 1967

CRE/BBC: *Five Views of Multi-Racial Britain* (London CRE, 1978)

Cronon, E. D., *Black Moses* (Madison, University of Wisconsin Press, 1955)

Cross, Colin, *The Fascists in Britain* (London, Barrie & Rockliff, 1961)

Cross, Colin, 'Britain's racialists', *New Society*, Vol. 5, June 1965

Cross, Colin, *The British Empire* (London, Hamlyn, 1972)

Cross, Crispin, *Ethnic Minorities in the Inner City: The Ethnic Dimension in Urban Deprivation in England* (London, Commission for Racial Equality, 1978)

Cruse, H., *The Crisis of the Negro Intellectual* (New York, William Morrow & Co. Inc., 1967)

Cumberland, R. *The West Indian: A Comedy* (London, 1775)

Cumpston, I. M. *Indians Overseas in British Territories, 1834–1854* (London, OUP, 1954)

Cundall, F., *The Governors of Jamaica in the Seventeeth Century* (London, 1936)

Dabydeen, D., *Hogarth's Blacks: Images of Black in Eighteenth Century English Art* (Dangaroo Press, 1985)

Dabydeen, D. (ed.), *The Black Presence in English Literature* (Manchester University Press, 1985)

Dahya, B., 'Yemenis in Britain: An Arab Community', *Race*, Vol. 6, no. 3, January 1965

Dahya, Z. 'Pakistani wives in Britain', *Race*, Vol. 6, no. 3, January 1965

Daniel, W. W., *Racial Discrimination in England* (Harmondsworth, Penguin, 1968)

Dasent, G. W., *Annals of an Eventful Life* (London, 1870)

Dashwood, A. 'Juries in a multi-racial society', *Criminal Law Review*, 1972

Daunton, M. J., 'Jack ashore, unionisation of seamen in Cardiff before 1914', *Welsh History Review*, Vol. 9, no. 2, 1978

Davies, C. S. L., 'Slavery and the Protector Somerset: The Vagrancy Act of 1547, *Economic History Review*, Vol. XIX, 1966

Davison, R. B., *West Indian Migrants* (London, OUP, 1962)

Davison, R. B., 'Labour supply under the Commonwealth Immigrants Act', *Industrial Welfare*, Vol. 44, no. 5, September–October 1962

Davison, R. B., 'Immigration and unemployment in the United Kingdom, 1955–1962', *British Journal of Industrial Relations*, Vol. 1, no. 1, February 1963

Davison, R. B., 'No place back home; a study of Jamaicans returning to Kingston, Jamaica', *Race*, Vol. 9, no. 4, April 1968

Davison, R. B., *Black Mother: Africa and the Atlantic Slave Trade* (Harmondsworth, Penguin Books, 1980)

Deakin, N., 'Immigration and British Politics', *Crucible*, May 1965

Deakin, N., *The Government's White Paper on Immigration: some comments on the section dealing with controls* (London, The Author, August 1965)

Deakin, N., *Colour and the British Electorate* (London, OUP, 1965)

Deakin, N., 'Britain – the 1966 General Election', *IRR Newsletter*, April 1966

Deakin, N., 'Colour and the 1966 General Election', *Race*, Vol. 8, no. 1, July 1966

Deakin, N., 'British Voters and the Immigration Issue', *IRR Newsletter*, March 1967 Supp.

Deakin, N., 'The Politics of the Commonwealth Immigrants Bill', *Political Quarterly*, Vol. 39, no. 1, January/March 1968

Deakin, N., 'Labour adopts a white Britain policy', *Venture*, Vol. 20, no. 4, April 1968

Deakin, N., 'The politics of integration: policies and practice', (London, IRR, 1969)

Deakin, N., 'Enoch's Flood', *Venture*, Vol. 21, no. 4, April 1969

Debrunner, H. W., *Presence and Prestige: Africans in Europe* (Basel Basler Afrika Bibliographien, 1979)

'Declaration', Black Trade Unionists Solidarity Movement, December 1981

Deedes, W., *Race Without Rancour* (London, Conservative Political Centre, August 1968)

Deer, N., *The History of Sugar*, 2 vols. (London, Chapman & Hall, 1949–50)

Defoe, Daniel, *Moll Flanders* (Abbey Classics Edition, London, n.d.)

De Muth, C. *Sus: A Report on the Vagrancy Act 1824* (London, Runnymede Trust, 1978)

Dennis, R., 'The Decline of Manufacturing Employment in Greater London 1966–74', *Urban Studies*, Vol. 15, no. 1 (University of Glasgow, 1978)

Desai, R., *Indian immigrants in Britain* (London, Oxford University Press, 1963)

De Silva, K. M., *Social Policy and Missionary Organisations in Ceylon, 1840–1855* (London, Longmans, 1965)

de Trafford, D. H., 'Racial integration in the field of employment', *Journal of the Royal Society of Arts*, Vol. 116, April 1968

'Devaluation of the British Passport', *Life*, Vol. 44, no. 5, March 1968

Dhesi, A., 'Some economic consequences of discrimination', *IRR Newsletter*, March 1969

Dhondy, M., 'The Strike at Imperial Typewriters', *Race Today*, July 1974

Dickey, A. F., 'English law and incitement to racial hatred', *Race*, Vol. 9, no. 3, January 1968

Dickey, A. F., 'Prosecutions under the Race Relations Act 1965', *Criminal Law Review*, 1968

Dickey, A. F., 'The Race Relations Act 1968', *IRR Newsletter*, November/December 1968

Dickey, A. F., 'The Race Relations Bill 1968', *IRR Newsletter*, April/May 1968

Dilke, Sir Charles, *Problems of Greater Britain* (London, Macmillan & Co. 1890)

Donnelly, L. (ed.), *Justice First* (London, Sheed & Ward, 1969)

Dorfman, G., *Government versus Trade Unionism in British Politics Since 1968* (London, Macmillan, 1979)

Dorfman, G., *British Trade Unionism Against the Trades Union Congress* (London, Macmillan, 1983)

Douglas, J. W. B., *Home and School: A Study of Ability and Attainment in the Primary School* (London, Panther, 1964)

Douglass, F. I., *Narrative of the Life of an American Slave* (Boston, Mass., Anti-Slavery Office, 1945)

Dow, G. A., *Slave Ships and Slaving* (Salem, Mass., Publications of the Marine Research Society, 1925)

Dowse, R. F., *Left in the Centre. The Independent Labour Party, 1893–1940* (London, Longmans, 1966)

Drake, St. Clair, J. G., *Value Systems, Social Structure and Race Relations in the British Isles* (Ph.D. Thesis, University of Chicago, 1954)

Drake, St. Clair, J. G., 'The "colour problem" in Britain: a study in social definitions', *Sociological Review*, Vol. 3, no. 2, December 1955

Drescher, S., 'Public Opinion and the Destruction of Colonial Slavery', in *Slavery and British Society, 1776–1846* (London, Macmillan, 1982)

Driver, G., 'Cultural competence, social power and school achievement: West Indian pupils in the West Midlands', *New Community*, Vol. VI, no. 3, 1978

Dromey, J. and Taylor, G., *Grunwick: The Workers' Story* (London, Lawrence & Wishart, 1978)

Drover, C., *Half-Caste* (London, Secker & Warburg, 1937)

DuBois, W. E. B., *The Souls of Black Folk* (Chicago, 1903)

DuBois, W. E. B., *Dusk of Dawn* (Harcourt Brace, New York, 1940)

DuBois, W. E. B., *The Autobiography of W. E. B. DuBois* (International Publishers, 1971)

Duffield, I., *Duse Mohamed Ali and the Development of Pan Africanism, 1866–1945* (Ph.D. Thesis, University of Edinburgh, 1971)

Duffield, I., 'Pan Africanism, rational and irrational', *Journal of African History*, Vol. XVIII, 1977

Duffield, I., 'Review of Reprints of *The Keys* and *The Black Man*', in *Journal of African History*, Vol. XIX, 1978

Duffield, I., *The Dilemma of Pan Africanism for Blacks in Britain, 1760–1950*, A paper presented to the International Conference on the History of Blacks in Britain, London, 28–30 September 1981

Dumbell, S., 'The beginnings of the Liverpool Cotton Trade', *Economic Journal*, Vol. XXXIV, 1924

Dummett, A., *A Portrait of Racism* (Pelican Books, 1973)

Dutt, R. P., 'Racialism and Reaction: notes of the month', *Labour Monthly*, Vol. 50, no. 6, June 1968

Dwarka Nath, *A History of Indians in British Guiana* (Edinburgh, 1950)

Edwards, A. J. and Batley, R., *The Politics of Positive Discrimination* (London, Tavistock, 1978)

Edwards, B., *The History of the British Colonies in the West Indies* (Dublin, Luke White, 1793)

Edwards, V. K., *The West Indian Language Issue in British Schools: Challenges and Responses* (London, Routledge & Kegan Paul, 1979)

Egan, P., *Life in London* (Sherwood Neely and Jones, 1821)

Eggington, J., *They Seek A Living* (London, Hutchinson, 1957)

Elkins, W. F., 'The Influence of Marcus Garvey on Africa; A British Report of 1922', *Science & Society*, Vol. XXXII, 1968

Elkins, W. F., 'Hercules and the Society of African Origin', *Caribbean Studies*, Vol. 1, no. 4, January 1972

Elmes, F., 'Coloured policemen', *Crime and Detection*, no. 1, June 1966

Elson, D. and Pearson, R., 'Nimble fingers make cheap workers: an analysis of women's employment in Third World export manufacturing', *Feminist Review*, no. 7, Spring 1981

Emecheta, B., *Second Class Citizen* (Fontana/Collins, 1974)

Engels, F., *The Origin of the Family, Private Property and the State* (London, Lawrence & Wishart, 1940)

Engels, F., *The Condition of the English Working Class* (Moscow, Progress Publishers, 1973)

Ennals, D., 'Labour's Race Relations Policy', *IRR Newsletter*, November/December 1968

Epps, A., *The Speeches of Malcolm X* (London, Peter Owen, 1969)

Equiano, O., *The Interesting Narrative of the Life of Olaudah Equiano or Gustavus Vassa, the African written by Himself*, 2 vols. (London, 1789)

Erickson, E. L., 'The Introduction of East Indian Coolies into the British West Indies', *Journal of Modern History*, June 1934

Esedebe, P. O., *A History of the Pan African Movement in Britain, 1900–1948*, (Ph.D. Thesis, University of London, 1968–69)

Evans, N., 'The South Wales Race Riots of 1919', *Journal of the Society for the Study of Welsh Labour History*, Spring 1980

Evans, P., *Immigration – the role of the Press*, (CIBA Foundation, London, Churchill 1966)

Evans, R. W., 'How the anomaly arose', *Venture*, Vol. 20, no. 4. April 1968

Fanon, F., *The Wretched of the Earth* (London, MacGibbon & Kee, 1965)

Field, J., 'The polls and race relations', *Race Today*, Vol. 1, no. 2, June 1969

Fielding, N., *The National Front* (London, Routledge & Kegan Paul, 1981)

File, N. and Power, C., *Black Settlers in Britain 1555 – 1958* (London, Heinemann Educational Books, 1981)

Flanders, A., *Industrial Relations: what is wrong with the system?* (London, Faber, 1965)

Fletcher, M. E., *Report of an Investigation into the Colour Problem in*

Liverpool and other Ports 1930 (Issued by the Liverpool Association for the Welfare of Half-caste Children, Liverpool, 1930)

Flett, H., 'Dispersal policies in council housing: arguments and evidence', *New Community*, Vol. VII, 1979

Fisher, G. and Joshua, H., 'Social policy and black youth', in E. Cashmore and B. Troyna (eds), *Black Youth in Crisis* (London, Allen & Unwin, 1982)

FitzHerbert, K., *West Indian Children in London* (London, G. Bell, 1967)

Fogelson, R. M., *Violence as a Protest: A Study of Riots and Ghettoes* (New York Garden City, Doubleday & Co., 1971)

Foner, N., 'Women, Work and Migration: Jamaicans in London', *New Community*, Vol. 5, nos. 1–2, 1976

Foner, N., *Jamaica Farewell* (London, Routledge & Kegan Paul, 1977)

Foot, P., *The Strike at Courtaulds, Preston* (London, IRR, July 1965)

Foot, P., *Immigration and Race in British Politics* (London, Penguin Books, 1965)

Ford, A. A., *Telling the Truth: the Life and Times of the British Honduran Forestry Unit in Scotland 1941–1944* (London, Karia Press, 1985)

Foster, W. Z., *History of the Communist Party of the United States* (New York, International Publishers, 1952)

Fox, A., *Industrial Sociology and Industrial Relations* (HMSO, 1966, Donovan Commission Research Paper no. 3)

FoxBourne, H. R., *English Merchants: Memoirs in Illustration of the Progress of British Commerce* (Edward Bentley, 1866)

Frost, T., *Forty Years Recollections: Literary and Political* (London, 1880)

Fryer, P., *Staying Power: The History of Black People in Britain* (London, Pluto Press, 1984)

Fuller, M., 'Young, Female and Black' in *Black Youth in Crisis* (Allen & Unwin, 1982)

Fyfe, C., *A History of Sierra Leone* (Oxford University Press, 1962)

Galenson, D., 'The Slave Trade to the English West Indies, 1673–1724', *Economic History Review*, 2nd ser., Vol. XXXII, 1979

Gallop, G. I., 'Introduction', *Pig's Meat: The Selected Writings of Thomas Spence, Radical and Pioneer Land Reformer* (Nottingham, 1982)

Gammage, R. G., *The History of the Chartist Movement* (London, Holyoake & Co., 1862)

Gandhi, M. K., *The Collected Works of Mahatma Gandhi* (Delhi, 1958)

Gangulee, N., *Indians in the Empire Overseas: A Survey* (London, 1947)

Garchedi, G., 'Authority and Foreign Labour: some notes on a later capitalist form of capital accumulation and state intervention', *Studies in Political Economy*, no. 2, 1979

Garvey, Amy Jacques, *Philosophy and Opinions of Marcus Garvey* (New York, Universal Publishing House, 1923)

Gayle, C. H., 'A Baptist Minister in Birmingham', *IRR Newsletter*, July/August 1966

Geiss, I., *The Pan African Movement* (London, Methuen & Co. Ltd, 1968)

Genovese, E., *Fruits of Merchant Capital: Slavery and Bourgeois Property in the Rise and Expansion of Capitalism* (Oxford University Press, 1983)

George, M. D., *English Social Life in the Eighteenth Century* (London, 1923)

George, M. D., *London Life in the Eighteenth Century* (London, Kegan Paul & Co., 1925)

Ghose, Z., *Confessions of a Native Alien* (London, Routledge & Kegan Paul, 1965)

Giles, R., *The West Indian Experience in British Schools: Multi-racial Education and Social Disadvantage in London* (London, Heinemann, 1977)

Gish, O., 'Colour and skill: British immigration, 1955–1968', *International Migration Review*, Vol. 3, no. 1, 1968

Glass, R. and Pollins, H., *Newcomers* (London Centre for Urban Studies and Allen & Unwin, 1960)

Goodman, B. (ed.), *The End of White World Supremacy: Four Speeches by Malcolm X* (New York, Merlin House, 1971)

Goodway, D., *London Chartism 1838–1848* (Cambridge University Press, 1982)

Gordon, Elise J., 'Mary Seacole – A Forgotten Nurse Heroine of the Crimea', *Midwife, Health Visitor and Community Nurse*, February 1975

Gorz, A., 'Immigrant labour', *New Left Review*, no. 61, 1970

Gottlieb, A. Z., *Indian and Pakistani immigrants in Great Britain since World War II* (Illinois, The Author, 1967)

Grant, J., *Sketches of London* (Sherwood Neely and Jones, 1821)

Gray, R., 'Race relations and the church in Britain', *Dublin Review*, Winter 1958–59

Greater London Council, *Racism Within Trade Unions* (Anti-Racist Trade Union Working Group, London GLC, November 1984)

Gregory, R., *India and East Africa* (Oxford Clarendon Press, 1971)

Grey, Earl, *The Colonial Policy of Lord John Russell's Administration* (London, 1853)

Griffith, J. A. G., *Coloured Immigrants in Britain* (London, OUP for the IRR, 1960)

Griffiths, P., *A Question of Colour* (London, Leslie Frewin, 1966)

Grigg, M., *The White Question* (London, Secker & Warburg, 1967)

Grimshaw, A. D., 'Factors contributing to colour violence in the United States and Britain', *Race*, Vol, 3, no. 2, May 1962

Gummer, S. and J. S., *When the Coloured People Come* (London, Oldbourne, 1966)

Gupta, P. S., *Imperialism and the British Labour Movement 1914–1964* (London, Macmillan, 1975)

Gwynn, J. B., 'Some economic aspects of immigration', *IRR Newsletter*, March 1965

Haig, Sir Wolseley (ed.), *The Cambridge History of India, III, Turks and Afghans* (Cambridge University Press, 1928)

Hall, S., *Policing The Crisis* (Macmillan, 1978)

Hammond, J. L. and B., *The Village Labourer 1760–1832* (London, Longmans & Co., 1911)

Hammond, J. L. and B., *The Town Labourer 1760–1832* (London, Longmans & Co., 1917)

Hammond, J. L. and B., *The Skilled Labourer, 1760–1832* (London, Longmans & Co., 1919)

Hancock, W. K., *Sonnets: The Sanguine Years, 1870–1914* (Cambridge, 1962)

Handysides, C. D., *West Indian integration in the Seventh Day Adventist Church in Britain*, B.Ed. Thesis, University of Reading, 1969

Harlow, V. T., *A History of Barbados, 1625–1685* (Oxford, 1926)

Harris, J. E., *The African Presence in Asia: Consequences of the East African Slave Trade* (Evanston, Ill., Northwestern University, 1971)

Harris, J. H., *Coolie Labour in the British Crown Colonies and Protectorates* (London, Edward Hughes & Co., 1910)

Harrison, B., 'Pubs', in H. J. Dyosand Michael Wolff, *The Victorian City: Images and Realities*, 2 Vols. (London, Henley and Burton, 1976)

Harrison, J. F. C., *The Second Coming: Popular Millenarianism, 1780–1850* (London & Henley, 1979)

Harrison, R. A., *Union Policy and Workplace Practice* (Runnymede Trust Industrial Unit, December 1970)

Hart, R., 'The Life and Resurrection of Marcus Garvey', *Race*, Vol. 9, 1967–68

Hartley, B., 'Immigrants and the youth service – eighteen months after the Hunt Report', *IRR Newsletter*, 1969

Hartmann, P. and Husband, C., 'The Mass Media and Racial Conflict' in S. Cohen and J. Young (eds), *The Manufacture of News*, (Constable, 1973)

Hartmann, P. and Husband, C., *Racism and the Mass Media* (London, Davis Poynter, 1974)

Harvey, T. and Brewin, T., *Jamaica in 1866: A Narrative of a Tour through the Island* (London, 1867)

Hashmi, F., *The Pakistani Family in Britain* (London, NCCI, 1967)

Hassan, L. and Dick, T., 'Health workers after the strike', *Race Today*, March/April 1983

Hatch, S., 'Coloured People in School Textbooks', *Race*, Vol. 4, no. 1, 1962

Hay, D. *et al.*, *Albions Fatal Tree: Crime and Society in Eighteenth Century England* (London, Allen & Lane, 1975)

Hebdige, D., *Subculture, the Meaning of Style* (London, Methuen, 1979)

Hecht, J. J., *Continental and Colonial Servants in Eighteenth Century England* (London, 1854)

Heginbotham, H., 'Young Immigrants and Work', *IRR Newsletter*, May 1967

Heineman, B., *The Politics of the Powerless* (London, Oxford University Press, 1972)

Helweg, A., *Sikhs in England* (Oxford University Press, 1979)

Henderson, I., *The Attitude and Policy of the Main Sections of the British Labour Movement to Imperial Issues, 1899–1924* (B.Litt., Thesis, Oxford University, 1965)

Henriques, F., *Family and Colour in Jamaica* (London, Eyre & Spottiswoode, 1953)

Hepple, B., 'Race Relations Act 1965', *Modern Law Review*, Vol. 29, no. 3, May 1966

Hepple, B., *Race, Jobs and the Law in Britain* (Allen Lane & Penguin Press, 1968)

Hepple, B., 'Street Report on anti-discrimination legislation and Wilson Report on Immigration appeals', *Modern Law Review*, Vol. 31, no. 3, May 1968

Hepple, B., 'Commonwealth Immigrants Act 1968', *Modern Law Review*, Vol. 31, July 1968

Hepple, B., 'The British Race Relations Acts, 1965 and 1968', *University of Toronto Law Journal*, 1969

Hepple, B., 'Race Relations Act 1968', *Modern Law Review*, Vol. 32, no. 2, March 1969

Hill, C. S., *Black and White in Harmony* (London, Hodder and Stoughton, 1958)

Hill, C. S., *West Indian Migrants and the London Churches* (London, OUP for the IRR, 1963)

Hill, C. S., 'Colour in Britain: a Christian viewpoint', *Congregational Monthly*, September 1965

Hill, C. S., *Immigration and Integration* (Oxford, Pergamon Press, 1970)

Hill, C. S., *Black Churches* (London, British Council of Churches, Community & Race Relations Unit, 1971)

Hill, C. and Matthews, D. (eds), *Race: a Christian Symposium* (London, Victor Gollancz, 1968)

Hill, R. A., 'The First England Years and After', in John Henrik Clarke (ed.) with the assistance of Amy Jacques Garvey, *Marcus Garvey and the Vision of Africa* (New York, 1974)

Hill, R. A., *Zion on the Zambesi, Dr. J. Albert Thorne, A Descendant of Africa, of Barbados and the African Colonial Enterprise: The Preliminary Stage 1894–97*, Paper presented to the International

Conference on Blacks in Britain, London, 28–30 September 1981

Hill, R. A., 'In England, 1932–1938' *Urgent Tasks*, no. 12, Summer 1981

Hill, R. A. (ed.), *The Marcus Garvey and Universal Negro Improvement Association Papers* (University of California Press 1983)

Hindell, Keith, 'The Genesis of the Race Relations Bill', *Political Quarterly*, October/December 1965

Hiro, D., 'The Asian Press in Britain', *New Society*, Vol. 9, June 1967

Hiro, D., 'Muslims in Britain', *New Society*, Vol. 10, 7 December 1967

Hiro, D., *Black British, White British* (London, Eyre & Spottiswoode, 1971)

Hobsbawm, E. J., *Primitive Rebels* (Manchester University Press, 1959)

Hobsbawm, E. J., *Industry and Empire* (London, Pelican Books, 1969)

Hobsbawm, E. J., *Labouring Men* (London, Wiedenfeld & Nicholson, 1973)

Hobsbawm, E. J., *The Age of Revolution* (London, Cardinal, 1973)

Holton, J. E., 'The status of the Coloured in Britain', *Phylon*, Vol. 22, no. 1, 1961

Hone, A., *For the Cause of Truth: Radicalism in London*, 1796–1821 (Oxford, 1892)

Hooker, J. R., *Black Revolutionary* (London, Pall Mall Press, 1967)

Hooker, J. R., *Henry Sylvester Williams: Imperial Pan Africanist* (London, Rex Collings, 1975)

Hooks, Bell, *Ain't I A Woman* (South End Press, 1981)

Hooper, R. (ed.), *Colour in Britain* (London, British Broadcasting Corporation, 1965)

Howard, R. M. (ed.), *Records and Letters of the Journal of the Longs of Longville, Jamaica and Hampton Lodge, Surrey* (London, 1925)

Hoyland, J. S., *Gopal Krishma Gokhale: His Life and Speeches* (Calcutta, YMCA Publishing House, 1933)

Hughes, J. L. and Larkin, J. F. (eds), *Tudor Royal Proclamations 1588–1603*, Vol. 3, 'Licensing Casper Van Senden to deport Negroes' (1601) Yale University Press, 1969

Hughes, R., 'Immigrants and the Churches', *Alta, The University of Birmingham Review*, no. 4, 1967–68

Humphrey, D. and John, G., *Because They're Black* (Penguin, 1971)

Humphrey, D., *Police Power and Black People* (London, Panther, 1972)

Humphrey, D. and Ward, M., *Passports and Politics* (Penguin Books, 1974)

Hunt, J., 'Race Relations in Britain: the decisive decade', *Patterns of Prejudice*, Vol. 1, no. 6, November/December 1967

Hunte, J. A., *Nigger Hunting in England* (London, April 1966)

Hunter, K., *History of Pakistanis in Britain* (London, The Author, 1962)

Husband, C. (ed.), *White Media and Black Britain* (London, Arrow, 1975)

Hussain, A., 'Pakistan takes immigration lightly', *New Society*, Vol. 6, November 1963

Huttenback, R. A., *Gandhi and South Africa: British Imperialism and the Indian Question 1860–1914* (Ithaca, 1971)

Huxley, E., *Back Street New Worlds* (London, Chatto and Windus, 1964)

Hyman, R., *Strikes* (Fontana/Collins, 1972)

Hynes, G., 'Why broadcast to immigrants? What is the role of television in a multi-racial society?', *Race Today*, Vol. 1, no. 1, May 1969

'Immigrants and the Police', *Race Today*, Vol. 1, no. 2, June 1969

'Immigration appeals – the long uncertain wait', *IRR Newsletter*, November/December 1968

Institute of Race Relations (and Southall Rights), *Southall: Birth of a Black Community* (London, 1981)

Jain, R. K., *South Indians on the Plantation Frontier in Malaya* (New Haven, 1970)

James, C. L. R., *World Revolution, 1917–1936. The Rise and Fall of the Communist International* (London, Secker & Warburg, 1937)

James, C. L. R., *Black Jacobins* (London, Secker & Warburg, 1938)

James, C. L. R., *A History of Negro Revolt* (London, 1938)

James, C. L. R., *State Capitalism and World Revolution* (Detroit, Facing Reality Publishing Committee, 1956)

James, C. L. R., *Beyond A Boundary* (London, Hutchinson, 1963)

James, C. L. R., *Nkrumah and the Ghana Revolution* (London, Allison and Busby, 1977)

James, C. L. R., *Notes on Dialectics* (London, Allison and Busby, 1983)

James, C. L. R., 'An accumulation of blunders', *New Society*.

(For a comprehensive bibliography of James' writings see: *At the Rendezvous with Victory* (London, Allison & Busby, 1984)

James, E., *The Reverend Gentleman: West Indians and the Church in Britain* (Southend-on-Sea Citizen Press, 1962)

James, S., *Sex, Race and Class* (Falling Wall Press & Race Today Publications, 1975)

James, S., *Women, the Unions and Work* (London, London Wages for Housework Committee and Falling Wall Press, 1976)

Jenkins, J. I., *The Coolie; His Rights and Wrongs* (London, Strahan & Co., 1871)

Jenner, P., 'Some Speculations on the economics of Immigration', CIBA Foundation (London, Churchill, 1966)

Jenner, P. and Cohen, B., 'Economic Effects of Immigration', *IRR Newsletter*, November/December 1966

Jessup, F. W. and Coles, E. K., *International and Inter-Racial Under-*

standing: the contribution of adult education (London, National Institute of Adult Education, September 1967)

John, De Witt, 'Southall, Part II: Analysis of General Election Results', *IRR Newsletter*, April 1966 Supplement

John, De Witt, *Indian Workers Associations in Britain* (London, OUP, 1969)

Johnson, B., *'I Think of My Mother': notes on the life and times of Claudia Jones* (London, Karia Press, 1985)

Johnson, R., 'Three Problematics: Elements on Theory of Working Class Culture', in *Working Class Culture* (Hutchinson, 1979)

Jones, C. *et al.*, *Race and the Press* (London, Runnymede Trust, 1971)

Jones, E., *Othello's Countrymen: the African in English Renaissance Drama* (Oxford University Press, 1965)

Jones, E., *The Elizabethan Image of Africa* (Charlottesville, University Press of Virginia, 1971)

Jones, K., *Immigrants and Social Services* (London, National Institute of Economic Review, 1967)

Jones, K. and Smith, A. D., *The Economic Impact of Commonwealth Immigration* (Cambridge, NIESR, 1970)

Jones, M., 'Turned Back at the Gate: How Our Officials Keep Out Commonwealth Immigrants', *New Statesman*, 10 March 1967

Joseph, G., 'The Incompatible Ménage à Trois: Marxism, Feminism and Racism', in Lydia Sargent (ed.), *Women and Revolution* (London, Pluto Press, 1981)

Joshua, H. and Wallace, T., *To Ride The Storm* (London, Heinemann Educational Books, 1983)

Karnik, V. B., *Indian Trade Unions – A Survey* (Bombay, Manaktalas, 1960

Katznelson, I., *Black Men, White Cities* (London, OUP, 1973)

Katznelson, I., 'Community, capitalist development and the emergence of class', *Politics and Society*, Vol. 4, no. 7, 1977

Keer, D., *Shahu Chhatrapati* (Bombay, Popular Prakashan, 1976)

Kettle, M. and Hodges, L., *Uprising: The Police, the People and the Riots in Britain's Cities* (London, Pan, 1982)

The Keys: Reprints of Vols. 1–7 with an Introductory Essay by R. J. MacDonald (New York, Kraus Thomson Organisation, 1976)

Khaliq, S. A., 'Pakistanis in Britain', *Plebs*, Vol. 58, no. 3, 1966

Kimble, D., *A Political History of Ghana. The Rise of Gold Coast Nationalism, 1850–1928* (Oxford, Clarendon Press, 1963)

Kinder, C., *West Indians in Moss Side: The Effectiveness of Voluntary Organisations in Integrating West Indians* (B.Litt. Thesis, Oxford University, 1966)

Kingsley, Charles, *Alton Locke, Tailor and Poet* (New York, Harper and Brothers, 1850)

Kingsley, Charles, *At Last: A Christmas in the West Indies* (London, 1871)

Kirkaldy, A. W., *British Shipping, its History, Organisation and Importance* (London, Kegan Paul, 1914)

Klass, M., *East Indians in Trinidad: A Study of Cultural Persistence* (New York and London, 1961)

Klugmann, J., *A History of the Communist Party of Great Britain* (London, 1968–69)

Knighton, W., *Forest Life in Ceylon* (London, Hurst & Blackett, 1854)

Knowles, K. G., *Strikes – A Study in Industrial Conflict* (Oxford, Basil Blackwell, 1952)

Knox, T. R., 'Thomas Spence: The Trumpet of Jubilee', *Past and Present*, Vol. 76, 1977

Kopelov, C., 'Education on racial issues', *IRR Newsletter*, April/May 1968

Kosmin, B. A., 'J. R. Archer 1863–1932: A Pan Africanist in the Battersea Labour Movement', *New Community*, Vol. VII, no. 3, 1979

Krasso, N., 'Trotsky's Marxism', *New Left Review*, no. 44, July–August 1967

Kushnick, L., 'The Act must be effective', *Venture*, Vol. 20, no. 4, April 1968

Kushnick, L., 'The race bill battle', *New Society*, Vol. 11, 27 June 1968

Kushnick, L., 'Creeping Racism in England', *Liberator*, Vol. 9, no. 8, August 1969

La Guerre, J. (ed.), *From Calcutta to Caroni* (London, Longman, 1974)

La Guerre, J., *The Social and Political Thought of the Colonial Intelligentsia* (Institute of Social and Economic Research, University of the West Indies, Mona, Jamaica, 1982)

Langley, J. A., *West African Aspects of Pan African Movements* (Ph.D. Thesis, Edinburgh University, 1968)

Langley, J. A., 'Pan Africanism in Paris, 1924–1936', *Journal of Modern African Studies*, Vol. 7, no. 1, 1969

Langley, J. A., *Pan Africanism and Nationalism in West Africa 1900–1945* (Oxford, Clarendon Press, 1973)

Langley, J. O., 'Garveyism and African Nationalism', *Race*, Vol. XI, no. 2, October 1969

Lash, C., 'The Trouble with Black Power', *New York Review of Books*, Vol. X, no. 4, February 1968)

Latimer, J., *Annals of Bristol in the Nineteenth Century* (Bristol, 1887)

Latimer, J., *The History of the Society of Merchant Venturers of the City of Bristol* (1903)

Law, I. and Henfrey, J., *A History of Racism in Liverpool, 1660–1950* (Liverpool, Merseyside Community Relations Council, 1981)

Law, I and Loy, L., *A History of Racism and Resistance in Liverpool*. Paper presented to the International Conference on the History of Blacks in Britain, London, 28–30 September 1981

Lawrence, D., 'Race Riots in Britain?' *Socialist Commentary*, March 1966

Layton-Henry, Z., *The Politics of Race in Britain* (London, Allen & Unwin, 1984)

Le Bon, G., *The Crowd: a Study of the Popular Mind* (London, T. Fisher Unwin, 1896)

Lee, F. F., 'Racial patterns in a British city: an institutional approach', *Phylon*, Vol. 21, no. 7, 1960

Lee, J. M., *Colonial Development and Good Government* (Oxford, Clarendon Press, 1967)

Leech, K., *Brick Lane 1978: The Events and Their Significance* (Birmingham, 1980)

'Legislation against racialism – Belgium, Britain, Canada', *Patterns of Prejudice*, Vol. 1, no. 1, 1967

Le Lohé, M., 'By-election in Bradford', *IRR Newsletter*, April/May 1968

Le Lohé, M. and Goldman, A., 'Race in local politics: the Rochdale Central Ward Election of 1968', *Race*, Vol. 10, no. 4, April 1969

Lenin, V. I., *Imperialism* (New York, Vanguard Press, 1926)

Lenin, V. I., *British Labour and British Imperialism* (London, Lawrence & Wishart, 1969)

Leonard, E. M., *The Early History of English Poor Relief* (Cambridge, 1906)

Lester, A., 'Racial Discrimination and the Law', *IRR Newsletter*, May/June 1965

Lester, A., 'Labour's White Problem', *Socialist Commentary*, June 1966

Lester, A., 'The Act and the British Constitution', *IRR Newsletter*, May/June 1968

Lester, A. and Bindman, G. I., *Race and the Law* (Penguin, 1972)

Lewis, G., 'Race Relations in Britain: A View from the Caribbean', *Race Today*, Vol. 1, no. 3, July 1969

Lewis, G. K., *Slavery, Imperialism and Freedom* (New York and London, Monthly Press, 1978)

Lewis, P. C., 'Cardiff Report – General Survey', *The Keys*, Vol. III, no. 2, October–December 1935

Lewis, P. C. and Brown, G. W., 'We too were in Cardiff', *The Keys*, Vol. III, no. 1, July–September 1935

Lewis, R. I., *Real Trouble! a Study of the Southall Trials* (London, Runnymede Trust, 1980)

Lindfors, Bernth, *The Hottentot Venus and Other Attractions in Nineteenth Century England*. Paper presented to the International Conference of Blacks in Britain, London, 28–30 September 1981

Little, K., *Negroes in Britain* (London, Kegan Paul, 1947)

Little, K., 'The Role of Voluntary Associations in West African Urbanization', *American Anthropologist*, Vol. 59, no. 4, 1957

Long, Edward, *The History of Jamaica* (London, T. Lowndnes, 1774)

Long, James (ed.), *Selections from Unpublished Records of Government 1748–1767 Relating Mainly to the Social Condition of Bengal* (Calcutta, 1869)

Lorimer, D., *Colour, Class and the Victorians* (London, Leicester University Press, 1978)

Lovell, J., *British Trade Unions, 1875–1933* (London, Macmillan, 1977)

Low, D., *Thieves Kitchen: The Regency Underworld* (London, Dent, 1982)

Lubbock, B., *Coolie Ships and Oil Sailers* (Glasgow, Brown, Son & Ferguson, 1935)

Lynch, H., *Edward Wilmot Blyden: Pan Negro Patriot 1832–1912* (Oxford University Press, 1967)

McCalman, I. D., 'Popular Radicalism and Freethought in Early Nineteenth Century London: A Study of Richard Carlile and His followers, 1815–32', Australian National University, M.A., 1975

McCalman, I. D., 'A Radical Underworld in Early Nineteenth-century London: Thomas Evans, Robert Wedderburn, George Cannon and their Circle, 1800–35', Monash University, Ph.D. Thesis 1984

McCalman, I. D., 'Unrespectable Radicalism: Infidels and Pornography in Early Nineteenth Century London', *Past and Present*, August 1984

McCarthy, W. E. J., *The Role of Shop Stewards in British Industrial Relations* (London, HMSO, 1966)

Maccoby, S., *English Radicalism, 1786–1832* (London, George Allen & Unwin, 1955)

McConville, M. and Baldwin, J., *Courts, Prosecutions and Convictions* (Oxford, Clarendon Press, 1981)

Macdonald, I., 'The Capitalist Way To Curb Discrimination', *Race Today*, August 1973

Macdonald, I. A., *Race Relations and Immigration Law* (London, Butterworths, 1969)

Macdonald, R. J., 'Dr. Harold Moody and the League of Coloured Peoples 1931–1947: A Retrospective View', *Race*, Vol. XIV, no. 3, 1973

Macdonald, R. J., 'The Wisers are Far Away . . . The Role of London's Black Press in the 1930s and 1940s'. Paper presented to the International Conference on the History of Blacks in Britain, London, September 1981

MacInnes, Colin, 'The Case of Michael X', *New Society*, Vol. 10, December 1967

MacInnes, Colin, *Visions of London* (London, McGibbon & Kee, 1969)

MacInnes, C. M., *Bristol, A Gateway of Empire* (Bristol, 1939)

McIntosh, N. and Smith, D. J., *The Extent of Racial Discrimination* (London, Butterworths, 1969)

McKay, C., *A Long Way From Home* (New York, Arno Press and New York Times, 1969)

Mackenzie, 'Radical Pan Africanism in the 1930s: A Discussion with C. L. R. James', *Radical History Review*, no. 24, Fall 1980

Mackey, H., 'The Complexion of the Accused': William Davidson, The Black Revolutionary in the Cato Street Conspiracy of 1820', *Negro Educational Review*, Vol. XXIII, 1972

Mackie, L. and Pattullo, P., *Women and Work* (London, Tavistock Publications, 1977)

McNeal, J., 'Education', in S. Abbott (ed.), *The Prevention of Racial Discrimination in Britain* (London, Oxford University Press, 1971)

McPherson, Sir John, *Development and Welfare in the West Indies, 1945–46* (HMSO, 1946)

Majumder, R. C., *History of the Freedom Movement in India* (Calcutta, Firma K. L. Mukhopadhyay, 1962)

Makonnen, Ras, *Pan Africanism From Within* (ed.) Kenneth King (London, OUP, 1973)

Malik, M. A., *From Michael de Freitas to Michael X* (London, Andre Deutsch, 1968)

Mangat, J. S., *A History of Asians in East Africa, c. 1886 to 1945* (Oxford 1945)

Manley, D. R., *The Social Structure of the Liverpool Negro Community with Special Reference to the Formation of Formal Associations* (Ph.D. Thesis, University of Liverpool 1958–59)

Mansukani, G. S., *The Quintessence of Sikhism* (Amritsar, Shiromani Gurdwara Parbandhak Committee, 1965)

Margery, P., *Industrial South Wales*, 1940

Mark, Sir Robert, *In the Office of Constable* (London, Collins, 1978)

Marquand, H. A., *An Industrial Survey of South Wales*, 3 vols. (University Press Board, 1937)

Marryat, J., *More Thoughts Occasioned by Two Publications* (J. W. Richardson, 1816)

Marsh, P., 'What Went Wrong at Woolf's' (Supplement to *IRR Newsletter*, January 1967)

Marshall, R., 'Equal Rights', *IRR Newsletter*, April/May 1968

Martin, L. L., 'West Indian Pupil Nurses and their problems in Training', *Nursing Times*, Vol. 61, August 1965

Martin, T., 'C. L. R. James and the Race Class Question', *Race*, Vol. XIV, 1972–73

Martin, T., *The Pan African Connection* (Cambridge, Mass., Shenkman, 1983)

Marx, Karl, *Capital*: A Critical Analysis of Capitalist Production, translated from the Third German Edition by Samuel Moore and Edward Aveling (eds) by Friederich Engels (Swan Sonnerschein & Co., Ltd, London 1896)

Marx, Karl, *Introduction to a Critique of Hegel's Philosophy of Right*

Masani, R. P., *Dadabhai Naoroji: The Grand Old Man of India* (London, Allen & Unwin, 1939)

Mason, D., *et al.*, *News from Notting Hill: the formation of a group ministry* (London, Epworth Press, 1967)

Mason, P., 'A democratic dilemma: consensus and leadership', *Race*, Vol. 10, no. 4, April 1969

Mathur, A. S. and J. S., *Trade Union Movement in India* (Allahabad, Chaitanya Publishing House, 1962)

Mathurin, O. C., *Henry Sylvester Williams and the Origins of the Pan African Movement, 1868–1911* (Greenwood Press, Westport and London, 1976)

Mattelart, A., *Mass Media, Ideologies and the Revolutionary Movement* (Harvester Press, 1980)

Maunder, W. F., 'The New Jamaican Emigration', *Social and Economic Studies*, Vol. 4, no. 1, March 1955

May, R. and Cohen, R., 'The Interaction Between Race and Colonialism: A Study of the Liverpool Race Riots of 1919', *Race and Class*, Vol. XVI, 1974

Maxwell, N., *The Power of Negro Action* (London, 1965)

Mehotra, S. R., *The Emergence of the Indian National Congress* (Delhi, Vikas Publications, 1971)

Menon, K. P. S., 'Indian Labour in Ceylon', *Ceylon Economic Journal*, December 1932

Merivale, H., *Lectures on Colonisation and Colonies* (London, 1839)

Miles, R., *Between Two Cultures? The Case for Rastafarianism* (Bristol SSRC Research Unit on Ethnic Relations, 1978)

Miles, R., *Racism and Migrant Labour* (London, Routledge & Kegan Paul, 1982)

Miles, R. and Phizacklea, A., *The TUC, Black Workers and Commonwealth Immigration 1954–1973* (Working Papers on Ethnic Relations no. 6 SSRC 1977)

Miles, R. and Phizacklea, A., *Racism and Political Action in Britain* (London, Routledge and Kegan Paul, 1979)

Miles, R. and Phizacklea, A., 'Working Class Racist Beliefs in the Inner City' in R. Miles and A. Phizacklea (eds), *Racism and Political Action in Britain* (London, Routledge & Kegan Paul, 1979)

Miles, R. and Phizacklea, A., *Labour and Racism* (London, Routledge & Kegan Paul, 1980)

Miles, R. and Phizacklea, A., 'The TUC and Black Workers 1974–1976', *British Journal of Industrial Relations*, Vol. XVI (2)

Miles, R. and Phizacklea, A., 'Class, Race Ethnicity and Political Action', *Political Studies*, Vol. XXV

Mill, J. S., 'The Nigger Question', *Fraser's Magazine*, January 1850

Millner, R., 'Racism and the law', *Labour Monthly*, July 1965

Milner, D., *Children and Race* (Penguin Books, 1975)

Mishan, E. J., 'Immigration: some economic effects', *Lloyds Bank Review*, no. 81, July 1966

Mishan, E. J., 'Immigration: long-run economic effects', *Lloyds Bank Review*, no. 87, January 1968

Mishan, E. J. and Needleman, L., 'Immigration, excess aggregate demand and the balance of payments', *Economica*, May 1966

Mitchell, H., *Caribbean Patterns* (W & R Chambers, London and Edinburgh, 1967)

Monolulu, Ras Prince, *I Gotta Horse* (London, Hurst & Blackett, 1950)

Moody, Harold, *Youth and Race* (British Christian Endeavour Union, London, 1936)

Moody, Harold, *Christianity and Race Relations* (London, Fellowship of Recognition Pamphlet Series no. 20, 1943)

Moody, Harold, *The Colour Bar* (London, St. Luke's College, New Mildmay Press, 1945)

Moore, R., 'Labour and Colour: 1965–1968', *IRR Newsletter*, October 1968

Moore, R. and Wallace, T., *Slamming The Door: The Administration of Immigration Control* (London, Martin Robertson, 1975)

Moreland, W. H. and Chatterjee, A. C., *A Short History of India* (London, 1936)

Moreley, J., 'Can white management cope with coloured workers?', *Business*, Vol. 96, no. 8, August 1966

Morris, M., *The General Strike* (Penguin Books, 1976)

Morris, R. J., *Class and Class Consciousness in the Industrial Revolution 1780–1850* (London, Macmillan, 1979)

Morris, Sam, 'Moody – the forgotten visionary', *New Community*, Vol. 3, Spring 1972

Mowat, C., *Britain Between The Wars* (London, Methuen, 1955)

Mukherjee, R., *The Rise and Fall of the East India Company* (London, Monthly Review Press, 1974)

Mullard, C., *Black Britain* (London, Allen & Unwin, 1973)

Mumford, L., *The City in History* (London, Secker & Warburg, 1961)

Musson, A. E., *British Trade Unions 1800–1875* (London, Macmillan, 1972)

Naipaul, V. S., *A House For Mr. Biswas* (London, Andre Deutsch, 1961)

Namier, L. B., *The Structure of Politics at the Accession of George III* (London, 1929)

Nanda, B. R., *Socialism in India* (London, Vikas Publications, 1972)

Nanda, B. R., *Gokhale, Gandhi and the Nehrus: Studies in Indian Nationalism* (London, Allen & Unwin, 1974)

Nanda, B. R., *Gokhale: The Indian Moderates and the British Raj* (Delhi and London, OUP, 1977)

Nandy, D., 'Immigrants and the election' *Labour Monthly*, October 1964

Nandy, D., 'Discrimination and the law', *Labour Monthly*, January 1967

Naoroji, Dadabhai, *Essays, Speeches, Addresses and Writings of Dadabhai Naoroji* (Bombay, Caxton Printing Works, 1887)

National Committee for Commonwealth Immigrants (NCCI), *Towards A Multi-Racial Society* (London, NCCI, 1967)

NCCI, *Survey of Four London Newspapers* (London, NCCI, 1967)

NCCI, *Copy of Resolutions on White Paper: immigration from the*

Commonwealth. Cmnd 2739, received from the Voluntary Liaison Committees (London, NCCI, 1965)

National Council for Civil Liberties, *Civil Liberty and the Police* (London, NCCL, 1963)

Navain, I., *The Politics of Racialism: A Study of the Indian Minority in South Africa* (Agra, 1962)

N'Dem, E., *Negro Immigrants in Manchester*, M.A. dissertation, University of London, 1953

Nehru, J., *Autobiography* (London, John Lane, 1936)

Nicholson, M., *Government–Trade Union Co-operation in Colonial Labour Development 1925–1945*, Institute of Commonwealth Studies (London, 1975)

Nicholson, M., *The TUC and the West Indies Royal Commission*, Institute of Commonwealth Studies (London, 1976)

Nield, B. and Saville, J., 'Saklatvala' in J. Saville and J. Bellamy (eds), *Dictionary of Labour Biography*, Vol. VI (Macmillan, 1982)

Nikolinakos, M., 'Notes towards a general theory of migration in late capitalism', *Race and Class*, Vol. 17, no. 1, 1975

Nkrumah, Kwame, *The Autobiography of Kwame Nkrumah* (Edinburgh, Thomas Nelson & Sons, 1957)

Nkrumah, K., *Dark Days in Ghana* (London, Lawrence & Wishart, 1968)

Omvedt, G., *We Will Smash This Prison!* (London, Zed Press, 1980)

Padmore, G., *The Life and Struggles of Negro Toilers* (London, RILU, 1931)

Padmore, G., *How Britain Rules Africa* (London, Wishart Books, 1936)

Padmore, G., *Africa and World Peace* (London, Secker & Warburg, 1937)

Padmore, G., *The Voice of Coloured Labour* (Manchester, Panaf Service, International African Service Bureau Publication no. 7, 1945)

Padmore, G. (ed.), *Colonial and Coloured Unity: A Programme of Action. History of the Pan African Congress* (Manchester, Pan African Federation, 1948)

Padmore, G., *Africa – Britain's Third Empire* (London, Dennis Dobson, 1949)

Padmore, G. *The Gold Coast Revolution* (London, Dennis Dobson, 1953)

Padmore, G., *Pan Africanism or Communism? The Coming Struggle For Africa* (London, Dennis Dobson, 1956)

Padmore, G. and Cunard, N., *The White Man's Duty* (Manchester, Pan African Service Ltd, 1945)

Padmore, G. (with Pizer, D.), *How Russia Transformed Her Colonial Empire* (London, Dennis Dobson, 1946)

Paine, S., *Exporting Workers: The Turkish Case* (Cambridge University Press, 1974)

Palme Dutt, R., *The Labour International Handbook* (London, The Labour Publishing Company, 1921)

Palme Dutt, R., *Britain's Crisis of Empire* (London, Lawrence & Wishart, 1949)

Pannell, N. and Brockway, F., *Immigration: What is the Answer* (London, Routledge & Kegan Paul, 1965)

Parekh, Bikhu (ed.), *Colour, Culture and Consciousness* (London, Allen & Unwin, 1974)

Pares, R., *War and Trade in the West Indies 1739–1763* (Clarendon Press, Oxford, 1936)

Pares, R., *A West India Fortune* (London, Longmans, Green & Co., 1950)

Parkinson, C. N., *The Rise of the Port of Liverpool* (Liverpool University Press, 1952)

Parmar, P. and Mirza, N., 'Growing angry, growing strong', *Spare Rib*, no. III, October 1981

Parsinnen, T. M., 'Thomas Spence and the Origins of English Land Nationalization', *Journal of the History of Ideas*, Vol. 34, 1973

Parsinnen, T. M., 'The Revolutionary Party in London', *Bulletin of the Institute of Historical Research*, Vol. XLV

Partington, M., 'Race Relations Act 1965: a too restricted view', *Criminal Law Review*, September 1967

Parvate, T. V., *Bal Gangadhar Tilak* (Ahmedabad, Navajivan Publishing House, 1958)

Parvate, T. V., *Mahadev Govind Ranade: A Biography* (London, Asia Publishing House, 1964)

Patel, P., 'The U.K. Commonwealth Immigrants Act 1968: An East African Asian's View', *Migration Today*, no. 10, April 1968

Patterson, O., *The Sociology of Slavery: an analysis of the origin, development and structure of Negro slave society in Jamaica* (London, MacGibbon & Kee, 1967)

Patterson, S., 'A recent West Indian immigrant group in Britain', *Race*, Vol. 1, no. 2, May 1960

Patterson, S., *Dark Strangers* (London, Tavistock Publications, 1963)

Patterson, O., 'West Indians returning home', *Race*, Vol. 10, no. 1, July 1968

Patterson, S., *Immigration and Race Relations in Britain 1960–1967* (London, OUP, 1969)

Patterson, S., *Immigrants in Industry* (London, OUP, 1968)

Peach, C., 'West Indian Migration to Britain: the economic factors', *Race*, Vol. 7, no. 1, July 1965

Peach, C., *West Indian Migration to Britain: A Social Geography* (London, OUP, 1968)

Pearson, D. G., 'West Indian Communal Associations: some observations', *New Community*, Vol. 5.

Pearson, N., ' "Colour" and the Police', *The Criminologist*, Vol. 3, no. 10, November 1968

Pelling, H., *A History of British Trade Unionism* (London, Macmillan Press, 1963)

Pelling, H., *The British Communist Party. A Historical Profile* (London, Adam & Charles Black, 1968)

Penson, L. M., 'The London West India interest in the eighteenth century', *English Historical Review*, Vol. XXXVI, 1921

Penson, L. M., *The Colonial Agents of the British West Indies* (London, University Press, 1924)

Peppard, N., 'Migration: some British and European comparisons', *Race*, Vol. 6, no. 2, October 1964

Perkins, Revd Erasmus, *A Few Hints Relative to the Texture of Mind and the Manufacture of Conscience* (T. Davison c. 1820)

Perkins, Revd E. (ed.), *The Trial of the Rev. Robert Wedderburn (A Dissenting Minister of the Unitarian Persuasion) for Blasphemy* 1820

Phillips, J., *Kwame Nkrumah and the Future of Africa* (London, Faber & Faber, 1960)

Phillips, U. B., *Life and Labour in the Old South* (Boston, 1929)

Phizacklea, A. and Miles, R., 'The Strike at Grunwick', *New Community*, Vol. VI, no. 3, 1978

Phizacklea, A. and Miles, R., 'Working class racist beliefs in the inner city' in R. Miles and A. Phizacklea (eds), *Racism and Political Action in Britain* (London, Routledge & Kegan Paul, 1979)

Pinchbeck, I., *Women Workers and the Industrial Revolution 1750–1850* (London, Virago, 1981)

Plamenatz, J., 'Strangers in our midst', *Race*, Vol. 7, no. 1, July 1965

Polak, H., *The Indians of South Africa: Helots within the Empire* (Madras, 1909)

Political and Economic Planning (PEP), *Racial Discrimination* (London, PEP, 1967)

Popkess, A., 'The Racial Disturbances in Nottingham', *Criminal Law Review*, October 1960

Poulantzas, N., *Political Power and Social Classes* (London, New Left Books, 1973)

Powell, E., 'Speech of 20 April 1968', *Race*, Vol. 10, no. 1, July 1968

Powell, E., *Freedom and Reality* (London, Batsford, 1969)

Prem, D., *The Parliamentary Leper: Colour and British Politics* (Delhi, Everest Press, 1966)

Prezworski, A., 'Proletariat into class: the process of class formation from Kautsky's "The Class Struggle" to recent controversies', *Politics and Society*, Vol. 4, no. 7, 1977

Prince, Mary, *The History of Mary Prince: A West Indian Slave related by herself* (London, Westleigh and Davis; Edinburgh, Waugh and Innis, 1831)

Prosser, D. C., 'The Absorption of immigrants: a brief survey of the work of some Roman Catholic organisations in Britain', *IRR Newsletter*, December 1964 supp.

Prothero, I. J., 'Chartism in London', *Past and Present*, no. 44, August 1969

Prothero, I. J., 'William Benbow and the concept of the "General Strike"', *Past and Present*, Vol. 6, 3, 1974

Prothero, I. J., *Artisans and Politics in Early Nineteenth Century London* (Dawson, 1979)

Pryce, Ken, *Endless Pressure: A Study of West Indian Life Styles in Bristol* (London, Penguin Books, 1979)

Quarles, B., *The Negro in the American Revolution* (University of North Carolina Press, Chapel Hill, 1961)

Quarles, B., *Black Abolitionists* (New York, OUP, 1969)

'Race Riots', *Clare Market Review*, Vol. 54, no. 1, 1958–59

Race Today, 'Black workers and the trade unions', August 1973

Race Today 'Black women and nursing: A job like any other', August 1974

Race Today, 'Black women and the wage', May 1975

Race Today, 'Caribbean women and the black community', May 1975

Race Today, 'The Grunwick Strike: The Bitter Lessons', November/December 1977

Race Today, 'The state of play at Fords', May/June 1982. For articles on Blacks and the British Police see: 'Up Against the Police', July/August 1976; 'Southall: What is to be done', May/June 1979; 'From Bobby to Babylon', May/June 1980, November 1980 and February/March 1982

Race Today Collective, *The Struggle of Asian Workers in Britain* (London, 1983)

Radin, B., 'Coloured workers and British Trade Unions', *Race*, Vol. VIII, no. 2, 1966

Ragatz, L., *The Fall of the Planter Class in the British Caribbean 1763–1833* (New York, 1928)

Ragatz, L., *Absentee Landlordism in the British Caribbean 1750–1833* (Reprinted from 'Agricultural History' 1931)

Ramana, M. V. V., *Non-Violence in Politics* (Delhi, Frank Bros. & Co., 1958)

Ramdin, Ron, *From Chattel Slave To Wage Earner: A History of Trade Unionism in Trinidad and Tobago* (London, Martin, Brian & O'Keeffe, 1982)

Ramsay, Revd J., *An Essay on The Treatment and Conversion of African Slaves in the British Sugar Colonies* (James Phillips, 1784)

Ransford, H. E., 'Isolation, Powerlessness and Violence', in A. D. Grimshaw (ed.), *Radical Violence in the United States* (Chicago, Aldine, 1969)

Rao, V. D., 'The Habshis: India's Unknown Africans', *Africa Report*, Vol. XVIII, no. 5, September–October 1973

Ratcliffe, P., *Racism and Reaction* (London, Routledge and Kegan Paul, 1981)

Raynor, J. and Harden, J., *Equality and City Schools: Readings in Urban Education*, Vol. 2 (London, Routledge and Kegan Paul, 1973)

Reed, M. L., *Wordsworth: The Chronology of the Early Years 1770–1799* (Cambridge, Harvard University Press, 1967)

Reid, I. (pseud.), 'Britain's Race White Paper', *Venture*, Vol. 17, no. 8, September 1965

Reid, J., 'Employment of Negroes in Manchester', *Sociological Review*, Vol. 4, no. 2, December 1956

Reid, W. H., *The Rise and Dissolution of the Infidel Societies in this Metropolis . . .* (London, 1800)

Rex, J., *Race, Colonialism and the City* (London, Routledge & Kegan Paul, 1973)

Rex, J., 'Race and the Inner City', BBC/CRE, 1978)

Rex, J., 'West Indian and Asian Youth', in *Black Youth in Crisis* E. Cashmore and B. Troyna, (eds), (London, Allen & Unwin, 1982)

Rex, J. and Moore, R., *Race, Community and Conflict* (London, Oxford University Press, 1967)

Reynolds, R., *My Life and Crimes* (London, Jarrolds, 1956)

Richmond, A., 'Economic Insecurity and Stereotypes as Factors in Colour Prejudice', *The Sociological Review*, Vol. XLII, no. 8, 1950

Richmond, A. H., 'Relation between skill and adjustment of a group of West Indian Negro Workers in England', *Occupational Psychology*, Vol. 25, no. 3, 1951

Richmond, A. H., *Colour Prejudice in Britain* (London, Routledge & Kegan Paul, 1954)

Richmond, A. H., 'Immigration as a social process: the case of coloured colonials in the U.K.', *Social and Economic Studies*, Vol. 5, no. 2, 1956

Roberts, B., 'The Debate on Sus' in *Black Youth in Crisis* (London, Allen & Unwin, 1982)

Roberts, B. C., *Labour in the Tropical Territories of the Commonwealth* (London, LSE/Gordon Bell & Sons Ltd, 1964)

Roberts, G. W., *Some Aspects of Emigration from the West Indies to the United Kingdom* (London, IRR, 1968)

Robinson, C. J., 'Coming to terms: the Third World and the Dialectic of Imperialism', *Race and Class*, Vol. XXII, no. 1, 1980

Robinson, C. J., 'Black Intellectuals at the British Core: 1920s–1930s'. Paper presented to the International Conference on the History of Blacks in Britain, London, September 1981

Robinson, C. J., *Black Marxism: The Making of the Black Radical Tradition* (London, Zed Press, 1983)

Robinson, K., *The Dilemmas of Trusteeship Aspects of British Colonial Policy Between the Wars* (London, Oxford University Press, 1965)

Rodney, W., *How Europe Underdeveloped Africa* (London, Bogle L'Ouverture Publications, 1972)

Rogers, J., *Connexions: foreign places, foreign faces* (Harmondsworth, Penguin Books, 1968)

Rose, E. J. B. *et al.*, *Colour and Citizenship* (London, published for the IRR by OUP, 1969)

Rose, H., 'The Police and the Coloured Communities', *IRR Newsletter*, October 1968

Rose, R., 'Race Relations: U.S. and U.K.', *Venture*, Vol. 17, no. 3, March 1965

Roth, S. J., 'British race legislation and international law', *Patterns of Prejudice*, Vol. 2, no. 3, May/June 1968

Rothermund, D., *The Phases of Indian Nationalism* (Bombay, Nachiketa Publications, 1970)

Rothermund, I., *The Philosophy of Restraints* (Bombay, Popular Prakashan, 1963)

Roux, E., *Time Longer Than Rope. A History of the Black Man's Struggle For Freedom in South Africa* (Madison, University of Wisconsin Press, 1964)

Rowbotham, S., *Hidden From History: rediscovering women in history from the seventeenth century to the present* (London, Pluto Press, 1977)

Rowbotham, S., *Beyond the Fragments: Feminism and the Making of Socialism* (London, Merlin, 1980)

Rubery, 'Structured labour markets, worker organisation and low pay', *Cambridge Journal of Economics*, Vol. 2, no. 1, 1978

Rubin, G., 'The Traffic in Women: notes on the political economy of sex' in R. Reiter (ed.), *Toward an Anthropology of Women* (Monthly Review Press, 1975)

Ruck, S. (ed.), *The West Indian Comes To England* (London, Routledge & Kegan Paul, 1960)

Rude, G., *Paris and London in the Eighteenth Century* (London, Collins, 1970)

Rude, G., *Protest and Punishment: The Story of the Social and Political Protesters Transported to Australia, 1788–1868* (Oxford, Clarendon Press, 1978)

Rude, G., *The Crowd in History: A Study of Popular Disturbances in France and England 1730–1848* (London, Lawrence & Wishart, 1981)

Rudkin, O., *Thomas Spence and His Connection* (London, Allen & Unwin, 1927)

Runnymede Trust, 'Trade Unions and Immigrant Workers', in *New Community*, Vol. IV, no. 1, 1974–75

Runnymede Trust and Radical Statistics Group, *Britain's Black Population* (London, Heinemann Educational Books, 1980)

Saha, P., *Shapurji Saklatvala: A Short Biography* (Delhi, People's Publishing House, 1970)

Saha, P., *Emigration of Indian Labour 1833–1900* (Delhi, People's Publishing House, 1970)

Sandhu, K. S., *Indians in Malaya: Immigration and Settlement 1786–1957* (London, 1969)

Saville, J. and Briggs, A. (eds), *Essays in Labour History* (London, Macmillan, 1967)

Scarman, Lord, *The Brixton Disorders 10–12 April 1981* (London, Pelican, 1981)

Scholes, Theophilius E. Samuel, *The British Empire and Alliances: or, Britain's Duty to her Colonies and Subject Races* (London, 1899)

Scholes, T. E. S., *Chamberlain and Chamberlainism: his Fiscal Proposals and Colonial Policy* (London, 1903)

Scholes, T. E. S., *Glimpses of the Ages: or, the 'Superior' and 'Inferior' Races, so-called, Discussed on the Light of Science and History*, 2 vols (London, 1905, 1908)

Scobie, E., *Black Britannia* (Chicago, Johnson Publishing Co., 1972)

Scoble, J., *Hill Coolies: a brief exposure of the deplorable condition of the hill coolies in British Guiana and Mauritius* (London, 1840)

Scott, N., 'Towards a framework for analysing the costs and benefits of labour migration', *International Institute for Labour Studies Bulletin*, no. 2, February 1967

Seacole, M., *Wonderful Adventures of Mary Seacole in Many Lands*. Edited by W.J.S. (London, James Blackwood, 1853)

de Selincourt, E., *The Letters of William and Dorothy Wordsworth: The Middle Years* (Oxford, Clarendon Press, 1937)

de Selincourt, E., *The Letters of William and Dorothy Wordsworth: The Later Years 1820–1850* (Oxford Clarendon Press, 1939)

Selvon, S., *The Lonely Londoners* (London, Allan Wingate, 1956)

Selvon, S., *Ways of Sunlight* (London, MacGibbon & Kee, 1957)

Senior, C. and Manley, D., *A Report on Jamaican Migration to Great Britain to the Jamaican* Executive Council, Kingston, (Jamaica) Government Printer, 1955

Sewell, W. G., *The Ordeal of Free Labour in the British West Indies* (New York, Harper & Bros., 1861)

Seymour-Ure, C., *The Political Impact of the Mass Media* (London, Constable, 1974)

Sharp, N., 'Cardiff's Coloured Population', *The Keys*, Vol. 1, no. 3, October 1933

Sheridan, R. B., 'The Commercial and financial Organisation of the British Slave Trade, 1750–1807', *Economic History Review*, 2nd Ser., Vol. XI, 1958–59

Sheridan, R. B., *Sugar and Slavery: An Economic History of the British West Indies 1623–1775* (Baltimore, Johns Hopkins University Press, 1973)

Sherwood, H. N., 'Paul Cuffe', *Journal of Negro History*, Vol. VIII

Sherwood, M., *Many Struggles: West Indian Workers and Service Personnel in Britain 1939–1945* (London, Karia Press, 1985)

Shepperson, G., 'Notes on Negro American influences on the emergence of African Nationalism', *Journal of African History*, 1960

Shepperson, G., 'Pan Africanism and "Pan Africanism": some historical notes', *Phylon*, Vol. XXIII, 1962

Shepperson, G., 'The Plantation Revolution and the Industrial Revolution, 1625–1775', *Caribbean Studies*, Vol. IX, no. 3, October 1969

Shirsat, K., *Kaka Joseph Baptista* (Bombay, Popular Prakashan, 1974)

Shyllon, F. O., *Black Slaves in Britain* (London, Oxford University Press, 1974)

Shyllon, F. O., 'The Black Presence and Experience in Britain'. Paper presented to the International Conference on the History of Blacks in Britain, London, September 1981

Sibly, J., 'Black country villages', *IRR Newsletter*, May/June 1965

Simmons, J., *From Empire to Commonwealth* (London, Odhams Press Ltd, 1960)

Sington, D., 'The policeman and the immigrant', *New Society*, Vol. 7, no. 178, February 1966

Sivanandan, A. V., 'Put Politics in Command', *Race Today*, August 1973

Sivanandan, A. V., 'Race, Class and the State: the black experience in Britain', *Race and Class*, Vol. 17, no. 4, 1976

Sivanandan, A. V., *From Immigration to Induced Repatriation* (Race and Class Pamphlet no. 5 1978)

Sivanandan, A. V., 'Imperialism and Disorganic Development in the Silicone Age', *Race and Class*, Vol. XXI, no. 2, 1979

Sivanandan, A. V., 'Asian and Afro-Caribbean Struggles: From Resistance to Rebellion', in *A Different Kind of Hunger* (London, Pluto Press, 1982)

Smart, W., *Economic Annals of the Nineteenth Century* (London, Macmillan, 1910)

Smelser, N., *The Theory of Collective Behaviour* (London, Routledge, 1962)

Smith, D. J., *Racial Disadvantage in Employment* (PEP Report, 1974)

Smith, D. J., *The Facts of Racial Disadvantage* (London, PEP Report, 1976)

Smith, D. J., *Racial Disadvantage in Britain* (Harmondsworth, Penguin, 1977)

Smith. E. W., *Aggrey of Africa. A Study in Black and White* (London, Student Christian Movement Press, 1930)

Smith, J. T., *Vagabondia or Anecdotes of Mendicant Wanderers through the Streets of London* (1817)

Smithies, B. and Fiddick, P., *Enoch Powell on Immigration* (London, Sphere, 1969)

Spearman, D., 'The Anti-Powell Post-bag', *IRR Newsletter*, June 1968

Spiers, M. and Le Lohe, M. J., 'Pakistanis in the Bradford municipal election of 1963', *Political Studies*, Vol. 12, 1964

Squire, L., 'Training immigrants within industry', *Race Today*, Vol. 1, no. 2, June 1969

Stalin, J., *Marxism And The National And Colonial Question* (London, Lawrence & Wishart, 1947)

Stanhope, J., *The Cato Street Conspiracy* (London, Jonathan Cape, 1962)

Stark, H. A., *Calcutta in Slavery Days* (Calcutta, 1917)

Steadman-Jones, G., *Outcast London* (Oxford, 1971)

Steel, D., *No entry: the background and implications of the commonwealth immigrants Act 1968* (London, Hurst, 1969)

Stephenson, P., *Young Coloured People in Coventry: is the youth service meeting the challenge?* (Coventry CRC, 1969)

Stevens, W., *A Memoir of Thomas Martin Wheeler* (London, John Bedford Leno, 1862)

Stevenson, D. and Wallis, P., 'Second Generation West Indians: A Study in Alienation', *Race Today*, August 1970

Suda, J. P., *The Indian National Movement* (Meerut City, Jai Prakash Nath & Co., 1969)

Sunday Times, *The Race Problem in Great Britain: Teachers Manual* (London, Sunday Times, 1966)

Tahmankar, D. V., *Lokamanya Tilak: Father of Indian Unrest and Maker of Modern India* (John Murray, 1956)

Tawney, R. H., *Religion and the Rise of Capitalism* (London, J. Murray, 1936)

Taylor, S., *The National Front in English Politics* (London, Macmillan, 1982)

Teear, L., *The Labour Party and Commonwealth Immigration*, M.A. Thesis, University of Sussex 1966

Tendulkar, B. G., *Mahatma: Life of Mohandas Karamchand Gandhi* (Bombay, 1951–54)

Thomas, B., *The Economics of the Immigration White Paper* (London, IRR, April 1966)

Thomas, G., 'The Council Election in Southall – May 1968', *IRR Newsletter*, July 1968

Thomas, R. P., and Bean, R. N., 'The fishers of men: the profits of the slave trade', *Journal of Economic History*, Vol. XXXIV, 1974

Thomas, T., *Indians Overseas: A Guide to Source Materials* (London, The British Library, 1982)

Thompson. D., *The Chartists* (London, M. T. Smith, 1984)

Thompson, E. P., *The Making of the English Working Class* (London, Victor Gollancz, 1963)

Thompson, E. P., 'The Moral Economy of the English Crowd in the Eighteenth Century', *Past and Present*, Vol. 50

Thompson, E. P., 'Eighteenth Century English Society: Class Struggle Without Class?', *Social History*, (iii) 1978

Thompson, E. P., *The Poverty of Theory* (London, Merlin Press, 1978)

Thornberry, C., 'Law, opinion and the immigrant', *Modern Law Review*, Vol. 25, no. 6, 1962

Thornberry, C., *The Stranger at the Gate: a study of the law on aliens and commonwealth citizens* (London, Fabian Society, 1964)

Thornberry, C., 'Law and race relations in Britain', *IRR Newsletter*, February 1965

Thornberry, C., 'Commitment or Withdrawal? The place of law in race relations in Britain', *Race*, Vol. 7, no. 1, July 1965

Thornberry, C., 'A note on the legal position of commonwealth immigrants and the White Paper proposals', *Race*, Vol. 7, no. 2, October 1965

Thornberry C., 'Some legal reflections on British immigration law', *IRR Newsletter*, March 1968

Thornton, A. P., *West India Policy Under the Restoration* (Oxford, Clarendon Press, 1956)

Thornton, A., *The Imperial Idea and its Enemies* (London, Macmillan, 1959)

Thornton, R. H., *British Shipping* (Cambridge University Press, 1939)

Tilly, C., 'Collective Violence in European Perspective', in I. K., Feierabend *et al.*, (eds), *Anger, Violence and Politics* (N.J., Prentice Hall, 1972)

Tilly, C. L. and R., *The Rebellious Century 1830–1930* (London, Dent, 1975)

Times News Team, *The Black Man in Search of Power* (London, Nelson, 1968)

Tinker, H., *A New System of Slavery* (London, Oxford University Press, 1974)

Tomlinson, S., 'West Indian Children and ESN Schooling', *New Community*, Vol. VI, no. 3, 1978

Torode, J., 'Race Moves in on the Unions', *New Society*, 17 June 1965

Touraine, A., *The Voice and the Eye* (Cambridge University Press, 1981)

Townsend, H. E. R., *Immigrant Pupils in England: The ILEA Response* (London, NFER, 1971)

Townsend, H. E. R. and Brittan, E. M., *Organisation in Multiracial Schools* (National Foundation for Educational Research in England and Wales, 1972)

The Trade Union Movement and Discrimination: A Collection of Papers presented to a Conference held at Ruskin College, Oxford, December 1970

Trillin, C., 'A reporter at large: colour in the mother country', *New Yorker*, 4 December 1965

Trollope, A., *The West Indies and the Spanish Main* (London, Chapman Hall, 1839)

Troyna, B., 'Differential Commitment to Ethnic Identity by Black Youth in Britain', *New Community*, Vol. VII, no. 3, 1979

TUC, *Black Workers: A TUC Charter for Equality of Opportunity* (London, 1981)

TUC Workbook on Racism (London, TUC Education Department, 1983)

Tumbor, H., *Television and the Riots* (Broadcasting Research Unit, 1982)

Tupper, E., *Seamen's Torch* (London, Hutchinson & Co., 1938)

Uberoi, N., 'Sikh Women in Southall', *Race*, Vol. 6, no. 1, July 1964

Ullman, V., *Martin K. Delany: The Beginnings of Black Nationalism* (Boston, Mass., Beacon Press, 1971)

Vaughan, D., *Negro Victory* (London, Independent Press Ltd, 1950)

Vaughan, J., *The Negro Presence in Reading*, M.Litt. Thesis, University of Oxford, 1959

Visram, R., *Ayahs, Lascars and Princes: Indians in Britain 1700–1947* (London, Pluto Press, 1986)

Wadsworth, A. P. and Mann, J., *The Cotton Trade and Industrial Lancashire 1600–1780* (Manchester University Press, 1931)

Wallas, G., *The Life of Francis Place, 1771–1854* (London, Longman & Co., 1898)

Wallman, S. (ed.), *Ethnicity at Work* (London, Macmillan Press, 1979)

Walsh, J. D., 'Methodism and the Mob in the Eighteenth Century', in J. D. Cumming and D. Baker (eds), *Popular Beliefs and Practices* (Cambridge, 1972)

Walshaw, R. S. and Jones, C., *Migration to and from Merseyside* (University Press of Liverpool, 1938)

Walston, H. D., 'Repatriation: why it is wrong', *Race Today*, Vol. 1, no. 1, May 1969

Walvin, J., *The Black Presence: A Documentary History of the Negro in England, 1555–1860* (London, Orbach & Chambers, 1971)

Walvin, J., *Black and White* (London, Allen Lane & Penguin Press, 1973)

Walvin, J. (ed.), *Slavery and British Society, 1776–1846* (London, Macmillan, 1982)

Walvin, J., 'The Propaganda of Anti-Slavery', in *Slavery and British Society* (London, Macmillan, 1982)

Ward, G., *Fort Grunwick* (London, Temple Smith, 1977)

Ward, J. T. (ed.), *Popular Movements, c. 1830–1850* (London, Macmillan, 1970)

Ward, J. T., *The Factory System* (Newton Abbott, David & Charles, 1970)

Ward, J. T., *Chartism* (London, Batsford, 1972)

Waskow, A. I., *From Race-Riot to Sit-In, 1919 and the 1960s* (New York, Garden Book, 1967)

Watson, A. R., *West Indian Workers in Great Britain* (Hodder & Stoughton, 1942)

Watson, J. L., *Between Two Cultures* (Oxford, Basil Blackwell, 1977).

Webb, S. and B., *History of Trade Unionism* (London, Longman & Co., 1894)

Wedderburn, R., *Truth, Self-supported; or, A refutation of certain doctrinal errors, generally adopted In the Christian Church* (G. Riebau, c. 1790)

Wedderburn, R., *The Axe Laid To the Root, or a Fatal Blow to Oppressors, being an address to the Planters and Negroes of the Island of Jamaica, No. 1* (1817)

Wedderburn, R., *The 'Forlorn Hope', or A Call to the Supine, To rouse from Indolence and assert Public Rights* (1817)

Wedderburn, R., *A Letter Addressed to the Rev. Solomon Herschell, The High Priest of Israel, The Chosen People of God concerning the origin of the Jewish Prophesies and their expected Messiah* (London, 1819)

Wedderburn, R., *A Few Plain Questions for an Apostate* (1819) and *A Few Lines for a Double-Faced Politician* (1819). PRO HO 42/202

Wedderburn, R., *The Horrors of Slavery: exemplified in the Life and History of the Rev. R. Wedderburn* (London, 1824)

Wells, R., *Insurrection: The British Experience* (Gloucester, 1983)

West, W., *Tavern Anecdotes and Reminiscences of the origins of signs, clubs, coffee houses . . .* (London, 1825)

Westergaard, J. and Resler, H., *Class in a Capitalist Society: A Study of Contemporary Britain* (London, Pelican Books, 1976)

Wheeler, T. M., 'Mr. William Cuffay', *Reynolds Political Instructor*, 13 April 1850

White, L. G., *Ships, Coolies and Rice* (London, 1936)

Wickenden, J., *Colour in Britain* (London, OUP for the IRR, 1958)

Wilberforce, R. I. and S., *The Life of William Wilberforce* (London, John Murray, 1838)

Wilkinson, G. T., *An Authentic History of the Cato Street Conspiracy with the Trials at large at the Conspirators for High Treason and Murder* (London, Thomas Kelly, 1820)

Williams, D. G. T., 'Racial Incitement and Public Order', *Criminal Law Review*, June 1966

Williams, E., *Capitalism and Slavery* (University of North Carolina Press, Chapel Hill, 1944)

Williams, E., *British Historians and the West Indies* (London, Andre Deutsch 1966)

Williams, E., *From Columbus to Castro: The History of the Caribbean 1492–1969* (London, Andre Deutsch, 1970)

Williams, E., *Inward Hunger* (London, Andre Deutsch, 1971)

Williams, H. M., 'Changes in pupils attitudes towards West African Negroes, following the use of two different teaching methods', *British Journal of Educational Psychology*, Vol. 31, 1961

Williams, R. C., 'The training of immigrant workers', *Race Today*, Vol. 1, no. 2, June 1969

Williamson, J., 'Threat of Racialism in Britain', *Political Affairs*, Vol. 45, no. 1, January 1966

Wilson, A., *Finding A Voice* (London, Virago, 1978)

Wilson, E., *Women & the Welfare State* (London, Tavistock Publications, 1977)

Wilson, E., *Only Halfway to Paradise: women in post-war Britain 1945–1968* (Tavistock, 1980)

Winthrop, D. J., *White Over Black: American Attitudes Towards the Negro, 1550–1812* (Chapel Hill, University of North Carolina Press, 1968)

Wolpert, S. A., *Tilak and Gokhale: Revolution and Reform in the Making of Modern India* (Berkeley and Los Angeles, University of California Press, 1962)

Wood, D., *Trinidad in Transition: The Years After Slavery* (London, OUP, 1968)

Wood, G. B., 'A Negro in the North of England', *Country Life Annual*, 1967

Wood, N., *Communism and the British Intellectuals* (London, Victor Gollancz, 1959)

Wordsworth, W., *Poetical Works* (Oxford Edition, London, 1904)

Wright, E. O., 'Class Boundaries in Advanced Capitalist Societies', *New Left Review*, no. 98, July/August 1976

Wright, P. L., *The Coloured Worker in British Industry* (Oxford University Press, 1968)

Young, K. and Connelly, Naomi, *Policy and Practice in the Multi-Racial City* (Policy Studies Institute, 1981)

Yult, W., *et al.*, 'Children of West Indian Immigrants, Intellectual Performance and Reading Attainment', *Journal of Child Psychology and Psychiatry*, 1975

Periodicals, Newspapers and Pamphlets

Action

American Anthropologist

American Sociological Review

Anti-Slavery Reporter

Army Quarterly

Black Dwarf

Black Liberator

Black Man

Black Trade Unionists Solidarity Movement: (Declaration and Newsletter)

British Journal of Educational Psychology

British Journal of Industrial Relations

Bulletin of the Institute of Historical Research

Bulletin of the Society for the Study of Labour History

Cambridge Journal of Economics

Caribbean Quarterly

Caribbean Studies

Caribbean Times

Clare Market Review

Cobbett's Weekly Political Register

Coloured American

Combat

Comet

Controversy

Courier

Criminal Law Review

The Criminologist

Dublin Review

Economica

Economic History Review

Economic Journal

The Economist

Educational Research

English Historical Review

Feminist Review

FOWAAD

Fraser's Magazine

Fraternity
Gentleman's Magazine
History Today
Institute of Race Relations
  Newsletter
International African Opinion
International Institute for Labour
  Studies Bulletin
International Migration Review
Journal of African History
Journal of Child Psychology and
  Psychiatry
Journal of the History of Ideas
Journal of Modern African Studies
Journal of Negro History
The Keys
Labour Monthly
Left
The Leveller
The Listener
Lloyd's Bank Review
Man
Midwife and Health Visitor
Migration Today
Modern Law Review
Negro Educational Review
New Age
New Leader
New Left Review
New Society
New Statesman
New Yorker
New York Times Review of Books
Northern Star
Nursing Times
Occupational Psychology
Past and Present
Peace News
Phylon
Political Affairs
Political Economy
Political Quarterly
Political Studies
Politics and Society
Population Studies
Race
Race and Class
Race Today

Regional Studies
The Republican
The Reasoner
Review of Reviews
Review of Security and the State
Reynolds Political Instructor
Science and Society
The Seaman
Social and Economic Studies
Social History
Sociological Review
Spare Rib
Studies in Political Economy
Tribune
Twentieth Century
Urban Studies
Venture
WASU Journal
West Africa

Newspapers
African Times and Orient Review
Birmingham Post
Bristol Post
Daily Herald
Daily Mirror
Daily Telegraph
Daily Worker
The Defender
Evening News
The Guardian
Hobart Mercury
Kensington News
Kensington Post
Lagos Standard
Liverpool Courier
Liverpool Echo
Manchester Guardian
Manchester Observer
Morning Chronicle
Morning Star
The Mirror
The New Times
News Chronicle
Northern Star
The Observer
Pall Mall Gazette
Port of Spain Gazette

Radical History Review
Socialist Commentary
Socialist Review
South Wales Echo
South Wales News
Sunday Telegraph
The Sunday Times

The Times
The Telegraph
Weekly Despatch
Westminster Gazette
West Indian Gazette
West Indian World
Woolers British Gazette

Index